23rd Annual Conference of the European Association for Machine Translation (EAMT2022)

Ghent, Belgium
1-3 June 2022

Editors:

Lieve Macken
Andrew Rufener
Joachim Van den Bogaert
Joke Daems
Arda Tezcan
Bram Vanroy
Margot Fonteyne
Loïc Barrault
Marta R. Costa-Jussà
Ellie Kemp
Spyridon Pilos
Christophe Declercq
Maarit Koponen
Mikel L. Forcada
Carolina Scarton
Helena Moniz

ISBN: 978-1-7138-5346-6

Printed from e-media with permission by:

Curran Associates, Inc.
57 Morehouse Lane
Red Hook, NY 12571

Some format issues inherent in the e-media version may also appear in this print version.

Association for Computational Linguistics
209 N. Eighth Street
Stroudsburg, Pennsylvania 18360

Phone: 1-570-476-8006
Fax: 1-570-476-0860

acl@aclweb.org

Additional copies of this publication are available from:

Curran Associates, Inc.
57 Morehouse Lane
Red Hook, NY 12571 USA
Phone: 845-758-0400
Fax: 845-758-2633
Email: curran@proceedings.com
Web: www.proceedings.com

EUROPEAN ASSOCIATION FOR MACHINE TRANSLATION

EAMT2022

Proceedings of the 23rd Annual Conference of the European Association for Machine Translation

1 – 3 June 2022
Ghent, Belgium

Edited by

Lieve Macken, Andrew Rufener, Joachim Van den Bogaert, Joke Daems, Arda Tezcan, Bram Vanroy, Margot Fonteyne, Loïc Barrault, Marta R. Costa-jussà, Ellie Kemp, Spyridon Pilos, Christophe Declercq, Maarit Koponen, Mikel L. Forcada, Carolina Scarton, Helena Moniz

Organised by

language and translation technology team

CROSSLANG

GHENT UNIVERSITY

Contents

Foreword from the General Chair

As president of the European Association for Machine Translation (EAMT) and General Chair of the 23rd Annual Conference of the EAMT, it is with great pleasure that I write these opening words to the Proceedings of EAMT 2022 (a first time for me!). The preparations for EAMT 2022 were initially started by the former President, Mikel Forcada, to whom I am deeply grateful for all the assistance and hand over.

A first note of appreciation and gratitude to the Executive Board Members who have moved to new plans in life, after long and outstanding dedicated service to the EAMT community. Firstly, Tony Clarke, EAMT treasurer for 23 years, in appreciation for his invaluable service as the longest-standing treasurer of our Association. To Andy Way, in appreciation for his years of service as secretary, president, conference organizer, and member of the Executive Board of our Association. To Viggo Hansen, our gratitude for his years of service as secretary, conference organizer, and member of the Executive Board of our Association.

One of the most significant milestones this year was the John Hutchins Machine Translation Archive new domain, an achievement built upon the hard work of our former president, Mikel Forcada, and a group of dedicated members, Barry Haddow, Leopoldo Pla, and Matt Post. The John Hutchins Machine Translation Archive is alive at: `https://mt-archive.net/`. We invite our community to visit John's archive!

A few lines more of gratitude to Matt Post, for being responsible for the import of the MT Archive conference proceedings into the ACL anthology. Our community is very thankful to Matt Post for the massive import work and patience along the way!

Now our EAMT 2022 event! After an online-edition in Lisbon, in 2020 (in which I had no opportunity to welcome you in person as a co-chair) and a cancellation in 2021, we now move forward to a fully and much hoped for live event in Ghent, Belgium! Winds of change in the pandemics are bringing a new hope. Embedded in this spirit, the local organizers are enthusiastic about hosting an in-person event, after the two-years interregnum, anticipating a much needed gathering of the community. Let us hope that these changes are here to stay.

Despite the positive changes in terms of covid, our community reached out to us requesting for support, specifically for freelance translators and/or members from low-income areas and war zones. For the first time, we have opened two calls for grants, encompassing, on one hand, students from Translation Studies and, on another, members from Middle East and African countries. A total of seven grants were given. We hope this initiative may mitigate the hard times we are living and may bring richer discussions into our EAMT 2022, diversifying geographically our membership.

EAMT 2022 will have a three-day, four-track programme put together by our chairs: Löic Barrault and Marta Costa-Jussà, research track co-chairs; Ellie Kemp and Spyridon Pilos, user track co-chairs; Maarit Koponen and Christophe Declercq, translator track co-chairs; and Mikel Forcada, as the projects/products track chair. Carolina Scarton, Secretary of EAMT, was the chair of the Best Thesis Award and also the technical coordinator of the reviewing process (our gratitude to Carolina who is always willing to support our community).

This year, the programme will also include two keynotes speakers, invited by Lieve Macken and Andrew Rufener (with our full support and enthusiasm), Laura Rossi (Medtronic) and Jörg Tiedemann (University of Helsinki), combining industry and academia visions on the field, a true honour to have them and to be able to discuss their talks in person.

EAMT 2022 brings a new breeze of hope and it is the result of the hard work of our local organizers from the Language and Translation Technology Team (LT3) of Ghent University and CrossLang. Our gratitude and appreciation to the LT3 team, Lieve Macken (co-chair), Joke Daems, Arda Tezcan, and Bram Vanroy; and to the CrossLang team, Andrew Rufener (co-chair), Joachim Van den Bogaert, and especially to Martine Massiera for her outstanding work taking care of our sponsors, registration process, all social events, and smoothly handling the logistics of the new calls for grants.

EAMT has been supported by generous sponsors in its initiatives along the years. This year is no exception. Our gratitude to our sponsors: Microsoft (platinum sponsor, who will also be giving a talk entitled "Microsoft and Translators' quest to break down language barriers"), Pangeanic and Yamagata (silver sponsors), STAR Group, Unbabel and Welocalize (bronze sponsors), Apertium (collaborator sponsor), Springer (best paper award supporter) and MultiLingual (media sponsor).

A final note to our participants! By the time I am writing these lines, there are already 113 participants and the number continues growing! Even in unstable times, this number is a very positive sign! We can finally meet in person! Let us take this opportunity to revive fruitful discussions, scientific collaborations, and constructive feedback in our community. I'm looking forward to seeing you all, finally!

Lisboa, 2022

Helena Moniz
President of the EAMT
General Chair of EAMT 2022
University of Lisbon / INESC-ID, Portugal

Message from the Organising Committee Chairs

It is with great pleasure that we finally welcome you in Ghent to attend the 23rd Annual Conference of the European Association for Machine Translation.

The idea of organizing the 23rd Annual Conference of EAMT in Ghent jointly by the LT3 research team and CrossLang emerged in 2019 at the Croke Park stadium in Dublin where we enjoyed the Gala Dinner of the MT Summit. Unfortunately, COVID-19 prevented us from organizing an on-site event and EAMT2021 was first postponed and eventually cancelled. We are therefore extremely pleased to be able to welcome you all in our beautiful city for EAMT2022 and to meet you all in person.

A lot can happen in two years. The venue we had originally booked, the Aula Academica of Ghent University, a historic building of 1826, was no longer available due to renovation work. As Ghent is a great mix of old and new, we instead welcome you in the trendy Zebrastraat and keep the historic part for the conference dinner, which will be organized in the church of Monasterium PoortAckere.

People also change jobs. With a new team (and a new EAMT president) we continued the preparations for the conference. We kept the basic format of previous editions, but added a second keynote speaker. This not only allowed us to find the optimal balance between academia and industry but also ensured gender balance. We are really looking forward to the talks of Jörg Tiedemann and Laura Rossi.

We did not opt for a hybrid conference as the advantages did not outweigh the disadvantages. As a compromise, we will record the oral sessions and make the recordings available after the conference.

We would express our sincerest gratitude to everyone who made EAMT2022 possible: Mikel Forcada as former president of EAMT; Helena Moniz as new president of EAMT; Carolina Scarton as EAMT Secretary; Löic Barrault and Marta Costa-Jussà as research track chairs; Ellie Kemp and Spyridon Pilos as user track co-chairs; Maarit Koponen and Christophe Declercq as translator track chairs.

We extend our thanks to our sponsors for their invaluable support: Microsoft (Platinum sponsor), Pangeanic and Yamagata (Silver sponsors), STAR Group, Unbabel and Welocalize (Bronze sponsors), Apertium (Collaborator sponsor), Springer (Supporter sponsor), and Multi-Lingual (media sponsor).

This conference would not have been possible without the hard work of all members of the joint organizing team: Andrew Rufener, Martine Massiera and Joachim Van den Bogaert of CrossLang; Lieve Macken, Joke Daems, Arda Tezcan, Bram Vanroy and Margot Fonteyne of the Language and Translation Technology Team (LT^3) of Ghent University. Sincere thanks as well to Sam Delmotte of Ghent University for recording the oral sessions.

Lieve Macken
Ghent University, LT^3

Andrew Rufener
CrossLang

On behalf of the local organizers

Preface by the Programme Chairs

On behalf of the programme chairs, a warm welcome to the 23rd annual conference of the European Association for Machine Translation in Ghent, Belgium. After all the restrictions, rescheduling and cancellations of events in the past couple of years, and after a prolonged period with almost all meetings online, we are delighted to finally be meeting our colleagues face-to-face again!

Following the approach which has proven so successful in the previous editions of EAMT, the conference programme consists of papers and posters divided into four tracks. These relate to research, users, translators and projects/products.

The research track this year was one of the most competitive tracks ever in the history of EAMT. Only 17 out of 39 papers were accepted (an acceptance rate of 44%), based on three-peer reviews. The papers describe state-of-the-art work being conducted and, therefore, are highly relevant to our community. Eight papers will be presented orally and nine as posters, as you may already find in the programme. We invite our community to reach out to the authors and discuss the relevant work conducted in such a demanding track.

The submissions for the user track in this edition mostly tackle the customer support domain - a particular focus of the oral sessions of the programme - and industry usage of MT. This track will discuss a number of practical issues for users. These range from the notion of "users" in a very challenging domain, to conversational data with strict time constraints, and the quality of the MT produced.

The translator's track, as is evident from the name, emphasises the perspective of translators on MT. This year, the track features three peer-reviewed papers, each of which addresses aspects of machine translation and post-editing carried out by translators in different settings. The diverging uses of post-editing and machine translation cover a survey of corporate use of post-editing and revision in the NMT era, post-editing practices for automatically generated subtitles, and annotation of post-editing and machine translation errors using speech-to-text technology.

Forty-four papers were submitted to the largest ever project/product track in the history of EAMT conferences. Of them, 41 were eventually accepted, some of them after an additional round of improvements with the general audience of EAMT in sight. As these lines are written, authors are preparing their posters, and also their poster booster slides, in anticipation of their (strictly-timed) two minutes of glory before the poster session.

In addition to the papers and posters relating to the different tracks, the programme also features two fascinating invited talks: Laura Rossi with her talk titled "I once said to my boss

'SMT will never work...' " and Jörg Tiedemann with "Democratizing machine translation with OPUS-MT".

We wish to thank the members of the scientific programme committee for their time and support, and for their invaluable expertise in peer-reviewing the submissions. Our thanks naturally go to all the authors, without whom the programme would not exist, the local organisers for all their hard work, as well as Carol Scarton, Helena Moniz and Mikel Forcada for their unfailing advice and support.

Löic Barrault
META AI Research

Ellie Kemp
CLEAR Global

Christophe Declercq
Univ. of Utrecht & Univ. College London

Mikel Forcada
Universitat d'Alacant

Marta Costa-jussà
META AI Research

Spyridon Pilos
European Court of Auditors

Maarit Koponen
University of Eastern Finland

EAMT 2022 Committees

General Chair

Helena Moniz, University of Lisbon, INESC-ID

Programme Chairs

Research track

Loïc Barrault, META AI Research
Marta R. Costa-jussà, META AI Research

User track

Ellie Kemp, CLEAR Global
Spyridon Pilos, European Court of Auditors

Translators' track

Christophe Declercq, Univ. of Utrecht & Univ. College London
Maarit Koponen, Univ. of Eastern Finland

Project/Product track

Mikel L. Forcada, Univ. d'Alacant

Thesis award

Carolina Scarton, Univ. of Sheffield

Organising committee

Lieve Macken, LT3, Ghent University (co-chair)
Andrew Rufener, CrossLang (co-chair)
Joachim Van den Bogaert, CrossLang
Joke Daems, LT3, Ghent University
Arda Tezcan, LT3, Ghent University
Bram Vanroy, LT3, Ghent University
Margot Fonteyne, LT3, Ghent University

Programme Committee

Research track

Duygu Ataman, New York University
Parnia Bahar, RWTH Aachen University
Anabela Barreiro, INESC-ID
Luisa Bentivogli, Fondazione Bruno Kessler
Magdalena Biesialska, Universitat Politècnica de Catalunya
José G. C. de Souza, Unbabel
Michael Carl, Kent State University
Sheila Castilho, Dublin City University
Mauro Cettolo, FBK - Fondazione Bruno Kessler
Colin Cherry, Google Research
Vishal Chowdhary, Microsoft
Chenhui Chu, Kyoto University
Raj Dabre, IIT Bombay
Mattia Antonino Di Gangi, AppTek
Miguel Domingo, Universitat Politècnica de València
Miquel Espla-Gomis, Universitat d'Alacant
Catarina Farinha, Unbabel
Mireia Farrús, Universitat de Barcelona
George Foster, Google
Mercedes García-Martínez, Pangeanic SL
Jesús González-Rubio, WebInterpret
Barry Haddow, The University of Edinburgh
Felix Hieber, Amazon
Matthias Huck, SAP SE
Shankar Kumar, Google
Ekaterina Lapshinova-Koltunski, Saarland University
Samuel Läubli, Zurich University of Applied Sciences
Lieve Macken, Ghent University
Andreas Maletti, Universität Leipzig
Joss Moorkens, Dublin City University
Mathias Müller, University of Zurich
Masaaki Nagata, NTT
Toshiaki Nakazawa, The University of Tokyo
Jan Niehues, Maastricht University
André Niyongabo, Polytechnic University of Catalonia
Constantin Orasan, University of Surrey
Pavel Pecina, Charles University
Stephan Peitz, Apple
Sergio Penkale, Unbabel
Andrei Popescu-Belis, HEIG-VD / HES-SO
Maja Popovic, ADAPT Centre @ DCU
Celia Rico, Universidad Complutense de Madrid, Spain
Matīss Rikters, Tilde
Rudolf Rosa, Charles University
Felipe Sánchez-Martínez, Universitat d'Alacant
Germán Sanchis-Trilles, Sciling S.L.

Yves Scherrer, University of Helsinki
Rico Sennrich, University of Zurich
Patrick Simianer, Lilt, Inc.
Katsuhito Sudoh, Nara Institute of Science and Technology
Aleš Tamchyna, Memsource a. s.
Jörg Tiedemann, University of Helsinki
Antonio Toral, University of Groningen
Marco Turchi, Fondazione Bruno Kessler
Vincent Vandeghinste, Instituut voor de Nederlandse Taal, Leiden & Centre for Computational Linguistics, KU Leuven
Sebastian Vincent, The University of Sheffield
Marion Weller-Di Marco, CIS - University of Munich
Deyi Xiong, Tianjin University
François Yvon, CNRS
Jiajun Zhang, Institute of Automation Chinese Academy of Sciences

User track

Nora Aranberri, University of the Basque Country
Adam Bittlingmayer, ModelFront
Vera Cabarrão, Unbabel
Federico Gaspari, Università per Stranieri "Dante Alighieri" di Reggio Calabria, Italy
Georg Kirchner, Dell Technologies
László János Laki, Hungarian Research Centre for Linguistics
Lena Marg, Welocalize
Mary Nurminen, Tampere University
Morgan O'Brien, Momentive AI
Niko Papula, Multilizer
Daniel Prou, European Commission
Steve Richardson, Brigham Young University
Laura Rossi, Medtronic
Marina Sánchez-Torrón, Unbabel
Yury Sharshov, TBSJ
Dimitar Shterionov, Tilburg University
Masaru Yamada, Rikkyo University

Translators' track

Khetam Al Sharou, Imperial College London
Dorothée Behr, GESIS - Leibniz Institute for the Social Sciences
Patrick Cadwell, Dublin City University
Ruben de La Fuente, PayPal
Gökhan Dogru, Universitat Autonoma de Barcelona
Maria Fernandez-Parra, Swansea University
Dorothy Kenny, Dublin City University
Caroline Lehr, Zurich University of Applied Sciences
Rudy Loock, Université de Lille, France, & CNRS "Savoirs, Textes, Langage" research unit
Antoni Oliver, Universitat Oberta de Catalunya
David Orrego-Carmona, Aston University
Alessandra Rossetti, Universiteit Antwerpen
Caroline Rossi, Université Grenoble Alpes
María Del Mar Sánchez Ramos, Universidad de Alcala
Vilelmini Sosoni, Ionian University

Thesis award

José G. C. de Souza, Unbabel
Vera Cabarrao, Unbabel Lda.; INESC-ID
Sheila Castilho, Dublin City University
Mirella De Sisto, Tilburg University
Mattia Antonino Di Gangi, AppTek
Miquel Esplà-Gomis, Universitat d'Alacant
Federico Gaspari, Dublin City University
Barry Haddow, University of Edinburgh
Ekaterina Lapshinova-Koltunski, Saarland University
Lieve Macken, Ghent University
Andre Martins, Unbabel
Maja Popovic, ADAPT Centre @ DCU
Celia Rico, Universidad Complutense de Madrid
Víctor M. Sánchez-Cartagena, Universitat d'Alacant
Marina Sánchez-Torrón, Unbabel
Arda Tezcan, Ghent University
Marco Turchi, Fondazione Bruno Kessler

Invited Speeches

Democratizing machine translation with OPUS-MT

Jörg Tiedemann, University of Helsinki, Finland

The demand for translation is ever growing and this trend will not stop. Being able to access the same kind of information is a fundamental prerequisite for equality in society and translation plays a crucial role when fighting discrimination based on language barriers. Efficient tools and a better coverage of the linguistic diversity in the World are necessary to cope with the amount of material that needs to be handled. Our mission is to support the development of high quality tools for automatic and computer-assisted translation by providing open services and resources that are independent of commercial interests and profit-driven companies. Equal information access is a human right and not only a privilege for people who can pay for it. In this talk I will discuss the current state of OPUS-MT, our project on open neural machine translation and the challenges that we try to tackle with multilingual NLP, transfer learning and data augmentation. I will report about on-going work on knowledge distillation, the creation of compact models for real-time translation and our work on modularization of neural MT.

"I once said to my boss 'SMT will never work...' "

Laura Rossi, Medtronic

I once said to my boss: 'SMT will never work...', yet here we are: after being statistical, MT became neural and even adaptive, and achieved levels of quality that were unthinkable 20 years ago, covering, in addition, more and more language pairs every day. Customizations of MT systems have turned into a commodity, made available through specialized companies, LSPs and even as a self-service model. MT is very well integrated in human translation workflows to lower prices and shorten turnarounds. So, what are users, and in particular corporate users, looking for next? What creates a differentiative and appealing offer? What makes them choose for one or the other vendor? The race is moving towards automation, integration, well-being and sustainability.

EAMT 2020 and EAMT 2021 Best Thesis Award — Anthony C Clarke Award

Despite not having an EAMT conference in 2021, we still had the EAMT Best Thesis Awards for PhD theses defended in 2020. Therefore, this EAMT 2022 proceedings contains the abstracts for the winners of both EAMT 2020 and EAMT 2021 Best Thesis Award (Anthony C Clarke Award).

Four PhD theses defended in 2020 were received as candidates for the 2020 edition of the Anthony C Clarke Award – EAMT Best Thesis Award, and all four were eligible. Eight EAMT Executive Committee members were recruited to examine and score the theses, considering how challenging the problem tackled in each thesis was, how relevant the results were for machine translation as a field, and what the strength of its impact in terms of scientific publications was. Two EAMT Executive Committee members also analysed all theses.

The scores of the best theses were extremely close, which made it very hard to select a single winner. A panel of seven EAMT Executive Committee members (Khalil Sima'an, Barry Haddow, Celia Rico, Lieve Macken, Carolina Scarton, Helena Moniz and Mikel L. Forcada) was assembled to process and discuss the reviews.

The panel has decided to have two ex aequo winners for the 2020 edition of the EAMT Best Thesis Award:

- **Maha Elbayad**: *Rethinking the Design of Sequence-to-Sequence Models for Efficient Machine Translation* (University Grenoble Alpes, France) — supervised by Laurent Besacier and Jakob Verbeek
- **Mattia Antonino Di Gangi**: *Neural Speech Translation: From Neural Machine Translation to Direct Speech Translation* (University of Trento, Italy) — supervised by Marcello Federico, Marco Turchi and Matteo Negri

Six PhD theses defended in 2021 were received as candidates for the 2021 edition of the Anthony C Clarke Award for the EAMT Best Thesis, and all six were eligible. 12 reviewers and five EAMT Executive Committee members were recruited to examine and score the theses, considering how challenging the problem tackled in each thesis was, how relevant the results were for machine translation as a field, and what the strength of its impact in terms of scientific publications was. Two EAMT Executive Committee members (Helena Moniz – EAMT President – and Carolina Scarton – EAMT Secretary) formed a panel to analyse all theses and discuss all reviews.

The year of 2021 was again a very good year for PhD theses in machine translation. The scores of the best theses were very close, which made it very hard to select a winner. After discussing all the theses and their reviews, the panel proposed a winner that was approved by the EAMT executive committee, represented by members André Martins, Barry Haddow, Celia Rico, Lieve Macken, Lucia Specia and Heidi Depraetere. The awardee of the 2021 edition of the EAMT Best Thesis is **Danielle Saunders'** thesis *Domain Adaptation for Neural Machine Translation* (University of Cambridge, UK), supervised by Professor Bill Byrne.

We are very grateful to all reviewers that helped in assessing the theses defended in 2021 and provided their invaluable and high quality feedback.

Carolina Scarton
EAMT Secretary
University of Sheffield, UK

Rethinking the Design of Sequence-to-Sequence Models for Efficient Machine Translation

Maha Elbayad[†]
LIG - Université Grenoble Alpes, France
Inria - Grenoble, France
maha.elbayad@inria.fr

In recent years, deep learning has enabled impressive achievements in Machine Translation. Neural Machine Translation (NMT) relies on training deep neural networks with large number of parameters on vast amounts of parallel data to learn how to translate from one language to another. One crucial factor to the success of NMT is the design of new powerful and efficient architectures. State-of-the-art systems are encoder-decoder models (Cho et al., 2014; Sutskever et al., 2014; Bahdanau et al., 2015; Gehring et al., 2017; Vaswani et al., 2017) that first encode a source sequence into a set of feature vectors and then decode the target sequence conditioning on the source features. In this thesis we question the encoder-decoder paradigm and advocate for an intertwined encoding of the source and target so that the two sequences interact at increasing levels of abstraction. For this purpose, we introduce Pervasive Attention, an NMT model with a computational graph different from existing encoder-decoder models. In Pervasive attention, the source and the target communicate and interact throughout the encoding process towards abstract features. To this end, our NMT model uses two-dimensional convolutional neural networks to process a grid of features where every position represents an interaction between a target and a source tokens.

To tackle a different aspect of efficiency in NMT systems, we explore the challenging task of online (also called simultaneous) machine translation (Fügen et al., 2007; Mieno et al., 2015; Dalvi et al., 2018; Ma et al., 2019) where the source is read incrementally and the decoder is fed partial contexts so that the model can alternate between reading and writing. To improve the translation's delay in online NMT systems, we first setup a common framework for online sequence-to-sequence models that will allow us to train existing deterministic decoders that alternate between reading the source and writing the target in a predetermined fashion, and dynamic decoders that condition their decoding path on the current input. We first prove the effectiveness of the deterministic online decoders and their ability to perform well outside the delay range they were optimized for. We then adapt Pervasive Attention models for the task of online translation with both a deterministic and a dynamic decoding strategy.

We also address the resource-efficiency of encoder-decoder models, namely Transformer models (Vaswani et al., 2017), state-of-the-art in a wide range of NLP tasks (Devlin et al., 2019; Yang et al., 2019; Liu et al., 2019; Ng et al., 2019). Models based on the Transformer architecture can grow deep, accumulating billions of parameters. We posit that going deeper in a neural network is not required for all instances, and design depth adaptive Transformer decoders. These decoders allow for anytime prediction and sample-adaptive halting mechanisms, to favor low cost predictions for low complexity instances, and save deeper predictions for complex scenarios.

Pervasive Attention models and our Online NMT framework are implemented on top of the Fairseq library (Ott et al., 2019) in our open-source code.[1]

Acknowledgements The author would like to thank her Ph.D. supervisors, Laurent Besacier and

[†] Now at Meta AI Research

[1] https://github.com/elbayadm/attn2d

Macken, Rufener, Van den Bogaert, Daems, Tezcan, Vanroy, Fonteyne, Barrault, Costa-jussà, Kemp, Pilos, Declercq, Koponen, Forcada, Scarton, Moniz (eds.)
Proceedings of the 23rd Annual Conference of the European Association for Machine Translation, p. 5–6
Ghent, Belgium, June 2022.

Jakob Verbeeek, and her thesis examiners, Holger Schwenk and Hermann Ney. The work presented in this thesis has been supported by the grant ANR-11-LABX-0025-01 "LabEx PERSYVAL". The work on Depth-adaptive Transformers was done during an internship at Facebook AI research hosted by Michael Auli.

References

Bahdanau, Dzmitry, Kyunghyun Cho, and Yoshua Bengio. 2015. Neural machine translation by jointly learning to align and translate. In *Proc. of ICLR*.

Cho, Kyunghyun, Bart Van Merriënboer, Caglar Gulcehre, Dzmitry Bahdanau, Fethi Bougares, Holger Schwenk, and Yoshua Bengio. 2014. Learning phrase representations using RNN encoder-decoder for statistical machine translation. In *Proc. of EMNLP*.

Dalvi, Fahim, Nadir Durrani, Hassan Sajjad, and Stephan Vogel. 2018. Incremental decoding and training methods for simultaneous translation in neural machine translation. In *Proc. of NAACL-HLT*.

Devlin, Jacob, Ming-Wei Chang, Kenton Lee, and Kristina Toutanova. 2019. Bert: Pre-training of deep bidirectional transformers for language understanding. In *Proc. of NAACL-HLT*.

Fügen, Christian, Alex Waibel, and Muntsin Kolss. 2007. Simultaneous translation of lectures and speeches. *Machine translation*.

Gehring, Jonas, Michael Auli, David Grangier, Denis Yarats, and Yann N. Dauphin. 2017. Convolutional sequence to sequence learning. In *Proc. of ICML*.

Liu, Yinhan, Myle Ott, Naman Goyal, Jingfei Du, Mandar Joshi, Danqi Chen, Omer Levy, Mike Lewis, Luke Zettlemoyer, and Veselin Stoyanov. 2019. Roberta: A robustly optimized BERT pretraining approach. *ArXiv preprint*.

Ma, Mingbo, Liang Huang, Hao Xiong, Renjie Zheng, Kaibo Liu, Baigong Zheng, Chuanqiang Zhang, Zhongjun He, Hairong Liu, Xing Li, Hua Wu, and Haifeng Wang. 2019. STACL: Simultaneous translation with implicit anticipation and controllable latency using prefix-to-prefix framework. In *Proc. of ACL*.

Mieno, Takashi, Graham Neubig, Sakriani Sakti, Tomoki Toda, and Satoshi Nakamura. 2015. Speed or accuracy? a study in evaluation of simultaneous speech translation. In *Proc. of INTERSPEECH*.

Ng, Nathan, Kyra Yee, Alexei Baevski, Myle Ott, Michael Auli, and Sergey Edunov. 2019. Facebook fair's wmt19 news translation task submission. In *Proc. of WMT*.

Ott, Myle, Sergey Edunov, Alexei Baevski, Angela Fan, Sam Gross, Nathan Ng, David Grangier, and Michael Auli. 2019. fairseq: A fast, extensible toolkit for sequence modeling. In *Proc. of NAACL-HLT*.

Sutskever, Ilya, Oriol Vinyals, and Quoc V. Le. 2014. Sequence to sequence learning with neural networks. In *Proc. of NeurIPS*.

Vaswani, Ashish, Noam Shazeer, Niki Parmar, Jakob Uszkoreit, Llion Jones, Aidan N. Gomez, Łukasz Kaiser, and Illia Polosukhin. 2017. Attention is all you need. In *Proc. of NeurIPS*.

Yang, Zhilin, Zihang Dai, Yiming Yang, Jaime Carbonell, Russ R Salakhutdinov, and Quoc V Le. 2019. Xlnet: Generalized autoregressive pretraining for language understanding. In *Proc. of NeurIPS*.

Neural Speech Translation: from Neural Machine Translation to Direct Speech translation

Mattia A. Di Gangi*
Fondazione Bruno Kessler (FBK)
ICT Doctoral School - University of Trento
via Sommarive, Povo, Trento, Italy
mattia.digangi@unitn.it

Speech-to-text translation, or simply speech translation (ST), is the task of translating automatically a spoken speech. The problem has classically been tackled by combining the technologies of automatic speech recognition (ASR) and machine translation (MT) with different degrees of coupling (Takezawa et al., 1998; Waibel et al., 1991). The most popular approach is to cascade ASR and MT systems, as it can make use of the state of the art in such mature fields (Black et al., 2002). The goal of this thesis was to develop the so-called approach of direct speech translation, which translates audio without intermediate transcription (Duong et al., 2016; Bérard et al., 2016; Weiss et al., 2017). Direct speech translation (DST) is based on the sequence-to-sequence learning technology that allowed the spectacular advances of the field of neural MT (NMT) but introducing its own challenges (Sutskever et al., 2014; Bahdanau et al., 2015).

We started with a study about the effects of NMT in cascaded ST, where we analyzed the translation errors of NMT and phrase-based MT (PBMT) for automatically transcribed input text. Our results showed that NMT achieves an overall higher quality also in this setting, but its ability to model a theoretically-unlimited context can introduce subtle errors. Indeed, we found that in PBMT the errors are localized in correspondence to the source error, whereas NMT can introduce errors far from the source-side error position.

Motivated by application needs, in a following work we studied how to use a single NMT system to translate effectively clean source text and automatic transcripts. We found that a simple training algorithm that fine-tunes the model on both kinds of inputs improves the translation quality of corrupted input without any degradation on clean input.

In a parallel research line, we were interested in making the training of RNN-based NMT more efficient, as it required at the time long training time also for relatively small datasets. For this, we proposed simple-recurrent NMT (SR-NMT), an encoder-decoder architecture that requires a fraction of parameters and computing power than LSTM-based NMT. It is built on top of simple recurrent units (Lei et al., 2017), which are faster to train but achieve a lower translation quality than LSTMs, particularly because they do not benefit from the addition of computation layers. On the other side, SR-NMT has been designed to be trained as a deep network and our results show how the performance improves significantly up to 8 layers in the encoder and in the decoder.

Our two research lines converge in our work on DST. We start with a participation in IWSLT 2018, which introduced a separate evaluation for direct models in order to encourage participants to explore this new and promising technology. From this participation we learn that training such kind of models is really difficult, findings confirmed by the very low results of all but the winning model. We hypothesize that such difficulty is due also to the low availability of training data for the task, which in fact requires source audio matched with its translation. It is much easier to find transcribed audio data and separate translated text.

In a first effort to overcome this data paucity, we propose MuST-C, a Multilingual Speech Translation Corpus (Di Gangi et al., 2019a). It is obtained from TED talks and provides the audio (in English) segmented into sentences matched with the cor-

*Now at AppTek GmbH

Macken, Rufener, Van den Bogaert, Daems, Tezcan, Vanroy, Fonteyne, Barrault, Costa-jussà, Kemp, Pilos, Declercq, Koponen, Forcada, Scarton, Moniz (eds.)
Proceedings of the 23rd Annual Conference of the European Association for Machine Translation, p. 7–8
Ghent, Belgium, June 2022.

responding audio transcripts and translations to 8 languages. MuST-C provides audio data ranging from 385 to 504 hours, according to the target language, filtered for achieving a high quality of parallel data.

With MuST-C available, we focused on deep learning methods for DST and proposed S-Transformer, an adaptation of Transformer to the task (Di Gangi et al., 2019b). The problems that S-Transformer aims to solve are the high resource burden in terms of computing power and training time of LSTM-based DST, and the difficulty of self-attention to model audio-like sequences, characterized by a very high number of time steps and low information density per step. The first problem is tackled effectively by the use of Transformer, which trains faster and scales better than LSTMs, while for modeling we used 2D CNNs, 2D self-attention, and time-biased self-attention, which help with both convergence time and translation quality.

Finally, we applied S-Transformer in a one-to-many multilingual fashion to make better use of the MusT-C data, as well as comparing character-level against BPE-level segmentation of the target sentence. Our results showed that the BPE-segmentation is generally better and achieves larger improvement also in the multilingual scenario. Moreover, we participated in the DST evaluation at IWSLT 2019 and 2020, where MuST-C became the main in-task training corpus, and our submissions' results were competitive with the ones of teams from the industry. The results and products of this thesis contributed to the fast development of the technology of DST and lowered the barrier of entry into the field by making data[1] and code[2] publicly available.

Acknowledgments

The author would like to thank his Ph.D. supervisors: Marcello Federico, Marco Turchi, and Matteo Negri; his thesis examiners: Evgeny Matusov, Jan Nieheus, and Loïc Barrault, as well as all the HLT-MT group at FBK. The author was financially supported by a Ph.D. scholarship from FBK. This thesis was partly financially supported by an Amazon AWS ML Grant.

[1] https://ict.fbk.eu/must-c/

[2] https://github.com/mattiadg/FBK-Fairseq-ST

References

Bahdanau, Dzmitry, Kyunghyun Cho, and Yoshua Bengio. 2015. Neural Machine Translation by Jointly Learning to Align and Translate. In *Proceedings of ICLR 2015*.

Bérard, Alexandre, Olivier Pietquin, Laurent Besacier, and Christophe Servan. 2016. Listen and Translate: A Proof of Concept for End-to-End Speech-to-Text Translation. In *NIPS Workshop on end-to-end learning for speech and audio processing*.

Black, Alan W, Ralf D Brown, Robert Frederking, Kevin Lenzo, John Moody, Alexander I Rudnicky, Rita Singh, and Eric Steinbrecher. 2002. Rapid Development of Speech-to-Speech Translation Systems. In *Seventh International Conference on Spoken Language Processing*.

Di Gangi, Mattia A., Roldano Cattoni, Luisa Bentivogli, Matteo Negri, and Marco Turchi. 2019a. Must-c: a Multilingual Speech Translation Corpus. In *Proceedings of NAACL 2019*, pages 2012–2017, Minneapolis, MN, USA.

Di Gangi, Mattia A., Matteo Negri, and Marco Turchi. 2019b. Adapting Transformer to End-to-End Spoken Language Translation. In *Proceedings of Interspeech 2019*, pages 1133–1137, Graz, Austria.

Duong, Long, Antonios Anastasopoulos, David Chiang, Steven Bird, and Trevor Cohn. 2016. An attentional Model for Speech Translation Without Transcription. In *Proceedings of NAACL 2016*, pages 949–959.

Lei, Tao, Yu Zhang, and Yoav Artzi. 2017. Training RNNs as Fast as CNNs. *arXiv preprint arXiv:1709.02755*.

Sutskever, Ilya, Oriol Vinyals, and Quoc V Le. 2014. Sequence to Sequence Learning with Neural Networks. In *Proceedings of NIPS 2014*.

Takezawa, Toshiyuki, Tsuyoshi Morimoto, Yoshinori Sagisaka, Nick Campbell, Hitoshi Iida, Fumiaki Sugaya, Akio Yokoo, and Seiichi Yamamoto. 1998. A Japanese-to-English speech translation system: ATR-MATRIX. In *Fifth International Conference on Spoken Language Processing*.

Waibel, Alex, Ajay N Jain, Arthur E McNair, Hiroaki Saito, Alexander G Hauptmann, and Joe Tebelskis. 1991. JANUS: a Speech-to-Speech Translation System Using Connectionist and Symbolic Processing Strategies. In *Proceedings of the ICASSP 1991*, pages 793–796.

Weiss, Ron J., Jan Chorowski, Navdeep Jaitly, Yonghui Wu, and Zhifeng Chen. 2017. Sequence-to-Sequence Models Can Directly Translate Foreign Speech. In *Proceedings of Interspeech 2017*, Stockholm, Sweden, August.

Domain Adaptation for Neural Machine Translation

Danielle Saunders*
Department of Engineering
University of Cambridge
Cambridge, UK
ds636@cantab.ac.uk

The development of deep learning techniques has allowed Neural Machine Translation (NMT) models to become extremely powerful, given sufficient training data and training time. However, such translation models struggle when translating text of a new or unfamiliar domain (Koehn and Knowles, 2017). A domain may be a well-defined topic, text of a specific provenance, text of unknown provenance with an identifiable vocabulary distribution, or language with some other stylometric feature.

NMT models can achieve good translation performance on domain-specific data via simple tuning on a representative training corpus. However, such data-centric approaches have negative side-effects, including over-fitting and brittleness on narrow-distribution samples and catastrophic forgetting of previously seen domains.

This thesis focuses instead on more robust approaches to domain adaptation for NMT. We consider the case where a system is adapted to a specified domain of interest, but may also need to accommodate new language, or domain-mismatched sentences. As well, the thesis highlights that lines of MT research other than performance on traditional 'domains' can be framed as domain adaptation problems. Techniques that are effective for e.g. adapting machine translation to a biomedical domain can also be used when making use of language representations beyond the surface-level, or when encouraging better machine translation of gendered terms.

Over the course of the thesis we pose and answer five research questions:

How effective are data-centric approaches to NMT domain adaptation? We find that simply selecting-domain relevant training data and fine-tuning an existing model achieves strong results, especially when a domain-specific data curriculum is used during training. However, we also demonstrate the side-effects of exposure bias and catastrophic forgetting.

Given an adaptation set, what training schemes improve NMT quality? We investigate two variations on the NMT adaptation algorithm, regularized tuning including Elastic Weighting Consolidation, and a new variant of Minimum Risk Training. We show they can mitigate the pitfalls of data-centric adaptation. Aside from avoiding the failure modes of data-centric methods, we show these methods may also give better model convergence.

Can domain adaptation help when the test domain is unknown? Most approaches to domain adaptation in the literature assume any unseen test data of interest has a known, fixed domain, with a matching set of tuning data. This thesis works towards relaxing these assumptions. We show that adapting sequentially across domains with regularization can achieve good cross-domain performance without knowing the specific test domain. We also explore domain adaptive model ensembling and automatic model selection. We find this can outperform oracle approaches, which select the best model for inference by using known provenance labels.

Can changing data representation have similar effects to changing data domain? Unlike data domain, data representation – for example, choice of subword granularity or use of syntactic annotation – does not change meaning or correspond to provenance. However, like domain, it can affect the information available to the model, and

*Now at RWS Language Weaver

Macken, Rufener, Van den Bogaert, Daems, Tezcan, Vanroy, Fonteyne, Barrault, Costa-jussà, Kemp, Pilos, Declercq, Koponen, Forcada, Scarton, Moniz (eds.)
Proceedings of the 23rd Annual Conference of the European Association for Machine Translation, p. 9–10
Ghent, Belgium, June 2022.

therefore impacts NMT quality for a given input. We combine multiple representations in a single model or in ensembles in a way reminiscent of multi-domain translation. In particular, we develop a scheme for ensembles of models producing multiple target language representations, and show that multi-representation ensembles improve syntax-based NMT.

Can gender bias in NMT systems be mitigated by treating it as a domain? We show that translation of gendered language is strongly influenced by vocabulary distributions in the training data, a hallmark of a domain. We also show that data selection methods have a strong effect on apparent NMT gender bias. We apply techniques from elsewhere in the thesis to tune NMT on a 'gender' domain, specifically regularized adaptation and multi-domain inference. We show this can improve gendered language translation while maintaining generic translation quality.

Human language itself is constantly adapting, and people's interactions with and expectations of MT are likewise evolving. With this thesis we hope to draw attention to the possible benefits and applications of different approaches to adapting machine translation. We hope that future work on adaptive NMT will focus not only on the language of immediate interest but the machine translation abilities or tendencies that we wish to maintain or abandon.

Acknowledgments

The author would like to thank her PhD supervisor, Bill Byrne. The work was supported by EPSRC grants EP/M508007/1 and EP/N509620/1, with some experiments performed using resources from the Cambridge Tier-2 system operated by the University of Cambridge Research Computing Service[1] funded by EPSRC Tier-2 capital grant EP/P020259/1.

References

Koehn, Philipp and Rebecca Knowles. 2017. Six Challenges for Neural Machine Translation *Proceedings of the First Workshop on Neural Machine Translation*, Vancouver, 28–39.

[1] `http://www.hpc.cam.ac.uk`

Research papers

Multi-Domain Adaptation in Neural Machine Translation with Dynamic Sampling Strategies

Minh-Quang Pham
Uni. Paris-Saclay, CNRS, LISN
F-91405 Orsay
pham@limsi.fr

Josep Crego
SYSTRAN ,
5 rue Feydeau, F-75002 Paris
crego@systrangroup.com

François Yvon
Uni. Paris-Saclay, CNRS, LISN
F-91405 Orsay, France
yvon@limsi.fr

Abstract

Building effective Neural Machine Translation models often implies accommodating diverse sets of heterogeneous data so as to optimize performance for the domain(s) of interest. Such multi-source / multi-domain adaptation problems are typically approached through instance selection or reweighting strategies, based on a static assessment of the relevance of training instances with respect to the task at hand. In this paper, we study dynamic data selection strategies that are able to automatically re-evaluate the usefulness of data samples in the course of training. Based on the results of multiple experiments, we show that our method offer a generic framework to automatically handle several real-world situations, from multi-source or unsupervised domain adaptation to multidomain learning.

1 Introduction

A typical setting in machine translation (MT) is to collect the largest possible collection of parallel data for the chosen language pair, with the intent to achieve optimal performance for the task of interest. In such situations, the training data distribution is opportunistic, while the test data distribution is chosen and fixed; a key aspect of training is then to mitigate the detrimental effects of a mismatch between these distributions. Single-source and multi-source[1] domain adaptation (DA) is a well-studied instance of this setting (see (Chu et al., 2017; Saunders, 2021) for a review), and so is multi-domain (MD) learning (Chu and Dabre, 2018; Zeng et al., 2018; Jiang et al., 2020; Pham et al., 2021). A related situation is multilingual MT (Firat et al., 2016; Ha et al., 2016; Johnson et al., 2017; Aharoni et al., 2019), where the diversity of training data not only corresponds to variations in the topic, genre, or register but also in language.

This problem is often approached by *static* instance selection or re-weighting strategies, where the available training data is used in proportion to its relevance for the testing conditions (Moore and Lewis, 2010; Axelrod et al., 2011). Finding the optimal balance of training data is however, a challenging task due, for instance, to the similarity between domains/languages, or to the regularization effects of out-of-domain data (Miceli Barone et al., 2017). A static policy may also be suboptimal when some target domains or languages are easier to train than others. Finally, improving the performance of the MT system in one domain will often hurt that of another (van der Wees et al., 2017; Britz et al., 2017) and improving model generalization across all domains (Koehn et al., 2018) may not achieve optimally for any particular domain.

Several recent proposals explore ways to instead consider *dynamic* data selection and sampling strategies: van der Wees et al. (2017) and Zhang et al. (2019) construct a static curriculum, while Wang et al. (2020a) and Wang et al. (2020b) build curricula that automatically adapt to the training data. In this paper, we contribute to this line of research in several ways.

- First, we propose a novel framework (*Multi-Domain Automated Curriculum*, MDAC for short), a variant of Differentiable Data Selec-

[1]In this paper, multi-source DA means having multiple domains to adapt from; this setting differs from multi-source translation, where several *source languages* are considered.

Macken, Rufener, Van den Bogaert, Daems, Tezcan, Vanroy, Fonteyne, Barrault, Costa-jussà, Kemp, Pilos, Declercq, Koponen, Forcada, Scarton, Moniz (eds.)
Proceedings of the 23rd Annual Conference of the European Association for Machine Translation, p. 13–22
Ghent, Belgium, June 2022.

tion (DDS) of Wang et al. (2020b), initially applied to multilingual NMT, that simultaneously accounts for the domain adaptation and the multidomain adaptation problems.

- We show that MDAC achieves performance that compare to fine-tuning strategies for DA (§ 5.1) and outperform some static data sampling strategies for multidomain settings (5.3).

- We show that our variant MDAC mitigates some failures of DDS in multidomain training.

- We illustrate the generality of differentiable data selection frameworks (both MDAC and DDS) on less common situations such as DA using unsupervised clustering (§ 5.5); DA using out-of-domain training data and small in-domain validation data (§ 5.4); and two-domain adaptation where the test distribution only mixes two of the training domain (§ 5.2).

2 Learning with multiple data sources

We conventionally define a domain d as a distribution $\mathcal{D}_d(x)$ over some feature space $\mathcal{X}$ that is shared across domains (Pan and Yang, 2010): in machine translation, $\mathcal{X}$ is the representation space for input sentences; each domain corresponds to a specific source of data, and may differ from other data sources in terms of textual genre, thematic content (Chen et al., 2016; Zhang et al., 2016), register, style (Niu et al., 2018), etc. Translation in domain d is formalized by a translation function $h_d(y|x)$ pairing sentences in a source language with sentences in a target language $y \in \mathcal{Y}$. h_d is usually assumed to be deterministic (hence $y = h_d(x)$) but may differ across domains.

It is usual in MT to opportunistically collect corpora from several domains, which means that training instances are distributed according to a mixture $\mathcal{D}^s$ such that $\mathcal{D}^s(x) = \sum_{d=1}^{n_d} \lambda^s(d)\mathcal{D}_d(x)$, with $\{\lambda^s(d), d = 1 \dots n_d\}$ the mixture weights satisfying $\sum_d \lambda^s(d) = 1$. In the sequel, boldface $\boldsymbol{\lambda}$ denotes a vector with $\lambda(d)$ the dth component of $\boldsymbol{\lambda}$.

The main challenge in this situation is to make the best of heterogeneous data, with the aim to achieve optimal performance for the target test conditions. These might correspond to data from just one of the training domains, as in standard supervised domain adaptation; a more difficult case is when the test data is from one domain unseen in training (unseen domain adaptation); in multidomain adaptation finally, the test distribution is itself a mixture of domains, some of which may also be observed in training. We thus assume that the test distribution takes the form $\mathcal{D}^t(x) = \sum_d \lambda^t(d)\mathcal{D}_d(x)$ - with only one non-null component in the case of domain adaptation (see Figure 1).

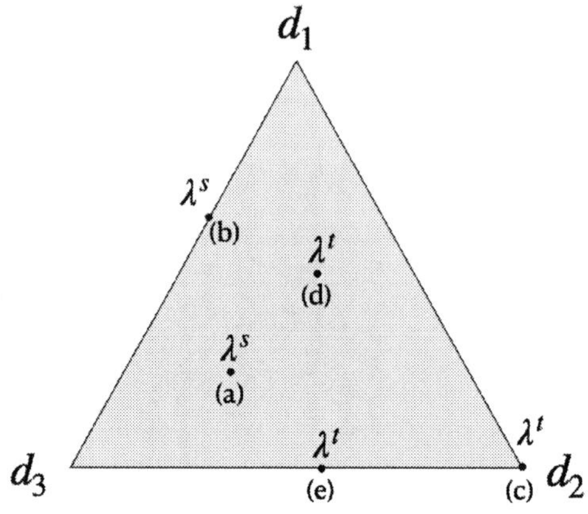

Figure 1: Training and testing with distribution mismatch. We consider three domains and represent $\boldsymbol{\lambda}^s$ and $\boldsymbol{\lambda}^t$ in the 3-dimensional simplex. Training with weights in (a) and testing with weights in (c) is supervised multi-source domain adaptation to domain 2 (d_2), while (b)-(c) is the unsupervised version, with no training data from d_2; training with weights in (a) and testing with weights in (d) is multi-domain learning, also illustrated with settings (a)-(e) (training domain d_1 is not seen in test), and (b)-(d) (test domain d_2 is unseen in training).

These situations have been amply documented from a theoretical perspective (Mansour et al., 2009b; Mansour et al., 2009a; Hoffman et al., 2018). A general recommendation in the DA setting is to adjust the sampling distribution used to optimize the system so as to compensate for the mismatch between $\mathcal{D}^s(x)$ and $\mathcal{D}^t(x)$. This can be approximated by reweighting instances, or more conveniently domains, which are selected during training with a probability $\lambda^l(d)$, with $\lambda^l(d) \neq \lambda^s(d)$.

A widely-used approach to supervised DA is *fine-tuning* (Luong and Manning, 2015), where $\boldsymbol{\lambda}^l$ varies during learning. With our notations, this approach first learns an initial parameter value with all the data ($\forall d, \lambda^l(d) = \lambda^s(d)$), then continues training with only batches from the test domain d_t ($\lambda^l(d) = \mathbb{I}(d = d_t)$), with $\mathbb{I}(A)$ the indicator function for predicate A. This strategy is potentially suboptimal as some out-of-domain samples may contribute to the final performance due to e.g. domain similarity. Optimizing the learning distribution in multidomain settings is even more challenging as the learner needs to take advantage of possible domains overlaps and also of the fact that some domains might be easier to learn than others.

3 Multi-Domain Automated Curriculum

3.1 Basic principles

Assuming training data in each of the n_d domains $d_1 \dots d_{n_d}$, the size of the training corpus in domain d is denoted N^s_d, and $N^s = \sum_d N^s_d$ is the total number of training samples. $\widehat{\mathcal{D}^l_d}$ and $\widehat{\mathcal{D}^t_d}$ denote the empirical train and test distributions for domain d and $\widehat{\mathcal{D}^u}(x; \boldsymbol{\lambda}^u) = \sum_d \lambda^u(d)\widehat{\mathcal{D}^u_d}(x)$ for $u \in \{l, t\}$. In our setting, $\boldsymbol{\lambda}^t$ and hence $\widehat{\mathcal{D}^t}(x; \boldsymbol{\lambda}^t)$ are fixed and predefined, approximated with an equivalent number of development corpora.

MDAC builds an adaptative training distribution $\boldsymbol{\lambda}^l$ that optimizes the data selection policy along with the training of the model. We parameterize $\boldsymbol{\lambda}^l$ by a differentiable function $\boldsymbol{\lambda}^l(\psi)$, which is described in § 4.4. We divide the training into many short sessions; in each session t, the model is trained with a static data distribution $\boldsymbol{\lambda}^l(\psi_t)$. After one learning session, we update the data distribution using the REINFORCE algorithm of Williams (1992). The evolution of ψ is thus defined by:

$$\psi_{t+1} = \psi_t + \mathbf{lr}_1 * \sum_{d=1}^{n_d} R(d) * \frac{\partial \lambda^l(d; \psi_t)}{\partial \psi},$$

where the reward $R(d)$ is computed as:

$$R(d) = J^t(\theta_{t+k}, \boldsymbol{\lambda}^t) - J^t(\theta_t, \boldsymbol{\lambda}^t), \qquad (1)$$

and where we also define:

$$\begin{aligned} \theta_{t+i} &= Update(\theta_{t+i-1}, [x^i_j, y^i_j]^N_{j=1}) \\ x^i_j, y^i_j &\sim \widehat{D^l_d}(x) \\ J^t(\theta, \boldsymbol{\lambda}^t) &= \sum_{d=1}^{n_d} \lambda^t(d) \sum_{x^t_d, y^t_d \in \widehat{D^t_d}} l(\theta, x^t_d, y^t_d). \end{aligned}$$

In these equations, N denotes the size of a batch; $\mathbf{lr}_1$ is the learning rate of the sampling distribution; $l(\theta, x, y)$ is the loss of the NMT model on sample (x, y); $J^t(\theta, \boldsymbol{\lambda}^t)$ is the weighted loss aggregated over n_d dev-sets corresponding to the n_d domains.

To compute the reward $R(d)$ associated to training the model with data from domain d, we simulate k training steps from the current checkpoint, using k batches sampled from $D^l(d)$ and computing the gain of the weighted dev-loss. This computation is inspired by the target prediction gain of Graves et al. (2017). However, where Graves et al. (2017) used accumulated gains from the past as rewards, we instead predict the usefulness of each domain for improving the future performance of the system given its current state. This is achieved by simulating a round of training with only the data from one domain. We also differ from these authors in the parameterization of the sampling distribution.

The work of Wang et al. (2020b) is also related: it is based on the bi-level optimization framework, which aims to find an optimal static distribution $\boldsymbol{\lambda}^l$ that will result in the best model with respect to a given target dev set at the end of training. These authors also derive a similar form of update for ψ. However, their reward is the cosine similarity between the gradient computed with the training data from one domain and the gradient computed with the dev set. We compare this approach with ours in the experiment section.

3.2 MDAC for (multi) domain adaptation

The setting developed in previous sections is quite general and can, in principle, accommodate the variety of situations mentioned above, and many more: basic DA, multidomain adaptation with various target distributions, possibly including domains unseen in training. In our experiments, we would like to better assess the potential of MDAC in these settings and seek to study the following questions:

- is MDAC a viable alternative to fine-tuning? In particular, does it enable to better take advantage of relevant data from other domains?
- is MDAC a viable option in multidomain adaptation scenarios?
- does MDAC enable to perform *unsupervised* (multi-)domain adaptation?

These questions are further explored in Section 5. We now turn to our experimental conditions.

4 Experimental settings

4.1 Data and metrics

We experiment with translation from English into French in 6 domains, corresponding to the following data sources: the UFAL Medical corpus V1.0 (MED)[2]; the European Central Bank corpus (BANK); the JRC-Acquis Communautaire corpus (LAW) (Steinberger et al., 2006); documentations for KDE, Ubuntu, GNOME and PHP from the Opus collection, merged in a IT-domain; TedTalks (TALK) (Cettolo et al., 2012), and the Koran (REL). Additional experiments use the News Commentary

[2]https://ufal.mff.cuni.cz/ufal_medical_corpus. We only use the in-domain (medical) subcorpora: PATR, EMEA, CESTA, ECDC.

	MED	LAW	BANK	IT	TALK	REL	NEWS
# lines	2609 (0.68)	501 (0.13)	190 (0.05)	270 (0.07)	160 (0.04)	130 (0.03)	260 (0)
# tokens	133 / 154	17.1 / 19.6	6.3 / 7.3	3.6 / 4.6	3.6 / 4.0	3.2 / 3.4	7.8 / 9.2
# types	771 / 720	52.7 / 63.1	92.3 / 94.7	75.8 / 91.4	61.5 / 73.3	22.4 / 10.5	-
# uniq	700 / 640	20.2 / 23.7	42.9 / 40.1	44.7 / 55.7	20.7 / 25.6	7.1 / 2.1	-

Table 1: Corpora statistics: number of parallel lines ($\times 10^3$) and proportion in the training domain mixture (exluding NEWS), number English and French tokens ($\times 10^6$), types and uniq types ($\times 10^3$): the latter are types that only appear in a given domain.

corpus (NEWS). Most corpora are available from the Opus website[3]. These corpora were deduplicated and tokenized with in-house tools; statistics are in Table 1. To reduce the number of types, we use Byte-Pair Encoding (Sennrich et al., 2016) with 30,000 merge operations on a corpus containing all sentences in both languages.We randomly select in each corpus a development and a test set of 1,000 lines and keep the rest for training. Validation sets are used to chose the best model according to the average BLEU score (Papineni et al., 2002).[4] Significance testing is performed using bootstrap resampling (Koehn, 2004), implemented in compare-mt[5] (Neubig et al., 2019). We report significant differences at the level of $p = 0.05$.

4.2 Baseline systems

Our baselines are standard for multidomain settings.[6] Using Transformers (Vaswani et al., 2017) implemented in OpenNMT-tf[7] (Klein et al., 2017), we build the following systems:

- Generic models trained with predefined mixtures of the training data taking the form:

$$\lambda_\alpha(d) = (\sum_{d=1}^{n_d} q_d^\alpha)^{-1}(q_d^\alpha) \quad q_d = \frac{|N_d^s|}{N^s} \quad (2)$$

  with $\alpha \in \{0, 0.25, 0.5, 0.75, 1.0\}$. We denote these as `Mixed-`$\alpha$ below. `Mixed-0` uses a uniform distribution, `Mixed-1.0` the empirical distribution of domains.

- fine-tuned models based on `Mixed-1.0`, further trained on each domain for at most 50 000 iterations, with early stopping when the dev BLEU stops increasing for 5 successive iterations. The fine-tuning (`FT-Full`) procedure updates all the parameters of the initial model, resulting in six systems, one per domain, with no parameter sharing across domains.

- systems trained with fixed mixtures with $\boldsymbol{\lambda}^l \in [\boldsymbol{\lambda}_0, \boldsymbol{\lambda}_{0.25}, \boldsymbol{\lambda}_{0.5}, \boldsymbol{\lambda}_{0.75}, \boldsymbol{\lambda}_{1.0}]$; these are used in the multidomain experiments of § 5.3;

- our implementations of dynamic sampling proposals from the literature: Curriculum Learning (CL) of Zhang et al. (2019) and Differential Data Selection (DDS) of Wang et al. (2020b) (see below);

All models use embeddings and hidden layers of dimension 512. Transformer models contain 8 attention heads in each of the 6+6 layers; the inner feedforward layer contains 2048 cells. Training lasts for 200K iterations, with batches of 12,288 tokens, Adam with parameters $\beta_1 = 0.9$, $\beta_2 = 0.98$, Noam decay ($warmup\_steps = 4000$), and a dropout rate of 0.1 in all layers.

4.3 CL and DDS re-implementations

We re-implement DDS in Tensorflow without any change in the choices of parameterization and hyper-parameters compared to the original code of Wang et al. (2020b).[8] We also re-implement the approach of Zhang et al. (2019) according to the authors' description. For each DA experiment, we combine the training data of all other domains into one corpus then compute the cross-entropy difference score of each source sentence of this combined dataset. We then sort and split the corpus into 9 shards and execute curriculum learning with 10 shards, using the in-domain data as the first shard.

4.4 MDAC systems

The behavior of MDAC only depends on (a) the initial domain distribution at the start of training $\boldsymbol{\lambda}^l_{t=0}$, and (b) the target (dev/test) distribution $\boldsymbol{\lambda}^t$. We thus report these systems as MDAC ($\boldsymbol{\lambda}^l_{t=0}$, $\boldsymbol{\lambda}^t$) and compare with DDS using the same settings.

In our work, we parameterize the distribution $\boldsymbol{\lambda}^l$ as follows (with $\beta = 2$ in all experiments):[9]

$$\lambda^l(d; \boldsymbol{\psi}) = \frac{\boldsymbol{\psi}[d]^\beta}{\sum_i \boldsymbol{\psi}[i]^\beta}.$$

[3] `http://opus.nlpl.eu`

[4] We use truecasing and `sacrebleu` (Post, 2018).

[5] `https://github.com/neulab/compare-mt`

[6] We however omit domain-specific systems trained only with the corresponding subset of the data, which are always inferior to the mix-domain strategy (Britz et al., 2017).

[7] `https://github.com/OpenNMT/OpenNMT-tf`

[8] `https://github.com/cindyxinyiwang/multiDDS`

[9] The *spherical softmax* in (de Brébisson and Vincent, 2016).

This parameterization avoids the "rich-get-richer" effect that we observe with $\boldsymbol{\lambda}(\boldsymbol{\psi}) = \text{softmax}(\boldsymbol{\psi})$, which yields gradients wrt. $\psi[d]$ that are proportional to $\exp(\psi[d])$ (see also Figure 2). Additional settings for the hyper-parameters of our method include the number of simulation steps $k = 10$ and the learning rate $\mathbf{lr}_{data} = 0.001$. We update the sampling distribution via 100 gradient descent iterations for almost all experimental settings except that for adaptation with automatic clusters (§ 5.5), where we use 20 gradient descent iterations to avoid converging to degenerate distributions. We split the training into 100 short sessions that last 2000 training steps each. The choice of those hyper-parameters is mostly heuristic except for the learning rate $\mathbf{lr}_{data}$ which is optimized via grid search over a set of values $\{0.001, 0.0025, 0.005\}$.

The computational cost of our approach is due to the simulation step, which is conducted after every 2,000 iterations to compute the reward of each domain (eq. (1)). During this step, we update the temporary checkpoint with k updates for each domain, which costs as much as k training updates. Therefore, we execute $k \times n_d$ updates after every 2,000 iterations. Our algorithm approximately costs $1 + \frac{k \times n_d}{2000}$ times as much as a standard training.

4.5 Experimental tasks

We evaluate our method in the 5 following conditions. In the *supervised domain adaptation task*, given the data from 6 domains (MED, BANK, LAW, IT, TALK, REL), we aim to build expert NMT models for each domain. To challenge the flexibility of the method, we also consider a *two-domain adaptation task*, where given the same 6 domains, we focus on adapting to a mixture of 2 domains. In the *multidomain adaptation task*, we use the same 6 domains to build one single NMT model that should perform optimally, assuming a uniform distribution of domains during the test. A fourth experiment (*unseen domain adaptation*), adds to the training data for 6 domains a small dev set in a new domain (NEWS): our target is a model which performs well for the unseen domain. Finally, in the *unsupervised domain adaptation task*, we cluster all available training data into 30 clusters using the KNN algorithm as in (Tars and Fishel, 2018), then learn mixture weights these clusters to one of 6 domains using the corresponding dev set. We compare MDAC to DDS for each of our 6 test sets.

5 Results and discussion

5.1 Domain Adaptation

In this setting, we aim to build an NMT model for one single domain: we accordingly set $\boldsymbol{\lambda}^t$ to a deterministic distribution $\boldsymbol{\lambda}_d$, where the target domain d has probability 1.

We consider three initializations for MDAC and DDS, using $\boldsymbol{\lambda}_0$, $\boldsymbol{\lambda}_1$ and $\boldsymbol{\lambda}_d$. According to Table 2, MDAC achieves the overall best performance when $\boldsymbol{\lambda}_{t=0} = \boldsymbol{\lambda}_0$. Doing so proves much better than initializing with $\boldsymbol{\lambda}_d$ for small domains: TALK, BANK and IT. Conversely, initializing with $\boldsymbol{\lambda}_d$ is beneficial when targeting large domains such as MED and LAW. The same conclusion holds for DDS.

We now compare the best MDAC system (using $\boldsymbol{\lambda}_{t=0} = \boldsymbol{\lambda}_0$) to full fine-tuning. According to Table 2, fine-tuning is better for large domains such as MED and LAW, while MDAC outperforms fine-tuning by approximately 1.2 BLEU for BANK and 1.0 BLEU for REL. This suggests that for small domains, out-of-domain data helps improve the generalization and that MDAC is able to exploit both the in-domain and the out-of-domain training data instead of edging out the out-of-domain training data as in fine-tuning. Results for DDS display similar trends but are always outperformed by MDAC. Results for CL, which does only well the large domain MED, lag somewhat behind.

5.2 Two-domain adaptation

In these control experiments, we showcase the flexibility of dynamic sampling and adapt to (arbitrary) pairs of target domains with equal weight, contrasting MDAC with DDS in Table 3. Here, MDAC significantly outperforms DDS in two settings (MED+IT and LAW+BANK) out of three.

5.3 Multi-domain NMT

We now turn to a more realistic scenario and consider multidomain NMT, which aims to train one single system with optimal performance averaged over 6 domains and targets a uniform test distribution $\boldsymbol{\lambda}^t = \boldsymbol{\lambda}_0$. In this situation, CL (Zhang et al., 2019) does not apply: we only contrast the performance of MDAC, DDS and several fixed training data distribution $\boldsymbol{\lambda}^l \in [\boldsymbol{\lambda}_0, \boldsymbol{\lambda}_{0.25}, \boldsymbol{\lambda}_{0.5}, \boldsymbol{\lambda}_{0.75}, \boldsymbol{\lambda}_{1.0}]$, where $\boldsymbol{\lambda}_\alpha$ is defined according to equation (2).

We again initialize MDAC and DDS with two distribution $\boldsymbol{\lambda}_0$ and $\boldsymbol{\lambda}_1$. According to Table 4, MDAC achieves the best performance with initial (uniform) $\boldsymbol{\lambda}_0$. The same conclusion holds for DDS. For this

domain $d=$	MED	LAW	BANK	TALK	IT	REL	avg.
FT-Full(d)	40.3	63.8	54.4	38.5	52.0	91.0	56.7
CL (d)	40.2	60.2	53.7	36.5	51.1	91.1	55.5
DDS (λ_0, λ_d)	39.6	60.1	55.0	38.5	52.5	92.0	56.3
MDAC (λ_0, λ_d)	39.6	62.5**	55.6*	38.5	52.4	92***	56.8
DDS (λ_1, λ_d)	39.7	53.9	49.6	37.9	43.1	64.3	48.1
MDAC (λ_1, λ_d)	40.2	59.9	52.6	38.5	50.7	79.8	53.6
DDS (λ_d, λ_d)	39.9	63.9	54.5	35.4	51.2	91.8	56.1
MDAC (λ_d, λ_d)	40.6	63.9	54.5	35.6	51.3	92.3	56.4

Table 2: Single domain adaptation. We report BLEU scores of each method for 6 target domains and their average: each column corresponds to a distinct system. (*) MDAC is significantly better than CL, fine-tuning and DDS with $p < 0.05$. (**) MDAC is significantly better than CL and DDS with $p < 0.05$. (***) MDAC is significantly better than CL, fine-tuning with $p < 0.05$.

configuration, MDAC outperforms static training distributions including $[\lambda_0, \lambda_{0.75}, \lambda_{1.0}]$ by a significant margin, and performs slightly better than $[\lambda_{0.25}, \lambda_{0.5}]$. Using MDAC thus dispenses with the empirical search of an optimal training mixture.

A second observation is that MDAC again outperforms DDS by a wide margin (+1.5 BLEU on average); the only domain where DDS does better is MED. Figure 2, which plots the evolution of the mixture weights during training, helps to understand the difference between the two methods. For DDS (Figure 2a), the sampling distribution quickly reaches a bi-modal regime in which only MED and REL have significant probability – hence the good performance on the former domain. In contrast, the distribution computed by MDAC evolves more smoothly; small domains such as BANK, IT, TALK and REL receive a larger part of training data in the early stages; their weights then slowly decrease as larger domains such as MED and LAW increase their share. This only happens at the end of training, when some NMT models might already be close to their peak performance for the small domains.

5.4 Unseen domain

The left part of Table 5 displays the performance on the unseen domain NEWS for systems trained with mixtures $\lambda^l \in [\lambda_0, \lambda_{0.25}, \lambda_{0.5}, \lambda_{0.75}, \lambda_{1.0}]$ and with dynamic data selection (MDAC and DDS). These systems have insignificant differences in BLEU, suggesting that dynamic mixtures do not improve the robustness of NMT systems against unseen domains. However, the performance of MDAC and DDS remains close to the best performance, showing that they also apply in such settings.

5.5 Automatic clustering

The right part of Table 5 reports the performance of NMT systems adapted to each domain. In comparison to Section 5.1, the training data is distributed in 30 automatic clusters instead of the 6 original domains. Splitting the train data into small groups gives the learner extra degrees of freedom when selecting the best distribution. However, as these clusters are built automatically, they are noisier in nature. According to results in Table 5, this scenario is hard both for DDS and MDAC, which performs much worse than for the supervised DA setting. This again signals the importance of initialization: analyzing the clustering, we find that the data for REL mostly correspond to one single cluster. With a uniform initialization, this cluster starts with a small weight and never succeeds in matching the good performance observed in the DA setting.

6 Related Work

Domain adaptation is an old problem that has been studied from many angles, both for SMT and NMT. A survey of supervised and unsupervised DA for NMT is in (Chu et al., 2017), where the authors distinguish between data-centric and model-centric DA, a view also adopted in the recent survey of Saunders (2021). Our approach to DA in this paper falls under the former category. We refer readers interested in DA to these papers.

Multidomain NMT (MDMT) aims to develop systems that simultaneously bode well for several domains. Like for DA, techniques for supervised MDMT combine one or several ingredients: (a) the specialization of data representations (Kobus et al., 2017) or of sub-networks (Pham et al., 2019) to differentiate the processing of each domain; (b) the use of adversarial techniques to neutralize differences between domains (Britz et al., 2017; Zeng et al., 2018); (c) the use of automatic domain identification e.g. (Jiang et al., 2020). Unsupervised MDMT is studied in (Farajian et al., 2017), as an instance of unsupervised DA.

Most approaches to adaptive/dynamic data selection take inspiration from Bengio et al. (2009), where the notion of curriculum learning is introduced. CL relies on the notion of the "easiness" of

domain $d =$	MED	LAW	BANK	TALK	IT	REL
DDS ($\boldsymbol{\lambda}_0, \boldsymbol{\lambda}_2$)	39.5	-	-	-	50.1	-
MDAC ($\boldsymbol{\lambda}_0, \boldsymbol{\lambda}_2$)	39.1	-	-	-	51.8*	-
DDS ($\boldsymbol{\lambda}_0, \boldsymbol{\lambda}_2$)	-	60.8	53.3	-	-	-
MDAC ($\boldsymbol{\lambda}_0, \boldsymbol{\lambda}_2$)	-	61.9*	54.5*	-	-	-
DDS ($\boldsymbol{\lambda}_0, \boldsymbol{\lambda}_2$)	-	-	-	37.9	-	91.3
MDAC ($\boldsymbol{\lambda}_0, \boldsymbol{\lambda}_2$)	-	-	-	36.9	-	90.4

Table 3: Adapting to two domains. For a given line, non empty columns correspond to the pair of target domains. (*) MDAC is significantly better than DDS with $p < 0.05$.

domain $d =$	MED	LAW	BANK	TALK	IT	REL	mean
Mixed-0	38.6	59.3	53.7	37.3	51.0	90.4	55.1
Mixed-0.25	38.9	59.6	53.3	37.6	50.5	90.6	55.1
Mixed-0.5	39.0	60.2	52.5	38.5	51.9	90.3	55.4
Mixed-0.75	39.4	59.9	51.9	38.8	50.0	87.6	54.6
Mixed-1	40.3	59.5	49.8	36.4	49.0	80.0	52.5
DDS ($\boldsymbol{\lambda}_0, \boldsymbol{\lambda}_0$)	40.1	56.9	50.7	37.4	46.8	92.0	54.0
MDAC ($\boldsymbol{\lambda}_0, \boldsymbol{\lambda}_0$)	38.5	60.3**	54.4*	37.3	51.3**	91.4*	55.5**
DDS ($\boldsymbol{\lambda}_1, \boldsymbol{\lambda}_0$)	40.6	55.5	48.0	36.2	46.9	60.1	47.9
MDAC ($\boldsymbol{\lambda}_1, \boldsymbol{\lambda}_0$)	40.2	59.3**	51.0**	36.9**	48.6**	80.7**	52.8**

Table 4: Multidomain adaptation. For a given line, all the columns *correspond to the same multi-domain system.* (*) MDAC is significantly better than Mixed-α with $p < 0.05$. (**) MDAC is significantly better than DDS with $p < 0.05$.

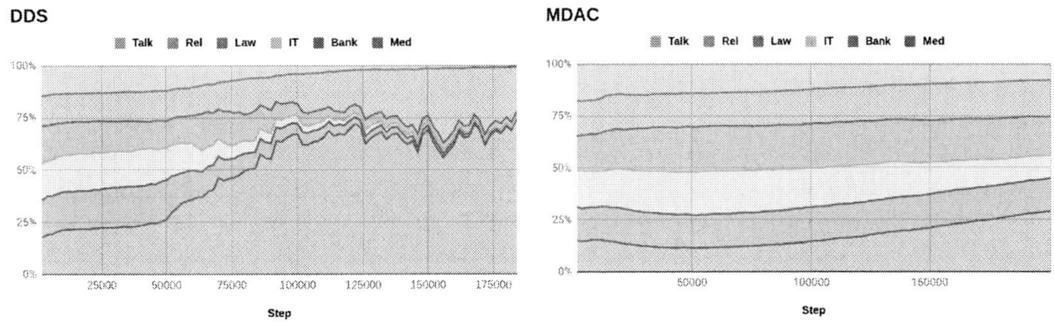

(a) DDS (b) MDAC

Figure 2: Evolution of the sampling distribution during training.

domain $d =$	NEWS
Unseen domain	
Mixed-0	25.7
Mixed-0.25	25.8
Mixed-0.5	26.5
Mixed-0.75	26.8
Mixed-1	26.9
DDS ($\boldsymbol{\lambda}_0, \boldsymbol{\lambda}_{news}$)	26.3
MDAC ($\boldsymbol{\lambda}_0, \boldsymbol{\lambda}_{news}$)	26.3

domain $d =$	MED	LAW	BANK	TALK	IT	REL	mean
Training with 30 clusters							
DDS ($\boldsymbol{\lambda}^*, \boldsymbol{\lambda}_d$)	38.3	60.1	50.3	35.8	49.1	90.1	53.9
MDAC ($\boldsymbol{\lambda}^*, \boldsymbol{\lambda}_d$)	39.2*	61.6*	52.0*	38.2*	49.1	89.7	55.0*

Table 5: Unseen domain adaptation (left) and automatic clustering adaptation (right). For a given line, each column corresponds to one distinct system. (*) MDAC is significantly better than DDS.

a sample to schedule the presentation of training data so as to start with the easiest examples and end with the hardest. Various ways to automate CL in the framework of multi-armed bandits are explored in (Graves et al., 2017), which has been an inspiration for our implementation. While the initial aim was primarily to improve and speed up training, CL has also proven useful for multidomain and multilingual MT, based on alternative definitions of "easiness". For instance, Zhang et al. (2019) study supervised DA and propose a curriculum approach which progressively augments the training data: early stages only use in-data, while less relevant[10] data are introduced in later stages. This is opposite to the policy of van der Wees et al. (2017), whose *gradual fine-tuning* progressively increases the focus on in-domain data.

Kumar et al. (2019) use reinforcement learning to learn the curriculum strategy: in this work, complexity corresponds to difficulty levels which are binned using contrastive data selection. The reward is based on the increase of the devset loss that results from the current data selection strategy. This technique is applied to multilingual NMT in (Kumar et al., 2021). Zhou et al. (2020) propose another CL-based approach which relies on *instance uncertainty* as a measure of their difficulty and presents data samples starting with the easiest. Another contribution of this work is a new stopping criterium. Closest to our problems, Wang et al. (2020a) adapt CL for multidomain NMT, where an optimal instance weighting scheme is found using Bayesian optimization techniques. Each step consists of (a) weighting instances based on relevance features, (b) fine-tuning a pretrained model using the weighted training set, and is applied to train a sequence of models. The one that maximizes the devset performance is finally retained.

7 Conclusion and outlook

In this study, we have presented a generic framework to perform multiple adaptation tasks for machine translation, ranging from supervised domain adaptation to multidomain NMT and unseen domain adaptation. In our experiments, we have shown that the same algorithm, aimed at automatically finding an effective data sampling scheme during the course of training, can be used in all these situations. This algorithm, we believe, provides us with a more sound approach to (multi-domain) DA than existing heuristics and dispenses with the costly search of optimal meta-parameters. Another contribution of our work is an experimental comparison of recent approaches to dynamic data selection.

Our future work will continue developing this approach and improve its effectiveness. One issue that we have left unaddressed is reward normalization, which is especially important in the early stages of training (Kumar et al., 2019). Another area where we need to progress is the unsupervised learning setting of § 5.5, where our results lag behind supervised DA. This might be due to the inability of our simplistic optimization strategy to handle situations where the number of clusters is large.

[10]Domain distance is computed with Lewis-Moore scores (based on the cross-entropy of in-domain LM).

References

Aharoni, Roee, Melvin Johnson, and Orhan Firat. 2019. Massively multilingual neural machine translation. In *Proceedings of the Conference of the North American Chapter of the Association for Computational Linguistics*, pages 3874–3884, Minneapolis, USA.

Axelrod, Amittai, Xiaodong He, and Jianfeng Gao. 2011. Domain adaptation via pseudo in-domain data selection. In *Proceedings of the Conference on Empirical Methods in Natural Language Processing*, pages 355–362, Edinburgh, UK.

Bengio, Yoshua, Jérôme Louradour, Ronan Collobert, and Jason Weston. 2009. Curriculum learning. In *Proceedings of the 26th International Conference on Machine Learning*, page 41–48, Montréal, Canada.

Britz, Denny, Quoc Le, and Reid Pryzant. 2017. Effective domain mixing for neural machine translation. In *Proceedings of the Second Conference on Machine Translation*, pages 118–126, Copenhagen, Denmark.

Cettolo, Mauro, Christian Girardi, and Marcello Federico. 2012. Wit^3: Web inventory of transcribed and translated talks. In *Proceedings of the 16th Conference of the European Association for Machine Translation*, pages 261–268, Trento, Italy.

Chen, Wenhu, Evgeny Matusov, Shahram Khadivi, and Jan-Thorsten Peter. 2016. Guided alignment training for topic-aware neural machine translation. In *Proceedings of the Conference of the Association for Machine Translation in the Americas*, Austin, USA.

Chu, Chenhui and Raj Dabre. 2018. Multilingual and multi-domain adaptation for neural machine translation. In *Proceedings of the 24st Meeting of the Association for Natural Language Processing*, pages 909—912, Okayama, Japan.

Chu, Chenhui, Raj Dabre, and Sadao Kurohashi. 2017. An empirical comparison of domain adaptation methods for neural machine translation. In *Proceedings of the 55th Annual Meeting of the Association for Computational Linguistics*, pages 385–391, Vancouver, Canada.

de Brébisson, Alexandre and Pascal Vincent. 2016. An exploration of softmax alternatives belonging to the spherical loss family. In Bengio, Y. and Y. LeCun, editors, *Proceedings of the 4th International Conference on Learning Representation*, San Juan, Puerto Rico.

Farajian, M. Amin, Marco Turchi, Matteo Negri, and Marcello Federico. 2017. Multi-domain neural machine translation through unsupervised adaptation. In *Proceedings of the Second Conference on Machine Translation*, pages 127–137, Copenhagen, Denmark.

Firat, Orhan, Kyunghyun Cho, and Yoshua Bengio. 2016. Multi-way, multilingual neural machine translation with a shared attention mechanism. In *Proceedings of the Conference of the North American Chapter of the Association for Computational Linguistics*, pages 866–875.

Graves, Alex, Marc G. Bellemare, Jacob Menick, Rémi Munos, and Koray Kavukcuoglu. 2017. Automated curriculum learning for neural networks. In Precup, D. and Y.-W. Teh, editors, *Proceedings of the 34th International Conference on Machine Learning*, volume 70, pages 1311–1320.

Ha, Thanh-He, Jan Niehues, and Alex Waibel. 2016. Toward multilingual neural machine translation with universal encoder and decoder. In *Proceedings of the 13th International Workshop on Spoken Language Translation*, Vancouver, Canada.

Hoffman, Judy, Mehryar Mohri, and Ningshan Zhang. 2018. Algorithms and theory for multiple-source adaptation. In Bengio, S., H. Wallach, H. Larochelle, K. Grauman, N. Cesa-Bianchi, and R. Garnett, editors, *Advances in Neural Information Processing Systems 31*, pages 8246–8256.

Jiang, Haoming, Chen Liang, Chong Wang, and Tuo Zhao. 2020. Multi-domain neural machine translation with word-level adaptive layer-wise domain mixing. In *Proceedings of the 58th Annual Meeting of the Association for Computational Linguistics*, pages 1823–1834, Online.

Johnson, Melvin, Mike Schuster, Quoc Le, Maxim Krikun, Yonghui Wu, Zhifeng Chen, Nikhil Thorat, Fernand a Viégas, Martin Wattenberg, Greg Corrado, Macduff Hughes, and Jeffrey Dean. 2017. Google's multilingual neural machine translation system: Enabling zero-shot translation. *Transactions of the Association for Computational Linguistics*, 5:339–351.

Klein, Guillaume, Yoon Kim, Yuntian Deng, Jean Senellart, and Alexander Rush. 2017. OpenNMT: Open-source toolkit for neural machine translation. In *Proceedings of ACL*, pages 67–72, Vancouver, Canada.

Kobus, Catherine, Josep Crego, and Jean Senellart. 2017. Domain control for neural machine translation. In *Proceedings of the International Conference Recent Advances in Natural Language Processing*, pages 372–378, Varna, Bulgaria.

Koehn, Philipp, Huda Khayrallah, Kenneth Heafield, and Mikel L. Forcada. 2018. Findings of the WMT 2018 shared task on parallel corpus filtering. In *Proceedings of the Third Conference on Machine Translation*, pages 726–739, Belgium, Brussels.

Koehn, Philipp. 2004. Statistical significance tests for machine translation evaluation. In *Proceedings of the Conference on Empirical Methods in Natural Language Processing*, pages 388–395, Barcelona, Spain.

Kumar, Gaurav, George Foster, Colin Cherry, and Maxim Krikun. 2019. Reinforcement learning based curriculum optimization for neural machine translation. In *Proceedings of the Conference of the North American Chapter of the Association for Computational Linguistics*, pages 2054–2061, Minneapolis, USA.

Kumar, Gaurav, Philipp Koehn, and Sanjeev Khudanpur. 2021. Learning policies for multilingual training of neural machine translation systems. *CoRR*, abs/2103.06964.

Luong, Minh-Thang and Christopher D. Manning. 2015. Stanford neural machine translation systems for spoken language domain. In *Proceedings of the International Workshop on Spoken Language Translation*, Da Nang, Vietnam.

Mansour, Yishay, Mehryar Mohri, and Afshin Rostamizadeh. 2009a. Domain adaptation with multiple sources. In Koller, D., D. Schuurmans, Y. Bengio, and L. Bottou, editors, *Advances in Neural Information Processing Systems 21*, pages 1041–1048.

Mansour, Yishay, Mehryar Mohri, and Afshin Rostamizadeh. 2009b. Multiple source adaptation and the Rényi divergence. In *Proceedings of the 25th Conference on Uncertainty in Artificial Intelligence*, pages 367–374.

Miceli Barone, Antonio Valerio, Barry Haddow, Ulrich Germann, and Rico Sennrich. 2017. Regularization techniques for fine-tuning in neural machine translation. In *Proceedings of the Conference on Empirical Methods in Natural Language Processing*, pages 1489–1494, Copenhagen, Denmark.

Moore, Robert C. and William Lewis. 2010. Intelligent selection of language model training data. In *Proceedings of ACL*, pages 220–224, Uppsala, Sweden.

Neubig, Graham, Zi-Yi Dou, Junjie Hu, Paul Michel, Danish Pruthi, Xinyi Wang, and John Wieting. 2019. compare-mt: A tool for holistic comparison of language generation systems. *CoRR*, abs/1903.07926.

Niu, Xing, Sudha Rao, and Marine Carpuat. 2018. Multi-task neural models for translating between styles within and across languages. In Bender, E., L. Derczynski, and P. Isabelle, editors, *Proceedings of the International Conference on Computational Linguistics*, pages 1008–1021, Santa Fe, USA.

Pan, Sinno Jialin and Qiang Yang. 2010. A survey on transfer learning. *IEEE Transactions on Knowledge and Data Engineering*, 22(10):1345–1359.

Papineni, Kishore, Salim Roukos, Todd Ward, and Wei-Jing Zhu. 2002. BLEU: a method for automatic evaluation of machine translation. In *Proceedings of the 40th Annual Meeting on Association for Computational Linguistics*, pages 311–318.

Pham, Minh Quang, Josep-Maria Crego, Jean Senellart, and François Yvon. 2019. Generic and Specialized Word Embeddings for Multi-Domain Machine Translation. In *Proceedings of the 16th International Workshop on Spoken Language Translation*, page 9p, Hong-Kong, China.

Pham, Minh Quang, Josep Crego, and François Yvon. 2021. Revisiting multi-domain machine translation. *Transactions of the Association for Computational Linguistics*, 9(0):17–35.

Post, Matt. 2018. A call for clarity in reporting BLEU scores. In *Proceedings of the Third Conference on Machine Translation*, pages 186–191, Brussels, Belgium.

Saunders, Danielle. 2021. Domain adaptation and multi-domain adaptation for neural machine translation: A survey. *CoRR*, abs/2104.06951.

Sennrich, Rico, Barry Haddow, and Alexandra Birch. 2016. Neural machine translation of rare words with subword units. In *Proceedings of the 54th Annual Meeting of the Association for Computational Linguistics (Volume 1: Long Papers)*, pages 1715–1725, Berlin, Germany.

Steinberger, Ralf, Bruno Pouliquen, Anna Widiger, Camelia Ignat, Tomaž Erjavec, Dan Tufis, and Dániel Varga. 2006. The JRC-Acquis: A multilingual aligned parallel corpus with 20+ languages. In *Proceedings of the Fifth International Conference on Language Resources and Evaluation*, Genoa, Italy.

Tars, Sander and Mark Fishel. 2018. Multi-domain neural machine translation. In Pérez-Ortiz, J.-A., F. Sánchez-Martínez, M. Esplà-Gomis, M. Popović, C. Rico, A. Martins, J. Van den Bogaert, and M. Forcada, editors, *Proceedings of the 21st Annual Conference of the European Association for Machine Translation*, pages 259–269, Alicante, Spain.

van der Wees, Marlies, Arianna Bisazza, and Christof Monz. 2017. Dynamic data selection for neural machine translation. In *Proceedings of the 2017 Conference on Empirical Methods in Natural Language Processing*, pages 1400–1410, Copenhagen, Denmark.

Vaswani, Ashish, Noam Shazeer, Niki Parmar, Jakob Uszkoreit, Llion Jones, Aidan N. Gomez, Łukasz Kaiser, and Illia Polosukhin. 2017. Attention is all you need. In Guyon, I., U. V. Luxburg, S. Bengio, H. Wallach, R. Fergus, S. Vishwanathan, and R. Garnett, editors, *Advances in Neural Information Processing Systems 30*, pages 5998–6008.

Wang, Wei, Ye Tian, Jiquan Ngiam, Yinfei Yang, Isaac Caswell, and Zarana Parekh. 2020a. Learning a multi-domain curriculum for neural machine translation. In *Proceedings of the 58th Annual Meeting of the Association for Computational Linguistics*, pages 7711–7723, Online.

Wang, Xinyi, Yulia Tsvetkov, and Graham Neubig. 2020b. Balancing training for multilingual neural machine translation. In *Proceedings of the 58th Annual Meeting of the Association for Computational Linguistics*, pages 8526–8537, Online.

Williams, Ronald J. 1992. Simple statistical gradient-following algorithms for connectionist reinforcement learning. *Machine learning*, 8(3-4):229–256.

Zeng, Jiali, Jinsong Su, Huating Wen, Yang Liu, Jun Xie, Yongjing Yin, and Jianqiang Zhao. 2018. Multi-domain neural machine translation with word-level domain context discrimination. In *Proceedings of the Conference on Empirical Methods in Natural Language Processing*, pages 447–457, Brussels, Belgium.

Zhang, Jian, Liangyou Li, Andy Way, and Qun Liu. 2016. Topic-informed neural machine translation. In *Proceedings of the International Conference on Computational Linguistics*, pages 1807–1817, Osaka, Japan.

Zhang, Xuan, Pamela Shapiro, Gaurav Kumar, Paul McNamee, Marine Carpuat, and Kevin Duh. 2019. Curriculum learning for domain adaptation in neural machine translation. In *Proceedings of the Conference of the North American Chapter of the Association for Computational Linguistics*, pages 1903–1915, Minneapolis, USA.

Zhou, Yikai, Baosong Yang, Derek F. Wong, Yu Wan, and Lidia S. Chao. 2020. Uncertainty-aware curriculum learning for neural machine translation. In *Proceedings of the 58th Meeting of the Association for Computational Linguistics*, pages 6934–6944, Online.

The use of online translators by students not enrolled in a professional translation program: beyond copying and pasting for a professional use

Rudy Loock
Benjamin Holt
Université de Lille and Savoirs, Textes, Langage CNRS research unit
651 Avenue des Nations-Unies 59100 Roubaix, France
rudy.loock@univ-lille.fr
benjamin.holt@univ-lille.fr

Sophie Léchauguette
Université de Lille and ULR 40 74 – CECILLE
651 Avenue des Nations-Unies 59100 Roubaix, France
sophie.lechauguette@univ-lille.fr

Abstract

In this paper, we discuss a use of machine translation (MT) that has been quite overlooked up to now, namely by students *not* enrolled in a professional translation program. A number of studies have reported massive use of free online translators (OTs), and it seems important to uncover such users' abilities and difficulties when using MT output, whether to improve their understanding, writing, or translation skills. We report here a study on students enrolled in a French 'applied languages program' (where students study two languages, as well as law, economics, and management). The aim was to uncover how they use OTs, as well as their (in)ability to identify and correct MT errors. Obtained through two online surveys and several tests conducted with students from 2020 to 2022, our results show an unsurprising widespread use of OTs for many different tasks, but also some specific difficulties in identifying MT errors, in particular in relation to target language fluency.

1 Introduction

Most professional translation training programs now include specific training on machine translation (MT) and post-editing (MTPE). MT-related skills, in connection with project management, are for instance an important component of the European Commission Directorate-General for Translation's competence framework for the European Master's in Translation network (DGT, 2017). A lot of research has already been done on such students' ability to post-edit MT output and on how to teach professional MT skills for the translation market. However, a professional use of MT is not restricted to the translation industry; for example, free OTs might also be used by tourism or international relations professionals, and before that by students of such disciplines. Not a lot of research has been done on this issue so far, and our work aims to help fill such a gap by studying how students enrolled in a French applied languages program, where they study two languages in addition to law, economics, and management, actually use OTs. We believe more research is necessary on the use of MT outside the translation industry, especially as no specific training is generally provided (see below), and as there is a link between MT use and language acquisition (Resende and Way, 2020, 2021). Also, raising awareness concerning the capabilities and limits of using OTs is all the more crucial these days because of (i) a real improvement in the quality of MT output since the advent of neural MT (NMT), and (ii) the biased perception of the general public, including students who never received any specific training. This bias is related, on the one hand, to contempt for the technology (see the numerous, supposedly funny MT fails all over the internet) and on the other hand to the belief that translators are obsolete because MT has reached "human parity".

Macken, Rufener, Van den Bogaert, Daems, Tezcan, Vanroy, Fonteyne, Barrault, Costa-jussà, Kemp, Pilos, Declercq, Koponen, Forcada, Scarton, Moniz (eds.)
Proceedings of the 23rd Annual Conference of the European Association for Machine Translation, p. 23–29
Ghent, Belgium, June 2022.

2 Research questions and methodology

A number of studies have shown that a very large majority of students regularly use OTs (e.g. O'Neill, 2019; Resende and Way, 2021; Loock and Léchauguette, 2021; Dorst et al., 2022), for both graded and non-graded work, and regardless of whether this is allowed by their institution. While these studies focus on students enrolled in language programs or with a background in humanities, there is no reason to consider that other students do not use OTs. And yet, this widespread use generally takes place without any specific training: according to Benites et al. (2021), for example, 77.1% of trainers in 4 Swiss universities (n=666) did not mention OTs, and 83.9% of the students (n=1,926) claimed that they had never received any specific guidelines on the use of MT. This makes MT a real "elephant in the classroom" (Loock et al., to appear). However, recently, researchers have been working on how to help MT users outside the translation industry adopt a critical approach (see Bowker and Buitrago Ciro (2019) for the research community, or Bowker (2020) for international business students for suggestions, which both put forward the concept "MT literacy", see below).

From this starting point, we decided to investigate the use of OTs by our students, in order to understand their uses and also to measure their efficiency when using MT output. To do so, we submitted groups of students to an online questionnaire (in 2020 and 2021) and to different types of exercises meant to evaluate their capacity to identify and correct errors in English-French MT output. This is ongoing research, as after a pilot study (Loock and Léchauguette, 2021) to get an overview of our starting point, we have been trying to find the best ways to train (and evaluate) our students' capacity to use OTs, hence regular tests since 2020. As discussed below, this is not an easy task, with students finding it hard to identify MT errors. The different tests aim to determine whether the language direction, the necessity to both identify and correct MT errors vs. only correct errors identified for them, the order of presentation for the original input and MT output, have an influence on our students' performance.

Our students' profile

Our students are applied languages students, which in the French academic context means that they major in English and another language, and attend economics, law, and management classes. The three-year program includes pedagogical translation classes from the second to the sixth semesters, in which they translate press texts, tourism brochures, extracts from websites, or infographics, with a pedagogical approach meant to help them develop their language skills. The classes do not focus on professional translation training. Specifically, our study was conducted on undergraduate students in their third and final year from the 2019–2020 to 2021–2022 academic years at the University of Lille, France. Most students go on to work in tourism, international relations, international commerce, and for some of them, the translation industry. All students who took part in our study are native speakers of French; international students' responses were not included in our analysis.

Methodology

Two groups of students anonymously completed an online survey in March 2020 (n=159) and in September 2021 (n=164). They were explicitly assured of the anonymity of their answers so that they could feel free to reply honestly (for some students – and some trainers – using OTs might be considered cheating). The questions dealt with which OTs were used, how they were used, why they were used, and overall satisfaction.

Between March 2020 and December 2021, three groups of students took a series of tests. They had to identify and/or correct errors in the MT output. The first test (part of our pilot study and conducted in March 2020) consisted in an English press text that had been machine translated into French with DeepL (https://www.deepl.com/translator). The instructions were to correct all accuracy and fluency errors in the MT output (no justifications were required). The evaluators had pre-identified a series of 20 errors (see examples in (1) and in Loock and Léchauguette, 2021 for a complete list) and the aim was to measure the number and types of errors identified and corrected by the students.

(1) a. The line in front of the Louis Vuitton store was barely a line by Paris standards.
MT output: La file d'attente devant le magasin Louis Vuitton était à peine plus longue que celle de Paris (accuracy issue)
Example of expected correction: La file n'avait rien de la file d'attente parisienne typique/ne ressemblait pas à une file d'attente parisienne traditionnelle
b. [I]t snakes around the back.
MT output: [E]lle serpente dans le dos (accuracy issue due to lexical ambiguity of *back*)

Example of expected correction: [E]lle serpente jusqu'à l'arrière du magasin.
c. after an 80-year-old Chinese tourist died of the virus
MT output: après qu'un touriste chinois de 80 ans soit mort du virus (grammar mistake, wrong mood)
Example of expected correction: après qu'un touriste chinois est mort/après la mort d'un touriste chinois

The second test (April 2021) introduced two changes: (i) the translation direction was now French→English, and (ii) a series of sentences were given instead of a text, with a hint that each sentence contained at least one error to be corrected – some examples are provided in (2):

(2) a. Ce dispositif, qui est rendu public seulement quelques jours avant son entrée en vigueur, vient contrarier de nombreux projets de départs organisés par les agences de voyages et les tour-opérateurs.
MT output: This device, which is made public only a few days before its entry into force, thwarts many departure projects organized by travel agencies and tour operators. (accuracy issue: lexical ambiguity of *dispositif*)
Example of expected correction: This system, which was made public a few days before being enforced, has hampered/thwarted many plans for departures organized by travel agencies and tour operators.
b. Fréquentation en berne, absence des touristes étrangers… L'année 2020 s'est révélée morne sur le plan touristique.
MT output: Attendance at half-mast, absence of foreign tourists... The year 2020 has turned out to be a dull year for tourism. (accuracy/fluency issue: literal translation of idiomatic expression)
Example of expected correction: With visits declining and no foreign tourists, 2020 has turned out to be a dismal year for tourism.

A third test (December 2021) introduced a new element: evaluators underlined parts of the French MT output with English as a source language (words, strings of words) meant to be corrected by the students (the identification part of the process was therefore done for them). Examples are provided in (3):

(3) a. "Do you get them from supermarket bins?" I asked them. They told me they regularly collected and redistributed the contents of the big skip-like bins behind supermarkets.
MT output: « **Les obtenez-vous** dans les poubelles des supermarchés ? » leur ai-je demandé. Ils m'ont dit qu'ils récupéraient et redistribuaient régulièrement le contenu **des grandes bennes à benne** derrière les supermarchés. (fluency issue: unnatural word order and choice of verb; nonsensical translation of *skip-like bins*)
Example of expected correction: « Vous les trouvez dans les poubelles des supermarchés ? » leur ai-je demandé. Ils m'ont répondu qu'ils récupéraient et redistribuaient régulièrement le contenu des grandes bennes à ordures derrière les supermarchés.
b. I had heard of people bin-diving before and I was captivated by their story.
MT output: J'avais déjà entendu parler de personnes **faisant de la plongée sous-marine** et j'ai été captivé par leur histoire. (accuracy issue : *bin-diving* interpreted as *scuba-diving*).
Example of expected correction: J'avais déjà entendu parler de personnes qui fouillaient dans les poubelles et j'ai été captivé par leur histoire.

A fourth test was implemented in April 2022 to test a new hypothesis: instead of presenting students with a table showing the original sentences in English on the left and the MT outputs on the right, the reverse was done to check whether reading the MT output first helps them to better identify fluency-related issues (avoiding a "priming effect", see discussion). The results of this test are being processed at the time of writing this paper.

All texts belonged to the press genre, a type of text that students are familiar with thanks to their translation classes, and all MT outputs were obtained via the free version of DeepL with no modifications whatsoever. The students were presented with the source text and the MT output side by side (the English original text on the left and the MT output on the right, except for the fourth test).

3 Results

In line with the few studies mentioned above, our results confirmed that our students are regular users of online translators: 83% in the first survey and 78% in the second answered that they used OTs on a regular basis, mostly DeepL (8 students out of 10) and Google Translate (3 students out of 10).
However, the mentioning of WordReference (https://www.wordreference.com) and Linguee (https://www.linguee.com/) in the category 'other OTs' indicates some confusion as to what an OT

– and therefore MT – is. According to our survey, students use OTs for many different kinds of tasks: translation tasks of course (80% of students), but also as writing aids (45% of students), e.g. when writing an essay, as a comprehension tool (50% of students), and as a grammatical tool (16% of students) for help with grammar exercises.

Students do not seem to be informed users, since they do not systematically provide enough context to obtain relevant MT output: only 5% of them actually copy/paste full texts; instead, they generally type words or parts of sentences (40% of students). Nevertheless, 80% are satisfied with what OTs have to offer (40% often, and another 40% sometimes). A large majority of students (93.8% in the first survey, 83.3% in the second one) thought that they were able to identify MT errors, either with no difficulty whatsoever or quite easily.

However, such confidence is blatantly contradicted by the results obtained in the different tests, with students clearly overestimating their ability to correct errors in the MT output. Out of the 20 errors identified by the evaluators in the first test, only 5.29 on average (1 out of 4) were correctly identified and corrected, with another 2.29 identified but wrongly corrected, meaning that 12.42 (nearly 2 out of 3) were simply overlooked by the students (n=159). In the second test, some improvement was noticed despite the fact that the MT output was now in a foreign language for the students (n=196). This time, thanks to the segmentation into sentences, an average of 10.2 errors out of 23 (that is a 44% success rate) were correctly identified. Still, more than half of the MT errors were overlooked, and only half (56%) of those identified were actually corrected in a relevant way. Finally, the third test, in which the students (n=158) only had to correct the pre-identified errors in the MT output, showed a real improvement with 67% of cases of relevant corrections.

In the different tests, a qualitative analysis of students' corrections showed that students tend to focus more on lexical choices than on the syntactic organization of the sentences, and are better at identifying accuracy issues than fluency issues.

4 Discussion

The results of our two surveys and series of tests clearly show that in spite of a very widespread use of OTs, for many different tasks ranging from understanding a text to actually translating it, our language students fail to use OTs effectively and are not sufficiently able to identify and correct errors in the MT output. In other words, they need to develop their "MT literacy", a concept put forward by Bowker and Buitrago Ciro (2019: 88) to refer to a series of skills in relation to users' capacity to understand how MT systems work, when it is relevant to use them, and when and how to modify MT output.

We can think of two possible explanations for our results which clearly show a lack of critical thinking when using OTs while "a healthy level of mistrust in [MT] output" or a kind of "healthy skepticism" (O'Brien and Ehrensberger-Dow, 2020) are required (OTs are no calculators). First, since our students find it particularly hard to identify MT errors related to the fluency of the target language, one might think they have a poor command of the target language's linguistic system, even when the target language is their native language. For example, the choice of a wrong mood in (2c) clearly shows that a grammatical rule is not known (74% of our students left the mood unchanged). Also, as we noticed direct calques that were left unchanged, it seems that our students are influenced, or "heavily primed", by the MT output that they see on the screen (see Carl and Schaeffer (2017) for the concept of priming). This has already been noted for professional post-editors, who "more easily accept sub-optimal translations which human translators, working from scratch, would otherwise not produce" (Carl and Schaeffer, 2017: 44). This might explain why our students are better at correcting MT errors when these have been identified for them (results of third test).

Specific training for an informed, professional, and critical use of OTs thus seems necessary. To address this need, we have introduced specific training in the translation class for our third-year students (hence perhaps the decrease from 93.8% to 83.3% between our two surveys in the rate of students who consider that they are able to identify MT errors). Our approach combines a theoretical and a practical approach. First, it seems important to address some technical considerations by defining what an OT is, how it differs from other online tools such as dictionaries or concordancers, and how it works (roughly) so that they understand why results vary from one OT to another and over time. Through comparisons between OTs, students can then be made aware of the importance of the corpus data behind the tool.

Also, thanks to the prolific scientific literature on the subject, a list of recurring MT errors can be provided to sensitize students to the limits of OTs. These cover language-independent errors: issues related to lexical/syntactic ambiguities, idiomatic expressions, word play, neologisms or rare words, proper names, omissions, production of non-existing words (Macken et al., 2019, De Clercq et al., 2021), algorithmic bias leading to lesser lexical variety (Vanmassenhove et al., 2019), gender bias (Salvodi et al., 2021), and literal translations leading to an over-/under-representation of some linguistic features in MT output (Loock, 2020; De Clercq et al., 2021). MT errors can also be language-dependent: for the English-French language pair, issues include the translation of compounds, the present perfect, or pronouns. All these issues (see Loock et al., to appear, for concrete examples) should not lead students to believe that MT output is systematically full of errors. However, they can help them become aware of the existence of so-called "machine translationese", and of the need for human intervention in the form of post-editing. Raising students' awareness of ethical considerations is also necessary for an informed use in a professional context other than the translation industry. These include confidentiality issues, the environmental impact of the technology (Strubell et al., 2019), and also the fact that MT engines are trained on data produced by human translators. Students should be sensitized to a "fair use" of OTs (Moorkens et al., 2020), and teaching institutions need to implement clear policies.

Practical training may include different activities, such as the correction of MT output, but also the comparison between output from different OTs, and between MT output and 'human' translation. Making students aware of functionalities that allow them to choose between alternative solutions can help them realize that the MT output on the screen is but one possibility among many: DeepL allows users to see other possible translations in a drop-down list when they click on a word in the MT output, and Google Translate provides alternative translations for the whole sentence. Such a dynamic approach to online translators, far from simply copying and pasting, then makes the use of OTs a decision-making process. The final goal should be to empower students with the skills necessary to use OTs independently and critically on their own.

Finally, we would like to stress that our students' difficulties in dealing with MT output are not isolated. MT is a challenge for everyone these days, and being able to use MT critically is also a challenge for translation students as well as translation professionals. The fact that MT errors have become more human-like with the development of NMT makes them harder to identify (and correct) for translation trainees (Yamada, 2019) and professionals (Castilho et al., 2017). Our non-translation students' difficulties should therefore come as no surprise, and it is actually incumbent upon trainers to ensure that OTs are integrated efficiently into students' set of online language tools alongside different types dictionaries (with or without concordancers and thesauruses), corpus tools, and grammar checkers.

5 Conclusion

In this paper, we cited our own studies that showed widespread use of OTs among students, combined with a striking inability of these same students to identify and correct errors in MT output. This led us to advocate for specific training on online translators/machine translation for students not enrolled in a professional translation program, for an informed, professional use. Like other studies, ours has shown that OTs are widely used by students, who nevertheless still need to develop their MT literacy. While a lot of attention has been paid to how to train translators translators-to-be, the use of machine translation by other categories of students is often overlooked (no training or guidelines by trainers or institutions), making the use of OTs an "elephant in the classroom".

In order to train students from all disciplines other than professional translation studies, specific pedagogical material is needed. In addition to the scientific literature mentioned above, some projects aim to make such material accessible, e.g., the European MultiTraINMT project (Machine Translation training for multilingual citizens, http://www.multitrainmt.eu) or the Machine Translation Literacy project (https://sites.google.com/view/machinetranslationliteracy/). As for the specific case of our students, an example-based methodology to sensitize them to recurring issues is being developed (Loock et al., to appear). Further research is however still needed to uncover the best way to introduce specific training on OTs: so far, as our findings demonstrate that students still encounter difficulties in identifying MT errors, training could emphasize the use of grammatical categories and sentence analysis as a means to strengthen students' fluency in the target language, be it their mother tongue or not. Being familiar with and using basic grammatical notions to analyze MT output is necessary for a professional use of OT.

References

Bowker, Lynne. 2020. Machine translation literacy instruction for international business students and business English instructors. *Journal of Business & Finance Librarianship*, 25(1-2): 25–43.

Bowker, Lynne, and Buitrago Ciro, J. 2019. *Machine Translation and global research: Towards improved machine translation literacy in the scholarly community*. Bingley: Emerald Publishing.

Carl, Michael, and Moritz J. Schaeffer. 2017. Why translation is difficult: A corpus-based study of non-literality in post-editing and from-scratch translation. *HERMES - Journal of Language and Communication in Business*, 56: 43–57.

Castilho, Sheila, Joss Moorkens, Federico Gaspari, Rico Sennrich, Vilelmini Sosoni, Yota Georgakopoulou, Pintu Lohar, Andy Way, Antonio Miceli Barone, and Maria Gialama. 2017. A comparative quality evaluation of PBSMT and NMT using professional translators. *Proceedings of the Machine Translation Summit XVI, Nagoya, Japan*, 116–131.

De Clercq, Orphée, Gert de Sutter, Rudy Loock, Bert Cappelle, and Koen Plevoets 2021. Uncovering machine translationese using corpus analysis techniques to distinguish between original and machine-translated French. Special issue of *Translation Quarterly*, 101: 21–45.

Delorme Benites, A., Cotelli Kureth, S., Lehr, C., and Steele, E. 2021. Machine translation literacy: a panorama of practices at Swiss universities and implications for language teaching. *CALL and professionalisation: short papers from EUROCALL 2021*: 80-87.

Directorate-General for Translation. 2017. European Master's in Translation competence framework. https://ec.europa.eu/info/sites/default/files/emt_competence_fwk_2017_en_web.pdf

Dorst, Aletta G., Susana Valdez, and Heather Bouman. 2022. Machine translation in the multilingual classroom. How, when and why do humanities students at a Dutch university use machine translation? *Translation and Translanguaging in Multilingual Contexts*, 8(1): 49–66.

Henshaw, Florencia, and Errol M. O'Neill. 2021. Is there a place for online translators in language courses? Panel discussion with Dr. Florencia Henshaw. IALLT (International Association for Language Learning Technology), Virtual Conference, June 17, 2021.

Loock, Rudy. 2018. Traduction automatique et usage linguistique : une analyse de traductions anglais-français réunies en corpus, *Meta: le journal de traducteurs/Meta: Translators' Journal* 63(3): 785–805.

Loock, Rudy. 2020. No more rage against the machine: How the corpus-based identification of machine-translationese can lead to student empowerment. *The Journal of Specialised Translation*, 34: 150–170.

Loock, Rudy, and Sophie Léchauguette 2021. Machine translation literacy and undergraduate students in applied languages: report on an exploratory study. *Revista Tradumàtica. Tecnologies de la Traducció*, 19: 204–225.

Loock, Rudy, Sophie Léchauguette, and Benjamin Holt. To appear. Dealing with the "elephant in the classroom": developing language students' machine translation literacy. *Australian Journal of Applied Linguistics.*

Macken, Lieve, Laura Van Brussel, and Joke Daems. 2019. NMT's wonderland where people turn into rabbits. A study on the comprehensibility of newly invented words in NMT output. *Computational Linguistics in the Netherlands Journal*, 9: 67–80.

Moorkens, Joss Dorothy, Kenny, and Félix do Carmo (eds) 2020. Fair MT: *Towards ethical, sustainable Machine Translation.* Special issue of *Translation Spaces*, 9(1).

Nunes Vieira, Lucas. 2020. Machine translation in the news: a framing analysis of the written press. *Translation Spaces*, 9(1): 98–122.

O'Neill, Errol M. 2019. Online translator, dictionary, and search engine use among L2 students. *CALL-EJ: Computer-Assisted Language Learning–Electronic Journal*, 20(1): 154–177.

Resende, Natália, and Andy Way. 2020. MTrill project: Machine Translation impact on language learning. *Proceedings of the 22nd Annual Conference of the European Association for Machine Translation*, 497–498.

Resende, Natália, and Andy Way. 2021. Can Google Translate rewire your L2 English processing? *Digital*, 1(1): 66–85.

Savlodi, Beatrice, Marco Gaido, Luisa Bentivogli, Matteo Negri, and Marco Turchi. 2021. Gender bias in machine translation. *Transactions of the Association for Computational Linguistics*, 9: 845–874.

Strubell, Emma, Ananya Ganesh, and Andrew McCallum. 2019. Energy and Policy Considerations for Deep Learning in NLP. *Proceedings of the 57th Annual Meeting of the Association for Computational Linguistics (ACL)*, Florence, Italy: 3645–3650.

Vanmassenhove, Eva, Dimitar Shterionov, and Andy Way. 2019. Lost in translation: Loss and decay of linguistic richness in machine translation. *Proceedings of Machine Translation Summit XVII v. 1: Research Track*, Dublin, Ireland, 222–232.

Yamada, Masaru. 2019. The impact of Google Neural Machine Translation on post-editing by student translators. *The Journal of Specialised Translation*, 31: 87–106.

Comparing and combining tagging with different decoding algorithms for back-translation in NMT: learnings from a low resource scenario

Xabier Soto, Olatz Perez-de-Viñaspre, Gorka Labaka, Maite Oronoz
HiTZ Basque Center for Language Technologies - Ixa, University of the Basque Country UPV/EHU
{xabier.soto, olatz.perezdevinaspre, gorka.labaka, maite.oronoz}@ehu.eus

Abstract

Recently, diverse refinements to the back-translation process have been proposed for improving the performance of Neural Machine Translation (NMT) systems, including the use of sampling instead of beam search as decoding algorithm, or appending a tag to the back-translated corpus. However, not all the combinations of the previous approaches have been tested, remaining unclear which is the best approach for developing a given NMT system. In this work, we empirically compare and combine existing techniques for back-translation in a real low resource setting: the translation of clinical notes from Basque into Spanish. Apart from automatically evaluating the NMT systems, we ask bilingual healthcare workers to perform a human evaluation, and analyze the different synthetic corpora by measuring their lexical diversity. For reproducibility and generalizability, we repeat our experiments for German to English translation using public data. The results suggest that in lower resource scenarios tagging only helps when using sampling for decoding, complementing the previous literature using bigger corpora from the news domain. When fine-tuning with a few thousand bilingual in-domain sentences, one of our proposed methods (tagged restricted sampling) obtains the best results both in terms of automatic and human evaluation.

1 Introduction

Neural Machine Translation (NMT) (Kalchbrenner and Blunsom, 2013; Sutskever et al., 2014) is the state-of-the-art approach for developing Machine Translation (MT) systems. However, as NMT is based on artificial neural networks, its performance is dependent on big quantities of bilingual sentences, which are not available for all language pairs and domains.

Back-translation (BT) (Sennrich et al., 2016a), based on the automatic translation of a corpus from the target language into the source language for augmenting the training data, has become a de facto standard for improving the performance of NMT models, provided that large monolingual corpora in the target language and domain are available.

When generating a translation, considering that looking for all the possible output sentences is practically infeasible, MT systems have to implement an efficient technique for selecting the most probable sentence according to the distribution of the training data. Typically, beam search (Tillmann and Ney, 2003) is used for generating both the output sentences of NMT systems and the synthetic sentences produced by BT systems.

Edunov et al. (2018) proposed to use sampling for BT as one way to further improve the performance of NMT systems. Specifically, their 'unrestricted sampling'[1] approach, consisting of randomly sampling from the output distribution, obtained the best results on average comparing to other decoding algorithms, including beam search.

On the contrary, Caswell et al. (2019) suggest that the improvement derived from using sampling

[1]In recent literature, unrestricted sampling is also referred as 'ancestral sampling'.

Macken, Rufener, Van den Bogaert, Daems, Tezcan, Vanroy, Fonteyne, Barrault, Costa-jussà, Kemp, Pilos, Declercq, Koponen, Forcada, Scarton, Moniz (eds.)
Proceedings of the 23rd Annual Conference of the European Association for Machine Translation, p. 31–40
Ghent, Belgium, June 2022.

for BT comes from the fact that the final NMT system can identify the synthetic corpus for having been generated by sampling instead of beam search, so they propose a simple alternative consisting of adding a tag to the corpus generated by the BT system using traditional beam search. They also tried to tag the output of the BT system using noising as proposed by Edunov et al. (2018), but they did not combine tagging with sampling.

Concurrent work by Graça et al. (2019) instead propose some variations to the sampling approach, consisting of disabling the label smoothing option when training the BT system, and restricting the sampling by setting a minimum value to the probability of the output sentences or limiting it to the top-k values. From these options, the last one obtained the best results, which we refer to as 'restricted sampling'.

Thus, we would have six options for generating the BT corpus, depending on which decoding algorithm is used, and whether tagging is used or not. From these combinations, the last two are proposed for the first time in this work:

1. beam search (Tillmann and Ney, 2003)
2. unrestricted sampling (Edunov et al., 2018)
3. restricted sampling (Graça et al., 2019)
4. tagged beam search (Caswell et al., 2019)
5. tagged unrestricted sampling (our contribution)
6. tagged restricted sampling (our contribution)

We compare these 6 methods both in terms of automatic evaluation of NMT systems, and lexical diversity (LD) of the synthetic corpora created by the BT systems. For MT automatic evaluation we use BLEU (Papineni et al., 2002), TER (Snover et al., 2006), chrF (Popović, 2015), and METEOR (Banerjee and Lavie, 2005); while for lexical diversity we measure TTR (Templin, 1975), Yule's I (Yule, 1944) and MTLD (McCarthy, 2005).

In the following, we briefly describe the lexical diversity metrics, for being less known.

TTR, standing for Type-Token Ratio, is the most common measure for lexical diversity. Its value is obtained by dividing the number of types — defined as the number of different words— by the total number of tokens or words in a given corpus. While easy to interpret, TTR is limited in the sense that their values differ significantly when changing the corpora size, thus it is only a valid metric for comparing lexical diversity of similar sized corpora.

Yule's I is the reversion of Yule's K, or "characteristic constant", which represents the variability of the lexical frequency as the analysed text from the corpus under study gets bigger. Yule's I and Yule's K are thought to be less sensitive to changes in the corpora size. However, both TTR and Yule's I are considered as better suited for small sized corpora.

MTLD or Measure of Textual, Lexical Diversity, sequentially measures the mean length of subsequent n-grams that have the same TTR value. As it is measured sequentially, it is less prone to changes in the values measured on different sized corpora, and it is considered as the most representative metric for measuring the lexical diversity of big corpora as the ones typically used in MT.

As a complement to our MT and LD metrics, we add the results coming from a preliminary human evaluation done by a bilingual biomedical expert. According to these results, we select the best two systems for translating clinical reports from Basque to Spanish, and ask bilingual healthcare workers to post-edit the outputs of these systems, as well as the system trained in the opposite direction.

Finally, we report an estimation of the carbon footprint produced when developing our systems, which can be considered for deciding which approach to take in future works.

2 Related Work

Apart from the works mentioned in the introduction proposing different methods for decoding or tagging the synthetic BT corpus (Edunov et al., 2018; Graça et al., 2019; Caswell et al., 2019), there is some other previous work on comparing different systems for BT.

Probably the most relevant work in this respect is the one that compares different techniques (i.e.: rule-based, statistical or neural MT) for generating the synthetic BT corpus. In this area, the work by Burlot and Yvon (2018) firstly compared the use of statistical (SMT) and neural (NMT) systems for BT, without observing significant differences. More similarly to our work, Soto et al. (2019) tried rule-based (RBMT), SMT and NMT for BT applied to the translation of clinical texts, obtaining better results with NMT, and specifically the Transformer architecture (Vaswani et al., 2017).

Poncelas et al. (2019) went one step further and not only compared the performance of different techniques for BT, but combined the synthetic corpora created by SMT and NMT systems, probing that the combination of the outputs of both systems was useful. Furthermore, Soto et al. (2020) compared and combined the outputs of RBMT, SMT and NMT systems for BT, also analysing the lexical diversity of the generated corpora. They observed that the combination of all systems was in general better than using the output of only one system, and tried to improve the performance by applying data selection (Biçici and Yuret, 2015; Poncelas et al., 2018) to the BT corpus, conditioned on the measured MT and LD metrics for each of the BT systems.

Regarding the use of tags for identifying the BT corpus, Marie et al. (2020) concluded that it was advisable to add a tag when the origin of the text was unknown, since systems using BT without a tag overfitted to the synthetic corpus, and even shown to be detrimental when used to translate text originally written in the source language.

Finally, our analysis of the lexical diversity of the BT data generated by different methods follows the work of Vanmassenhove et al. (2019), where the authors study the loss of lexical diversity of a given corpus after being translated with SMT and NMT systems. Therefore, in our work we measure the lexical diversity of the BT corpora according to the same metrics they calculate.

3 Material and methods

We test the six methods presented in the introduction for a real use case: the translation of clinical notes from Basque to Spanish (eu–es). This work is part of an ongoing project that aims to implement an MT system in the Basque public health service (Osakidetza), so Basque speaking healthcare workers can write their reports in Basque without compromising the safety of their patients.[2]

The first step in this project is the compilation of a Basque/Spanish (eu/es) parallel corpus of health records to be used for fine-tuning and evaluation, while previously collected Spanish monolingual corpora will be used for BT. Since these corpora are private, we reproduce our experiments in a similar setting for translating biomedical texts from German to English (de–en), using only publicly available data.

For both language pairs, we preprocess our corpora by tokenizing and truecasing through Moses tools.[3] Further, we apply BPE (Sennrich et al., 2016b) for 90,000 (eu/es) and 40,000 (de/en) iterations. The number of BPE steps for eu/es was optimized in previous experiments, while the de/en one was taken from a reference system (Bawden et al., 2020) that will be described in Section 3.2.

For training all our systems, we use the Transformer architecture as implemented in Fairseq (Ott et al., 2019), with 6 encoder-decoder layers and an embedding size of 512.

All the systems were trained for 30 epochs, except the es–eu system that was trained for 50 epochs due to applying the BPE-dropout (Provilkov et al., 2020) regularization technique, as this setting obtained better results on preliminary experiments. In the future, we plan to do the same for the best performing eu–es systems. For de/en, we opt to use regular BPE for better reproducibility.

In the following subsections, we describe the data used for each language pair.

3.1 eu–es corpora

In the eu–es scenario we define four types of data: 1) out-of-domain bilingual sentences, 2) bilingual clinical terms, 3) bilingual clinical notes, and 4) monolingual health records in Spanish. We use the sets 1–3 to train the BT system (es–eu), and later train the final eu–es systems adding the monolingual corpora through BT.

In both translation directions, we apply regular fine-tuning, dividing the training process in two steps: 1) pretraining, using all except the bilingual clinical notes, and 2) fine-tuning, continuing the training of the pretrained systems with the bilingual in-domain sentences. In this case, we pretrain+fine-tune the systems for 30+30 epochs.

Table 1 sums up the domain, languages, number of sentences and use of each of our corpora.

[2] It is expected that the output of the MT system will be post-edited before making it available to Spanish monolingual healthcare workers.

[3] `https://github.com/moses-smt/mosesdecoder/blob/master/scripts/tokenizer/tokenizer.perl` and `https://github.com/moses-smt/mosesdecoder/blob/master/scripts/recaser/truecase.perl` respectively

Domain	Languages	Sentences	Use
out-of-domain	eu/es	4,896,719	pretrain
clinical terms	eu/es	924,804	pretrain
clinical notes	eu/es	28,602	fine-tune
health records	es	4,946,293	back-tr.

Table 1: Characteristics and use of the eu/es corpora.

In the following lines, we present some of the details of the training corpora, as enumerated in the beginning of this subsection.

3.1.1 Out-of-domain bilingual sentences

In this work, we use around 5 million out-of-domain sentences. Among these, around 3 million sentences are from the news domain, formed by the 3 times repetition of a corpus from the Basque public broadcast service EiTB (Etchegoyhen et al., 2016), along with a more recent one from the same source (Etchegoyhen and Gete, 2020). The remaining 2 million sentences are from different domains as administrative (IVAP), consumer magazines (Eroski), online magazines (Irrika), translation memories (EIZIE), movie synopses, web crawling (San Vicente and Manterola, 2012) and literature (Sarasola et al., 2015).

We also include as out-of-domain data the sentences extracted from documents published in Osakidetza's website, since their domain is not close to the clinical notes focus of our study. These documents are available online,[4] and for this work we omitted the administrative ones (in Spanish: '*Planes y programas anuales y plurianuales*' and '*Memorias Osakidetza*').

3.1.2 Bilingual clinical terms

For adapting the pretraining systems to the clinical domain, we leverage clinical terminology available in Basque and Spanish. Most of the 900,000 bilingual terms come from the automatic translation of SNOMED CT into Basque (Perez-de-Viñaspre, 2017), while another 30,000 are manual translations into Basque of ICD-10 concept descriptions in Spanish made available for the WMT Biomedical shared task (Bawden et al., 2020).

Finally, around 200 terms related to the COVID-19 pandemic are compiled, coming around half of them from an interim release of SNOMED CT that was made available in the beginning of the pandemic,[5] and translated into Basque by a translator of Osakidetza. The remaining terms were collected by Elhuyar.[6]

3.1.3 Bilingual clinical notes

For fine-tuning and evaluation, we use the bilingual corpus compiled in the project with Osakidetza, where 149 Basque speaking healthcare workers volunteered writing their clinical notes in Basque and Spanish.

These sentences are classified among 5 types: 1) discharge reports, 2) progress reports, 3) hospitalization reports, 4) informative permissions and 5) others. Since the main aim of Osakidetza is to translate discharge and progress reports, only sentences coming from these document types are used for evaluation.

The documents were written by professionals of different specialties (e.g.: pediatrics), from where 2,000 sentences were reserved half for validation and another half for testing purposes. The remaining 28,602 were used for fine-tuning.

3.1.4 Monolingual health records in Spanish

In addition to the collected bilingual data, from previous projects developed with Osakidetza we had access to discharge reports from Galdakao-Usansolo hospital, adding up to around 2 million non-repeated sentences; as well as discharge (1 million) and progress (2 million) reports from Basurto hospital.

Both the bilingual and monolingual corpora from Osakidetza were provided to us without any personally identifiable information (names, surnames, etc.), and it was further de-identified by shuffling the sentences coming from each source. The authors had to sign a non-disclosure commitment before getting access to this private data.

3.2 de–en corpora

For generalization and reproducibility, we also perform our experiments using available data in de–en, as well as clinical notes in English for BT. The bilingual data is the same used for training the baseline systems in the WMT Biomedical shared task (Bawden et al., 2020), consisting of around 3 million sentences extracted from the UFAL cor-

[4]`https://www.osakidetza.euskadi.eus/profesionales/-/publicaciones-profesionales/`, accessed on October 1, 2020.

[5]`https://www.snomed.org/news-and-events/articles/march-2020-interim-snomedct-release-COVID-19`

[6]We can make them available upon permission from Elhuyar.

pus[7] after removing the "Subtitles" subset. For evaluation we use Khresmoi,[8] also used in Bawden et al. (2020), where 500 sentences are defined for validation and 1,000 sentences for testing.

For evaluation, and when generating the synthetic corpus through beam search, we use a beam size of 16.[9] This value, along with the 40,000 BPE iterations mentioned above, were optimized for the en–de language pair in Bawden et al. (2020).

Finally, for BT we use the discharge reports in English available in MIMIC III (Johnson et al., 2016).[10] After removing the headers containing unnecessary information, deleting the tags for identifying dates, and erasing the empty lines, this monolingual corpus is reduced to around 2 million sentences. We choose to not perform sentence splitting to avoid introducing errors associated with this process. As a consequence, before translating this corpus we filter out the sentences longer than 1,000 BPE (sub)words using Moses cleaning corpus tool.[11] Note that, although there are longer sentences in the training corpus, fairseq skips by default all the sentences longer than 1,024 tokens, so the maximum sentence length of the training corpus is similar to the one of the monolingual corpus used for BT. All the necessary scripts for reproducing the de-en experiments can be found in `https://gitlab.com/xabiersotol/bt_tagging_and_decoding`.

4 Results and discussion

4.1 MT automatic evaluation

Table 2 presents the MT automatic evaluation scores of the es–eu and en–de systems used for back-translating the monolingual corpora from the clinical domain. Note that both target languages Basque and German are morphologically richer than the corresponding source languages, so metrics like BLEU, based on word-level accuracy, underestimate the actual MT quality comparing to the same systems trained in the opposite direction ('pretraining+fine-tuning' for eu–es and 'pretraining' for de–en in Table 3).

[7] `https://ufal.mff.cuni.cz/ufal_medical_corpus`

[8] `https://lindat.mff.cuni.cz/repository/xmlui/handle/11234/1-2122`

[9] Beam size is 10 for evaluation in the eu/es language pair.

[10] `https://mimic.physionet.org/gettingstarted/access/`

[11] `https://github.com/moses-smt/mosesdecoder/blob/master/scripts/training/clean-corpus-n.perl`

	BLEU↑	TER↓	METEOR↑	CHRF↑
es–eu	33.88	49.27	47.02	61.02
en–de	29.96	52.63	47.64	60.60

Table 2: MT scores of the back-translation systems.

Table 3 shows the MT evaluation scores of the final eu–es and de–en systems. The first rows for each language pair present the results before adding the BT corpus, while the next lines present the values obtained when applying each of the decoding algorithms tested in this work, whether using tagging or not. In the case of eu–es, we include the scores before and after fine-tuning.

	System	BLEU↑	TER↓	MET.↑	CHRF↑
eu–es	pretraining	26.99	58.61	47.70	53.35
	+fine-tuning	46.67	38.74	63.56	66.46
	+BT (beam search)	44.11	41.54	61.48	66.24
	+fine-tuning	51.37	35.15	67.11	70.10
	+BT (tag. beam search)	41.29	44.45	59.47	64.22
	+fine-tuning	51.99	34.96	67.27	70.11
	+BT (unr. sampling)	43.48	41.39	61.36	65.94
	+fine-tuning	52.68	33.84	67.93	71.06
	+BT (tag. unr. sampl.)	42.07	44.33	59.97	65.13
	+fine-tuning	52.42	34.75	67.51	70.72
	+BT (res. sampling)	44.69	40.83	62.23	66.85
	+fine-tuning	52.90	33.96	68.23	71.12
	+BT (tag. res. sampl.)	42.13	43.71	60.22	65.40
	+fine-tuning	**53.10**	**33.55**	**68.30**	**71.34**
de–en	pretraining	42.34	38.55	39.91	67.93
	+BT (beam search)	**44.67**	**37.46**	**40.97**	**69.62**
	+BT (tag. beam search)	44.40	37.63	40.79	69.41
	+BT (unr. sampling)	42.47	41.17	39.58	67.65
	+BT (tag. unr. sampl.)	43.14	38.42	40.35	68.59
	+BT (res. sampling)	40.03	45.73	38.60	66.42
	+BT (tag. res. sampl.)	43.27	38.28	40.51	68.68

Table 3: MT scores of the final eu–es and de–en systems

Beyond the scope of this work, we want to start highlighting that for the eu–es direction, fine-tuning with less than 30,000 sentences (row 2) obtains higher improvements than any of the BT methods (rows starting with '+BT') tried in this work, with the only exception of the chrF value for restricted sampling.

Focusing on the methods under study after fine-tuning, we observe that one of the new combinations tried in this work, tagged restricted sampling, obtains the best scores according to all the MT metrics in the eu–es direction, closely followed by restricted sampling and unrestricted sampling, inverting the order of these two according to TER.

Looking to the generated translations, we see that, regardless of the decoding algorithm, the systems before fine-tuning and not using tagging hallucinate '¡/- ... -/¿' style marks when translating sentences corresponding to typical headers like

'CURRENT DISEASE' or 'TREATMENT'. Analyzing the training corpora, we detect this kind of marked headers in the reports coming from Basurto Hospital, so we will remove these tags in future developments. However, we want to highlight that, not only fine-tuning with clean bilingual data, but also tagging the BT corpora, had the effect of removing this particular noise.

Regarding the de–en direction, where, conditioned by the privacy of clinical data, the size of the training corpora is smaller than for the eu–es counterpart, traditional beam search still obtains the best results, followed by tagged beam search. Most interestingly, we see that, in this particular setting, the effect of tagging is only beneficial when using sampling for BT, complementing the hypothesis of Caswell et al. (2019), that presents tagged back-translation as a "simpler alternative to noising". With these results, we show that both tagging and sampling can be orthogonal methods to improve the performance in lower resource settings.

For complementing the de/en MT scores calculated in biomedical data from Khresmoi, we test these same systems with clinical data from HimL,[12] to analyze possible distortions by the slight domain mismatch between the bilingual biomedical data from WMT Biomedical shared task and the monolingual clinical data from MIMIC III. For converting the HimL data from .sgm to raw text we use the tool available on Nematus.[13] Later we tokenize, truecase and apply BPE as done for the rest of the de/en data. Table 4 presents the results on HimL.[14]

	System	BLEU↑	TER↓	MET.↑	CHRF↑
	en–de pretraining	24.71	59.50	41.06	52.30
de–en	pretraining	32.39	50.96	33.52	55.95
	+BT (beam search)	**33.58**	**49.93**	**34.96**	**57.89**
	+BT (tag. beam search)	33.31	50.01	34.36	57.29
	+BT (unr. sampling)	28.70	59.68	31.36	53.12
	+BT (tag. unr. sampl.)	32.42	51.23	33.89	56.42
	+BT (res. sampling)	29.04	58.71	31.90	54.12
	+BT (tag. res. sampl.)	33.31	50.26	34.40	57.06

Table 4: MT scores of the de/en systems on HimL

We observe that beam search also obtains the best results on HimL data in the de–en direction, again followed by tagged beam search for BLEU, TER and chrF, being the results of tagged restricted sampling equal to the latter according to BLEU, and slightly better in terms of METEOR. The main difference comes from the worst results obtained by unrestricted sampling, which in this setting achieves the lowest scores according to all metrics, confirming the hypothesis that unrestricted sampling only works with big corpora.

4.2 Lexical diversity derived from BT

Table 5 presents the LD values measured on the BT corpora created by each of the methods under study, including the results on the original monolingual corpora for reference.

Language	Corpus	MTLD	Yule's I	TTR
es	original	13.99	0.668	0.438
eu	BT (beam search)	13.71	0.863	0.578
	BT (tag. beam search)	14.72	0.799	0.387
	BT (unr. sam.)	13.99	7.628	65.22
	BT (tag. unr. sam.)	14.84	7.123	41.69
	BT (res. sam.)	13.73	2.545	5.851
	BT (tag. res. sam.)	14.72	2.359	3.748
en	original	14.14	0.347	0.129
de	BT (beam search)	14.50	0.899	0.754
	BT (tag. beam search)	15.37	0.841	0.521
	BT (unr. sam.)	15.15	8.376	93.62
	BT (tag. unr. sam.)	15.86	7.890	62.19
	BT (res. sam.)	14.39	3.374	12.64
	BT (tag. res. sam.)	15.15	3.167	8.566

Table 5: Lexical diversity scores of the monolingual corpora before and after BT using different decoding algorithms, whether tagging or not. Yule's I and TTR values are multiplied by 100 for improved readability.

Comparing the results on each language, we surprisingly see that the MTLD values increase when adding a tag to the BT corpus, while Yule's I and TTR metrics follow our intuition and decrease when adding the same prefix to each sentence coming from BT. Focusing on the more linguistically relevant LD scores without tagging, we observe that, as expected, unrestricted sampling obtains the highest scores in each language for all metrics. By definition, translations generated through restricted sampling are less diverse than the ones produced by unrestricted sampling, since the former will generally produce words that appear more in the training corpus. Considering these LD results, a human MT evaluation is needed in the eu–es direction to see if the higher MT scores for restricted sampling correspond to an actual increase on MT quality or, as it happens with beam search, these higher MT scores are an artifact of automatic

[12] http://www.himl.eu/test-sets

[13] https://github.com/EdinburghNLP/nematus/blob/master/data/strip_sgml.py

[14] Specifically, on the 1044 sentences coming from the NHS subset, since the remaining sentences from Cochrane are used for validation purposes.

metrics that use to overestimate systems that tend to output more frequent words.

4.3 Preliminary human evaluation

Before carrying out a proper human evaluation by the same healthcare workers who compiled the bilingual clinical eu/es data, we make a first estimation by asking a bilingual biomedical expert to blindly evaluate the quality of the 3 systems that obtained higher MT automatic scores in the eu–es setting, namely 1) tagged restricted sampling, 2) restricted sampling and 3) unrestricted sampling.

For assessing the quality of these systems we focus on the adequacy of the generated translations, comparing their semantics with the ones of the corresponding source sentences and checking the reference translations in case of doubt. Table 6 shows the number of sentences from the first 100 non-repeated sentences of the test set identified as totally correct in terms of meaning for each of the best performing systems in the eu–es direction.

tag. res. sam.	res. sam.	unr. sam.
83	75	83

Table 6: Number of sentences perfectly translated from the first 100 non-repeated sentences of the test set for each of the best ranked systems in the eu–es direction.

We clearly observe that restricted sampling, which obtained the second best MT automatic scores but the lowest LD scores according to the most relevant MTLD metric, gets significantly lower adequacy scores (75/100) in this preliminary human evaluation, while tagged restricted sampling and unrestricted sampling obtain the same number of totally correct translations (83/100). This confirms our intuition that, in the absence of a human evaluation, LD metrics can be used as a proxy to assess the MT quality of different systems trained with the same corpus.

4.4 Human evaluation

In this section we present the results of the human evaluation performed by 37 bilingual healthcare workers. For doing this, we use PET[15] tool, asking each evaluator to post-edit 100 out of 500 sentences translated by the es–eu system and the best performing eu–es systems. Each of these 500 sentences was post-edited by 3 different evaluators. Considering that some of the sentences were translated equally by the two eu–es systems, 22 volunteers evaluated the eu–es translations, while 15 post-edited the outputs of the es–eu system.

[15] `https://github.com/wilkeraziz/PET`

Table 7 presents the post-editing times registered for each system. For a better comparison, we normalize the post-editing time by sentence length in the second column.

	Seconds	Seconds/Word
es–eu	65.88	7.19
eu–es (tag. res. sam.)	23.23	2.67
eu–es (unr. sam.)	22.78	2.66

Table 7: Average post-editing times by the best performing eu–es systems and the es–eu system, before and after normalizing per sentence length.

Comparing the results in each direction, we see that post-editing times are much larger for es–eu translation, while the difference between the two eu–es systems is very small, especially after normalization.

Table 8 shows the calculated HTER values, by distinguishing its post-edition types corresponding to insertions (INS), deletions (DEL), substitutions (SUB) and shifts (SHIFT).

	HTER (ALL)	HTER (INS)	HTER (DEL)	HTER (SUB)	HTER (SHIFT)
es–eu	12.47	0.95	3.39	7.21	0.92
eu–es (t.r.s.)	5.50	0.54	2.60	2.17	0.20
eu–es (u.s.)	6.24	0.60	3.00	2.30	0.35

Table 8: HTER values by the best performing eu–es systems and the es–eu system, disaggregated by post-edition types.

As it happened with post-editing times, we observe that the HTER values are higher for the es–eu direction. On the other hand, while post-editing times were slightly higher for the 'tagged restricted sampling' system, we see that this system outperforms the 'unrestricted sampling' system regarding HTER and all its post-edition types.

Finally, Table 9 shows the average keystrokes registered by PET in all its 3 main values.

	VISIBLE	KEYSTROKES	ALLKEYS
es–eu	7.32	10.20	11.13
eu–es (t.r.s.)	3.23	4.21	4.42
eu–es (u.s.)	4.16	5.41	5.63

Table 9: Registered keystrokes for the best performing eu–es systems and the es–eu system, where "VISIBLE": letters + digits + spaces + symbols; "KEYSTROKES": "VISIBLE" + erase; and "ALLKEYS": "KEYSTROKES" + navigation + commands.

Again, for the eu–es direction, we see that the 'tagged restricted sampling' system obtains better results than the 'unrestricted sampling' system in terms of keystrokes, so we select this system for a final error analysis.

4.5 Error analysis

Table 10 shows the number of omissions, additions, mistranslations and shift errors by the best performing 'tagged restricted sampling' system in the eu–es direction, distinguishing between single and multiple word errors.

	Omissions	Additions	Mistransl.	Shifts
TOTAL	51	6	103	4
Single words	35	4	80	1
Multiple words	16	2	23	3

Table 10: Classification of the MT errors for the best performing eu–es system (tagged restricted sampling).

We observe that most of the errors correspond to mistranslations, approximately doubling the omissions, and being the additions and shifts very scarce. For the most common omissions and mistranslations, most of the time these errors are related to a single word, especially for the latter.

From the omitted words, 12 are articles, while one of the added words is also an article. Among the mistranslations, there are 15 clinical terms translated as acronyms, 8 abbreviations, 3 missing accents and 3 singular/plural mismatches. Notice that all of these errors will not substantially alter the sentence meaning.

4.6 Carbon footprint

To conclude this section, answering to the call made by Strubell et al. (2019), we report the carbon footprint derived from training our systems. For doing that, we obtain the training times from the log files for each system, accordingly calculate the consumed power, and then estimate the corresponding CO_2 emissions.

Table 11 shows the measured time, power consumption and CO_2 emissions estimated for each of the developed systems. Each experiment was done using a single Nvidia Titan V GPU with a maximum power of 250W. We estimate the CO_2 emissions by applying equations (1) and (2) in Strubell et al. (2019), considering only the power consumed by our GPUs. Note that the training of the es–eu system is done for 50 epochs, while the rest are performed for 30 epochs.

For interpreting these results, it must be considered that the default implementation of fairseq is not optimized to use the maximum power of the GPUs at any time, so the presented values must be taken with caution as a clear overestimation. We leave as future work modifying the fairseq hyperparameters to make a more efficient use of our GPUs, at the same time adjusting our estimation of the generated CO_2 emissions.

System	Time (h)	Power (kWh)	CO_2e (lbs)
es–eu	81.93	32.36	30.88
eu–es	38.66	15.27	14.57
eu–es + BT (b.s.)	71.90	28.40	27.10
eu–es + BT (t.b.s.)	65.92	26.04	24.84
eu–es + BT (u.s.)	75.66	29.89	28.51
eu–es + BT (t.u.s.)	70.33	27.78	26.50
eu–es + BT (r.s.)	70.83	27.98	26.69
eu–es + BT (t.r.s.)	67.96	26.85	25.61
en–de	42.30	16.71	15.94
de–en	37.31	14.74	14.06
de–en + BT (b.s.)	51.53	20.35	19.42
de–en + BT (t.b.s.)	53.08	20.97	20.00
de–en + BT (u.s.)	54.37	21.48	20.49
de–en + BT (t.u.s.)	55.94	22.10	21.08
de–en + BT (r.s.)	52.26	20.64	19.69
de–en + BT (t.r.s.)	53.47	21.12	20.15
TOTAL			**355.53**

Table 11: Training time, power consumption and estimated CO_2 emissions for each system. 't.' stands for tagged; 'b.s.' for 'beam search'; 'u.s.' for 'unrestricted sampling'; and 'r.s.' for 'restricted sampling'.

5 Conclusions and future work

In this work, we have empirically compared and combined different methods for BT applied to the MT of clinical texts. One of the new combinations tried in this work, tagged restricted sampling, obtained the best automatic scores according to all the metrics studied in the eu–es direction, confirmed by the HTER and keystroke results from the human evaluation performed by bilingual healthcare workers.

In the simulated low resource de–en scenario, traditional beam search still obtained the best MT results, followed by tagged beam search. This confirms the generalized agreement that sampling is only helpful when large monolingual data are available. Moreover, we observe that tagging only helps when using sampling for decoding the BT systems, complementing previous work that proposed tagging the synthetic corpora as an alternative to the use of sampling. However, to drive more generalizable conclusions it would be necessary to try these methods on more diverse scenarios.

Considering the LD metrics, the decoding algorithm that obtained the best MT results in the eu–es scenario (restricted sampling) obtained one of the lowest MTLD scores. In a preliminary human evaluation done by a bilingual biomedical expert to assess the 3 systems that obtained higher MT evaluation scores, restricted sampling obtained significantly worse results than unrestricted sampling, even that the latter obtained lower MT automatic scores. This is a sign that LD metrics can be used as a complement to the MT automatic evaluation scores for identifying the best performing systems.

Finally, we have estimated the carbon footprint derived from our experiments. We will consider these values to study possible ways of reducing or neutralizing our carbon footprint.

Acknowledgements

We thank the healthcare workers who volunteered compiling the bilingual clinical domain corpus and taking part in the human evaluation. We also thank Nora Aranberri and Ekain Arrieta for helping us with the human evaluation, as well as Marco Turchi and Luisa Bentivogli for fruitful discussions. This work was supported by the Spanish Ministry of Economy and Competitiveness (MINECO) [grant number BES-2017-081045]; DOTT-HEALTH project (MCIU / AEI / FEDER, UE) [grant number PID2019-106942RB-C31]; and both by the Spanish Ministry of Science and Innovation and the European Commission in a CHIST-ERA project (FEDER, ANTIDOTE PCI2020-120717-2).

References

Banerjee, Satanjeev, and Alon Lavie. 2005. METEOR: An Automatic Metric for MT Evaluation with Improved Correlation with Human Judgments. In *Proceedings of the ACL Workshop on Intrinsic and Extrinsic Evaluation Measures for Machine Translation and/or Summarization*, Ann Arbor, Michigan, USA. 65–72.

Bawden, Rachel, Giorgio Maria Di Nunzio, Cristian Grozea, Inigo Jauregi Unanue, Antonio Jimeno Yepes, Nancy Mah, David Martinez, Aurélie Névéol, Mariana Neves, Maite Oronoz, Olatz Perez-de-Viñaspre, Massimo Piccardi, Roland Roller, Amy Siu, Philippe Thomas, Federica Vezzani, Maika Vicente Navarro, Dina Wiemann, and Lana Yeganova. 2020. Findings of the WMT 2020 Biomedical Translation Shared Task: Basque, Italian and Russian as New Additional Languages. In *Proceedings of the Fifth Conference on Machine Translation*, online. 660–687.

Biçici, Ergun, and Deniz Yuret. 2015. Optimizing instance selection for statistical machine translation with feature decay algorithms. *Transactions on Audio, Speech and Language Processing*, 23(2):339–350.

Burlot, Franck, and François Yvon. 2018. Using Monolingual Data in Neural Machine Translation: a Systematic Study. In *Proceedings of the Third Conference on Machine Translation: Research Papers*, Brussels, Belgium. 144–155.

Caswell, Isaac, Ciprian Chelba, and David Grangier. 2019. Tagged back-translation. In *Proceedings of the Fourth Conference on Machine Translation (Volume 1: Research Papers)*, Florence, Italy. 53–63.

Edunov, Sergey, Myle Ott, Michael Auli, and David Grangier. 2018. Understanding back-translation at scale. In *Proceedings of the 2018 Conference on Empirical Methods in Natural Language Processing*, Brussels, Belgium. 489–500.

Etchegoyhen, Thierry, Andoni Azpeitia, and Naiara Pérez. 2016. Exploiting a Large Strongly Comparable Corpus. In *Proceedings of the Tenth International Conference on Language Resources and Evaluation*, Porotoroz, Slovenia. 3523–3529.

Etchegoyhen, Thierry, and Harritxu Gete. 2020. Handle with Care: A Case Study in Comparable Corpora Exploitation for Neural Machine Translation. In *Proceedings of the 12th Language Resources and Evaluation Conference*, Marseille, France. 3799–3807.

Graça, Miguel, Yunsu Kim, Julian Schamper, Shahram Khadivi, and Hermann Ney. 2019. Generalizing back-translation in neural machine translation. In *Proceedings of the Fourth Conference on Machine Translation (Volume 1: Research Papers)*, Florence, Italy. 45–52.

Johnson, Alistair E.W., Tom J. Pollard, Lu Shen, Li-wei H. Lehman, Mengling Feng, Mohammad Ghassemi, Benjamin Moody, Peter Szolovits, Leo Anthony Celi, and Roger G. Mark. 2016. Mimic-iii, a freely accessible critical care database. *Scientific Data*, 3(160035).

Kalchbrenner, Nal, and Phil Blunsom. 2013. Recurrent continuous translation models. In *Proceedings of the 2013 Conference on Empirical Methods in Natural Language Processing*, Seattle, Washington, USA. 1700–1709.

Marie, Benjamin, Raphael Rubino, and Atsushi Fujita 2020. Tagged Back-translation Revisited: Why Does It Really Work? In *Proceedings of the 58th Annual Meeting of the Association for Computational Linguistics*, online. 5990–5997.

McCarthy, Philip M. 2005. *An Assessment of the Range and Usefulness of Lexical Diversity Measures and the Potential of the Measure of Textual, Lexical Diversity*. Ph.D. thesis, University of Memphis, Tennessee, USA.

Ott, Myle, Sergey Edunov, Alexei Baevski, Angela Fan, Sam Gross, Nathan Ng, David Grangier, and Michael Auli. 2019. fairseq: A Fast, Extensible Toolkit for Sequence Modeling. In *Proceedings of the 2019 Conference of the North American Chapter of the Association for Computational Linguistics (Demonstrations)*, Minneapolis, Minnesota, USA. 48–53.

Papineni, Kishore, Salim Roukos, Todd Ward, and Wei-Jing Zhu. 2002. BLEU: a method for automatic evaluation of machine translation. In *Proceedings of the 40th annual meeting on association for computational linguistics*, Philadelphia, Pennsylvania, USA. 311–318.

Perez-de-Viñaspre, Olatz. 2017. *Automatic medical term generation for a low-resource language: translation of SNOMED CT into Basque*. Ph.D. thesis, University of the Basque Country, Donostia, Spain.

Poncelas, Alberto, Gideon Maillette de Buy Wenniger, and Andy Way. 2018. Feature decay algorithms for neural machine translation. In *Proceedings of the 21st Annual Conference of the European Association for Machine Translation*, Alacant, Spain, 239–248.

Poncelas, Alberto, Maja Popović, Dimitar Shterionov, Gideon Maillette de Buy Wenniger, and Andy Way. 2019. Combining PBSMT and NMT Back-translated Data for Efficient NMT. In *Proceedings of the International Conference on Recent Advances in Natural Language Processing*, Varna, Bulgaria. 922–931.

Popović, Maja. 2015. chrF: character n-gram F-score for automatic MT evaluation. In *Proceedings of the Tenth Workshop on Statistical Machine Translation*, Lisbon, Portugal. 392–395.

Provilkov, Ivan, Dmitrii Emelianenko, and Elena Voita. 2020. BPE-Dropout: Simple and Effective Subword Regularization. In *Proceedings of the 58th Annual Meeting of the Association for Computational Linguistics*, online. 1882–1892.

San Vicente, Iñaki, and Iker Manterola. 2012. PaCo2: A Fully Automated tool for gathering Parallel Corpora from the Web. In *Proceedings of the Eighth International Conference on Language Resources and Evaluation*, Istanbul, Turkey. 1–6.

Sarasola, Ibon, Pello Salaburu, and Josu Landa. 2015. *Hizkuntzen Arteko Corpusa (HAC)*. University of the Basque Country UPV/EHU (Euskara Institutua), Bilbo, Spain.

Sennrich, Rico, Barry Haddow, and Alexandra Birch. 2016. Improving neural machine translation models with monolingual data. In *Proceedings of the 54th Annual Meeting of the Association for Computational Linguistics (Volume 1: Long Papers)*, Berlin, Germany. 86–96.

Sennrich, Rico, Barry Haddow, and Alexandra Birch. 2016. Neural Machine Translation of Rare Words with Subword Units. In *Proceedings of the 54th Annual Meeting of the Association for Computational Linguistics (Volume 1: Long Papers)*, Berlin, Germany. 1715–1725.

Snover, Matthew, Bonnie Dorr, Richard Schwartz, Linnea Micciulla, and John Makhoul. 2006. A study of translation edit rate with targeted human annotation. In *Proceedings of the 7th Conference of the Association for Machine Translation in the Americas*, Cambridge, USA. 223–231.

Soto, Xabier, Olatz Perez-De-Viñaspre, Maite Oronoz, and Gorka Labaka. 2019. Leveraging SNOMED CT terms and relations for machine translation of clinical texts from Basque to Spanish. In *Proceedings of the Second Workshop on Multilingualism at the Intersection of Knowledge Bases and Machine Translation*, Dublin, Ireland. 8–18.

Soto, Xabier, Dimitar Shterionov, Alberto Poncelas, and Andy Way. 2020. Selecting Backtranslated Data from Multiple Sources for Improved Neural Machine Translation. In *Proceedings of the 58th Annual Meeting of the Association for Computational Linguistics*, online. 3898–3908.

Strubell, Emma, Ananya Ganesh, and Andrew McCallum. 2019. Energy and Policy Considerations for Deep Learning in NLP. In *Proceedings of the 57th Annual Meeting of the Association for Computational Linguistics*, Florence, Italy. 3645–3650.

Sutskever, Ilya, Oriol Vinyals, and Quoc V. Le. 2014. Sequence to sequence learning with neural networks. In *Advances in neural information processing systems*, Montréal, Canada. 3104–3112.

Templin, Mildred C. 1975. *Certain Language Skills in Children: Their Development and Interrelationships*. University of Minnesota Press, Minneapolis, Minnesota, USA.

Tillmann, Christoph, and Hermann Ney. 2003. Word reordering and a dynamic programming beam search algorithm for statistical machine translation. *Computational Linguistics*, 29(1):97–133.

Vanmassenhove, Eva, Dimitar Shterionov, and Andy Way. 2019. Lost in Translation: Loss and Decay of Linguistic Richness in Machine Translation. In *Proceedings of Machine Translation Summit XVII: Research Track*, Dublin, Ireland. 222–232.

Vaswani, Ashish, Noam Shazeer, Niki Parmar, Jakob Uszkoreit, Llion Jones, Aidan N. Gomez, Łukasz Kaiser, and Illia Polosukhin. 2017. Attention is all you need. In *Advances in Neural Information Processing Systems*, Long Beach, California, USA. 5998–6008.

Yule, George U. 1944. *The Statistical Study of Literary Vocabulary*. Cambridge University Press, Cambridge, UK.

Passing Parser Uncertainty to the Transformer: Labeled Dependency Distributions for Neural Machine Translation

Dongqi Pu **Khalil Sima'an**
dongqi.me@gmail.com k.simaan@uva.nl
Institute for Logic, Language and Computation
University of Amsterdam

Abstract

Existing syntax-enriched neural machine translation (NMT) models work either with the single most-likely unlabeled parse or the set of n-best unlabeled parses coming out of an external parser. Passing a single or n-best parses to the NMT model risks propagating parse errors. Furthermore, unlabeled parses represent only syntactic groupings without their linguistically relevant categories. In this paper we explore the question: Does passing both parser uncertainty and labeled syntactic knowledge to the Transformer improve its translation performance? This paper contributes a novel method for infusing the whole labeled dependency distributions (LDD) of the source sentence's dependency forest into the self-attention mechanism of the encoder of the Transformer. A range of experimental results on three language pairs demonstrate that the proposed approach outperforms both the vanilla Transformer as well as the single best-parse Transformer model across several evaluation metrics.

1 Introduction

Neural Machine Translation (NMT) models based on the seq2seq schema, e.g., Kalchbrenner and Blunsom (2013); Cho et al. (2014); Sutskever et al. (2014); Bahdanau et al. (2014), first encode the source sentence into a high-dimensional content vector before decoding it into the target sentence.

Several prior studies (Shi et al., 2016; Belinkov and Bisk, 2018) have pointed out that although NMT models may induce aspects of syntactic relations, they still cannot capture the subtleties of syntactic structure that should be useful for accurate translation, particularly by bridging long distance relations.

Previous work provides support for the hypothesis that explicit incorporation of source syntactic knowledge could result in better translation performance, e.g., Eriguchi et al. (2016); Bastings et al. (2017). Most models condition translation on a single best parse **syn**:

$$\arg\max_{\mathbf{t}} P(\mathbf{t}|\mathbf{s}, \mathbf{syn}) \quad (1)$$

where **s** and **t** are the source and target sentences respectively. Other models incorporate the n-best parses or forest (without parser probabilities and labels), e.g., Neubig and Duh (2014). The idea here is that the syntactically richer input (**s**, **syn**) should be better than the bare sequential word order of **s**, leading to a more accurate and sharper translation distribution $P(\mathbf{t}|\mathbf{s}, \mathbf{syn})$.

While most syntax-enriched strategies result in performance improvements, there are two noteworthy gaps in the literature addressing source syntax. Firstly, none of the existing works conditions on the probability distributions over source syntactic relations. And secondly, none of the existing approaches conditions on the dependency labels, thereby conditioning only on the binary choice whether there is an unlabeled dependency relation between two words.

Tu et al. (2010); Ma et al. (2018); Zaremoodi and Haffari (2018) showed that the whole dependency forest provides better performance than a single best parse approach. In this paper we go

Macken, Rufener, Van den Bogaert, Daems, Tezcan, Vanroy, Fonteyne, Barrault, Costa-jussà, Kemp, Pilos, Declercq, Koponen, Forcada, Scarton, Moniz (eds.)
Proceedings of the 23rd Annual Conference of the European Association for Machine Translation, p. 41–50
Ghent, Belgium, June 2022.

one step further and propose that *a syntactic parser is more useful if it conveys to the NMT model also its remaining uncertainty, expressed as the whole probability distributions over dependency relations rather than a mere forest.*

To the best of our knowledge, there is no published work that incorporates a parser's distributions over dependency relations into the Transformer model (Vaswani et al., 2017), let alone incorporating distributions over labeled dependency relations into NMT models at large.

This paper contributes a generic approach for infusing labeled dependency distributions into the encoder's self-attention layer of the Transformer. We represent a labeled dependency distributions as a three-dimensional tensor of parser probabilities, where the first and second dimensions concern word-positions and the third concerns the dependency labels.

The resulting tensor is infused into the computation of the multi-head self-attention, where every head is made to specialize in a specific dependency class. We contribute empirical evidence that passing uncertainty to the Transformer and passing labeled dependencies both give better performance than passing a single unlabeled parse, or an unlabeled/labeled set of dependency relations with uniform probabilities.

2 Related Work

The role of source syntactic knowledge in better reordering was appreciated early on during the Statistical Machine Translation (SMT) era. For example, Mylonakis and Sima'an (2011) propose that source language parses should play a crucial role in guiding the reordering within translation, and do so by integrating constituency labels of varying granularity into the source language. Although, NMT encoders have been claimed to have the ability to learn syntax, work on RNNs-based models shows the value of external source syntax in improving translation performance, e.g., Eriguchi et al. (2016), by refining the encoder component, leading to a combination of a tree-based encoder and a sequential encoder.

Noteworthy to recall here that the attention mechanism was originally aimed to capture all word-to-word relations, including syntactic-semantic relations. whereas, the work of Bastings et al. (2017) has shown that a single unlabeled dependency parse, encoded utilizing Graph Convolutional Networks (GCNs), can help improve MT performance. Ma et al. (2018) and Zaremoodi and Haffari (2018) attempt to incorporate parse forests into RNNs-based NMT models, mitigating parsing errors by providing more candidate options. However, these two works only rely on the binary (unlabeled) relations in all the sub-trees, ignoring the elaborate probability relations between word positions and the type of these relations.

Although the Transformer (Vaswani et al., 2017) is considered to have a better ability to implicitly learn relations between words than the RNNs-based models, existing work (Zhang et al., 2019; Currey and Heafield, 2019) shows that even incorporating a single best parse could improve the Transformer translation performance. Followup work (Bugliarello and Okazaki, 2020; Peng et al., 2021) provides similar evidence by changing the Transformer's self-attention mechanism based on the distance between the input words of dependency relations, exploiting the single best unlabeled dependency parse.

The work of Pham et al. (2019) suggests that the benefits of incorporating a single (possibly noisy) parse (using data manipulation, linearized or embedding-based method) can be explained as a mere regularization effect of the model, which does not help the Transformer to exploit the actual syntactic knowledge. Interestingly, Pham et al. (2019) arrive at a similar hypothesis, but they concentrate on exploring how to train one of the heads of the self-attention in the Transformer for a combined objective of parsing and translation. The parsing-translation training objective focuses the self-attention of a single head at learning the distribution of unlabeled dependencies while learning to translate as well, i.e., the distribution is not taken as source input but as a gold training objective. By training a single head with syntax, they leave all other heads without direct access to syntax.

Our work confirms the intuition of Pham et al. (2019) regarding the utility of the parser's full dependency distributions, but in our model these distributions are infused directly into the self-attention while maintaining a single training objective (translation). Furthermore, we propose that only when the full probability distribution matrices over labeled dependency relations is infused directly into the transformer's self-attention mechanism (not as training objective), syntax has a chance to teach the Transformer to better learn syntax-informed self-attention weights.

3 Proposed Approach

A parser can be seen as an external expert system that provides linguistic knowledge to assist the NMT models in explicitly taking into account syntactic structure. For some sentences, the parser could be rather uncertain and spread its probability over multiple parses almost uniformly, but in the majority of cases the parser could have a rather sharp distribution over the alternative parses. Therefore, simply passing a dependency forest amounts merely to passing all alternative parses accompanied with zero information on parser confidence (maximum perplexity) to the Transformer NMT model, which does not help it to distinguish between the parsing information of the one input from that of another. This could increase the complexity of learning the NMT model unnecessarily.

An alternative is then to use for each sentence a dependency distribution in the form of conditional probabilities, which could be taken to represent the degree of confidence of the parser in the individual dependency relations. Furthermore, we propose that each dependency relation type (label), provides a more granular local probability distribution that could assist the Transformer model in making more accurate estimation of the context vector. This might enhance the quality of encoding the source sentence, particularly because the Transformer model relies on a weak notion or word order, which is input in the form of positional encoding outside the self-attention mechanism.

Note that the word-to-word dependency probabilities is not equivalent to using a distribution over dependency parses. This is because in some cases the word-to-word dependencies (just like word-to-word attention) could combine together into general graphs (not necessarily trees). We think that using relations between pairs of words (rather than upholding strict tree or forest structures) fits well with the self-attention mechanism.

3.1 Dependency Distributions

Denote with $|T|$ target sentence length and with $\text{encode}(\cdot)$ the NMT model's encoder. We contrast different syntax-driven models:

$$P(\mathbf{t}|\mathbf{s}, \mathbf{syn}) \approx \prod_{i=1}^{|T|} P(t_i|t_{<i}, \text{encode}(\mathbf{s}, \mathbf{syn})) \quad (2)$$

with **syn** $\in$ {**{L,U}DD**, **U{L,U}DD**, **{L,U}DP**}, where **{L,U}DD** is the labeled/unlabeled dependency distribution[1], **U{L,U}DD** the uniform labeled/unlabeled dependency distribution[2], and **{L,U}DP** the 1-best labeled/unlabeled dependency parse. We also use **LDA** to stand for a model were the attention weights are fixed equal to **LDD** (i.e., not learned).

Our primary idea is to exert a soft influence on the self-attention in the encoder of the Transformer to allow it to fit its parameters with both syntax and translation awareness together. For infusing the labeled dependency distributions, we start with "matrixization" of labeled dependency distributions, which results in a compact tensor representation suitable for NMT models.

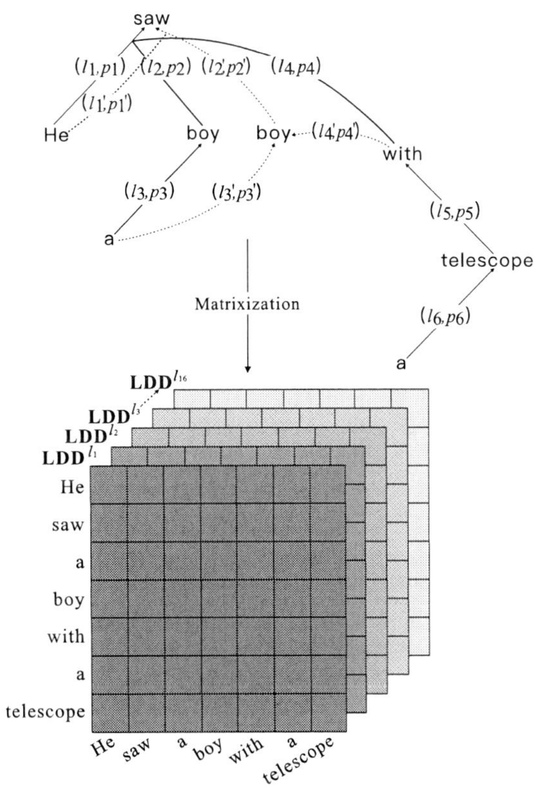

Figure 1: Labeled dependency distributions

Figure 1 illustrates by example how we convert the labeled dependency distribution (**LDD**) into a three-dimensional **LDD** tensor. The x-axis and y-

[1]Unlabeled dependency distribution is the sum of labeled dependency distributions on the z-axis, which is the same as 1-best unlabeled dependency parse.

[2]It is used for the purpose of ablation experiments, that is, the value of each point in the 3-dimensional tensor is identical.

axis of the tensor are the words in the source sentence, and the z-axis represents the type of dependency relation. Each point representing a conditional probability $p(i,j,l) = p(s_j, l|s_i) \in [0,1] \subseteq \mathbb{R}$ of source word s_i modifying another source word s_j with relation l.

LDD Matrix for a specific label l: The matrix $\mathbf{LDD}^l$ extracted from the **LDD** tensor for a dependency label l is defined as the matrix in which every entry (i,j) contains the probability of a word s_i to modify word s_j with dependency relation l.

3.2 Parser-Infused Self-attention

Inspired by Bugliarello and Okazaki (2020), we propose a novel Transformer NMT model that incorporates the **LDD** into the first layer of the encoder side. Figure 2 shows our LDD sub-layer.

The standard self-attention layer employs a multi-head attention mechanism of h heads. For an input sentence of length T, the input of self-attention head h_i in the LDD layer is the word embedding matrix $\mathbf{X} \in \mathbb{R}^{T \times d_{\text{model}}}$ and the dependency distribution matrix $\mathbf{LDD}^{l_i} \in \mathbb{R}^{T \times T}$ for label l_i assigned to head h_i uniquely[3]. Hence, when we refer to head h_i, we refer also to its uniquely assigned dependency label l_i, but we omit l_i to avoid complicating the notation.

As usual in multi-head self-attention (h being the number of heads) for head h_i, first it linearly maps three input vectors, $\mathbf{q}, \mathbf{k}, \mathbf{v} \in \mathbb{R}^{1 \times d_{\text{model}}}$ for each token, resulting in three matrices $\mathbf{Q}^{h_i} \in \mathbb{R}^{T \times d}$, $\mathbf{K}^{h_i} \in \mathbb{R}^{T \times d}$, and $\mathbf{V}^{h_i} \in \mathbb{R}^{T \times d}$, where d_{model} is the dimension of input vectors, and $d = d_{\text{model}}/h$. Subsequently, an attention weight for each position is obtained by:

$$\mathbf{S}^{h_i} = \frac{\mathbf{Q}^{h_i} \cdot \mathbf{K}^{h_i \top}}{\sqrt{d}} \quad (3)$$

At this point we infuse the resulting self-attention weight matrix $\mathbf{S}^{h_i}$ for head h_i with the specific **LDD** matrix $\mathbf{LDD}^{l_i}$ for label l_i using element-wise multiplication. Assuming that $d^{l_i}_{p,q} \in \mathbf{LDD}^{l_i}$, this is to say:

$$n^{h_i}_{p,q} = s^{h_i}_{p,q} \times d^{l_i}_{p,q}, \text{ for } p,q = 1,...,T \quad (4)$$

The purpose of element-wise multiplication is to nudge the attention mechanism to "dynamically" learn weights that optimize the translation objective but also diverge the least from the parser probabilities in the dependency distribution matrix.

Next, the resulting weights are softmaxed to obtain the final syntax-infused distribution matrix for head h_i and the label attached to this head l_i:

$$\mathbf{N}^{h_i} = \text{softmax}(\mathbf{S}^{h_i} \odot \mathbf{LDD}^{l_i}) \quad (5)$$

We stress that every attention head is infused with a different dependency relation matrix $\mathbf{LDD}^{l_i}$ for a particular dependency relation l_i. By focusing every head on a different label we hope to "soft label", or specialize, it for that label.

Now that we have syntax-infused weights $\mathbf{N}^{h_i}$ we multiply them with the value matrix $\mathbf{V}^{h_i}$ to get the attention weight matrix of the attention head h_i for the relation l_i.

$$\mathbf{M}^{h_i} = \mathbf{N}^{h_i} \cdot \mathbf{V}^{h_i} \quad (6)$$

Subsequently, the multi-head attention linearly maps the concatenation of all the heads with a parameter matrix $\mathbf{W}^o \in \mathbb{R}^{d_{\text{model}} \times d_{\text{model}}}$, and sends this hidden representation to the standard Transformer encoder layers for further computations.

$$\text{MultiHead}(\mathbf{Q},\mathbf{K},\mathbf{V}) = \text{Concat}(\mathbf{M}^{h_i},...,\mathbf{M}^{h_m})\mathbf{W}^o \quad (7)$$

Finally, the objective function for training our model with syntax knowledge is identical to that of the vanilla Transformer (Vaswani et al., 2017):

$$\text{Loss} = -\sum_{t=1}^{T}[y_t \ln(o_t) + (y_t - 1)\ln(1 - o_t)] \quad (8)$$

Where y_t and o_t are, respectively, the true and the model-predicted value at state t, and T represents the number of states. The syntactic distribution matrices are not the object of optimization in the model, so it is incorporated into the model in the form of a parameter-free matrix.

4 Experiments and Analysis

Experimental Setup We establish seven distinct sets of experiments, refer to Table 1. To be specific, we will conduct particular experiments to validate the empirical performance under both medium size and small size training parallel corpora. Apart from the different network structures used in the models, the number of network layers are identical in the same language pair translation experiments for all models. Additionally,

[3]We group the original dependency labels into 16 alternative group labels. The grouping is provided in Appendix A.

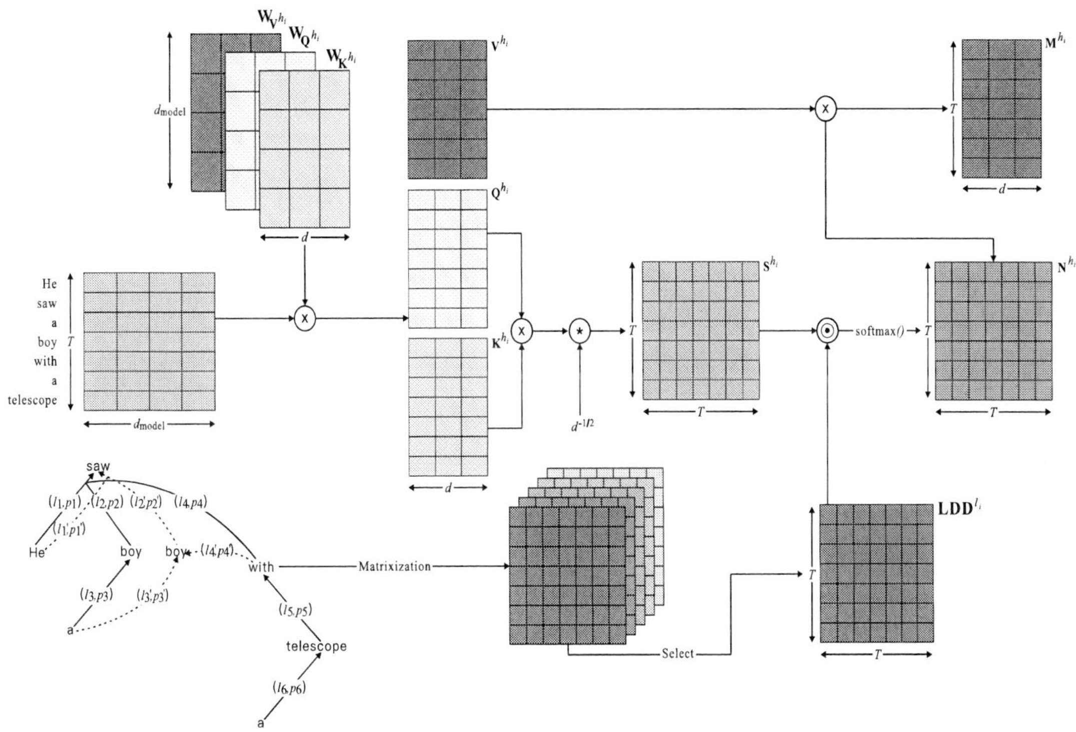

Figure 2: Labeled dependency distribution sub-layer ($\mathbf{LDD}^{l_i}$ for head h_i)

the seven models in each experiment will use the same parameter settings, loss function, and optimizer algorithm. Experiments will employ BLEU-{1,4} score (Papineni et al., 2002), RIBES score (Isozaki et al., 2010), TER score (Snover et al., 2006), and BEER score (Stanojevic and Sima'an,, 2014) as criteria for evaluating the model's effectiveness.

Parser: We employ an external dependency parser *SuPar* (Zhang et al., 2020) to automatically parse the source sentences. Since this parser was trained using the biaffine method (Dozat and Manning, 2016), we can extract dependency distributions by changing its source code.

Data: We evaluate the translation tasks for three language pairs from three different language families: English-Chinese (En→Zh), English-Italian (En→It), and English-German (En→De). We chose $dev2010$ and $test2010$ as our validation and test datasets from IWSLT2017 En→De and En→It tasks. In En→Zh, we randomly selected a 110K subset from the IWSLT2015 dataset as training set and used $dev2010$ as validation set, $tst2010$ as test set. Table 2 exhibits the division and statistics of the datasets.

For training only, we first filtered out the source sentences that SuPar cannot parse and sentences that exceed 256 tokens in length. And then, we used SuPar[4] to parse each source language sentence to obtain the labeled dependency distributions and applied Spacy[5] to tokenize the source and target languages, respectively. Finally, we replaced words in the corpus with "<unk>" for words with frequency less than two counts, and for each mini-batch sentences, added "<bos>","<eos>" tokens at the beginning and end, and for sentences with inconsistent lengths per mini-batch, added a corresponding number of "<pad>" tokens at the end of the sentences to keep the batch length consistent.

Hyperparameters: In the low-resource experiments, the batch size was 256, the number of layers for the encoder and decoder was 4, and the number of warm-up steps was 400. In the medium-resource experiments, their values were 512, 6, 4000, respectively. For the rest, we use the base configuration of the Transformer (Vaswani et al., 2017): All experiments were optimized using Adam (Kingma and Ba, 2015) (where β_1 was 0.9, β_2 was 0.98, ϵ was 10-9) and the initial learning rate was set to 0.0001, gradually reduced during training as follows:

[4]https://github.com/yzhangcs/parser
[5]https://spacy.io/

Table 1: Five sets of experimental group description

Experimental group	Description
Baseline (BL)	The original Transformer model.
+Labeled dependency attention only (LDA)	Replace **S** matrix directly with the labeled dependency distributions.
+1-best labeled dependency parse (LDP)	Incorporate 1-best dependency tree with specific (e.g. l_1) label.
+1-best unlabeled dependency parse (UDP)	Incorporate 1-best (regardless the type of dependency relations) dependency tree.
+Uniform labeled dependency distributions (ULDD)	Incorporate uniform labeled dependency distributions.
+Uniform unlabeled dependency distributions (UUDD)	Incorporate uniform unlabeled dependency distributions.
+Labeled dependency distributions (LDD)	Incorporate labeled dependency distributions with standard Transformer self-attention.

Table 2: Datasets statistics

Task	Corpus	Training set	Validation set	Test set
English → German	Multi30k	29000	1014	1000
	IWSLT 2017	206112	888	1568
English → Italian	IWSLT 2017	231619	929	1566
English → Chinese	IWSLT 2015	107860	802	1408

$$\mathrm{lr} = d_{\mathrm{model}}^{-0.5} \cdot \min(\mathrm{step\_num}^{-0.5}, \mathrm{step\_num} \cdot \mathrm{warmup\_steps}^{-1.5}) \tag{9}$$

The number of heads in multi-head attention was set to 8 (16 in LDD layer), the dimension of the model was 512, the dimension of inner fully-connected layers was set to 2048, and the loss function was the cross-entropy loss function. The checkpoint with the highest BLEU-4 score on the validation set was saved for model testing during training. The number of epochs was set to 50 (one epoch represents a complete training produce). In order to prevent over-fitting, we set the dropout rate (also in our LDD layer) to 0.1.

4.1 Experimental Results

The experimental results for each model under low- and medium-resource scenarios are shown in Tables 3 to 6. The first group represents the baseline model, while the remaining groups represent the control models. It is necessary to note that the last group is the model proposed in this paper.

As compared to the baseline model, either form of modeling the syntactic knowledge of the source language could be beneficial to the NMT models. Whether it was in the choice of lexical (BLEU-1) or in the order of word (RIBES), there was a certain degree of improvement, which also supports the validity and rationality of incorporating syntactic knowledge. The proposed model (LDD) achieved the best score in at least three of the five different evaluation metrics, regardless of the language translation tasks. The proposed model consistently reached the highest results on BLEU-4, which increased by at least one point when compared to the baseline model, with an average increase rate of more than 5%. Furthermore, in most translation experiments, incorporating labeled dependency distributions provided better outcomes than the 1-best unlabeled dependency parse system (UDP)[6]. This indicates the efficacy of providing more parsing information, particularly the dependency probabilities. In the low resource scenarios, the models of incorporating syntactic knowledge

Table 3: Multi30k evaluation results (En → De)

Model	BLEU-1	RIBES	BLEU-4	TER	BEER
BL	**58.13**	78.86	30.14	62.95	0.59
+LDA	54.10	**80.10**	30.49	63.47	**0.61**
+LDP	54.26	79.58	30.71	79.58	0.61
+UDP	55.84	78.96	31.05	63.38	0.60
+ULDD	52.20	79.50	27.80	63.02	0.59
+UUDD	53.38	79.75	29.09	63.34	0.60
+LDD	55.65	79.97†‡	**31.29**†‡	**62.66**†‡	**0.61**
LDD compared to BL	$-\Delta 2.48$	$+\Delta 1.11$	$+\Delta 1.15$	$+\Delta 0.29$	$+\Delta 0.02$
LDD compared to UDP	$-\Phi 0.19$	$+\Phi 1.01$	$+\Phi 0.24$	$+\Phi 0.72$	$+\Phi 0.01$

[1] The black bold in the table represents the best experimental results under the same test set.
[2] Δ and Φ represent the improvement of our model compared to baseline and 1-best unlabeled parse system respectively.
[3] $\dagger$ and $\ddagger$ indicate statistical significance ($p<0.05$) against baseline and 1-best unlabeled parse system via T-test and Kolmogorov-Smirnov test respectively.

Table 4: IWSLT2017 evaluation results (En → De)

Model	BLEU-1	RIBES	BLEU-4	TER	BEER
BL	51.63	68.64	26.13	83.34	0.53
+LDA	49.89	69.04	26.16	83.53	0.53
+LDP	51.12	68.91	26.38	83.93	0.53
+UDP	50.90	69.20	26.39	84.65	0.53
+ULDD	50.80	**69.56**	25.10	82.76	0.53
+UUDD	48.85	68.90	25.41	86.19	0.53
+LDD	**54.98**†‡	68.83†	**27.78**†‡	**81.85**†‡	**0.54**
LDD compared to BL	$+\Delta 3.35$	$+\Delta 0.19$	$+\Delta 1.65$	$+\Delta 1.49$	$+\Delta 0.01$
LDD compared to UDP	$+\Phi 4.08$	$-\Phi 0.37$	$+\Phi 1.39$	$+\Phi 2.80$	$+\Phi 0.01$

[1] The black bold in the table represents the best experimental results under the same test set.
[2] Δ and Φ represent the improvement of our model compared to baseline and 1-best unlabeled parse system respectively.
[3] $\dagger$ and $\ddagger$ indicate statistical significance ($p<0.05$) against baseline and 1-best unlabeled parse system via T-test and Kolmogorov-Smirnov test respectively.

[6] All previous work uses only 1-best unlabeled parse, which is also our main comparison object. We will refer to it as 1-best parse or 1-best tree below.

Table 5: IWSLT2017 evaluation results (En → It)

Model	BLEU-1	RIBES	BLEU-4	TER	BEER
BL	54.14	68.58	27.11	77.52	0.56
+LDA	51.25	**69.90**	26.13	81.23	0.56
+LDP	51.72	68.26	25.65	80.03	0.55
+UDP	53.17	**69.90**	28.13	**76.18**	0.56
+ULDD	51.30	67.83	25.23	80.62	0.54
+UUDD	54.00	66.83	25.23	78.41	0.55
+LDD	**56.73**†‡	69.69†	**29.34**†‡	76.34†	**0.57**
LDD compared to BL	+Δ2.59	+Δ1.11	+Δ2.23	+Δ1.18	+Δ0.01
LDD compared to UDP	+Φ3.56	−Φ0.21	+Φ1.21	−Φ0.16	+Φ0.01

[1] The black bold in the table represents the best experimental results under the same test set.

[2] Δ and Φ represent the improvement of our model compared to baseline and 1-best unlabeled parse system respectively.

[3] † and ‡ indicate statistical significance ($p<0.05$) against baseline and 1-best unlabeled parse system via T-test and Kolmogorov-Smirnov test respectively.

Table 6: IWSLT2015 evaluation results (En → Zh)

Model	BLEU-1	BLEU-4	TER	BEER
BL	46.53	18.31	67.96	0.20
+LDA	44.91	18.25	70.96	0.20
+LDP	47.34	18.85	70.02	0.20
+UDP	46.92	19.71	**67.29**	0.20
+ULDD	40.67	17.89	77.04	0.19
+UUDD	34.14	18.05	79.27	0.18
+LDD	**47.62**†‡	**20.25**†‡	67.38†	0.20
LDD compared to BL	+Δ1.09	+Δ1.94	+Δ0.58	+Δ0.00
LDD compared to UDP	+Φ0.70	+Φ0.54	−Φ0.09	+Φ0.00

[1] The black bold in the table represents the best experimental results under the same test set.

[2] Δ and Φ represent the improvement of our model compared to baseline and 1-best unlabeled parse system respectively.

[3] † and ‡ indicate statistical significance ($p<0.05$) against baseline and 1-best unlabeled parse system via T-test and Kolmogorov-Smirnov test respectively.

paid less attention to the neighboring words in the corpus sentence because syntactic knowledge may assist models in focusing on distant words with syntactic relations, which was reflected in the decrease of BLEU-1 scores. This problem was alleviated in the richer-resource scenarios, which also showed that the robustness of the models improved.

For ablation experiments, passing the uniform dependency distributions verifies our hypothesis. A uniform probability tensor cannot provide valuable information to the Transformer model and risks misleading the model, resulting in the worst performance. Another notable finding is that simply incorporating labeled dependency distributions (replacing the **K** and **Q** matrices in the attention matrices) as dependency attention outperformed the baseline model on average. The benefit of this strategy is that by replacing **K** and **Q** matrices and their associated calculation process can drastically decrease the number of parameters and computing requirements.

4.2 Qualitative Analysis

BLEU-4 Scores Comparison: We also attempted to visualize the results to understand the performance of the proposed model better. In Figure 3, although the 1-best parse model performs better than the baseline model, the model we propose has higher scores than the baseline model and the 1-best parse model in all the median, upper and lower quartile scores. From the original scatter diagram, we can observe the scatter distribution of the proposed model at the upper position in general, indicating that, our model can earn higher scores for translated results than the baseline model and 1-best parse model.

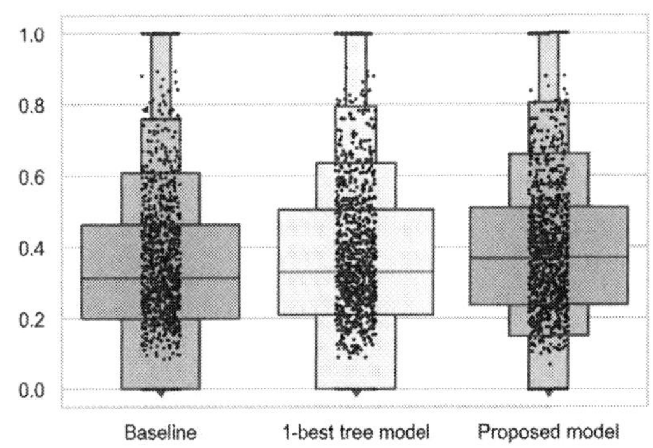

Figure 3: Box plot of baseline model, 1-best tree model and proposed model results

Impact of Sentence Length: We investigated translation performance for different target sentence lengths, by grouping the target sentences in the IWSLT datasets by sentence length intervals. We choose to group the target sentence lengths rather than source sentence lengths because, cf. Moore (2002), the source sentence and target sentence lengths are proportional. Second, since the target languages are different, and the source language is English, we are particularly concerned about the change in the length of sentences across different target languages.

Overall, our model outperformed the baseline system and 1-best parse system, as shown in Figure 4. Among them, the increase in the length range (20,30], (30,40] and (40,50] were more pronounced over the baseline system and 1-best parse system. The BLEU-4 scores of both our model and 1-best parse model were in danger of slipping

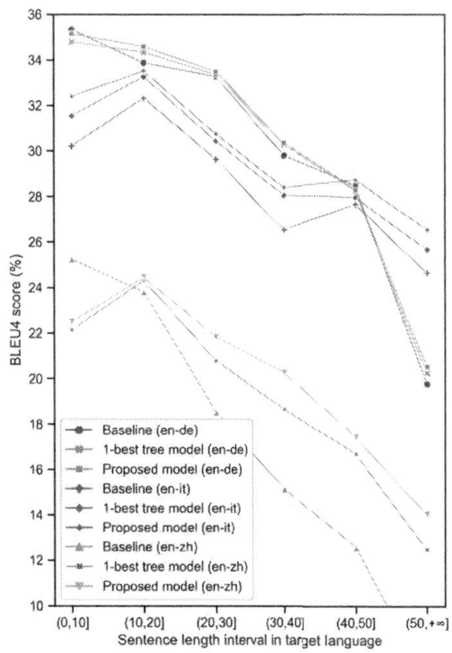

Figure 4: BLEU-4 comparison in sentences length

below the baseline model in the sentence length interval (0,10]. Corpus analysis shows that this length interval contains many fragments, remaining after slicing long sentences. Because the syntactic structures of these fragments were incomplete, they may negatively impact on the model's translation performance. As sentence length increased further, all models saw substantial declines in BLEU-4 scores, following similar downward patterns. When the sentence length exceeds 50, the BLEU-4 scores of our method remained significantly different from both the baseline model and the 1-best parse model. These showed that our proposed model has better translation performance in lengthy sentences, but BLEU-4 scores were still relatively low, indicating that the NMT models have much room for improvement.

Attention Weights Visualization: The final layer's attention weights of the 1-best parse model and the model we proposed are depicted in Figures 5 and 6, respectively. Judging from the comparison of the figures, we find that there are certain consistencies; for example, each word has higher attention weights to the words around it. However, the distinction is also discernible.

Specifically, for the word "A", the word "A" and the word "man" have a syntactic relation, which was represented in both figures. However, the 1-best parse model also provided "staring" a higher

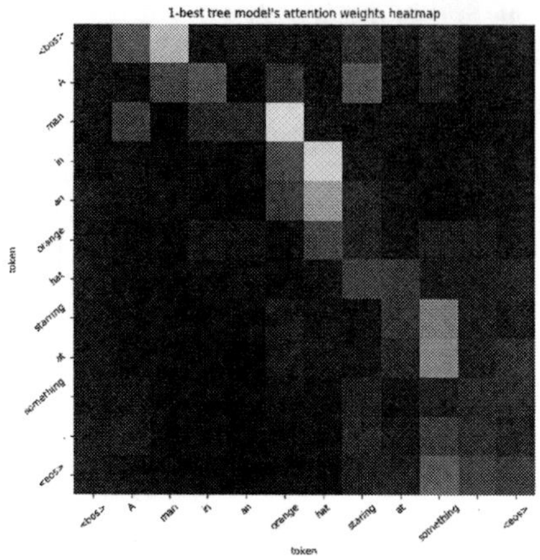

Figure 5: An example of 1-best parse model's attention weights

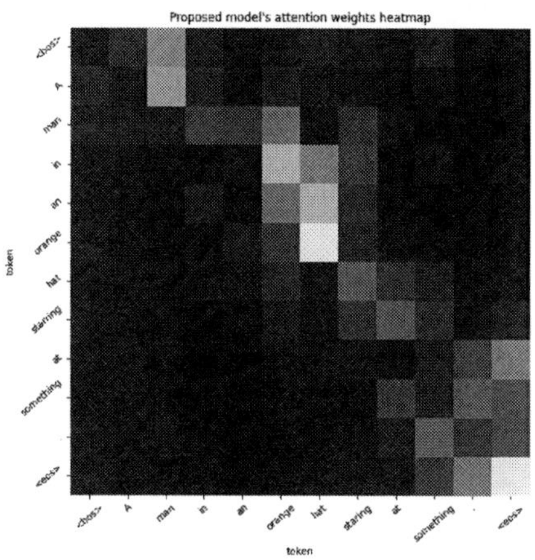

Figure 6: An example of proposed model's attention weights

attention weight, which is contrary to the syntactic structures, and the model we proposed resolved this problem. For the word "man", the 1-best parse model did not pay proper attention to distance but with syntactic relation word "staring", on the contrary, in the proposed model, "staring" was paid attention with a very high value. In a nutshell, both the 1-best parse model and the proposed model are better than the baseline model in terms of attention alignment which demonstrates that the syntactic knowledge contained in dependency distributions can guide the weight computation of the attention mechanism, directing it to pay more attention to words with syntactic relations, thereby improving the alignment quality to a certain extent.

5 Conclusion

This paper presented a novel supervised conditional labeled dependency distributions Transformer network (LDD-Seq). This method primarily improves the self-attention mechanism in the Transformer model by converting the dependency forest to conditional probability distributions; each self-attention head in the Transformer learns a dependency relation distribution, allowing the Transformer to learn source language's dependency constraints, and generates attention weights that are more in line with the syntactic structures. The experimental outcomes demonstrated that the proposed method was straightforward, and it could effectively leverage the source language dependency syntactic structures to improve the Transformer's translation performance without increasing the complexity of the Transformer network or interfering with the highly parallelized characteristic of the Transformer model.

References

Bahdanau, Dzmitry, Kyunghyun Cho, and Yoshua Bengio. 2014. Neural machine translation by jointly learning to align and translate. *arXiv preprint arXiv:1409.0473*.

Bastings, Jasmijn and Ivan Titov and Wilker Aziz and Diego Marcheggiani and Khalil Sima'an. 2017. Graph Convolutional Encoders for Syntax-aware Neural Machine Translation. *Proceedings of the 2017 Conference on Empirical Methods in Natural Language Processing*. 1957–1967.

Belinkov, Yonatan and Yonatan Bisk. 2018. Synthetic and Natural Noise Both Break Neural Machine Translation. *International Conference on Learning Representations*.

Bugliarello, Emanuele and Naoaki Okazaki. 2020. Enhancing Machine Translation with Dependency-Aware Self-Attention. *Proceedings of the 58th Annual Meeting of the Association for Computational Linguistics*, Online. 1618–1627.

Chen, Kehai and Rui Wang and Masao Utiyama and Eiichiro Sumita and Tiejun Zhao. 2018. Syntax-directed attention for neural machine translation. *Proceedings of the AAAI Conference on Artificial Intelligence*.

Cho, Kyunghyun and Bart van Merriénboer and Caglar Gulcehre and Dzmitry Bahdanau and Fethi Bougares and Holger Schwenk and Yoshua Bengio. 2014. Learning Phrase Representations using RNN Encoder–Decoder for Statistical Machine Translation. *Proceedings of the 2014 Conference on Empirical Methods in Natural Language Processing (EMNLP)*. 1724–1734.

Currey, Anna and Kenneth Heafield. 2019. Incorporating Source Syntax into Transformer-Based Neural Machine Translation. *Proceedings of the Fourth Conference on Machine Translation (Volume 1: Research Papers*. 24–33.

Deguchi, Hiroyuki and Akihiro Tamura and Takashi Ninomiya. 2019. Dependency-based self-attention for transformer NMT. *Proceedings of the International Conference on Recent Advances in Natural Language Processing (RANLP 2019)*. 239–246.

Dozat, Timothy and Christopher D Manning. 2016. Deep biaffine attention for neural dependency parsing. *arXiv preprint arXiv:1611.01734*.

Duan, Sufeng and Hai Zhao and Junru Zhou and Rui Wang. 2019. Syntax-aware transformer encoder for neural machine translation. *2019 International Conference on Asian Language Processing (IALP)*. IEEE. 396–401.

Eriguchi, Akiko and Kazuma Hashimoto and Yoshimasa Tsuruoka. 2016. Tree-to-Sequence Attentional Neural Machine Translation. *Proceedings of the 54th Annual Meeting of the Association for Computational Linguistics (Volume 1: Long Papers)*, Berlin, Germany 823–833.

Isozaki, Hideki and Tsutomu Hirao and Kevin Duh and Katsuhito Sudoh and Hajime Tsukada. 2010. Automatic evaluation of translation quality for distant language pairs. *Proceedings of the 2010 Conference on Empirical Methods in Natural Language Processing*. 944–952.

Kalchbrenner, Nal and Phil Blunsom. 2013. Recurrent Continuous Translation Models. *Proceedings of the 2013 Conference on Empirical Methods in Natural Language Processing*. 1700–1709.

Kingma, Diederik P and Jimmy Ba. 2015. Adam: A Method for Stochastic Optimization. *ICLR (Poster)*.

Ma, Chunpeng and Akihiro Tamura and Masao Utiyama and Tiejun Zhao and Eiichiro Sumita. 2018. Forest-Based Neural Machine Translation. *Proceedings of the 56th Annual Meeting of the Association for Computational Linguistics (Volume 1: Long Papers)*, Melbourne, Australia. 1253–1263.

Moore, Robert C. 2002. Fast and accurate sentence alignment of bilingual corpora. *Conference of the Association for Machine Translation in the Americas*. Springer. 135–144.

Omote, Yutaro and Akihiro Tamura and Takashi Ninomiya. 2019. Dependency-based relative positional encoding for transformer NMT. *Proceedings of the International Conference on Recent Advances in Natural Language Processing (RANLP 2019)*. 854–861.

Mylonakis, Markos and Khalil Sima'an. 2011. Learning hierarchical translation structure with linguistic annotations. *Proceedings of the 49th Annual Meeting of the Association for Computational Linguistics: Human Language Technologies*. 642–652.

Neubig, Graham and Kevin Duh. 2014. On the elements of an accurate tree-to-string machine translation system. *Proceedings of the 52nd Annual Meeting of the Association for Computational Linguistics (Volume 2: Short Papers)*. 143–149.

Papineni, Kishore and Salim Roukos and Todd Ward and Wei-Jing Zhu. 2002. Bleu: a method for automatic evaluation of machine translation. *Proceedings of the 40th annual meeting of the Association for Computational Linguistics*. 311–318.

Peng, Ru and Tianyong Hao and Yi Fang. 2021. Syntax-aware neural machine translation directed by syntactic dependency degree. *Neural Computing and Applications*. 16609–16625.

Pham, Thuong Hai and Dominik Macháček and Ondřej Bojar. 2019. Promoting the Knowledge of Source Syntax in Transformer NMT Is Not Needed. *Computación y Sistemas*. 923–934.

Shi, Xing and Inkit Padhi and Kevin Knight. 2016. Does String-Based Neural MT Learn Source Syntax? *Proceedings of the 2016 Conference on Empirical Methods in Natural Language Processing*, Austin, Texas. 1526–1534.

Snover, Matthew and Bonnie Dorr and Richard Schwartz and Linnea Micciulla and John Makhoul. 2006. A study of translation edit rate with targeted human annotation. *Proceedings of the 7th Conference of the Association for Machine Translation in the Americas: Technical Papers*. 223–231.

Stanojević, Miloš and Khalil Sima'an. 2014. Fitting Sentence Level Translation Evaluation with Many Dense Features. *Proceedings of the 2014 Conference on Empirical Methods in Natural Language Processing (EMNLP)*, Doha, Qatar. 202–206.

Sutskever, Ilya and Oriol Vinyals and Quoc V Le. 2014. Sequence to sequence learning with neural networks. *Advances in neural information processing systems*.

Tu, Zhaopeng and Yang Liu and Young-Sook Hwang and Qun Liu and Shouxun Lin. 2010. Dependency forest for statistical machine translation. *Proceedings of the 23rd International Conference on Computational Linguistics (Coling 2010)*. 1092–1100.

Vaswani, Ashish and Noam Shazeer and Niki Parmar and Jakob Uszkoreit and Llion Jones and Aidan N Gomez and Łukasz Kaiser and Illia Polosukhin. 2017. Attention is all you need. *Advances in neural information processing systems*. 5998–6008.

Zaremoodi, Poorya and Gholamreza Haffari. 2018. Incorporating Syntactic Uncertainty in Neural Machine Translation with a Forest-to-Sequence Model. *Proceedings of the 27th International Conference on Computational Linguistics*. 1421–1429.

Zhang, Tianfu and Heyan Huang and Chong Feng and Longbing Cao. 2021. Self-supervised bilingual syntactic alignment for neural machine translation. *Proceedings of the AAAI Conference on Artificial Intelligence*. 14454–14462.

Zhang, Meishan and Zhenghua Li and Guohong Fu and Min Zhang. 2019. Syntax-Enhanced Neural Machine Translation with Syntax-Aware Word Representations. *Proceedings of the 2019 Conference of the North American Chapter of the Association for Computational Linguistics: Human Language Technologies, Volume 1 (Long and Short Papers*, Minneapolis, Minnesota. 1151–1161.

Zhang, Yu and Zhenghua Li and Min Zhang. 2020. Efficient Second-Order TreeCRF for Neural Dependency Parsing. *Proceedings of the 58th Annual Meeting of the Association for Computational Linguistics*, Online. 3295–3305.

A Appendix: Dependency group labels

Table A: 16 alternative dependency group labels

Dependency group labels	Original dependency labels
l_1	root
l_2	aux, auxpass, cop
l_3	acomp, ccomp, pcomp, xcomp
l_4	dobj, iobj, pobj
l_5	csubj, csubjpass
l_6	nsubj, nsubjpass
l_7	cc
l_8	conj, preconj
l_9	advcl
l_{10}	amod
l_{11}	advmod
l_{12}	npadvmod, tmod
l_{13}	det, predet
l_{14}	num, number, quantmod
l_{15}	appos
l_{16}	punct

How well do real-time machine translation apps perform in practice? Insights from a literature review

Mark Pluymaekers
Zuyd University of Applied Sciences
Brusselseweg 150, 6217 HB Maastricht (NL)
mark.pluymaekers@zuyd.nl

Abstract

Although more and more professionals are using real-time machine translation during dialogues with interlocutors who speak a different language, the performance of real-time MT apps has received only limited attention in the academic literature. This study summarizes the findings of prior studies (N = 34) reporting an evaluation of one or more real-time MT apps in a professional setting. Our findings show that real-time MT apps are often tested in realistic circumstances and that users are more frequently employed as judges of performance than professional translators. Furthermore, most studies report overall positive results with regard to performance, particularly when apps are tested in real-life situations.

1 Introduction

In 1997, Mark Seligman wrote that "the Internet offers a tremendous opportunity for experiments with real-time machine translation (MT) of dialogues" (Seligman, 1997). In December of the same year, SYSTRAN and AltaVista launched "the first widely available, real-time, high-speed and free translation service on the Internet" (Yang & Lange, 1998). Now, 25 years later, the Google Translate app has been downloaded more than 1 billion times from the Google App Store (Pitman, 2021). Since 2011, the app offers a conversation mode, which enables users to have utterances within a dialogue translated in real-time so that their conversation partners can understand them. Other apps such as iTranslate, TripLingo and Microsoft Translator can also be used to support synchronous dialogue between interlocutors who do not speak the same language (Tao, 2022).

To the best of our knowledge, there are no publicly available data on the frequency with which MT apps are used for real-time translation and the contexts in which this occurs. However, given the popularity of these apps, it can be expected that a large number of synchronous dialogues are translated every day, and that this happens not only in informal situations, but also in professional contexts. This raises the question of how well real-time MT apps perform in these kinds of situations. Traditionally, the academic literature has paid more attention to the quality of written translations that have been produced using MT than to the output of real-time MT apps. This study aims to boost research into the performance of real-time MT apps by summarizing the findings of earlier studies in which the performance of such apps was evaluated in a professional context.

2 MT quality assessment

The quality of MT output has been a hotly debated topic for decades, and a wide variety of methods for its assessment have been proposed (cf. Castilho et al., 2018). When classifying these methods, authors commonly distinguish between automated metrics and human metrics (e.g., Rivera-Trigueros, 2021; Chatzikoumi, 2020). Automated metrics include Word Error Rates (WERs), precision, recall, and BLEU scores, all of which are calculated on the basis of a comparison between MT output and a reference translation created by a professional human translator.

Macken, Rufener, Van den Bogaert, Daems, Tezcan, Vanroy, Fonteyne, Barrault, Costa-jussà, Kemp, Pilos, Declercq, Koponen, Forcada, Scarton, Moniz (eds.)
Proceedings of the 23rd Annual Conference of the European Association for Machine Translation, p. 51–60
Ghent, Belgium, June 2022.

Human metrics are further subdivided by Chatzikoumi (2020) into metrics in which human experts express a direct judgement concerning the translation quality and metrics in which no direct judgement is expressed. When experts are asked to indicate the adequacy or fluency of a machine translated text on a 5-point scale, for example, they make an explicit quality judgement. When, on the other hand, they classify the translation errors occurring in the MT output, they provide useful information for improving the application without explicitly judging the quality of the output. Measuring the post-editing effort required to reach an acceptable quality level for the target text (e.g. Lacruz et al., 2014) also provides an indirect indication of MT quality.

There are several reasons why most of the metrics discussed above can be considered less suitable for assessing real-time MT that is used to support synchronous dialogues. First of all, post-editing does not occur in such situations, so post-editing effort cannot be used as a quality indicator. In the absence of a human-generated reference translation, automated metrics can also not be calculated. Technically speaking, human experts could judge the quality of the output after the dialogue has taken place, but they would be at a disadvantage due to the limited length and disfluent nature of the source texts, particularly when speech input is used (Przybocki et al., 2011).

Moreover, it is important to acknowledge that MT quality assessment can have different purposes. Many of the metrics above were primarily developed to identify areas of improvement for MT applications that are 'under construction' (Dorr et al., 2011). For professionals contemplating the use of real-time MT in their daily professional routines, however, improving the application is not the main priority. They want to know whether using MT will enhance the quality of their interactions with patients, students or business partners who speak a different language. In some cases, they might even wonder whether the use of MT is ethically responsible given the prevalence of errors in MT output and the potentially damaging consequences of such errors in certain contexts (Vieira et al., 2020).

Taken together, these considerations suggest that the evaluation of real-time MT might best be approached from the perspective of 'fitness for purpose', which is achieved when the quality of a translation is 'good enough' for the end user to understand the information content and pragmatic intent of a translated message (Moorkens et al., 2018; Directorate General for Translation, 2016). Although this concept has featured prominently in both practical and academic discourse about translation quality for quite some time (Jiménez-Crespo, 2018), it is not yet standard practice to ask end users to assess the quality of (post-edited) MT output (cf. Van Egdom & Pluymaekers, 2019).

This raises the question to what extent existing studies into the performance of real-time MT apps are guided by the concept of fitness for purpose, and how fitness for purpose is operationalized in evaluation methods used in these studies. For the current paper, we are specifically interested in the answers to the following questions:

RQ1: To what extent are real-time MT applications tested in authentic professional situations?

RQ2: Which quality indicators are most commonly used and how are they operationalized?

RQ3: Who judges the performance of real-time MT apps?

RQ4: Which overall picture concerning the performance of real-time MT apps emerges from the research conducted so far?

We hope to find these answers by conducting a systematic literature review of prior studies (N = 34) which report an evaluation of a real-time MT app that was or could be used to facilitate a synchronous dialogue between interlocutors who did not speak the same language. More information about our methodology is provided in the next chapter.

3 Method

For our literature review, we collected papers published in peer-reviewed journals or conference proceedings which assessed the quality of linguistic material that was translated in real-time by an MT application and that was related to actual or potential dialogues in professional settings (e.g., healthcare, education or tourism). Studies that focused on other types of linguistic material (e.g., websites or leaflets) or only described a real-time MT system without reporting an evaluation were excluded from the sample. Subsequently, the studies included in the sample were coded on a number of key variables derived from the research questions stated above. The following sections describe the sampling method, the coding procedure and the statistical analyses.

3.1 Sampling

In compiling the sample, we followed a multi-step approach (see Figure 1). First, we conducted an initial search in four scientific databases (EBSCO-host, PubMed, Web of Science and Google Scholar), which were selected for reasons of practicality (i.e., accessibility via the university library) as well as quality (cf. Creswell, 2014; Gusenbauer & Haddaway, 2020). In each database, we used the following Boolean combination of search words:

("mobile translat*" OR "real-time translat*" OR "automatic translat*") OR ("translat* tool" OR "translat* app") AND ("quality" OR "evaluation" OR "usability") NOT "knowledge translation"

Depending on the search functionalities of the database, this query was applied to the abstract, the title and the abstract, or the entire text. The relevance of the articles that came up in the search results was assessed in two steps. On the basis of the abstracts, 23 articles were marked as potentially relevant. After reading the complete articles, we decided that 10 of them indeed corresponded to the inclusion criteria outlined above.

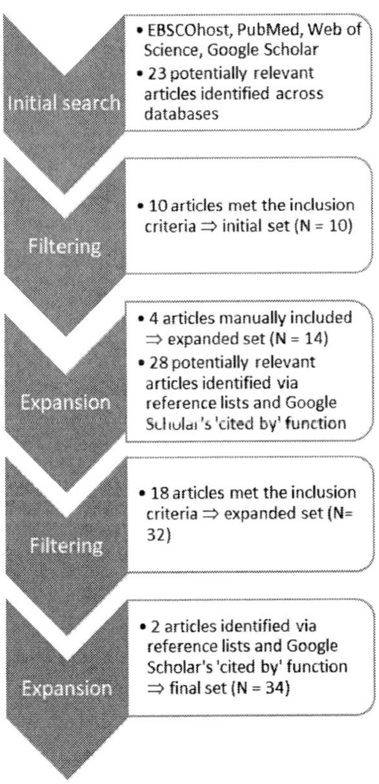

Figure 1: Overview of the sampling process

In the next step, we expanded the sample by (1) manually adding 4 articles that we had found earlier and (2) investigating studies that were either included in the reference list of one of the articles in the initial set or that referred to one of the articles in the initial set. By doing so, we identified 28 potential additions to the sample, 18 of which met the screening criteria. For the newly added articles (4+18), we repeated the reference check described above, which led to the identification of 2 more articles. After this, saturation was achieved, resulting in a final sample of 34 articles (see Appendix A). More information about the characteristics of these articles (year of publication, the number and types of applications tested, language combinations etc.) will be provided in section 4.1 below.

3.2 Coding

All articles were coded by two independent coders using the coding scheme presented in Table 1.

Year of publication	
Publication type	☐ Conference paper ☐ Journal article
Professional domain	☐ Healthcare ☐ ICT ☐ Education ☐ Tourism ☐ Other, namely:
# of applications	
Application type	☐ Existing generic ☐ Existing domain-specific ☐ Tailor-made
Modality	☐ Text-to-text ☐ Text-to-speech ☐ Speech-to-text ☐ Speech-to-speech
Language combination(s)	
Test type(s)	☐ Real-life situation ☐ Scenario-based simulation ☐ Corpus-based simulation
Data collection method(s)	☐ Survey ☐ Interview ☐ Focus group ☐ Content analysis ☐ Observation ☐ Other, namely:
Judge(s)	☐ Provider ☐ Recipient ☐ User (no provider-recipient relationship) ☐ Professional translator ☐ Native speaker / bilingual ☐ Other, namely:

Quality indicator(s)	#	Variable	Operatio-nalization
	1		
	2		
	3		
Overall evaluation	☐ Positive ☐ Negative ☐ Mixed		

Table 1: Coding scheme

Any disagreements between the two coders were discussed until consensus was reached. Most variables in the table are more or less self-explanatory, but there are three variables we wish to elaborate on here. First of all, *application type* was included to be able to distinguish between MT applications created for general purposes (e.g., Google Translate), MT applications created for specific professional domains (e.g., Canopy Medical Translator) and MT applications created by the authors of the article. With respect to *test type*, we noticed during the screening process that not all applications are tested in situations that involve actual dialogue; Sometimes, frequently occurring utterances from professional dialogues are provided to the application to assess the quality of the translation (referred to as 'corpus-based simulation' in Table 1). If actual dialogues are involved in the test, they can be either real-life dialogues or dialogues from a role-playing scenario scripted by the researchers. Finally, for the variable *judge* we decided to distinguish between providers and recipients of care, service or education, as our initial observations suggested that providers may be asked more frequently to assess the performance of MT apps than recipients.

3.3 Analysis

The outcomes of the coding process were entered into an SPSS data file containing mainly nominal variables recording the presence or absence of certain methodological features (e.g., whether recipients were asked to judge the performance of the app or whether focus groups were used to collect data). To gain insight into the sample characteristics and answer the research questions, frequency tables were created. To assess whether the overall judgement regarding the performance of the app differed as a function of methodological choices made, we used Chi-squared tests.

4 Results

4.1 Sample characteristics

All studies in the sample were published between 2005 and 2022. Figure 2 shows how the studies were distributed over the years. 28 studies (82%) were published in peer-reviewed journals, while 6 (18%) appeared in conference proceedings. The majority of the studies (27 or 79%) focused on one real-time MT application; 5 studies (15%) made a comparison between two applications while only 2 studies (Hwang et al., 2022 and Panayiotou et al., 2020) included three applications in their evaluation. Existing general-purpose applications were tested most frequently (18 studies or 53%), followed by apps that were created by the authors themselves and existing domain-specific applications, which were tested in 12 (35%) and 8 (24%) studies respectively. Most evaluations were conducted in the context of healthcare (28 studies or 82%). A wide variety of tested language combinations could be observed in the sample, although the majority of studies (24 or 71%) looked at one or two combinations, and English was part of the tested language combinations in 25 of the 34 studies (74%).

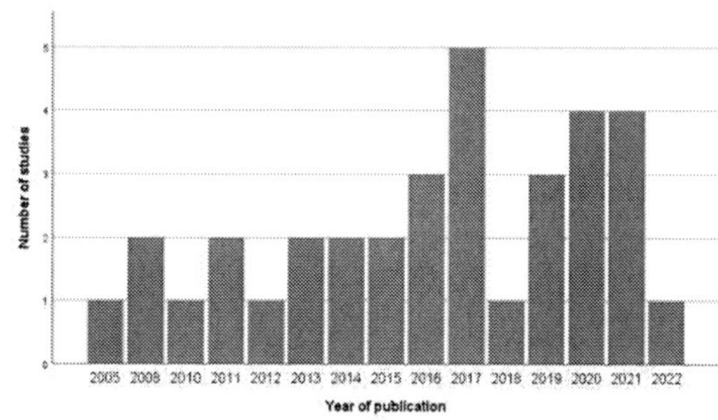

Figure 2: Number of studies by year of publication

4.2 Test types and data collection methods

Of the 34 studies in the sample, 32 used a single test type. The two exceptions were Calefato et al. (2016) and Haith-Cooper (2014), who conducted both a scenario-based and a corpus-based simulation. Far more common was the use of multiple data collection methods, which was observed in 18 of the 34 studies (53%). Tables 2 and 3 show which test types and data collection methods were used most frequently.

As Table 2 shows, most studies made an attempt to conduct a test in more or less authentic circumstances, be it in real life or during a scenario-based simulation. As can be seen in

Table 3, quantitative data collection methods such as surveys, content analysis (e.g., counting the number of correctly translated words or sentences) and observation (e.g., measuring how long it took participants to accomplish a certain task) were more popular than qualitative data collection methods, such as interviews and focus groups.

Test type	Number of studies
Real-life situation	16 (47%)
Scenario-based simulation	15 (44%)
Corpus-based simulation	5 (15%)

Table 2: Test types and the number of studies they were used in (including percentages)

Data collection method	Number of studies
Surveys	23 (68%)
Content analysis	13 (38%)
Observation	12 (35%)
Interviews	8 (24%)
Focus groups	3 (9%)

Table 3: Data collection methods and the number of studies they were used in (including percentages)

4.3 Quality indicators and judges

The majority of the studies (27 or 79%) employed multiple quality indicators to assess the performance of the MT app(s) under study. For judges, this was not the case, as 20 studies (59%) relied on a single category of judges. The quality indicator used most often was usability or ease of use, although it was used in only half of the studies in the sample. Similarly, providers were the most frequently employed judges, but they were still only involved in 18 out of the 34 studies (53%). Tables 4 and 5 summarize the frequency information for the different quality indicators and categories of judges.

Table 4 shows that many different quality indicators were used, some of which showed conceptual overlap even though they were referred to using different terms. That is why we decided to group them together in the table. It should be noted, however, that many studies did not provide explicit definitions of their quality indicators and that there was little uniformity in the way that variables such as *ease of use* or *accuracy* were measured. With respect to the judges, providers were more frequently asked to provide their opinion than recipients, and professional translators were involved in only a handful of studies.

Quality indicator	Number of studies
Usability / ease of use	17 (50%)
Accuracy / adequacy / acceptability	16 (47%)
Satisfaction / meeting needs	11 (32%)
Usefulness / helpfulness / effectiveness	10 (29%)
Intention to use / actual use	8 (24%)
Time / efficiency / duration	7 (21%)
Comprehensibility / intelligibility	5 (15%)
Objective outcome quality	4 (12%)
Other	16 (47%)

Table 4: Quality indicators and the number of studies they were used in (including percentages)

Judge	Number of studies
Provider	18 (53%)
Recipient	13 (38%)
Native speaker / bilingual	8 (24%)
Translator / translation student	3 (9%)
User	3 (9%)
Other	5 (15%)

Table 5: Categories of judges and the number of studies they were used in (including percentages)

4.4 Overall performance

Of the 34 studies in the sample, 22 (65%) reported overall positive results with regard to the performance of the MT app(s) under study. 8 studies (24%) yielded mixed results, while only 4 studies (12%) were unequivocally negative in their final judgement. Mixed results mainly stemmed from differences between tested apps or variants of apps (e.g., Bouillon et al., 2017; Turner et al., 2019; Starlander et al., 2005) or different outcomes for different quality indicators (e.g., Seligman & Dillinger, 2015; Herrmann-Werner et al., 2021; Calefato et al., 2016).

Because of small cell sizes, the number of meaningful Chi-squared tests that we could run was limited. However, the outcomes of the tests that we did conduct show that an overall positive evaluation occurred more often than expected if the app was created by the authors themselves ($\chi^2(2) = 6.09$, $p < 0.05$) and if the test involved real-life situations ($\chi^2(2) = 7.55$, $p < 0.05$). Conversely, a negative overall evaluation occurred more often than expected if accuracy was used as a quality indicator ($\chi^2(2) = 7.32$, $p < 0.05$).

5 Conclusions and discussion

The aim of this study was to gain insight into (1) how the performance of real-time MT apps has been evaluated in previous research and (2) which overall picture concerning the performance of real-time MT apps emerges from the research conducted so far. To this end, we conducted a literature review in which we coded 34 published studies reporting an evaluation of real-time MT apps and their output.

Based on the results, we can conclude that the vast majority of studies have tested the app(s) during actual dialogues between interlocutors who did not speak each other's language (RQ1). In about half of those studies, a predefined scenario was used; in the other half, participants used the app(s) during their daily work. The most commonly used quality indicators were the perceived ease of use, the accuracy of the translations, the satisfaction with the user experience, and the perceived usefulness (RQ2). Therefore, it should not come as a surprise that users (both providers and recipients) were frequently employed as judges. Professional translators were involved in only a handful of studies (RQ3). Finally, 22 of the 34 studies came to a positive overall conclusion regarding the performance of the tested app(s). Only 4 studies reported mainly negative results (RQ4).

These outcomes suggest that fitness-for-purpose has indeed been an important guiding principle in previous studies that evaluated real-time MT apps. This is understandable, as many quality indicators used for the evaluation of written MT output are less applicable when MT is used to support synchronous dialogue. In addition, many studies were conducted with a view to a concrete professional context (e.g., communication between doctors and patients), which can explain why the focus was mainly on the course and the outcome of the dialogue as a whole, and less on the literal content of individual utterances within that dialogue.

At the same time, there are a number of observations that are cause for concern, both from a methodological as well as from a practical point of view. First of all, many studies are not clear about the definitions of their quality indicators, and even the most commonly used dependent variables are operationalized in many different ways. This not only reduces the comparability of studies, but also the possibility for professionals to make an evidence-based decision regarding the best app for their specific purpose. A similar point can be made with regard to the wide variety of language combinations examined and the lack of standardization in test scenarios. These methodological choices also add variance to the data that can obscure insight into the overall performance of the apps under investigation.

Another striking finding is that providers of care, education or services are asked about their experiences more often than recipients. One could argue that real-time MT apps are more likely to benefit recipients, as they can remove language barriers and increase the likelihood that recipients' wishes and concerns are well understood by providers. However, if a doctor or teacher feels that a dialogue that was supported by a real-time MT app has gone well, that does not necessarily mean that the other party involved in the dialogue has also experienced it that way. Therefore, it is advisable to always involve both parties in future evaluations.

Finally, only a few studies have attempted to establish objectively whether the translated dialogue also led to the desired outcome – in most cases, a correct diagnosis (e.g., Bouillon et al., 2017; Leite et al., 2016; Spechbach et al., 2019; Starlander et al., 2005). Although determining the correctness or objective desirability of an outcome is not possible in all professional situations, especially in contexts such as healthcare and education, one would expect that more attention would be devoted to what ultimately matters: A patient who recovers and a student who learns.

Of course, our study also has its limitations. Because reference lists played an important role in identifying potentially relevant studies, it is possible that we have overlooked previous research from certain professional domains. Since the majority of the studies in our sample (82%) were conducted in the context of healthcare, we could not compare the performance of real-time MT apps – nor the expectations of their users – across professional domains. In addition, some features of previous studies were not explicitly coded, such as the distinction between fixed-phrase translators and MT apps that can handle unrestricted input. Moreover, because the final sample was relatively small, we were only able to make a limited number of comparisons in our statistical analyses.

Therefore, we hope that future studies can investigate more systematically which variables explain the differences in performance between real-time MT apps. In addition, the various definitions and operationalizations of quality indicators can be mapped, so that more insight is gained into their interrelationships and conceptual overlap. Finally, it may be possible to develop and validate a more or less standardized test protocol that can increase the comparability of future studies.

Acknowledgement

The author would like to thank Magda de Bruin for her contribution to the coding process.

References

Bouillon, P., Gerlach, J., Spechbach, H., Tsourakis, N., & Halimi Mallem, I. S. (2017). Babeldr vs Google Translate: A user study at Geneva university hospitals (HUG). In *20th Annual Conference of the European Association for Machine Translation (EAMT)*.

Calefato, F., Lanubile, F., Conte, T., & Prikladnicki, R. (2016). Assessing the impact of real-time machine translation on multilingual meetings in global software projects. *Empirical Software Engineering, 21(3)*, 1002-1034.

Castilho, S., Doherty, S., Gaspari, F., & Moorkens, J. (2018). Approaches to human and machine translation quality assessment. In J. Moorkens, S. Castilho, F. Gaspari and S. Doherty (Eds.), *Translation quality assessment*. Cham: Springer, pp. 9–38.

Chatzikoumi, E. (2020). How to evaluate machine translation: A review of automated and human metrics. *Natural Language Engineering*, 26(2), 137–161.

Creswell, J.W. (2014). *Research design: Qualitative, Quantitative, and Mixed Methods Approaches.* Los Angeles: Sage.

Directorate-General for Translation (2016). DGT guidelines for evaluation of outsourced translation. *Ares (2016) 3157529.*

Dorr B., Snover M. and Madnani N. (2011). Chapter 5.1 introduction. In Olive J., McCary J. and Christianson C. (Eds.), *Handbook of Natural Language Processing and Machine Translation.* DARPA Global Autonomous Language Exploitation. New York: Springer, pp. 801–803

Gusenbauer, M., & Haddaway, N. R. (2020). Which academic search systems are suitable for systematic reviews or meta-analyses? Evaluating retrieval qualities of Google Scholar, PubMed, and 26 other resources. *Research synthesis methods, 11(2)*, 181-217.

Haith-Cooper, M. (2014). Mobile translators for non-English-speaking women accessing maternity services. *British Journal of Midwifery, 22(11)*, 795-803.

Herrmann-Werner, A., Loda, T., Zipfel, S., Holderried, M., Holderried, F., & Erschens, R. (2021). Evaluation of a Language Translation App in an Undergraduate Medical Communication Course: Proof-of-Concept and Usability Study. *JMIR mHealth and uHealth, 9(12)*, e31559.

Hwang, K., Williams, S., Zucchi, E., Chong, T. W., Mascitti-Meuter, M., LoGiudice, D., ... & Batchelor, F. (2022). Testing the use of translation apps to overcome everyday healthcare communication in Australian aged-care hospital wards—An exploratory study. *Nursing open.*

Jiménez-Crespo, M. A. (2018). Crowdsourcing and translation quality: Novel approaches in the language industry and translation studies. In J. Moorkens, S. Castilho, F. Gaspari and S. Doherty (Eds.), *Translation quality assessment*. Cham: Springer, pp. 69-93.

Lacruz I., Denkowski M. and Lavie A. (2014). Cognitive demand and cognitive effort in post-editing. In *Proceedings of the Third Workshop on Post-Editing Technology and Practice. 11th Conference of the Association for Machine Translation in the Americas, Vancouver, BC, Canada.*

Leite, F. O., Cochat, C., Salgado, H., da Costa, M. P., Queirós, M., Campos, O., & Carvalho, P. (2016). Using Google Translate© in the hospital: a case report. *Technology and Health Care, 24(6)*, 965-968.

Moorkens, J., Castilho, S., Gaspari, F. and Doherty, S. (Eds.) (2018). *Translation quality assessment.* Cham: Springer.

Panayiotou, A., Hwang, K., Williams, S., Chong, T. W., LoGiudice, D., Haralambous, B., ... & Batchelor, F. (2020). The perceptions of translation apps for everyday health care in healthcare workers and older people: A multi-method study. *Journal of Clinical Nursing, 29(17-18)*, 3516-3526.

Pitman, J. (2021, 28 April). Google Translate: One billion installs, one billion stories. Retrieved from https://blog.google/products/translate/one-billion-installs/ on 25 March 2022.

Przybocki M., Le A., Sanders G., Bronsart S., Strassel S. and Glenn M. (2011). Chapter 5.4.3 Post-editing. In Olive J., McCary J. and Christianson C. (Eds.), *Handbook of Natural Language Processing and Machine Translation.* DARPA Global Autonomous Language Exploitation. New York: Springer

Rivera-Trigueros, I. (2021). Machine translation systems and quality assessment: a systematic review. *Language Resources and Evaluation*, 1-27.

Seligman, M. (1997). Interactive real-time translation via the Internet. *Working Notes, Natural Language Processing for the World Wide Web*, 24-26.

Seligman, M., & Dillinger, M. (2015). Evaluation and Revision of a Speech Translation System for Health Care. In *Proceedings of International Workshop for Spoken Language Translation 2015* (pp. 3-4).

Spechbach, H., Gerlach, J., Karker, S. M., Tsourakis, N., Combescure, C., & Bouillon, P. (2019). A speech-enabled fixed-phrase translator for emergency settings: Crossover study. *JMIR medical informatics, 7(2)*, e13167.

Starlander, M., Bouillon, P., Rayner, M., Chatzichrisafis, N., Hockey, B. A., Isahara, H., ... & Santaholma, M. (2005). Breaking the language barrier: machine assisted diagnosis using the medical speech translator. *Studies in health technology and informatics, 116*, 811-816.

Tao, U. (2022, 25 January). Top ten free translator apps 2022. Retrieved from https://www.timekettle.co/blogs/tips-and-tricks/top-10-free-translator-apps-2020 on 25 March 2022.

Turner, A. M., Choi, Y. K., Dew, K., Tsai, M. T., Bosold, A. L., Wu, S., ... & Meischke, H. (2019). Evaluating the usefulness of translation technologies for emergency response communication: A scenario-based study. *JMIR public health and surveillance, 5(1)*, e11171.

Van Egdom, G. M. W., & Pluymaekers, M. (2019). Why go the extra mile? How different degrees of post-editing affect perceptions of texts, senders and products among end users. *Journal of specialised translation, 31*, 158-176.

Vieira, L. N., O'Hagan, M., & O'Sullivan, C. (2021). Understanding the societal impacts of machine translation: a critical review of the literature on medical and legal use cases. *Information, Communication & Society*, 24(11), 1515-1532.

Yang, J., & Lange, E. D. (1998). SYSTRAN on AltaVista. A user study on real-time machine translation on the Internet. In *Conference of the Association for Machine Translation in the Americas* (pp. 275-285). Springer, Berlin, Heidelberg.

Appendix A. Overview of studies included in the literature review.

Ahmed, A. N., Chit, S. C., & Omar, M. (2016). Design and evaluation of a multilanguage instant messaging application. *Proceedings of Knowledge Management International Conference 2016*, Chiang Mai, Thailand.
Aiken, M., & Park, M. (2020). A Comparison of two Multilingual Meeting Systems. *International Journal of Computer and Technology, 20*, 38-44.
Albrecht, U. V., Behrends, M., Matthies, H. K., & von Jan, U. (2013). Usage of multilingual mobile translation applications in clinical settings. *JMIR mHealth and uHealth, 1(1)*, e2268.
Beh, T. H. K., & Canty, D. J. (2015). English and Mandarin translation using Google Translate software for pre-anaesthetic consultation. *Anaesthesia and intensive care, 43(6)*, 792.
Bouillon, P., Gerlach, J., Spechbach, H., Tsourakis, N., & Halimi Mallem, I. S. (2017). Babeldr vs Google Translate: A user study at Geneva university hospitals (HUG). In *20th Annual Conference of the European Association for Machine Translation (EAMT).*
Calefato, F., Lanubile, F., Conte, T., & Prikladnicki, R. (2016). Assessing the impact of real-time machine translation on multilingual meetings in globalsoftware projects. *Empirical Software Engineering, 21(3)*, 1002-1034.
Chen, X., Acosta, S., & Barry, A. E. (2017). Machine or human? Evaluating the quality of a language translation mobile app for diabetes education material. *JMIR diabetes, 2(1)*, e13.
Day, K. J., & Song, N. (2017). Attitudes and concerns of doctors and nurses about using a translation application for in-hospital brief interactions with Korean patients. *BMJ Health & Care Informatics, 24(3).*
Ehsani, F., Kinzey, J., Zuber, E., Master, D., & Sudre, K. (2008). Speech to speech translation for nurse patient interaction. In *Coling 2008: Proceedings of the workshop on Speech Processing for Safety Critical Translation and Pervasive Applications* (pp. 54-59).
Freyne, J., Bradford, D., Pocock, C., Silvera-Tawil, D., Harrap, K., & Brinkmann, S. (2018). Developing digital facilitation of assessments in the absence of an interpreter: participatory design and feasibility evaluation with allied health groups. *JMIR formative research, 2(1)*, e8032.
Haith-Cooper, M. (2014). Mobile translators for non-English-speaking women accessing maternity services. *British Journal of Midwifery, 22(11)*, 795-803.
Herrmann-Werner, A., Loda, T., Zipfel, S., Holderried, M., Holderried, F., & Erschens, R. (2021). Evaluation of a Language Translation App in an Undergraduate Medical Communication Course: Proof-of-Concept and Usability Study. *JMIR mHealth and uHealth, 9(12)*, e31559.

Hwang, K., Williams, S., Zucchi, E., Chong, T. W., Mascitti-Meuter, M., LoGiudice, D., ... & Batchelor, F. (2022). Testing the use of translation apps to overcome everyday healthcare communication in Australian aged-care hospital wards—An exploratory study. *Nursing open.*

Janakiram, A. A., Gerlach, J., Vuadens-Lehmann, A., Bouillon, P., & Spechbach, H. (2020). User Satisfaction with a Speech-Enabled Translator in Emergency Settings. *Digital Personalized Health and Medicine*, 1421-1422.

Kaliyadan, F. & Sreekanth, G. (2010). The use of Google language tools as an interpretation aid in cross-cultural doctor–patient interaction: a pilot study. *Informatics in primary care, 18(2)*, 141-43.

Kapoor, R., Truong, A. T., Vu, C. N., & Truong, D. T. (2020). Successful Verbal Communication Using Google Translate to Facilitate Awake Intubation of a Patient With a Language Barrier: A Case Report. *A&A Practice, 14(4)*, 106-108.

Leite, F. O., Cochat, C., Salgado, H., da Costa, M. P., Queirós, M., Campos, O., & Carvalho, P. (2016). Using Google Translate© in the hospital: a case report. *Technology and Health Care, 24(6)*, 965-968.

Narang, B., Park, S. Y., Norrmén-Smith, I. O., Lange, M., Ocampo, A. J., Gany, F. M., & Diamond, L. C. (2019). The use of a mobile application to increase access to interpreters for cancer patients with limited English proficiency: a pilot study. *Medical care, 57(Suppl 6 2)*, S184.

Ozaki, S., Matsunobe, T., Yoshino, T., & Shigeno, A. (2011). Design of a face-to-face multilingual communication system for a handheld device in the medical field. In *International Conference on Human-Computer Interaction* (pp. 378-386). Springer, Berlin, Heidelberg.

Panayiotou, A., Hwang, K., Williams, S., Chong, T. W., LoGiudice, D., Haralambous, B., ... & Batchelor, F. (2020). The perceptions of translation apps for everyday health care in healthcare workers and older people: A multi-method study. *Journal of Clinical Nursing, 29(17-18)*, 3516-3526.

Patil, S., & Davies, P. (2014). Use of Google Translate in medical communication: evaluation of accuracy. *BMJ, 349*.

Ross, R. K., Lake, V. E., & Beisly, A. H. (2021). Preservice teachers' use of a translation app with dual language learners. *Journal of Digital Learning in Teacher Education, 37(2)*, 86-98.

Şahin, M., & Duman, D. (2013). Multilingual Chat through Machine Translation: A Case of English-Russian. *Meta: journal des traducteurs/Meta: Translators' Journal, 58(2)*, 397-410.

Seligman, M., & Dillinger, M. (2015). Evaluation and Revision of a Speech Translation System for Health Care. In *Proceedings of International Workshop for Spoken Language Translation 2015* (pp. 3-4).

Şentürk, E., Orhan-Sungur, M., & Özkan-Seyhan, T. (2021). Google Translate: Can It Be a Solution for Language Barrier in Neuraxial Anaesthesia? *Turkish Journal of Anaesthesiology and Reanimation, 49(2)*, 181.

Silvera-Tawil, D., Pocock, C., Bradford, D., Donnell, A., Freyne, J., Harrap, K., & Brinkmann, S. (2021). Enabling Nurse-Patient Communication With a Mobile App: Controlled Pretest-Posttest Study With Nurses and Non–English-Speaking Patients. *JMIR nursing, 4(3)*, e19709.

Soller, R. W., Chan, P., & Higa, A. (2012). Performance of a new speech translation device in translating verbal recommendations of medication action plans for patients with diabetes. *Journal of diabetes science and technology, 6(4)*, 927-937.

Spechbach, H., Gerlach, J., Karker, S. M., Tsourakis, N., Combescure, C., & Bouillon, P. (2019). A speech-enabled fixed-phrase translator for emergency settings: Crossover study. *JMIR medical informatics, 7(2)*, e13167.

Stankevičiūtė, G., Kasperavičienė, R., & Horbačauskienė, J. (2017). Issues in machine translation: a case of mobile apps in the Lithuanian and English language pair. *International journal on language, literature and culture in education, 4*, 75-88.

Starlander, M., Bouillon, P., Flores, G., Rayner, M., & Tsourakis, N. (2008). Comparing two different bidirectional versions of the limited-domain medical spoken language translator MedSLT. In *Proceedings of the 12th Annual conference of the European Association for Machine Translation* (pp. 176-181).

Taicher, B. M., Alam, R. I., Berman, J., & Epstein, R. H. (2011). Design, implementation, and evaluation of a computerized system to communicate with patients with limited native language proficiency in the perioperative period. *Anesthesia & Analgesia, 112(1)*, 106-112.

Turner, A. M., Choi, Y. K., Dew, K., Tsai, M. T., Bosold, A. L., Wu, S., ... & Meischke, H. (2019). Evaluating the usefulness of translation technologies for emergency response communication: A scenario-based study. *JMIR public health and surveillance, 5(1)*, e11171.

Villalobos, O., Lynch, S., DeBlieck, C., & Summers, L. (2017). Utilization of a mobile app to assess psychiatric patients with limited English proficiency. *Hispanic Journal of Behavioral Sciences, 39(3)*, 369-380.

Searching for COMETINHO: The Little Metric That Could

Ricardo Rei[*,1,2,3] **Ana C Farinha**[*,1] **José G. C. de Souza**[*,1]
Pedro G. Ramos[2] **André F. T. Martins**[1,3,4] **Luisa Coheur**[2,3] **Alon Lavie**[1]
[1]Unbabel [2]INESC-ID [3]Instituto Superior Técnico [4]Instituto de Telecomunicações
{ricardo.rei, catarina.farinha, jose.souza}@unbabel.com

Abstract

Recently proposed neural-based machine translation evaluation metrics, such as COMET and BLEURT, exhibit much higher correlations with human judgments than traditional lexical overlap metrics. However, they require large models and are computationally very costly, preventing their application in scenarios where one has to score thousands of translation hypotheses (e.g. outputs of multiple systems or different hypotheses of the same system, as in minimum Bayes risk decoding). In this paper, we introduce several techniques, based on pruning and knowledge distillation, to create more compact and faster COMET versions—which we dub COMETINHO. First, we show that just by optimizing the code through the use of *caching* and *length batching* we can reduce inference time between 39% and 65% when scoring multiple systems. Second, we show that pruning COMET can lead to a 21% model reduction without affecting the model's accuracy beyond 0.015 Kendall τ correlation. Finally, we present DISTIL-COMET, a lightweight distilled version that is 80% smaller and 2.128x faster while attaining a performance close to the original model. Our code is available at: `https://github.com/Unbabel/COMET`

* Corresponding authors.

1 Introduction

Traditional metrics for machine translation (MT) evaluation rely on lexical similarity between a given hypothesis and a reference translation. Metrics such as BLEU (Papineni et al., 2002) and CHRF (Popović, 2015) remain popular due to efficient memory usage and fast computational performance, even though several studies have shown that they correlate poorly with human judgements, specially for high quality MT (Ma et al., 2019; Mathur et al., 2020a).

In contrast, neural fine-tuned metrics on top of pre-trained models such as mBERT (Devlin et al., 2019) and XLM-R (Conneau et al., 2020) (e.g BLEURT (Sellam et al., 2020) and COMET (Rei et al., 2020) have demonstrated significant improvements in comparison to other metrics (Mathur et al., 2020b; Kocmi et al., 2021; Freitag et al., 2021b). The improvements made them good candidates for revisiting promising research directions where the metric plays a more central role in candidate selection during decoding, such as N-best reranking (Ng et al., 2019; Bhattacharyya et al., 2021; Fernandes et al., 2022) and minimum Bayes risk (MBR) decoding (Eikema and Aziz, 2021; Müller and Sennrich, 2021). Nonetheless, the complexity of such strategies using metrics based on large transformer models can become impractical for a large set of MT hypotheses.

In this paper, we describe several experiments that attempt to reduce COMET computational cost and model size to make it more efficient at inference. Our techniques are particularly useful in settings where we have multiple translations from different systems on the same source sentences. Since the models are based on triplet encoders, we will first analyse the impact of *embedding caching*

Macken, Rufener, Van den Bogaert, Daems, Tezcan, Vanroy, Fonteyne, Barrault, Costa-jussà, Kemp, Pilos, Declercq, Koponen, Forcada, Scarton, Moniz (eds.)
Proceedings of the 23rd Annual Conference of the European Association for Machine Translation, p. 61–70
Ghent, Belgium, June 2022.

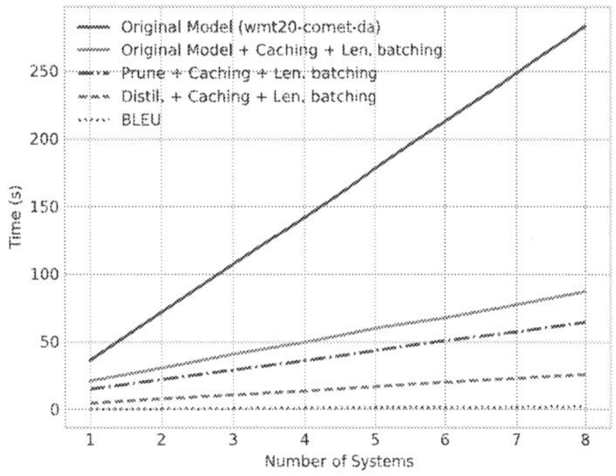

Figure 1: Comparison between the vanilla COMET, COMET with caching and length batching, PRUNE-COMET and DISTIL-COMET. We report the average of 5 runs for each model/metric for a varying number of systems. All experiments were performed using the German→English WMT20 Newstest, with a `NVIDIA GeForce GTX 1080 TI` GPU and a constant batch size of 16. For comparison we also plot the runtime of BLEU in a `Intel(R) Core(TM) i7-6850K CPU @ 3.60GHz`.

and *length batching*. Then, we will try to further reduce the computational cost by using *weight pruning* and *knowledge distillation*. Our results show that embedding caching and length batching alone can boost COMET performance 39.19% when scoring one system and 65.44% when scoring 8 systems over the same test set. Furthermore, with knowledge distillation we are able to create a model that is 80% smaller and 2.128x faster with a performance close to the original model and above strong baselines such as BERTSCORE and PRISM. Figure 1 shows time differences for all proposed methods when evaluating a varying number of systems.

2 Related Work

In the last couple of years, learned metrics such as COMET (Rei et al., 2020) and BLEURT (Sellam et al., 2020) proved to achieve high correlations with human judgments (Mathur et al., 2020b; Freitag et al., 2021a; Kocmi et al., 2021). They are cast as a regression problem and capture the semantic similarity between the translated text and a reference text, going beyond the simple surface/lexical similarities—the base of popular metrics like BLEU (Papineni et al., 2002) and CHRF (Popović, 2015). The fact that COMET and BLEURT metrics leverage large pre-trained multilingual models was a huge turning point. By using contextual embeddings trained on a different task, researchers were able to overcome the scarcity of data in MT evaluation (as well as in other tasks in which data is also limited). With such multilingual models, high-quality MT evaluation is now a possibility, even for language pairs without labeled data available (i.e. zero-shot scenarios). However, this multilingual property usually comes with a trade-off. For example, for cross-lingual transfer task, gains in performance (higher accuracy with human labels) only occur by adding new language pairs until a certain point, after which adding more languages actually decreases the performance, unless the model capacity is also increased (a phenomena called "the curse of multilinguality" (Conneau et al., 2020).

Besides the curse of multilinguality phenomena, the NLP community has been motivated to build larger and larger transformer models because, generally, the bigger the model the better it performs. This was demonstrated in several tasks like the ones in the GLUE benchmark (Goyal et al., 2021) and in multilingual translation tasks (Fan et al., 2020). Hence, models are achieving astonishing sizes like BERT with 340M parameters (Devlin et al., 2019), XLM-R$_{XXL}$ with 10.7B parameters (Goyal et al., 2021), M2M-100 with 12B parameters (Fan et al., 2020), and GPT-3 with 175B parameters (Brown et al., 2020). However, this growth comes with computational, monetary and environmental costs. For example, training a model with 1.5B parameters costs from 80k dollars up to 1.6M dollars[1] when doing hyper-parameter tuning and performing multiple runs per setting (Sharir et al., 2020). Such scale makes running similar experiments impractical to the majority of research groups, and the high energy and high response latency of such models are preventing them from being deployed in production (e.g. (Sun et al., 2020)).

To deal with the above problem, it is necessary to apply techniques for making models more compact, such as pruning, distillation, quantization, among others. In a recent review (Gupta and Agrawal, 2022) summarizes these techniques for increasing inference efficiency, i.e., for making the model faster, consuming fewer computational resources, using less memory, and less disk space. DistilBERT (Sanh et al., 2019) is a successful example: using distillation with BERT as the

[1]Estimates from (Sharir et al., 2020) calculated using internal AI21 Labs data; cloud solutions such as GCP or AWS can differ.

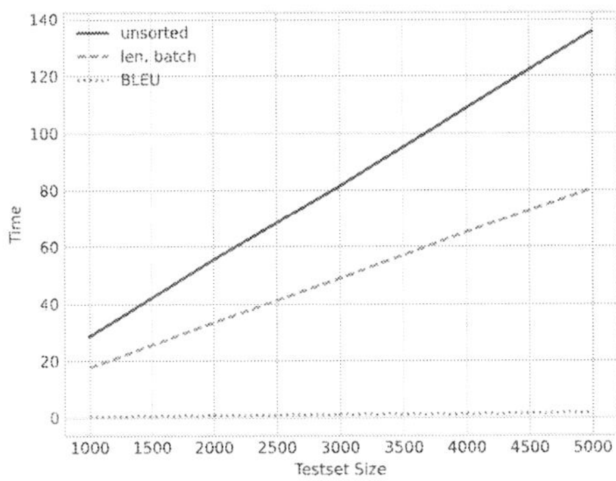

Figure 2: Runtime (in seconds) varying number of examples, with a `NVIDIA GeForce GTX 1080 TI` GPU and a constant batch size of 16. The time is calculated with the average of 10 runs using the default COMET model `wmt20-comet-da`. For comparison we also plot the runtime of BLEU in a `Intel(R) Core(TM) i7-6850K CPU @ 3.60GHz`.

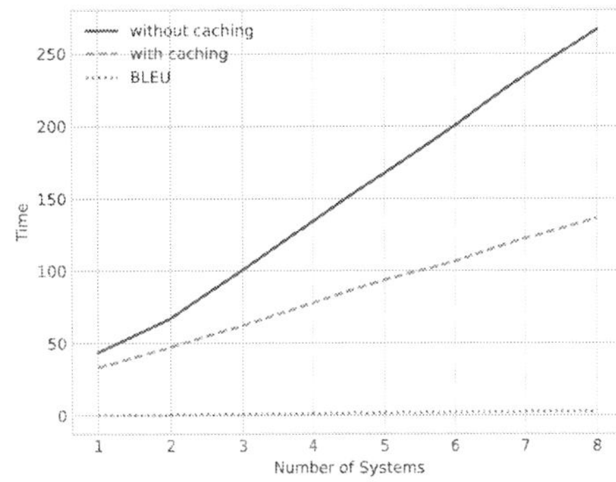

Figure 3: Runtime (in seconds) varying number of systems for the `de-en` WMT20 Newstest, with a `NVIDIA GeForce GTX 1080 TI` GPU and a constant batch size of 16. The time is calculated with the average of 5 runs using the default COMET model `wmt20-comet-da`. For comparison we also plot the runtime of BLEU in a `Intel(R) Core(TM) i7-6850K CPU @ 3.60GHz`.

teacher and reducing the amount of layers from the regular 12 to only 6, the model retains 97% of BERT's performance while reducing the size by 40% and being 60% faster. The authors have also shown that when used for a mobile application (iPhone), the DistilBERT was 71% faster than BERT. Another example, closer to our research, is the metric obtained from using synthetic data and performing distillation using a new variation of BLEURT as the teacher (Pu et al., 2021). The resulting metric obtains up to 10.5% improvement over vanilla fine-tuning and reaches 92.6% of teacher's performance using only a third of its parameters. Nonetheless, the architecture of BLEURT-based models requires that the reference is always encoded together with MT hypothesis which is extremely inefficient in use cases such as MBR, where the metric has a $\mathcal{O}(N^2)$ complexity (with N being the number of hypotheses), and system scoring where for a fixed source and reference we can have several translations being compared.

3 Length Sorting and Caching

Before exploring approaches that reduce the number of model parameters, we experiment with techniques to optimize the inference time computational load. One which is commonly used is to sort the batches according to sentence length to reduce tensor padding (Pu et al., 2021). Since COMET receives three input texts (source, hypothesis and reference), for simplicity, we do length sorting according to the source length. Figure 2 shows the speed difference between an unsorted test set with varying size and length-based sorting.

As previously pointed out, COMET metrics are based on triplet encoders[2] which means that the source and reference encoding does not depend on the provided MT hypothesis as opposed to other recent metrics such as BLEURT (Sellam et al., 2020) which have to repetitively encode the reference for every hypotheses. With that said, using COMET we only need to encode each unique sentence (source, hypothesis translation or reference translation) once. This means that we can cache previously encoded batches and reuse their representations. In Figure 3, we show the speed gains, in seconds, when scoring multiple systems over the same test set. This reflects the typical MT development use case in which we want to select the best among several MT systems.

These two optimizations altogether are responsible for reducing the inference time of COMET from 34.7 seconds to 21.1 seconds while scoring 1 system (39.19% faster) and from 265.9 seconds to 91.9 seconds when scoring 8 systems (65.44% faster). For all experiments performed along the rest of the paper we always use both optimization on all COMET models being compared.

[2]A triplet encoder, is a model architecture where three sentences are encoded independently and in parallel. Architectures such as this have been extensively explored for sentence retrieval applications due to its efficiency (e.g. Sentence-BERT (Reimers and Gurevych, 2019))

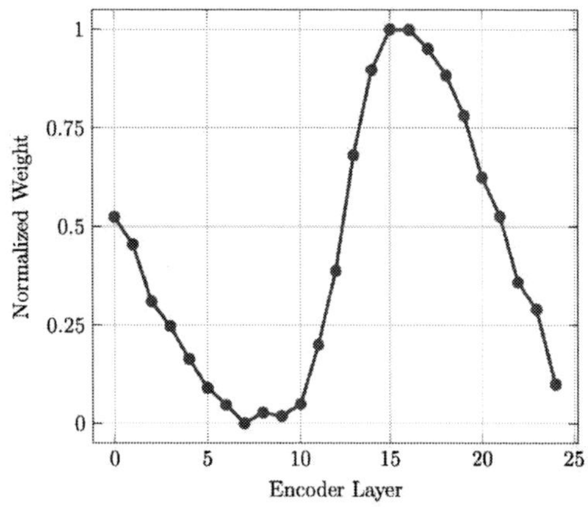

Figure 4: Normalized weights distribution for the COMET default model (wmt20-comet-da). As we can observe layers between 15-19 are the most relevant ones with a normalized weight between 0.75 and 1. The representations learnt by layers 15-19 depend on previous layers but we can prune the top layers (20-25) without impacting the layers that the model deemed more relevant.

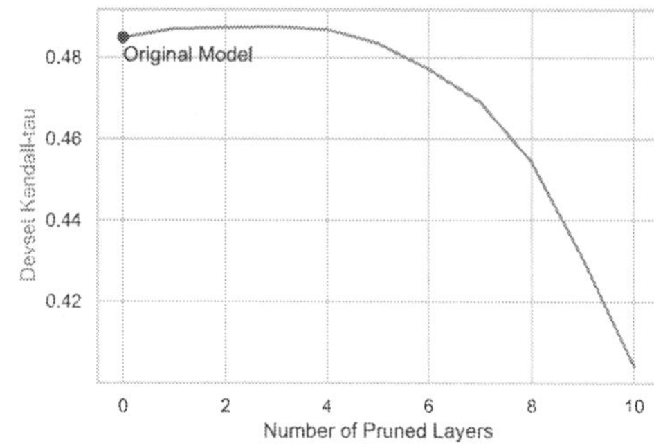

Figure 5: Impacts in performance of Layer Pruning for the WMT 2020 development set. We can observe that removing up to 5 layers does not affect model performance but provides a 10% reduction in model size.

4 Model Pruning

Model pruning has been widely used in natural language processing to remove non-informative connections and thus reducing model size (Zhu and Gupta, 2018). Since most COMET parameters come from the XLM-R model, we attempt to reduce its size. We start with layer pruning by removing the top layers of XLM-R. Then we experiment with making its encoder blocks smaller either by reducing the size of the feed-forward hidden layers or by removing attention heads. The main advantage of these approaches is their simplicity: within minutes we are able to obtain a new model with reduced size and memory footprint with minimal performance impact.

For all the experiments in this section, we used the development set from the Metrics shared task of WMT 2020. This set contains direct assessment annotations (DA; (Graham et al., 2013)) for English→German, English→Czech, English→Polish and English→Russian. We use these language pairs because they were annotated by experts exploring *document context* and in a *bilingual setup* (without access to a reference translation)[3]. Nonetheless, in Section 6 we show the resulting model performance on all language pairs from WMT 2021 for both DA and multidimensional quality metric annotations (MQM; (Lommel et al., 2014)).

4.1 Layer Pruning

In large pre-trained language models, different layers learn representations that capture different levels of linguistic abstractions, which can impact a downstream task in different ways (Peters et al., 2018; Tenney et al., 2019). In order to let the model learn the relevance of each layer during training, (Peters et al., 2018) proposed a layer-wise attention mechanism that pools information from all layers. This method has been adopted in COMET.

After analyzing the weights learnt by COMET (wmt20-comet-da) for each layer of XLM-R (Figure 4), we realized that the topmost layers (20-25) are not the most relevant ones. This means that we can prune those layers without having an impact on the most relevant features.

Each removed layer decreases the number of total parameters by 2.16%. Figure 5 shows the impacts in performance after removing a varying number of layers. As we can observe, performance starts to decrease only after removing 5 layers. Yet, removing 5 layers already produces a 10.8% reduction in model parameters. Surprisingly, removing the last layer (pruning 1 layer) slightly improves the performance in terms of Kendall-tau (Kendall, 1938).

4.2 Transformer Block Pruning

The Transformer architecture is composed of several encoder blocks (layers) stacked on top of the other. In the previous section, we reduce model

[3]In the WMT 2020 findings paper (Mathur et al., 2020b), most metrics showed suspiciously low correlations with human judgements based on crowd-sourcing platforms such as Mechanical Turk. Thus, we decided to focus just on 4 language pairs in which annotations are deemed as trustworthy.

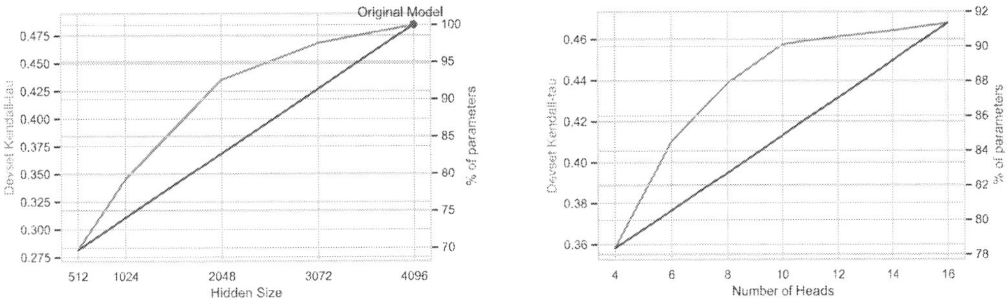

(a) Feed-forward hidden size pruning.

(b) Attention head pruning.

Figure 6: Impact of gradient based pruning techniques on model size (in blue) and performance on the WMT 2020 development set (in green). Note that in Figure (a) we apply pruning just for the feed-forward hidden size. In Figure (b) pruning is applied to several heads while freezing the hidden size to 3072 (3/4 of the original hidden size of XLM-R).

size by removing the topmost blocks (depth pruning). In this section we reduce the size of each block instead (width pruning).

Each transformer block is made of two components: a *self-attention* (composed of several attention heads) and a *feed-forward neural network*. In XLM-R-large, each block is made of 16 self-attention heads followed by a feed-forward of a single hidden layer with 4092 parameters.

Using the `TextPruner` toolkit[4], we can easily prune both the attention heads and the feed-forward hidden sizes. Figure 6a shows the impact of pruning the hidden sizes from 4096→{512, 1024, 2048, 3072} while Figure 6b shows the impact of reducing the attention heads from 16→{4, 6, 8, 10, 12, 14}.

4.3 Pruned-COMET

After experimenting with these three different pruning techniques, we created a pruned version of COMET in which we keep only 19 XLM-R layers, we reduced the feed-forward hidden size by 3/4 (3072 hidden size) and we removed 2 heads (out of 16). According to our experiments above, the resulting model's performance drop should be almost the same as the original model but the resulting model is 21.1% smaller.

The resulting model is able to score 1000 samples in just 19.74 seconds, while the original model takes around 31.32 seconds. It is important to notice that most of the XLM-R parameters come from its huge embedding layer. Since the embedding size memory does not affect the inference time, the obtained 20% reduction in parameters translates into speed improvements of around 36.97%.[5]

5 Distillation

Another commonly used way to compress neural networks is through knowledge distilation (Bucilua et al., 2006; Hinton et al., 2015) in which, for large amounts of unlabeled data, a smaller neural network (the student) is trained to mimic a more complex model (the teacher).

As the teacher network, we used an ensemble of 5 COMET models trained with different seeds (Glushkova et al., 2021). The student network follows the same architecture as the original model and the same hyper-parameters. However, instead of using XLM-R-large, it uses a distilled version with only 12 layers, 12 heads, embeddings of 384 features, and intermediate hidden sizes of 1536. This model has only 117M parameters compared to the 560M parameters from the large model.

Regarding the unlabeled data for distillation, we extracted 25M sentence pairs from OPUS (Tiedemann, 2012) ranging a total of 15 language pairs. To guarantee high quality parallel data we used Bicleaner tool (Ramírez-Sánchez et al., 2020) with a threshold of 0.8. Then, using pre-trained MT models available in Hugging Face Transformers, we created 2 different translations for each source: one using a bilingual model (in theory a high quality translation) and another using pivoting (which can be thought as lower quality). Finally, we scored all the data using our teacher ensem-

[4]`https://textpruner.readthedocs.io/en/latest/`

[5]Experiments performed in a `NVIDIA GeForce GTX 1080 TI` GPU and a constant batch size of 16. The resulting time is the average of 5 runs.

Table 1: Kendall's tau correlation on high resource language pairs using the MQM annotations for both News and TED talks domain collected for the WMT 2021 Metrics Task.

		zh-en		en-de		en-ru		
Metric	**# Params**	**News**	**TED**	**News**	**TED**	**News**	**TED**	**avg.**
BLEU	-	0.166	0.056	0.082	0.093	0.115	0.067	0.097
CHRF	-	0.171	0.081	0.101	0.134	0.182	0.255	0.154
BERTSCORE	179M	0.230	0.131	0.154	0.184	0.185	0.275	0.193
PRISM	745M	0.265	0.139	0.182	0.264	0.219	0.292	0.229
BLEURT	579M	**0.345**	**0.166**	**0.253**	**0.332**	**0.296**	**0.347**	**0.290**
COMET	582M	0.336	0.159	0.227	0.290	0.284	0.329	0.271
PRUNE-COMET	460M	0.333	0.157	0.219	0.293	0.274	0.319	0.266
DISTIL-COMET	119M	0.321	0.161	0.202	0.274	0.263	0.326	0.258

Table 2: Kendall's tau-like correlations on low resource language pairs using the DARR data from WMT 2021 Metrics task.

Metric	**# Params**	**zu-xh**	**xh-zu**	**bn-hi**	**hi-bn**	**en-ja**	**en-ha**	**en-is**	**avg.**
BLEU	-	0.381	0.1887	0.070	0.246	0.315	0.124	0.278	0.229
CHRF	-	0.530	0.301	0.071	0.327	0.371	0.186	0.373	0.308
BERTSCORE	179M	0.488	0.267	0.074	0.365	0.413	0.161	0.354	0.303
BLEURT	579M	**0.563**	**0.362**	**0.179**	0.498	0.483	0.186	0.469	0.391
COMET	582M	0.550	0.285	0.156	**0.526**	**0.521**	**0.234**	**0.474**	**0.392**
PRUNE-COMET	460M	0.541	0.264	0.163	0.519	0.513	0.197	0.439	0.377
DISTIL-COMET	119M	0.488	0.254	0.135	0.498	0.471	0.145	0.419	0.344

ble. The resulting corpus contains 45M tuples with (`source`, `translation`, `reference`, `score`).

The resulting model which name DISTIL-COMET, scores 1000 sentences in 14.72 seconds resulting in a 53% speed improvement over the original model[3].

6 Correlation with Human Judgements

In this section, we show results for {PRUNE and DISTIL}-COMET in terms of correlations with MQM annotations from WMT 2021 Metrics task for two different domains: News and TED talks. Since these annotations only cover high-resource language pairs (English→German, English→Russian, Chinese→English), we also evaluate models on low resource language pairs using DA Relative Ranks from WMT 2021, namely we test these models for: Hindi↔Bengali, Zulu↔Xhosa, English→Hausa, English→Icelandic, English→Japanese. For a detailed comparison, we also present results for CHRF (Popović, 2015) and BLEU (Papineni et al., 2002), two computationally efficient lexical metrics, and other neural metrics such as PRISM[6] (Thompson and Post, 2020), BLEURT (Sellam et al., 2020) and BERTSCORE (Zhang et al., 2020).

From Table 1, we can observe that PRUNE-COMET has minimal performance drops compared with vanilla COMET with only 80% of its parameters. DISTIL-COMET performance is on average 0.013 Kendall's bellow vanilla COMET for high resources languages, which is impressive for a model that only has 20% of COMET's parameters. For low-resource languages, we can observe bigger performance differences between COMET, PRUNE-COMET, and DISTIL-COMET which confirm results by (Pu et al., 2021) that shows that smaller MT evaluation models are limited in their ability to generalize to several language pairs. Nonetheless, when comparing with other recently proposed metrics such as PRISM and BERTSCORE, {PRUNE and DISTIL}-COMET have higher correlations with human judgements for both high and low resource language pairs. The only exception is BLEURT which shows stronger correlations than COMET on high-resource language pairs and com-

[6] PRISM does not support the low-resource language pairs used in our experiments, thus we only report PRISM correlations with MQM data

petitive performance in low-resource ones.[7]

7 Use Case: Minimum Bayes Risk Decoding

In minimum Bayes risk (MBR) decoding, a machine translation evaluation metric can be used as the utility function for comparing the translation hypotheses. This kind of approach, also known as "consensus decoding", derived from the idea that the top ranked translation is the one with the highest average score when compared to all other hypotheses. This process requires that each hypothesis translation be compared to every other hypotheses in an hypotheses candidate list. Having faster neural metrics could directly impact research and computational performance of using MBR decoding approaches with such metrics.

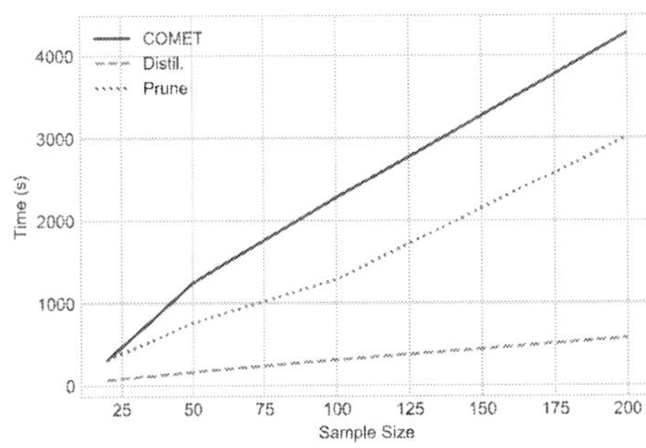

Figure 7: Runtime for performing MBR with a different number of samples using one `NVIDIA GeForce GTX 1080 TI GPU`.

Using COMET models with distillation or pruning can have a considerable effect at the performance of MBR decoding using such models as the utility function. Figure 7 shows that DISTIL-COMET is always substantially faster than the original COMET model especially for larger candidate list sizes such as 200 candidates. Likewise, PRUNE-COMET performs better than the original model but its performance is also considerably higher than DISTIL-COMET.

Regarding the two COMET variants there is a clear trade-off that needs to be taken into consideration, as evidenced by the results in Section 6: while DISTIL-COMET is faster, PRUNE-COMET is more accurate, leaving the choice of each model to use up to the most important aspect for the application. In the case of MBR decoding, this might depend on the hardware available for performing the computations.

[7] For a more detailed comparison between COMET and BLEURT metrics we refer the reader to the WMT 2021 Metrics shared task results paper (Freitag et al., 2021b) where both metrics ended up statistically tied for most language pairs and domains.

8 Conclusion and Future Work

In this paper we presented two simple optimizations that lead to significant performance gains on neural metrics such as COMET and two approaches to reduce its number of parameters. Together these techniques achieve impressive gains in performance (both speed and memory) at a very small cost in performance.

To showcase the effectiveness of our methods, we presented DISTIL-COMET and PRUNE-COMET. These models were obtained using COMET knowledge distillation and pruning respectively. To test the proposed models, we used the data from the WMT 2021 Metrics task which covers low resource languages as well as high resource languages. Overall the results of PRUNE-COMET are stable across the board with only a small degradation compared to the original metric. Knowledge distillation leads to much higher compression rates but seems to confirm previous findings (Pu et al., 2021) which suggest the lack of model capacity when it comes to the multilingual generalization for low resource languages.

A primary avenue for future work is to study how decreasing the model size can further impact on robustness of the metric, inspired by recent studies which identified weaknesses of COMET metrics when dealing with numbers and named entities (Freitag et al., 2021b; Amrhein and Sennrich, 2022). Also, in this work we explored knowledge distillation directly from the teacher output but an interesting avenue for improving the quality of the student model is to explore alternative distillation approaches that learn directly from internal representations of the teacher model such as self-attention distillation (Wang et al., 2020).

Acknowledgments

We would like to thank João Alves and Craig Stewart and the anonymous reviewers for useful feedback. This work was supported by the P2020 Program through project MAIA (contract No 045909) and by the European Union's Horizon 2020 research and innovation program (QUARTZ grant agreement No 951847).

References

Amrhein, Chantal and Rico Sennrich. 2022. Identifying Weaknesses in Machine Translation Metrics Through Minimum Bayes Risk Decoding: A Case Study for COMET. *CoRR*, abs/2010.11125.

Bhattacharyya, Sumanta, Amirmohammad Rooshenas, Subhajit Naskar, Simeng Sun, Mohit Iyyer, and Andrew McCallum. 2021. Energy-based reranking: Improving neural machine translation using energy-based models. In *Proceedings of the 59th Annual Meeting of the Association for Computational Linguistics and the 11th International Joint Conference on Natural Language Processing (Volume 1: Long Papers)*, pages 4528–4537, Online, August. Association for Computational Linguistics.

Brown, Tom B., Benjamin Mann, Nick Ryder, Melanie Subbiah, Jared Kaplan, Prafulla Dhariwal, Arvind Neelakantan, Pranav Shyam, Girish Sastry, Amanda Askell, Sandhini Agarwal, Ariel Herbert-Voss, Gretchen Krueger, Tom Henighan, Rewon Child, Aditya Ramesh, Daniel M. Ziegler, Jeffrey Wu, Clemens Winter, Christopher Hesse, Mark Chen, Eric Sigler, Mateusz Litwin, Scott Gray, Benjamin Chess, Jack Clark, Christopher Berner, Sam McCandlish, Alec Radford, Ilya Sutskever, and Dario Amodei. 2020. Language models are few-shot learners. *CoRR*, abs/2005.14165.

Bucilua, Cristian, Rich Caruana, and Alexandru Niculescu-Mizil. 2006. Model compression. In *Proceedings of the 12th ACM SIGKDD International Conference on Knowledge Discovery and Data Mining*, KDD '06, page 535–541, New York, NY, USA. Association for Computing Machinery.

Conneau, Alexis, Kartikay Khandelwal, Naman Goyal, Vishrav Chaudhary, Guillaume Wenzek, Francisco Guzmán, Edouard Grave, Myle Ott, Luke Zettlemoyer, and Veselin Stoyanov. 2020. Unsupervised cross-lingual representation learning at scale. In *Proceedings of the 58th Annual Meeting of the Association for Computational Linguistics*, pages 8440–8451, Online, July. Association for Computational Linguistics.

Devlin, Jacob, Ming-Wei Chang, Kenton Lee, and Kristina Toutanova. 2019. BERT: Pre-training of deep bidirectional transformers for language understanding. In *Proceedings of the 2019 Conference of the North American Chapter of the Association for Computational Linguistics: Human Language Technologies, Volume 1 (Long and Short Papers)*, pages 4171–4186, Minneapolis, Minnesota, June. Association for Computational Linguistics.

Eikema, Bryan and Wilker Aziz. 2021. Sampling-based minimum bayes risk decoding for neural machine translation. *CoRR*, abs/2108.04718.

Fan, Angela, Shruti Bhosale, Holger Schwenk, Zhiyi Ma, Ahmed El-Kishky, Siddharth Goyal, Mandeep Baines, Onur Celebi, Guillaume Wenzek, Vishrav Chaudhary, Naman Goyal, Tom Birch, Vitaliy Liptchinsky, Sergey Edunov, Edouard Grave, Michael Auli, and Armand Joulin. 2020. Beyond english-centric multilingual machine translation. *CoRR*, abs/2010.11125.

Fernandes, Patrick, Antonio Farinhas, Ricardo Rei, José G. C. de Souza, Perez Ogayo, Neubig Graham, and André F. T. Martins. 2022. Quality-Aware Decoding for Neural Machine Translation. In *Accepted at the 2022 Annual Conference of the North American Chapter of the Association for Computational Linguistics*, Seattle, Washington, july. Association for Computational Linguistics.

Freitag, Markus, George Foster, David Grangier, Viresh Ratnakar, Qijun Tan, and Wolfgang Macherey. 2021a. Experts, Errors, and Context: A Large-Scale Study of Human Evaluation for Machine Translation. *Transactions of the Association for Computational Linguistics*, 9:1460–1474, 12.

Freitag, Markus, Ricardo Rei, Nitika Mathur, Chi-kiu Lo, Craig Stewart, George Foster, Alon Lavie, and Ondřej Bojar. 2021b. Results of the WMT21 metrics shared task: Evaluating metrics with expert-based human evaluations on TED and news domain. In *Proceedings of the Sixth Conference on Machine Translation*, pages 733–774, Online, November. Association for Computational Linguistics.

Glushkova, Taisiya, Chrysoula Zerva, Ricardo Rei, and André F. T. Martins. 2021. Uncertainty-aware machine translation evaluation. In *Findings of the Association for Computational Linguistics: EMNLP 2021*, pages 3920–3938, Punta Cana, Dominican Republic, November. Association for Computational Linguistics.

Goyal, Naman, Jingfei Du, Myle Ott, Giri Anantharaman, and Alexis Conneau. 2021. Larger-scale transformers for multilingual masked language modeling. In *Proceedings of the 6th Workshop on Representation Learning for NLP (RepL4NLP-2021)*, pages 29–33, Online, August. Association for Computational Linguistics.

Graham, Yvette, Timothy Baldwin, Alistair Moffat, and Justin Zobel. 2013. Continuous measurement scales in human evaluation of machine translation. In *Proceedings of the 7th Linguistic Annotation Workshop and Interoperability with Discourse*, pages 33–41, Sofia, Bulgaria, August. Association for Computational Linguistics.

Gupta, Manish and Puneet Agrawal. 2022. Compression of deep learning models for text: A survey. *ACM Trans. Knowl. Discov. Data*, 16(4), jan.

Hinton, Geoffrey, Oriol Vinyals, and Jeffrey Dean. 2015. Distilling the knowledge in a neural network. In *NIPS Deep Learning and Representation Learning Workshop*.

Kendall, M. G. 1938. A new measure of rank correlation. *Biometrika*, 30(1/2):81–93.

Kocmi, Tom, Christian Federmann, Roman Grundkiewicz, Marcin Junczys-Dowmunt, Hitokazu Matsushita, and Arul Menezes. 2021. To ship or not to ship: An extensive evaluation of automatic metrics for machine translation. In *Proceedings of the Sixth Conference on Machine Translation*, pages 478–494, Online, November. Association for Computational Linguistics.

Lommel, Arle, Aljoscha Burchardt, and Hans Uszkoreit. 2014. Multidimensional quality metrics (MQM): A framework for declaring and describing translation quality metrics. *Tradumàtica: tecnologies de la traducció*, 0:455–463, 12.

Ma, Qingsong, Johnny Wei, Ondřej Bojar, and Yvette Graham. 2019. Results of the WMT19 metrics shared task: Segment-level and strong MT systems pose big challenges. In *Proceedings of the Fourth Conference on Machine Translation (Volume 2: Shared Task Papers, Day 1)*, pages 62–90, Florence, Italy, August. Association for Computational Linguistics.

Mathur, Nitika, Timothy Baldwin, and Trevor Cohn. 2020a. Tangled up in BLEU: Reevaluating the evaluation of automatic machine translation evaluation metrics. In *Proceedings of the 58th Annual Meeting of the Association for Computational Linguistics*, pages 4984–4997, Online, July. Association for Computational Linguistics.

Mathur, Nitika, Johnny Wei, Markus Freitag, Qingsong Ma, and Ondřej Bojar. 2020b. Results of the WMT20 metrics shared task. In *Proceedings of the Fifth Conference on Machine Translation*, pages 688–725, Online, November. Association for Computational Linguistics.

Müller, Mathias and Rico Sennrich. 2021. Understanding the properties of minimum bayes risk decoding in neural machine translation. In *Proceedings of the Joint Conference of the 59th Annual Meeting of the Association for Computational Linguistics and the 11th International Joint Conference on Natural Language Processing (ACL-IJCNLP 2021)*.

Ng, Nathan, Kyra Yee, Alexei Baevski, Myle Ott, Michael Auli, and Sergey Edunov. 2019. Facebook FAIR's WMT19 news translation task submission. In *Proceedings of the Fourth Conference on Machine Translation (Volume 2: Shared Task Papers, Day 1)*, pages 314–319, Florence, Italy, August. Association for Computational Linguistics.

Papineni, Kishore, Salim Roukos, Todd Ward, and Wei-Jing Zhu. 2002. Bleu: a method for automatic evaluation of machine translation. In *Proceedings of the 40th Annual Meeting of the Association for Computational Linguistics*, pages 311–318, Philadelphia, Pennsylvania, USA, July. Association for Computational Linguistics.

Peters, Matthew E., Mark Neumann, Mohit Iyyer, Matt Gardner, Christopher Clark, Kenton Lee, and Luke Zettlemoyer. 2018. Deep contextualized word representations. In *Proceedings of the 2018 Conference of the North American Chapter of the Association for Computational Linguistics: Human Language Technologies, Volume 1 (Long Papers)*, pages 2227–2237, New Orleans, Louisiana, June. Association for Computational Linguistics.

Popović, Maja. 2015. chrF: character n-gram F-score for automatic MT evaluation. In *Proceedings of the Tenth Workshop on Statistical Machine Translation*, pages 392–395, Lisbon, Portugal, September. Association for Computational Linguistics.

Pu, Amy, Hyung Won Chung, Ankur Parikh, Sebastian Gehrmann, and Thibault Sellam. 2021. Learning compact metrics for MT. In *Proceedings of the 2021 Conference on Empirical Methods in Natural Language Processing*, pages 751–762, Online and Punta Cana, Dominican Republic, November. Association for Computational Linguistics.

Ramírez-Sánchez, Gema, Jaume Zaragoza-Bernabeu, Marta Bañón, and Sergio Ortiz-Rojas. 2020. Bifixer and Bicleaner: two open-source tools to clean your parallel data. In *Proceedings of the 22nd Annual Conference of the European Association for Machine Translation*, pages 291–298, Lisboa, Portugal, November. European Association for Machine Translation.

Rei, Ricardo, Craig Stewart, Ana C Farinha, and Alon Lavie. 2020. COMET: A neural framework for MT evaluation. In *Proceedings of the 2020 Conference on Empirical Methods in Natural Language Processing (EMNLP)*, pages 2685–2702, Online, November. Association for Computational Linguistics.

Reimers, Nils and Iryna Gurevych. 2019. Sentence-BERT: Sentence embeddings using Siamese BERT-networks. In *Proceedings of the 2019 Conference on Empirical Methods in Natural Language Processing and the 9th International Joint Conference on Natural Language Processing (EMNLP-IJCNLP)*, pages 3982–3992, Hong Kong, China, November. Association for Computational Linguistics.

Sanh, Victor, Lysandre Debut, Julien Chaumond, and Thomas Wolf. 2019. Distilbert, a distilled version of bert: smaller, faster, cheaper and lighter. In *NeurIPS EMC2̂ Workshop*.

Sellam, Thibault, Dipanjan Das, and Ankur Parikh. 2020. BLEURT: Learning robust metrics for text generation. In *Proceedings of the 58th Annual Meeting of the Association for Computational Linguistics*, pages 7881–7892, Online, July. Association for Computational Linguistics.

Sharir, Or, Barak Peleg, and Yoav Shoham. 2020. The cost of training NLP models: A concise overview. *CoRR*, abs/2004.08900.

Sun, Zhiqing, Hongkun Yu, Xiaodan Song, Renjie Liu, Yiming Yang, and Denny Zhou. 2020. MobileBERT: a compact task-agnostic BERT for resource-limited devices. In *Proceedings of the 58th Annual*

Meeting of the Association for Computational Linguistics, pages 2158–2170, Online, July. Association for Computational Linguistics.

Tenney, Ian, Dipanjan Das, and Ellie Pavlick. 2019. BERT rediscovers the classical NLP pipeline. In *Proceedings of the 57th Annual Meeting of the Association for Computational Linguistics*, pages 4593–4601, Florence, Italy, July. Association for Computational Linguistics.

Thompson, Brian and Matt Post. 2020. Automatic machine translation evaluation in many languages via zero-shot paraphrasing. In *Proceedings of the 2020 Conference on Empirical Methods in Natural Language Processing (EMNLP)*, pages 90–121, Online, November. Association for Computational Linguistics.

Tiedemann, Jörg. 2012. Parallel data, tools and interfaces in OPUS. In *Proceedings of the Eighth International Conference on Language Resources and Evaluation (LREC'12)*, pages 2214–2218, Istanbul, Turkey, May. European Language Resources Association (ELRA).

Wang, Wenhui, Furu Wei, Li Dong, Hangbo Bao, Nan Yang, and Ming Zhou. 2020. Minilm: Deep self-attention distillation for task-agnostic compression of pre-trained transformers. In Larochelle, H., M. Ranzato, R. Hadsell, M.F. Balcan, and H. Lin, editors, *Advances in Neural Information Processing Systems*, volume 33, pages 5776–5788. Curran Associates, Inc.

Zhang, Tianyi, Varsha Kishore, Felix Wu, Kilian Q. Weinberger, and Yoav Artzi. 2020. Bertscore: Evaluating text generation with bert. In *International Conference on Learning Representations*.

Zhu, Michael and Suyog Gupta. 2018. To prune, or not to prune: Exploring the efficacy of pruning for model compression. In *6th International Conference on Learning Representations, ICLR 2018, Vancouver, BC, Canada, April 30 - May 3, 2018, Workshop Track Proceedings*. OpenReview.net.

Studying Post-Editese in a Professional Context: A Pilot Study

Lise Volkart
FTI/TIM, University of Geneva
Switzerland
lise.volkart@unige.ch

Pierrette Bouillon
FTI/TIM, University of Geneva
Switzerland
pierrette.bouillon@unige.ch

Abstract

The past few years have seen the multiplication of studies on post-editese, following the massive adoption of post-editing in professional translation workflows. These studies mainly rely on the comparison of post-edited machine translation and human translation on artificial parallel corpora. By contrast, we investigate here post-editese on comparable corpora of authentic translation jobs for the language direction English into French. We explore commonly used scores and also proposes the use of a novel metric. Our analysis shows that post-edited machine translation is not only lexically poorer than human translation, but also less dense and less varied in terms of translation solutions. It also tends to be more prolific than human translation for our language direction. Finally, our study highlights some of the challenges of working with comparable corpora in post-editese research.

1 Introduction

Much progress has been made since the seminal paper by Baker (1993) introduced the notion of *translation universals* and suggesting "to capture" the differences between original and translated language using comparable electronic corpora. Corpora of translated texts have been widely studied since then and research by Olohan and Baker (2000), Cappelle and Loock (2013) and Volansky et al. (2019), among others, have revealed the existence of translationese features. Following this, a new type of corpus-based translation studies has recently emerged together with the boom of neural machine translation (NMT) systems and their large integration into professional translation workflows. Those new studies are interested in the phenomenon of *machine translationese* and *post-editese*, the latter being defined as "the expected unique characteristics of a post-edited text that set it apart from a [human] translated text" (Daems et al., 2017). Our study falls within this area of research and focuses of post-editese in professional context.

First, we provide a short literature review of previous work on post-editese that will allow us to highlight the novel aspects of our research, as well as the common components that could constitute the basis for the development of a consistent methodology for the study of post-editese. Subsequently, we present the main goals of our study, as well as our research questions. We then describe the comparable corpus used for our pilot study and discuss the main advantages and drawbacks of such a corpus for the study of post-editese. Following this, we describe the experiments conducted and results obtained. Finally, we provide a summary of our findings and some perspectives for the future continuation of this work.

2 Related work

This section presents some of the recent studies investigating the differences between human and raw and/or post-edited machine translation output.

Čulo and Nitzke (2016) conducted a study on terminological variation and cognate translations in human translation (HT) and post-edited machine translation (PEMT) produced by students on a text of approximately 150 words. They observed less

Macken, Rufener, Van den Bogaert, Daems, Tezcan, Vanroy, Fonteyne, Barrault, Costa-jussà, Kemp, Pilos, Declercq, Koponen, Forcada, Scarton, Moniz (eds.)
Proceedings of the 23rd Annual Conference of the European Association for Machine Translation, p. 71–79
Ghent, Belgium, June 2022.

variation in PEMT than in HT and a priming effect of machine translation (MT) in PEMT on the terminological level. They also found that PEMT tends to contain more cognate translations.

Similar results were observed by Martikainen and Kübler (2016) in their study comparing two different corpora (each approximately 500 000 words) of medical summaries translated from English into French with or without statistical machine translation (SMT). They noted differences between HT and PEMT regarding the frequencies of certain words or phrases, as well as a tendency towards standardization of the translations in PEMT, as indicated by an over-representation of the most frequent translation solutions. They also observed a higher number of cognate translation or formal equivalences in PEMT. Finally, they pointed out that HT had a greater expanding ratio than PEMT, meaning that HT tends to produce longer translations.

Daems et al. (2017) attempted to investigate if HT and PEMT could be identified as such by human evaluators as well as by a classifier, which would indicate the existence of a post-editese phenomenon. Neither the human evaluators, nor the classifier were able to accurately distinguish HT from PEMT. However, the methodology applied to build the classifier brought to light some features that might be useful to discriminate HT and PEMT, such as type-token ratio, average word length, ratio of long words or the percentage of frequent words.

In his study conducted with translation students between 2016 and 2018, Farrel (2018) compared HT and PEMT of Wikipedia abstracts from English into Italian. While analyzing a set of 41 source n-grams, he noted that the most frequent HT solutions tend to be over-represented in PEMT showing "an apparent normalization and homogenization of the choices made by post-editors" compared to HT.

In consecutive studies, Castilho et al. (2019) and Castilho and Resende (2022) investigated post-editese features on a news corpus and two literary excerpts (approximately 5000 to 6000 tokens each) by comparing the source, MT, HT and PEMT versions for the language direction English into Brazilian Portuguese. Three translation universals (simplification, explicitation and convergence) were investigated through features such as lexical richness, lexical density, mean sentence length, length ratio, number of pronouns and variance scores for the different features. Some significant differences between HT and PEMT were observed for certain features, but the results were not homogeneous across the different datasets. For the variance scores, they observed that MT and PEMT tended to converge for the scores investigated, meaning that they are more similar to each other than they are to the source or HT. Although they are good indicators of the existence of a form of post-editese, these mixed results demonstrate that the candidate features of post-editese can be highly influenced by the corpus under investigation.

Toral (2019) also investigated the simplification translation universal, together with normalization and interference, using lexical richness, lexical density, length ratio and comparison of part-of-speech (PoS) sequences. The experiment was conducted on three different datasets (ranging from 100 to 1000 sentence pairs), five language directions (involving EN, DE, ES, FR, ZH) and three types of MT architectures (rule-based, SMT and NMT). He observed that PEMT texts tended to be lexically simpler, to have a lower lexical density and to have sentences closer to the source text in terms of length. PoS sequences also tended to be more similar to the typical PoS sequences of the source language. According to the author, these results are evidences of the existence of the post-editese that is a form of exacerbated translationese.

The above-mentioned studies present a certain number of similarities both in terms of the corpora or the features under investigation. For instance, it can be noted that they are all, except for one, based on parallel target corpora, i.e., translations of the same source text produced with different translation modes (MT/PEMT and HT). As for the features under investigation, we remark a strong representation of features related to lexical richness and diversity (i.e., type/token ratio or the variation of translation solutions), as well as to target text length (i.e., word length, sentence length ratio, text length).

3 Goals and research questions

The aim of our study is to investigate whether some of the findings of previous studies on post-editese can be confirmed on a corpora of authentic HT and PEMT translation projects for the language direction English into French. We intend to apply some of the metrics that have proven to be good indicators of post-editese so far and compare our results with the existing hypothesis on post-editese. We also propose the use of a novel metric borrowed from translation process research to study post-editese through the lens of translation variation between HT and PEMT. With this work, we hope to contribute to the development of a consistent and reliable methodology for the study of post-editese and to encourage additional work on authentic data in this domain.

The following research questions have guided our work:

Does the use of PEMT instead of HT affect the final translation in terms of:

- Lexical richness and lexical density?
- Sentence length ratio?
- Diversity of translation solutions?

4 Corpus

4.1 Choice of corpus design

As described in the previous section, many studies on post-editese rely on parallel target corpora (i.e., a HT and a PEMT of one single source corpora). Such corpora have to be (at least partially) artificially created for research purposes, as no one would produce twice a translation of the same text with two different translation modes in a professional context. Results obtained on such datasets might be difficult to generalize and may not accurately reflect the phenomena as it occurs in the professional context. An example of this issue can be seen in Castilho et al. (2019) and Castilho and Resende (2022) where the results exhibit a large divergence for certain metrics depending on the text genre of the dataset. Furthermore, some artificially created parallel datasets may not be homogeneous in terms of translators/post-editors profile (professional vs non-professionals) or of source language quality (original vs translated language) such as in Toral (2019). Finally, artificial parallel corpora might contain data that would not be translated with the help of NMT in a professional context

To avoid such issues, we decided to use comparable corpora, i.e. a HT and a PEMT of two different, but comparable, source corpora. This choice of working with comparable corpora allows us to work on authentic data produced in a professional context by translators in their usual working conditions, instead of data especially created for research purposes. With this design, we ensure the reliability and the coherence of our corpora in terms of the MT system used, the professional status and the experience of the post-editors/translators, as well as the level of post-editing (light or full) , with aim to gain insights into post-editese features as they may appear in production scenarios. However, these advantages go hand in hand with a number of challenges. First, such corpora are difficult to obtain, languages services being often reluctant to share their translation memories. Second, comparability of the corpora cannot be guaranteed as sources are different and the comparison between HT and PEMT has to be carefully conducted to avoid any misinterpretation of results. Finally, the corpus should ideally include data of several language services and several domains to allow generalization of the results.

4.2 Building of the corpus

The corpus was built from a collection of authentic translation/post-editing projects handled by the language service of the European Investment Bank (EIB). We limited our selection to the "press release" domain where NMT is now systematically used in combination with full post-editing. We extracted a number of projects handled before (i.e., human translated in a CAT-tool with translation memory) and after NMT integration (i.e., NMT post-edited in the same CAT-tool also with translation memory). For all projects, the language direction was English into French.

Translation units were extracted for both translation modes to obtain two corpora each comprising two sub-corpora (source and target). Fuzzy matched segments were removed from PEMT projects to exclude any eventual human translated segment. For this pilot experiment, we studied HT and PEMT output as they were before the final revision stage that is normally performed before delivery of the translation. In future studies, we also plan to study the corpora of revised HT and PEMT.

We performed several cleaning steps such as removing URLs, non-alphabetical segments and duplicates segment pairs. Statistics on the corpora at this stage are presented in Table 1. Apart from the corpora length difference, a large discrepancy in the average source segments length between HT and PEMT can be observed, with PEMT having on average longer segments. This difference can be easily explained by the fact that short segments

Sub-corpus	Trans. mode	# segments	# tokens	av. sent. length
Source	HT	3,440	47,781	13.91
	PEMT	1,981	41,577	21.01
Target	HT	3,440	62,588	18.20
	PEMT	1,981	56,734	28.64

Table 1: Number of segments, number of tokens and average sentence length (in tokens, excl. punctuation) for each sub-corpus and each translation mode **before** the sampling by length.

Sub-corpus	Trans. mode	# segments	# tokens	av. sent. length
Source	HT	1,894	40,518	21.43
	PEMT	1,814	40,830	22.53
Target	HT	1,894	52,772	27.87
	PEMT	1,814	55,585	30.64

Table 2: Number of segments, number of tokens and average sentence length (in tokens, excl. punctuation) for each sub-corpus and each translation mode **after** the sampling by length.

have higher chances of being matched in the translation memory and thus less likely to be sent to MT. Short and very short segments (less than 6 tokens) are then almost systematically "human-translated" and therefore under-represented in the PEMT corpora as illustrated by the source segments length distribution presented in Figure 1. In this distribution, we also observed that segments with a length between 6 and 15 tokens are twice as many in the HT compared to PEMT. To make our corpora more comparable, we decided to sample them according to source segments length. Segment pairs with a source shorter than 6 tokens were removed from both corpora (apart from the issue of comparability, these segments are mainly headers, and therefore not particularly interesting for our analysis). Then, half of the segment pairs for which the source contained between 6 and 15 tokens were randomly selected and removed from the HT corpora. Finally, we also removed segment pairs with a source longer that 60 tokens as they are over-represented in the PEMT corpus. This sampling step resulted in two corpora of comparable size with comparable source segments length distribution as shown in Table 2 and Figure 2.

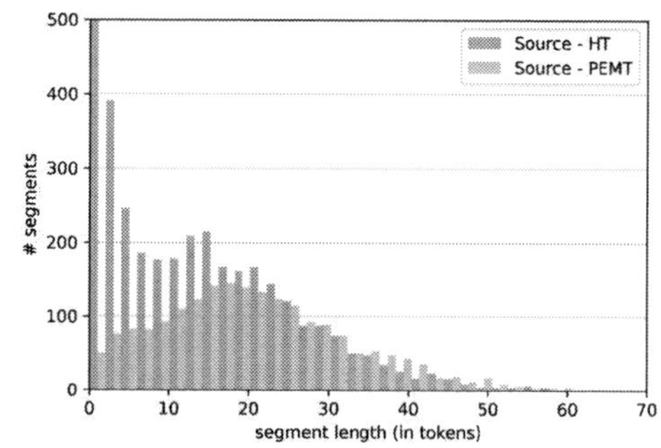

Figure 1: Source segment length distribution **before** sampling by length.

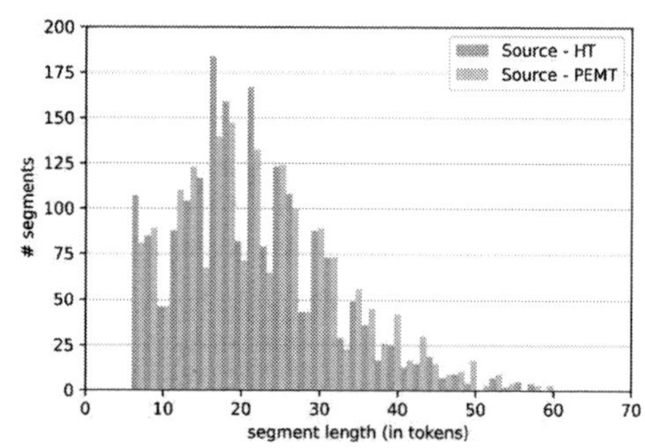

Figure 2: Source segment length distribution **after** sampling by length.

4.3 Corpus analysis

4.3.1 Lexical richness

Lexical richness (or lexical diversity) was investigated in post-editese research using type/token ratio (TTR) by Toral (2019), Castilho et al. (2019) and Castilho and Resende (2022), who all formulated the hypothesis that it would be lower for PEMT texts due to the influence of the MT output, which tends to be less lexically diverse than HT, as pointed out by Vanmassenhove et al. (2019). This hypothesis was confirmed by Toral (2019), but only partially confirmed by Castilho et al. (2019) and Castilho and Resende (2022). Considering these results, we also expected PEMT to be lexically poorer than HT. In our study, we measured lexical richness using standardized type/token ratio (STTR) (Scott, 2019) (also called MSTTR (Malvern and Richards, 2002)) that has the advantage of being less sensitive to corpus size and therefore allows a comparison of corpora of different lengths (Brezina, 2018). This score is obtained by averaging all TTR scores computed for every non-overlapping window of 1000 words in the corpus (Brezina, 2018).

STTR was computed for HT and PEMT target corpora but also for their respective sources in order to ensure that any potential difference between PEMT and HT was not due to a difference in the sources.

Table 3 presents the STTR scores for source and target HT and PEMT as well as the relative difference between HT and PEMT.

Sub-corpus	HT	PEMT	Rel. diff.
Source	0.44	0.42	-4.38%
Target	0.44	0.41	*-6.08%

Table 3: STTR scores for HT and PEMT corpora for source and target and relative difference between each translation mode for each sub-corpus. The higher the score the higher the lexical richness. *Indicates significance at $p < 0.001$, significance was tested on successive TTR scores using Mann-Whitney non-parametric test, as data were not normally distributed.

Looking at the target corpora only, STTR was significantly lower for PEMT, which is in line with our hypothesis that PEMT tends to be lexically poorer compared to HT, similar the results of other studies. However, this difference has to be considered together with the relative difference in STTR scores on the source side. Indeed, the PEMT source sub-corpora had also a lower STTR than the HT source corpora. This difference in source could explain the difference observed in the target, but only to a certain extent, as the STTR difference was more pronounced in the target. Even if the difference in lexical richness in the source corpora makes it difficult to measure with precision the influence of the translation mode on the lexical richness in the target, our results are in favour of the hypothesis that PEMT produces lexically poorer translations compared to HT.

4.3.2 Lexical density

Lexical density is a commonly used metric in post-editese research for the measurement of the amount of information present in a text, but with contradictory outcomes (see Toral, 2019; Castilho et al., 2019 and Castilho and Resende, 2022). It corresponds to the ratio between the number of content words (adjectives, adverbs, nouns and verbs) and the total number of words. We used SpaCy[1] English and French small models to tag our corpora and identify the content words. Table 4 shows lexical density scores for HT and PEMT as well as their relative difference.

Sub-corpus	HT	PEMT	Rel. diff.
Source	0.58	0.61	*+4.55%
Target	0.56	0.56	+0.34%

Table 4: Lexical density scores for HT and PEMT corpora for source and target and relative difference between each translation mode for each sub-corpus. The higher the score the higher the lexical density. *Indicates significance at $p < 0.001$. Significance was tested with a permutation test as described in Koplenig (2019), with 10 000 permutations.

The lexical density score was slightly higher for PEMT than for HT in the target sub-corpora, but this difference was not statistically significant. However, the difference between HT and PEMT sources is statistically significant ($p < 0.001$) with a lexical density lower for the HT source. A comparison of source and target for both translation modes showed that lexical density was lower in the target for both translation modes, but the loss in lexical density was more important in PEMT. These results indicate a tendency toward a lower lexical density in PEMT compared to HT, similar to the results of Toral (2019) and partially to those of Castilho et al. (2019) and Castilho and Resende (2022).

4.3.3 Expanding ratio

Expanding and length ratios are commonly used metrics to identify post-editese features (see Toral, 2019; Castilho et al., 2019 and Castilho and Resende, 2022). Toral (2019) computed the absolute value of the length ratio (with the length measured in characters) and found out that MT and PEMT are closer to the source text than HT in terms of length for all but one dataset, thus indicating that PEMT exhibits signs of an interference from the source text in terms of length. Martikainen and Kübler (2016) reached a similar conclusion when computing the so-called expanding ratio ("coefficient de foisonnement") on their corpora of HT, statistical machine translation (SMT) and post-

[1]https://spacy.io/models, accessed on 14th march 2022

edited SMT (PESMT). Similarly to the length ratio, the expanding ratio represents the length variation between source and target but is computed from the length measured in words (Cochrane, 1995; Cochrane, 2000). On their corpora, Martikainen and Kübler (2016) noted that SMT and PESMT have a lower expanding ratio than HT, meaning that they are shorter and therefore closer to the length of the source. This can be interpreted as a sign of interference of MT as SMT systems are known to produce output with a length similar to the source (Toral, 2019). However, this is not the case with NMT, which tends to reproduce the target length seen in the training data (Lakew et al., 2019). Therefore, we do not expect to find a significant difference between the expanding ratio of HT and PEMT. We computed the expanding ratio at sentence level with the length measured in characters according to the following formula:

$$ER = \frac{Length_{target} - Length_{source}}{Length_{source}} \times 100$$

Table 5 presents the average expanding ratio for HT and PEMT and the relative difference between both.

HT	PEMT	Rel. diff.
30.77%	37.18%	*+21.11%

Table 5: Average expanding ratios for HT and PEMT corpora and relative difference. The higher the ratio, the longer the translated segment compared to its source. *Indicates significance at $p < 0.001$. Significance was tested using Mann-Whitney non-parametric test, as data were not normally distributed.

The obtained expanding ratio for HT is not surprising as translations from English into French are typically longer than the source and can exhibit an expanding ratio from 10% to 30%, depending on the type of texts (Cochrane, 2000). However, for PEMT this ratio is much higher (+21.11% compared to HT), meaning that PEMT, for the same source segment length, tends to produce longer translations than HT[2].

We propose two possible explanations that require further investigation: 1) either the NMT system produces a raw MT close to the HT in terms of length (i.e., it reproduces the length observed in the training data) and the post-editors tend to add elements rather than to remove some, or 2) this particular NMT system tends to favor longer target segments.

4.3.4 Adverb word translation entropy

Several studies have shown that the use of MT and PE can lead to an overrepresentation of the most frequent translation solutions compared to HT (Martikainen and Kübler, 2016; Farrel, 2018). As already highlighted by several authors (Farrel, 2018; Čulo and Nitzke, 2016; Toral, 2019), this homogenization of the translation solutions could be the result of a priming effect of the raw MT output as MT systems tend to favour the most frequent translation solutions found in the training data (Vanmassenhove et al., 2019).

To measure the eventual loss in translation solutions variation we use a metric borrowed from translation process research, the word translation entropy (HTra), introduced by Carl et al. (2016) as part of a methodology to measure translation literality (Carl and Schaeffer, 2017). This metric is used to assess how many different translations a given source text word has across different target texts (Carl and Schaeffer, 2017). Htra is computed as the sum over all observed word translation probabilities $p(s \rightarrow t_i)$ of a given source text word s into target text word $t_i...n$ multiplied with their information content $I(p) = -log_2(p)$ (Carl et al., 2016) as shown in the following equation:

$$HTra(s) = -\Sigma_i^n{=1}p(s \rightarrow t_i) \times log_2(p(s \rightarrow t_i))$$

According to Carl and Schaeffer (2017), HTra measures the entropy of the lexical variation in the translation. This metric was used by several authors in translation process research to measure translation variation of a source word across different target translations and to draw correlations between HTra and different cognitive effort measures (see for instance Carl and Schaeffer 2017; Wei 2021). We consider that HTra could be a good measure to compare translation solution variation between HT and PEMT as it reflects the amount of translation alternatives, while also capturing the weight of these alternatives (Bangalore et al., 2016). As translation solutions have to be partially manually extracted, computing HTra for all content word categories is a time-consuming

[2] As source segments are on average slightly longer in the PEMT subcorpora, we tested the correlation between source segments length and expanding ratio. Pearson's correlation coefficient revealed a very weak negative correlation (-0.07) between source segment length and expanding ratio, therefore discarding the potential bias from the source segment length differences between HT and PEMT subcorpora.

task. For this reason, we started by computing the entropy for a number of frequent adverbs in the corpus. We chose the adverbs as it is a category in which several translation equivalences are generally available.

To select the adverbs for which the entropy will be computed, we extracted all the adverbs occurring at least once in both source corpora (HT and PEMT). From this list, we selected the top 30 most frequent adverbs (in both corpora combined) and computed the HTra for the 20 adverbs with the closest incidence in HT and PEMT source corpora to avoid any HTra discrepancy due to a large presence of a certain adverbs in one corpus but not in the other. Using the SketchEngine[3] corpus tool we extracted all segment pairs in which a selected adverb occurs in the source for HT and PEMT and manually extracted all the possible translations and their frequency in each sub-corpora. Table 6 shows the HT and PEMT entropy scores for all selected adverbs as well as the average HTra obtained in both sub-corpora for the sample of adverbs.

Adverb	HT	PEMT
currently	1.22	0.44
especially	1.75	1.56
fully	1.28	1.69
particularly	1.75	0.95
already	0.67	1.31
forward	1.55	1.81
only	2.23	2.09
nearly	1.31	0.72
therefore	2.46	1.66
here	1.30	1.39
just	2.41	1.66
now	2.36	2.01
further	3.42	2.46
often	0.00	0.00
also	1.58	1.46
very	1.02	1.16
most	0.47	0.35
about	2.82	2.42
all	0.00	1.92
more	1.80	1.30
Average	**1.57**	**1.42**

Table 6: HTra scores for the selected adverbs for HT and PEMT. The higher the HTra, the higher the variation of translation solutions, a score of 0 indicates that there is only one translation solution in the whole corpus.

[3]https://www.sketchengine.eu/

The average HTra for the selected adverbs was lower for PEMT than for HT, indicating that translation solutions were less varied in PEMT. However, this difference was not statistically significant, possibly due to the reduced number of adverbs considered and their relatively low frequency in the corpora. Nevertheless, this difference can be considered as an indication of a tendency of PEMT to produce less varied translations. Further research on the HTra of adverbs and other categories is needed to confirm these observations.

5 Conclusion and Future Work

In this study, we applied some of the metrics commonly used in post-editese research to comparable corpora of authentic HT and PEMT jobs for the language direction English into French. The aim of our study was to investigate if findings of previous studies could be confirmed on such a corpora. We studied the effect of the translation mode (HT or PEMT) on lexical richness, lexical density, expanding ratio and adverb translation entropy. Below is a summary of our main findings:

Lexical richness: PEMT exhibits lower lexical richness than HT. This difference can partly be explained by the difference in lexical richness observed in the source corpora. However, the amplitude of these differences suggests an effect of the translation mode on lexical richness, with PEMT producing lexically poorer translations. Those results are coherent with previous finding on machine translationese and post-editese (see for instance Toral, 2019; Vanmassenhove et al., 2019)

Lexical density: our results indicate a tendency toward a lower lexical density in PEMT compared to HT. This is in line with the findings of Toral (2019), but, once again, the differences between target corpora are difficult to interpret due to the differences already existing in the source corpora.

Expanding ratio: the expanding ratio is much higher for PEMT than HT, which means that for a given source sentence length, PEMT tends to produce longer target sentences. Further investigation with access to raw MT output is needed to uncover the reasons behind this target length discrepancy between HT and PEMT.

Adverb word translation entropy: the HTra computed for the list of selected adverbs reveals that PEMT presents less variation in the translation solutions of adverbs, supporting the conclusion made by Farrel (2018) or Čulo and Nitzke

(2016) that PEMT leads to more uniform translations.

This pilot study shows that some of the previously identified post-editese features can be found in authentic PEMT jobs and proposes the use of a novel metric for measuring the translation variation in PEMT. In addition, our study highlights the complexity of investigating post-editese on parallel corpora. Apart from the difficulty of gaining access to authentic data (including raw MT), the question of the comparability of the corpora represents a major challenge. The fact that HT and PEMT are not obtained from the same source corpus complicates the interpretation and the generalization of the results. Increasing the size and the diversity of the corpora, as well as developing techniques to increase corpus comparability, might be interesting options to overcome these challenges. Access to raw MT output could also be very helpful to facilitate the interpretation of the results. Despite the challenges faced, we are still convinced that the study of post-editese on authentic data is essential to fully understand the implications and potential consequences on the language use of the currently massive adoption of NMT in the translation industry. In the next stage of our research, we will increase the size of our corpora by adding data from other language services and other domains. We also plan to investigate the HTra metric more in depth by calculating scores for other categories and by checking their correlation with human judgement.

Acknowledgement

We would like to thank the EIB for sharing their data with us.

References

Baker, Mona. 1993. Corpus Linguistics and Translation Studies: Implications and applications. *Text and Technology. In Honour of John Sinclair*, 233–250.

Bangalore, Srinivas, Bergljot Behrens, Michael Carl, Maheshwar Ghankot, Arndt Heilmann, Jean Nitzke, Moritz Schaeffer and Annegret Sturm. 2016. Syntactic variance and priming effects in translation. *New directions in empirical translation process research*, 211–238.

Brezina, Vaclav. 2018. Statistics in corpus linguistic: A practical guide. Cambridge University Press.

Capelle, Bert and Rudy Loock. 2013. Is there interference of usage constraints?: A frequency study of existential there is and its French equivalent il y a in translated vs. non-translated texts *Target. International Journal of Translation Studies*, 2(25):252–275.

Carl, Michael and Moritz Schaeffer. 2017. Why translation is difficult: A corpus-based study of non-literality in post-editing and from-scratch translation. *HERMES-Journal of Language and Communication in Business*, 43–57.

Carl, Michael, Srinivas Bangalore and Moritz Schaeffer. 2016. The CRITT translation process research database. *New directions in empirical translation process research*, 13–54.

Castilho, Sheila and Natàlia Resende. 2022. Post-Editese in Literary Translations. *Information*, 2(13):66.

Castilho, Sheila, Natàlia Resende and Ruslan Mitkov. 2019. What Influences the Features of Post-editese? A Preliminary Study. *Proceedings of the Human-Informed Translation and Interpreting Technology Workshop (HiT-IT 2019)*, Varna, Bulgaria, 19–27.

Cochrane, Guylaine. 1995. Le foisonnement, phénomène complexe. *TTR: traduction, terminologie, rédaction*, 2(8):175–193.

Cochrane, Guylaine. 2000. Le foisonnement dans les textes de spécialité, illusion d'optique ou réalite quantifiable ? Université Laval.

Čulo, Oliver and Jean Nitzke. 2016. Patterns of Terminological Variation in Post-editing and of Cognate Use in Machine Translation in Contrast to Human Translation. *Proceedings of the 19th Annual Conference of the European Association for Machine Translation*, 106–114, Riga, Lettonie.

Daems, Joke, Orphée De Clercq and Lieve Macken. 2017. Translationese and Post-editese: How comparable is comparable quality? *Linguistica Antverpiensia, New Series: Themes in Translation Studies*, 16:89–103.

Farrel, Michael. 2018. Machine Translation Markers in Post-Edited Machine Translation Output. *Proceedings of the 40th Conference Translating and the Computer*, London, United-Kingdom, 50–59.

Koplenig, Alexander. 2011. A non-parametric significance test to compare corpora. *PLoS ONE*, 9(14).

Lakew, Surafel M., Mattia Di Gangi and Marcello Federico, 2019. Controlling the output length of neural machine translation.

Malvern, David and Brian Richards. 2002. Investigating accommodation in language proficiency interviews using a new measure of lexical diversity. *Language Testing*, 1(19):85–104.

Martikainen, Hanna and Nathalie Kübler. 2016. Ergonomie cognitive de la post-édition de traduction automatique : enjeux pour la qualité des traductions. *ILCEA*

Olohan, Maeve and Mona Baker. 2000. Reporting that in translated English. Evidence for subconscious processes of explicitation? *Across languages and cultures*, 2(1):141–158.

Scott, Mike. *Wordsmith Tools Manual*. https://lexically.net/downloads/version7/HTML/index.html.

Toral, Antonio. 2019. Post-editese: an Exacerbated Translationese. *Proceedings of MT Summit XVII*, Dublin, Ireland. 273–281.

Vanmassenhove, Eva, Dimitar Shterionov and Andy Way. 2019. Lost in Translation: Loss and decay of Linguistic Richness in Machine Translation. *Proceedings of MT Summit XVII*, Dublin, Ireland, 222–232.

Volansky, Vered, Noam Ordan and Shuly Wintner. 2015. On the Features of Translationese. *Digital Schorlarship in the HUmanities*, 30(1): 222–232.

Wei, Yuxiang. 2021. Entropy and Eye Movement: A Micro-analysis of Information Processing in Activity Units During the Translation Process. *Explorations in Empirical Translation Process Research*, 165–202.

Diformer: Directional Transformer for Neural Machine Translation

Minghan Wang[1], **Jiaxin Guo**[1], **Yuxia Wang**[2], **Daimeng Wei**[1], **Hengchao Shang**[1], **Yinglu Li**[1], **Chang Su**[1], **Yimeng Chen**[1], **Min Zhang**[1], **Shimin Tao**[1], **Hao Yang**[1]
[1]Huawei Translation Services Center, Beijing, China
[2]The University of Melbourne, Melbourne, Australia
{wangminghan,guojiaxin1,weidaimeng,shanghengchao,
liyinglu,suchang8,chenyimeng,zhangmin186,
taoshimin,yanghao30}@huawei.com
yuxiaw@student.unimelb.edu.au

Abstract

Autoregressive (AR) and Non-autoregressive (NAR) models have their own superiority on the performance and latency, combining them into one model may take advantage of both. Current combination frameworks focus more on the integration of multiple decoding paradigms with a unified generative model, e.g. Masked Language Model. However, the generalization can be harmful on the performance due to the gap between training objective and inference. In this paper, we aim to close the gap by preserving the original objective of AR and NAR under a unified framework. Specifically, we propose the Directional Transformer (Diformer) by jointly modelling AR and NAR into three generation directions (left-to-right, right-to-left and straight) with a newly introduced direction variable, which works by controlling the prediction of each token to have specific dependencies under that direction. The unification achieved by direction successfully preserves the original dependency assumption used in AR and NAR, retaining both generalization and performance. Experiments on 4 WMT benchmarks demonstrate that Diformer outperforms current united-modelling works with more than 1.5 BLEU points for both AR and NAR decoding, and is also competitive to the state-of-the-art independent AR and NAR models.

1 Introduction

Machine translation can be considered as a conditional generation task, which has been dominated by neural networks, especially after Transformer (Vaswani et al., 2017). Conventional autoregressive (AR) NMT models obtain the impressive performance, but it's time-consuming to decode token one by one sequentially (Sutskever et al., 2014; Bahdanau et al., 2015). Aiming at fast inference, non-autoregressive (NAR) NMT models enhance the parallelizability by reducing or removing the sequential dependency on the translation prefix inside the decoder, but suffering from performance degradation owing to the multi-modality problem, which is still an open-question (Gu et al., 2018; Shu et al., 2020; Ghazvininejad et al., 2020; Lee et al., 2018; Ghazvininejad et al., 2019; Stern et al., 2019; Welleck et al., 2019; Gu et al., 2019a; Gu et al., 2019b).

It's always non-trivial to balance high performance and low latency in a single model perfectly. Therefore, another branch focuses on the **unified-modeling** of multiple decoding paradigms so that decoding with AR or NAR in different scenarios (AR for quality-first and NAR for speed-first) with one model can be achieved (Mansimov et al., 2020; Tian et al., 2020; Qi et al., 2021), making the performance and speed can be pursued more practically.

Whereas, challenges still exist. For example, a generalized conditional language model is often required to support the generation with customized orders or positions (Mansimov et al., 2020; Tian et al., 2020), which actually prevents the model from being fully trained on specific decoding method, leading to the declines in overall performance. In addition, in some works, AR and NAR decoding

Macken, Rufener, Van den Bogaert, Daems, Tezcan, Vanroy, Fonteyne, Barrault, Costa-jussà, Kemp, Pilos, Declercq, Koponen, Forcada, Scarton, Moniz (eds.)
Proceedings of the 23rd Annual Conference of the European Association for Machine Translation, p. 81–90
Ghent, Belgium, June 2022.

may needs to be trained separately in the stage of pretraining or fine-tuning (Qi et al., 2021), making the training more expensive.

To ameliorate these issues, we propose Directional Transformer (Diformer) which resolve the unification of AR and NAR in a more practical way. First of all, we abandon the compatible of multiple flexible decoding strategies, but focusing on the modeling of some commonly used strategies that have good performance. For the AR decoding, it has been proved that monotonic linear generation is still considered as the best strategy (Mansimov et al., 2020; Tian et al., 2020), so we choose to only model the left-to-right (L2R) and right-to-left (R2L) generation. For the NAR decoding, we choose to follow the stream of masked-language model, like mask-predict in CMLM (Ghazvininejad et al., 2019) or parallel easy-first in Disco (Kasai et al., 2020), since they are simpler than insertion-based method but still being effective.

To this end, we unify two decoding paradigms into three generation directions — **L2R**, **R2L** and **straight**, and formulate it through a new objective named as **Directional Language Model (DLM)**, making the prediction of tokens conditioned on contexts controlled by a newly introduced direction variable. It ties AR and NAR into a unified generation framework while still preserving the original dependency assumptions of AR and NAR, retaining both generalization and performance. Meanwhile, all directions can be trained simultaneously with the time spent equally to the training of an independent NAR model, which greatly reduces the training cost compared to two-stages methods.

Experimental results on the WMT14 En↔De and WMT16 En↔Ro datasets for all three directions indicate that Diformer performs better than previous unification-based works by more than 1.5 BLEU points. Comparing to other state-of-the-art independent AR and NAR models, Diformer is also competitive when decoding in the same mode. We summarize contributions of our work as:

- We unify the AR and NAR decoding into three generation direction and formulate it with the **Directional Language Model**.
- We propose the Diformer, a Transformer-based model that can be trained with DLM, where all direction can be trained simultaneously.
- Experiments on WMT14 En↔De and WMT16 En↔Ro demonstrate the ability of Diformer with competitive results compared to unified or independent models.

1.1 Related Work

(Mansimov et al., 2020) unifies decoding in directed and undirected models by a generalized framework, in which the generating process is factorized as the position selection and the symbol replacement, where the first step is achieved by Gibbs sampling or learned adaptive strategies, the second step can be handled by a masked language model pretrained on monolingual corpora and fine-tuned on the NMT task. Their model supports at least 5 decoding strategies including hand-crafted and learned, all of them can be used for both linear time decoding (AR) and constant time decoding (NAR).

Similarly, (Tian et al., 2020) unified AR and NAR by adapting permutation language modeling objective of XLNet to conditional generation, making it possible to generate a sentence in any order. The model is evaluated to decode in monotonic and non-monotonic AR, semi-AR and NAR with at least 8 position selection strategies including pre-defined and adaptive.

Both of them achieves the compatible to customized decoding through position selection and applying the selected positions/orders on a generalized generative model, which leads to the gap between training and inference. In contrast to the position selection, we directly model the decoding process with three generation directions in a task-specific manner, thereby without introducing additional complexity to the task and close the gap between training objective and inference strategy. We consider it is worthwhile to obtain performance improvements by abandon some flexibility.

2 Method

2.1 Background

Before the description of Diformer, the conventional AR model and the iterative mask prediction based NAR model that applied in Diformer will be introduced first.

The likelihood of an AR model is a factorization following the product rule, assuming each token is conditioned on all previous generated context.

Taking the L2R and R2L AR model as examples:

$$\mathcal{L}_{\text{L2R}} = \sum_{i=1}^{N} \log P(y_i | y_{1:i-1}, X; \theta) \quad (1)$$

$$\mathcal{L}_{\text{R2L}} = \sum_{i=1}^{N} \log P(y_i | y_{i+1:N}, X; \theta) \quad (2)$$

where X is the source text, $y_{1:i-1}$ and $y_{i+1:N}$ are previous outputs in opposite direction, θ is the learnable parameters, N is the target length.

In the iterative-refinement based NAR model like CMLM (Ghazvininejad et al., 2019), the conditional dependency is loosed, assuming the prediction of target token can be independent with each other, but conditioned on the output tokens (context) from last iteration:

$$\mathcal{L}_{\text{CMLM}} = \sum_{y_i \in Y_{\text{mask}}^{(t)}} logP(y_i | X, Y_{\text{obs}}^{(t)}; \theta). \quad (3)$$

where t is the iteration step $t = \{1, ..., T\}$, Y_{obs} are observable tokens (context), $Y_{\text{mask}} = Y \setminus Y_{\text{obs}}$ are masked tokens for predicting. In each iteration, $N\frac{T-t}{T}$ of predicted tokens with low confidence will be re-masked and predicted again in the next iteration, conditioned on remaining high-confidence predictions as observable context until the last iteration. At the initial iteration, the model determines the target length N based on the source text $P(N|X)$ and makes the first step prediction with $N - 2$ mask symbols as well as [BOS] and [EOS] input to the decoder, equivalent to merely conditioned on the source.

Instead of using the global context, in DisCo (Kasai et al., 2020), the target token at each position is predicted with different context, namely, the disentangled context. In such case, all tokens can be used for training and updated at each iteration during inference:

$$\mathcal{L}_{\text{DisCo}} = \sum_{i=1}^{N} logP(y_i | X, Y_{\text{obs}}^{i,t}; \theta), \quad (4)$$

where $Y_{\text{obs}}^{i,t}$ is the context only for y_i. The parallel easy-first decoding strategy is proposed (we call it easy first in following sections for simplicity) to improve the decoding efficiency, where the context of each token is composed by predictions at *easier* positions determined in the first iteration:

$$Y_{\text{obs}}^{i,t} = \{y_j^{t-1} | z(j) < z(i)\}, \quad (5)$$

where $z(i)$ denotes the descending ordered rank of the probability P_i computed in the first iteration. During the training of CMLM and DisCo, a subset of tokens are selected as the context, CMLM updates parameters only with the loss on masked tokens while DisCO uses all tokens for updating.

In the Diformer, we aim to unify the two exclusive dependency assumptions (Yang et al., 2019) of AR and NAR essentially by proposing a new training objective and model architecture that can make them trained jointly.

2.2 Directional Language Model

We aim to unify the AR and NAR decoding into three generation directions — L2R, R2L and straight, i.e. making prediction on the target token at the rightward, leftward and the original position. How to realize this goal is an open-question. In this work, we achieve it by explicitly providing a direction instruction and corresponded contexts to the model. Taking an example on the target sequence $Y = [A, B, C, D, E]$, the probability of $y_3 = C$ generated from three directions can be expressed as:

$$P_3 = \begin{cases} P(y_3 = C | X, \{A, B\}) & \text{L2R} \\ P(y_3 = C | X, \{D, E\}) & \text{R2L} \\ P(y_3 = C | X, \{A, B, ?, D, E\}) & \text{straight} \end{cases}$$

where ? can be a mask symbol performing like a placeholder.

Formally, given the target sequence $Y = [y_1, ..., y_N]$, token y_i can be generated **from** direction $z_i \in \mathcal{Z} = \{R, S, L\}$ (i.e. L2R, straight and R2L) given the context Y_{z_i} and X:

$$P(y_{z_i} | X, Y_{z_i}),$$

where Y_{z_i} is determined by the direction z_i:

$$Y_{z_i} = \begin{cases} y_{1:i-1} & z_i = R \\ y_{i+1:N} & z_i = L \\ Y_{\text{obs}}^i & z_i = S \end{cases}$$

When $z_i = R$ or L, the model works exactly same to the conventional AR model by conditioning on previously generated tokens at leftwards or rightwards. When $z_i = S$, the model works in an iterative-refinement manner (e.g. mask-predict in CMLM or parallel easy-first in DisCO) by conditioning on a partially observed sequence Y_{obs}^i with multiple tokens being masked including y_i, same as the disentangled context in DisCo.

We can thereby formulate the objective of directional language model as the expectation over all possible generation directions on each token:

$$P(Y|X) = \mathbb{E}_{z_i \in \mathcal{Z}}\left[\prod_{i=1}^{N} P(y_{z_i}|X, Y_{z_i})\right] \quad (6)$$

The expectation can be approximated with sampling, similar to the permutation language model in (Yang et al., 2019; Tian et al., 2020), where a permutation of the sequence is sampled during training, we, instead, sample the direction **for each token**. In this way, the factorization of DLM incorporates both conditional dependency assumption of AR, and conditional independence assumption of NAR, thereby makes the training objective closely related to the decoding methods.

Training The sampling of direction in DLM allows us to train the generation of all directions simultaneously, we introduce the detailed method in this section.

As we all know that the training of Transformer (Vaswani et al., 2017) can be paralleled with teacher forcing, achieved by feeding $y_{1:N-1}$ (context) to the model at once and computing the loss on $y_{2:N}$ (target). The context and target sequence can be easily created by a shifting operation that aligns y_{i-1} to y_i.

Diformer can also be trained in a similar way, but before that, we have to make a slight change when implementing the computation of the likelihood in Eq 6 due to the difficulty of creating the context sequence Y_{z_i} with complicated dependencies. The original equation aims to compute the likelihood on the ground-truth sequence Y where each token is conditioned on a customized context determined by the sampled direction, meaning that the context sequence cannot be shared as Transformer does. Creating specialized context for every token is non-trivial especially when encountered with position changing caused by the shifting when $z_i = R$ or L.

For the convenience of the implementation, we fix the input sequence $y_{1:N}$ and create a new target sequence Y^* where tokens are accordingly shifted with the sampled directions:

$$P(Y^*|X) = \prod_{i=1}^{N} P(y_j|X, Y_{z_i}), \quad (7)$$

where $j = i + 1$ for $z_i = R$, $j = i - 1$ for $z_i = L$ and $j = i$ for $z_i = S$. When training on large corpus with random sampling on directions, we can say that $P(Y^*|X) \approx P(Y|X)$ theoretically.

Formally, let the source and target sequence as $X = [x_1, ..., x_{|X|}]$ and $Y = [y_1, ..., y_N]$ where N is the target length. Then, we uniformly sample a direction instruction sequence $Z = [z_1, ..., z_N]$ with N elements, where z_1 and z_N are fixed to be R and L as they are [BOS] and [EOS], which can only be used to predict tokens inside the sequence for the AR setting, and can never be masked in the NAR setting.

The input sequence Y_{in} is created by directly copying from ground-truth Y, which will be masked accordingly in the decoder to create the disentangled context.

According to the sampled direction sequence Z, we can now create the modified target sequence Y^* by shifting tokens in Y based on z_i, which is shown in Figure 1.

To be compatible with the NAR decoding, we also predict the target length $P(N|X)$ with the same way as (Ghazvininejad et al., 2019). Note that the predicted length is only used for NAR decoding, the AR decoding still terminates when [EOS] or [BOS] is generated for L2R and R2L setting.

Finally, the cross-entropy loss is used for both generation ($\mathcal{L}_{\text{DLM}}$) and length prediction ($\mathcal{L}_{\text{LEN}}$) task, the overall loss can be obtained by adding them together:

$$\mathcal{L}_{\text{Diformer}} = \mathcal{L}_{\text{DLM}} + \lambda \mathcal{L}_{\text{LEN}}, \quad (8)$$

where λ is the factor on which the best performance can be obtained with the value of 0.1, after searched from 0.1 to 1.0 in the experiment.

2.3 Directional Transformer

Diformer is mainly built upon the Transformer (Vaswani et al., 2017) architecture but with several modifications for the compatible of the multi-directional generation, especially for avoiding the information leakage during training.

Specifically, we directly use the standard Transformer encoder in the Diformer, except that an additional MLP layer is added on top of it for length prediction. For the decoder, several modifications are performed: 1) We introduce an additional embedding matrix to encode the direction instruction. 2) The original uni-directed positional embedding is expended to a bi-directed positional embedding. 3) We follow the work in DisCo to disentangle

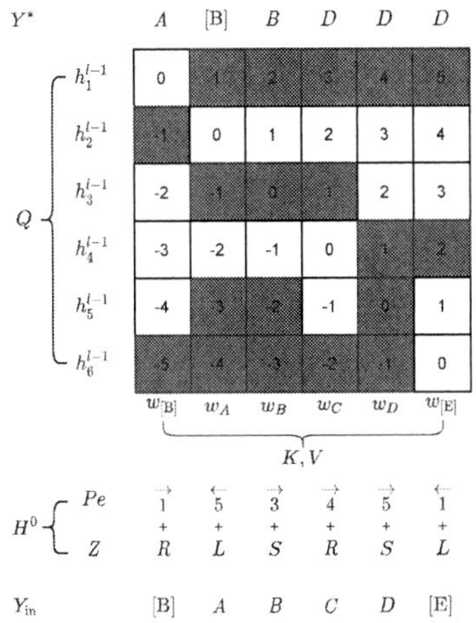

Figure 1: An example of training Diformer with DLM, where values in grids are the relative distance of K, V w.r.t Q, attention masks are indicated by dark grids.

the context by de-contextualizing K, V only with word embedding, and replacing the input of Q in the first layer only with direction and position signal. 4) To compensate the removed positional information in K, V, we integrate the relative positional embedding in the self-attention, successfully resolved the problem on information leakage and the compatible of bi-directional generation.

Directional Embeddings An embedding matrix is used to map the categorical variable z_i into the hidden space, denoted as δ, $\delta(z_i) \in \mathbb{R}^{d_{\text{model}}}$ where d_{model} is hidden size of the model. For simplicity, we directly use z_i to represent the embedded direction at position i in following sections.

The joint training of L2R and R2L can be problematic with the positional embedding of the original Transformer since the index is counted in a uni-directed order, which can be used for cheating under the bi-directional scenario since future positional index can leak information of the sentence length.

To solve this, we propose to make the positional embedding directed, achieved by encoding the position index counted oppositely based on the direction with separate parameters:

$$p_{z_i} = \begin{cases} \overrightarrow{Pe}(\overrightarrow{i}) & z_i = R \text{ or } z_i = S \\ \overleftarrow{Pe}(\overleftarrow{i}) & z_i = L \end{cases}$$

where $\overrightarrow{Pe}$ and $\overleftarrow{Pe}$ are different embedding matrics to encode position indices counting from L2R ($\overrightarrow{i}$) or R2L ($\overleftarrow{i}$) accordingly. More detailed description can be found in Figure 1.

Finally, we add encoded position and direction embeddings together as the initial hidden-state $h_i^{l=0}$ for the computation of $Q^{l=0}$ in the first self-attention layer $h_i^0 = p_{z_i} + z_i$:

Directional Self-Attention In DisCo, to prevent the information leakage from the disentangled context, the input representation for computing K, V is de-contextualized by directly reusing the projection of input embeddings $k_i, v_i = \text{Proj}(w_i + p_i)$. In Diformer, we have to further remove the positional information since the directed positional embedding can still be used for cheating in the computation of self-attention across layers.

Completely removing the the positional information on K, V and only using the word-embedding w_i can be harmful to the performance. Therefore, we propose an alternative solution by replacing the removed absolute positional embedding with the relative positional embedding proposed in (Shaw et al., 2018) for two reasons: 1) The relative position is computed in a 2 dimensional space, meaning that p_{ij} and p_{kj} for token y_j is not shared between y_i and y_k, which satisfies our requirements that each token in the context should have the position information only used for y_i but not shared for y_k. 2) The position information is only injected during the computation of self-attention without affecting the original word embedding used in K, V.

Formally, we directly use the method in (Shaw et al., 2018) but replace the hidden representation for computing K, V with word embeddings:

$$h_i^{l'} = \sum_{j=1}^{N} \alpha_{ij}(w_j W^V + p_{ij}^V) \quad (9)$$

$$\alpha_{ij} = \frac{\exp e_{ij}}{\sum_{k=1}^{N} \exp e_{ik}} \quad (10)$$

$$e_{ij} = \frac{h_i^{(l-1)} W^Q (w_j W^K + p_{ij}^K)^\top}{\sqrt{d_{\text{head}}}} \quad (11)$$

where $h_i^{l'}$ is the output of the self-attention in current layer, w_j is the word embedding, p_{ij}^V, p_{ij}^K are embedded relative positions, W^Q, W^K, W^V are parameters for Q, K and V, h_i^{l-1} is the last layer's hidden state, d_{head} is the hidden size of a single head. Two parameter matrics are used as embeddings — Re^K and Re^V, with the shape of $[2k+1, d_{\text{head}}]$, where k is the max length. p_{ij} is obtained by embedding the distance between i and j clipped by the maximum length k.

Finally, a customized attention mask (see Figure 1) is created during training to simulate specific dependencies based on the sampled direction sequence Z with following rules:

- If $z_i = R$, all tokens for $j > i$ will be masked.
- If $z_i = L$, all tokens for $j < i$ will be masked.
- If $z_i = S$, y_i and a subset of randomly selected tokens will be masked following the method in (Ghazvininejad et al., 2020), excluding [BOS] and [EOS].

Inference Diformer can generate a sequence with 4 modes including L2R and R2L for AR decoding, mask-predict and parallel easy-first for NAR decoding.

For the AR decoding, the model works exactly same as the conventional Transformer, except that for each step, a fixed direction $z_i = R$ or L should also be also be given, together with previously generated tokens, making it a pure-linear autoregressive generation. Beam search can be directly used in both L2R and R2L decoding. For the NAR decoding, the model uses mask-predict or easy-first by applying specific masking operation during each iteration, where all tokens are assigned with $z = S$. Length beam can be used to further improve the performance. Detailed examples are shown in the Appendix.

More importantly, we find that the multi-directional property of Diformer can be used for reranking, which is quite beneficial for the NAR decoding. Specifically, compared to other NAR models that uses an external AR model for reranking, Diformer can do it all by its own without introducing additional computational costs. For example, it first refines 5 candidates with 8 iterations and performs reranking with the rest of 2 iterations by re-using the encoder states and scoring candidates with L2R and R2L modes, which is equivalent to the computational cost of a 10-stepped refinement reported in CMLM. The scores computed in two directions are averaged to obtain the final rank. Experimental results show that 8 steps of refinement + 2 steps of reranking obtains significant performance improvements compared to 10 steps of refinement without re-ranking. It can also be used for AR decoding, where all tokens are scored under the reversed direction, e.g. generating with L2R and scoring with R2L. We name this method as **self-reranking**.

3 Experiments

3.1 Experimental Setup

Data We evaluate Diformer on 4 benchmarks including WMT14 En↔De (4.5M sentence pairs) and WMT16 En↔Ro (610k sentence pairs). The data is preprocessed in the same way with (Vaswani et al., 2017; Lee et al., 2018), where each sentence is tokenized with Moses toolkit (Koehn et al., 2007) and encoded into subwords using BPE (Sennrich et al., 2016). We follow (Gu et al., 2018; Ghazvininejad et al., 2019; Zhou et al., 2020) to create the knowledge distilled (KD) data with L2R Transformer-big and Transformer-base for En↔De and En↔Ro, the reported performance in the overall results are all obtained by training on the KD data.

Configuration We follow the same configurations with previous works (Vaswani et al., 2017; Ghazvininejad et al., 2019; Ghazvininejad et al., 2020) on hyperparameters: $n_{(encoder+decoder)\_layers} = 6 + 6$, $n_{heads} = 8$, $d_{hidden} = 512$, $d_{FFN} = 2048$. For customized components in Diformer, we tune the max relative distance k in [1,8,16,256] and find that $k = 256$ obtains best performance. Adam (Kingma and Ba, 2015) is used for optimization with 128k tokens per batch on 8 V100 GPUs. The learning rate warms up for 10k steps to 5e-4 and decays with inversed-sqrt. Models for En↔De and En↔Ro are trained for 300k and 100k steps, last 5 checkpoints are averaged for final evaluation. We set beam size as 4 and 5 for AR and NAR decoding. When decoding in NAR mode, we set the max iteration for mask-predict and easy-fist decoding as 10 without using any early-stopping strategy. For fair comparison, we reduce the max iteration to 8 when decoding with self-reranking in NAR model. Our model is implemented with PyTorch and fairseq (Ott et al., 2019). BLEU (Papineni et al., 2002) is used for evaluation.

3.2 Results & Analysis

We perform experiments on Diformer to evaluate its performance on three generation directions with four decoding strategies. We mainly compare Diformer to three types of models: 1) the unified-models that is able to decode with multiple strategies, 2) pure AR model, i.e. standard Transformer, 3) pure NAR models. (see Table 1)

	En-De		De-En		En-Ro		Ro-En	
	AR	NAR	AR	NAR	AR	NAR	AR	NAR
AR Models								
T-big (Vaswani et al., 2017)	28.4	-	-	-	-	-	-	-
T-base (Vaswani et al., 2017)	27.3	-	-	-	-	-	-	-
T-big (our impl, En↔De teacher)	28.52	-	32.10	-	-	-	-	-
T-base (our impl, En↔Ro teacher)	27.67	-	31.12	-	35.29	-	34.02	-
T-base + distill	28.41	-	31.69	-	35.21	-	33.87	-
NAR models								
NAT (Gu et al., 2018)	-	19.17	-	23.20	-	29.79	-	31.44
iNAT (Lee et al., 2018)	-	21.61	-	25.48	-	29.32	-	30.19
InsT (Stern et al., 2019)	27.29	27.41	-	-	-	-	-	-
CMLM (Ghazvininejad et al., 2019)	-	27.03	-	30.53	-	33.08	-	33.31
LevT (Gu et al., 2019b)	-	27.27	-	-	-	-	-	33.26
DisCO (Kasai et al., 2020)	-	27.34	-	31.31	-	33.22	-	33.25
Unified models								
(Mansimov et al., 2020)	25.66	24.53	30.58	28.63	-	-	-	-
(Tian et al., 2020)	27.23	26.35	-	-	-	-	-	-
Diformer (ours)								
- L2R	28.35/**28.68**	-	31.58/31.76	-	35.06/35.16	-	33.84/**33.92**	-
- R2L	28.58/28.50	-	**32.00**/31.78	-	**35.17**/35.13	-	33.90/33.90	-
- mask-predict	-	27.51/**27.99**	-	31.05/31.35	-	33.62/**34.37**	-	32.68/33.11
- easy-first	-	27.35/27.84	-	31.21/**31.68**	-	33.58/34.23	-	32.97/**33.34**

Table 1: This table shows the overall performance of Diformer compared to the AR, NAR and unified models when decoding with AR or NAR strategies. T-big/-base is the abbreviation of Transformer-big/-base. The BLEU score using self-rerank (right) or not (left) is separated by /.

Comparison with unified models For the comparison to unified-models (Mansimov et al., 2020; Tian et al., 2020), Diformer outperforms others in all generation directions, by obtaining more than 1.5 BLEU.

As discussed in the section 1, their support on multiple generation strategies is achieved by applying certain position selection strategy on the masked language model or generating with certain permutation with the permutation language model. This creates the gap between the training and inference since a specific decoding strategy might not be fully trained with the generalized objective as analyzed in (Mansimov et al., 2020). So, compared to both, we use the task-specific modelling in exchange for better performance by abandon certain flexibility, thus makes the learned distribution to be same with the one used in decoding, which answers why Diformer performs better.

Comparison with AR models For the En↔De dataset, since we use a larger teacher model (Transformer-big), therefore, we only compare Diformer with same sized Transformer-base trained on the raw and distilled data. The Diformer outperforms Transformer trained on the raw data with a large margin and reaches the same level to the one trained on distilled data. Interesting, the best performance of Diformer are usually obtained by the R2L decoding and the reranked results on L2R, the reason of it will be further discussed in ablation study sections. For the En↔Ro dataset, Diformer can also obtain similar performance compared to the same sized Transformer trained on the distilled data produced by a same sized teacher.

Comparison with NAR models Diformer is also competitive to a series of NAR models including iterative-refinement based and fully NAR models. We speculate the strong performance of Diformer comes from the joint training of AR and NAR, since it is similar to the multi-task scenario, where tasks are closely correlated but not same. This could be beneficial for the task that is more difficult i.e. NAR, because the learned common knowledge on AR tasks could be directly used in it. By applying the self-reranking method, Diformer could obtain additional 0.5 BLEU over the strong baseline.

3.3 Ablation Study

In this section, we perform extra experiments to investigate factors that could influence the performance of Diformer and the mechanism behind it. All experiments of ablation study are performed on the WMT14 En→De dataset.

The influence of Knowledge Distillation We train Diformer not only with distilled data but also with raw data as shown in table 2. The degrada-

Data Condition	R	L	mask-predict	easy-first
T-base (our impl)				
Raw data	27.67	-	-	-
Distilled data	28.41	-	-	-
Diformer				
Raw data	27.21	27.08	24.12	24.18
Raw data (fixed right)	27.63	-	-	-
Distilled data	28.35	28.55	27.51	27.35

Table 2: This table shows the performance of Transformer and Diformer trained on raw and distilled data where T-base represents for Transformer-base. An additional experiment with fixed $z_i = R$ for all tokens is also presented.

max k	R	L	mask-predict	easy-first
256	28.35	28.58	27.51	27.35
16	28.51	28.48	27.25	27.32
8	28.13	28.25	26.58	26.71
1	26.81	26.85	18.78	19.53

Table 3: This table shows the performance of Diformer with different max k.

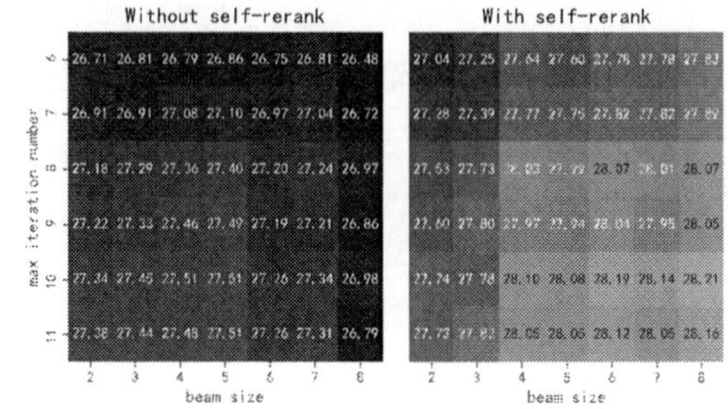

Figure 2: The heatmap shows the BLEU score decoded with mask-predict when using self-reranking or not under different max iteration number and length beam size.

tion of NAR decoding when training on raw data is not surprising which is a common problem faced by all NAR models. However, the performance of AR decoding also degrades. We speculate that on the raw data, the difficulty of learning to generate from straight and R2L increased significantly, making the model to allocate more capacity to fit them, resulting in the negative influence on the performance of L2R. We verify this by fixing $z_i = R$ for all tokens and train the model on raw data. The result confirms it because the performance recovers to its original level. On the contrary, the knowledge distilled data is cleaner and more monotonous (Zhou et al., 2020), making it easier to learn for all directions, and allows the model to allocate balanced capacity on each direction. As for the better performance obtained by R2L decoding, we consider the reason is that, the R2L is able to learn the distilled data generated by the L2R teacher in a complementary manner, making it more efficient to learn the knowledge that cannot be learned by L2R due to the same modeling method.

The Importance of Relative Position We also demonstrate the importance of the relative positional embedding by evaluating the model with different maximum relative distance k and obtain the same conclusion (Shaw et al., 2018) — the distance should be at least 8. Meanwhile, we observe that NAR is more sensitive to the positional information, which is reasonable, since the decoding of NAR is conditioned on the bi-directional context, where the positional information contains both distance and direction thereby is more important compared to that in AR.

Improvements of Self-Reranking As shown in the overall results, self-reranking is a useful method to improve the performance especially for NAR decoding. For the AR decoding, the improvements is not that significant since the outputs are already good enough for L2R or R2L, the tiny gap between reranking and generation direction cannot provide enough help, which indicates that using self-reranking for AR is not that profitable compared to NAR.

We further investigate its ability on NAR decoding (mask-predict) given different max iteration number and length beam size, as shown in Figure 2. It clearly shows that without reranking, the incorrect selection on beam candidates may even reduce the performance with larger beam size. The use of self-reranking actually lets the performance and beam-size positively correlated, meaning that exchanging 2 steps of iteration with self-reranking can be profitable with larger beam size. In practical usage of self-reranking, it is critical to find the optimal combination by balancing the beam size and max iteration number so that both high performance and low latency can be obtained.

Efficiency of the Model Since our model involves both AR and NAR decoding, we also make a compression on the decoding speed with CMLM. We evaluate this on a single V100 GPU, the decoding speed is computed by generated sentences per second recorded by the fairseq. Table 4 shows the result including the speed up under different iteration number and beam-size compared with AR baseline. When decoding with mask-predict and with same configurations, Diformer has sim-

Model	Beam Size	Iteration	Speed Up	BLEU
Transformer	5	T	1.0	28.41
CMLM (MP)	1	4	13.21	25.12
CMLM (MP)	5	4	3.39	25.94
CMLM (MP)	5	10	1.49	27.09
Diformer (MP)	1	4	14.82	25.25
Diformer (MP)	5	4	3.27	26.48
Diformer (MP)	5	10	1.58	27.51
Diformer (MP+SR)	5	4+2	2.4	27.60
Diformer (MP+SR)	5	8+2	1.57	27.99

Table 4: This table presents the compression of the Diformer and CMLM on the decoding efficiency as well as the performance. MP represents for mask-predict and SR stands for self-reranking. For the Diformer decoding with MP+SR, number of iteration is composed with real generation steps and reranking steps.

ilar decoding speed and performance compared with CMLM. With the help of self-reranking, the performance of Diformer can be significantly improved without introducing additional latency compared to decoding with equivalent iterations without self-reranking.

4 Conclusion

In this paper, we present Directional Transformer which is able to model the autoregressive and non-autoregressive generation with a unified framework named Directional Language Model which essentially links two types of conditional language model with three generation directions. Compared to previous works, Diformer exchanges the generalization on decoding strategies for better performance and thereby only support 4 decoding strategies. Experimental results on WMT14 En↔De and WMT16 En↔Ro demonstrate that the unification of AR and NAR can be achieved by Diformer without losing any performance. The bidirectional property of Diformer allows it to perform self-reranking which is especially useful for NAR decoding to improve performance with no additional computational cost.

Except from machine translation, Diformer can be easily extended to other tasks like language modeling by removing the dependency on X. It has the potential to unify the representation learning and generation with a single model, which is actually our ongoing work.

References

Bahdanau, Dzmitry, Kyunghyun Cho, and Yoshua Bengio. 2015. Neural machine translation by jointly learning to align and translate. In Bengio, Yoshua and Yann LeCun, editors, *3rd International Conference on Learning Representations, ICLR 2015, San Diego, CA, USA, May 7-9, 2015, Conference Track Proceedings*.

Ghazvininejad, Marjan, Omer Levy, Yinhan Liu, and Luke Zettlemoyer. 2019. Mask-predict: Parallel decoding of conditional masked language models. In Inui, Kentaro, Jing Jiang, Vincent Ng, and Xiaojun Wan, editors, *Proceedings of EMNLP-IJCNLP 2019, Hong Kong, China, November 3-7, 2019*, pages 6111–6120. Association for Computational Linguistics.

Ghazvininejad, Marjan, Vladimir Karpukhin, Luke Zettlemoyer, and Omer Levy. 2020. Aligned cross entropy for non-autoregressive machine translation. In *Proceedings of the 37th International Conference on Machine Learning, ICML 2020, 13-18 July 2020, Virtual Event*, volume 119 of *Proceedings of Machine Learning Research*, pages 3515–3523. PMLR.

Gu, Jiatao, James Bradbury, Caiming Xiong, Victor O. K. Li, and Richard Socher. 2018. Non-autoregressive neural machine translation. In *6th International Conference on Learning Representations, ICLR 2018, Vancouver, BC, Canada, April 30 - May 3, 2018, Conference Track Proceedings*. OpenReview.net.

Gu, Jiatao, Qi Liu, and Kyunghyun Cho. 2019a. Insertion-based decoding with automatically inferred generation order. *Trans. Assoc. Comput. Linguistics*, 7:661–676.

Gu, Jiatao, Changhan Wang, and Junbo Zhao. 2019b. Levenshtein transformer. In Wallach, Hanna M., Hugo Larochelle, Alina Beygelzimer, Florence d'Alché-Buc, Emily B. Fox, and Roman Garnett, editors, *Advances in Neural Information Processing Systems 32: Annual Conference on Neural Information Processing Systems 2019, NeurIPS 2019, December 8-14, 2019, Vancouver, BC, Canada*, pages 11179–11189.

Kasai, Jungo, James Cross, Marjan Ghazvininejad, and Jiatao Gu. 2020. Non-autoregressive machine translation with disentangled context transformer. In *Proceedings of the 37th International Conference on Machine Learning, ICML 2020, 13-18 July 2020, Virtual Event*, volume 119 of *Proceedings of Machine Learning Research*, pages 5144–5155. PMLR.

Kingma, Diederik P. and Jimmy Ba. 2015. Adam: A method for stochastic optimization. In Bengio, Yoshua and Yann LeCun, editors, *3rd International Conference on Learning Representations, ICLR 2015, San Diego, CA, USA, May 7-9, 2015, Conference Track Proceedings*.

Koehn, Philipp, Hieu Hoang, Alexandra Birch, Chris Callison-Burch, Marcello Federico, Nicola Bertoldi, Brooke Cowan, Wade Shen, Christine Moran, Richard Zens, Chris Dyer, Ondrej Bojar, Alexandra Constantin, and Evan Herbst. 2007. Moses: Open source toolkit for statistical machine translation. In Carroll, John A., Antal van den Bosch, and

Annie Zaenen, editors, *ACL 2007, June 23-30, 2007, Prague, Czech Republic*. The Association for Computational Linguistics.

Lee, Jason, Elman Mansimov, and Kyunghyun Cho. 2018. Deterministic non-autoregressive neural sequence modeling by iterative refinement. In Riloff, Ellen, David Chiang, Julia Hockenmaier, and Jun'ichi Tsujii, editors, *Proceedings of the 2018 Conference on Empirical Methods in Natural Language Processing, Brussels, Belgium, October 31 - November 4, 2018*, pages 1173–1182. Association for Computational Linguistics.

Mansimov, Elman, Alex Wang, Sean Welleck, and Kyunghyun Cho. 2020. A generalized framework of sequence generation with application to undirected sequence models.

Ott, Myle, Sergey Edunov, Alexei Baevski, Angela Fan, Sam Gross, Nathan Ng, David Grangier, and Michael Auli. 2019. fairseq: A fast, extensible toolkit for sequence modeling. In Ammar, Waleed, Annie Louis, and Nasrin Mostafazadeh, editors, *Proceedings of NAACL-HLT 2019, Minneapolis, MN, USA, June 2-7, 2019, Demonstrations*, pages 48–53. Association for Computational Linguistics.

Papineni, Kishore, Salim Roukos, Todd Ward, and Wei-Jing Zhu. 2002. Bleu: a method for automatic evaluation of machine translation. In *Proceedings of the 40th Annual Meeting of the Association for Computational Linguistics, July 6-12, 2002, Philadelphia, PA, USA*, pages 311–318. ACL.

Qi, Weizhen, Yeyun Gong, Jian Jiao, Yu Yan, Weizhu Chen, Dayiheng Liu, Kewen Tang, Houqiang Li, Jiusheng Chen, Ruofei Zhang, Ming Zhou, and Nan Duan. 2021. BANG: bridging autoregressive and non-autoregressive generation with large scale pretraining. In Meila, Marina and Tong Zhang, editors, *Proceedings of ICML 2021, 18-24 July 2021, Virtual Event*, volume 139 of *Proceedings of Machine Learning Research*, pages 8630–8639. PMLR.

Sennrich, Rico, Barry Haddow, and Alexandra Birch. 2016. Neural machine translation of rare words with subword units. In *Proceedings of ACL 2016, August 7-12, 2016, Berlin, Germany, Volume 1: Long Papers*. The Association for Computer Linguistics.

Shaw, Peter, Jakob Uszkoreit, and Ashish Vaswani. 2018. Self-attention with relative position representations. In Walker, Marilyn A., Heng Ji, and Amanda Stent, editors, *Proceedings of the 2018 Conference of NAACL-HLT, New Orleans, Louisiana, USA, June 1-6, 2018, Volume 2 (Short Papers)*, pages 464–468. Association for Computational Linguistics.

Shu, Raphael, Jason Lee, Hideki Nakayama, and Kyunghyun Cho. 2020. Latent-variable non-autoregressive neural machine translation with deterministic inference using a delta posterior. In *The Thirty-Fourth AAAI Conference on Artificial Intelligence, AAAI 2020, New York, NY, USA, February 7-12, 2020*, pages 8846–8853. AAAI Press.

Stern, Mitchell, William Chan, Jamie Kiros, and Jakob Uszkoreit. 2019. Insertion transformer: Flexible sequence generation via insertion operations. In Chaudhuri, Kamalika and Ruslan Salakhutdinov, editors, *Proceedings of ICML 2019, 9-15 June 2019, Long Beach, California, USA*, volume 97 of *Proceedings of Machine Learning Research*, pages 5976–5985. PMLR.

Sutskever, Ilya, Oriol Vinyals, and Quoc V. Le. 2014. Sequence to sequence learning with neural networks. In Ghahramani, Zoubin, Max Welling, Corinna Cortes, Neil D. Lawrence, and Kilian Q. Weinberger, editors, *Advances in Neural Information Processing Systems 27: Annual Conference on Neural Information Processing Systems 2014, December 8-13 2014, Montreal, Quebec, Canada*, pages 3104–3112.

Tian, Chao, Yifei Wang, Hao Cheng, Yijiang Lian, and Zhihua Zhang. 2020. Train once, and decode as you like. In Scott, Donia, Núria Bel, and Chengqing Zong, editors, *Proceedings of COLING 2020, Barcelona, Spain (Online), December 8-13, 2020*, pages 280–293. International Committee on Computational Linguistics.

Vaswani, Ashish, Noam Shazeer, Niki Parmar, Jakob Uszkoreit, Llion Jones, Aidan N. Gomez, Lukasz Kaiser, and Illia Polosukhin. 2017. Attention is all you need. In Guyon, Isabelle, Ulrike von Luxburg, Samy Bengio, Hanna M. Wallach, Rob Fergus, S. V. N. Vishwanathan, and Roman Garnett, editors, *Advances in Neural Information Processing Systems 30: Annual Conference on Neural Information Processing Systems 2017, December 4-9, 2017, Long Beach, CA, USA*, pages 5998–6008.

Welleck, Sean, Kianté Brantley, Hal Daumé III, and Kyunghyun Cho. 2019. Non-monotonic sequential text generation. In Chaudhuri, Kamalika and Ruslan Salakhutdinov, editors, *Proceedings of ICML 2019, 9-15 June 2019, Long Beach, California, USA*, volume 97 of *Proceedings of Machine Learning Research*, pages 6716–6726. PMLR.

Yang, Zhilin, Zihang Dai, Yiming Yang, Jaime G. Carbonell, Ruslan Salakhutdinov, and Quoc V. Le. 2019. Xlnet: Generalized autoregressive pretraining for language understanding. In Wallach, Hanna M., Hugo Larochelle, Alina Beygelzimer, Florence d'Alché-Buc, Emily B. Fox, and Roman Garnett, editors, *Advances in Neural Information Processing Systems 32: Annual Conference on Neural Information Processing Systems 2019, NeurIPS 2019, December 8-14, 2019, Vancouver, BC, Canada*, pages 5754–5764.

Zhou, Chunting, Jiatao Gu, and Graham Neubig. 2020. Understanding knowledge distillation in non-autoregressive machine translation. In *8th International Conference on Learning Representations, ICLR 2020, Addis Ababa, Ethiopia, April 26-30, 2020*. OpenReview.net.

Multilingual Neural Machine Translation With the Right Amount of Sharing

Taido Purason
University of Tartu
Tartu, Estonia
taido.purason@ut.ee

Andre Tättar
University of Tartu
Tartu, Estonia
andre.tattar@ut.ee

Abstract

Large multilingual Transformer-based machine translation models have had a pivotal role in making translation systems available for hundreds of languages with good zero-shot translation performance. One such example is the universal model with shared encoder-decoder architecture. Additionally, jointly trained language-specific encoder-decoder systems have been proposed for multilingual neural machine translation (NMT) models. This work investigates various knowledge-sharing approaches on the encoder side while keeping the decoder language- or language-group-specific. We propose a novel approach, where we use universal, language-group-specific and language-specific modules to solve the shortcomings of both the universal models and models with language-specific encoders-decoders. Experiments on a multilingual dataset set up to model real-world scenarios, including zero-shot and low-resource translation, show that our proposed models achieve higher translation quality compared to purely universal and language-specific approaches.

1 Introduction

Multilingual neural machine translation has been a fundamental topic in recent years, especially for zero- and few-shot translation scenarios. Traditionally, universal NMT models (see Fig. 1a) have

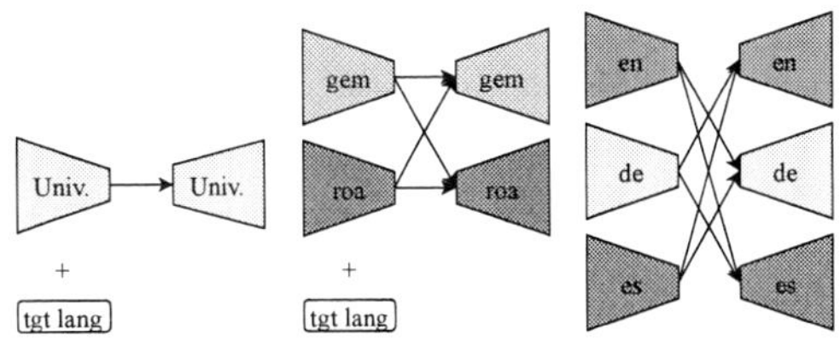

(a) Universal model **(b)** Model with language-group-specific modules **(c)** Model with language-specific modules

Figure 1: Different granularities of the modular architecture. *roa* – Romance; *gem* – Germanic; *tgt lang* – Target language token added to indicate the language of the output sentence.

been used to produce zero-shot or low-resource translations (Johnson et al., 2016). However, previous research has established that universal NMT models with shared encoder-decoder architecture have some disadvantages: (1) high-resource language pairs tend to suffer loss in translation quality (Arivazhagan et al., 2019); (2) the vocabulary of the model increases greatly, especially for languages that do not share an alphabet such as English and Japanese; (3) the need to retrain from scratch when a new language does not share the model's vocabulary.

Recently, there has been renewed interest in multilingual systems, which have jointly trained language-specific encoders-decoders (see Fig. 1c) which we call the modular architecture (Lyu et al., 2020). The goal of these models has been to achieve a better overall translation quality compared to universal or uni-directional NMT models. However, there is a disadvantage: lower zero-shot translation quality compared to universal models. To combat this problem, shared encoder/decoder layers (also called *interlingua* layers) have been proposed (Liao et al., 2021).

Macken, Rufener, Van den Bogaert, Daems, Tezcan, Vanroy, Fonteyne, Barrault, Costa-jussà, Kemp, Pilos, Declercq, Koponen, Forcada, Scarton, Moniz (eds.)
Proceedings of the 23rd Annual Conference of the European Association for Machine Translation, p. 91–100
Ghent, Belgium, June 2022.

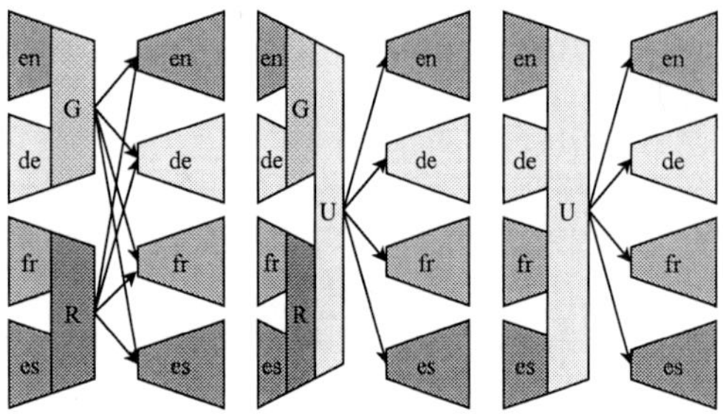

(a) Language group sharing

(b) Language group and universal sharing (tiered)

(c) Universal sharing (between all languages)

Figure 2: Different types of encoder layer sharing in the modular architecture. Note that the width of layers in the figure does not correspond to the actual width but rather reflects the sharing extent, i.e. all layers in the encoder have the same width dimension. *U* – universal, *G* – Germanic, *R* – Romance.

In this paper, we focus on improving the overall translation quality by using different knowledge- and layer-sharing methods. More specifically, we investigate the effect of sharing encoder layers to improve the generalizability and quality of NMT models. Secondly, we present novel language group based models that are inspired by the universal and modular systems. We propose (1) various degrees of granularity (or specificity) of modules (illustrated in Fig. 1); (2) layer sharing, including combining layers of various granularities into a tiered architecture (illustrated by Fig. 2). Our methods show better translation quality in all testing scenarions compared to the universal model without increasing training or inference time by having variable degrees of modularity or sharing in the encoder.

Our research looks beyond zero-shot and high-resource NMT performance – we set up our experiments to investigate model performance for many data scenarios like zero-shot and low- to high-resource settings. We use a combination of Europarl (Koehn, 2005), EMEA (Tiedemann, 2012), and JRC-Acquis (Steinberger et al., 2006) datasets for training and evaluation and six languages grouped into two language groups: Germanic (German, English, Danish) and Romance (French, Spanish, Portuguese). The results show that our approaches can provide an improvement to universal models in all data scenarios. Furthermore, our approaches improve the zero-shot and low-resource translation quality of the modular architecture without harming the high-resource language translation quality.

The main contributions of our paper are:

- We introduce a novel language-group-specific modular encoder and decoder architecture (Fig. 1b).
- Showing that different architectures of shared encoder layers (Fig. 2) improve the low-resource MT quality of the modular model while also improving the high-resource MT quality that suffers in the universal NMT setting.
- We empirically show what effect sharing encoder layers has and present a detailed analysis that supports layer sharing.

2 Related Works

Multilingual neural machine translation models follow the encoder-decoder architecture and approaches following this architecture can vary in the amount of parameter sharing (Dabre et al., 2020).

The most straightforward approach with no parameter sharing would be having a system of uni-directional models. While it is feasible with a small amount of high-resource languages, it becomes problematic in scenarios with low-resource languages or a large number of languages. Firstly, the number of uni-directional models in the system grows quadratically with the number of languages, harming maintainability. Secondly, there is no transfer learning between language pairs due to separate models, which means that low-resource languages generally have low translation quality. These issues are addressed by pivoting with some success, however, it does not come without trade-offs (Habash and Hu, 2009). The main problem with pivoting is that it is not possible to fully utilize all the training data since we only use training data that contains the pivot language. Furthermore, due to multiple models being potentially used for a translation, the translation is slower, and there is a chance of error propagation and loss of information.

The most widely used approach in multilingual NMT uses a fully shared (universal) model, which has a single encoder and decoder shared between all the languages and uses a token added to the input sentence to indicate the target language (Johnson et al., 2016). Arivazhagan et al. (2019) identified that the universal model suffers from the capacity bottleneck: with many languages in the model, the translation quality begins to deteriorate.

This especially harms the translation quality of high-resource language pairs. Zhang et al. (2020) further confirmed this and suggested deeper and language-aware models as an improvement. Still, the problem of low maintainability remains, since adding the languages to the model is not possible without retraining the whole model. Furthermore, adding languages with different scripts likely results in lower translation quality since the vocabulary can not be altered.

Escolano et al. (2019) suggested a proof-of-concept model with language-specific encoders and decoders that started bilingual and was incrementally trained to include other languages. Escolano et al. (2020) further improved on it and proposed a joint training procedure that produced a model that outperformed the universal model in translation quality. Furthermore, their proposed model is expandable by incrementally adding new languages without affecting the existing languages' translation quality. Lyu et al. (2020) investigated the performance of the modular model from the industry perspective. They found that the modular model often outperforms single direction models thanks to transfer learning while being a competitor to the universal model as well due to the additional capacity of language-specific modules.

Modular models can contain shared modules as well. Liao et al. (2021) set out to improve the zero-shot performance of modular models, which is often worse than the zero-shot performance of universal models. They achieve this by sharing upper layers of language-specific encoders between all languages. The current paper is an extension of that work. While Liao et al. (2021) used English-centric training data and denoising autoencoder task to achieve universal interlingua, in this paper we are not using an autoencoder task, since our data is not one language centric.

Introducing language-specific modules into a universal model can be a good way to increase the capacity of the model without significantly increasing training or inference time. An example of a system that utilizes this is described in Fan et al. (2020). They use language-specific and language group layers in the decoder of the model following the universal architecture model to provide more capacity. They also note that language-specific layers are more effective when applied to the decoder. Liao et al. (2021) also found that sharing in decoder is not beneficial when there are shared layers in the encoder. These are also the main motivations for focusing on sharing encoder layers in this paper.

3 Experiment setup

3.1 Data

Our aim was to create a dataset that resembles a real-world scenario where language pairs with varying amounts of data are encountered. The data is collected from Europarl (Koehn, 2005), EMEA (Tiedemann, 2012), and JRC-Acquis (Steinberger et al., 2006). The training dataset is created by sampling from the aforementioned datasets so that the training dataset is composed of 70% Europarl, 15% EMEA, and 15% JRC-Acquis. The test set is composed of completely multi-parallel sentences.

Language combination	Direction (lang. group)	
	intra	inter
high–high	1,000,000	1,000,000
high–mid	500,000	500,000
mid–mid	500,000	100,000
low–high	100,000	10,000
low–mid	100,000	0
low–low	0	0

Table 1: Dataset size rules per language type pair and language group. intra – translation within language group, inter – translating between language groups

The dataset is composed of English, German, Danish, French, Spanish, and Portuguese. For creating the dataset and defining models, these are divided into Germanic (English, German, Danish) and Romance (French, Spanish, Portugese) language groups. We define high-resource (English, German, French), medium-resource (Spanish), and low-resource (Danish, Portuguese) languages that produce high-resource (1,000,000 lines), higher medium resource (500,000 lines), lower medium resource (100,000 lines), low-resource (10,000 lines), and zero-shot (0 lines) language pairs when combined according to the rules in Table 1. With these rules, we also give low and medium resource language directions less training sentences if they consist of languages from different language groups compared to the pairs consisting of the same language group languages. The resulting dataset composition from these rules is visible in Table 2. The test set consists of 2000 multi-parallel sentences for each language pair from the same distribution as the training data. Since the training dataset is cre-

src	tgt						
	en	de	da	fr	es	pt	all
en	–	1,000,000	100,000	1,000,000	500,000	10,000	2,610,000
de	1,000,000	–	100,000	1,000,000	500,000	10,000	2,610,000
da	100,000	100,000	–	10,000	0	0	210,000
fr	1,000,000	1,000,000	10,000	–	500,000	100,000	2,610,000
es	500,000	500,000	0	500,000	–	100,000	1,600,000
pt	10,000	10,000	0	100,000	100,000	–	220,000
all	2,610,000	2,610,000	210,000	2,610,000	1,600,000	220,000	9,860,000

Table 2: Dataset sizes (number of sentence pairs) per language pair.

ated by randomly sampling data for each language pair, it is not completely multi-parallel, however, it probably contains many multi-parallel lines. The validation dataset is created for all non-zero-shot pairs with size per language pair defined by $n_{\text{test}}(\text{langpair}) = \max(n_{\text{train}}(\text{langpair}) \cdot 0.0006, 100)$.

The dataset size is quite small compared to data used for training state-of-the-art models mainly due to limited computational resources. However, we believe that it still allows us to draw conclusions that can be applied at larger scales.

3.2 Model architecture

Previous research has investigated sharing layers of the modular architecture (Liao et al., 2021). In this work, we mainly focus on layer sharing in the encoders. The layers are shared in 2 ways: (1) inside language groups (Fig. 2a), and (2) between all languages (universally, Fig. 2c). These two methods are also combined into a tiered architecture (Fig. 2b). We also experiment with different levels of granularity of modules and introduce language-group-specific modules referred to as *group modular* model (Fig. 1b).

As baselines, we use a modular architecture without layer sharing (Fig. 1c) and a universal architecture with one encoder and decoder shared between all languages (Fig. 1a).

All of the models in our experiments follow the transformer base architecture (Vaswani et al., 2017) (6 encoder layers, 6 decoder layers). In addition to dropout of 0.1, attention and activation dropout of 0.1 are used. The embeddings are shared within a language module (encoder-decoder) for language-specific modular models and within a language group module for group modular models. For the universal model, all embeddings are shared.

3.3 Segmentation model training

We use Byte Pair Encoding (BPE) (Sennrich et al., 2016) implemented in SentencePiece (Kudo and Richardson, 2018) as the segmentation algorithm. For the language-specific encoder-decoder approach, we train a BPE model with a vocabulary size of 16,000 for each of the languages. In the group-specific approach, we have a BPE model for each of the language groups with a vocabulary size of 32,000. For the universal model, we have a single unified BPE model with vocabulary size of 32,000. For training the BPE models, we use character coverage of 1.0 and training data consisting of the training set of the corresponding languages.

3.4 Model training

Fairseq (Ott et al., 2019) is used to implement training and models. We made the code for our custom implementations publicly available[1].

For the following experiments, we set the convergence criteria to be 5 epochs of no improvement in the validation set loss. To evaluate the experiments, we always use the best epoch according to the validation loss.

The learning rate is selected from {0.0002, 0.0004, 0.0008} by the highest BLEU score on the validation set after 20 training epochs. Gradient accumulation frequency is selected using BLEU score on the validation set after convergence from 8, 16, 32, 48. For all experiments in this paper, the total maximum batch size is 384,000 tokens (max tokens in a batch multiplied by the gradient accumulation frequency and the number of GPUs).

From the initial experiments, learning rate of 0.0004 and gradient accumulation frequency of 48 is selected. For all experiments, Adam optimizer (Kingma and Ba, 2015), inverse square root learning-rate scheduler with 4,000 warm-up steps, and label smoothing (Szegedy et al., 2016) of 0.1

[1] https://github.com/TartuNLP/fairseq/tree/modular-layer-sharing

Architecture	Language pair resource					
	zero-shot	low	medium-low	medium-high	high	all
Universal	33.62	38.12	39.64	43.64	42.32	39.87
Group modular (GM)						
EA3–6	**35.03**	**39.48**	40.89	44.66	43.31	**41.06**
EA5–6	34.52	39.23	40.78	44.59	43.19	40.88
No sharing	33.76	38.90	40.75	44.60	43.32	40.73
Language modular (LM)						
EA3–6	34.73	38.79	**40.91**	44.68	43.36	40.90
EG3–4 EA5–6	34.57	38.61	40.76	**44.91**	**43.59**	40.90
EG 3–6	34.37	38.56	40.56	44.90	43.42	40.78
EA5–6	33.81	38.28	40.32	44.75	43.38	40.54
EG5 EA6	33.51	38.07	40.33	44.72	43.41	40.46
EG5–6	33.59	37.85	40.32	44.69	43.44	40.43
No sharing	32.14	37.19	39.92	44.74	43.50	40.02

Table 3: Average test set BLEU scores per language pair resource. EG - encoder layer shared within language group, EA - encoder layer shared between all languages. Best score(s) per resource (column) in bold.

are used.

The training approach is similar to the proportional approach in Lyu et al. (2020). The batches are created according to the granularity of the modules, so that the correct module can be chosen for each batch. For the modular models with language-specific encoders-decoders, each batch contains only samples from one language pair. For the group-specific models, the batch contains data from one group pair. We determined by preliminary experiments that gradient accumulation is necessary for the modular models to learn, which we speculate is due to language-specific modules and the aforementioned batch creation strategy. Since the universal model does not have that constraint, a lower gradient accumulation frequency of 8 is used. For group-specific and universal models, target language tokens are added to the input sentence.

We used one NVIDIA A100 GPU for training the models. All models were trained with mixed precision.

3.5 Evaluation

BLEU (Papineni et al., 2001) score is used as the primary metric for translation quality. It is calculated using SacreBLEU[2] (Post, 2018). Beam search with beam size of 5 is used for decoding. Since there are 30 language pairs in total, we group the languages depending on the size of the language pair dataset and mostly look at average test set BLEU scores for analysis.

4 Results

4.1 Main results

As a baseline, we trained a universal and a modular model. We then trained modular models with 2 uppermost or 4 uppermost layers of the encoder shared universally, language-group-specifically or tiered (bottom half of the shared layers shared group-specifically, the rest universally). We also explore language-group-specific modules (group modular model). The main results are visible in Table 3 (evaluation results of individual directions are in Appendix B). Note that the ordering of rows in the table corresponds to the increasing order of total number of parameters which can be found in Appendix A.

4.1.1 No sharing

We can firstly observe that the modular model without any sharing (LM No sharing) performs worse on zero-shot and low-resource language pairs than the universal model (by 1.48 and 0.93 BLEU points, respectively). However, when looking at the medium-high and high resource directions, the modular model performs achieves a higher translation quality (by 1.10 and 1.18 BLEU points, respectively). The translation quality in the medium-low language pairs is similar between the universal and baseline modular model.

4.1.2 Sharing 2 layers

Compared to the baseline modular model (LM No sharing), the modular model with 2 shared encoder layers (LM EA5–6) performs better on

[2]signature: `refs:1|case:mixed|eff:no|tok:13a|smooth:exp|version:2.0.0`

zero-shot, low, and medium-low resource language pairs on average, with medium-high and high resource language translation quality only slightly decreasing. Overall, we can observe 0.52 BLEU point increase in translation quality of the shared layer model compared to the modular model.

We can also see that with sharing 2 upper layers in language groups (LM EG5–6) or tiered (LM EG5 EA6), the results are similar, but on average lower by 0.11 and 0.08 BLEU points, respectively. Sharing layers group-specifically gives a similar effect to sharing layers between all languages on average. With group-specific sharing, the lower resource languages have a slightly lower BLEU score, and the higher resource languages have a slightly higher BLEU score compared to the universal layer sharing. We can see the same trend with tiered sharing.

Comparing the language modular models with 2 shared layers to the universal model, the group sharing (LM EG5–6) and tiered (LM EG5 EA6) have slightly worse translation quality in zero- and low-resource language pairs on average, however they outperform the universal model in all of the other higher resource directions. The model with 2 universally shared layers outperforms the universal model in all resource levels. On average, the universally shared modular model (LM EA5–6) outperforms the universal model by 0.67 BLEU points.

4.1.3 Sharing 4 layers

We can see that sharing 4 layers provides better translation quality on average than sharing 2 layers. All of the models (LM EG3–6, LM EG3–4 EA5–6, LM EA3–6) outperform the universal model in all resource types. The universally shared model (LM EA3–6) performs the best out of the three on average in the zero, low, and medium-low resource directions, while the tiered model (LM EG3–4 EA5–6) has the best higher resource performance, even outperforming the baseline modular model, although only by a small margin. Overall, the two aforementioned models have the highest average BLEU score of the language modular models, outperforming the baseline modular model by 0.88 points and the universal model by 1.03 points. Both of them outperform the universal model in the zero-shot direction: the universally shared modular model (LM EA3–6) by 1.11 BLEU points and the tiered modular model (LM EG3–4 EA5–6) by 0.95 BLEU points.

4.1.4 Group modules

When looking at models with group-specific modules (group modular in Table 3), we can see that they outperform the universal model and the baseline language modular model (LM No sharing) on average. The improvement over the baseline modular model comes mostly from the increase in translation quality in low-resource directions and the improvement over the universal model from higher-resource directions, as we also observed in the previous results. We can also observe that the group modular models outperform the universal model at all resource levels.

The group modular model also benefits from having layers shared between all languages. The average BLEU score increases when shared layers are added to the group modular model, which can mainly be attributed to the increase in zero-shot and low resource translation quality.

The group modular model with 4 encoder layers (GM EA3–6) shared is the best performing model in zero-shot and low-resource directions, outperforming the universal model by 1.41 BLEU points in zero-shot and 1.36 BLEU points in low-resource directions on average. On average, it outperforms the baseline language modular model by 1.04 BLEU points and the baseline universal model by 1.19 BLEU points. Complete evaluation results are presented in Appendix B.

Although we used language group modules and language group sharing in our experiments, we failed to find any meaningful effect on the translation quality when translating between language groups versus translating between languages in the same group.

4.2 Sharing between all languages

The previous experiments have shown that group sharing and tiered architectures were only slightly different from sharing between all languages. Furthermore, the number of shared layers affects the result more than the type of sharing. Hence, we continue with experiments on sharing the language modular model layers between all languages to further study the effect of number of encoder layers shared on BLEU scores. The results can be seen in Table 4.

We can see that, on average, sharing more layers increases the BLEU score steadily until 5 upper encoder layers are shared. Compared to sharing 5 upper layers, sharing all 6 layers slightly de-

Enc. shared layer(s)	Language pair resource					
	zero-shot	low	medium-low	medium-high	high	all
No sharing	32.14	37.19	39.92	44.74	**43.50**	40.02
6	33.07	37.63	40.09	44.67	43.35	40.23
5–6	33.81	38.28	40.32	44.75	43.38	40.54
4–6	34.16	38.43	40.41	44.85	43.43	40.68
3–6	34.73	38.79	**40.91**	44.68	43.36	40.90
2–6	**34.97**	**39.03**	40.81	**44.94**	43.44	**41.03**
1–6	34.61	38.70	40.79	44.60	43.23	40.80

Table 4: Average test set BLEU scores for experiments with encoder layer sharing between all languages in the language modular model.

creases the BLEU scores in all language resource types. This could be attributed to: (1) 1 language-specific layer can better transform the language-specific embeddings to a joint representation than none or (2) more capacity with 5 layers shared and 1 language-specific compared to sharing all 6.

The modular model with encoder layers 2–6 shared provides a very close BLEU score to the best performing model from the previous set of experiments (GM EA3–6). It should be noted however that none of the shared layer models outperform the plain modular model in high resource languages on average, although the difference is quite small. Detailed evaluation results with all translation directions for this model are available in Appendix B.

4.3 Effect of joint embeddings

Since the universal model uses joint embeddings and vocabulary and the modular model uses language-specific embeddings, we investigate whether this could be the reason for the better performance of the latter. We train a modular model with shared embeddings, vocabulary, and encoder layers while still using language-specific decoders. The results in Table 5 show that on average the modular model with shared encoder layers still outperforms the universal model in all resource types even with shared vocabulary and embeddings. Although the selection of training data for the SentencePiece model did not take the language data imbalance into account, we can see that using a unified segmentation model and vocabulary does not significantly decrease the translation quality.

5 Discussion and future work

Multilingual NMT is a complex problem. On the one hand, we face the problem of poor low-resource MT performance of the fully modular model, and on the other hand, we have the capacity issues of the universal model. Our experiments show that we can achieve the best of both worlds with models that combine aspects of both universal and modular NMT architectures.

Although including shared layers in the modular model has kept the translation quality of higher resource language pairs the same or slightly decreased it, there has been a substantial improvement in the translation quality of low and zero resource language pairs compared to the plain modular model. Furthermore, compared to the universal model, these shared layer modular models substantially increase translation quality in all types of language resource directions.

Language-group-specific modules are worth considering as an architecture, as they provide better translation quality in all language resource types compared to the universal model while having fewer parameters in total than models with language-specific modules. Even with language group modules, the zero-shot and low-resource translation quality benefits from layers shared between all languages.

The layer sharing strategy ultimately depends on the available computational and data resources. Having language-specific modules could become memory inefficient in massively multilingual scenarios. Hence, having language group modules or layer sharing is a good compromise between capacity and model size. Approaching the problem from the perspective of the universal model, using some degree of modularization is a good way of increasing capacity without sacrificing zero-shot performance or training time.

Our work also leaves room for future research. While we focused on encoder layer sharing, decoder layer sharing is a direction that we want to investigate in future work comprehensively. Incrementally adding languages is also an important aspect of modular models and should be investigated. In our work, we had a relatively small

Architecture	Language pair resource					
	zero-shot	low	medium-low	medium-high	high	all
Universal	33.62	38.12	39.64	43.64	42.32	39.87
Language modular						
shared enc. + emb. + voc.	**34.65**	**39.01**	40.67	44.43	43.06	40.77
shared enc.	34.61	38.70	**40.79**	**44.60**	**43.23**	**40.80**

Table 5: Average test set BLEU scores for embedding sharing experiments. shared enc. – shared encoder; shared enc. + emb. + voc. – shared encoder, shared embeddings (incl. decoder embeddings) and joint vocabulary.

dataset compared to many state-of-the-art systems, so it would be beneficial to see how our approaches work in a scenario with significantly more data. As previously mentioned, using significantly more languages in the system could also set more constraints on our approaches and would be a promising direction for future works since it could highlight differences between our proposed methods better.

6 Conclusion

In this paper, we propose multiple ways of improving universal models and models with language-specific encoders-decoders by combining features of both. We experimented with language- and language-group-specific modules and sharing layers of the encoders between all languages, groups of languages, or combining them into a tiered architecture. We found that having some layers universally shared (between all languages) benefits the zero-shot and low-resource translation quality of the modular architectures while not hurting the translation quality of high-resource directions. The modular models with some universally shared layers outperform the universal models in all language-resource types (from zero to high). Our best model outperforms the baseline language modular model by 1.04 BLEU points and the universal model by 1.19 BLEU points on average.

References

Arivazhagan, Naveen, Ankur Bapna, Orhan Firat, Dmitry Lepikhin, Melvin Johnson, Maxim Krikun, Mia Xu Chen, Yuan Cao, George Foster, Colin Cherry, Wolfgang Macherey, Zhifeng Chen, and Yonghui Wu. 2019. Massively Multilingual Neural Machine Translation in the Wild: Findings and Challenges. 7.

Dabre, Raj, Chenhui Chu, and Anoop Kunchukuttan. 2020. A Survey of Multilingual Neural Machine Translation. *ACM Computing Surveys*, 53(5).

Escolano, Carlos, Marta R. Costa-jussà, and José A. R. Fonollosa. 2019. From Bilingual to Multilingual Neural Machine Translation by Incremental Training. In *Proceedings of the 57th Annual Meeting of the Association for Computational Linguistics: Student Research Workshop*, pages 236–242, Stroudsburg, PA, USA. Association for Computational Linguistics.

Escolano, Carlos, Marta R. Costa-jussà, José A. R. Fonollosa, and Mikel Artetxe. 2020. Multilingual Machine Translation: Closing the Gap between Shared and Language-specific Encoder-Decoders. 4.

Fan, Angela, Shruti Bhosale, Holger Schwenk, Zhiyi Ma, Ahmed El-Kishky, Siddharth Goyal, Mandeep Baines, Onur Celebi, Guillaume Wenzek, Vishrav Chaudhary, Naman Goyal, Tom Birch, Vitaliy Liptchinsky, Sergey Edunov, Edouard Grave, Michael Auli, and Armand Joulin. 2020. Beyond English-Centric Multilingual Machine Translation. 10.

Habash, Nizar and Jun Hu. 2009. Improving Arabic-Chinese Statistical Machine Translation using English as Pivot Language. In *EACL 2009 - 4th Workshop on Statistical Machine Translation, Proceedings of theWorkshop*.

Johnson, Melvin, Mike Schuster, Quoc V. Le, Maxim Krikun, Yonghui Wu, Zhifeng Chen, Nikhil Thorat, Fernanda Viégas, Martin Wattenberg, Greg Corrado, Macduff Hughes, and Jeffrey Dean. 2016. Google's Multilingual Neural Machine Translation System: Enabling Zero-Shot Translation. 11.

Kingma, Diederik P. and Jimmy Lei Ba. 2015. Adam: A method for stochastic optimization. In *3rd International Conference on Learning Representations, ICLR 2015 - Conference Track Proceedings*.

Koehn, Philipp. 2005. Europarl : A Parallel Corpus for Statistical Machine Translation. *MT Summit*, 11.

Kudo, Taku and John Richardson. 2018. SentencePiece: A simple and language independent subword tokenizer and detokenizer for neural text processing. In *EMNLP 2018 - Conference on Empirical Methods in Natural Language Processing: System Demonstrations, Proceedings*.

Liao, Junwei, Yu Shi, Ming Gong, Linjun Shou, Hong Qu, and Michael Zeng. 2021. Improving Zero-shot Neural Machine Translation on Language-specific Encoders- Decoders. In *2021 International Joint*

Conference on Neural Networks (IJCNN)*, pages 1–8. IEEE, 7.

Lyu, Sungwon, Bokyung Son, Kichang Yang, and Jaekyoung Bae. 2020. Revisiting Modularized Multilingual NMT to Meet Industrial Demands. In *Proceedings of the 2020 Conference on Empirical Methods in Natural Language Processing (EMNLP)*, pages 5905–5918, Online, 11. Association for Computational Linguistics.

Ott, Myle, Sergey Edunov, Alexei Baevski, Angela Fan, Sam Gross, Nathan Ng, David Grangier, and Michael Auli. 2019. Fairseq: A fast, extensible toolkit for sequence modeling. In *NAACL HLT 2019 - 2019 Conference of the North American Chapter of the Association for Computational Linguistics: Human Language Technologies - Proceedings of the Demonstrations Session*.

Papineni, Kishore, Salim Roukos, Todd Ward, and Wei-Jing Zhu. 2001. BLEU: a Method for Automatic Evaluation of Machine Translation. In *Proceedings of the 40th Annual Meeting on Association for Computational Linguistics - ACL '02*, page 311, Morristown, NJ, USA. Association for Computational Linguistics.

Post, Matt. 2018. A Call for Clarity in Reporting BLEU Scores. In *WMT 2018 - 3rd Conference on Machine Translation, Proceedings of the Conference*, volume 1.

Sennrich, Rico, Barry Haddow, and Alexandra Birch. 2016. Neural machine translation of rare words with subword units. In *54th Annual Meeting of the Association for Computational Linguistics, ACL 2016 - Long Papers*, volume 3.

Steinberger, Ralf, Bruno Pouliquen, Anna Widiger, Camelia Ignat, Tomaž Erjavec, Dan Tufiş, and Dániel Varga. 2006. The JRC-Acquis: A multilingual aligned parallel corpus with 20+ languages. In *Proceedings of the 5th International Conference on Language Resources and Evaluation, LREC 2006*.

Szegedy, Christian, Vincent Vanhoucke, Sergey Ioffe, Jon Shlens, and Zbigniew Wojna. 2016. Rethinking the Inception Architecture for Computer Vision. In *Proceedings of the IEEE Computer Society Conference on Computer Vision and Pattern Recognition*, volume 2016-December.

Tiedemann, Jörg. 2012. Parallel data, tools and interfaces in OPUS. In *Proceedings of the 8th International Conference on Language Resources and Evaluation, LREC 2012*.

Vaswani, Ashish, Noam Shazeer, Niki Parmar, Jakob Uszkoreit, Llion Jones, Aidan N. Gomez, Łukasz Kaiser, and Illia Polosukhin. 2017. Attention is all you need. In *Advances in Neural Information Processing Systems*, volume 2017-December.

Zhang, Biao, Philip Williams, Ivan Titov, and Rico Sennrich. 2020. Improving Massively Multilingual Neural Machine Translation and Zero-Shot Translation.

A Number of parameters

The number of parameters of the models can be seen in Table 6.

Architecture	Total params.	Inference params.
Universal	60,526,080	60,526,080
Group modular		
EA3-6	108,442,624	60,526,080
EA5-6	114,747,392	60,526,080
No sharing	121,052,160	60,526,080
Language modular		
EA3-6	250,938,368	52,331,008
EA5-6 EG3-4	257,243,136	52,331,008
EG3-6	263,547,904	52,331,008
EA5-6	282,462,208	52,331,008
EA6 EG5	285,614,592	52,331,008
EG5-6	288,766,976	52,331,008
No sharing	313,986,048	52,331,008

Table 6: Number of parameters

B Detailed evaluation results

Tables 7, 8, 9, 10, and 11 provide detailed evaluation results for selected experiments.

src	tgt					
	en	de	da	fr	es	pt
en	–	38.84	40.39	48.60	51.07	45.32
de	46.41	–	32.44	38.60	39.08	34.41
da	45.60	30.57	–	36.77	37.32	32.77
fr	49.28	32.19	31.65	–	42.95	39.65
es	52.06	32.66	32.63	44.02	–	41.13
pt	49.17	31.37	31.74	43.25	44.09	–

Table 7: Universal model test set BLEU scores.

src	tgt					
	en	de	da	fr	es	pt
en	–	1.30	2.14	1.25	1.30	-0.30
de	1.44	–	0.98	1.31	1.15	-0.38
da	0.56	-0.32	–	-1.56	-1.60	-2.93
fr	1.07	0.73	1.03	–	1.04	0.16
es	1.61	0.98	1.17	0.50	–	0.12
pt	-1.49	-2.84	-2.55	-0.77	-0.60	–

Table 8: Improvement of the baseline language modular model over the universal model on test set in BLEU points.

src	tgt					
	en	de	da	fr	es	pt
en	–	0.76	1.78	1.44	0.55	1.29
de	1.00	–	1.52	1.12	1.13	1.37
da	0.98	0.91	–	1.41	0.87	1.28
fr	0.79	0.82	1.62	–	0.75	1.51
es	1.31	1.11	1.87	1.25	–	0.98
pt	1.38	1.14	1.65	1.34	0.95	–

Table 9: Improvement of the group modular model with layers 3–6 shared (group modular EA3–6) over the universal model on test set in BLEU points.

src	tgt					
	en	de	da	fr	es	pt
en	–	0.84	1.75	1.49	1.10	-0.62
de	1.40	–	1.30	1.19	1.43	-0.44
da	2.30	1.25	–	1.93	1.59	0.35
fr	0.94	0.88	2.10	–	1.26	0.18
es	1.70	1.06	1.79	1.26	–	0.22
pt	1.73	0.80	1.70	1.07	1.33	–

Table 10: Improvement of the modular model with layers 2–6 shared (EA2–6) over the universal model on test set in BLEU points.

Lang. pair	Universal	Group modular			Language modular						
		EA3–6	EA5–6	–	EA3–6	EG3–4 EA5–6	EG3–6	EA5–6	EG5 EA6	EG5–6	–
en–de	38.84	39.6	39.57	39.77	39.96	40.11	39.8	39.67	39.96	39.83	**40.14**
de–en	46.41	47.41	47.25	47.32	47.76	47.8	47.78	**47.88**	47.56	47.72	47.85
en–da	40.39	42.17	41.99	42.37	42.36	42.65	42.5	42.52	42.45	**42.68**	42.53
da–en	45.6	46.58	46.77	46.62	47.86	**47.91**	47.52	46.93	47	47.23	46.16
en–fr	48.6	50.04	50.04	49.9	49.78	**50.15**	49.78	49.77	50.08	49.84	49.85
fr–en	49.28	50.07	49.84	50.32	50.43	50.56	50.49	**50.57**	50.27	50.45	50.35
en–es	51.07	51.62	52.03	52.01	51.92	52.22	52.34	52.18	52.03	52.07	**52.37**
es–en	52.06	53.37	53.27	53.58	53.72	53.77	53.84	**53.89**	53.69	53.7	53.67
en–pt	45.32	**46.61**	46.49	46.12	45.11	44.73	44.58	45.04	45.07	44.54	45.02
pt–en	49.17	**50.55**	50.39	50.53	50.13	49.95	49.95	48.97	48.82	48.87	47.68
de–da	32.44	33.96	33.66	33.56	34.08	**34.11**	33.67	33.93	33.75	33.58	33.42
da–de	30.57	31.48	31.42	31.21	**31.89**	31.53	31.27	30.85	30.8	30.95	30.25
de–fr	38.6	39.72	39.7	39.7	39.56	39.92	39.72	39.77	39.72	**39.97**	39.91
fr–de	32.19	**33.01**	32.72	32.93	32.68	32.98	32.97	32.64	32.89	32.83	32.92
de–es	39.08	40.21	40.12	40.2	39.94	**40.44**	40.28	40.18	40.07	40.06	40.23
es–de	32.66	**33.77**	33.61	33.29	33.44	33.63	33.76	33.66	33.55	33.45	33.64
de–pt	34.41	**35.78**	35.72	35.14	34.27	34.35	34.28	34.59	34.33	34.18	34.03
pt–de	31.37	**32.51**	32.35	32.17	31.55	31.51	31.52	30.38	30.03	30.02	28.53
da–fr	36.77	38.18	37.91	37.94	37.99	38	**38.26**	37.03	36.78	36.82	35.21
fr–da	31.65	33.27	32.54	31.49	**33.67**	33.11	32.8	33.65	33.37	32.66	32.68
da–es	37.32	38.19	38.31	37.84	38.47	38.56	**38.59**	37.39	37.09	37.52	35.72
es–da	32.63	34.5	33.41	32.46	34.52	**34.81**	33.78	34.62	34.14	34.23	33.8
da–pt	32.77	**34.05**	33.78	33.5	33.19	32.57	32.72	31.79	31.66	31.74	29.84
pt–da	31.74	**33.39**	32.57	31.24	32.76	32.34	32.38	31.44	31.13	30.86	29.19
fr–es	42.95	43.7	43.78	43.78	43.86	**44.18**	44.09	43.73	43.83	43.86	43.99
es–fr	44.02	**45.27**	44.74	44.76	45.18	45.21	45.08	44.88	45.14	44.98	44.52
fr–pt	39.65	**41.16**	41.08	40.84	40.13	39.57	39.79	39.88	39.97	39.64	39.81
pt–fr	43.25	**44.59**	44.27	44.24	44.19	43.94	43.79	43.16	43.14	42.99	42.48
es–pt	41.13	42.11	42.15	**42.38**	41.65	41.39	41.36	41.19	41.42	41.04	41.25
pt–es	44.09	45.04	44.88	44.78	**45.09**	44.95	44.61	44.06	44.1	44.46	43.49

Table 11: Test set BLEU scores for the main experiments. The best result of each row is in bold.

Literary translation as a three-stage process: machine translation, post-editing and revision

Lieve Macken, Bram Vanroy, Luca Desmet and Arda Tezcan
LT[3], Language and Translation Technology Team
Ghent University
Belgium
{firstname.lastname}@ugent.be

Abstract

This study focuses on English-Dutch literary translations that were created in a professional environment using an MT-enhanced workflow consisting of a three-stage process of automatic translation followed by post-editing and (mainly) monolingual revision. We compare the three successive versions of the target texts. We used different automatic metrics to measure the (dis)similarity between the consecutive versions and analyzed the linguistic characteristics of the three translation variants. Additionally, on a subset of 200 segments, we manually annotated all errors in the machine translation output and classified the different editing actions that were carried out. The results show that more editing occurred during revision than during post-editing and that the types of editing actions were different.

1 Introduction

With the current quality of neural machine translation (NMT) systems, the question arises whether post-editing NMT output is a viable alternative to human translation for real large-scale translation tasks. In this paper, we present the results of a case study on literary translations. We collaborated with Nuanxed, a book translation company, which uses an MT-enhanced workflow consisting of a three-stage process of automatic translation followed by post-editing and revision.

In this case study, we compare three successive versions of the target texts as they proceed through the translation process: the machine translation, the post-edited and the (mainly) monolingually revised translation. We used different automatic metrics to measure the (dis)similarity between the consecutive versions and to analyze the linguistic characteristics of the three translation variants. To assess the quality of the MT output and to get an insight into the editing actions that were carried out, a fine-grained manual annotation was carried out on a subset of 200 segments.

2 Related research

Although employing Machine Translation (MT) for more creative text types such as literature may not seem to be a natural fit, several researchers looked into the feasibility of using MT for literary texts, first with statistical (Besacier and Schwartz, 2015; Toral and Way, 2015) and later with neural machine translation systems (Toral and Way, 2018; Kuzman et al., 2019; Toral et al., 2020).

To assess the usefulness of MT for literary texts, researchers often compare raw (unedited) machine translations of literary texts with their human-translated (HT) counterparts. Three successive studies were conducted to assess the quality of generic NMT systems for English-Dutch literary texts, the language pair we also focus on in this study (Tezcan et al., 2019; Fonteyne et al., 2020; Webster et al., 2020). According to these studies, the main issues found in literary NMT are different types of mistranslations, coherence issues, and style & register problems. The percentage of NMT sentences that were free of errors varied and averages ranged from 44% to 25% in different studies, with a notable exception of the NMT version of Jane Austen's *Sense and Sensibility* in which only 5% of all machine-translated sentences were error-free. It thus seems that NMT quality is highly de-

Macken, Rufener, Van den Bogaert, Daems, Tezcan, Vanroy, Fonteyne, Barrault, Costa-jussà, Kemp, Pilos, Declercq, Koponen, Forcada, Scarton, Moniz (eds.)
Proceedings of the 23rd Annual Conference of the European Association for Machine Translation, p. 101–110
Ghent, Belgium, June 2022.

pendent on the source text and that some literary texts are more challenging for automatic translation systems than others. When comparing linguistic characteristics of NMT and HT, the machine translations were less lexically rich, showed a lower level of lexical and semantic cohesion and tended to follow the structures of the source sentences more closely, whereas the human translations showed the ability to deviate from the source structure (Webster et al., 2020). It is thus clear that in order to obtain high-quality literary translations, human intervention in the form of a post-editing (PE) step is needed.

Daems and colleagues investigated whether post-edited MT output differs from HT in English-to-Dutch texts (2017), and called this (dis)similarity between PE and HT 'post-editese'. The authors did not find proof of this. Neither humans nor computer systems were able to distinguish between the two types of translation, although the authors note that this may be due to a rather limited dataset size. They considered features such as average word and sentence length, average tf-idf, perplexity, type-token ratio, number of verb phrases/passives, parse tree depth, and so on. Working with different language combinations and architectures, Toral (2019) came to a different conclusion. He found that PE is indeed notably different from HT in terms of a limited set of features, namely lower lexical variety (type-token ratio) and density (content words ratio), sentence length inference of ST, and POS sequence perplexity. It must be noted however, that not only the language pairs differed in the studies of Daems et al. (2017) and Toral (2019), and hence the MT quality, but also the proficiency level and the degree of postediting that was requested (light or full). It is thus difficult to draw conclusions about the existence of post-editese.

Neither Daems and colleagues nor Toral investigated post-editese in literary texts. Castilho and Resende (2022), however, found some evidence for post-editese in literary translation of English into Brazilian Portuguese but note that such observations depend on the literary genre. Statistical differences between HT and PE were found, especially in the thriller genre (The Girl on the Train; TGOTT) and only barely in children's literature (Alice's Adventures in Wonderland; AW), which is explained by the emphasis on the author's figurative style in the latter book. Post-editese effects for lexical density (simplification), length ratio (text length of PE vs HT; explicitation), personal pronoun ratio (explicitation), and convergence (translated texts are more similar to each other than original texts are to each other) (partially) were found for TGOTT, but only evidence for convergence was discovered in AW.

Guerberof-Arenas and Toral (2020) focused on creativity, one of the distinguishing features of literary texts. They analyzed both creativity and acceptability in MT, PE and HT texts. The translation and post-edited version were created by two professional translators specialized in literary translation. To quantify acceptability they counted the number of errors in the different translations. Interestingly, they found that the HT translations contained slightly more errors than the PE translations, with HT having lowest number fluency errors and PE having the lowest number of accuracy errors. To measure translational creativity they selected 48 English source sentences that contained units of high creativity potential (in which translators most likely depart from the source text structure): metaphorical expressions, imagery and abstraction, idioms, comparisons, verbal phrases or complex syntactic structures. They quantified creativity by investigating creative shifts, which can be defined as "abstracting, modifying or concretising source text ideas in the target text" (Bayer-Hohenwarter, 2011, p. 663). When comparing the three types of shifts in the HT and PE condition, no major differences were found for abstractness and modification, but the HT contained more instances of concretisation.

The work of Daems et al. (2017) mentioned above built on earlier work on 'translationese' (Gellerstam, 1986). In the field of translation studies, it is generally accepted that a translated text is different from an original text in the same language, almost as if it is a genre on its own. Baker (1993, p. 243-245) discusses six "universal features of translation" that may mark translated texts: explicitness, disambiguation and simplification, a focus on grammaticality (especially in interpreting), avoiding repetitions by omission or rewording, exaggeration of target language features, and finally unexpected distributions of certain language features with respect to the source text (ST) and original texts in the target language. This phenomenon where translation is considered different from original text is often referred to as 'translationese', and researchers have investigated its existence, both via human perception and computer models.

Kruger (2017), however, made an interesting point by suggesting that some of these translationese features might also be the consequence of the editorial intervention subsequent to translation. Evidence for features commonly denoted as translationese such as increased explicitness, simplification and normalisation were also found in a parallel corpus of monolingual edited texts and their unedited counterparts. It thus seems that translation and linguistic editing share certain similarities.

In the publishing sector, it is quite common that many actors play a role in the production of a translation. For example, Moe and colleagues (2021) explain that in Slovenia language revisors correct the grammar and style of translations, usually without having access to the source texts. They may change the text's structure, syntax and word order and replace words and phrases to make the text more suitable. Different terms are used to refer to this process: linguistic revision/editing, copy-editing and translation revision. Mossop states that both editing and revision "involve checking linguistic correctness as well as the suitability of a text's style for its future readers and for the use they will make of it" (Mossop et al., 2020, p. 1). Translation revision can be considered the broader term as it also comprises a bilingual component, although different revision procedures exist (Ipsen and Dam, 2016) and the process can be predominantly monolingual (the revisor focuses on the target text and only refers back to the source text if a passage is problematic) or bilingual (the revisor systematically compares the source and target text).

3 Method

3.1 Data

The data we received from the company consists of an English novel (68,762 source words) and three Dutch translations: the machine translation generated by DeepL[1], the post-edited (PE) version and the revised (REV) version. An NDA was signed between the researchers and the company. The post-editor worked in a standard CAT tool that divides the text in sentences and displays both the source and target segments side-by-side. The post-editor thus worked on a segment-by-segment basis to edit the machine translation suggestions. The revisor received the post-edited translation in Microsoft Word. Revision in this case is mainly a monolingual process, which aims at improving the reading experience or, in the case of audio-books, the listening experience. The revisor could consult the source text whenever there was a need. The post-editor was Flemish, the revisor Dutch. Both the post-editor and the revisor were paid by the hour, so there was no real time pressure. For this study, we used the first chapter of the book. We used YouAlign[2] to align all versions at sentence level and manually verified the sentence alignments. The data set consists of 578 aligned segments (7,921 source words; 9,419 source tokens).

3.2 Automated evaluation

Automatic evaluation metrics for MT play a central role in rapid assessment of MT quality. A key characteristic of almost all automatic MT evaluation metrics is that they assess MT quality by calculating the similarity between the MT output to a reference translation. We use automatic MT evaluation metrics with a different goal, namely to measure the (dis)similarity between the consecutive versions of the texts produced in the target language, i.e. the machine translations (MT), the post-edited (PE) and the revised translations (REV).

In literature, we can find various metrics that differ with regard to the approach they take to measure the similarity between two texts. To obtain a nuanced picture, we use a variety of MT evaluation metrics, which focus on different dimensions, such as Translation Edit Rate (TER) (Snover et al., 2006), CharCut (Lardilleux and Lepage, 2017), COMET (Rei et al., 2020) and BERTScore (Zhang et al., 2019). While CharCut and TER measure the amount of editing required to transform one text into another in terms of character- and token-level edit operations respectively, COMET and BERTScore target the semantic aspect of translation quality by calculating the distance between vector representations of sentences and tokens, respectively. Additionally, we use ASTrED (Vanroy, 2021), which has been originally proposed to quantify syntactic similarity between a source sentence and its (human) translation. By working on a deeper linguistic level, ASTrED compares the

[1] `https://www.deepl.com/`, translations created end 2021

[2] `https://youalign.com/`

edit distance between the dependency structures of two sentences, while also taking word alignment information into account. Word alignments were automatically created with AwesomeAlign (Dou and Neubig, 2021). For this metric, we only used sentences that were translated as single sentences, without splitting or merging (156 in total of the manually verified subset, see below).

Besides analysing the degree of similarity between the different versions of the target texts, we were also interested in how well the lexical richness of the original novel was captured in the three versions. With the assumption that an increase in number of types with respect to number of tokens indicates a greater lexical richness in a given text, we calculated type-token ratio (TTR) and Mass index (Mass, 1972), which, unlike TTR, is not sensitive to text variations in text length. We calculated TTR and Mass index values of each document separately.

Word translation entropy, finally, is a formula to measure lexical variation by taking into account for each source word how many translations it has or can have in a given corpus based on its word alignments, and the distribution of those translations (Schaeffer et al., 2016). Put differently, it quantifies how certain or unambiguous the translation of a token is. A higher value indicates more uncertainty, i.e., a less straightforward lexical choice. In this study, we use this formula to measure average word translation entropy (AWTE) on document level, by measuring entropy for each source word (English) of the first chapter of the novel taking into account the three different translations in Dutch.

All data sets were tokenized prior to performing automatic measurements, using the Stanza Toolkit (Qi et al., 2020). While the MT metrics were calculated using the data with the original casing, to obtain more accurate results, we used the lowercased version of each document to measure lexical richness.

3.3 Manual evaluation

The first 200 segments (3,222 source tokens) of the data set were manually annotated. The manual annotation task consists of three separate sub-tasks: labelling of errors in the MT output, labelling of PE and REV actions and labelling of remaining errors in the final translation. The first sub-task allows us to assess the quality of the NMT system on the literary text; the second and third sub-tasks give us insights in the post-editing and revision actions and allow us to assess the quality of the final translation.

To label the MT errors we used the SCATE MT error taxonomy tailored to the annotation of literary MT on document level (Tezcan et al., 2019). This taxonomy is based on the well-known distinction between accuracy and fluency and is hierarchical in nature. According to this taxonomy accuracy and fluency errors can be annotated on the same text span, e.g. when a mistranslation error (accuracy error) causes a logical problem (fluency error). However, to minimize the annotation workload, we decided to only label the accuracy errors in this case. We also reduced the number of error labels by merging a number of error categories that were present in the original taxonomy.

To classify the PE and REV actions from a linguistic perspective, a classification scheme was devised based on the work of Desmet (2021) and Vandevoorde et al. (2021). The categorization scheme contains four main categories (*lexico-semantic*, *syntax & morphology*, *style* and *spelling & punctuation*), which are further subdivided in subcategories (see Table 1). All PE and REV actions were also labelled from a translation quality perspective. We distinguished the following four categories to label a post-editing action for its correctness and necessity: *MT error correction*, *consistency*, *preferential* and *undesirable* change. When labelling revision actions, the label *PE error correction* was added to this list to indicate undesirable changes made by the post-editor that were corrected by the revisor. In the final translation we also labelled all MT and PE errors that were not corrected.

Detailed annotation guidelines were drafted to ensure consistency between annotators. To facilitate the manual annotation process, the WebAnno[3] annotation tool was used. Figure 1 shows a full example of the annotation process. Two errors were labelled in the MT version: the phrase *met een opgewonden glimlach* (*with an excited smile*) is placed in a wrong position in the clause and *glinsteren* is a wrong translation for *glimpse*. The post-editor corrected these two MT errors and made two preferential changes: *zojuist* was replaced by a synonym (*net*) and *the red of Rudolph's nose* is changed into *Rudolph's red nose*. The revisor

[3]https://webanno.github.io/webanno/

Lexico-semantic	Syntax & morphology
Addition	Agreement
Coherence marker	Number
Explicitation	Diminutive
Implicitation	Comparison
Deletion	Tense
Synonym	Other
Collocation & idiom	
Specific	**Spelling & punctuation**
Vague	Capitalization
Other	Compound
	Linking word punctuation
Style	Punctuation linking word
Word order	Punctuation added
Structural change	Punctuation deleted
Shorter	Other
Split sentence	
Merged sentence	
Other	

Table 1: Linguistic typology

made additional changes: *glimlach* was replaced by a diminutive *lachje*, the proper name *Rudolph* was spelled in Dutch, and the preposition *tussen* was replaced by another preposition *door*. The revisor also made some structural changes and split the long sentence and rephrased the last clause making it a less literal translation.

Figure 1: Example of annotations made in Webanno

To help the annotators to spot the differences between the MT output and the PE version or the PE and the REV, we used Charcut (Lardilleux and Lepage, 2017), which creates an HTML document in which differences between two versions are visualized (see Figure 2).

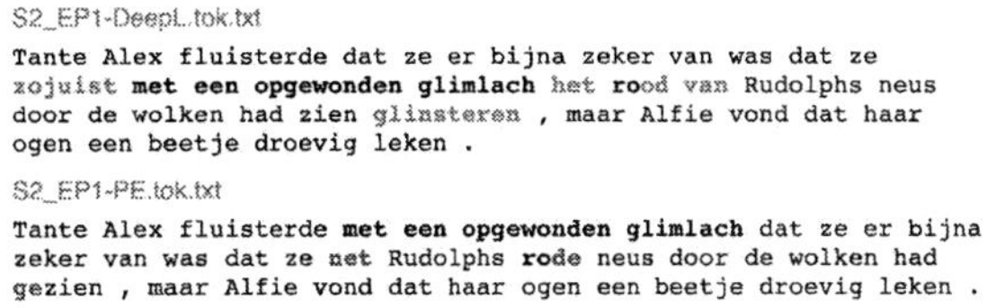

Figure 2: Example of Charcut visualizations (MT–PE)

4 Results

4.1 Automated evaluation

First, we use five automatic metrics that target different aspects of (dis)similarity, as described in Section 3.2, between the consecutive versions of the texts produced in the target language. The results are presented in Table 2.

	MT-PE	PE-REV	MT-REV
CharCut ↓	0.126	0.148	0.240
TER ↓	0.215	0.251	0.355
BERTScore ↑	0.941	0.936	0.900
COMET ↑	0.835	0.765	0.620
ASTrED ↓	0.305	0.307	0.332

Table 2: Overview of automated evaluation results. Up arrow: higher value means more similar; down arrow: lower value means more similar.

According to all automatic metrics used in this analysis, each consecutive modification made to the MT output, i.e. post-editing and revision, results in observable differences for all measured aspects, namely the degree of editing (CharCut and TER), semantic (BERTScore and COMET) and syntactic (ASTrED) similarity. Moreover, the level of (dis)similarity between the different document pairs seems to be different. As shown by the results of all five metrics, the similarity between the MT output and post-edited version (MT-PE) is higher compared to the similarity between post-edited and revised translations (PE-REV). Moreover, the similarity between the MT output and the revised translations is the lowest in comparison to the analyses made on other document pairs.

To measure lexical richness, we calculated TTR and Mass index for the chapter in English (SRC) and all three versions of the translated text in Dutch. These results are provided in Table 3, together with the unique and total number of tokens for each text.

These results show that, compared to the original text in English, all three translations in Dutch have a higher number of tokens and unique tokens.

	SRC	MT	PE	REV
# unique tokens	1820	1922	1962	2022
# tokens	9419	9285	9429	9632
TTR	0.182	0.196	0.198	0.199
MASS	0.020	0.020	0.019	0.019

Table 3: Summary of lexical richness measures

Moreover, these numbers increase with a similar ratio after each consecutive modification made on the MT output, resulting in a difference of 347 tokens and 100 unique tokens between the revised translations and the MT output. The post-editing and revision steps also make the translations lexically more rich, as observed by the TTR measurements. TTR is also observed to be higher in all three versions of the target text compared to the original novel. However, these observations are not confirmed by the Mass index scores, which indicate similar levels of lexical richness in all four documents.

In a final analysis we measure AWTE by comparing the MT output, the PE and REV translations to the original novel in English. To increase our confidence about the differences between the AWTE values (as word alignment was an automatic process), for each comparison, we use translation options with the minimum probability threshold of 0.01 and we repeat the calculations by increasing the minimum frequency threshold for the set of source words (up to 10, which covers 64% of all source tokens) we take into consideration. While a minimum threshold frequency of 1 covers all the source words in the source text, a threshold of n calculates AWTE only for the subset of source words that appear at least n times in the source text. The AWTE measurements made on the three document pairs are shown in Figure 3.

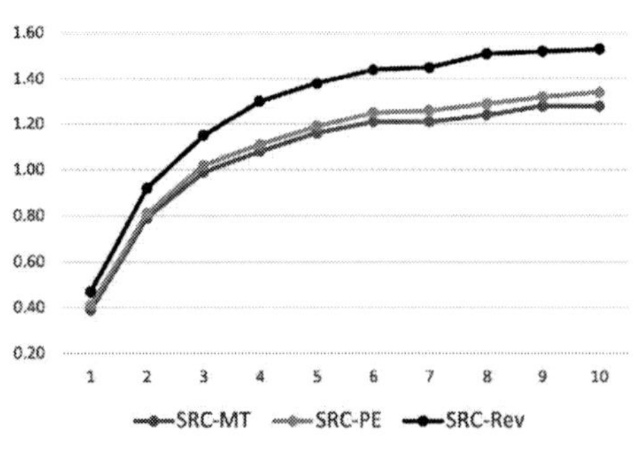

Figure 3: Average word translation entropy values

These results show that, for all minimum frequency thresholds, AWTE increases with each consecutive modification made to the MT output. Furthermore, the revision step increases AWTE to a larger extent, compared to post-editing, resulting in a higher level of uncertainty on average for the lexical choices made for translating source words during this operation.

4.2 Manual evaluation

Given that DeepL is a generic MT system and thus not tailored to literary texts, the overall quality of the machine-translated text can be deemed relatively good. The subset contained 275 MT errors, which is on average 1.38 error per sentence. Fifty-five sentences (27.5%) were free of errors. Table 4 shows the distribution of the 275 MT errors. In terms of accuracy, 152 errors were found, half of which were mistranslations. The NMT system wrongly translated words (e.g. *short crust pastry – korstdeeg*) and tenses (e.g. *was rolling out – rolde ... uit*), or used a translation of a word or phrase that was incorrect in the given context (word sense e.g. *ports – poorten* (meaning: *porto's*)), which sometimes led to illogical constructions, or even changed the meaning of the entire sentence. The machine moreover appeared to have difficulties translating multiword expressions and idioms as well (e.g. *going to see a man about a dog* was translated literally). The second largest category was capitalization and punctuation errors, which almost solely consisted of missing quotation marks that were not copied from source to target text by the machine. Also quite often, source text information was omitted (e.g. the verb *to sprinkle* was deleted in *as Fergus reminded him* ***to sprinkle*** *– zoals Fergus hem herinnerde)*; additions, on the other hand, did not occur in the subset.

In terms of fluency, the most problematic category was spelling and punctuation. The majority of these errors were related to quotation marks, missing commas and capitalization problems (*kerstman (Santa)* starts with a lowercase letter whereas *Kerstmis (Christmas)* starts with a capital letter in Dutch, which is confusing for the NMT system). Stylistic problems were often-occurring as well, when the MT contained disfluent constructions that are not wrong from a grammatical point of view, but could nonetheless be translated in a more idiomatic and fluent way. These were in most cases very literal translations of English constructions (e.g. *said Fergus with a laugh – zei Fergus met een lach*). Lastly, a number of lexical problems were found: when a word was not an entirely wrong translation of the source word in the context, but nevertheless did not entirely fit in the Dutch sentence either (e.g. *the **glow** of his screen – het **schijnsel** van zijn scherm vs. de **gloed** van zijn scherm*).

Accuracy	152	Fluency	123
Mistranslation	77	Coherence	13
Multiword	15	Discourse marker	1
Word sense	15	Coreference	2
Other	47	Tense	0
Addition	0	Other	10
Omission	21	Lexicon	18
Untranslated	7	Grammar & syntax	10
Do not translate	1	Style	35
Capitalization & punctuation	46	Disfluent	33
		Repetition	0
		Other	2
		Spelling & punctuation	47
		Capitalisation	13
		Compound	4
		Punctuation	23
		Other	7

Table 4: MT errors in the manually annotated subset of 200 segments

Table 5 shows the PE and REV quality label distribution. The revisor carried out more editing actions (569) than the post-editor (501), and these in themselves were of a different nature. While the post-editor focused on correcting MT errors (219; 44% of all post-edits), e.g. by adding ST information missing from the MT output, and on making preferential improvements (224), the revisor mainly sought to further improve the overall quality and readability of the text: 492 (86%) of the revisor's edits were preferential changes to make the text more coherent and understandable (by means of explicitations and structural changes as well as splitting of sentences; see Figure 4 for details). Often an MT error was corrected by the post-editor and further improved by the revisor, as can be seen in the example in Figure 1: the post-editor corrected the word order error of the MT and made sure that phrase *met een opgewonden glimlach* correctly modifies the verb. The revisor further improved the translation by replacing *glimlach* by the diminutive *lachje*.

Some MT errors were not spotted by the post-editor but corrected by the revisor, and most of the errors introduced during post-editing were corrected in the revision step as well. A very small number of MT errors (7) seeped through into the final text (e.g. *Christmas play – kerstspel* (*Christmas game*)), and 6 post-editor errors were left uncorrected (e.g. *buddy up – vrienden worden* (*became friends*; ST meaning: *to pair together with someone*)). Finally, 8 revisor changes were deemed undesirable, mostly due to the information presented in the final target text no longer being consistent with the information in the source text. As always some of these are, however, debatable. In the following example the subject of *saw* has been made implicit by the post-editor and was wrongly interpreted by the revisor:

- ST: *Aunty Alex also understood about all the things that Alfie could see and hear, **like when he saw the lady** who used to live upstairs at their old flat, until she died.*

- PE: *Tante Alex begreep ook alles wat Alfie kon zien en horen, zoals de mevrouw die boven in hun oude flat woonde, tot ze stierf.*
  *(Aunty Alex also understood everything that Alfie could see and hear, **like the lady** who lived upstairs in their old flat, until she died.)*

- REV: *Bovendien kon tante Alex alles horen en zien wat Alfie kon zien en horen, net zoals de mevrouw die boven hun oude flat gewoond had tot ze doodging.*
  *(Moreover, aunty Alex could hear and see everything that Alfie could see and hear, **just like the lady** who had lived upstairs from their old flat until she died.)*

As can be seen in Figure 4 both the post-editor and the revisor made lexico-semantic changes for the most part (45% and 44% respectively), of which using synonyms or other words are in the lead. Spelling and punctuation changes represent 24% of all post-edits and were mainly corrections of MT errors; of the revisor changes, 21% were spelling and punctuation changes, although these largely consisted of *mama/papa* being preferentially spelled into *mamma/pappa*. When we look in more detail at the different editing actions, it is clear that the revisor carried out different types of editing actions and made a lot of explicitations, split long sentences, made more structural changes (compared to the post-editor), added more coherence markers and made the translation sometimes more specific and sometimes more vague. These edits greatly improve the readability of the translation and tailor it to the target audience.

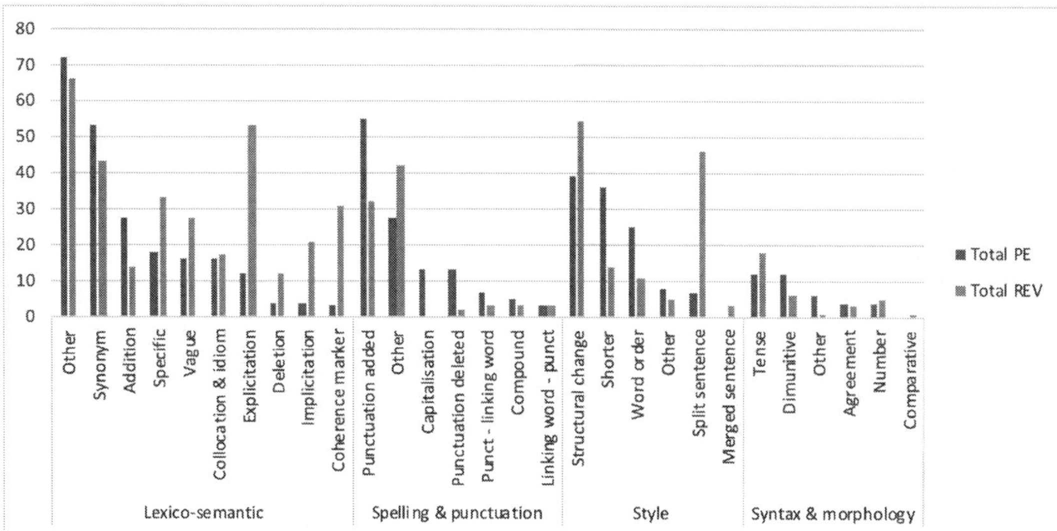

Figure 4: Linguistic classification of the post-editing (PE) and revision (REV) actions

Quality Label	PE	REV
Consistency	13	0
MT error correction	219	32
PE error correction	NA	37
Preferential	224	492
Undesirable	45	8
Total	**501**	**569**

Table 5: Quality labels assigned to the post-editing (PE) and revision (REV) actions

5 Discussion

In this paper, we examined the possibility of using an MT-enhanced translation workflow for the translation of literary texts in a real-life professional translation scenario. We examined three different versions of the target texts as they proceed through the translation process: the MT output, the post-edited version and the revised translation.

DeepL was used as MT engine to translate an English novel into Dutch. MT quality was in line with expectations with 27.5% error-free sentences. The three main error types were various kinds of mistranslations, disfluent sentence constructions and different types of spelling and punctuation problems. DeepL failed to correctly copy quotation marks from source to target, a problem that can potentially be fixed by applying a number of post-processing rules. Mistranslations and disfluent constructions have been reported in earlier research as the main error types and require more attention from the post-editor.

Forty-four percent of all post-editing actions were corrections of MT errors, 24% of all post-edits were preferential changes, 9% of all post-edits were labelled as 'undesirable'. Apart from adding missing punctuation marks, the post-editor mainly carried out lexico-semantic changes (replacing words with better alternatives or synonyms) and stylistic operations (restructuring MT fragments or coming up with shorter translation solutions). Most MT errors were solved in the post-editing step. Only 5.6% of all editing actions during revision were related to MT errors; another 5.5% were corrections of problems introduced during post-editing. The majority of the revisor's edits (86%) were thus preferential in nature. The revisor made slightly more edits than the post-editor. The revisor, just like the post-editor, mainly made lexico-semantic changes, but the subcategories were different. The revisor often made information and relations that the reader might be able to infer from the context explicit as can be seen from subcategories 'explicitation' and 'coherence marker' in Figure 4. The revisor also made a lot of stylistic changes and restructured fragments and even split sentences in 23% of all segments.

Post-editing and revision can be considered two different cognitive processes. Post-editing is by nature a bilingual process in which the post-editor can be primed both by the MT suggestion and the source segment. Moreover, as the post-editor worked in a traditional CAT tool, in which the text is segmented at sentence level, it might be more difficult to focus on the flow of the target text.

Revision was mainly a monolingual process, carried out in Microsoft Word, in which it is easier to focus on the translated text as a standalone product. It is remarkable, however, that the revisor carried out many edits that fall within two subcategories that are often considered as 'translationese', e.g. increased explictness (subcategories 'explicitation' and 'coherence marker') and simplification (subcategory 'split sentence'). We consider this as an indication that monolingual editing and translation indeed share certain similarities as Kruger (2017) suggested.

The automatic evaluation confirmed that more editing took place in the revision step than in the post-editing step. The degree of similarity between the MT, the PE and the REV version was assessed based on the amount of editing, and semantic and syntactic similarity measures. All measures confirmed that the degree of similarity between MT and PE was higher than the degree of similarity between PE and REV. The lowest similarity scores were obtained when comparing the MT with the revised version. As a side note we would like to point out that in MT research it is common practice to use automatic evaluation metrics to compare the MT output with an independent reference translation, often without knowing how this reference translation was created. It might as well be that the reference translation being used is the output of a two-stage process of human translation followed by revision, which, depending on the amount of editing that took place, may have altered the human translation to a large extent.

Another feature that has been widely studied in previous research is lexical richness. In this study, we quantified lexical richness by means of TTR, Mass index and average word translation entropy. Some results were inconclusive (higher TTR values, but lower or similar Mass index values). Average word translation entropy showed a clearer picture, with the revised version having the highest values. It thus seems that the revised version exhibits many characteristics that have been attributed to human translations: a higher degree of explicitation and simplification, more lexical variety and translations that deviate more from the source structure (compared to MT). This study, however, cannot provide a conclusive answer to the question of whether the implemented three-stage process of automatic translation followed by post-editing and revision is a viable alternative to human translation followed by revision. This can only be measured by means of comparative translation reception studies in which the reading (or listening) experience is measured.

One of the major limitations of this study is that we only had data of one post-editor and one revisor. Moreover, the post-editor and the revisor had different experience levels, with the post-editor having less experience in the literary domain. Studying the edits of two different persons most probably changes the distribution of the edits. It would therefore be interesting to replicate this study with more post-editors and more revisors and on different language pairs. In future work we also intend to zoom in on the sentences with high creativity potential as was done by Guerberof-Arenas and Toral (2020) and examine in more detail the creative shifts in the post-edited and revised version.

References

Baker, Mona. 1993. Corpus linguistics and translation studies. *Text and technology*, John Benjamins. 233–250.

Bayer-Hohenwarter, Gerrit. 2011. "Creative Shift" as a Means of Measuring and Promoting Translational Creativity *Meta: Translators' Journal*, 56(3):663–692.

Besacier, Laurent and Lane Schwartz. 2015. Automated Translation of a Literary Work: A Pilot Study. *Proceedings of the Fourth Workshop on Computational Linguistics for Literature*, Association for Computational Linguistics. 114-122.

Castilho, Sheila and Natália Resende. 2022. Post-Editese in Literary Translations. *Information*, 13(2):66.

Daems, Joke, Orphée De Clercq, and Lieve Macken. 2017. Translationese and Post-Editese: How Comparable is Comparable Quality. *Linguistica Antverpiensia*, 16:89–103.

Desmet, Luca. 2021. *An exploratory study of professional post-edits by English-Dutch DGT translators.* Master's thesis, Ghent University.

Dou, Zi-Yi, and Graham Neubig. 2021. Word Alignment by Fine-tuning Embeddings on Parallel Corpora. *Proceedings of the 16th Conference of the European Chapter of the Association for Computational Linguistics: Main Volume*, online. 2112–2128.

Fonteyne, Margot, Arda Tezcan and Lieve Macken. 2020. Literary Machine Translation under the Magnifying Glass: Assessing the Quality of an NMT-Translated Detective Novel on Document Level.

Proceedings of The 12th Language Resources and Evaluation Conference, Marseille, France. 3790–3798.

Gellerstam, Martin. 1986. Translationese in Swedish novels translated from English. *Scandinavian Symposium on Translation Theory*, Lund.

Guerberof-Arenas, Ana and Antonio Toral. 2020. The impact of post-editing and machine translation on creativity and reading experience. *Translation Spaces*, 9 (2):255–282.

Ipsen, A. Helene and Helle V. Dam. 2016 Translation Revision: Correlating Revision Procedure and Error Detection. *HERMES - Journal of Language and Communication in Business*, 55: 143–156.

Kruger, Haidee. 2017. The effects of editorial intervention: Implications for studies of the features of translated language. In G. De Sutter, M.A. Lefer and I. Delaere (Eds.), *Empirical translation studies: New methodological and theoretical traditions*, De Gruyter Mouton. 113–156.

Kuzman, Taja, Špela Vintar and Mihael Arčan. 2019. Neural Machine Translation of Literary Texts from English to Slovene. *Proceedings of the Qualities of Literary Machine Translation*, Dublin, Ireland. 1–9.

Lardilleux, Adrien, and Yves Lepage. 2017. CHARCUT: Human-Targeted Character-Based MT Evaluation with Loose Differences. *Proceedings of the 14th International Workshop on Spoken Language Translation*, Tokyo, Japan. 146–153.

Mass, Heinz-Dieter. 1972. Über den zusammenhang zwischen wortschatzumfang und länge eines textes. *Zeitschrift für Literaturwissenschaft und Linguistik 2, no. 8:73.*

Moe, Marija Zlatnar, Tamara Mikolič Južnič, and Tanja Žigon. 2021. Who determines the final version? The roles of translators, language revisers and editors in the publishing of a literary translation. *Across Languages and Cultures*, 22 (1):14–44.

Mossop, Brian, Jungmin Hong and Carlos Teixeira. 2020. *Revising and editing for translators* (4th edition). Routledge, Taylor and Francis: London; New York.

Qi, Peng, Yuhao Zhang, Yuhui Zhang, Jason Bolton, and Christopher D. Manning. 2020. Stanza: A Python Natural Language Processing Toolkit for Many Human Languages. *ACL System Demonstrations*.

Rei, Ricardo, Craig Stewart, Ana C. Farinha, and Alon Lavie. 2020. COMET: A neural framework for MT evaluation. *Proceedings of the 2020 Conference on Empirical Methods in Natural Language Processing (EMNLP)*, online. 2685–2702.

Schaeffer, Moritz, Barbara Dragsted, Kristian Tangsgaard Hvelplund, Laura Winther Balling, and Michael Carl. 2016. Word translation entropy: Evidence of early target language activation during reading for translation. *New directions in empirical translation process research*. Springer, Cham, Switzerland. 183–210.

Snover, Matthew, Bonnie Dorr, Rich Schwartz, Linnea Micciulla and John Makhoul. 2006. A study of translation edit rate with targeted human annotation. *Proceedings of the 2006 Conference of the Association for Machine Translation in the Americas*, Cambridge, MA, USA. 223–231.

Tezcan, Arda, Joke Daems and Lieve Macken. 2019. When a 'sport' is a person and other issues for NMT of novels. *Proceedings of the Qualities of Literary Machine Translation*, Dublin, Ireland. 40–49.

Toral, Antonio. 2019. Post-editese: An Exacerbated Translationese. *Proceedings of Machine Translation Summit XVII: Research Track*, Dublin, Ireland. 273–281.

Toral, Antonio, Antonio Oliver, and Pau Ribas Ballestí. 2020. Machine Translation of Novels in the Age of Transformer. J. Porsiel (Ed.), *Maschinelle Übersetzung für Übersetzungsprofis*, BDÜ Fachverlag. 276–295.

Toral, Antonio and Andy Way. 2015. Machine-assisted translation of literary text: A case study. *Translation Spaces*, John Benjamins. 4(2):240–267.

Toral, Antonio and Andy Way. 2018. What Level of Quality Can Neural Machine Translation Attain on Literary Text? In J. Moorkens et al. (Eds.), *Translation Quality Assessment: From Principles to Practice*, Springer. 263–287.

Vandevoorde, Lore, Roxana Weintraub and Marta Arabadjieva. 2021. *Sustained quality in Council translations: assessing the importance of human translation actions*. Council of the European Union. Translation Service.

Vanroy, Bram. 2021. *Syntactic Difficulties in Translation*. Ph.D. thesis, Ghent University.

Webster, Rebecca, Margot Fonteyne, Arda Tezcan, Lieve Macken and Joke Daems. 2020. Gutenberg Goes Neural: Comparing Features of Dutch Human Translations with Raw Neural Machine Translation Outputs in a Corpus of English Literary Classics. *Informatics*, 7(3).

Zhang, Tianyi, Varsha Kishore, Felix Wu, Kilian Q. Weinberger, and Yoav Artzi. 2020. BERTScore: Evaluating text generation with BERT. *Proceedings of ICLR 2020*, online.

On the Interaction of Regularization Factors in Low-resource Neural Machine Translation

Àlex R. Atrio[1,2] and **Andrei Popescu-Belis**[1,2]

[1]HEIG-VD / HES-SO
Yverdon-les-Bains
Switzerland

[2]EPFL
Lausanne
Switzerland

{alejandro.ramirezatrio, andrei.popescu-belis}@heig-vd.ch

Abstract

We explore the roles and interactions of the hyper-parameters governing regularization, and propose a range of values applicable to low-resource neural machine translation. We demonstrate that default or recommended values for high-resource settings are not optimal for low-resource ones, and that more aggressive regularization is needed when resources are scarce, in proportion to their scarcity. We explain our observations by the generalization abilities of sharp vs. flat basins in the loss landscape of a neural network. Results for four regularization factors corroborate our claim: batch size, learning rate, dropout rate, and gradient clipping. Moreover, we show that optimal results are obtained when using several of these factors, and that our findings generalize across datasets of different sizes and languages.

1 Introduction

The training of neural machine translation (NMT) models is governed by many hyper-parameters, which play a central role in the performances of the trained models, especially their generalization abilities. While most of the NMT frameworks recommend default values for the hyper-parameters, when it comes to low-resource settings, fewer guidelines are available.

This study systematically explores the roles and interactions of a subset of hyper-parameters in low-resource NMT settings, namely those acting as *regularization factors*. Regularizers do not fall under a single theoretical definition: Goodfellow et al. (2016, page 224) view them as a collection of methods "intended to reduce generalization error but not training error." We present here a unified perspective on several regularizers which act upon the estimation of the gradients during back-propagation. Using the distinction made by Keskar et al. (2016) between flat and sharp basins in the loss landscape, we argue that noisier estimates of the gradients can increase the likelihood of finding flatter minima, which have better generalization abilities. Specifically, we defend three claims:

1. NMT models benefit from more aggressive regularization when the amount of training data is small. We demonstrate this for four different regularizers: batch size, learning rate, dropout, and gradient clipping. We compare the default regularization hyper-parameters of the OpenNMT-py framework for mid-to-high resources – comparable to those of the original Transformer (Vaswani et al., 2017) – with the ones we optimized for a low-resource setting (Sections 4-7).

2. The combination of different regularization sources is preferable over their individual use. When used together, an amount of regularization from each of the four factors under study outperforms the use of any single one alone, and the best scores are robust with respect to the variation of each factor (Section 8).

3. Regularization factors optimized on one low-resource dataset are beneficial for low-resource datasets in other languages, and benefit from more aggressive regularization as the amount of training data decreases. We demonstrate this by comparing our default and optimized settings on data samples of varying sizes from our main corpus and four additional low-size datasets (Section 9).

Macken, Rufener, Van den Bogaert, Daems, Tezcan, Vanroy, Fonteyne, Barrault, Costa-jussà, Kemp, Pilos, Declercq, Koponen, Forcada, Scarton, Moniz (eds.)
Proceedings of the 23rd Annual Conference of the European Association for Machine Translation, p. 111–120
Ghent, Belgium, June 2022.

2 Background and Related Work

2.1 Regularizers and the Loss Landscape

In the absence of a general treatment of regularization factors, most studies combine them empirically and search only a very small part of the hyper-parameter space. Kukačka et al. (2017) provide a taxonomy of regularization factors, but continue to define them simply as techniques to improve generalization. Similarly, in their survey, Moradi et al. (2020) consider as regularization any "component of the learning process or prediction procedure that is added to alleviate data shortage," but do not provide a common measure of regularization or consider the combination of factors.

Peng et al. (2015) study regularization techniques independently as well as in combination, still without a common theoretical underpinning. On two NLP tasks, they observe that using two factors – namely, L2 norm of weights and embeddings, and dropout – is better than using either by itself. Moreover, when using both factors, if one is set to its optimal value obtained when used alone, the other one must be lowered.

We adopt here the perspective put forward by Keskar et al. (2016), among others, who explain the *generalization gap* between values of regularization factors in terms of the topography of the loss landscape. Given a minimum of the loss function, the slower this function varies around its neighborhood (hence creating flat basins in the topography), the *flatter* (or less sharp) is the region. Models that are optimized in flatter regions tend to generalize better, and moderately less accurate gradients give models a higher probability of finding these flatter regions.

Here, we narrow down our perspective to a set of regularization factors that concern the estimation of the gradients of the loss function, as they are used during training with back-propagation. According to the above perspective, models trained with noisier gradient estimates are more likely than models trained with precise ones to find *flat* minima of the loss function, as their identification requires less precision. Additionally, a moderate amount of noise confers "exploratory abilities" that allow the search to exit sharper basins. Therefore, there is an optimal amount of noise in the gradient estimation: with too much noise, training is hampered or becomes impossible, but with too little noise, the model is likely to get trapped into sharp minimizers with low generalization abilities.

For instance, in the case of batch size (a frequently studied regularization factor), Goodfellow et al. (2016, Chapter 8.1.3) explain that models trained with smaller batch sizes tend to optimize into low-precision regions because they use noisier gradient estimates than when training with larger batch sizes.

Hypothesizing that noisier gradients improve the chance of a model to optimize into flatter regions, Smith and Le (2017) and Smith et al. (2017) propose a gradient noise scale to measure how learning rate (another regularization factor) should be adjusted to the batch size, on image data. They estimate the average gradient noise g for each batch as $g = \epsilon(N/B - 1) \approx \epsilon N/B$ where ϵ is the learning rate, N the size of the training set, and B the batch size, assuming that $N \gg B$. This shows that "increasing the batch size and decaying the learning rate are quantitatively equivalent" (Smith et al., 2017, Sec. 1).

Jastrzębski et al. (2018) also note that the proportionality of batch size and learning rate is crucial for gradient descent convergence, and the ability of the resulting model to generalize well. In particular, higher ratios seem to lead to flatter minima, which lead to better generalization, similar to what Keskar et al. (2016) observed. Specifically whether the relation between batch size and learning rate is linear, squared, or otherwise, has not been conclusively determined (Krizhevsky, 2014; Hoffer et al., 2017; Popel and Bojar, 2018). The roles of the batch size and learning rate have often been discussed from the perspective of computer vision, but different studies have made different observations, and the debate has not been settled yet (Dinh et al., 2017; Hoffer et al., 2017; Goyal et al., 2017; Li et al., 2017; Kawaguchi et al., 2017). As for dropout and gradient clipping, which are additional regularization factors, they have not been considered yet in relation to flat and sharp minimizers. We will consider here that the claim that less accurate gradients lead to flatter minima applies to them too: for dropout, due to removing some components of the sums; and for clipping, by affecting the norm of the gradient.

2.2 Regularization Factors for NMT

Recent NMT models are based on the Transformer (Vaswani et al., 2017), a deep encoder-decoder neural network which is quite sensitive to the hyper-parameters governing regularization factors during training. We discuss here the four parameters that we study in this paper.

Batch size. As we saw, models trained with smaller batch sizes have better generalization capabilities. However, batch size is not only a regularization factor, but has an influence on training speed: larger batches accelerate training by making a better use of the GPU memory.

Learning rate is a positive scalar that controls how much the weights are updated. We use the dynamic learning schedule known as 'noam' (Vaswani et al., 2017, Eq. 3). During its initial steps, known as *warmup*, the learning rate increases linearly from zero, reaching its highest value at the last warmup step w. Afterwards, it decays proportionally to the inverse square root of the step number s. At each step, this is multiplied by a factor based on the output size of the embedding layer d_{model} (512 in Transformer-Base). Moreover, following OpenNMT-py's recommendation, we include a *scaling factor* (*sf*), which we set by default to 2. The learning rate lr at each step s:

$$lr(s) = sf \cdot d_{model}^{-0.5} \cdot min\left(s^{-0.5},\ s \cdot w^{-1.5}\right) \quad (1)$$

Dropout (Srivastava et al., 2014) consists of a masking noise: a probability that a unit is randomly turned off during training. It is applied on the output of each hidden layer, including the output of the attention layers, but not the embedding layer, so no loss of input or output data occurs. This encourages each hidden unit to perform well regardless of other units (Goodfellow et al., 2016, Chapter 7.12).

Gradient clipping consists of renormalizing the gradient g to a threshold v if it exceeds it, i.e. if $||g|| > v$, then $g \leftarrow gv/||g||$ (same direction but bounded norm). Therefore, the smaller the value of v, the more aggressively we clip the gradients, and the more regularization is applied (Goodfellow et al., 2016, Chapter 10.11.1).

2.3 Role of Regularization for NMT

Popel and Bojar (2018) report that BLEU scores increase with batch size in a Transformer-based NMT system, although with diminishing returns, and recommend setting a large batch size. They observed moderate changes across a large range of learning rates, and found thresholds beyond which training was much slower or diverged. They made similar observations for warmup steps, concluding that the search space for learning rate and warmup steps was wide. Their experiments were performed on large datasets, leaving their questions open for low-resource settings.

Ott et al. (2018) observe that training time with very large datasets can be shortened when using larger batch sizes: they accumulate batches from 25k tokens per batch to 400k. When paired with an increased learning rate schedule (noam's times two) they do not report performance loss.

Sennrich and Zhang (2019) found that smaller batch sizes (1k-4k) were beneficial for low-resource NMT, and studied a variety of regularization factors for recurrent neural networks. However, the regularization factors were not disentangled, and their effects on Transformer-based NMT are difficult to extrapolate.

Araabi and Monz (2020) studied the Transformer's hyper-parameters in several low-resource settings. They observed improvements for larger batch sizes on the larger datasets, but did not observe improvements with smaller batch sizes on smaller datasets, or changes to optimal number of warmup steps or learning rate. They concluded to the need for larger batches from the Transformer. However, due to the late position of the batch size and learning rate in their order of optimization of the hyper-parameters, their regularizing effects cannot be precisely determined.

Xu et al. (2020) computed gradients while accumulating minibatches, and observed that increasing batch size stabilizes gradient direction up to a certain point, which allowed them to dynamically adjust batch sizes while training. Miceli Barone et al. (2017) observed improvements when combining dropout with L2-norm during fine-tuning, and concluded that "multiple regularizers outperform a single one."

In previous work, we observed improvements of scores and training time when using smaller batch sizes, with a Transformer on a low-resource dataset (Atrio and Popescu-Belis, 2021). We found a minimum value of the batch size below which training diverged, but did not study other regularization factors and interactions between them.

Studies on the optimization and effects of regularization factors thus remain scarce. Many previous studies optimize parameters in sequence. While this strategy is certainly a faster approach to optimization, it does not shed full light on each factor in isolation, as we do below in Sections 4 to 7, or in combination, as we study in Sections 8

Dataset	Src-tgt	Lines	Words (tgt)
WMT20 Low-res	HSB-DE	60k	823k
=	=	40k	550k
=	=	20k	273k
NewsComm. v13	DE-EN	120k	3M
TED Talks	SK-EN	61k	1.3M
=	SL-EN	19k	443k
=	GL-EN	10k	214k

Table 1: Numbers of lines of the original corpora used in our experiments. Sections 4-8 use only the first dataset. We do not use monolingual or back-translated data, and train our tokenizers using only each parallel corpus.

and 9.

3 Data and Systems

We train our NMT systems with the Upper Sorbian (HSB) to German (DE) training data of the WMT 2020 Low-Resource Translation Task (Fraser, 2020). We also use the HSB-DE development and test sets provided by the WMT 2020 and 2021 Low-Resource Translation Tasks (Fraser, 2020; Libovický and Fraser, 2021), each consisting of 2k sentences. As length-based filtering does not show significant differences, we do not filter our data. Additionally, in Section 9, we train systems for translation from Galician (GL), Slovenian (SL), and Slovak (SK) into English (EN), using tokenized and cleaned transcriptions of TED Talks (Qi et al., 2018).[1] Finally, we train a larger German to English system using 120k lines from News Commentary v13 (Bojar et al., 2018), and sample 1,500 lines each for development and testing. Table 1 presents these resources.

Tokenization into subwords is done with a Unigram LM model (Kudo, 2018) from SentencePiece.[2] For each language pair we build a shared vocabulary of 10k subwords using only the parallel corpus, with character coverage of 0.98, *nbest* of 1 and *alpha* of 0.

We use the Transformer-Base architecture (Vaswani et al., 2017) implemented in OpenNMT-py (Klein et al., 2017; Klein et al., 2020).[3] Our default setting of hyper-parameters is the one recommended by OpenNMT-py[4] which is close to the original Transformer (Vaswani et al., 2017). The regularization factors appear with relatively low strengths in this setting, as is usual when large datasets are available. The setting includes the 'noam' learning rate schedule with a scaling factor of 2 and a dropout rate of 0.1. For Adam, $\beta_1 = 0.9$, $\beta_2 = 0.998$ and $\epsilon = 10^{-8}$.

We train our models for a maximum of 100 hours, although they generally converge earlier. When comparing batch sizes in Section 4, it could be argued that epochs might provide a fairer comparison, but we measure real clock time as the most relevant measure for practitioners.

A batch consists of lines (tokenized sentences) that are translated one by one, with a fixed maximum length of 512 tokens for Transformer-Base. Lines are padded if shorter, and filtered out if longer. We train all models on two GPUs with 11 GB of memory each (GeForce RTX 1080Ti). Each device processes several batches, depending on the batch size, which are afterwards accumulated and used to update the model. The *effective batch size* and the `batch_size` parameter of OpenNMT-py are two different values: the former is $G \times A \times$ `batch_size`, where G is the number of GPUs and A the number of accumulated batches, here equal to two.[5] Throughout the paper, we report the `batch_size` parameter, but the effective batch size is in fact four times larger.

We generate translations with a beam size of seven, with consecutive ensembles of four checkpoints. For each model we report the highest BLEU score (Papineni et al., 2002) calculated with SacreBLEU (Post, 2018) on detokenized text[6] as well as the chrF score (Popović, 2015). We test the statistical significance of differences in scores at the 95% confidence level using paired bootstrap resampling from SacreBLEU.

4 Batch Size

In this section we train models with batch sizes ranging from 500 to 10,000, with all other hyper-parameters set to default. Models with batch sizes of 100 and 250 were also trained, but did not converge. The largest tested batch size is the largest value supported by our GPUs.

The BLEU and chrF scores in Table 2 show that lowering the batch size improves quality of NMT,

[1] `https://github.com/neulab/word-embeddings-for-nmt`

[2] `https://github.com/google/sentencepiece`

[3] We make public our configuration files and package requirements at `https://github.com/AlexRAtrio/reg-factors`.

[4] `https://opennmt.net/OpenNMT-py/FAQ.html#how-do-i-use-the-transformer-model`

[5] `https://forum.opennmt.net/t/epochs-determination/3119`

[6] `https://github.com/mjpost/sacrebleu` with the signature nrefs:1|bs:1000|seed:12345|case:mixed|eff:no|tok:13a|smooth:exp|version:2.0.0.

Batch Size	train		dev		test	
	Xent	Acc.	BLEU	chrF	BLEU	chrF
0.5k	0.02	99.93	50.54*	73.35	43.95^	69.25
1k	0.01	99.94	**52.02**	**74.63**	**44.40**^	**70.02**
3k	0.01	99.96	50.16*	73.38	43.91^	69.16
6k	0.01	99.97	49.66+	73.09	42.55−	68.85
9k	0.01	99.96	49.42+	73.10	42.22−	68.40
10k	0.01	99.97	48.46	72.49	42.19−	68.38

Table 2: HSB-DE scores with various batch sizes, all other settings being default ones. Values with the same color or symbol are *not* significantly different. The highest scores are in bold.

likely due to the regularizing effect of a less accurate gradient, according to our theoretical perspective. In particular, we observe improved results with a batch size smaller than 3,000 (+1.71 BLEU) and an optimal size around 1,000 (+2.21), with scores gradually decreasing as batch size increases. These results are in line with previous observations (Sennrich and Zhang, 2019; Atrio and Popescu-Belis, 2021).

There is no clear correlation between the training accuracy or cross-entropy loss and the generalization capacity, i.e. the scores on the development and test sets. The lower scores of models trained with larger batch sizes are likely not due to overfitting, because the *testing* curves of these models do not show any decrease late in the training. This further supports the claim that better generalization abilities are due to flat minima (Keskar et al., 2016, Section 2.1).

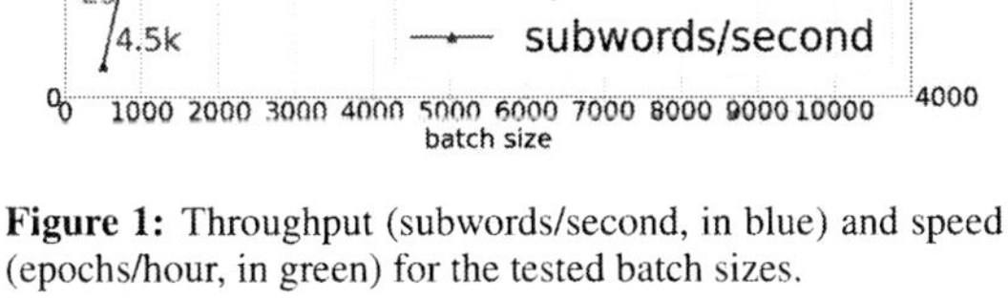

Figure 1: Throughput (subwords/second, in blue) and speed (epochs/hour, in green) for the tested batch sizes.

Our results are competitive with the comparable baselines from the WMT20 shared task on low-resource NMT for HSB-DE (Fraser, 2020), which used the same parallel data.[7] The baseline BLEU scores of Knowles et al. (2020), Libovický et al. (2020) and Kvapilíková et al. (2020) were respectively 44.1, 43.4, and 38.7 on the test set.

Regularization through smaller batch sizes thus provides visible improvements with respect to the default setting. Larger batch sizes, however, exploit more fully the memory of the GPUs, which enables higher throughput in terms of subwords processed per second, as illustrated in Figure 1, although this does not increase linearly: instead, we observe diminishing returns as batch size increases. Still, while a batch size of 10k has the lowest BLEU scores, it nearly doubles the throughput with respect to the highest-scoring batch size (1k). Due to differences in hardware and software, these values are difficult to compare to other studies, but the trends are similar to those observed by Popel and Bojar (2018, Section 4.1).

If the regularization attained with lower batch sizes can also be obtained by using other regularization factors, this would allow the use of larger batch sizes for a more efficient training. Therefore, in the next sections, we will compare a large batch size (10k) and the optimal, regularized one (1k), and verify that none of the other regularization factors that will be optimized have an impact on speed.

5 Learning Rate

Previous studies by Smith et al. (2017) and Smith and Le (2017) have shown that the regularization effects of the batch size and of the learning rate may be comparable. In this section, we study the role of varying schedules of the learning rate (5.1) and the effect of resetting the schedule in mid-training, i.e. suddenly increasing the learning rate before another decrease (5.2).

5.1 Regularization through Learning Rate

Since all our models have the same dimension of embeddings (d_{model} in Eq. 1 above), the only variables influencing the learning rate in the 'noam' schedule are the number of warmup steps and the scaling factor (Vaswani et al., 2017, Eq. 3). We test two different values for the former: 8k (default) and 16k. For the latter, we test even values from 2 (default) to 14. Figure 2 displays some tested schedules, including our default one (8k, 2) and the 'noam' original one (4k, 1).

The results in Table 3 show that both batch sizes reach similar maximal scores (46.20 and 46.29),

[7] Some of these systems used in fact larger monolingual HSB, DE and/or CS datasets for training their tokenizers, while we only used 60k lines of parallel HSB-DE text.

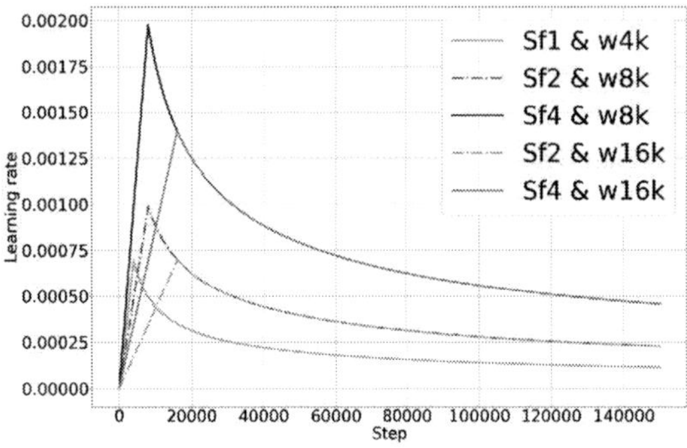

Figure 2: 'Noam' learning rate schedules with different scaling factors (*sf*) and numbers of warmup steps (*w*).

although with different scaling factors: 6 for a batch size of 1k vs. 10 for a batch size of 10k. The improvement is 1.8 BLEU points for a batch size of 1k, and 4.1 for 10k. As a batch size of 1k is already a strong regularization factor, a smaller value of the learning rate (hence less regularization through this factor) is sufficient, compared to the case of a larger batch size.

War mup	2	4	6	8	10	12	14
8k	44.40	**45.42**	38.90	0.65	0.18	0.05	0.60
16k	43.96	45.74	46.20*	46.07*	45.79*	45.24*	42.24
8k	42.19	44.59	45.27⋆	**45.93**–	45.87–	45.34⋆	45.31⋆
16k	41.70	44.36	45.32+	45.89^	**46.29**^	45.69+	45.69+

Table 3: BLEU scores on the HSB-DE test set for batch sizes of 1k (top) and 10k (bottom) and various learning schedules. We denote scores that are *not* significantly different row-wise with the same color or symbol.

The models trained with the larger batch size (10k) are more stable when learning rates increase (larger scaling factors) likely due to more accurate estimates of the gradients (compare lines 1 vs. 3, and 2 vs. 4). Similarly, these models have a higher maximal learning rate beyond which they diverge (compare in Table 3 the large difference between lines 1 and 2 with the small difference between lines 3 and 4). This shows the importance of increasing the number of warmup steps as the scaling factor increases, to avoid reaching high maxima of the learning rate (the peaks visible on the schedules in Figure 2). Moreover, the regularization provided by other factors (in this case, batch size) needs to be taken into account when increasing the amount of regularization from the learning rate. Finally, as long as the maximal learning rate remains below the values that make a model diverge, the BLEU scores do not change significantly when the scaling factor increases above a certain value, as also observed by Popel and Bojar (2018, 4.6, Fig. 7).

5.2 Resetting the LR during Training

From the perspective of the loss landscape, we hypothesize that introducing more noise into the gradient when the scores have already leveled-off, namely by resetting the learning rate schedule, should increase the probability for the weights to escape the sharp minima basins and avoid falling back into them, which should improve the generalization abilities of the trained model. Since a model trained with a smaller batch size has a higher chance, during the first part of training, to fall into flat minima due to an increased gradient noise (Smith et al., 2017), we expect the larger batch sizes to benefit more from this strategy than the smaller ones.

Batch size		Hours 50	100 no lr reset	100 reset lr
1k	BLEU	44.25	44.40	**45.85**
	chrF	69.78	70.02	70.84
	Train. Acc.	99.93	99.94	99.84
	Xent	0.02	0.01	0.02
	Δ		*+0.15*	***+1.60***
10k	BLEU	41.60	42.19	**45.25**
	chrF	68.03	68.38	70.57
	Train. Acc.	99.94	99.97	99.92
	Xent	0.01	0.01	0.01
	Δ		*+0.59*	***+3.65***

Table 4: BLEU and chrF scores on the HSB-DE test set, training accuracy and cross-entropy on the training set, and change of BLEU scores when continuing training until 100 hours vs. resetting the learning rate at 50h.

In Table 4 we provide the scores after training for 50 hours (half of their training time); the scores after 100 hours when continuing to train from the 50-hour checkpoint; and the final score after training for 50 hours with a schedule reset at the 50-hour checkpoint. The results corroborate our hypothesis: both batch sizes benefit significantly from the strategy of resetting the learning rate, and the large batch size more than the smaller one ((+3.65 vs. +1.6 BLEU points). As both models reached their highest BLEU scores before 25 hours, the difference is likely not due to that fact that the first model saw more times the training data thanks to its higher throughput. Furthermore, after increasing the learning rate mid-training, both the loss and training accuracy worsen or remain stable, while BLEU scores improve, likely due to reaching flatter basins, not lower minima.

6 Dropout Rate

The dropout of a certain proportion of neurons during training is another frequent source of regularization. As this amounts to removing certain terms from the summation of gradients, its role can also be considered from the perspective of flat vs. sharp minimizers.

Dropout							
0.1	0.2	0.3	0.4	0.5	0.6	0.7	0.8
44.40*	45.35+	**45.39**+	44.87*	44.54*	42.58	37.69	19.83
42.19	43.76	44.74	**45.40**^	45.39^	45.26^	42.91	35.52

Table 5: Dropout scores on the HSB-DE test set for 1k (top) and 10k (bottom) batch sizes. We denote row-wise lack of significant differences with the same color or symbol. Dropout rates of 0.9 have considerably lower scores.

BLEU scores in Table 5 show that the model trained with a larger batch size – hence subject to less regularization – requires a more aggressive dropout of around 0.4–0.6 in order to reach its highest scores, with respect to a model trained with a smaller batch size, which reaches its highest score for 0.2–0.3. This is consistent with our previous findings from Section 5.1 and Table 3, which also showed that the model subject to less regularization from a factor (larger batch size) required more regularization from another factor in order to reach its highest scores.

7 Gradient Clipping

Finally, we experiment with our fourth regularization factor: gradient clipping. Since it directly involves constraining the norm of the gradient, the perspective based on flat vs. sharp basins in the loss landscape also holds for it.

Batch size	Drop out	Gradient Clipping				
		None	20	10	5	2.5
1k	0.1	44.40	44.75	**44.92**	44.74	44.54
10k	0.1	42.19	**42.41**	42.01	42.30	42.20
	0.2	43.76	44.15	**44.34**	43.98	43.85
	0.3	44.74	**45.36**	44.72	44.75	44.99
	0.4	45.40	**45.56**	45.30	45.45	45.48

Table 6: BLEU scores on the HSB-DE test set for batch sizes of 10k and 1k on the test set, with a dropout rate of 0.1 (default), for several upper limits of the gradients.

As in the previous sections, we compare models trained with batch sizes of 1k and 10k, but observe no statistically significant differences between them when using default values for other hyper-parameters, with BLEU scores shown in Table 6 – although values of 10 or 20 are always among the best. This is likely because default settings do not feature enough regularization (i.e., they do not increase enough the gradient's norm) for the gradients to be affected by clipping. For this reason, we perform additional experiments with a batch size of 10k (due to its advantage for speed) with more regularizing dropout values of 0.2, 0.3, and 0.4, and scaling factor of 6 and 10. Regarding the models with increasing dropout rate, we only observe a statistically significant difference between the best and worst results (for dropout of 0.2), the best and two worst results (for 0.3), and no differences at all (for 0.4). We conclude that gradient clipping only marginally affects training in these settings.

8 Combining Regularization Factors

We will now show that a combination of regularization factors can produce higher scores than individual factors used separately, and that the maximal scores are stable when varying the strengths of regularizers around their optimal values. The batch size is fixed at 10k, since this enables a higher training speed than 1k with similar best scores, provided that other regularization factors are used, as shown in Tables 3, 4 and 5. The number of warmup steps is fixed at 16k since we showed in Section 5.1 that this parameter mainly limits the peaks of the learning rate and thus prevents models from diverging early in the training. Our search space for the other regularization factors is shown in Table 8.

Factor	Value	Xent	Tr. acc.	BLEU	chrF	Δ
Defaults	-	0.01	99.97	42.19	68.38	-
Batch size	1k	0.02	99.94	44.40	70.02	+2.21
S.f.	10	0.01	99.94	45.93	70.74	+3.74
S.f. + w.s.	10+16k	0.01	99.94	46.29	71.22	+4.10
L.r. reset	50%	0.01	99.92	45.25	70.57	+3.06
Dropout	0.4	0.07	99.46	45.40	71.00	+3.21
Clipping	10	0.01	99.96	42.41	68.43	+0.22
Combination	Table 8	0.03	99.78	**47.11**	**71.88**	**+4.92**
+ l.r. reset	-	0.06	99.30	**47.20**	**71.80**	**+5.01**

Table 7: HSB-DE scores on the test set when the regularization factors are used either independently (lines 2–6) or in combination (line 7), in the latter case with the optimal values from Table 8. The last column shows increases in BLEU scores over the default settings.

We present in Table 7 the highest scores achieved using individual regularization factors, along with those from the default setup (first line) and from the combination of factors (last two lines). Regularization factors are already present in the default setup, but at low strengths.

The comparison of scores in Table 7 shows that each factor used independently allows the model to outperform the default setting by 2–4 BLEU points. However, the use of a combination of factors achieves the highest score of 47.20 BLEU points (+ 5.01), which is significantly above all others. In the case of resetting the learning rate, although this has a visible effect when used with default parameters, its effect is much smaller when used jointly with other regularization factors, likely because a flat basin is found before the reset. Moreover, the combination of factors results in a higher loss and a lower accuracy on the train set than the default setup or factors used individually, which supports our interpretation of the improvement based on flatter minima.

Table 8 shows that the best scores reached with increased regularization are quite stable when varying the intensity of the factors. The optimal region of the scaling factor is around 10, with a relatively flat neighborhood, similar to the case when it was optimized individually (Section 5). Optimal dropout rates are now around 0.3–0.5, compared to 0.4–0.6 when used individually (Section 6). Finally, gradient clipping has only a marginal effect in combination with other factors, presumably because it cannot help to increase the gradients.

Grad clipping	**Scaling factor**	**Dropout** 0.1	0.3	0.5	0.7
None	2	42.19	44.74	45.39	42.91
	6	45.32	46.70	46.22	43.66
	10	46.29	47.06	46.93	43.18
	14	45.69	46.84	47.07	43.61
	18	45.26	46.89	46.67	43.19
5	2	41.39	44.47	45.05	43.48
	6	45.20	46.62	46.70	43.88
	10	45.65	**47.11**	46.76	44.04
	14	45.57	**47.11**	47.06	43.63
	18	44.72	46.59	47.02	42.72

Table 8: HSB-DE BLEU scores for a combination of the scaling factor, gradient clipping, and dropout rate, for a batch size of 10k and 16k warmup steps. The highest scores are in bold.

9 Testing on Additional Corpora

In this section, we confirm our claims using additional low-resource datasets. We consider two smaller samples with 40k and 20k lines from the HSB-DE corpus, as well as parallel datasets for Galician, German, Slovak and Slovenian (see Section 3). We do not optimize regularization factors on each dataset, but only use the optimal hyper-parameters found above on HSB-DE with 60k lines.

Table 9 demonstrates that these hyper-parameter values bring significant improvements of BLEU and chrF scores over the baseline for all datasets (four different source languages). When comparing HSB-DE datasets of different sizes, we find that as the amount of data decreases, the positive effects of our regularization parameters increase, with up to 21% improvement in BLEU scores for the smallest subset. Furthermore, we also observe an increase in the loss over all datasets with the optimized setup, which shows that the reason why their less accurate gradients generalize better is not due to finding lower but rather flatter minima of loss.

10 Conclusion

We presented a unified perspective on the role of four regularization factors in low-resource settings: batch size, learning schedule, gradient clipping and dropout rate. The results support our claim that more regularization is beneficial in such settings, with respect to the default values that are recommended for high-resource settings. We first substantiated the claim for each factor taken individually, and then showed that a combination of factors leads to improved scores and is robust when factors vary. Finally, we showed that our findings generalize across different low-resource sizes and

Corpus	**Lines**	**Default** Xent	Tr. Acc.	BLEU	chrF	**Optimized** Xent	Tr. Acc.	BLEU	chrF	**%Δ** BLEU
HSB-DE	*60k*	*0.01*	*99.97*	*42.19*	*68.38*	*0.06*	*99.30*	***47.20***	*71.80*	***+11.87***
HSB-DE	40k	0.01	99.98	32.38	60.68	0.03	99.80	**37.63**	65.12	**+16.21**
HSB-DE	20k	0.01	99.98	22.93	51.42	0.02	99.93	**27.84**	56.27	**+21.41**
DE-EN	120k	0.10	98.20	29.94	56.81	0.60	84.71	**35.77**	61.44	**+19.47**
SK-EN	61k	0.02	99.89	25.61	46.42	0.40	89.29	**29.71**	49.67	**+16.01**
SL-EN	19k	0.01	99.93	15.53	34.99	0.09	98.89	**18.43**	37.75	**+18.67**
GL-EN	10k	0.01	99.98	16.00	34.52	0.04	99.69	**19.04**	37.84	**+19.00**

Table 9: BLEU scores on test sets of different corpora and subsets of our main HSB-DE corpus (first line), comparing our default setup and our optimized setup as presented in Section 8.

languages. Overall, we interpreted the results from the perspective of the loss landscape, and argued that more regularization is beneficial because the noise it introduces in the estimation of gradients leads to finding flatter minima of the loss, which have better generalization abilities. We hope that better insights on the loss landscape of the Transformer will confirm our theoretical interpretation, and that the observations put forward in this paper will also help practitioners with setting hyperparameters for low-resource NMT systems.

11 Acknowledgments

We thank the Swiss National Science Foundation (DOMAT grant n. 175693, On-demand Knowledge for Document-level Machine Translation) and Armasuisse (FamilyMT project). We especially thank Dr. Ljiljana Dolamic (Armasuisse) for her support in the FamilyMT project. We are also grateful to the anonymous reviewers and to Giorgos Vernikos for their helpful suggestions.

References

Araabi, Ali and Christof Monz. 2020. Optimizing Transformer for low-resource neural machine translation. In *Proceedings of the 28th International Conference on Computational Linguistics*, pages 3429–3435, Barcelona, Spain.

Atrio, Àlex R. and Andrei Popescu-Belis. 2021. Small batch sizes improve training of low-resource neural MT. In *Proceedings of the 18th International Conference on Natural Language Processing (ICON)*, Patna, India.

Bojar, Ondřej, Christian Federmann, Mark Fishel, Yvette Graham, Barry Haddow, Philipp Koehn, and Christof Monz. 2018. Findings of the 2018 conference on machine translation (WMT18). In *Proceedings of the Third Conference on Machine Translation: Shared Task Papers*, pages 272–303, Belgium, Brussels.

Dinh, Laurent, Razvan Pascanu, Samy Bengio, and Yoshua Bengio. 2017. Sharp minima can generalize for deep nets. In *International Conference on Machine Learning*, pages 1019–1028.

Fraser, Alexander. 2020. Findings of the WMT 2020 shared tasks in unsupervised MT and very low resource supervised MT. In *Proceedings of the Fifth Conference on Machine Translation*, pages 765–771.

Goodfellow, Ian, Yoshua Bengio, and Aaron Courville. 2016. *Deep Learning*. MIT Press.

Goyal, Priya, Piotr Dollár, Ross Girshick, Pieter Noordhuis, Lukasz Wesolowski, Aapo Kyrola, Andrew Tulloch, Yangqing Jia, and Kaiming He. 2017. Accurate, large minibatch SGD: Training Imagenet in 1 hour. *arXiv preprint arXiv:1706.02677*.

Hoffer, Elad, Itay Hubara, and Daniel Soudry. 2017. Train longer, generalize better: Closing the generalization gap in large batch training of neural networks. In *Proceedings of the 31st International Conference on Neural Information Processing Systems*, NIPS'17, page 1729–1739.

Jastrzębski, Stanislaw, Zachary Kenton, Devansh Arpit, Nicolas Ballas, Asja Fischer, Yoshua Bengio, and Amos Storkey. 2018. Width of minima reached by stochastic gradient descent is influenced by learning rate to batch size ratio. In *Proceedings of 27th International Conference on Artificial Neural Networks*, Lecture Notes in Computer Science, pages 392–402. Springer, Cham.

Kawaguchi, Kenji, Leslie Pack Kaelbling, and Yoshua Bengio. 2017. Generalization in deep learning. *arXiv preprint arXiv:1710.05468*.

Keskar, Nitish Shirish, Dheevatsa Mudigere, Jorge Nocedal, Mikhail Smelyanskiy, and Ping Tak Peter Tang. 2016. On large-batch training for deep learning: Generalization gap and sharp minima. *arXiv preprint arXiv:1609.04836*.

Klein, Guillaume, Yoon Kim, Yuntian Deng, Jean Senellart, and Alexander Rush. 2017. OpenNMT: Open-source toolkit for NMT. In *Proceedings of the 55th Annual Meeting of the Association for Computational Linguistics, System Demonstrations*, pages 67–72.

Klein, Guillaume, François Hernandez, Vincent Nguyen, and Jean Senellart. 2020. The OpenNMT neural machine translation toolkit: 2020 edition. In *Proceedings of the 14th Conference of the Association for Machine Translation in the Americas*, pages 102–109.

Knowles, Rebecca, Samuel Larkin, Darlene Stewart, and Patrick Littell. 2020. NRC systems for low resource German-Upper Sorbian machine translation 2020: Transfer learning with lexical modifications. In *Proceedings of the Fifth Conference on Machine Translation*, pages 1112–1122.

Krizhevsky, Alex. 2014. One weird trick for parallelizing convolutional neural networks. *arXiv preprint arXiv:1404.5997*.

Kudo, Taku. 2018. Subword regularization: Improving neural network translation models with multiple subword candidates. In *Proceedings of the 56th Annual Meeting of the Association for Computational Linguistics*, pages 66–75.

Kukačka, Jan, Vladimir Golkov, and Daniel Cremers. 2017. Regularization for deep learning: A taxonomy. *arXiv preprint arXiv:1710.10686*.

Kvapilíková, Ivana, Tom Kocmi, and Ondřej Bojar. 2020. CUNI systems for the unsupervised and very low resource translation task in WMT20. In *Proceedings of the Fifth Conference on Machine Translation*, pages 1123–1128.

Li, Hao, Zheng Xu, Gavin Taylor, Christoph Studer, and Tom Goldstein. 2017. Visualizing the loss landscape of neural nets. *arXiv preprint arXiv:1712.09913*.

Libovický, Jindřich, Viktor Hangya, Helmut Schmid, and Alexander Fraser. 2020. The LMU Munich system for the WMT20 very low resource supervised MT task. In *Proceedings of the Fifth Conference on Machine Translation*, pages 1104–1111.

Libovický, Jindřich and Alexander Fraser. 2021. Findings of the WMT 2021 shared tasks in unsupervised MT and very low resource supervised MT. In *Proceedings of the Sixth Conference on Machine Translation*.

Miceli Barone, Antonio Valerio, Barry Haddow, Ulrich Germann, and Rico Sennrich. 2017. Regularization techniques for fine-tuning in neural machine translation. In *Proceedings of the 2017 Conference on Empirical Methods in Natural Language Processing*, pages 1489–1494, Copenhagen, Denmark.

Moradi, Reza, Reza Berangi, and Behrouz Minaei. 2020. A survey of regularization strategies for deep models. *Artificial Intelligence Review*, 53(6):3947–3986.

Ott, Myle, Sergey Edunov, David Grangier, and Michael Auli. 2018. Scaling neural machine translation. In *Proceedings of the Third Conference on Machine Translation: Research Papers*, pages 1–9, Belgium, Brussels.

Papineni, Kishore, Salim Roukos, Todd Ward, and Wei-Jing Zhu. 2002. Bleu: a method for automatic evaluation of machine translation. In *Proceedings of the 40th Annual Meeting of the Association for Computational Linguistics*, pages 311–318, Philadelphia, PA, USA.

Peng, Hao, Lili Mou, Ge Li, Yunchuan Chen, Yangyang Lu, and Zhi Jin. 2015. A comparative study on regularization strategies for embedding-based neural networks. In *Proceedings of the 2015 Conference on Empirical Methods in Natural Language Processing*, pages 2106–2111, Lisbon, Portugal.

Popel, Martin and Ondřej Bojar. 2018. Training tips for the Transformer model. *The Prague Bulletin of Mathematical Linguistics*, 110(1):43–70, 4.

Popović, Maja. 2015. chrF: character n-gram f-score for automatic MT evaluation. In *Proceedings of the Tenth Workshop on Statistical Machine Translation*, pages 392–395, Lisbon, Portugal.

Post, Matt. 2018. A call for clarity in reporting BLEU scores. In *Proceedings of the Third Conference on Machine Translation: Research Papers*, pages 186–191, Belgium, Brussels.

Qi, Ye, Devendra Sachan, Matthieu Felix, Sarguna Padmanabhan, and Graham Neubig. 2018. When and why are pre-trained word embeddings useful for neural machine translation? In *Proceedings of the 2018 Conference of the North American Chapter of the Association for Computational Linguistics*, pages 529–535, New Orleans, LA, USA.

Sennrich, Rico and Biao Zhang. 2019. Revisiting low-resource neural machine translation: A case study. In *Proceedings of the 57th Annual Meeting of the Association for Computational Linguistics*, pages 211–221, Florence, Italy.

Smith, Samuel L and Quoc V Le. 2017. A bayesian perspective on generalization and stochastic gradient descent. *arXiv preprint arXiv:1710.06451*.

Smith, Samuel L, Pieter-Jan Kindermans, Chris Ying, and Quoc V Le. 2017. Don't decay the learning rate, increase the batch size. *arXiv preprint arXiv:1711.00489*.

Srivastava, Nitish, Geoffrey Hinton, Alex Krizhevsky, Ilya Sutskever, and Ruslan Salakhutdinov. 2014. Dropout: a simple way to prevent neural networks from overfitting. *The journal of machine learning research*, 15(1):1929–1958.

Vaswani, Ashish, Noam Shazeer, Niki Parmar, Jakob Uszkoreit, Llion Jones, Aidan N Gomez, Lukasz Kaiser, and Illia Polosukhin. 2017. Attention is all you need. In *Advances in Neural Information Processing Systems 30*, pages 5998–6008.

Xu, Hongfei, Josef van Genabith, Deyi Xiong, and Qiuhui Liu. 2020. Dynamically adjusting Transformer batch size by monitoring gradient direction change. In *Proceedings of the 58th Annual Meeting of the Association for Computational Linguistics*, pages 3519–3524.

Controlling Extra-Textual Attributes about Dialogue Participants: A Case Study of English-to-Polish Neural Machine Translation

Sebastian T. Vincent, Loïc Barrault, Carolina Scarton
Department of Computer Science, University of Sheffield
Regent Court, 211 Portobello, Sheffield, S1 4DP, UK
{stvincent1, l.barrault, c.scarton}@shef.ac.uk

Abstract

Unlike English, morphologically rich languages can reveal characteristics of speakers or their conversational partners, such as gender and number, via pronouns, morphological endings of words and syntax. When translating from English to such languages, a machine translation model needs to opt for a certain interpretation of textual context, which may lead to serious translation errors if extra-textual information is unavailable. We investigate this challenge in the English-to-Polish language direction. We focus on the underresearched problem of utilising external metadata in automatic translation of TV dialogue, proposing a case study where a wide range of approaches for controlling attributes in translation is employed in a multi-attribute scenario. The best model achieves an improvement of $+5.81$ chrF++/$+6.03$ BLEU, with other models achieving competitive performance. We additionally contribute a novel attribute-annotated dataset of Polish TV dialogue and a morphological analysis script used to evaluate attribute control in models.

1 Introduction

In some languages, dialogue explicitly expresses certain information about the interlocutors: for example, while in English words describing the speaker "I" and the interlocutor "you" are ambiguous w.r.t. their gender, number and formality, languages such as Polish, German or Spanish will mark for one or more of these attributes. In industrial settings such as dubbing and speech translation, there is an abundance of available metadata about the interlocutors, such as their genders, that could be used to help resolve these ambiguities.

Field	Value
source	"Are you blind?"
spoken by (=speaker)	"Anne"
speaker's gender	"feminine"
spoken to (=interlocutor(s))	["Mark", "Colin"]
interlocutor(s)' gender	"masculine"
formality	"informal"

Table 1: A TV segment along with available metadata.

Table 1 shows an example of such a TV segment: the English sentence *'Are you blind?'*, should translate to Polish as *'Jesteście ślepi?'* as the addressee is a group of men and the setting is informal; however, when spoken e.g. formally to a mixed-gender group of people, the correct translation would read *'Są państwo ślepi?'*, using a different verb inflection and an honorific *państwo*. Since the contextual information required to resolve the ambiguity in this example does not belong to the text itself, traditional models do not use it. This yields hypotheses which introduce some assumptions about that context, typically reflecting biases present in the (often unbalanced) training data. To avoid this, a better solution is to resolve such ambiguities by using both the available metadata and the source text as translation input. Alternatively, when such information is unavailable, all possible contextual variants could be provided as output, passing the choice from the model to the user (Jacovi et al., 2021; Schioppa et al., 2021).

In the context of the gender of the speaker and interlocutor, prior research has explored two ways

Macken, Rufener, Van den Bogaert, Daems, Tezcan, Vanroy, Fonteyne, Barrault, Costa-jussà, Kemp, Pilos, Declercq, Koponen, Forcada, Scarton, Moniz (eds.)
Proceedings of the 23rd Annual Conference of the European Association for Machine Translation, p. 121–130
Ghent, Belgium, June 2022.

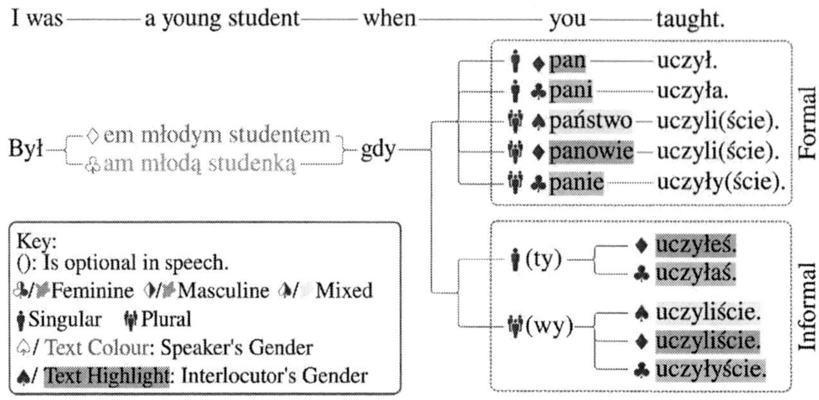

Figure 1: Example of an ambiguous English sentence with all plausible translations to Polish. There are a total of 18 equally plausible possible hypotheses based on the combination of contexts.

in which such information influences a text (Rabinovich et al., 2017; Vanmassenhove et al., 2018). Firstly, naturally occurring texts satisfy grammatical agreement between the gender of the speaker and interlocutor and the utterances which describe them. How this agreement is expressed in speech varies among different languages (Stahlberg et al., 2007). Polish is a *grammatical gender language*: every noun is assigned a gender, and grammatical forms must agree with that noun. In contrast, English is a *natural gender language*, with "no grammatical markings of sex" (Stahlberg et al., 2007, p. 165). Secondly, gender can be seen as a demographic factor that influences the way people express themselves (e.g. word choice). Hereinafter we refer to the former as *grammatical agreement* and the latter as *behavioural agreement.*

In this work, we seek to build machine translation (MT) models that satisfy grammatical agreement. Given an English sentence and a set of attributes (e.g. the gender of the speaker and number of interlocutors), an MT system must translate this sentence into Polish with a correct grammatical agreement to all attributes but introduce no markings of behavioural agreement.

We explore the agreement to one SPEAKER attribute: the gender of the speaker (SPGENDER), and three INTERLOCUTOR attributes: the gender(s) and number of interlocutor(s) (ILGENDER, ILNUMBER), as well as the desired FORMALITY of addressing the interlocutor(s). Figure 1 exemplifies the extent of ambiguity these attributes introduce in English-to-Polish translation.

The **main contributions** of our work are: (1) a novel English-Polish parallel corpus of TV dialogue annotated for SPGENDER, ILGENDER, ILNUMBER and FORMALITY; (2) a tool for analysing attributes expressed in Polish utterances; (3) the examination of a wide range of approaches to attribute control in NMT, showing that at least four of them can be reliably used for incorporating extra-linguistic information within English-to-Polish translation of dialogue.

The paper is structured as follows. Section 2 discusses previous work. Section 3 presents the problem definition, focusing on Polish as the target language. The creation of the parallel English-Polish corpus of dialogue utterances that mark subsets of the investigated attributes is presented in Section 4.1. How the MT models are trained to control the four extra-textual attributes is discussed in Section 4.3, whilst the results are presented in Section 4.2. Finally, we describe conclusions and potential directions for future work in Section 6.

2 Related Work

The state-of-the-art in MT is currently represented by neural MT (NMT) (Sutskever et al., 2014; Bahdanau et al., 2015) implemented via the Transformer architecture (Vaswani et al., 2017). Despite their unparalleled performance, these models are limited by ignoring the extra-textual context (e.g. speaker's gender). Consequently, much recent work aims to control NMT with various attributes. In particular, attention has been paid to tasks such as multilingual NMT (Johnson et al., 2017), by specifying the target language in the input; formality or politeness transfer (e.g. Sennrich et al. (2016)); controlling the gender of the speaker and/or interlocutor (Elaraby et al., 2018; Vanmassenhove et al., 2018; Moryossef et al., 2019); length and verbosity (Lakew et al., 2019; Lakew et al., 2021); or constraining the vocabulary (Ailem et al., 2021).

Attribute control in NMT is most commonly facilitated with a *tagging* (or *side constraints*) approach, whereby a set of terms is added to the vocabulary, each embedding a certain type. These are trained alongside token embeddings and used in various ways during inference. Controlling multiple attributes with this approach has not been excessively studied (Schioppa et al., 2021), but can be facilitated by simply concatenating the tags (Takeno et al., 2017). However, for a set of equally important attributes, their ordering should not matter, but a tagging approach by design requires tags to be ordered in a specific way. Combining attributes by averaging their embeddings has also been explored in previous work (cf. Lample et al. (2019), Schioppa et al. (2021)), where authors incorporated the resulting vectors either into the input of the Encoder or the Decoder or directly into the model (Michel and Neubig, 2018; Schioppa et al., 2021).

Typically, attribute-controlling neural models are fully supervised, requiring annotated training data. Such annotations can be obtained directly, e.g. from metadata (Vanmassenhove et al., 2018); although most available corpora are unannotated. Sennrich et al. (2016) and Elaraby et al. (2018) automatically annotate the data using morphosyntactic parsers based on rules, validating agreement to the attribute in question in target-side sentences. To verify that the rules capture the attribute completely, a precision/recall score is computed against a manually labelled test set.

3 Problem Specification

Recognising the small number of studies within machine translation research on the English-to-Polish language direction, as well as our capacity (thanks to the available parsers and native speakers to validate their performance), we decide to focus the study on this language pair. Polish is a West Slavic language spoken by over 50M people over the world (Jassem, 2003). It uses an expanded version of the Latin alphabet and is characterised by a complex inflectional morphology (Feldstein, 2001). It is a grammatical gender language (Koniuszaniec and Błaszkowska, 2003) meaning all forms dependent on pronouns must agree to their gender and number. It uses a West Slavic system of honorifics *pani, pan, panie, panowie, państwo* (henceforth *Pan+*) (Stone, 1977). Being a null-subject language (Sigurðsson and Egerland, 2009), it does not require that pronouns signifying the speaker or the interlocutor are explicit, **unless** they belong to the *Pan+* group (Keown, 2003).

English lacks a grammatical gender or a system of honorifics, and the pronoun "you" is used for both plural and singular second person addressees. It is therefore ambiguous w.r.t. some expressions describing the speaker or the interlocutor, which we capture into four attributes, as follows (the attributes are summarised in Table 2).

SPEAKER attributes The gender of all forms dependent on the pronoun *ja* "I" must match the gender of the speaker SPGENDER $\in \{feminine, masculine\}$. This includes past and future verbal expressions (e.g. *byłam* 'I was$_{\text{fem}}$' vs. *byłem* 'I was$_{\text{masc}}$'), adjectives (e.g. *piękna* 'pretty$_{\text{fem}}$' vs. *piękny* 'pretty$_{\text{masc}}$') and nouns (e.g. *wariatka* 'lunatic$_{\text{fem}}$' vs. *wariat* 'lunatic$_{\text{masc}}$') that describe the speaker.

INTERLOCUTOR attributes All word forms dependent on the pronoun *ty/wy/Pan+* "you", including the pronoun itself, must match:

- the gender of the interlocutor (ILGENDER); this includes cases analogous to SPGENDER, extended to e.g. vocatives (e.g. *Ty wariatko/cie!* 'You lunatic$_{\text{fem/masc}}$!');
- the number of interlocutors (ILNUMBER); this includes verbs and pronouns in second person;
- the formality in addressing the interlocutor (FORMALITY)[1]; this entails using an inflection of the pronoun Pan+ consistent with ILGENDER and ILNUMBER where applicable, or using polite forms (e.g. *Proszę wejść.* 'Come in.').

Attribute	Abbreviation	Type
SPEAKER		
SPGENDER	*<sp:feminine>*	Feminine speaker
	<sp:masculine>	Masculine speaker
INTERLOCUTOR		
ILGENDER	*<il:feminine>*	Feminine interlocutor(s)
	<il:masculine>	Masculine interlocutor(s)
	<il:mixed>	Mixed-gender interlocutor(s)
ILNUMBER	*<singular>*	One interlocutor
	<plural>	Multiple interlocutors
FORMALITY	*<informal>*	Informal
	<formal>	Formal

Table 2: Attributes and types controlled in the experiment.

[1] While we define formality as binary, it can be more complex e.g. Japanese in Feely et al. (2019).

Throughout this paper, when discussing *gender* we refer solely to grammatical gender rendered in utterances. In the Polish language, the grammatical system of gender in first and second person is a dichotomy of masculine and feminine variants, lacking alternatives for people who identify as neither. We discuss potential solutions to this issue in directions for future work (§6).

4 Experimental Setup

4.1 Data Collection

We collect pre-training data from two corpora: the English-to-Polish part of OpenSubtitles18 (Lison and Tiedemann, 2016) and the Europarl (Koehn, 2005) corpus. The data quantities can be found in Table 3 (column "`pretrain`").

		`pretrain`	`finetune`	`amb_test`
train	#sents	10.8M	2.9M	–
	#tokens	82.1M	26M	–
dev	#sents	3K	3.5K	–
	#tokens	23.3K	48.7K	–
test	#sents	–	3.5K	1K
	#tokens	–	47.7K	10.3K

Table 3: Quantities of unique data used for: model pre-training (`pretrain`), model fine-tuning (`finetune`) and the test set for calculation of restricted impact (`amb_test`). Values are averaged for source and target text.

Corpus Extraction for Fine-tuning We extract the fine-tuning data directly from the pre-training corpus; each sample is paired with an annotation of up to four types of attributes. For that purpose we implement a set of morphosyntactic rules for the Polish SpaCy model (Tuora and Kobyliński, 2019) which uses the Morfeusz2 morphological analyser (Kieras and Wolinski, 2017).[2] Since attribute annotations vary at sentence level, we produce sentence-level annotations (instead of word- or scene-level). For both speaker and interlocutor gender attributes, the masculine gender makes up over 60% of the corpus. Altogether, a total of 34.33% of the corpus marks at least one of the attributes. Figure 2 shows how linguistic categories contributed to extracting each attribute.

Similarly to Elaraby et al. (2018) and Gonen and Webster (2020), we observe that certain nouns marked as describing the speaker or interlocutor have a fixed gender irrespective of that person's gender and are therefore inadequate determinants of their gender (e.g. *coward* "tchórz" is always masculine). We could not find a reliable (complete nor heuristic) method to resolve this other than creating a "stopwords" list of all inflexible nouns. The process is now performed in two steps: we first extract a list of sentences containing gender-marked words and then filter out those that were selected based on our "stopwords" list of inflexible nouns.

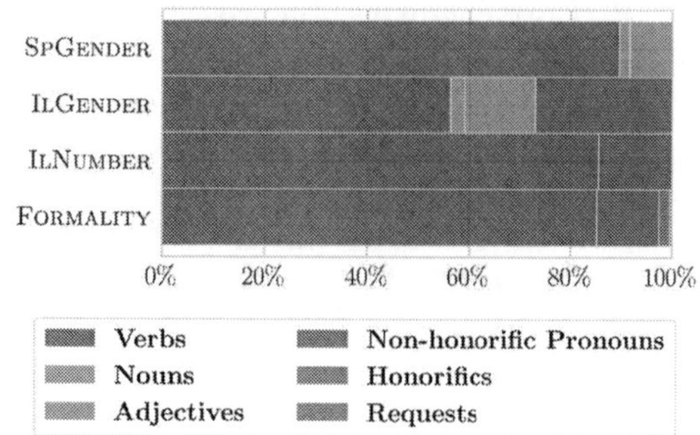

Figure 2: Contributions of each grammatical category to each attribute in the extracted corpus.

We extract 223.0K noun-dependent sentences with 9K unique lemmatised nouns in the first pass, build the "stopwords" list of 6.8K words and end up with 67.3K sentences.

Parser Rules We identify sentences marking for SpGender by finding tokens in first person singular and verifying that their head marks feminine or masculine gender. Formality is identified through the use of the inflected pronouns in the *Pan+* set (unless it is used as a title, e.g. in *'Ms Smith'*). Formal requests are selected by finding *proszę* (*'please'*) in the target sentence but not in the source. IlGender is trivially inferred in formal cases; for informal language, we match structures analogous to those for the SpGender and extend them to comparative phrases and vocatives. IlNumber follows from the plurality of second-person verbs as well as the use of the pronoun *ty* (*'you'*, singular) or *wy* (*'you'*, plural).

Parser Performance To measure the effectiveness of the parser, a native Polish speaker with expertise in NLP manually annotated a random sample of 1K sentence pairs from the training corpus for the provided attribute types. Given a sample, the annotator was instructed to identify a type from each attribute, and then highlight a part of the Polish sentence proving its occurrence. Preci-

[2]The code is available at `https://github.com/st-vincent1/grammatical_agreement_eamt/`.

Count			Context				Example	
`train`	`dev`	`test`	SpGender	IlGender	IlNumber	Formality	*English*	*Polish*
419.9K	0.8K	0.8K	*sp:feminine*	*	*	*	I'm an amateur.	Jestem amator**ką**.
743.6K	0.8K	0.8K	*sp:masculine*	*	*	*	I'm all alone.	Jestem całkiem **sam**.
9.3K	0.2K	0.2K	*	*il:feminine*	*plural*	*informal*	You're smitten.	Jeste**ście** odurz**one**.
73.8K	0.2K	0.2K	*	*il:masculine*	*plural*	*informal*	Have you met Pete?	Pozna**liście** Pete'a?
315.9K	0.2K	0.2K	*	×	*plural*	*informal*	You need to leave.	Musi**cie** wyjść.
326.8K	0.2K	0.2K	*	×	*singular*	*informal*	I got you something.	Przyniosłem **ci** coś.
273.0K	0.2K	0.2K	*	*il:feminine*	*singular*	*informal*	Are you sick?	Jesteś chor**a**?
498.7K	0.2K	0.2K	*	*il:masculine*	*singular*	*informal*	Understand?	Zrozumia**łeś**?
0.7K	0.1K	0.1K	*	*il:feminine*	*plural*	*formal*	Please, let me explain.	Wyjaśnię **paniom**.
2.7K	0.2K	0.2K	*	*il:masculine*	*plural*	*formal*	Aren't you?	**Panowie** nie są?
5.7K	0.2K	0.2K	*	*il:mixed*	*plural*	*formal*	You are wrong.	Myl**ą** się **państwo**.
63.0K	0.2K	0.2K	*	*il:feminine*	*singular*	*formal*	Martini for you?	Dla **pani** martini?
144.0K	0.2K	0.2K	*	*il:masculine*	*singular*	*formal*	Let me have your coat.	Wezmę **pański** płaszcz.
33.5K	0.2K	0.2K	*	×	×	*formal*	Go ahead.	**Proszę** kontynu**ować**.

Table 4: Training data quantities for all combinations of contexts with examples for each combination, with relevant grammatical expressions highlighted. Since Speaker and Interlocutor contexts are always independent, the counts include cases where they co-occur. * = this attribute *may* occur in this place; × = this attribute is never expressed within this category.

sion and recall scores were measured between the judgements of the parser and the annotator. The parser (hereinafter *Detector*) scored near-perfectly (**99.82%** precision and **99.17%** recall averaged over all attributes) and proved suitable for the tasks of both extracting the corpus and evaluating attribute controlling. Beyond input errors leading to incorrect parsing, we observed two consistent cases of failure:

- when the interlocutor is addressed in plural but is in fact singular (in cases like "$\text{Go}_{\text{singular}}$ help her. Maybe you [two] $\text{will}_{\text{plural}}$ figure it out together." the addressee may be interpreted as *plural* instead of *singular* depending on the majority of grammatical matches for each type);
- some tag questions (e.g. "prawda?") or expressions (e.g. the words "kimś" ('$\text{someone}_{\text{instr.}}$'), "czymś" ('$\text{something}_{\text{instr.}}$')) are consistently incorrectly analysed for dependencies, which sometimes leads to triggering of incorrect rules.

Data Selection and Annotation Table 4 shows particular groups of contexts, their typical expression, and total count in the corpus.[3] Similarly to Sennrich et al. (2016), we mask the annotations of half the training samples every epoch at random and give half of the unannotated sentence pairs a random set of attributes. This helps preserve the translation quality of the model's outputs when insufficient context is given.

Our development and test sets are balanced across the 14 context groups (cf. table 4). We gather a total of 4K unique examples for each set. When evaluating each implemented approach, we provide two results: when *complete context* is given, or when an *isolated attribute* type is provided. Consider a complete-context test case within the IlNumber group of

<il:feminine>,*<plural>*,*<formal>* I like you.

The input for the isolated attribute is as follows:

<plural> I like you.

that is, we omit all types but those belonging to the examined attribute. For the *complete context* case we provide the full input. To evaluate each individual type (e.g. *<il:feminine>* or *<formal>*), in the isolated attribute case we gather all development/test cases which match the selected type, with a total count of minimum 200 examples (for *<il:mixed>*) up to 1200 (for *<plural>*).

4.2 Model Settings

We use the Transformer architecture (Vaswani et al., 2017) implemented in PyTorch (Paszke et al., 2019). Similarly to Lakew et al. (2021), we test a range of model alterations.

We split them into two categories: Types as Tags (Tag*) and Embedded Types (Emb*). We scale each approach that was originally proposed as a way of controlling a single attribute to a multi-attribute scenario: for Tag*, we supply multiple tags in a random order, and for Emb* we average the embeddings (see Table 5).

[3]Note that IlGender, IlNumber, Formality are co-dependent, since they all concern the same entity (the interlocutor), and thus different combinations of their types lead to different grammatical expressions.

Approach	Multi-attribute solution	Embedding size	Input space occupied
Types as Tags			
TAGENC▲ (Sennrich et al., 2016)			n_{types}
TAGDEC (Takeno et al., 2017)	$++$	$n_{types} * d_{model}$	$n_{types} + 1$
TAGENCDEC▲ (Lakew et al., 2021)			$2 * n_{types} + 1$
Embedded Types			
EMBPWSUM (Lakew et al., 2021)			0
EMBADD (Schioppa et al., 2021)			0
EMBENC (Ours)	$\frac{\sum types}{n_{types}}$	$n_{types} * d_{model}$	1
EMBSOS (Lample et al., 2019)			0
EMBENCSOS (Ours)			1
OUTBIAS▲ (Michel and Neubig, 2018)	$\frac{\sum types}{n_{types}}$	$n_{types} * len_{vocab}$	0

Table 5: Comparison of examined approaches. $++$ = concatenation. ▲ = Approach originally proposed for single-attribute control and extended by us.

Types as Tags We encode each type of each attribute as a special vocabulary token (e.g. $<singular>$, cf. Table 2). During fine-tuning, these *tags* are concatenated to the source or target[4] sentences and trained like other tokens. We use three settings:

- TAGENC: appending the tags to the source sentence (Sennrich et al., 2016).
- TAGDEC: prepending the tag to the target sentence (Takeno et al., 2017).
- TAGENCDEC: applying tags to both sentences (Niu and Carpuat, 2020).

Average Embedding As an alternative to sequential tagging, embedded types T can be averaged and supplied as a single vector $\overline{E(T)}$ (Lample et al., 2019). We test five settings:

- EMBPWSUM: adding $\overline{E(T)}$ position-wise to each input token (Lakew et al., 2021).
- EMBADD: adding $\overline{E(T)}$ position-wise to Encoder outputs (Schioppa et al., 2021).
- EMBENC: concatenating $\overline{E(T)}$ to the input (cf. Dai et al. (2019), but in our approach the embedding is not trained adversarially).
- EMBSOS: replace the start-of-sequence ($<sos>$) token in the Decoder input with $\overline{E(T)}$ (Lample et al., 2019).
- EMBENCSOS: as an additional setting, we test combining EMBENC and EMBSOS.

As a special case, we test OUTBIAS: adding a type embedding as a bias on the final layer of the Decoder (Michel and Neubig, 2018). We omit the *black-box injection* method of Moryossef et al. (2019) due to its inapplicability to ILGENDER in plural and to FORMALITY. Our baseline is the pre-trained model without attribute information.

4.3 Training Details

We preprocess the corpus with Moses tools for detokenisation and normalising punctuation[5], and by running a short set of custom rules. We train a joint sub-word segmentation model of 16K tokens with SentencePiece (Kudo and Richardson, 2018) and encode both sides of the corpus. We follow the standard training regimen for a 6-layer Transformer (Vaswani et al., 2017) with an input length limit of 100 tokens; this model has just over 52.3M trainable parameters. All training is done on a single 32GB GPU. As the decoding algorithm, we use beam search with a beam size of 5. We pre-train the model until a patience criterion of the chrF++ (Popović, 2017) validation score not increasing for 5 consecutive validation steps (which occur every 3/4th epoch). This happens around the 24th epoch, or after 66 hours of training.

Each of the nine architectural upgrades is a copy of the pre-trained model expanded with the relevant component and fine-tuned. The fine-tuning process exposes the model to the fine-tuning corpus in 10 epochs; performance is validated every half epoch. We select the best checkpoint based on the highest chrF++ score on the development set.

4.4 Evaluation

We consider the following criteria in evaluation:

1. **Translation Quality.** Attribute-controlled

[4]During inference, we supply tags by forcibly decoding the relevant type tokens, followed by a $<null>$ token, before the main decoding step commences.

[5]https://github.com/alvations/sacremoses

	isolated attribute			*complete context*			
Model	chrF++↑	BLEU↑	*Agree*↑ (%)	chrF++↑	BLEU↑	*Agree*↑ (%)	AMBID↑
Baseline	46.60	23.13	74.35	46.60	23.13	74.35	–
TAGENC	**48.95**	**25.52**	99.03	**52.41**	**29.16**	**99.39**	**95.87**
TAGDEC	48.65	**25.40**	99.21	50.83	27.65	96.84	93.15
TAGENCDEC	48.28	25.26	99.35	51.01	28.15	**99.26**	82.66
EMBPWSUM	46.03	22.37	100	51.90	28.69	97.90	88.67
EMBADD	47.45	23.61	**99.96**	51.77	28.56	98.24	87.76
EMBENC	47.72	24.39	83.42	52.23	**28.98**	**99.30**	**95.58**
EMBSOS	48.28	24.90	**99.91**	**52.38**	**29.09**	98.47	92.07
EMBENCSOS	48.60	25.08	**99.87**	51.94	28.77	98.55	92.37
OUTBIAS	48.59	24.98	96.71	49.32	26.11	86.25	94.05

Table 6: Translation performance of all models; "*isolated attribute*" means that only one (the investigated) attribute was revealed to the model. The highlighted scores include the best one in the column and all statistically equivalent results according to a bootstrap resampling method ($p < 0.05$).

translations should be of quality no worse than translations of the non-specialised model.

2. **Grammatical Agreement.** Attribute-controlled hypotheses should completely agree to the specified type where necessary.
3. **Restricted Impact.** Grammatical agreement should only affect words that explicitly render the attributes. Therefore, if no attribute is to be expressed in the hypotheses, then they should be no different from baseline hypotheses.

We evaluate translation quality with chrF++ (Popović, 2017)[6] and BLEU (Papineni et al., 2002). Grammatical agreement is quantified with the help of the *Detector*. For every attribute, we calculate how many hypotheses agree to the correct type t and to the incorrect type $\hat{t}$. Let hyp_t be a hypothesis translated using type t as context, and $agree(hyp, t)$ denote that the *Detector* has found evidence of type t expressed in hyp. We express the total agreement score as:

$$Agree = \frac{agree(hyp_t, t)}{agree(hyp_t, t) + agree(hyp_t, \hat{t})}$$

Finally, we quantify restricted impact with a custom metric, which measures that attribute-independent sentences do not carry any attribute-reliant artifacts; we define this metric, AMBID, as:

$$\text{chrF++}(\text{NMT}(src_a, A), \text{NMT}(src_a, \widehat{A}))$$

where A is a set of attribute types and $\widehat{A}$ is the reverse set.[7] We use an attribute-ambivalent test set of a 1K sentences to calculate this score (Table 3, column "amb_test").

[6]For clarity, we normalise chrF++ scores to a [0, 100] range.

[7]For the type triplet ILGENDER we assume that $\widehat{il{:}masculine}$ = *il:feminine*, $\widehat{il{:}mixed}$ = *il:feminine*, $\widehat{il{:}feminine}$ = *il:masculine*.

5 Results

We report quantitative results in Table 6.

Grammatical Agreement The *Agree* column in Table 6 shows the agreement scores given by the *Detector*. In the isolated attribute scenario, all methods but OUTBIAS and EMBENC achieve near-perfect agreement scores. The agreement scores in the *complete context* scenario remain high for other models except TAGDEC, and pick up for EMBENC, suggesting that controlling several attributes generally has no negative impact on individual attributes.

Translation Quality Attribute-controlling models achieve significant gains over baseline for both the isolated attribute and complete context scenarios, and the gains are consistently higher in the latter, suggesting that exposing the models to more context yields better translations. TAGENC achieves the highest improvement over the baseline in terms of chrF++/BLEU for complete context (+5.81 chrF++/+6.03 BLEU). The gains in translation quality are correlated with agreement scores, except for EMBPWSUM, for which the isolated attribute scenario leads to a near-perfect agreement but low quality scores. Further investigation shows that this model learned to overproduce context-sensitive words when given a context of only a subset of types (e.g. translating "you" as "I" to introduce SPGENDER marking), leading to high agreement scores but degradation in quality. This highlights the importance of pairing an accuracy measure with a translation quality metric.

To investigate how successful the models are at modelling each context group individually, we report the mean chrF++ scores obtained for each

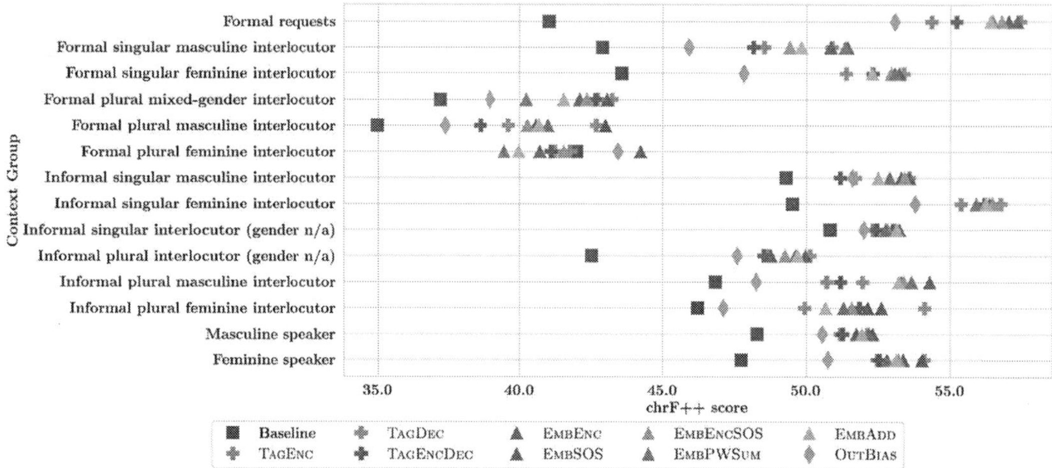

Figure 3: Translation quality (chrF++) for each contextual group.

group's test set (Figure 3). All contextual models bring significant improvements over the baseline except in the *Formal plural feminine interlocutor group*, for which there was little training data (cf. Table 4); improvements are consistently greater for feminine than masculine groups. No single model performs consistently better than others than others, but TAGDEC, EMBPWSUM and OUTBIAS fall behind on most groups. Finally, we observe no significant gain generally from including information in both the Encoder and the Decoder.

Restricted Impact The AMBID scores shown in Table 6 reveal that TAGENC and EMBENC introduce the least variation in attribute-ambivalent utterances, suggesting that adding contextual information to the Encoder input only helps limit creation of unwanted artifacts. The distance of only 4.13 chrF++ points to the ideal score of 100 for the highest-scoring model suggests good separation of grammatical and behavioural agreement. Some separation-specific modelling may further improve this score, but it was outside the scope of this work.

General Discussion The results suggest that TAGENC is the most reliable approach to the presented problem, followed by EMBSOS and EMBENC. Notably, we find other methods dubbed as superior to TAGENC in previous work (EMBADD, TAGDEC and TAGENCDEC) to underperform in our case.

6 Conclusions and Future Work

In this work, we have highlighted the problem of grammatical agreement in translation of TV dialogue in the English-to-Polish language direction. We have created and described a dataset annotated for four speaker and interlocutor attributes that directly influence grammar in dialogue: speaker's gender, interlocutor's gender and number and formality relations between them. We have presented a selection of models capable of controlling these attributes in translation, yielding a performance gain of up to +5.81chrF++/+6.03BLEU over the baseline (non-controlling) model. Finally, we have produced a tool that produces an accuracy score for agreement to each type.

Considering all criteria of evaluation, we have identified TAGENC as the best performing approach, with EMBENC, and EMBSOS also achieving competitive performance. TAGENC may be more attractive in scenarios where interventions in the model architecture are impossible as it can be implemented via data preprocessing alone, but the other two have a more scalable design (cf. §2). Finally, contrary to some previous work, we found no advantages stemming from including the contextual information in the Decoder as well as the Encoder.

Future Work NMT research should strive to move beyond seeing gender as a dichotomous phenomenon (Savoldi et al., 2021). Within this paper we did not consider the scenarios with non-binary interlocutors due to i) lack of available data and ii) lack of consensus regarding non-binary gender expression in the Polish language (Misiek, 2020). However, our work can be applied to non-binary expression once data and more studies are available. Furthermore, the influence in NMT of other extra-textual attributes (e.g. multimodal ones, like spatial information, or emergent ones, such as personal attributes) is yet to be explored. It remains an open question whether such attributes should all be considered individually, or whether there is a way of identifying and/or using them implicitly.

Acknowledgements

This work was supported by the Centre for Doctoral Training in Speech and Language Technologies (SLT) and their Applications funded by UK Research and Innovation [grant number EP/S023062/1].

References

Ailem, Melissa, Jingshu Liu, and Raheel Qader. 2021. Encouraging neural machine translation to satisfy terminology constraints. In *Findings of the Association for Computational Linguistics: ACL-IJCNLP 2021*, pages 1450–1455, Online, August. Association for Computational Linguistics.

Bahdanau, Dzmitry, Kyung Hyun Cho, and Yoshua Bengio. 2015. Neural machine translation by jointly learning to align and translate. *3rd International Conference on Learning Representations, ICLR 2015 - Conference Track Proceedings*, pages 1–15.

Dai, Ning, Jianze Liang, Xipeng Qiu, and Xuanjing Huang. 2019. Style transformer: Unpaired text style transfer without disentangled latent representation. In *Proceedings of the 57th Annual Meeting of the Association for Computational Linguistics*, pages 5997–6007, Florence, Italy, July. Association for Computational Linguistics.

Elaraby, Mostafa, Ahmed Y. Tawfik, Mahmoud Khaled, Hany Hassan, and Aly Osama. 2018. Gender aware spoken language translation applied to English-Arabic. *2nd International Conference on Natural Language and Speech Processing, ICNLSP 2018*, pages 1–6.

Feely, Weston, Eva Hasler, and Adrià de Gispert. 2019. Controlling Japanese honorifics in English-to-Japanese neural machine translation. In *Proceedings of the 6th Workshop on Asian Translation*, pages 45–53, Hong Kong, China, November. Association for Computational Linguistics.

Feldstein, Ron F. 2001. *A Concise Polish Grammar*. Slavic and East European Language Research Center (SEELRC), Duke University, 2001.

Gonen, Hila and Kellie Webster. 2020. Automatically identifying gender issues in machine translation using perturbations. In *Findings of the Association for Computational Linguistics: EMNLP 2020*, pages 1991–1995, Online, November. Association for Computational Linguistics.

Jacovi, Alon, Ana Marasović, Tim Miller, and Yoav Goldberg. 2021. Formalizing Trust in Artificial Intelligence: Prerequisites, Causes and Goals of Human Trust in AI. In *Proceedings of the 2021 ACM Conference on Fairness, Accountability, and Transparency*, FAccT '21, page 624–635, New York, NY, USA. Association for Computing Machinery.

Jassem, Wiktor. 2003. Polish. *Journal of the International Phonetic Association*, 33(1):103–107.

Johnson, Melvin, Mike Schuster, Quoc V. Le, Maxim Krikun, Yonghui Wu, Zhifeng Chen, Nikhil Thorat, Fernanda Viégas, Martin Wattenberg, Greg Corrado, Macduff Hughes, and Jeffrey Dean. 2017. Google's Multilingual Neural Machine Translation System: Enabling Zero-Shot Translation. *Transactions of the Association for Computational Linguistics*, 5:339–351.

Keown, Anne. 2003. Motivations for Polish pronouns of address. *Glossos*, 4(4).

Kieras, Witold and Marcin Wolinski. 2017. Morfeusz 2–analizator i generator fleksyjny dla jezyka polskiego. *Jezyk Polski*, 97(1):75–83.

Koehn, Philipp. 2005. Europarl: A Parallel Corpus for Statistical Machine Translation. In *Conference Proceedings: the tenth Machine Translation Summit*, pages 79–86, Phuket, Thailand. AAMT, AAMT.

Koniuszaniec, G and Hanka Błaszkowska. 2003. Language and gender in Polish. *Gender across Languages*, 3:259–285.

Kudo, Taku and John Richardson. 2018. SentencePiece: A simple and language independent subword tokenizer and detokenizer for neural text processing. In *Proceedings of the 2018 Conference on Empirical Methods in Natural Language Processing: System Demonstrations*, pages 66–71, Brussels, Belgium, November. Association for Computational Linguistics.

Lakew, Surafel Melaku, Mattia Di Gangi, and Marcello Federico. 2019. Controlling the Output Length of Neural Machine Translation. *arXiv*.

Lakew, Surafel M., Marcello Federico, Yue Wang, Cuong Hoang, Yogesh Virkar, Roberto Barra-Chicote, and Robert Enyedi. 2021. Machine translation verbosity control for automatic dubbing. *ICASSP, IEEE International Conference on Acoustics, Speech and Signal Processing - Proceedings*, 2021-June:7538–7542.

Lample, Guillaume, Sandeep Subramanian, Eric Michael Smith, Ludovic Denoyer, Marc'Aurelio Ranzato, and Y. Lan Boureau. 2019. Multiple-attribute text rewriting. *7th International Conference on Learning Representations, ICLR 2019*, pages 1–20.

Lison, Pierre and Jörg Tiedemann. 2016. OpenSubtitles2016: Extracting large parallel corpora from movie and TV subtitles. In *Proceedings of the Tenth International Conference on Language Resources and Evaluation (LREC'16)*, pages 923–929, Portorož, Slovenia, May. European Language Resources Association (ELRA).

Michel, Paul and Graham Neubig. 2018. Extreme adaptation for personalized neural machine translation. In *Proceedings of the 56th Annual Meeting of the Association for Computational Linguistics (Volume 2: Short Papers)*, pages 312–318, Melbourne, Australia, July. Association for Computational Linguistics.

Misiek, Szymon. 2020. Misgendered in Translation?: Genderqueerness in Polish Translations of English-language Television Series. *Anglica. An International Journal of English Studies*, pages 165–185.

Moryossef, Amit, Roee Aharoni, and Yoav Goldberg. 2019. Filling gender & number gaps in neural machine translation with black-box context injection. In *Proceedings of the First Workshop on Gender Bias in Natural Language Processing*, pages 49–54, Florence, Italy, August. Association for Computational Linguistics.

Niu, Xing and Marine Carpuat. 2020. Controlling neural machine translation formality with synthetic supervision. *AAAI 2020 - 34th AAAI Conference on Artificial Intelligence*, 2(1):8568–8575.

Papineni, Kishore, Salim Roukos, Todd Ward, and Wei-Jing Zhu. 2002. Bleu: a method for automatic evaluation of machine translation. In *Proceedings of the 40th Annual Meeting of the Association for Computational Linguistics*, pages 311–318, Philadelphia, Pennsylvania, USA, July. Association for Computational Linguistics.

Paszke, Adam, Sam Gross, Francisco Massa, Adam Lerer, James Bradbury, Gregory Chanan, Trevor Killeen, Zeming Lin, Natalia Gimelshein, Luca Antiga, Alban Desmaison, Andreas Köpf, Edward Yang, Zach DeVito, Martin Raison, Alykhan Tejani, Sasank Chilamkurthy, Benoit Steiner, Lu Fang, Junjie Bai, and Soumith Chintala. 2019. PyTorch: An imperative style, high-performance deep learning library. *Advances in Neural Information Processing Systems*, 32(NeurIPS).

Popović, Maja. 2017. chrF++: words helping character n-grams. In *Proceedings of the Second Conference on Machine Translation*, pages 612–618, Copenhagen, Denmark, September. Association for Computational Linguistics.

Rabinovich, Ella, Shachar Mirkin, Raj Nath Patel, Lucia Specia, and Shuly Wintner. 2017. Personalized machine translation: Preserving original author traits. *15th Conference of the European Chapter of the Association for Computational Linguistics, EACL 2017 - Proceedings of Conference*, 1:1074–1084.

Savoldi, Beatrice, Marco Gaido, Luisa Bentivogli, Matteo Negri, and Marco Turchi. 2021. Gender Bias in Machine Translation. *Transaction of the Association for Computational Lignuistics (TACL)*.

Schioppa, Andrea, David Vilar, Artem Sokolov, and Katja Filippova. 2021. Controlling Machine Translation for Multiple Attributes with Additive Interventions. In *Proceedings of the 2021 Conference on Empirical Methods in Natural Language Processing*, pages 6676–6696, Online and Punta Cana, Dominican Republic, 11. Association for Computational Linguistics.

Sennrich, Rico, Barry Haddow, and Alexandra Birch. 2016. Controlling politeness in neural machine translation via side constraints. *2016 Conference of the North American Chapter of the Association for Computational Linguistics: Human Language Technologies, NAACL HLT 2016 - Proceedings of the Conference*, pages 35–40.

Sigurðsson, Halldór Ármann and Verner Egerland. 2009. Impersonal null-subjects in Icelandic and elsewhere*. *Studia Linguistica*, 63(1):158–185.

Stahlberg, Dagmar, F Braun, L Irmen, and Sabine Sczesny. 2007. Representation of the sexes in language. *Social Communication*, pages 163–187.

Stone, Gerald. 1977. Address in the Slavonic Languages. *The Slavonic and East European Review*, 55(4):491–505.

Sutskever, Ilya, Oriol Vinyals, and Quoc V. Le. 2014. Sequence to sequence learning with neural networks. *Advances in Neural Information Processing Systems*, 4(January):3104–3112.

Takeno, Shunsuke, Masaaki Nagata, and Kazuhide Yamamoto. 2017. Controlling Target Features in Neural Machine Translation via Prefix Constraints. *Afnlp*, pages 55–63.

Tuora, Ryszard and Łukasz Kobyliński. 2019. Integrating Polish Language Tools and Resources in Spacy. In *Proceedings of PP-RAI 2019 Conference*, pages 210–214.

Vanmassenhove, Eva, Christian Hardmeier, and Andy Way. 2018. Getting gender right in neural machine translation. *Proceedings of the 2018 Conference on Empirical Methods in Natural Language Processing, EMNLP 2018*, pages 3003–3008.

Vaswani, Ashish, Noam Shazeer, Niki Parmar, Jakob Uszkoreit, Llion Jones, Aidan N. Gomez, Lukasz Kaiser, and Illia Polosukhin. 2017. Attention is all you need. *Advances in Neural Information Processing Systems*, pages 5999–6009.

Auxiliary Subword Segmentations as Related Languages for Low Resource Multilingual Translation

Nishant Kambhatla **Logan Born** **Anoop Sarkar**
School of Computing Science
Simon Fraser University
8888 University Drive, Burnaby BC, Canada
{nkambhat, loborn, anoop}@sfu.ca

Abstract

We propose a novel technique of combining multiple subword tokenizations of a single source-target language pair for use with multilingual neural translation training methods. These alternate segmentations function like related languages in multilingual translation, improving translation accuracy for low-resource languages and producing translations that are lexically diverse and morphologically rich. We also introduce a cross-teaching technique which yields further improvements in translation accuracy and cross-lingual transfer between high- and low-resource language pairs. Compared to other strong multilingual baselines, our approach yields average gains of +1.7 BLEU across the four low-resource datasets from the multilingual TED-talks dataset. Our technique does not require additional training data and is a drop-in improvement for any existing neural translation system.

1 Introduction

Multilingual neural machine translation (NMT, Dong et al. 2015; Johnson et al. 2017) models are capable of translating from multiple source and target languages. Besides allowing efficient parameter sharing (Aharoni et al., 2019) these models facilitate inherent transfer learning (Zoph et al., 2016; Firat et al., 2016) that can especially benefit low resource languages (Nguyen and Chiang, 2017; Gu et al., 2018; Neubig and Hu, 2018; Tan et al., 2019). A common technique to address lexical sharing and complex morphology in multilingual NMT is to decompose longer words into shorter subword units (Sennrich et al., 2016). Since subword units are produced using heuristic methods, not all subwords are created equally. This can put low- and extremely low-resource languages at a disadvantage, even when these languages are paired with a suitable high resource language. To diminish the impact of rare subwords in NMT, Kambhatla et al. (2022) leverage ciphertexts to augment the training data by constructing multiple-views of the source text. "Soft" decomposition methods based on transfer learning (Wang et al., 2018) address the problem of sub-optimal word segmentation with shared character-level lexical and sentence representations across multiple source languages (Gu et al., 2018). Wang et al. (2021) addressed this problem with a multiview-subword regularization technique that also improves the effectiveness of cross-lingual transfer in pretrained multilingual representations by simultaneously finetuning on different input segmentations from a heuristic and a probabilistic tokenizer. While subword regularization methods (Kudo, 2018; Provilkov et al., 2020) have been widely explored in NMT, this work is the first to study them together with multilingual training methods.

Concretely, we construct pairs of "related languages" by segmenting an input corpus twice, each time with a different vocabulary size and algorithm for finding subwords; we use these "languages" (really, views of the same language) for multilingual training of an NMT model. We propose *Multi-Sub training*, a method that combines multilingual NMT training methods with a diverse set of auxiliary subword segmentations which func-

Macken, Rufener, Van den Bogaert, Daems, Tezcan, Vanroy, Fonteyne, Barrault, Costa-jussà, Kemp, Pilos, Declercq, Koponen, Forcada, Scarton, Moniz (eds.)
Proceedings of the 23rd Annual Conference of the European Association for Machine Translation, p. 131–140
Ghent, Belgium, June 2022.

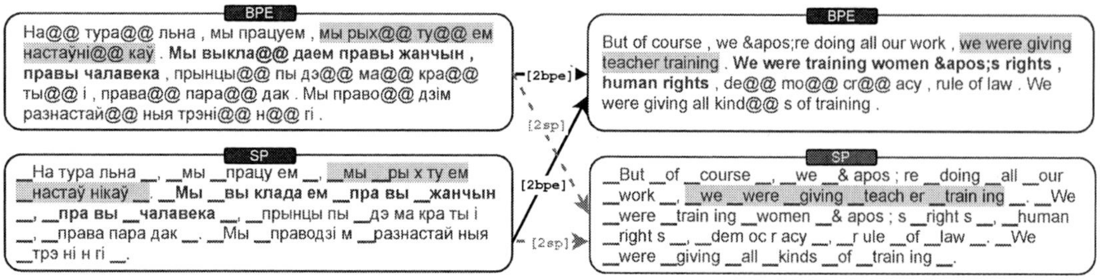

Figure 1: An illustration of the interaction between the primary (BPE) and auxiliary (SP) subwords for the same sample from the `be-en` dev set where each type of segmentation is treated as a separate language. The model is taught to translate into a specific segmentation via multilingual training using the target "language" tags `[2bpe]` and `[2sp]`. The sentence in bold type font shows both variants of the source sentence translating to the same target sentence. The colored spans show different segmentations of the same word(s) in source/target.

tion like related languages in a multilingual setting since they have distinct but partially-overlapping vocabularies and share the same underlying lexical and grammatical features. Our model is able to transfer information between segmentations analogous to the way information is transferred between typologically similar languages.

We also introduce a *cross-teaching* technique in which a model is trained to translate source sentences from one subword tokenization into target sentences from a different subword tokenization. By using Multi-Sub training together with cross-teaching, we obtain strong results on four low-resource languages in the multilingual TED talks dataset outperforming strong multilingual baselines, with the most significant improvements in the lowest-resource languages. In addition to improving the BLEU scores, our technique captures word compositionality better leading to improved lexical diversity and morphological richness in the target language. Multi-Sub with cross-teaching is better at clustering different languages in the sentence embedding space than previous methods including Multi-Sub without cross-teaching.

2 Auxiliary Segmentation as a Related Language

Pairing related languages is common in multilingual NMT[1]: Nguyen and Chiang (2017) combine Uzbek/Turkish and Uzbek/Uyghur; Johnson et al. (2017) study multilingual translation to and from English with pairs such as Spanish/Portuguese or Japanese/Korean. Neubig and Hu (2018) pair low resource languages like Azerbaijani with a related "helper" language like Turkish.

We take these techniques as motivation for the present work. Our principal contribution is to rethink what it means to use "related" languages in a multilingual translation model. Beyond simply employing *other* languages from the same family, or those with high lexical overlap, we show that a model trained on different segmentations *of the same language* can produce improvements in translation quality.

Rather than segmenting a corpus with a single tokenizer prior to training a translation model, we produce multiple segmentations using different tokenizers. Consider the example sentences in Figure 1. On both the source and target sides, the same sentence is represented using both Byte-pair Encodings (BPEs, Sennrich et al. 2016, with a "@@" separator) and in parallel as sentencepieces (SP, Kudo 2018, with a "_" separator). Each segmentation uses a different vocabulary size, which guarantees that their subword sequences are to some extent distinct. The two tokenizations still resemble one other in many ways: (i) they have a non-trivial degree of lexical overlap (mostly between subwords which do not fall along word boundaries); (ii) they share the same grammatical structure, as both represent the same underlying language; and (iii) both sequences have the same semantic interpretation. We thus refer to the two segmentations as a pair of "related languages".

Applying two segmentations to a parallel corpus yields a total of four "languages": the source and target represented as BPE subwords, and the same represented using SP subwords. We obtain two source "languages" (each containing data from both high and low resource languages) and two target "languages". Using this four way configuration, we train a model following a common multi-

[1] Here we do not distinguish between languages which are related in the linguistic sense (having some genetic affiliation) and those which are related in a more pragmatic sense of having high lexical overlap.

lingual training method (Johnson et al., 2017): depending on the segmentation we want to translate into, we prepend a target token **[2bpe]** or **[2sp]** to the source side. We explore two different multilingual training configurations:

[BPE+SP]: In this setting, a source sentence in a particular segmentation is translated into the target with the same segmentation. Specifically, this model is trained multilingually on the pairs

BPE [src] → BPE [tgt]

SP [src] → SP [tgt]

Cross-teaching: In addition to [BPE+SP], in this setting, each source sentence with a particular segmentation is translated into the target with alternate segmentation. This multilingual model is therefore trained on the following pairs:

BPE [src] → SP [tgt]

SP [src] → BPE [tgt]

Using multilingual training, our model is able to *transfer* information between BPE and SP segmentations in much the same way that conventional multilingual models transfer information between languages with a shared linguistic affiliation. Unlike data augmentation techniques which generate synthetic training data, Multi-Sub training uses only the content of the original training corpus. Furthermore, contrary to other works which employ multiple segmentations (Wang et al., 2018; Wu et al., 2020), Multi-Sub training and cross-teaching do not affect model architecture and do not require specialised training. Thus Multi-Sub training can be used as a simple, drop-in improvement to an existing neural translation model.

3 Experiments

3.1 Experimental Setup

Data Following prior work on low-resource and multilingual NMT (Neubig and Hu, 2018, Wang et al., 2018) we use the multilingual Ted talks dataset (Qi et al., 2018). We use four low resource languages (LRL): Azerbaijani (az), Belarusian (be), Galician (gl) and Slovak (sk), and four high resource languages (HRL): Turkish (tr), Russian (ru), Brazilian-Portuguese (pt), and Czech (cs). In all experiments and baselines, each LRL is paired with the related HRL and English is the target language.

Table 1 shows general statistics for each dataset. Based on the size of the training data, we consider az, be and gl as extremely low-resource while sk is a slightly higher-resource dataset.

LRL	#train	#dev	#test	HRL	#train
az	5.9k	671	903	tr	182k
be	4.5k	248	664	ru	208k
gl	10.0k	682	1007	pt	185k
sk	61.5k	2271	2445	cs	103k

Table 1: Statistics from our low resource language (LRL) and high resource language (HRL) datasets.

Model Details Our model comprises a single bi-directional LSTM as encoder and decoder, with 128-dimensional word embeddings and 512-dimensional hidden states. We are careful to keep this configuration consistent with our baseline model (Neubig and Hu, 2018) to ensure a fair comparison. We use `fairseq`[2] to implement the baseline as well as our proposed models. We set dropout probability to 0.3, and use an adam optimizer with a learning rate of 0.001. In practice, we train a Multi-Sub model until convergence, and then use this model to continue training on cross-teaching data until convergence. For inference, we use beam size 5 with length penalty. We use `sacrebleu`[3] (Post, 2018) to report BLEU (Papineni et al., 2002) scores on the detokenized translations. We perform statistical significance tests for our results based on bootstrap resampling (Koehn, 2004) using `compare-mt` toolkit.[4]

For fair comparison with prior work, we use BPE (Subword-nmt, Sennrich et al. 2016) as our primary segmentation toolkit and sentencepiece (SP, Kudo 2018) as our auxiliary tokenizer. We only use the BPE segmentations to tune our model via validation. In other words, while we train on both BPE and SP, we save model checkpoints that are optimized for BPE tokenized inputs.[5]

Following Neubig and Hu (2018), we separately learn 8k BPE subwords on each of the source and target languages. When combining an LRL and a HRL, we take the union of the vocabulary on the source side and the target side separately. We use the same procedure with the SP tokenizer using a subword vocabulary size of 4k. To train BPE and SP together, we take the union of the vocabularies

[2] `https://github.com/pytorch/fairseq`

[3] SacreBLEU signature: BLEU+CASE.MIXED+NUMREFS.1 +SMOOTH.EXP+TOK.13A+VERSION.1.4.14

[4] `https://github.com/neulab/compare-mt`

[5] Our model can handle sentencepiece inputs as well. For a model that performs *equally* well on BPE and SP, construct a validation set with equal number of source sentences with both segmentations and save the checkpoints optimized for the validation metric. We chose BPE segments for validation to be comparable with previous work.

Lex Unit	Model	tr/az	ru/be	pt/gl	cs/sk
Word	Lookup	7.66	13.03	28.65	25.24
Sub-joint	Lookup	9.40	11.72	22.67	24.97
Sub-sep	UniEnc (Gu et al., 2018)	4.80	8.13	14.58	12.09
Sub-sep	Lookup (Neubig and Hu, 2018)[6]	10.8	16.2	27.7	28.4
Sub-sep	Adaptation (All→Bi) (ibid.)	11.7	18.3	28.8	28.2
Word	SDE (Wang et al., 2018)	11.82	18.71	**30.30**	28.77
Sub-sep	SDE (ibid.)	12.35	16.30	28.94	28.35
Multi-Sub	Lookup [BPE + SP] (Ours)	12.0*	18.5**	28.6*	**28.8**†
(BPE 8k + SP 4k)	Lookup + Cross-teaching (Ours)	**12.7****	**18.8****	29.6**	28.6†

Table 2: All models are trained on a LRL and a related HRL with English as the target language with LSTMs. BLEU scores are reported on the test set of the LRL. The sub-sep lookup model (Neubig and Hu, 2018) is our primary baseline (shaded in grey). Our best results compared to the baseline are underlined. Bolding indicates best overall results on the datasets. We indicate statistical significance w.r.t primary baseline with † ($p < 0.05$), ∗ ($p < 0.001$) and ∗∗ ($p < 0.0001$).

of the source and target sides separately, resulting in a vocabulary which is union of the BPE and SP subword vocabularies of each side.

3.2 Main results

We compare the results of our *Multi-Sub* models against various baselines in Table 2. *Sub-sep* models use a union of subword vocabularies learned separately for each of the source and target languages; the union is performed separately for the source and target sides yielding two separate vocabularies. *Sub-joint* refers to subword vocabularies learned jointly on the concatenation of all of the source and target languages. Such models consistently perform worse than their *sub-sep* counterparts for all datasets, as the HRL tends to occupy a larger share of the vocabulary and leaves the LRL with both a smaller vocabulary as well as smaller subwords. Our reimplementation of the *sub-sep* model (Neubig and Hu, 2018) mitigates this by (separately) learning the same number of subwords for the HRL and LRL. Using words instead of subwords performs on par with the *sub-sep* model for `gl` → `en` but worse for other languages.

We see that our model, Multi-Sub, handily outperforms all of these baselines. Compared to the *de-facto* sub-sep model (highlighted in grey, and used as the baseline in the rest of the paper), Multi-Sub without cross-teaching gains +1.2 BLEU points on `az` and `be`, and +0.9 on `gl`. The improvement on `cs` is not large, but is significant at +0.4 BLEU.

We also compare our approach against more sophisticated models, such as soft decoupled encoding (SDE, Wang et al. 2018) which shares lexical and latent semantic representations across multiple source languages. Our modest Multi-Sub model with cross-teaching outperforms SDE (with *words* as lexical units) on three out of four languages, with the largest gain being +0.9 BLEU on `az` → `en`. Multi-Sub consistently and significantly outperforms *subword*-level SDE on all language pairs with gains ranging from +0.4 BLEU to +2.5 BLEU. Note that although Multi-Sub is -0.7 BLEU behind *word-level* SDE on `gl`, it outperforms sub-sep by +2.6 BLEU and *subword-level* SDE by +2.5 BLEU.

Overall, our models are consistently better than the sub-sep baseline. For most languages, substantial improvements over the baseline come when the Multi-Sub model is combined with cross-teaching.

3.3 Comparison with Subword Regularization

Table 3 contrasts Multi-Sub against BPE-dropout (Provilkov et al., 2020), a subword regularization technique.[7] For comparison we report results from the baseline sub-sep model with and without subword regularization. Our implementation applies BPE-dropout to the training data with probability $p = 0.1$, and the model and training are otherwise identical to sub-sep.

Although subword regularization improves upon the baseline model, the difference is small, likely because of the small amount of data avail-

[6]The numbers are from our reimplementation of Neubig and Hu (2018). Original BLEU scores on this dataset were az: 10.9, be: 15.8, gl: 27.3, sk: 25.5 while a reimplementation by Wang et al. (2018) yields az: 10.9, be: 16.17, gl: 28.1, sk: 28.5. Our implementation matches the performance on all test sets except for gl where we lag by 0.5 points.

[7]Using only one tokenizer (either BPE or SP) with different subword sizes closely resembles subword regularization. Using SP and BPE, on the other hand, results in different word-boundary markers that makes our technique distinct.

	tr/az	ru/be	pt/gl	cs/sk
Sub-sep	10.8	16.2	27.7	28.4
+ SR	11.0	16.6	28.4	28.2
Multi-sub	**12.7**	**18.8**	**29.6**	**28.8**

Table 3: Comparing subword regularization (SR) with our best results. We use BPE-dropout (Provilkov et al., 2020) at $p = 0.1$.

able for the LRLs. By contrast our Multi-Sub technique yields much larger gains.

Discussion BPE-dropout (Provilkov et al., 2020) is a subword regularization technique that exposes the model to learn better word compositionalities by probabilistically producing multiple segmentations for each word. Multi-Sub, on the other hand, uses a secondary subword segmentation of lower vocabulary size and leverages its compositionalities as a related language to learn better representations. In Multi-Sub with cross-teaching, the model learns to produce four way translations on the same source and target languages: BPE [src] $\rightarrow$ {BPE [tgt] , SP [tgt]} and SP [src] $\rightarrow$ {BPE [tgt] , SP [tgt]}. Although this method is deterministic, and the model learns from only two unique subword sequences instead of one (e.g. sub-sep), this inter-segmentation interaction through multilingual training helps the model learn better compositionalities and morphology. See Section 4.2 for a discussion on the linguistic complexity of the output translations.

3.4 Choice of Auxiliary Subwords

Our primary subword tokenizer is BPE with 8000 subwords; we use sentencepiece (SP) as our auxiliary subword tokenizer. To choose the right auxiliary subword vocabulary size, we experiment with three different sizes (6k, 4k and 2k) on `tr/az` and `ru/be` datasets. To determine the optimal vocabulary size, we focus on two key aspects of the candidate segmentations: translation quality and average sentence length. Figure 2 presents a summary of our results.

On both datasets, subword vocabularies of sizes 6k and 4k yield slightly lower BLEU scores than the baseline with 8k subwords; the drop is minimal (`az`: 10.4 vs. 10.1, `be`: 15.6 vs. 15.5 for 6k and 4k). Performance is substantially worse on the same datasets with 2k subwords (7.2 for `az` and 14.1 for `be`) so we reject the 2k setting.

Next, we compare the average sentence lengths

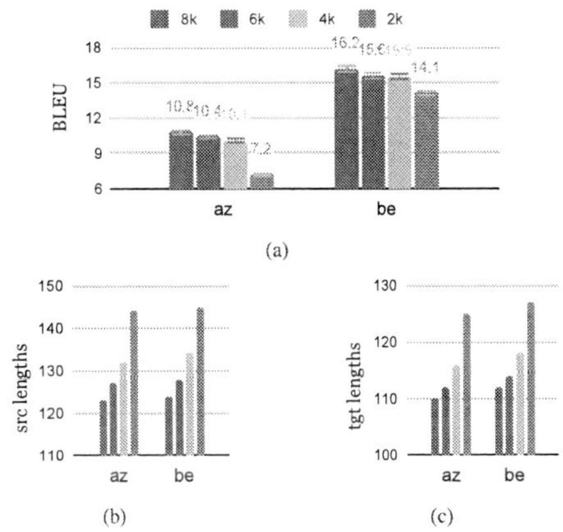

Figure 2: Effect of auxiliary subword vocabulary size on BLEU (a) and sentence length (b, c) in `tr/az` and `ru/be`.

in the subword-tokenized training data (both source and target sides) across different subword vocabulary sizes. At a vocabulary size of 6k, sentence length does not vary substantially from the length found with 8k subwords (Figure 2(b, c)). 4k subwords yield a more significant increase in sentence length on both source (`tr/az`: +9, `ru/be`: +10) and target sides for both datasets. This is favourable since this guarantees as many new subwords as possible in the sentence without increasing its length dramatically. On the basis of these results, we have chosen 4k SP subwords for our auxiliary segmentations.

4 Analysis

4.1 Correlation to Data Availability

Using a secondary subword model as a related language yields different degrees of improvement in different languages. We investigate whether these variations correlate with the degree to which the LRL is "low-resource".

We report (Table 4) the amount of training data available for the LRL, the word-level vocabulary size of each LRL (v_{LRL}), and the ratio of this size to the vocabulary size of the corresponding HRL

	#train	v_{LRL}	$\frac{v_{LRL}}{v_{HRL}}$	BLEU Δ
az	5.94k	13.1k	11.29	+1.90
be	4.50k	9.9k	11.43	+2.61
gl	10.03k	10.9k	27.69	+1.90
sk	61.50k	48.5k	80.01	+0.40

Table 4: Comparison of size of training data in LRL with the BLEU improvements. Column 4 shows the ratio of the word vocabularies of LRL (v_{LRL}) to HRL (v_{HRL}). The ratios are multiplied by 100 for readability.

		Model	BLEU	TTR	RTTR	LTTR	MTTR ↓	HD-D	MTLD	MTLD-A	MTLD-Bi	Yule's K ↓
Az→En		Reference	–	0.1845	22.98	0.8248	0.0417	0.8738	106.60	108.47	108.17	80.68
	1	Base	10.8	0.0855	10.9615	0.7466	0.0600	0.7750	33.9342	38.3466	38.1259	170.4321
	2	BPE 8k + SP 4k	12.0	0.0971	12.2866	0.7591	0.0572	0.7936	40.0937	44.7958	44.8005	152.0778
	3	2 + Cross-teach	12.7	**0.0993**	**12.4746**	**0.7610**	**0.0569**	**0.7961**	**41.3529**	**45.4622**	**45.3590**	**149.4563**
Be→En		Reference	–	0.1863	20.83	0.8219	0.0434	0.8687	102.95	104.44	104.3692	85.73
	1	Base	16.2	0.1149	13.0503	0.7714	0.0556	0.8045	51.1452	52.4293	52.6571	139.7345
	2	BPE 8k + SP 4k	18.5	0.1225	13.7806	0.7777	0.0542	0.8017	51.9363	52.9719	53.0382	147.5613
	3	2 + Cross-teach	18.8	**0.1249**	**14.0746**	**0.7799**	**0.0536**	**0.8071**	**54.8368**	**55.6391**	**55.7884**	**142.6042**
Gl→En		Reference	–	0.1484	19.45	0.8043	0.0462	0.8643	91.22	94.81	94.67	87.92
	1	Base	27.7	0.1329	17.1629	0.7924	0.0492	0.8312	72.9798	73.9316	73.8523	120.5782
	2	BPE 8k + SP 4k	28.6	0.1365	17.6551	0.7952	0.0485	0.8328	**76.0790**	**75.5915**	**75.5815**	119.1850
	3	2 + Cross-teach	29.6	**0.1366**	**17.7624**	**0.7955**	**0.0484**	**0.8307**	74.6902	73.7315	73.7201	**112.5075**
Sk→En		Reference	–	0.1253	25.5328	0.8047	0.0423	0.8689	95.38	102.52	102.24	86.20
	1	Base	28.4	0.0935	18.9185	0.7769	0.0484	0.8383	72.7529	74.8386	74.9117	112.8484
	2	BPE 8k + SP 4k	28.8	**0.0954**	19.3010	**0.7787**	**0.0480**	**0.8411**	**74.5821**	**76.1596**	**76.2799**	**110.8807**
	3	2 + Cross-teach	28.6	0.0947	**19.3118**	0.7784	**0.0480**	0.8379	72.8657	74.7803	74.8770	114.8330

Table 5: Lexical diversity of the reference human translations vs. model outputs in different settings for each LRL.

(v_{HRL}). The ratio v_{LRL}/v_{HRL} is directly proportional to the number of training samples in the LRLs. This ratio has a generally *negative* correlation to the BLEU gains in our models—the more training data is available, the smaller the improvements. This strongly suggests that using auxiliary subwords as a foreign language is a technique best suited to low resource languages.

4.2 Linguistic Complexity

While estimating linguistic complexity is a multifarious task, lexical and morphological diversity are two of its major components. In this section we perform an exhaustive assessment of our models' translations using lexical diversity metrics (Section 4.2.1) and morphological inflectional diversity metrics (Section 4.2.2).

4.2.1 Lexical Richness

We use several metrics to quantify lexical diversity across translations from different models.[8] The metrics include type-token ratio (TTR) and its variants—Root TTR (RTTR, Guiraud 1960), Log TTR (LTTR), and (MATTR, Covington and McFall 2010)—hypergeometric distribution D (HDD, McCarthy and Jarvis 2007), measure of textual, lexical diversity (MTLD, McCarthy 2005) and Yule's K (Yule, 2014). The scores for these measures are presented in Table 5 for our model outputs and for the reference human translations.

On average, Multi-Sub training with cross-teaching significantly improves the lexical diversity of the generated translations. Improvements in lexical diversity correlate with BLEU scores in all languages (which need not be the case, cf. Vanmassenhove et al. 2021), implying that our methods produce translations which are not only more accurate, but also richer and more varied in terms of vocabulary. These effects are most pronounced in the lowest-resource languages, `az` and `be`, where cross-teaching yields improvements in every metric relative to both the baseline and Multi-Sub training without cross-teaching. In `gl`, cross-teaching yields improvements in all metrics except MTLD and its variants, which are optimized by Multi-Sub training without cross-teaching. `Sk` is unique in that the greatest improvements for most metrics come from Multi-Sub training without cross-teaching. This parallels the pattern observed in the BLEU scores (Table 4), and confirms our earlier claim that cross-teaching is most effective in cases of extreme data scarcity, while Multi-Sub training without cross-teaching works better for high resource languages.

4.2.2 Morphological Richness

To examine the morphological complexity of the translations produced by our models, we averaged the inflectional diversity of the lemmas. Following Vanmassenhove et al. (2021), we used the Spacy-udpipe lemmatizer to retrieve all lemmas.[9]

Shannon Entropy (H, Shannon 1948) is used to measure the variety of inflected forms associated with a given lemma (higher entropy means more variation). Entropy is averaged across each lemma

[8] The intent of this section is not to claim that LD metrics are potential indicators of proficiency, quality or sophistication; they simply represent qualities which may be desirable for certain applications, cf. Vanmassenhove et al. (2021)

[9] `https://github.com/TakeLab/spacy-udpipe`

	Model	BLEU	H ↑	D ↓
Az→En	Reference	–	69.26	54.75
1	Base	10.8	64.12	59.14
2	BPE 8k + SP 4k	12.0	63.67	59.67
3	2 + Cross-teach	12.7	**65.62**	**57.97**
Be→En	Reference	–	71.24	53.97
1	Base	16.2	64.12	59.14
2	BPE 8k + SP 4k	18.5	67.32	67.78
3	2 + Cross-teach	18.8	**67.78**	**57.52**
Gl→En	Reference	–	68.27	55.88
1	Base	27.7	66.64	56.95
2	BPE 8k + SP 4k	28.6	**66.93**	56.95
3	2 + Cross-teach	29.6	66.20	**56.92**
Sk→En	Reference	–	69.03	55.41
1	Base	28.4	62.96	59.18
2	BPE 8k + SP 4k	28.8	**63.41**	58.91
3	2 + Cross-teach	28.6	62.50	**59.37**

Table 6: Morphological diversity measures comparing our model outputs against the human references.

in the model outputs.

Simpson's Diversity Index (D, Simpson 1949) measures the probability that two randomly-sampled items have the same label; large values imply homogeneity (most items belong to the same category). We measure morphological diversity by computing the probability that two instances of a given lemma represent the same inflected form.

The results in Table 6 parallel the lexical diversity evaluation: in the extremely low-resource languages `az` and `be`, cross-teaching yields a clear improvement in both the entropy and diversity index of the output translations. The model thus employs a greater variety of inflectional forms, which provides more choices to the decoder (Vanmassenhove et al., 2021) (c.f. Fig. 8). In slightly higher-resource languages like `sk`, the impact of cross-teaching is less pronounced: the best diversity index is in `gl`, but Multi-Sub training without cross-teaching yields the best entropy. Multi-Sub training without cross-teaching also yields the greatest degree of morphological diversity in `sk`.

Model	**gl**	**sk**
Base	0.39	0.11
Multi-Sub/Cross-teaching	**0.51***†	**0.12**†

Table 7: F1 scores on zero-shot NER in `sk` and `gl`. † means the best result comes from cross-teaching; ∗ means the best result comes without cross-teaching.

4.3 Improved Cross-lingual Transfer

Downstream Task: NER Multi-Sub training improves the usefulness of subword embeddings

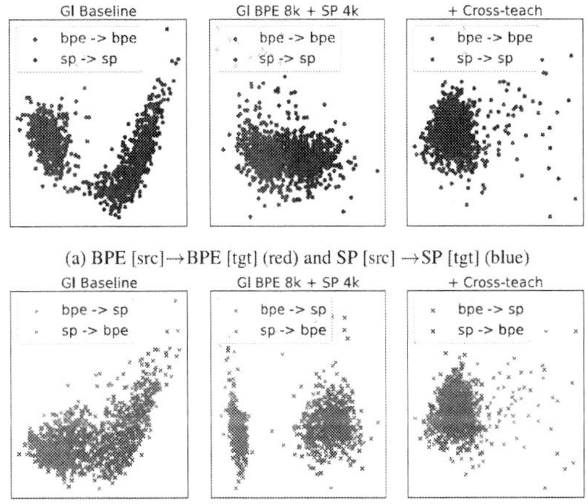

(a) BPE [src]→BPE [tgt] (red) and SP [src] →SP [tgt] (blue)

(b) BPE [src]→SP [tgt] (red) and SP [src] →BPE [tgt] (blue)

Figure 3: PCA decomposition of Galician sentence representations in the baseline (left), Multi-Sub (center), and cross-teaching (right) settings. Multi-Sub training can reduce separation between tokenizations, while the addition of cross-teaching eliminates separation entirely.

for downstream tasks. We train NER models on `pt` and `cs` using the pre-trained embeddings from our translation models; then, following Sharoff 2017, we evaluate each of these models on the corresponding LRL.[10] Since the NER models are never trained on LRL data, this is a zero-shot evaluation where model performance should reflect the degree of multilinguality in the pre-trained embeddings. Table 7 reports F1 scores for this task. We observe that Multi-Sub training on its own can yield significant performance improvements (as in `gl`), but cross-teaching is sometimes required to obtain optimal results (as in `sk`). Together with the results in Figure 3, this suggests that cross-teaching can play a crucial role in facilitating cross-lingual transfer.

Visualizations of Sentence Embeddings We find that cross-teaching significantly reduces the separation between different tokenizations in the sentence representations of certain languages. Figure 3 shows the distribution of sentence representations produced by our two tokenizers. In the baseline, BPE-tokenized sentences are clearly separated from (parallel) SP-tokenized sentences; in the Multi-Sub setting we observe less separation, although distinct clusters of BPE and SP inputs are still clearly visible. By contrast, in the cross-teaching setting, there is significant overlap be-

[10] `cs` training data taken from Sevcíková et al. 2007, `sk` test data from Piskorski et al. 2017, and `pt`/`gl` training and test data from Garcia and Gamallo 2014

gl (src)	en (ref.)	sub-sep	SDE	multi-sub+cross-teach
Se queres saber sobre o clima, preguntas a un climatólogo.	If you want to know about climate, you ask a climatologist.	If you want to know about climate, you're asking a college friend.	If you want to know about climate, they ask for a weather.	If you want to know about the climat, you ask a climatologist.

Table 8: Example of translations of the same source sentence from `gl`→`en` test set with different models.

tween the representations of BPE and SP inputs.

This suggests that cross-teaching serves to eliminate "monolingual" subspaces (that is, subspaces representing a single tokenization) in favor of representing all input languages in the same joint space. On the basis of this result, we argue that cross-teaching is an effective technique for increasing the degree of multilinguality in a translation model.[11]

5 Qualitative Analysis

We list translations for the baseline *sub-sep* and SDE models along with our Multi-Sub model in Table 8. While sub-sep results in an entirely unrelated translation of the `gl` word climatólogo, SDE produces a related word weather. Multi-Sub, however, produces an accurate translation of the word which is climatologist.

6 Related Work

Several techniques have been proposed to improve lexical representations for multilingual machine translation. Zoph et al. (2016) propose to first train a HRL parent model, then transfer some of the learned parameters to the LRL child model to initialize and constrain training. Similarly, Nguyen and Chiang (2017) pair related languages together and transfer source word embeddings from parent-HRL words to their child-LRL equivalents. Johnson et al. (2017); Neubig and Hu (2018), on the other hand, learn a joint vocabulary over several languages and train a single NMT model on the concatenated data. Gu et al. (2018) introduce a latent embedding space shared by all languages to enhance parameter sharing in lexical representation. Wang et al. (2018); Gao et al. (2020) use a similar idea but use character n-gram encodings (SDE) instead of the conventional subword/word embeddings. By contrast Multi-Sub does not involve any architectural changes and improves the representation of low-resource languages by training on multiple segmentations of the same corpus.

Subword-regularization methods (Kudo, 2018; Provilkov et al., 2020) share the motivation of alleviating sub-optimal subwords by exposing a model to multiple segmentations of the same word. However, our method is substantially different in that (i) we use two completely different subword algorithms with different vocabulary sizes (*contra* Wang et al. 2021), and (ii) we do not rely on expensive sampling procedures (*contra* Kudo 2018) or additional data to learn an LM. Especially for low-resource languages, our method not only improves translation quality but also enhances a model's cross-lingual transfer capabilities. Finally, this simple architecture-agnostic technique can act as drop-in improvement for existing methods.

7 Conclusion

This work introduces Multi-Sub training with cross-teaching—a novel technique that combines multiple alternative subword tokenizations of a source-target language pair—to improve the representation of low-resource languages. Our proposed methods obtain significant gains on low-resource datasets from multilingual TED-talks. We performed exhaustive analysis to show that our methods also increase the lexical and morphological diversity of the output translations, and produce better multilingual representations which we demonstrate by performing zero-shot NER by exploiting representations from a high resource language. Multi-Sub training and cross-teaching are simple architecture-agnostic steps which can be easily applied to existing single or multilingual neural machine translation models and do not require any external data.

Acknowledgements

N.K would like to thank Kumar Abhishek for the numerous discussions that helped shape this paper. The research was partially supported by

[11] In this respect, cross-teaching has a similar effect to BPE-dropout (Provilkov et al., 2020), which serves to eliminate monolingual subspaces at the level of subword embeddings (but recall our prior comments on the distinction between BPE-dropout and Multi-Sub in Section 3.3).

the Natural Sciences and Engineering Research Council of Canada grants NSERC RGPIN-2018-06437 and RGPAS-2018-522574 and a Department of National Defence (DND) and NSERC grant DGDND-2018-00025 to the third author.

References

Aharoni, Roee, Melvin Johnson, and Orhan Firat. 2019. Massively multilingual neural machine translation. In *Proceedings of the 2019 Conference of the North American Chapter of the Association for Computational Linguistics: Human Language Technologies*.

Covington, Michael A, and Joe D McFall. 2010. Cutting the gordian knot: The moving-average type–token ratio (mattr). *Journal of quantitative linguistics*, 17(2):94–100.

Dong, Daxiang, Hua Wu, Wei He, Dianhai Yu, and Haifeng Wang. 2015. Multi-task learning for multiple language translation. In *Proceedings of the 53rd Annual Meeting of the Association for Computational Linguistics and the 7th International Joint Conference on Natural Language Processing*, Beijing, China.

Firat, Orhan, Kyunghyun Cho, and Yoshua Bengio. 2016. Multi-way, multilingual neural machine translation with a shared attention mechanism. In *Proceedings of the 2016 Conference of the North American Chapter of the Association for Computational Linguistics: Human Language Technologies*.

Gao, Luyu, Xinyi Wang, and Graham Neubig. 2020. Improving target-side lexical transfer in multilingual neural machine translation. In *Findings of the Association for Computational Linguistics: EMNLP 2020*.

Garcia, Marcos, and Pablo Gamallo. 2014. Multilingual corpora with coreferential annotation of person entities. In *Proceedings of the Ninth International Conference on Language Resources and Evaluation (LREC'14)*, Reykjavik, Iceland. European Language Resources Association (ELRA).

Gu, Jiatao, Hany Hassan, Jacob Devlin, and Victor OK Li. 2018. Universal neural machine translation for extremely low resource languages. In *Proceedings of the 2018 Conference of the North American Chapter of the Association for Computational Linguistics: Human Language Technologies*.

Guiraud, P. 1960. *Problèmes et Méthodes de la Statistique Linguistique*. Presses universitaires de France.

Johnson, Melvin, Mike Schuster, Quoc V Le, Maxim Krikun, Yonghui Wu, Zhifeng Chen, Nikhil Thorat, Fernanda Viégas, Martin Wattenberg, Greg Corrado, et al. 2017. Google's multilingual neural machine translation system: Enabling zero-shot translation. *Transactions of the Association for Computational Linguistics*, 5:339–351.

Kambhatla, Nishant, Logan Born, and Anoop Sarkar. 2022. CipherDAug: Ciphertext Based Data Augmentation for Neural Machine Translation. In *Proceedings of the 60th Annual Meeting of the Association for Computational Linguistics (Volume 1: Long Papers)*.

Koehn, Philipp. 2004. Statistical significance tests for machine translation evaluation. In *Proceedings of the 2004 Conference on Empirical Methods in Natural Language Processing*, Barcelona, Spain.

Kudo, Taku. 2018. Subword regularization: Improving neural network translation models with multiple subword candidates. In *Proceedings of the 56th Annual Meeting of the Association for Computational Linguistics*.

McCarthy, Philip M. 2005. *An assessment of the range and usefulness of lexical diversity measures and the potential of the measure of textual, lexical diversity (MTLD)*. Ph.D. thesis, The University of Memphis.

McCarthy, Philip M, and Scott Jarvis. 2007. vocd: A theoretical and empirical evaluation. *Language Testing*, 24(4):459–488.

Neubig, Graham, and Junjie Hu. 2018. Rapid adaptation of neural machine translation to new languages. In *Proceedings of the 2018 Conference on Empirical Methods in Natural Language Processing*.

Nguyen, Toan Q, and David Chiang. 2017. Transfer learning across low-resource, related languages for neural machine translation. In *Proceedings of the Eighth International Joint Conference on Natural Language Processing*.

Papineni, Kishore, Salim Roukos, Todd Ward, and Wei-Jing Zhu. 2002. Bleu: a method for automatic evaluation of machine translation. In *Proceedings of the 40th annual meeting of the As-*

sociation for Computational Linguistics, pages 311–318.

Piskorski, Jakub, Lidia Pivovarova, Jan Šnajder, Josef Steinberger, and Roman Yangarber. 2017. The first cross-lingual challenge on recognition, normalization, and matching of named entities in slavic languages. In *Proceedings of the 6th Workshop on Balto-Slavic Natural Language Processing*, Valencia, Spain.

Post, Matt. 2018. A call for clarity in reporting BLEU scores. In *Proceedings of the Third Conference on Machine Translation: Research Papers*, Belgium, Brussels. Association for Computational Linguistics.

Provilkov, Ivan, Dmitrii Emelianenko, and Elena Voita. 2020. Bpe-dropout: Simple and effective subword regularization. In *Proceedings of the 58th Annual Meeting of the Association for Computational Linguistics*, pages 1882–1892.

Qi, Ye, Devendra Sachan, Matthieu Felix, Sarguna Padmanabhan, and Graham Neubig. 2018. When and why are pre-trained word embeddings useful for neural machine translation? In *Proceedings of the 2018 Conference of the North American Chapter of the Association for Computational Linguistics: Human Language Technologies, Volume 2 (Short Papers)*, pages 529–535.

Sennrich, Rico, Barry Haddow, and Alexandra Birch. 2016. Neural machine translation of rare words with subword units. In *Proceedings of the 54th Annual Meeting of the Association for Computational Linguistics*, pages 1715–1725.

Sevcíková, Magda, Zdenek Zabokrtský, and Oldrich Kruza. 2007. Named entities in czech: Annotating data and developing NE tagger. In *Text, Speech and Dialogue, 10th International Conference, TSD 2007, Pilsen, Czech Republic, September 3-7, 2007, Proceedings*, volume 4629 of *Lecture Notes in Computer Science*, pages 188–195. Springer.

Shannon, Claude E. 1948. A mathematical theory of communication. *Bell Syst. Tech. J.*, 27(3):379–423.

Sharoff, Serge. 2017. Toward pan-Slavic NLP: Some experiments with language adaptation. In *Proceedings of the 6th Workshop on Balto-Slavic Natural Language Processing*, Valencia, Spain. Association for Computational Linguistics.

Simpson, Edward H. 1949. Measurement of diversity. *nature*, 163(4148):688.

Tan, Xu, Jiale Chen, Di He, Yingce Xia, Tao Qin, and Tie-Yan Liu. 2019. Multilingual neural machine translation with language clustering. In *Proceedings of the 2019 Conference on Empirical Methods in Natural Language Processing and the 9th International Joint Conference on Natural Language Processing (EMNLP-IJCNLP)*, pages 963–973.

Tweedie, Fiona J, and R Harald Baayen. 1998. How variable may a constant be? measures of lexical richness in perspective. *Computers and the Humanities*, 32(5):323–352.

Vanmassenhove, Eva, Dimitar Shterionov, and Matthew Gwilliam. 2021. Machine translationese: Effects of algorithmic bias on linguistic complexity in machine translation. In *Proceedings of the 16th Conference of the European Chapter of the Association for Computational Linguistics: Main Volume*, pages 2203–2213, Online..

Wang, Xinyi, Hieu Pham, Philip Arthur, and Graham Neubig. 2018. Multilingual neural machine translation with soft decoupled encoding. In *International Conference on Learning Representations*.

Wang, Xinyi, Sebastian Ruder, and Graham Neubig. 2021. Multi-view subword regularization. In *Proceedings of the 2021 Conference of the North American Chapter of the Association for Computational Linguistics: Human Language Technologies*, pages 473–482, Online.

Wu, Lijun, Shufang Xie, Yingce Xia, Yang Fan, Jian-Huang Lai, Tao Qin, and Tieyan Liu. 2020. Sequence generation with mixed representations. In *Proceedings of the 37th International Conference on Machine Learning*, volume 119 of *Proceedings of Machine Learning Research*, pages 10388–10398. PMLR.

Yule, C Udny. 2014. *The statistical study of literary vocabulary*. Cambridge University Press.

Zoph, Barret, Deniz Yuret, Jonathan May, and Kevin Knight. 2016. Transfer learning for low-resource neural machine translation. In *Proceedings of the 2016 Conference on Empirical Methods in Natural Language Processing*, pages 1568–1575.

Fast-Paced Improvements to Named Entity Handling for Neural Machine Translation

Pedro Mota, Vera Cabarrão, Eduardo Farah
Unbabel, Lisbon, Portugal
{pedro.mota, vera.cabarrao, eduardo.farah}@unbabel.com

Abstract

In this work, we propose a Named Entity (NE) handling approach to improve translation quality within an existing Natural Language Processing (NLP) pipeline without modifying the Neural Machine Translation (NMT) component. Our approach seeks to enable fast delivery of such improvements and alleviate user experience problems related to NE distortion. We implement separate NE recognition and translation steps. Then, a combination of standard entity masking technique and a novel *semantic equivalent* placeholder guarantees that both NE translation is respected and the best overall quality is obtained from NMT. The experiments show that translation quality improves in 38.6% of the test cases when compared to a version of the NLP pipeline with less-developed NE handling capability.

1 Introduction

NE play a crucial role in many downstream NLP tasks. There is extensive research showing that properly handling NE improves the performance of systems performing Question Answering (Talmor and Berant, 2019), Summarization (Zhou et al., 2021), and Information Retrieval (Wang et al., 2021). In this paper, we focus on NMT, another task that benefits from NE modeling (Shavarani and Sarkar, 2021). NMT models are prone to disturb NE, leading to critical quality issues in the translation. Overcoming such problems is challenging since it is hard to have good coverage of all possible entities in the training data. This is due to the open-ended nature of NE as well as their domain specificity. For example, for the `Organization (ORG)` category, new entities appear daily in a variety of domains. Moreover, NE are linguistically complex structures that can occur in ambiguous contexts. This impairs the ability of models to generalize and instead learn unwanted biases (Hassan Awadalla et al., 2018; Modrzejewski et al., 2020). This causes NE to be hallucinated towards frequent realizations, omitted, or incorrectly translated. Figure 1 shows some examples of this issue in the output translation of an English $\rightarrow$ French NMT model. This occurs despite the model having 65×10^6 parameters and being trained with 100 million sentence pairs.

The NMT community has long been familiar with the NE handling problem (Koehn and Knowles, 2017). This has spurred research on how to address such model limitations. Invariably, all works resort to either incorporating new modeling features in existing NMT architectures (Li et al., 2019; Modrzejewski et al., 2020) or integrating with external knowledge sources to bridge the NE gap (Zhao et al., 2020a; Feng et al., 2021).

In spite of the achievements of the previously mentioned works, they have the drawback of requiring a model-specific solution. In a commercial setting, this is problematic since NE handling, at least for some categories, might come only as an afterthought. Having the NLP pipeline already in place entails that rolling out changes can be slow due to the high number of existing models. It should be noted that there are also time and budget constraints regarding the model size and volume of training data in order to make a NMT system economically viable. This blocks translation quality improvements related to NE handling.

Macken, Rufener, Van den Bogaert, Daems, Tezcan, Vanroy, Fonteyne, Barrault, Costa-jussà, Kemp, Pilos, Declercq, Koponen, Forcada, Scarton, Moniz (eds.)
Proceedings of the 23rd Annual Conference of the European Association for Machine Translation, p. 141–149
Ghent, Belgium, June 2022.

	DATE distortion
Input:	However, on *18 February 2022* you again contacted us.
Translation:	Cependant, le *18 février*, vous nous avez à nouveau contactés.
	PERSON distortion
Input:	Hi *Zéphyrin*
Translation:	Bonjour *Zécerin*

Figure 1: Examples of NE distortions by NMT.

In this paper, we propose an alternative perspective to NE handling. We argue that it is important to deliver, as fast as possible, translation quality improvements to end-users, avoiding critical communication issues. To achieve this, we describe a process that enables NE handling to be deployed in an NLP pipeline without changing the NMT component. In an NMT industry scenario, this is relevant since flexibility in model architecture is necessary to accommodate different use cases. Thus, the decoupling of NE handling is desirable to not add extra requirements to the NMT component.

In particular, we first carry out a NE recognition pre-processing step. Then, we obtain the corresponding translation for that entity. Finally, we resort to a semantically-equivalent mask that the NMT can properly handle. When it is not possible to generate a semantically-equivalent entity, we default to the standard placeholding method from NMT. This affords a good trade-off between translation quality and the NLP pipeline run-time.

2 Related Work

The standard approach to NE handling within a NLP pipeline corresponds to introducing NE information and forwarding it to the NMT component. The end goal is to allow the model to improve the NE translation quality. In previous work, there are different approaches to make use of this NE information, which we summarize below.

A possible approach is the placeholder method (Wang et al., 2017; Post et al., 2019), where source sentences are masked by a generic entity token, exposed to the NMT model during training. After translation, the masks are placed back into the target sentence, based on an index or alignment. Li et al. (2016; 2019) extend this approach to overcome the limitation of dealing with rare words in this setting. This is done with a dedicated character-level sequence-to-sequence model for NE translation. A NE recognition step is also added to enable the use of category-specific entity tokens. NEs are crawled from the training data and their translation extracted from Wikipedia. The NE translation pairs are then used to train both the character-level and NMT models.

Another line of research uses entity embeddings to convey word-level NE category information to guide the NMT model. An example is source factors (Sennrich and Haddow, 2016), which take the form of supplementary embeddings that are added or concatenated to existing word embeddings in the model. Ugawa (2018) combines this with an additional Long Short-Term Memory (LSTM) (Hochreiter and Schmidhuber, 1996) layer to better handle NE. This contrasts with the work from Modrzejewski et al. (2020), where better translation quality is achieved by directly combining source factors in a Transformer network (Vaswani et al., 2017). SemKGE (Moussallem et al., 2019) take a similar approach but construct the embeddings differently. These map subject-relation-object triples from a Knowledge Graph (KG) (Vrandečić and Krötzsch, 2014) into a continuous vector space to obtain Knowledge Graph Embeddings (KGE) (Bordes et al., 2013). To this end, a supervised fastText (Joulin et al., 2017) classifier determines a set of referring expressions of NE from the KG and uses them to initialize the embedding weights of the NMT model. Zhao et al. (2020b) use a similar methodology but focus on dealing with the drawback of only taking into account NE that appear in both the KG and the training dataset. To leverage the remaining relevant information in the KG, phrase translation pairs are first extracted from the training data. The pairs that appear in the KGs are considered seed pairs in a KGEs semantic space. This semantic space is then used to compare new NE with the seed pairs. If KGE are close, then a synthetic sentence pair is generated by replacing the original NE with the new ones.

Continuing the entity embedding research line, Xie et al. (2022) take it a step further and provide a generic recipe to achieve a single end-to-end NE-aware NMT model, which avoids the overhead of separate NE handling steps. Moreover, there is no extra cost at inference time since the NE components can be disabled. To achieve this, an enhanced encoder and decoder are trained in a multi-task framework by combining translation and NE recognition in a focal loss (Lin et al., 2017).

Given the current state-of-the-art, we conclude that previous approaches introduce coupling to the NMT architecture by either changing it or jointly training new embeddings. While this brings advantages in many scenarios, we argue that it is also valuable to address the use case where a large NLP pipeline already exists and fast incremental improvements to NE need to be delivered by means of new categories. In this context, we build upon the placeholder approach, where we are willing to sacrifice *translation quality* for a *translation guarantee* that certain words are perfectly translated. We extend this approach to better reconcile these two competing aspects as well as study the more complex case where the NE require translation.

3 Named Entity Handling

In our approach, we first start by performing a NE recognition pre-processing step (Section 3.1). Then, we obtain the corresponding translation for a given target language (Section 3.2). We forward all the previous information to a NE handler step that obtains the best possible quality from the existing NMT model while guaranteeing that the expected translation appears in the output translation.

3.1 Recognition

For this step, we combined regex and neural network-based approaches to identify NE in a source sentence. This way we can capture NE with a structured format as well as context dependent ones. We support the following categories:

- **Regex**: `GLOSSARY`, `IP-ADDRESS`, `EMAIL`, `ALPHANUMERIC-ID`, `PHONE-NUMBER`, `BANK-NUMBER`, `CURRENCY`, `NUMBER`, `PERCENTAGE`, `URL`, and `DATE` (numerical).
- **Neural**: `PERSON`, `COUNTRY`, `Products & Organizations (PRO-ORG)`, and `DATE` (alphanumerical).

The `GLOSSARY` category is a manually curated list of terminology that must be enforced in a particular domain. The `ALPHANUMERIC-ID` captures NEs such as promotional codes. The regex `DATE` category matches numerical dates (e.g.: `yy/mm/dd`). The neural `DATE` covers the numbers and text case such as "January 1st, 2022". The `PRO-ORG` is a merge between two different categories, Products, and Organizations since it is often the case that they are almost indistinguishable.[1] The remaining categories are self-explanatory.

3.2 Translation

Different translation needs stem from the different possible NE categories as well as the language pair. For a set of categories, the NE should be kept as in the original text and should not be translated. This is the case for `URL`, `PRO-ORG`, `PHONE-NUMBER`, `IP-ADDRESS`, `BANK-NUMBER`, (generally) `PERSON`, `NUMBER`, `PERCENTAGE`, `DATE` (numerical), `CURRENCY`, `ALPHANUMERIC-ID`, and `EMAIL`.

When the NE cannot be copied, it is necessary to provide a suitable translation. For cases where the NE can be translated without context, a dictionary-based approach can be suitable. This is the case for the `COUNTRY` category since there is a limited number of possible realizations. Moreover, building the dictionaries for a variety of language pairs is feasible through available resources such as KGs. Another option can be to outsource the NE translation to an external NMT provider such as Google, Amazon, or Microsoft. A use case for this is the `DATE` (alphanumerical) category since there is some variety in the day, month, and year structure as well as language-specific punctuation rules that make it hard to translate. Using an external service can be a solution in this case, because the provider can afford to have very large generic models (trained on large amounts of data), making them more robust to some NE categories.

Depending on the target language, a category might require or not translation. This is the case of `PERSON`, which requires transliteration if the source and target scripts do not match, namely in Arabic, Russian, and Greek. The strategies described above can still be applied. The dictionary approach can be supported by character transliteration tools when a name cannot be found.

[1]For example, the search engine *Google* is also the name of the organization.

3.3 Neural Machine Translation Integration

The output of the previous steps is a set of word spans with the NE category and expected translation. In the next section, we describe how to integrate this output with NMT to obtain a more robust NE handling strategy.

3.3.1 Named Entity Masking

It is plausible that a particular realization of a NE will not be present in the training data of the NMT model, leading to a poor quality translation. For example, the PERSON category has a wide variety of realizations since it varies according to the language, can have abbreviations, and many possible combinations of first, second, and last names.

To overcome the previous problem, we propose the use of a *semantic equivalent* version to mask the original NE. This is akin to the standard masking in NMT, which corresponds to a context-free replacement of a class of input tokens with a single mask token. The idea is to collapse distributionally similar tokens into a single token that the decoder can then be trained to reliably copy to the translation. Then, a demasking step replaces the token placeholder with either a copy of the source match value or the translation obtained from a dictionary. This feature is commonly available in NMT industry to satisfy the requirement of being able to enforce domain-specific terminology. The advantage of using a semantic equivalent mask is that it does not change the underlying meaning of the sentence. Thus, we can avoid degrading the translation quality in other parts of the sentence since the NMT has access to all the necessary linguistic information. To achieve this we only need to search for a semantic equivalent that the NMT is likely to correctly translate. To this end, we came up with a list of plausible candidates and empirically observe if NMT was able to translate them.

Despite increased translation robustness, there is still no guarantee that the NMT will output the semantic equivalent mask. When this is the case, we argue that it is likely that NMT distorted the mask. To repair the translation we trigger an entity fallback mechanism. This mechanism resorts to standard masking using the available default entity token placeholder. This is also useful in situations where generating a semantic equivalent is not possible. For example, for the COUNTRY category, one can easily find the necessary translation for a variety of languages. The obstacle is that gender is hard to obtain, especially because it depends on the target language. Thus, we can first check if the raw sentence translation contains the expected NE translation; if it does not, then resort to entity fallback. The drawback of this strategy is that it will hide linguistic information from the NMT. Thus, errors such as agreement in gender are expected.

The previously described strategy achieves improvements on both translation *quality* and translation *guarantee* aspects. This occurs because we use a semantic equivalent mask to have the best possible quality from the existing NMT and only resort to the entity fallback guarantee after checking that the expected translation was not output.

3.3.2 Semantic Equivalent Generation

To apply the previous strategy, it is necessary to define a semantic equivalent NE generation process. This is not straightforward since the required linguistic features might not be available and vary across categories and languages. For example, for the PERSON category, we need to determine the gender (female, male, or unisex). Despite being an open-ended NE, it is still possible to get good coverage by leveraging resources available online.[2] From these resources, we can build a name lookup table with the gender information. For PERSON NE containing more than one word, we heuristically check each word in the lookup table and return the first match. Another linguistic feature that the PERSON category can have is if it corresponds to a family name. Although we do not try to identify this feature, we generate a semantic equivalent family name if we find a title (e.g.: "Mr."; "Mrs.").

Putting all NE handling steps together, we provide two examples of our approach in Figure 2. In the PERSON category example, the semantic equivalent masking was able to repair the NE distortion described in the beginning of this paper (Figure 1). In the COUNTRY category example, the NMT did not output the expected translation, causing a critical error. After re-translating with the default entity token $MASK, we were able to guarantee that "Japão" appeared in the final output. It should be noted that there is an agreement error: the preposition "na" is in the feminine form and it should be in the masculine one ("no"). Despite this error, this is less critical than omitting the NE, and, thus, the overall translation quality was improved.

[2] For example, https://github.com/lead-ratings/gender-guesser

	PERSON Example
Input:	Hi Zéphyrin
NE Recognition:	Hi **Zéphyrin**
NE Translation:	Hi **[Zéphyrin→Zéphyrin]**
Semantic Equivalent:	Hi **[Thomas→Thomas]**
NMT:	Bonjour **Thomas**
Output:	Bonjour **Zéphyrin**
	COUNTRY Example
Input:	I understand that currently you are in Japan
NE Recognition:	I understand that currently you are in **Japan**
NE Translation:	I understand that currently you are in **[Japan→Japão]**
NMT:	Entendo que, atualmente, está no país
Retranslation:	I understand that currently you are in **[$MASK→Japão]**
	Entendo que, atualmente, está na **$MASK**
Output:	Entendo que, atualmente, está na **Japão**

Figure 2: NE handling pipeline.

4 Experiments

We carry experiments in all NE handling steps, namely: recognition (Section 4.1), NE translation (Section 4.2), and NMT integration (Section 4.3).

4.1 Named Entity Recognition Experiments

The following sections describe the evaluation of NE recognition step.

4.1.1 Experimental Setup

Our NLP pipeline is deployed in a commercial setting, thus, there are requirements constraining the model to have a small memory footprint and fast inference time. The architecture of the neural network is a stack combining GloVe word embeddings (Pennington et al., 2014), an LSTM layer, a hierarchical character-level BiLSTM-CRF (Lample et al., 2016), and a final CRF (Lafferty et al., 2001) layer on top. We use word embeddings of size 100 and the remaining layers have 256 hidden units. Training runs for up to 120 epochs, on batch size 32, and learning rate 0.1.

The training data is from the customer support domain, in the travel, technology, and education topics. The data was annotated by a linguist expert, taking approximately 3 weeks. In total, 46168 English sentences were annotated. This experiment focuses on the following categories: PERSON, COUNTRY, PRO-ORG, and DATE. The number of instances for each categories is: 5968, 397, 695, 17057, and 2178, respectively.

We compare our performance with two out-of-the-box models: spaCy 3.2.1 (Honnibal et al., 2020), *en_core_web_sm* model, and Stanza 1.3.0 (Qi et al., 2020), OntoNotes-based model. To measure performance, we use precision, recall, and F_1 metrics in a 10-fold cross-validation setup.

4.1.2 Experimental Results

The results are depicted in Table 1 and show that our custom model performs significantly better than the out-of-the-box models, with differences up to 72.6 in F_1. Between spaCy and Stanza, we observe that the latter generally performs better. It is also possible to observe that there are some NE categories that are easier to recognize for our custom model. This is the case of PERSON, and DATE, which shows that there is a lot of structure for these categories in our domain. In the remaining categories, the main issues we detected were variance in context (PRO-ORG), making it hard for the model to generalize, and a low number of occurrences (COUNTRY, and DATE), limiting the ability to learn the category during training.

Given the previous results, we conclude that in our use case of customer support domain it is worth paying the acquisition cost of the manually annotated NE data since it provides a great performance boost over out-of-the-box models.

4.2 Named Entity Translation Experiments

We now report the experimental results for the NE translation step.

Category	Metric	spaCy	Stanza	Custom
PERSON	Pre	35.7±1.9	71.1±3.4	97.4±0.8
	Rec	57.1±2.4	56.8±1.4	97.4±2.8
	F_1	43.9±1.9	63.1±1.8	96.3±1.6
COUNTRY	Pre	23.4±5.7	61.9±5.3	93.1±4.0
	Rec	7.5±1.9	6.2±2.5	76.5±8.9
	F_1	11.2±2.4	11.1±4.2	83.7±5.9
PRO-ORG	Pre	40.8±2.9	62.4±3.8	85.9±1.6
	Rec	30.8±1.3	36.2±1.5	88.4±2.5
	F_1	35.0±1.2	45.8±1.8	87.1±1.4
DATE	Pre	25.4±2.3	31.4±2.8	87.7±9.1
	Rec	78.6±4.5	63.7±2.7	95.3±2.3
	F_1	38.4±2.8	41.9±2.6	91.0±5.1

Table 1: NE recognition experimental results.

4.2.1 Experimental Setup

As mentioned in Section 3.2, in language pairs with different scripts, like English → Russian, the PERSON category might need translation. In this context, we collected 784 sentences containing the PERSON category and asked a Russian native speaker to provide the transliteration. Then, we measured the accuracy performance for the following approaches: one-to-one character mapping, Polyglot (Chen and Skiena, 2016), name dictionary (Merhav and Ash, 2018), and NMT providers (Google, Amazon, and Microsoft). In the name dictionary approach, we fallback to character mapping if the name is not in the dictionary.

4.2.2 Experimental Results

The results in Table 2 show that the most competitive approaches are the name dictionary and Google, with an accuracy up to 31.9% higher. For the name dictionary approach, we observe that the majority of the errors occur (95.3%) when the name was not present in the dictionary, resulting to a fall back to the character mapping strategy.

	%Accuracy
Character Mapping	50.4
Polyglot	46.2
Name Dictionary	**82.3**
Google	81.3
Amazon	75.8
Microsoft	74.5

Table 2: Name translation results.

The main difficulty we observed in this task stems from the fact that name transliteration needs to follow very specific rules. These introduce many exceptions to the standard character mapping, which explains its low results. An example of such rules is that the character "ы" can never go at the end of a name ("й" should be used instead). This makes the standard mapping from "y" fail for names like "Rey".

4.3 Neural Machine Translation Experiments

To understand the impact on quality of extending our NLP pipeline with new categories, we performed several experiments for the PERSON, COUNTRY and DATE (alphanumerical) categories.

4.3.1 Experimental Setup

The datasets are from the same domain as in previous experiments and the evaluations were done by expert linguists with fluent knowledge of the language pairs evaluated. To this end, we marked if the translation was better, the same, or worse than the previous version of the pipeline. We consider that the quality is better if errors in the original NMT are corrected or if the translation is more adequate. We consider translations as the same if both are equivalent. Finally, we consider that translations are worse if new errors are introduced. The experiments were carried out in a total of 2130 sentences in 7 language pairs (English source).

Regarding the baseline NMT, we trained bilingual models following the training procedure for the Transformer-base architecture (Vaswani et al., 2017). We first train a generic model using data available in the Opus platform (Tiedemann, 2012); the data volume is in the order of magnitude of hundreds of millions. Then, the model is fine-tuned with domain data; the data volume is in the order of magnitude of hundreds of thousands. The improved NE handling used the semantic equivalent (PERSON), Google NMT provider (DATE), and dictionary (COUNTRY) translation strategies.

4.3.2 Experimental Results

The obtained results are described in Table 3. Overall, it can be observed that the percentage of improved sentences is higher than the percentage of damaged sentences across all categories and languages. This validates that our NE handling strategy is beneficial. The majority of the cases marked as worse are due to incorrectly identified NE in the recognition step.

Category	Target	%Better	%Same	%Worse	#Sentences
PERSON	German	14.9	80.1	4.9	141
	French	22.5	77.4	0.0	31
	Dutch	45.4	38.3	16.1	99
	Brazilian	93.3	5.15	1.52	330
DATE	German	59.5	25.6	14.8	168
	French	68.5	21.1	10.3	194
	Portuguese	65.0	20.4	14.5	240
COUNTRY	German	8.3	87.9	3.8	346
	French	3.5	96.3	0.3	400
	Dutch	5.0	95.0	0.0	40
	Italian	2.7	97.3	0.0	73
	Brazilian	9.7	90.3	0.0	31
	Portuguese	6.3	87.5	6.3	16
	Turkish	4.8	95.2	0.0	21

Table 3: NMT quality experimental results.

The highest improvements were obtained for the PERSON category in Brazilian Portuguese with 98% of sentences showing better quality. In this particular case, the majority of these improvements are related to punctuation and register. For the other languages, the main difference was avoiding name omissions and hallucinations.

For the DATE category, the improvements were similar across all evaluated languages with gains up to 68.5% in the test cases. This shows that this category is prone to be distorted by the NMT. Looking at the sentences where it performed worse, a more in-depth analysis showed that the main issues were related to the translation of ordinal numbers, as well as the wrong preposition before the date, a consequence of using the generic entity token mask.

In what respects COUNTRY, it is possible to conclude that this is the category with the lowest percentage of improvements. The majority of sentences remained the same. This is because the entity fallback mechanism was not triggered often, which is in line with the fact that this is a NE with a limited number of realizations. This highlights the importance of entity fallback since otherwise, we could be introducing many agreement errors unnecessarily. In the few cases where the quality slightly decreased, the root cause was mainly the use of wrong prepositions before the NE when a valid translation did not match the dictionary.

5 Conclusions and Future Work

In this work, we presented a NE handling process, with the ultimate goal of bootstrapping an existing NLP pipeline to improve translation quality. This problem was tackled from a perspective of allowing such improvements to be delivered without having to change one of the main components of the pipeline, the NMT. By having this decoupling, the improvements can be delivered fast, enhancing the user experience in situations where NE translation errors can lead to catastrophic communication errors. Our process is based on dedicated recognition and NE translation steps. Integration into the existing NMT is done through semantic equivalent masking and an entity fallback mechanism. To evaluate NE recognition, we compared our domain custom model against two out-of-the-box models. The results show that the trade-off between recognition performance and data acquisition costs justifies a custom model for our use case. To evaluate our overall approach, we compared the translation quality of NE of the existing pipeline with the improved version. It was possible to observe that we achieved *translation quality* improvements while affording *translation guarantee* at the same time, validating our approach.

We also want to highlight that our approach allows us to easily anonymize Personally Identifiable Information (PII) data by exposing the NE mask rather than its original text. This is a concern for us since our NLP pipeline supports a feedback loop between NMT and human post-edition. The semantic equivalent mask is advantageous in this scenario since it allows editors to review more natural-looking sentences and without the cognitive overhead of processing a generic placeholder.

Regarding future work, one of the concerns is how to extend the generation of semantic equivalent NE to categories other than PERSON. The main obstacle is identifying the necessary linguistic properties for the generation in all necessary target languages. Another concern is the scalability of the NE recognition component. Thus far, our solution has been efficient since we have an overarching domain that ties in otherwise different topics. When moving to a completely different domain, we want to investigate how to keep this efficiency in collecting new data while leveraging the existing model.

6 Acknowledgements

This work was supported by national funds in Portugal through Fundação para Ciência e a Tecnologia (FCT), with reference UIDB/50021/2020 and through FCT and Agência Nacional de Inovação with the Project Multilingual AI Agents Assistants (MAIA), contracted number 045909.

References

Bordes, Antoine, Nicolas Usunier, Alberto Garcia-Duran, Jason Weston, and Oksana Yakhnenko. 2013. Translating Embeddings for Modeling Multi-relational Data. In *Proceedings of NIPS 2013, International Conference on Neural Information Processing Systems*, pages 2787–2795.

Chen, Yanqing and Steven Skiena. 2016. False-friend detection and entity matching via unsupervised transliteration. *arXiv preprint arXiv:1611.06722*.

Feng, Steven Y., Varun Gangal, Jason Wei, Sarath Chandar, Soroush Vosoughi, Teruko Mitamura, and Eduard Hovy. 2021. A survey of data augmentation approaches for NLP. In *Proceedings of ACL 2021, Annual Meeting of the Association for Computational Linguistics*, pages 968–988.

Hassan Awadalla, Hany, Anthony Aue, Chang Chen, Vishal Chowdhary, Jonathan Clark, Christian Federmann, Xuedong Huang, Marcin Junczys-Dowmunt, Will Lewis, Mu Li, Shujie Liu, Tie-Yan Liu, Renqian Luo, Arul Menezes, Tao Qin, Frank Seide, Xu Tan, Fei Tian, Lijun Wu, Shuangzhi Wu, Yingce Xia, Dongdong Zhang, Zhirui Zhang, and Ming Zhou. 2018. Achieving human parity on automatic chinese to english news translation. arXiv:1803.05567.

Hochreiter, Sepp and Jürgen Schmidhuber. 1996. Lstm can solve hard long time lag problems. In *Proceedings of NIPS 1996, International Conference on Neural Information Processing Systems*, page 473–479.

Honnibal, Matthew, Ines Montani, Sofie Landeghem, and Adriane Boyd. 2020. spaCy: Industrial-strength natural language processing in python. To appear.

Joulin, Armand, Edouard Grave, Piotr Bojanowski, and Tomas Mikolov. 2017. Bag of tricks for efficient text classification. In *Proceedings of EACL 2017, European Chapter of the Association for Computational Linguistics*, pages 427–431.

Koehn, Philipp and Rebecca Knowles. 2017. Six challenges for neural machine translation. In *Proceedings of the WNMT 2017, Workshop on Neural Machine Translation*, pages 28–39.

Lafferty, John D., Andrew McCallum, and Fernando C. N. Pereira. 2001. Conditional random fields: Probabilistic models for segmenting and labeling sequence data. In *Proceedings of the ICML 2001, International Conference on Machine Learning*, pages 282–289.

Lample, Guillaume, Miguel Ballesteros, Sandeep Subramanian, Kazuya Kawakami, and Chris Dyer. 2016. Neural architectures for named entity recognition. In *Proceedings of NAACL 2016, North American Chapter of the Association for Computational Linguistics*, pages 260–270.

Li, Xiaoqing, Jiajun Zhang, and Chengqing Zong. 2016. Towards zero unknown word in neural machine translation. In *Proceedings of the IJCAI 2016, International Joint Conference on Artificial Intelligence*, page 2852–2858.

Li, Xiaoqing, Jinghui Yan, Jiajun Zhang, and Chengqing Zong. 2019. Neural name translation improves neural machine translation. In Chen, Jiajun and Jiajun Zhang, editors, *Proceedings of CWMT 2019, China Workshop on Machine Translation*, pages 93–100.

Lin, Tsung-Yi, Priya Goyal, Ross Girshick, Kaiming He, and Piotr Dollár. 2017. Focal loss for dense object detection. In *Proceedings of ICCV 2017, International Conference on Computer Vision*, pages 2999–3007.

Merhav, Yuval and Stephen Ash. 2018. Design challenges in named entity transliteration. In *Proceedings of CLNLP 2018, International Conference on Computational Linguistics*, pages 630–640.

Modrzejewski, Maciej, Miriam Exel, Bianka Buschbeck, Thanh-Le Ha, and Alexander Waibel. 2020. Incorporating external annotation to improve named entity translation in NMT. In *Proceedings of EACL 2020, Annual Conference of the European Association for Machine Translation*.

Moussallem, Diego, Axel-Cyrille Ngonga Ngomo, Paul Buitelaar, and Mihael Arcan. 2019. Utilizing knowledge graphs for neural machine translation augmentation. In *Proceedings of K-CAP, International Conference on Knowledge Capture*, page 139–146.

Pennington, Jeffrey, Richard Socher, and Christopher D. Manning. 2014. Glove: Global vectors for word representation. In *Proceedings of EMNLP 2014, Empirical Methods in Natural Language Processing*, pages 1532–1543.

Post, Matt, Shuoyang Ding, Marianna Martindale, and Winston Wu. 2019. An exploration of placeholding in neural machine translation. In *Proceedings of MT-Summit 2019, Machine Translation Summit*, pages 182–192.

Qi, Peng, Yuhao Zhang, Yuhui Zhang, Jason Bolton, and Christopher D. Manning. 2020. Stanza: A python natural language processing toolkit for many human languages. In *Proceedings of the ACL 2020, Annual Meeting of the Association for Computational Linguistics*, pages 101–108.

Sennrich, Rico and Barry Haddow. 2016. Linguistic input features improve neural machine translation. In *Proceedings of WMT 2016, Conference on Machine Translation*, pages 83–91.

Shavarani, Hassan S. and Anoop Sarkar. 2021. Better neural machine translation by extracting linguistic information from BERT. In *Proceedings of EACL 2021, European Chapter of the Association for Computational Linguistics*, pages 2772–2783.

Talmor, Alon and Jonathan Berant. 2019. MultiQA: An empirical investigation of generalization and transfer in reading comprehension. In *Proceedings of ACL 2019, Annual Meeting of the Association for Computational Linguistics*, pages 4911–4921.

Tiedemann, Jörg. 2012. Parallel data, tools and interfaces in OPUS. In *Proceedings of LREC 2012, International Conference on Language Resources and Evaluation*, pages 2214–2218.

Ugawa, Arata, Akihiro Tamura, Takashi Ninomiya, Hiroya Takamura, and Manabu Okumura. 2018. Neural machine translation incorporating named entity. In *Proceedings of CLNLP 2018, International Conference on Computational Linguistics*, pages 3240–3250.

Vaswani, Ashish, Noam Shazeer, Niki Parmar, Jakob Uszkoreit, Llion Jones, Aidan N Gomez, Łukasz Kaiser, and Illia Polosukhin. 2017. Attention is all you need. In *Proceedings of NIPS 2017, International Conference on Neural Information Processing Systems*, pages 5998–6008.

Vrandečić, Denny and Markus Krötzsch. 2014. Wikidata: A free collaborative knowledgebase. *Communications of the ACM*, 57(10):78–85.

Wang, Yuguang, Shanbo Cheng, Liyang Jiang, Jiajun Yang, Wei Chen, Muze Li, Lin Shi, Yanfeng Wang, and Hongtao Yang. 2017. Sogou neural machine translation systems for WMT17. In *Proceedings of the WMT 2017, Conference on Machine Translation*, pages 410–415.

Wang, Xinyu, Yong Jiang, Nguyen Bach, Tao Wang, Zhongqiang Huang, Fei Huang, and Kewei Tu. 2021. Improving named entity recognition by external context retrieving and cooperative learning. In *Proceedings of ACL 2021, Annual Meeting of the Association for Computational Linguistics*, pages 1800–1812.

Xie, Shufang, Yingce Xia, Lijun Wu, Yiqing Huang, Yang Fan, and Tao Qin. 2022. End-to-end entity-aware neural machine translation. *Machine Learning*, pages 1–23.

Zhao, Yang, Lu Xiang, Junnan Zhu, Jiajun Zhang, Yu Zhou, and Chengqing Zong. 2020a. Knowledge graph enhanced neural machine translation via multi-task learning on sub-entity granularity. In *Proceedings of CLNLP 2020, International Conference on Computational Linguistics*, pages 4495–4505.

Zhao, Yang, Jiajun Zhang, Yu Zhou, and Chengqing Zong. 2020b. Knowledge graphs enhanced neural machine translation. In *Proceedings of IJCAI 2020, International Joint Conference on Artificial Intelligence*, pages 4039–4045.

Zhou, Hao, Weidong Ren, Gongshen Liu, Bo Su, and Wei Lu. 2021. Entity-aware abstractive multi-document summarization. In *Proceedings of ACL 2021, Annual Meeting of the Association for Computational Linguistics*, pages 351–362.

Synthetic Data Generation for Multilingual Domain-Adaptable Question Answering Systems

Alina Kramchaninova, Arne Defauw
CrossLang
Kerkstraat 106, 9050 Gentbrugge, Belgium
{firstname.lastname}@crosslang.com

Abstract

Deep learning models have significantly advanced the state of the art of question answering systems. However, the majority of datasets available for training such models have been annotated by humans, are open-domain, and are composed primarily in English. To deal with these limitations, we introduce a pipeline that creates synthetic data from natural text. To illustrate the domain-adaptability of our approach, as well as its multilingual potential, we use our pipeline to obtain synthetic data in English and Dutch. We combine the synthetic data with non-synthetic data (SQuAD 2.0) and fine-tune multilingual BERT models on the question answering task. Models trained with synthetically augmented data demonstrate a clear improvement in performance when evaluated on the domain-specific test set, compared to the models trained exclusively on SQuAD 2.0. We expect our work to be beneficial for training domain-specific question-answering systems when the amount of available data is limited.

1 Introduction

Recent advances in tackling the problem of question answering (QA) rely on large-scale, open-domain datasets (Bartolo et al., 2021), annotated by humans and composed primarily in English (e.g. SQuAD 1.0 (Rajpurkar et al., 2016), and SQuAD 2.0 (Rajpurkar et al., 2018)). Despite some indications of poor robustness and generalisation (Bartolo et al., 2021), models trained on such datasets are capable of providing topic-agnostic, general-purpose assistance to their users (Ruder and Sil, 2021).

Nevertheless, most industrial applications of QA systems are domain-specific, and often need to be able to operate in multilingual environments. Data collection and manual composition of datasets for each domain and language is most definitely a laborious task, not to mention that certain domains are of little academic or commercial interest and are only of use for some low-resource communities (Rogers et al., 2021). Moreover, while the current synthetic data generation systems focus on augmenting QA data in the SQuAD format,[1] little research has been done on either the generation of synthetic data from natural plain text, or in multiple languages.

Furthermore, most machine reading comprehension (MRC) benchmarks focus primarily on the creation of questions with multi-word factoid answers (e.g. SQuAD 2.0 pairs each factoid question with a Wikipedia paragraph), as well as unanswerable questions (Liu et al., 2020). However, in a real-world scenario, a QA system should ideally be able to provide a response on semantically complex questions such as "I am an EU citizen living in the UK. What changes for me after Brexit?", and questions containing grammar and spelling errors (e.g. questions asked by a non-native speaker, or containing mistakes caused by dyslexia).

In this work, we introduce a domain-adaptable end-to-end pipeline for generic synthetic data generation that requires no manual textual preprocessing, and allows for the integration of mul-

[1] A tuple (c, q, a) where c refers to the context—text segment in which the answer a to the question q should be found.

Macken, Rufener, Van den Bogaert, Daems, Tezcan, Vanroy, Fonteyne, Barrault, Costa-jussà, Kemp, Pilos, Declercq, Koponen, Forcada, Scarton, Moniz (eds.)
Proceedings of the 23rd Annual Conference of the European Association for Machine Translation, p. 151–160
Ghent, Belgium, June 2022.

tilingual features. We utilise this pipeline to create domain-specific training sets in English (EN) and Dutch (NL) from the web scraped data of the Single Digital Gateway and Your Europe portal,[2] which provides information on rules and procedures for citizens and businesses in the EU, in all European languages. We combine the obtained data with SQuAD 2.0 in English and its machine-translated-into-Dutch version to fine-tune multiple instances of a BERT (Bidirectional Encoder Representations from Transformers) model (Devlin et al., 2019) on the QA task. We then cross-evaluate the performance of these models on the relevant test sets, and observe improvements on the QA task when evaluated on the domain-specific test sets, while remaining competitive against models trained on the SQuAD-only counterparts in both languages.

2 Related Work

Existing approaches to synthetic data generation often view question and answer generation as dual tasks (Tang et al., 2017; Shakeri et al., 2020), where one task can improve the other and vice-versa. Roundtrip consistency (Alberti et al., 2019) is one of the methods that combines question generation and question answering models to, first, generate a question conditioned on a pre-selected answer span and its context, and then match against it an answer predicted by a QA system. If there is a match, the triplet (i.e. context, question and answer) is considered valid.

Cloze generation (Dhingra et al., 2018) is a more intuitive approach: it logically splits a document in ratio of 20:80, with the introduction being the first 20% of the input text. It is assumed that the introduction contains answer candidates that are likely to occur in the remainder of the document. Potential answer candidates are consequently selected by matching multi-word spans between introductory sentences and the rest of the text.

These approaches, however, focus on potential answers that are primarily named entities or noun phrases (Tang et al., 2017; Alberti et al., 2019; Puri et al., 2020; Shakeri et al., 2020). For our use-case, we are interested in finding answers of longer spans that might contain administrative procedures in a multilingual setting (e.g. answers to such questions as "how do I request an international passport?" or "Waar kan ik mijn wagen registreren?" - "Where can I register my car?"). Moreover, we are interested in finding right answers in a document that might contain multiple procedures, i.e. the introduction might not match the subsequent content at all, unlike the assumption of the methods proposed in (Dhingra et al., 2018).

OG	Results tend to be scattered across different websites that often lack any guarantee of quality or reliability, and significant *information gaps* remain in many areas, leaving important questions unanswered
MT	Resultaten zijn meestal verspreid over verschillende websites die vaak geen enkele garantie voor kwaliteit of betrouwbaarheid hebben, en er blijven op veel gebieden aanzienlijke *informatielacunes*, waardoor belangrijke vragen onbeantwoord blijven
OG	information gaps
MT	informatie hiaten

Table 1: Translation of Segments via Google Translate

In this work we propose the use of a combination of question generation (QG), question paraphrasing (QP) and unsupervised filtering methods to solve these limitations of previous work. We present techniques for building models and filtering methods in any language using machine translation (MT). For both QP and QG we rely on a T5 model (Raffel et al., 2019) fine-tuned on the respective downstream task (we refer to Section 3).

With regard to the sub-task of QP, we note that on its own it is not an area of active research, although paraphrasing as a data augmentation technique has been explored in both academic (Witteveen and Andrews., 2019) and applied contexts. For instance, Rasa Open Source,[3] a framework for building chatbots and voice-based virtual assistance, researches paraphrasing as a data augmentation technique, to ensure the recognition and anticipation of different variations of the same intent,[4] as small variations in questions, e.g. the use of synonyms, may yield different answers (Dong et al., 2017).

Although multilingual QA remains a relatively unexplored problem, there exist various datasets for the fine-tuning and evaluation of multilingual

[2]https://ec.europa.eu/growth/single-market/single-digital-gateway_en

[3]https://rasa.com/open-source

[4]https://forum.rasa.com/t/paraphrasing-for-nlu-data-augmentation-experimental/27744

QA systems, such as the human-composed TyDi QA (Clark et al., 2020), or MLQA (Lewis et al., 2020) that was created using translation alignments.

Whereas MT may appear as a possible solution to the scarcity of the data for each domain and language, three issues remain. First, and the most evident one, is the quality of MT output, e.g. such problems as the preservation of the word order of the source language might occur (Clark et al., 2020). The second issue lies in the potential misalignment of answer spans (Carrino et al., 2020; Lee et al., 2018) caused by differences between translations of answer segments within the context, and outside of it (see Table 1 where 'OG' stands for 'original' and 'MT' for 'machine-translated'). The bigram "information gaps" was translated to "informatielacunes" within context, but to "informatie hiaten" as a standalone term.[5] As a consequence, it becomes more difficult to determine the offsets (i.e. the position in the context) of such answer spans, and potentially renders the segment useless. Lastly, it must be noted that even though there exist large language models that can generalise across languages, language similarity (Pires et al., 2019) is an important factor that affects the performance of certain architectures across multiple languages.

3 Methodology

We developed a synthetic data generation pipeline that converts plain text into question answering pairs via the following steps: passage detection, keyword filtering, question generation and question paraphrasing.

3.1 Passage Detection

For our use-case, we extracted text from html pages scraped from the web using the Trafilatura[6] library. Next, a rule-based approach was used to parse plain text into chunks (paragraphs and sentences) that can be used as input for the question generator (see Section 3.3). First, we split the text extracted via the Trafilatura library using the newline delimiter, after which we evaluated the start and end characters of each resulting text chunk: if a chunk ends with a question mark or colon, we concatenated the chunk with the subsequent chunk; if it starts with a character that indicates enumeration (e.g. a dash, an asterisk...), the chunk was concatenated with the previous chunk. Chunks containing less than one sentence were discarded. This rule-based approach discards any processing noise that might have occurred during the extraction of text, and delivers semantically charged, coherent paragraphs.

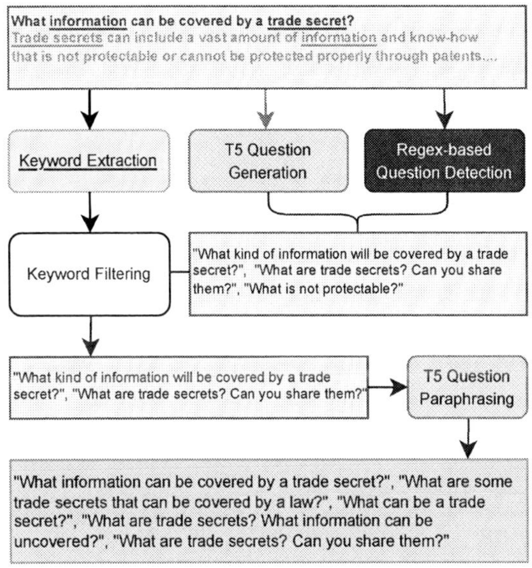

Figure 1: Synthetic Data Generation Pipeline

Consequently, via a sentence-splitter[7] we split the obtained paragraphs into sentences. Both paragraphs and the sentences they contain are fed to the QG model (see Section 3.3): in this way, due to the length differences of sentences and paragraphs, we generate QA pairs of different degrees of complexity. To recreate the SQuAD format for the composition of the synthetic data, for each resulting QA pair, where the input to the QG model is considered the answer, and the output the corresponding question, we also add its context. If the input (i.e. the resulting answer) to the QG model is a paragraph, the context is the document containing that paragraph. If the input is a sentence, the context is the paragraph containing that sentence.

3.2 Keyword Filtering

Once we have obtained the to-be-processed chunks (sentences and paragraphs), we use the YAKE! (Campos et al., 2020) library to extract the most meaningful n-grams from each chunk, one at a

[5] Similarly, in morphologically rich languages, standalone terms could be translated to their base forms while inflected within a context.

[6] `https://github.com/adbar/trafilatura`

[7] `https://pypi.org/project/sentence-splitter`

time. The library implements an unsupervised approach that can be applicable to various languages, without a need for external knowledge such as dictionaries or corpora. YAKE! builds upon features extracted from the document (or text chunk in our case) such as casing, word frequency, word relatedness to the document, and how often a candidate n-gram appears within different sentences. YAKE! then heuristically combines these features to calculate a score for each n-gram—the lower the score, the more meaningful the keyword. From this list of generated n-grams, we compute the average score and select the entities with a lower than average score. This final list for each text chunk is cached and used to filter question candidates of the corresponding chunk, after both the QG (see Section 3.3) and QP (see Section 3.4) steps.

3.3 Question Generation

For question generation we used a pre-trained T5 model fine-tuned on the downstream task of QG. For our English pipeline, we used an existing and publicly available T5 based QG model[8]. For QG in Dutch, we fine-tuned a pretrained multilingual T5 model (mT5) (Xue et al., 2020) on the downstream task of QG on the following datasets machine-translated (see Section 3.5) into Dutch[9]: SQuAD 2.0 (Rajpurkar et al., 2018), RACE (Lao et al., 2017), CoQA (Reddy et al., 2019), and MSMARCO (Bajaj et al., 2016). The mT5-Base model pre-trained on 101 languages, is a 580-million parameter model, the fine-tuning of which is very expensive memory-wise. To limit the resources used, we pruned the model by removing the unused vocabulary from other languages than the desired one (Dutch) via an update of the tokenizer and embedding layer.

The potential answers (paragraphs and sentences) obtained via the passage detection step (Section 3.1) are used as input to these T5 based QG models, resulting in a QA pair. By adding the context (i.e. the document if the input chunk is a paragraph, a paragraph if the input chunk is a sentence, also see Section 3.1), we further obtain a synthetic data point in the SQuAD format.

Although sometimes overlooked in the literature, we did not discard questions already present in the web scraped data, but extracted them using a pre-defined regular expression (regex), e.g. "What information can be covered by a trade secret?" in Figure 1. If a question is detected in a given paragraph, it is split into two at the end index of the detected question, and the first part is cached as a question instance, while the second part is considered being the answer to the question.

[8]https://huggingface.co/valhalla/t5-small-e2e-qg

[9]See https://huggingface.co/datasets/iarfmoose/question_generator for the original EN dataset.

Your Europe	EN	NL
Documents	308	171
Total Q before Key. Filt.	57,182	38,751
Q via Regex	20	16
+ QG (sentence)	3,861	439
+ QP (sentence)	18,828	2,080
+ QG (paragraph)	701	86
+ QP (paragraph)	3,900	304
= Total Q after Key. Filt.	27,310	2,925

Table 3: Synthetic data overview.

Q	welke nationaliteit is verantwoordelijk voor sociale zekerheid?
A	Welk land er verantwoordelijk is voor uw sociale zekerheid, dus ook uw gezinstoelagen (kinderbijslag, opvoedingstoelagen, ouderschapsverlof enz.), hangt in de EU af van uw economische situatie en uw woonplaats, niet van uw nationaliteit.

Table 2: Accepted semantically incorrect synthetic question

We then used the keyword filter, described in the previous section, to decide which generated and/or detected questions are kept and eventually paraphrased (see Section 3.4). In other words, if a generated or detected question contains any word from the keyword list, the question is considered valid.

We empirically observed that the quality of the generated questions in Dutch is vastly dependent on the quality of the translation. However, unlike previous work that focuses on evaluating the quality of generated questions (Chen et al., 2020), (Chan and Fan, 2019), in our training set we allow questions that are grammatically incorrect or contain made up or confusing words, e.g. the word "land" (country) was replaced by the word "nationaliteit" (nationality) in Table 2.

3.4 Question Paraphrasing

In a similar way as for the QG sub-task, we used an existing T5 model fine-tuned on the downstream task of QP. For English we used an existing QP

Type	Text
Context	YES - A medicine available in one EU country might not be sold in another EU country, or it might be sold under a different brand name. When asking for a prescription from your doctor that you intend to dispense in another EU country, you should ensure they use the common name for the prescribed product wherever possible. This will enable a pharmacist in another EU country to prescribe you the equivalent product in that country. To find out if your medicine is available in other EU countries, you can check with your country's national contact point for cross-border healthcare. \n This depends on national law in each European country and will therefore vary throughout the EU. Check with the National Enforcement body in the country concerned or a national consumer centre for more information.\n YES — in all EU countries. Switzerland still applies restrictions on Bulgarian, Croatian and Romanian nationals.\n Ask the host-country liaison office for posted workers. \n Whenever certain conditions have to be fulfilled before you become entitled to health coverage, the national health insurance body examining your claim must take account of periods of insurance, residence or employment completed under the legislation of other EU countries. This ensures that you will not lose your healthcare coverage when changing jobs or moving to another country. \n You can get child benefits from Switzerland or Germany; you won't get full benefits from more than one country. If entitlement in both countries is based on work, even if your children live in yet another country, you will get your benefits from whichever of the two countries where you work that pays the most.
Question	I am unemployed and I come from Bulgaria. Am I allowed to look for work in another EU country and have my benefits transferred there?
Answer	YES — in all EU countries. Switzerland still applies restrictions on Bulgarian, Croatian and Romanian nationals.
$QA_{S, EN\text{-}NL}$	Switzerland or Germany
$QA_{SGP, EN\text{-}NL}$	YES — in all EU countries

Table 4: Your Europe test example.

model[10] fine-tuned on the Quora Question Pairs (QQP) dataset[11]. For Dutch, we fine-tuned a separate mT5 model on the machine-translated QQP dataset.

The detected and/or generated questions that have passed the keyword filter (see Section 3.3) are fed to these QP models individually, without any consideration for the answer or the context. We once again applied the keyword filter to select the most meaningful paraphrased questions.

3.5 Machine Translation

In order to obtain multilingual datasets for the QG and QP task, we rely on transformer-based neural MT models provided via the CEF eTranslation service.[12]. The CEF eTranslation sevice provides translation in 24 official European languages.

4 Experiments

We fine-tuned the multilingual distilled version of BERT (Sanh et al., 2019) (mDistilBERT) on the QA task using the synthetic data obtained using the methods described in Section 3 and the SQuAD 2.0 datasets (we refer to Section 4.1). Full overview of the training data, its sources and size, can be found in Tables 3 and 5. As multilingual BERT models are known to perform better on tasks in English (Riabi et al., 2021), we performed separate experiments with English and Dutch data, as well as experiments with the bilingual data combined. All models were tested on four test sets, two in each language.

4.1 Datasets

Train sets SQuAD 2.0 is a benchmark dataset for question-answering systems. In addition to the 86,821 question answering pairs, the dataset contains 43,498 unanswerable questions. As we are interested in creating a robust QA model that will be able to detect answers in a document, and not interested in unanswerable questions, we omit the latter type of questions, resulting in a non-synthetic training set of length 86,821 for English.

For our Dutch experiments, we used the publicly available machine-translated version of SQuAD 2.0.[13] This dataset contains 53,376 positive and 41,768 negative examples, the latter being omitted.

We further create a synthetic dataset from the web scraped data from the Your Europe portal using the pipeline described in Section 3. In Table 3 we show statistics of our resulting synthetic dataset, and the number of questions (and corresponding answers and context) generated in each step. The second row of Table 3 show the number of documents scraped for both English and Dutch. Next, the total number of questions generated via QG, QP and regex is shown, before filtering via keyword extraction (Total Q before Key. Filt.). The

[10]https://github.com/ramsrigouthamg/Paraphrase-any-question-with-T5-Text-To-Text-Transfer-Transformer-
[11]https://quoradata.quora.com/First-Quora-Dataset-Release-Question-Pairs
[12]https://ec.europa.eu/cefdigital/wiki/display/CEFDIGITAL/eTranslation

[13]https://gitlab.com/niels.rouws/dutch-squad-v2.0

Dataset	$QA_{S, EN}$	$QA_{SG, EN}$	$QA_{SGP, EN}$	$QA_{S, NL}$	$QA_{SGP, NL}$	$QA_{S, EN\text{-}NL}$	$QA_{SGP, EN\text{-}NL}$
S_{EN}	**114,131**	86,821	86,821	-	-	86,821	**59,511**
QG_{EN}	-	**27,310**	4,582	-	-	-	4,582
QP_{EN}	-	-	22,728	-	-	-	22,728
S_{NL}	-	-	-	**56,301**	53,376	53,376	**50,451**
QG_{NL}	-	-	-	-	541	-	541
QP_{NL}	-	-	-	-	2,384	-	2,384
Total	114,131	114,131	114,131	56,301	56,301	140,197	140,197

Table 5: Overview of data composition per trained model. Numbers in bold refer to the randomly oversampled (columns $QA_{S, EN}$, $QA_{SG, EN}$, $QA_{S, NL}$) and undersampled data (column $QA_{SGP, EN\text{-}NL}$).

following rows show the resulting number of questions, after keyword filtering (see Section 3.2), created in each step of the pipeline, both when using sentences and paragraphs as input chunks to the pipeline.

We may observe a difference in the number of generated synthetic questions in English and Dutch. This is primarily caused by the quality of generated and paraphrased questions filtered via keyword extraction: due to the compounding nature of the Dutch language, a great number of questions were filtered out, e.g. if the word "huwelijksaanvraag" (marriage application) is in the original text segment while the generated question might contain the word "huwelijksaangifte" (marriage declaration).

Test sets We evaluate both on the SQuAD 2.0 dataset, and on a domain-specific test set. For the evaluation on SQuAD in English, we held out 5,875 positive examples from the original dataset, while for the evaluation in Dutch, 3,522 positive examples were selected from the machine-translated-into-Dutch SQuAD 2.0 dataset.

To test our pipeline in a setting that would be as close as possible to real-world scenarios, we used a subset of the Your Europe data that was excluded from the training set, and similarly not used as input to the synthetic data generation pipeline. We specifically chose the pages that contained Frequently Asked Questions (FAQ) to retrieve 333 English questions and 265 Dutch questions, and the corresponding answers. These questions were not simplistic call-to-action questions, but mostly compound questions such as "I work in Germany, my husband works in Switzerland, and we live with our children in Austria. Where can we get child benefits from?" The QA pairs were then manually evaluated to ensure that every question is paired with a semantically correct answer.

As the QA pairs were mostly gathered from the FAQ pages of the Your Europe portal, we decided to create an artificial context for each QA pair: we randomly selected five potential answers from other QA pairs, and randomly concatenated them to the single right answer for the given question. An example of such a context and its corresponding QA pair can be seen in Table 4.

4.2 Models

For an objective evaluation of the impact of the different steps of our pipeline for synthetic data generation on the performance of QA models, we have trained several QA models on various combinations of data (see Table 5). In the column 'Dataset' we refer to SQuAD (S) and synthetic training datasets that consist of generated (QG) and paraphrased questions (QP) per language, as indicated in the name of each dataset, we also refer to Table 3.

The model names (first row of Table 5) equally contain the language code of the corresponding dataset, although every fine-tuned QA model uses the same base language model (mDistilBERT) in order to objectively compare the results of each model.

In Table 5, the resulting English QA model $QA_{SGP, EN}$ is trained on both the English SQuAD dataset (86,821 segments=S_{EN}) and the full set of English synthetic data (27,310 segments=QG_{EN}+QP_{EN}), where 'S' stands for SQuAD, 'G' for segments obtained via QG and regex, and 'P' for segments obtained via QP. Similarly, $QA_{S, EN}$ was trained exclusively on the non-synthetic SQuAD training data, randomly oversampled to 114,131 segments to prevent potential differences in performance due to the size of the training data. To analyse the importance of

Context	Bills can be introduced to Parliament in a number of ways; the Scottish Government can introduce new laws or amendments to existing laws as a bill; a committee of the Parliament can present a bill in one of the areas under its remit; a member of the Scottish Parliament can introduce a bill as a private member; or a private bill can be submitted to Parliament by an outside proposer. Most draft laws are government bills introduced by ministers in the governing party. Bills pass through Parliament in a number of stages:
Question	A member of what parliament can introduce a bill as a public member?
$QA_{S,\,EN}$	Scottish
$QA_{SG,\,EN}$	Scottish Government can introduce new laws or amendments to existing laws as a bill ; a committee of the Parliament can present a bill in one of the areas under its remit ; a member of the Scottish Parliament can introduce a bill as a private member
$QA_{SGP,\,EN}$	a member of the Scottish Parliament can introduce a bill as a private member

Table 6: Predictions of different QA models, trained only using SQuAD data ($QA_{S,\,EN}$) and QA models trained on a combination of SQuAD and synthetic data ($QA_{SG,\,EN}$ and $QA_{SGP,\,EN}$), on a segment from the held out EN SQuAD test set.

Model	BLEU	F1	SemSim
$QA_{S,\,EN}$	**0.2033**	**0.2538**	**0.4420**
$QA_{SG,\,EN}$	0.1673	0.2120	0.4138
$QA_{SGP,\,EN}$	0.1789	0.2272	0.4175
$QA_{S,\,EN\text{-}NL}$	**0.2058**	**0.2580**	**0.4382**
$QA_{SGP,\,EN\text{-}NL}$	0.1795	0.2293	0.4219

Table 7: Scores obtained by the various QA models on the held out EN SQuAD test set

Model	BLEU	F1	SemSim
$QA_{S,\,NL}$	0.1866	0.2315	0.4779
$QA_{SGP,\,NL}$	**0.1928**	**0.2369**	**0.4863**
$QA_{S,\,EN\text{-}NL}$	**0.1733**	**0.2132**	**0.4559**
$QA_{SGP,\,EN\text{-}NL}$	0.1478	0.1828	0.4427

Table 8: Scores obtained by the various QA models on the held out NL SQuAD test set

Model	BLEU	F1	SemSim
$QA_{S,\,EN}$	0.0772	0.1165	0.1995
$QA_{SG,\,EN}$	0.1438	0.1898	0.2813
$QA_{SGP,\,EN}$	**0.1557**	**0.1997**	**0.3145**
$QA_{S,\,EN\text{-}NL}$	0.0712	0.1107	0.1734
$QA_{SGP,\,EN\text{-}NL}$	**0.1903**	**0.2588**	**0.4018**

Table 9: Scores obtained by the various QA models on the EN domain-specific (Your Europe) test set

Model	BLEU	F1	SemSim
$QA_{S,\,NL}$	0.0681	0.1033	0.1635
$QA_{SGP,\,NL}$	**0.1650**	**0.2236**	**0.3320**
$QA_{S,\,EN\text{-}NL}$	0.0706	0.1001	0.1429
$QA_{SGP,\,EN\text{-}NL}$	**0.1892**	**0.2556**	**0.3689**

Table 10: Scores obtained by the various QA models on the NL domain-specific (Your Europe) test set

QP as a pipeline feature, we also performed an ablation study, training $QA_{SG,\,EN}$ on SQuAD data in combination with the oversampled synthetic QG_{EN} dataset.

An identical strategy was applied in order to obtain the Dutch QA models $QA_{S,\,NL}$ and $QA_{SGP,\,NL}$. Similarly, for our bilingual models, we combined the English and Dutch versions of SQuAD, and synthetic datasets to train the bilingual $QA_{S,\,EN\text{-}NL}$ and $QA_{SGP,\,EN\text{-}NL}$ models. Note that for a fair comparison of models trained exclusively on SQuAD ($QA_{S,\,EN\text{-}NL}$) with $QA_{SGP,\,EN\text{-}NL}$, we randomly undersampled the English and Dutch SQuAD dataset in this case.

4.3 Metrics

The performance of the various QA models listed in Table 5 was evaluated using the following metrics: sentence BLEU (Papineni et al., 2002), Rouge-L (Lin, 2004) that measures the longest common subsequence to calculate f1-measure, and the cosine similarity calculated using multilingual Sentence-BERT embeddings (Reimers and Gurevych, 2019). We use these metrics to measure the predicted answer against the gold standard answer.

5 Discussion of Results

In this section we compare the performance of the QA models trained on both non-synthetic (i.e. SQuAD) and synthetic data, and models trained exclusively on non-synthetic data. As discussed in Section 4.2, we present results for both English and Dutch. We also evaluate the performance of a bilingual QA model.

In Table 7 we show the scores of our QA models trained on EN and a combination of EN and NL data obtained on the held out EN SQuAD test set. We observe that $QA_{S,\,EN}$ trained on the

EN SQuAD data, achieved the best performance. Nevertheless, despite slightly lower scores, models trained on the combination of SQuAD and synthetic data, do not demonstrate a large regression in performance. This is also illustrated by the example shown in Table 6: we notice that predictions by $QA_{SG,\,EN}$ and $QA_{SGP,\,EN}$ tend to be of longer spans, causing this small drop in performance when evaluated on the gold standard answer 'Scottish'. Similar results are obtained for the QA models trained on NL and a combination of EN and NL data (Table 8), although in this case the $QA_{SGP,\,NL}$ model achieves slightly better scores than the model trained on non-synthetic data only ($QA_{S,\,NL}$).

More interestingly, in Tables 9 and 10, we present the results on the domain-specific (Your Europe) test sets for EN and NL. We observe that models trained on non-synthetic data only ($QA_{S,\,EN}$, $QA_{S,\,NL}$, $QA_{S,\,EN\text{-}NL}$) demonstrate an overall lower performance compared to the models also trained on synthetic data ($QA_{SG,\,EN}$, $QA_{SGP,\,EN}$, $QA_{SGP,\,NL}$ and $QA_{SGP,\,EN\text{-}NL}$). Comparing scores achieved by $QA_{SG,\,EN}$ and $QA_{SGP,\,EN}$ we can also conclude that adding synthetic segments obtained via QP results in an increase in performance, consistent across all metrics. Finally, from these results we also see that bilingual models trained on synthetic and non-synthetic data achieve better performance than their monolingual version (i.e. $QA_{SGP,\,EN}$ and $QA_{SGP,\,NL}$ versus $QA_{SGP,\,EN\text{-}NL}$).

6 Conclusion

In this paper we presented a novel multilingual domain-adaptable pipeline for the generation of synthetic training data for QA models. Our experiments demonstrate that models trained with synthetic data achieved improved performance on domain-specific test sets that included not solely factual, but semantically complex questions, both in English and Dutch. As our pipeline incorporates two mT5 models fine-tuned on task- and language-specific datasets, we demonstrate that it is possible to make use of MT and apply our approach to any language supported by mT5.

One of the remaining challenges of this approach is the quality monitoring of the generated synthetic questions, especially for languages other than English. It would be useful to experiment with more advanced filtering methods than the method based on keyword extraction proposed in this work. For instance, a semantic similarity feature could potentially detect questions that might not include specific keywords, but also questions containing synonyms of extracted keywords or semantically close paraphrases. We also assume that it would be useful to introduce an additional feature to evaluate the chunks that are processed by our pipeline for synthetic data generation, as not every input paragraph or sentence would serve as an answer to a potential question in a real-world scenario.

Acknowledgements

This work was performed in the framework of the CEFAT4Cities project (2019-EU-IA-0015), funded by the CEF Telecom programme (Connecting Europe Facility).

References

Alberti, Chris, Daniel Andor, Emily Pitler, Jacob Devlin, and Michael Collins 2019. Synthetic QA Corpora Generation with Roundtrip Consistency. In *Proceedings of the 57th Annual Meeting of the Association for Computational Linguistics*, pages 6168–6173, Florence, Italy. Association for Computational Linguistics.

Bajaj, Payal, Daniel Campos, Nick Craswell, Li Deng, Jianfeng Gao, Xiaodong Liu, Rangan Majumder, Andrew McNamara, Bhaskar Mitra, Tri Nguyen, Mir Rosenberg, Xia Song, Alina Stoica, Saurabh Tiwary, and Tong Wang. 2016. MS MARCO: A Human Generated MAchine Reading COmprehension Dataset. *ArXiv*, abs/1611.09268.

Bartolo, Max, Tristan Thrush, Robin Jia, Sebastian Riedel, Pontus Stenetorp, and Douwe Kiela 2021. Improving Question Answering Model Robustness with Synthetic Adversarial Data Generation. In *Proceedings of the 2021 Conference on Empirical Methods in Natural Language Processing*, pages 8830–8848, Online and Punta Cana, Dominican Republic. Association for Computational Linguistics.

Campos, Ricardo, Vítor Mangaravite, Arian Pasquali, Alípio Jorge, Celia Nunes, and Adam Jatowt. 2020. Yake! keyword extraction from single documents using multiple local features. In *Information Sciences*.

Carrino, Casimiro Pio, Marta R. Costa-jussa, José A. R. Fonollosa. 2020. Automatic Spanish Translation of the SQuAD Dataset for Multilingual Question Answering. *ArXiv*, abs/1912.05200.

Chan, Ying-Hong, and Yao-Chung Fan. 2019. A Recurrent BERT-based Model for Question Generation. In *Proceedings of the 2nd Workshop on Machine*

Reading for Question Answering, pages 154–162, Hong Kong, China. Association for Computational Linguistics.

Chen, Yu, Lingfei Wu, Mohammed J. Zaki. 2020. Reinforcement Learning Based Graph-to-Sequence Model for Natural Question Generation. *ArXiv*, abs/1908.04942.

Clark, Jonathan H., Eunsol Choi, Michael Collins, Dan Garrette, Tom Kwiatkowski, Vitaly Nikolaev, and Jennimaria Palomaki. 2020. TyDi QA: A Benchmark for Information-Seeking Question Answering. In *Transactions of the Association for Computational Linguistics*, 8:454–470.

Devlin, Jacob, Ming-Wei Chang, Kenton Lee, and Kristina Toutanova. 2019. BERT: Pre-training of Deep Bidirectional Transformers for Language Understanding. In *Proceedings of the 2019 Conference of the North American Chapter of the Association for Computational Linguistics: Human Language Technologies*, Volume 1 (Long and Short Papers), pages 4171–4186, Minneapolis, Minnesota. Association for Computational Linguistics.

Dhingra, Bhuwan, Danish Danish, and Dheeraj Rajagopal. 2018. Simple and Effective Semi-Supervised Question Answering. In *Proceedings of the 2018 Conference of the North American Chapter of the Association for Computational Linguistics: Human Language Technologies*, Volume 2 (Short Papers), pages 582–587, New Orleans, Louisiana. Association for Computational Linguistics.

Dong, Li, Jonathan Mallinson, Siva Reddy, and Mirella Lapata. 2017. Learning to Paraphrase for Question Answering. In *Proceedings of the 2017 Conference on Empirical Methods in Natural Language Processing*, pages 875–886, Copenhagen, Denmark. Association for Computational Linguistics.

Klein, Tassilo, and Moin Nabi. 2019. Learning to Answer by Learning to Ask: Getting the Best of GPT-2 and BERT Worlds. *ArXiv*, abs/1911.02365.

Lai, Guokun, Qizhe Xie, Hanxiao Liu, Yiming Yang, and Eduard Hovy. 2017. RACE: Large-scale ReAding Comprehension Dataset From Examinations. In *Proceedings of the 2017 Conference on Empirical Methods in Natural Language Processing*, pages 785–794, Copenhagen, Denmark. Association for Computational Linguistics.

Lee, Kyungjae, Kyoungho Yoon, Sunghyun Park, and Seung-won Hwang. 2018. Semi-supervised Training Data Generation for Multilingual Question Answering. In *Proceedings of the Eleventh International Conference on Language Resources and Evaluation (LREC 2018)*, Miyazaki, Japan. European Language Resources Association (ELRA).

Lewis, Patrick, Barlas Oguz, Ruty Rinott, Sebastian Riedel, and Holger Schwenk. 2020. MLQA: Evaluating Cross-lingual Extractive Question Answering. In *Proceedings of the 58th Annual Meeting of the Association for Computational Linguistics*, pages 7315–7330, Online. Association for Computational Linguistics.

Lin, Chin-Yew. 2004. ROUGE: A Package for Automatic Evaluation of Summaries. In *Text Summarization Branches Out*, pages 74–81, Barcelona, Spain. Association for Computational Linguistics.

Liu, Dayiheng, Yeyun Gong, Jie Fu, Yu Yan, Jiusheng Chen, Jiancheng Lv, Nan Duan, and Ming Zhou. 2020. Tell Me How to Ask Again: Question Data Augmentation with Controllable Rewriting in Continuous Space. In *Proceedings of the 2020 Conference on Empirical Methods in Natural Language Processing (EMNLP)*, pages 5798–5810, Online. Association for Computational Linguistics.

Papineni, Kishore, Salim Roukos, Todd Ward, and Wei-Jing Zhu. 2002. Bleu: a Method for Automatic Evaluation of Machine Translation. In *Proceedings of the 40th Annual Meeting of the Association for Computational Linguistics*, pages 311–318, Philadelphia, Pennsylvania, USA. Association for Computational Linguistics.

Pires, Telmo, Eva Schlinger, and Dan Garrette. 2019. How Multilingual is Multilingual BERT? In *Proceedings of the 57th Annual Meeting of the Association for Computational Linguistics*, pages 4996–5001, Florence, Italy. Association for Computational Linguistics.

Puri, Raul, Ryan Spring, Mohammad Shoeybi, Mostofa Patwary, and Bryan Catanzaro. 2020. Training Question Answering Models From Synthetic Data. In *Proceedings of the 2020 Conference on Empirical Methods in Natural Language Processing (EMNLP)*, pages 5811–5826, Online. Association for Computational Linguistics.

Radford, Alec, Jeff Wu, Rewon Child, David Luan, Dario Amodei, and Ilya Sutskever. 2019. Language Models are Unsupervised Multitask Learners.

Raffel, Colin, Noam Shazeer, Adam Roberts, Katherine Lee, Sharan Narang, Michael Matena, Yanqi Zhou, Wei Li, and Peter J. Liu. 2019. Exploring the limits of transfer learning with a unified text-to-text transformer. *ArXiv*, abs/1910.10683.

Rajpurkar, Pranav, Jian Zhang, Konstantin Lopyrev, and Percy Liang. 2016. Squad: 100,000+ questions for machine comprehension of text. In *Proceedings of the 2016 Conference on Empirical Methods in Natural Language Processing*, pages 2383–2392.

Rajpurkar, Pranav, Robin Jia, and Percy Liang. 2018. Know what you don't know: Unanswerable questions for squad. *ArXiv*, abs/1806.03822.

Reddy, Siva, Danqi Chen, and Christopher D. Manning. 2019. CoQA: A Conversational Question Answering Challenge. *ArXiv*, abs/1808.07042.

Reimers, Nils, and Iryna Gurevych. 2019. Sentence-BERT: Sentence Embeddings using Siamese BERT-Networks. In *Proceedings of the 2019 Conference on Empirical Methods in Natural Language Processing and the 9th International Joint Conference on Natural Language Processing (EMNLP-IJCNLP)*, pages 3982–3992, Hong Kong, China. Association for Computational Linguistics.

Riabi, Arij, Thomas Scialom, Rachel Keraron, Benoît Sagot, Djamé Seddah, and Jacopo Staiano. 2021. Synthetic Data Augmentation for Zero-Shot Cross-Lingual Question Answering. In *Proceedings of the 2021 Conference on Empirical Methods in Natural Language Processing*, pages 7016–7030, Online and Punta Cana, Dominican Republic. Association for Computational Linguistics.

Rogers, Anna, Matt Gardner, and Isabelle Augenstein. 2021. QA Dataset Explosion: A Taxonomy of NLP Resources for Question Answering and Reading Comprehension. *ArXiv*, abs/2107.12708.

Ruder, Sebastian and Avi Sil. 2021. Multi-Domain Multilingual Question Answering. In *Proceedings of the 2021 Conference on Empirical Methods in Natural Language Processing: Tutorial Abstracts*, pages 17–21, Punta Cana, Dominican Republic & Online. Association for Computational Linguistics.

Sanh, Victor, Lysandre Debyt, Julien Chaumond and Thomas Wolf. 2019. DistilBERT, a distilled version of BERT: smaller, faster, cheaper and lighter. *arxiv pre-print arXiv:1910.01108.*

Shakeri, Siamak, Cicero Nogueira dos Santos, Henry Zhu, Patrick Ng, Feng Nan, Zhiguo Wang, Ramesh Nallapati, and Bing Xiang. 2020. End-to-end synthetic data generation for domain adaptation of question answering systems. *ArXiv*, abs/2010.06028.

Tang, Duyu, Nan Duan, Tao Qin, and Ming Zhou. 2017. Question answering and question generation as dual tasks. *ArXiv*, abs/1706.02027.

Witteveen, Sam and Martin Andrews. 2019. Paraphrasing with Large Language Models. In *Proceedings of the 3rd Workshop on Neural Generation and Translation*, pages 215–220, Hong Kong. Association for Computational Linguistics.

Xue, Linting, Noah Constant, Adam Roberts, Mihir Kale, Rami Al-Rfou, Aditya Siddhant, Aditya Barua and Colin Raffel. 2020. mT5: A massively multilingual pre-trained text-to-text transformer. *ArXiv*, abs/2010.11934.

Automatic Discrimination of Human and Neural Machine Translation: A Study with Multiple Pre-Trained Models and Longer Context

Tobias van der Werff
Bernoulli Institute
University of Groningen
t.n.van.der.werff@student.rug.nl

Rik van Noord
CLCG
University of Groningen
rikvannoord@gmail.com

Antonio Toral
CLCG
University of Groningen
a.toral.ruiz@rug.nl

Abstract

We address the task of automatically distinguishing between human-translated (HT) and machine translated (MT) texts. Following recent work, we fine-tune pre-trained language models (LMs) to perform this task. Our work differs in that we use state-of-the-art pre-trained LMs, as well as the test sets of the WMT news shared tasks as training data, to ensure the sentences were not seen during training of the MT system itself. Moreover, we analyse performance for a number of different experimental setups, such as adding *translationese* data, going beyond the sentence-level and normalizing punctuation. We show that (i) choosing a state-of-the-art LM can make quite a difference: our best baseline system (DEBERTA) outperforms both BERT and ROBERTA by over 3% accuracy, (ii) adding *translationese* data is only beneficial if there is not much data available, (iii) considerable improvements can be obtained by classifying at the document-level and (iv) normalizing punctuation and thus avoiding (some) shortcuts has no impact on model performance.

1 Introduction

Generally speaking, translations are either performed manually by a human, or performed automatically by a machine translation (MT) system. There exist many use cases in Natural Language Processing in which working with a human-translated text is not a problem, as they are usually of high quality, but in which we would like to filter out automatically translated texts. For example, consider training an MT system on a parallel corpus crawled from the Internet: we would preferably only keep the high-quality human-translated sentences.

In this paper, we will address this task of discriminating between human-translated (HT) and machine-translated texts automatically. Studies that have analysed MT outputs and HTs comparatively have found evidence of systematic differences between the two (Ahrenberg, 2017; Vanmassenhove et al., 2019; Toral, 2019). These outcomes provide indications that an automatic classifier should in principle be able to discriminate between these two classes, at least to some extent.

There is previous related work in this direction (Arase and Zhou, 2013; Aharoni et al., 2014; Li et al., 2015), but they used Statistical Machine Translation (SMT) systems to get the translations, while the introduction of Neural Machine Translation (NMT) has considerably improved general translation quality and has led to more natural translations (Toral and Sánchez-Cartagena, 2017). Arguably, the discrimination between MT and HT is therefore more difficult with NMT systems than it was with previous paradigms to MT.

We follow two recent publications that have attempted to distinguish NMT outputs from HTs (Bhardwaj et al., 2020; Fu and Nederhof, 2021) and work with MT outputs generated by state-of-the-art online NMT systems. Additionally, we also build a classifier by fine-tuning a pre-trained language model (LM), given the fact that this approach obtains state-of-the-art performance in many text-based classification tasks.

Macken, Rufener, Van den Bogaert, Daems, Tezcan, Vanroy, Fonteyne, Barrault, Costa-jussà, Kemp, Pilos, Declercq, Koponen, Forcada, Scarton, Moniz (eds.)
Proceedings of the 23rd Annual Conference of the European Association for Machine Translation, p. 161–170
Ghent, Belgium, June 2022.

The main differences with previous work are:

- We experiment with state-of-the-art LMs, instead of only using BERT- and ROBERTA-based LMs;
- We empirically check the performance impact of adding *translationese* training data;
- We go beyond sentence-level by training and testing our best system on the document-level;
- We analyse the impact of punctuation shortcuts by normalizing the input texts;
- We use the test sets of WMT news shared task as our data sets, to ensure reproducibility and that the MT system did not see the translations during its training.

The rest of the paper is organised as follows. Section 2 outlines previous work on the topic. Section 3 details our methodology, focusing on the data sets, classifiers and evaluation metrics. Subsequently, Section 4 presents our experiments and their results. These are complemented by a discussion and further analyses, in Section 5. Finally, Section 6 presents our conclusions and suggestions for future work. All our data, code and results is publicly available at `https://github.com/tobiasvanderwerff/HT-vs-MT`

2 Related Work

Analyses Previous work has dealt with finding systematic and qualitative differences between HT and MT. Ahrenberg (2017) compared manually an NMT system and a HT for one text in the translation direction English-to-Swedish. They found that the translation by NMT was closer to the source and exhibited a more restricted repertoire of translation procedures than the HT. Related, an automatic analysis by Vanmassenhove et al. (2019) found that translations by NMT systems exhibit less lexical diversity than HTs. A contemporary automatic analysis corroborated the finding about less lexical diversity and concluded also that MT led to translation that had lower lexical density, were more normalised and had more interference from the source language (Toral, 2019).

SMT vs HT classification Given these findings, it is no surprise that automatic classification to discriminate between MT and HT has indeed been attempted in the past. Most of this work targets SMT since it predates the introduction of NMT and uses a variety of approaches. For example, Arase and Zhou (2013) relied on fluency features, while Aharoni et al. (2014) used part-of-speech tags and function words, and Li et al. (2015) parse trees, density and out-of-vocabulary words. Their methods reach quite high accuracies, though indeed rely on SMT systems, which are of considerable lower quality than the current NMT ones.

NMT vs HT classification To the best of our knowledge only two publications have tackled this classification with the state-of-the-art paradigm, NMT (Bhardwaj et al., 2020; Fu and Nederhof, 2021). We now outline these two publications and place our work with respect to them.

Bhardwaj et al. (2020) work on automatically determining if a French sentence is HT or MT, with the source sentences in English. They test a variety of pre-trained language models, either multilingual –XLM-R (Conneau et al., 2020) and mBERT (Devlin et al., 2019a)– or monolingual for French: CamemBERT (Martin et al., 2020) and FlauBERT (Le et al., 2020). Moreover, they test their trained models across different domains and MT systems used during training. They find that pre-trained LMs can perform this task quite well, with accuracies of over 75% for both in-domain and cross-domain evaluation. Our work follows theirs quite closely, though there are a few important differences. First, we use publicly available WMT data, while they use a large private data set, which unfortunately limits reproducibility. Second, we analyze the impact of punctuation-type "shortcuts", while it is unclear to what extent this gets done in Bhardwaj et al. (2020).[1] Third, we also test our model on the document-level, instead of just the sentence-level.

Fu and Nederhof (2021) work on the WMT18 news commentary data set for translating Czech, German and Russian into English. By fine-tuning BERT they obtain an accuracy of 78% on all languages. However, they use training sets from WMT18, making it highly likely that Google Translate (which they use to get the translations) has seen these sentences during training.[2] This means that the MT outputs they get are likely of higher quality than it would be the case in a

[1]They do apply 12 conservative regular expressions, but, as there is no code available, it is unclear what these are and what impact this had on their results.

[2]This likely does not apply to Bhardwaj et al. (2020), as they use a private data set.

real-world scenario, and thus closer to HT, which would make the task unrealistically harder for the classifiers. On the other hand, an accuracy of 78% is quite high on this challenging task, so perhaps this is not the case. This accuracy might even be suspiciously high: it could be that the model overfit on the Google Translations, or that the data contains artifacts that the model uses as a shortcut.

Original vs MT Finally, there are three related works that attempt to discriminate between MT and original texts written in a given language, rather than human translations as is our focus. Nguyen-Son et al. (2019a) tackles this by matching similar words within paragraphs and subsequently estimating paragraph-level coherence. Nguyen-Son et al. (2019b) approaches this task by round-trip translating original and machine-translated texts and subsequently using the similarities between the original texts and their round-trip translated versions. Nguyen-Son et al. (2021) extends the former work improving the detection of MT even if a different system is used.

3 Method

3.1 Data

We will experiment with the test sets from the WMT news shared tasks.[3] We choose this data set mainly for these four reasons:

(i) it is publicly available so it guarantees reproducibility;

(ii) it has the translation direction annotated, hence we can inspect the impact of having original text or human-translated text (i.e. *translationese*) in the source side;

(iii) the data sets are also available at the document-level, meaning we can train and evaluate systems that go beyond sentence-level;

(iv) these sets are commonly used as test sets, so it is unlikely that they are used as training data in online MT systems, which we use in our experiments.

We will use the German-English data sets, and will focus on the translation direction German-to-English. This language pair has been present the longest at WMT's news shared task, from 2008 till the present day. Hence, it is the language pair

[3]For example, `https://www.statmt.org/wmt20/translation-task.html`

Data set	# SNT$_O$	# SNT$_T$	# DOC$_O$	# DOC$_T$
WMT08	361	0	15	0
WMT09	432	448	17	21
WMT10	500	505	15	22
WMT11	601	598	16	18
WMT12	611	604	14	18
WMT13	500	500	7	9
WMT14	1,500	1,503	96	68
WMT15	736	1,433	33	48
WMT16	1,499	1,500	87	68
WMT17	1,502	1,502	66	64
WMT18 (dev)	1,498	—	69	—
WMT19 (test)	2,000	—	145	—
WMT08-17	8,242	8,593	366	336
WMT14-17	5,237	5,938	282	248

Table 1: Statistics of the data sets. # SNT stands for number of sentences, # DOC for number of documents, O for number of sentences or documents in which the source side is original, while T stands for *translationese*. WMT08-17 and WMT14-17 indicate the sizes of the two training sets used.

with the most test data available. We use 2008 to 2017 as training, 2018 as dev and 2019 as test. Full statistics are shown in Table 1.

Translationese For each of these sets, roughly half of the data was originally written in our source language (German) and human-translated to our target language (English), while the other half was originally written in our target language (English) and translated to our source language (German) by a human translator. We thus make a distinction between text that originates from text written in the source language (German), and text that originates from a previous translation (i.e. English to German). We will refer to the latter as *translationese*.

Half of the data can thus be considered a different category: the source sentences are actually not original, but a translation, which means that the machine-translated output will actually be an automatic translation of a human translation, instead of an automatic translation of original text. In that part of the data, the texts in the HT category are not human translations of original text, but the original texts themselves. Since this data might exhibit different characteristics, given that the translation direction is the inverse, we only use the sentences and documents that were originally written in German for our dev and test sets (indicated with O in Table 1). Moreover, we empirically evaluate in Section 4 whether removing the extra *translationese* data from the training set is actually beneficial for the classifier.

MT Since we are interested in contrasting HT vs state-of-the-art NMT, we automatically translate the sentences using a general-purpose and widely used online MT system, DeepL.[4] We translate from German to British English,[5] specifically. We use this MT system for the majority of our experiments, though we do experiment with cross-system classification by testing on data that was translated with other MT systems, such as Google Translate, using their paid API.[6] We manually went through a subset of the translations by both DeepL and Google Translate and indeed found them to be of high quality.

To be clear, in our experiments, the machine translations actually double the size of the train, dev and test sets as indicated in Table 1. For each German source sentence, the data set now contains a human translation (HT, taken from WMT) and a machine translated variant (MT, from DeepL or Google), which are labelled as such. As an example, if we train on both the *original* and *translationese* sentence-level data of WMT08-17, we actually train on $8,242 \cdot 2 + 8,593 \cdot 2 = 33,670$ instances. Note that this also prevents a bias in topic or domain towards either HT or MT.

Ceiling To get a sense of what the upper ceiling performance of this task will be, we check the number of cases where the machine translation is the exact same as the human translation. For DeepL, this happened for 3.0% of the WMT08-17 training set sentences, 3.1% of the dev set and 3.9% of the test set. For Google, the percentages are 2.4%, 2.0% and 3.5%, respectively.[7] Of course, in practice, it is likely impossible to get anywhere near this ceiling, as the MT system also sometimes offers arguably better translations (see Section 5 for examples).

[4]`https://www.deepl.com/translator` - used in November 2021.

[5]DeepL forces the user to choose a variety of English (either British or American). This implies that the MT output could be expected to be (mostly) British English while the HT is a mix of both varieties. Hence, one could argue that variety is an aspect that could be picked up by the classifier. We also use Google Translate, which does not allow the user to select an English variety.

[6]We noticed that the free Python library *googletrans* had clearly inferior translations. The paid APIs for Google and DeepL obtain COMET (Rei et al., 2020) scores of 59.9 and 61.9, respectively, while the *googletrans* library obtains 21.0.

[7]If we apply a bit more fuzzy matching by only keeping ascii letters and numbers for each sentence, the percentages go up by around 0.5%.

Parameter	Range
Learning rate	$5 \times 10^{-6}, \mathbf{10^{-5}}, 3 \times 10^{-5}$
Batch size	$\{\mathbf{32}, 64\}$
Warmup	$\{\mathbf{0.06}\}$
Label smoothing	$\{\mathbf{0.0}, 0.1, 0.2\}$
Dropout	$\{0.0, \mathbf{0.1}\}$

Table 2: Hyperparameter range and final values (bold) for our final DEBERTA models. Hyperparameters not included are left at their default value.

3.2 Classifiers

SVM We will experiment with a number of different classifiers. As a baseline model, we use a linear SVM with unigrams and bigrams as features trained with `scikit-learn` (Pedregosa et al., 2011), for which the data is tokenized with `Spacy`.[8] The use of a SVM is mainly to find out how far we can get by just looking at the superficial lexical level. It also allows us to identify whether the classifier uses any shortcuts, i.e. features that are not necessarily indicative of a human or machine translation, but due to artifacts in the data sets, which can still be picked up as such by our models. An example of this is punctuation, which was mentioned in previous work (Bhardwaj et al., 2020). MT systems might normalize uncommon punctuation,[9] while human translators might opt for simply copying the originally specified punctuation in the source sentence (e.g. quotations, dashes). We analyse the importance of normalization in Section 5.

Fine-tuning LMs Second, we will experiment with fine-tuning pre-trained language models.[10] Fu and Nederhof (2021) only used BERT (Devlin et al., 2019b) and Bhardwaj et al. (2020) used a set of BERT- and ROBERTA-based LMs, but there exist newer pre-trained LMs that generally obtain better performance. We will empirically decide the best model for this task, by experimenting with a number of well-established LMs: BERT (Devlin et al., 2019b), RoBERTa (Liu et al., 2019), DeBERTa (He et al., 2021b; He et al., 2021a), XLNet (Yang et al., 2019), BART (Lewis et al., 2020) and Longformer (Beltagy et al., 2020). For all these models, we only tune the batch size and learning rate. The

[8]`https://spacy.io/`

[9]The normalisation of the punctuation as a pre-processing step when training an MT system is a widespread technique, so that e.g. «, », ″, “ and „ are all converted to e.g. ″.

[10]Implemented using HuggingFace (Wolf et al., 2020).

		Acc.
BART-large	Lewis et al. (2020)	64.9
BERT-large	Devlin et al. (2019b)	61.9
DEBERTA-v3-large	He et al. (2021a)	68.6
Longformer-large	Beltagy et al. (2020)	63.5
ROBERTA-large	Liu et al. (2019)	65.5
XLNET-base	Yang et al. (2019)	62.3
DEBERTA-v3-large (optim)		68.9

Table 3: Best **development set** results (all in %) for MT vs HT classification for a number of pre-trained LMs. On the test set, DEBERTA-v3-large (optim) obtains an accuracy of 66.1.

Trained on → ↓ Evaluated on	DeepL Acc.	Google Acc.
DeepL	66.1 ± 1.1	56.3 ± 0.3
Google	63.8 ± 1.6	64.9 ± 1.1
FAIR (Ng et al., 2019)	62.6 ± 1.9	57.7 ± 1.8
RWTH (Rosendahl et al., 2019)	61.9 ± 1.5	58.3 ± 1.8
PROMT (Molchanov, 2019)	50.3 ± 0.9	52.1 ± 3.3
online-X	57.5 ± 1.1	56.6 ± 3.4

Table 4: Test set scores (all in %) for training and testing our best DEBERTA across different MT-systems (DeepL and Google) and 4 WMT19 submissions. online-X refers to an anonymous online MT system evaluated at WMT19.

best model from these experiments is then tuned further (on the dev set). We tune a single parameter at a time and do not perform a full grid search due to efficiency and environmental reasons. Hyperparameter settings and range of values experimented with are shown in Table 2.

Evaluation We evaluate the models looking at the accuracy and F1-score. When standard deviation is reported, we averaged over three runs. For brevity, we only report accuracy scores, as we found them to correlate highly with the F-scores. We include additional metrics, such as the F-scores, on our GitHub repository.

4 Experiments

SVM The SVM classifier was trained on the training set WMT08–17_O (i.e. part of the data set with original source side), where the MT output was generated with DeepL. It obtained an accuracy of 57.8 on dev and 54.9 on the test set. This is in line with what would be expected: there is some signal at the lexical level, but other than that the task is quite difficult for a simple SVM classifier.

Finding the best LM As previously indicated, we experimented with a number of pre-trained LMs. For efficiency reasons, we perform these experiments with a subset of the training data (WMT14-17_O, i.e. with only translations from original text). The results are shown in Table 3. We find the best performance by using the DeBERTa-v3 model, which quite clearly outperformed the other LMs. We obtain a 6.7 point absolute increase in accuracy over BERT (61.9 to 68.6), the LM used by Fu and Nederhof (2021)), and a 3.7 point increase over the second best performing model, BART-large. We tune some of the remaining hyperparameters further (see Table 2) and obtain an accuracy of 68.9. We will use this model in our next experiments.

Cross-system performance A robust classifier that discriminates between HT and MT should not only recognize MT output that is produced by a particular MT system (the one the classifier is trained on), but should also work across different MT systems. Therefore, we test our DeepL-trained classifier on the translations of Google Translate (instead of DeepL) and vice versa. In this experiment we train the classifier on all the training data (i.e. WMT08-17_{O+T}) and evaluate on the test set.

In Table 4, we find that this cross-system evaluation leads to quite a drop in accuracy: 2.3% for DeepL and even 8.6% for Google. It seems that the classifier does not just pick up general features that discriminate between HTs and NMT outputs, but also MT-system specific features that do not always transfer to other MT systems.

In addition, we test both classifiers on a set of MT systems submitted to WMT19. We pick the two top and two bottom submissions according to the human evaluation (Barrault et al., 2019). The motivation is to find out how the classifiers perform on MT outputs of different levels of translation quality. We also notice a considerable drop in performance here. Interestingly, the classifiers perform best on the high-quality translations of FAIR and RWTH (81.6 and 81.5 human judgment scores at WMT19, respectively), and perform considerably worse on the two bottom-ranked WMT19 systems (71.8 and 69.7 human judgment scores). It seems that the classifier does not learn to recognize lower-quality MT outputs if it only saw higher-quality ones during training.

This inability to deal with lower-quality MT when trained only on high-quality MT seems counterintuitive and was quite surprising to us. After all, the difference between high-quality MT and human translation tends to be more subtle than in the case of low-quality MT. However,

	Dev	Test
WMT14-17$_{O+T}$	71.1 ± 1.3	64.9 ± 0.6
WMT14-17$_{O}$	68.9 ± 1.4	64.0 ± 1.1
WMT08-17$_{O+T}$	71.2 ± 0.9	66.1 ± 1.1
WMT08-17$_{O}$	71.5 ± 0.8	66.3 ± 0.5
WMT08-17$_{T}$	63.7 ± 0.8	59.5 ± 0.3

Table 5: Dev and test scores for training our best DEBERTA model on either WMT14-17 or WMT08-17 translated with DeepL, compared with training on the same data sets but not adding the *translationese data* (T) and only using T.

the learned features most useful for distinguishing high-quality MT from HT are likely different in nature than the features that are most useful for distinguishing low-quality MT from HT (e.g., simple lexical features versus features related to word ordering). From this perspective, feeding low-quality MT to a system trained on high-quality MT can be seen as an instance of out-of-distribution data that is not modelled well during the training stage. Nevertheless, this featural discrepancy could likely be resolved by supplying additional examples of low-quality MT to the classifier at training time.

Removing translationese data In our previous experiment we used the full training data (i.e. WMT08-17$_{O+T}$). However, most of the WMT data sets only consist for 50% of sentences that were originally written in German; the other half were originally written in English (see Section 3.1). We ask the question whether this additional data (which we refer to as *translationese*) is actually beneficial to the classifier. On the one hand, it is in fact a different category than human translations from original text. On the other, its usage allows us to double the amount of training data (see Table 1).

In Table 5 we show that the extra data helps if there is not much training data available (WMT14-17), but that this effect disappears once we increase the amount of training data (WMT08-17). In fact, the *translationese* data seems to be clearly of lower quality (for this task), since a model trained on only this data (WMT08-17$_{T}$), which is of the same size as the WMT08-17$_{O}$ experiments, results in quite a drop in accuracy (59.5 vs 66.3 on the test set). We have also experimented with pre-training on WMT08-17$_{O+T}$ and then fine-tuning on WMT08-17$_{O}$. Our initial results were mixed, but we plan on investigating this in future work.

Beyond sentence-level In many practical use-cases, we actually have access to full documents, and thus do not have to restrict ourselves to looking at just sentences. This could lead to better performance, since certain problems of NMT systems only come to light in a multi-sentence setting (Frankenberg-Garcia, 2021). Since WMT also contains document-level information, we can simply use the same data set as before. Due to the number of instances being very low at document level (see Table 1), and to the fact that the addition of *translationese* data showed to be beneficial with limited amounts of training data (see Table 5), we use all the data available for our document-level experiments, i.e. WMT08-17$_{O+T}$.

We have four document-level classifiers: (i) a SVM, similar to the one used in our sentence-level experiments, but for which each training instance is a document; (ii) majority voting atop our best sentence-level classifier, DEBERTA, i.e. we aggregate its sentence-level predictions for each document by taking the majority class; (iii) DEBERTA fine-tuned on the document-level data, truncated to 512 tokens; and (iv) Longformer (Beltagy et al., 2020) fine-tuned on the document-level data, as this LM was designed to handle documents.

For document-level training, we use gradient accumulation and mixed precision to avoid out-of-memory errors. Additionally, we truncate the input to 512 subword tokens for the DEBERTA model. For the dev and test set, this means discarding 11% and 2% of the tokens per document on average, respectively.[11] A potential approach for dealing with longer context without resorting to truncation is to use a sliding window strategy, which we aim to explore in future work.

The results are presented in Table 6. First, we observe that the document-level baselines obtain, as expected, better accuracies than their sentence-level counterparts (e.g. 60.7 vs 54.9 for SVM and 72.5 vs 66.1 for DEBERTA on test). Second, we observe large differences between dev and test, as well as large standard deviations. The instability of the results could be due, to some extent, to the low number of instances in these data sets (138 and 290, as shown in Table 1). Moreover, the test set is likely harder in general than the dev set, since it on average has fewer sentences per document (13.8 vs 21.7).

[11]The median subword token count in the HT document-level data is 376, with a minimum of 47 and maximum of 3,254.

	DeepL		Google	
	Dev	Test	Dev	Test
SVM	74.8	60.7	84.7	64.8
DEBERTA (mc)	84.7±8.0	72.5±5.2	93.2±1.1	67.6±3.4
DEBERTA	91.1 ± 2.4	76.8±4.4	95.9 ± 1.5	60.8±1.2
Longformer	80.2 ± 2.7	82.0±7.2	94.2±1.3	63.2±0.9

Table 6: Accuracies of training and evaluating on document-level DeepL and Google data. For DEBERTA, we try two versions: a sentence-level model applied to each sentence in a document followed by majority classification (mc), and a model trained on full documents (truncated to 512 tokens).

5 Discussion & Analysis

Thus far we have reported results in terms of an automatic evaluation metric: classification accuracy. Now we would like to delve deeper by conducting analyses that allow us to obtain further insights. To this end, we exploit the fact that the SVM classifier outputs the most discriminative features for each class: HT and MT.

5.1 Punctuation Normalization

In this first analysis we looked at the best features of the SVM to find out whether there is an obvious indication of "shortcuts" that the pre-trained language models can take. The best features for both HT and MT are shown in Table 8.

For comparison, we also show the best features after applying Moses' (Koehn et al., 2007) punctuation normalization,[12] which is commonly used as a preprocessing step when training MT systems. Indeed, there are punctuation-level features that by all accounts should not be indicative of either class, but still show up as such. The backtick (`) and dash symbol (–) show up as the best unigram features indicating HT, but are not present after the punctuation is normalized.

Now, to be clear, one might make a case of still including these features in HT vs MT experiments. After all, if this is how MT sentences can be spotted, why should we not consider them? On the other hand, the shortcuts that work for this particular data set and MT system (DeepL) might not work for texts in different domains or texts that are translated by different MT systems. Moreover, the shortcuts might obscure an analysis of the more interesting differences between human and machine translated texts.

[12]https://github.com/moses-smt/mosesdecoder/blob/master/scripts/tokenizer/normalize-punctuation.perl

	Original	Normalized
Sent-level		
SVM	54.9	54.5
DEBERTA-v3	66.1 ± 1.1	67.0 ± 0.6
Doc-level		
SVM	60.7	60.0
DEBERTA (majority)	72.5 ± 5.2	72.0 ± 4.1
DEBERTA	76.8 ± 4.4	77.2 ± 4.7
Longformer	82.0 ± 7.2	83.7 ± 2.1

Table 7: Test set accuracies of training and evaluating on sentence-level and document-level data on either the original or normalized (by Moses) input texts, translated with DeepL.

In any case, we want to determine the impact of punctuation-level shortcuts by comparing the original scores versus the scores of our classifiers trained on punctuation-normalized texts. The results of our baseline and best sentence- and document-level systems with and without normalization are shown in Table 7. We observe that, even if the two best unigram features were initially punctuation, normalizing does not affect performance in a major way. There is even a small increase in performance for DEBERTA-v3 and Longformer, though likely not significant.

5.2 Unigram Analysis

In our second analysis we manually went through the data set to analyse the 10 most indicative unigram features for MT (before normalization).[13] Interestingly, some are due to errors by the human translator: the MT system correctly used *schoolyard* instead of the split *school yard*, and it also used the correct name *Olympiakos Piraeus* instead of the incorrect *Olypiacos Piraeus* (typo in the first word). Some are indeed due to a different (and likely better) lexical choice by the human translator, though the translation is not necessarily wrong: *competing gang* instead of *rival gang*, *espionage scandal* instead of *spy affair*, *judging panel* instead of *jury* and *radiation* instead of *rays*. Finally, the feature *disclosure* looks to be an error on the MT side. It occurs a number of times in the machine-translated version of a news article discussing Wikileaks, in which the human translator chose the correct *Wikileaks publication* instead of *Wikileaks disclosure* and *whistleblower activists* instead of *disclosure activists*.

[13]Of course, since we only look at unigrams here, and the performance of the sentence-level SVM is not very high anyway, all these features have in common that they do not necessarily generalize to other domains or MT-systems.

Before normalization				After normalization			
Most indicative for MT		Most indicative for HT		Most indicative for MT		Most indicative for HT	
1-grams	2-grams	1-grams	2-grams	1-grams	2-grams	1-grams	2-grams
olympiakos	are said	`	the riders	olympiakos	" proctor	u.s.	the riders
affair	" proctor	–	the 2015	affair	are said	program	consequently ,
forsa	2010 ,	u.s.	consequently ,	forsa	book "	nearly	the 2015
rival	per cent	nearly	projects ,	rays	2010 ,	anticipated	. the
rays	almost the	program	. the	rival	per cent	everybody	projects ,
schoolyard	the flat	anticipated	life "	disclosure	almost the	premier	<93>the hunting
disclosure	in view	<93>the	- weiss	jury	be put	lama <92>s	a part
jury	with industry	premier	a part	succeed	and later	weiss	as for

Table 8: Best features (1-gram and 2-gram models) in the SVM classifier per class, before and after normalizing punctuation.

For the best unigrams indicative of HT, there are some signs of simplification by the MT system. It never uses *nearly* or *anticipate*, instead generally opting for *almost* and *expected*. Similarly, human translators sometimes used *U.S.* to refer to the United States, while the MT system always uses *US*. The fact that we used British English for the DeepL translations might also play a role: *program* is indicative for HT since the MT system generally used *programme*.

6 Conclusions

In this paper we trained classifiers to automatically distinguish between human and machine translations for German-to-English. Our classifiers are built by pre-training state-of-the-art language models. We use the test sets of the WMT shared tasks, to ensure that the machine translation systems we use (DeepL and Google) did not see the data already during training. Throughout a number of experiments, we show that: (i) the task is quite challenging, as our best sentence-level systems obtain around 65% accuracy, (ii) using *translationese* data during training is only beneficial if there is limited data available, (iii) the accuracy drops considerably when performing cross MT-system evaluating, (iv) accuracy improves when performing the task on the document-level and (v) normalizing punctuation (and thus avoiding certain shortcuts) does not have an impact on model performance.

In future work, we aim to do a number of things. For one, we want to experiment with both translation directions and different source languages instead of just German. Second, we want to perform cross-domain experiments (as in Bhardwaj et al. (2020)), as we currently only looked at news texts.[14] Third, we want to look at the effect of the source language: does a monolingual model that is trained on English translations from German still work on translations into English from different source languages? This can shed on light on the question in what sense general source language-independent features that discriminate between HT and MT are actually identified by the model. Fourth, we plan to also use the source sentence, with a multilingual pre-trained LM, following Bhardwaj et al. (2020). This additional information is expected to lead to better results. While the source sentence is not always available, there are real-world cases in which it is, e.g. filtering crawled parallel corpora. Fifth, we would like to expand the task to a 3-way classification, as in the least restrictive scenario, given a text in a language, it could be either originally written in that language, human translated from another language or machine translated from another language.

7 Acknowledgements

The authors received funding from the European Union's Connecting Europe Facility 2014-2020 - CEF Telecom, under Grant Agreement No. INEA/CEF/ICT/A2020/2278341 (MaCoCu). This communication reflects only the authors' views. The Agency is not responsible for any use that may be made of the information it contains. We thank the Center for Information Technology of the University of Groningen for providing access to the Peregrine high performance computing cluster. Finally, we thank all our MaCoCu colleagues for their valuable feedback throughout the project.

[14]Note that this domain has a real-world application: the detection of fake news, given the fact that MT could be use to spread such news in other languages (Bonet-Jover, 2020).

References

Aharoni, Roee, Moshe Koppel, and Yoav Goldberg. 2014. Automatic detection of machine translated text and translation quality estimation. In *Proceedings of the 52nd Annual Meeting of the Association for Computational Linguistics (Volume 2: Short Papers)*, pages 289–295.

Ahrenberg, Lars. 2017. Comparing machine translation and human translation: A case study. In *Proceedings of the Workshop Human-Informed Translation and Interpreting Technology*, pages 21–28, Varna, Bulgaria, September. Association for Computational Linguistics, Shoumen, Bulgaria.

Arase, Yuki and Ming Zhou. 2013. Machine translation detection from monolingual web-text. In *Proceedings of the 51st Annual Meeting of the Association for Computational Linguistics (Volume 1: Long Papers)*, pages 1597–1607.

Barrault, Loïc, Ondřej Bojar, Marta R. Costa-jussà, Christian Federmann, Mark Fishel, Yvette Graham, Barry Haddow, Matthias Huck, Philipp Koehn, Shervin Malmasi, Christof Monz, Mathias Müller, Santanu Pal, Matt Post, and Marcos Zampieri. 2019. Findings of the 2019 conference on machine translation (WMT19). In *Proceedings of the Fourth Conference on Machine Translation (Volume 2: Shared Task Papers, Day 1)*, pages 1–61, Florence, Italy, August. Association for Computational Linguistics.

Beltagy, Iz, Matthew E Peters, and Arman Cohan. 2020. Longformer: The long-document transformer. *arXiv preprint arXiv:2004.05150*.

Bhardwaj, Shivendra, David Alfonso Hermelo, Phillippe Langlais, Gabriel Bernier-Colborne, Cyril Goutte, and Michel Simard. 2020. Human or neural translation? In *Proceedings of the 28th International Conference on Computational Linguistics*, pages 6553–6564, Barcelona, Spain (Online), December. International Committee on Computational Linguistics.

Bonet-Jover, Alba. 2020. The disinformation battle: Linguistics and artificial intelligence join to beat it.

Conneau, Alexis, Kartikay Khandelwal, Naman Goyal, Vishrav Chaudhary, Guillaume Wenzek, Francisco Guzmán, Edouard Grave, Myle Ott, Luke Zettlemoyer, and Veselin Stoyanov. 2020. Unsupervised cross-lingual representation learning at scale. In *Proceedings of the 58th Annual Meeting of the Association for Computational Linguistics*, pages 8440–8451, Online, July. Association for Computational Linguistics.

Devlin, Jacob, Ming-Wei Chang, Kenton Lee, and Kristina Toutanova. 2019a. BERT: Pre-training of deep bidirectional transformers for language understanding. In *Proceedings of the 2019 Conference of the North American Chapter of the Association for Computational Linguistics: Human Language Technologies, Volume 1 (Long and Short Papers)*, pages 4171–4186, Minneapolis, Minnesota, June. Association for Computational Linguistics.

Devlin, Jacob, Ming-Wei Chang, Kenton Lee, and Kristina Toutanova. 2019b. BERT: Pre-training of deep bidirectional transformers for language understanding. In *Proceedings of the 2019 Conference of the North American Chapter of the Association for Computational Linguistics: Human Language Technologies, Volume 1 (Long and Short Papers)*, pages 4171–4186, Minneapolis, Minnesota, June. Association for Computational Linguistics.

Frankenberg-Garcia, Ana. 2021. Can a corpus-driven lexical analysis of human and machine translation unveil discourse features that set them apart? *Target. International Journal of Translation Studies*, 09.

Fu, Yingxue and Mark-Jan Nederhof. 2021. Automatic classification of human translation and machine translation: A study from the perspective of lexical diversity. In *Proceedings for the First Workshop on Modelling Translation: Translatology in the Digital Age*, pages 91–99, online, May. Association for Computational Linguistics.

He, Pengcheng, Jianfeng Gao, and Weizhu Chen. 2021a. Debertav3: Improving deberta using electra-style pre-training with gradient-disentangled embedding sharing. *arXiv preprint arXiv:2111.09543*.

He, Pengcheng, Xiaodong Liu, Jianfeng Gao, and Weizhu Chen. 2021b. DeBERTa: Decoding-enhanced BERT with disentangled attention. In *International Conference on Learning Representations*.

Koehn, Philipp, Hieu Hoang, Alexandra Birch, Chris Callison-Burch, Marcello Federico, Nicola Bertoldi, Brooke Cowan, Wade Shen, Christine Moran, Richard Zens, Chris Dyer, Ondřej Bojar, Alexandra Constantin, and Evan Herbst. 2007. Moses: Open source toolkit for statistical machine translation. In *ACL Companion Volume Proceedings of the Demo and Poster Sessions*, pages 177–180, Prague, Czech Republic, June.

Le, Hang, Loïc Vial, Jibril Frej, Vincent Segonne, Maximin Coavoux, Benjamin Lecouteux, Alexandre Allauzen, Benoit Crabbé, Laurent Besacier, and Didier Schwab. 2020. FlauBERT: Unsupervised language model pre-training for French. In *Proceedings of the 12th Language Resources and Evaluation Conference*, pages 2479–2490, Marseille, France, May. European Language Resources Association.

Lewis, Mike, Yinhan Liu, Naman Goyal, Marjan Ghazvininejad, Abdelrahman Mohamed, Omer Levy, Veselin Stoyanov, and Luke Zettlemoyer. 2020. BART: Denoising sequence-to-sequence pre-training for natural language generation, translation, and comprehension. In *Proceedings of the 58th Annual Meeting of the Association for Computational Linguistics*, pages 7871–7880, Online, July. Association for Computational Linguistics.

Li, Yitong, Rui Wang, and Hai Zhao. 2015. A machine learning method to distinguish machine translation from human translation. In *Proceedings of the 29th Pacific Asia Conference on Language, Information and Computation: Posters*, pages 354–360.

Liu, Yinhan, Myle Ott, Naman Goyal, Jingfei Du, Mandar Joshi, Danqi Chen, Omer Levy, Mike Lewis, Luke Zettlemoyer, and Veselin Stoyanov. 2019. Roberta: A robustly optimized bert pretraining approach. *arXiv preprint arXiv:1907.11692*.

Martin, Louis, Benjamin Muller, Pedro Javier Ortiz Suárez, Yoann Dupont, Laurent Romary, Éric de la Clergerie, Djamé Seddah, and Benoît Sagot. 2020. CamemBERT: a tasty French language model. In *Proceedings of the 58th Annual Meeting of the Association for Computational Linguistics*, pages 7203–7219, Online, July. Association for Computational Linguistics.

Molchanov, Alexander. 2019. Promt systems for wmt 2019 shared translation task. In *Proceedings of the Fourth Conference on Machine Translation (Volume 2: Shared Task Papers, Day 1)*, pages 302–307, Florence, Italy, August. Association for Computational Linguistics.

Ng, Nathan, Kyra Yee, Alexei Baevski, Myle Ott, Michael Auli, and Sergey Edunov. 2019. Facebook FAIR's WMT19 news translation task submission. In *Proceedings of the Fourth Conference on Machine Translation (Volume 2: Shared Task Papers, Day 1)*, pages 314–319, Florence, Italy, August. Association for Computational Linguistics.

Nguyen-Son, Hoang-Quoc, Tran Phuong Thao, Seira Hidano, and Shinsaku Kiyomoto. 2019a. Detecting machine-translated paragraphs by matching similar words. *arXiv preprint arXiv:1904.10641*.

Nguyen-Son, Hoang-Quoc, Tran Phuong Thao, Seira Hidano, and Shinsaku Kiyomoto. 2019b. Detecting machine-translated text using back translation. *arXiv preprint arXiv:1910.06558*.

Nguyen-Son, Hoang-Quoc, Tran Thao, Seira Hidano, Ishita Gupta, and Shinsaku Kiyomoto. 2021. Machine translated text detection through text similarity with round-trip translation. In *Proceedings of the 2021 Conference of the North American Chapter of the Association for Computational Linguistics: Human Language Technologies*, pages 5792–5797.

Pedregosa, F., G. Varoquaux, A. Gramfort, V. Michel, B. Thirion, O. Grisel, M. Blondel, P. Prettenhofer, R. Weiss, V. Dubourg, J. Vanderplas, A. Passos, D. Cournapeau, M. Brucher, M. Perrot, and E. Duchesnay. 2011. Scikit-learn: Machine learning in Python. *Journal of Machine Learning Research*, 12:2825–2830.

Rei, Ricardo, Craig Stewart, Ana C Farinha, and Alon Lavie. 2020. COMET: A neural framework for MT evaluation. In *Proceedings of the 2020 Conference on Empirical Methods in Natural Language Processing (EMNLP)*, pages 2685–2702, Online, November. Association for Computational Linguistics.

Rosendahl, Jan, Christian Herold, Yunsu Kim, Miguel Graça, Weiyue Wang, Parnia Bahar, Yingbo Gao, and Hermann Ney. 2019. The RWTH Aachen University machine translation systems for WMT 2019. In *Proceedings of the Fourth Conference on Machine Translation (Volume 2: Shared Task Papers, Day 1)*, pages 349–355, Florence, Italy, August. Association for Computational Linguistics.

Toral, Antonio and Víctor M. Sánchez-Cartagena. 2017. A multifaceted evaluation of neural versus phrase-based machine translation for 9 language directions. In *Proceedings of the 15th Conference of the European Chapter of the Association for Computational Linguistics: Volume 1, Long Papers*, pages 1063–1073, Valencia, Spain, April. Association for Computational Linguistics.

Toral, Antonio. 2019. Post-editese: an exacerbated translationese. In *Proceedings of Machine Translation Summit XVII: Research Track*, pages 273–281, Dublin, Ireland, August. European Association for Machine Translation.

Vanmassenhove, Eva, Dimitar Shterionov, and Andy Way. 2019. Lost in translation: Loss and decay of linguistic richness in machine translation. In *Proceedings of Machine Translation Summit XVII: Research Track*, pages 222–232, Dublin, Ireland, August. European Association for Machine Translation.

Wolf, Thomas, Lysandre Debut, Victor Sanh, Julien Chaumond, Clement Delangue, Anthony Moi, Pierric Cistac, Tim Rault, Rémi Louf, Morgan Funtowicz, Joe Davison, Sam Shleifer, Patrick von Platen, Clara Ma, Yacine Jernite, Julien Plu, Canwen Xu, Teven Le Scao, Sylvain Gugger, Mariama Drame, Quentin Lhoest, and Alexander M. Rush. 2020. Transformers: State-of-the-art natural language processing. In *Proceedings of the 2020 Conference on Empirical Methods in Natural Language Processing: System Demonstrations*, pages 38–45, Online, October. Association for Computational Linguistics.

Yang, Zhilin, Zihang Dai, Yiming Yang, Jaime Carbonell, Russ R Salakhutdinov, and Quoc V Le. 2019. Xlnet: Generalized autoregressive pretraining for language understanding. *Advances in neural information processing systems*, 32.

A Taxonomy and Study of Critical Errors in Machine Translation

Khetam Al Sharou[1] and **Lucia Specia**[1, 2]
[1]Language and Multimodal AI Lab, Imperial College London, UK
[2]Computer Science Department, University of Sheffield, UK
{k.al-sharou, l.specia}@imperial.ac.uk

Abstract

Not all machine mistranslations are of equal scale of severity. For example, mistranslating a date or time in an appointment, mistranslating a number or currency in a contract, or hallucinating profanity may lead to catastrophic consequences for the users. The severity of the errors is an important but overlooked aspect of machine translation (MT) quality evaluation. In this paper, we present the results of our effort to bring awareness to the problem of critical translation errors. We study, validate and extend an initial taxonomy of critical errors with the view of providing guidance for critical error analysis, annotation and mitigation. We test the extended taxonomy for three language pairs to examine to what extent it generalises across languages. We provide an account of factors that affect annotation tasks along with recommendations on how to improve annotation practice in future work. We also study patterns in the source text that can lead to critical errors. Detecting such linguistic patterns could be used to improve the performance of MT systems, especially for user-generated content.

1 Introduction

Machine Translation (MT) has now become ubiquitous in many online platforms (e.g. social networks) and generally used without any human post-editing due to cost, timeliness, and accessibility. The rapid development and adoption of MT has advanced efforts to improve and standardise MT evaluation, and increased discussion on how we should evaluate MT (Dorr et al., 2011; García, 2014; Ulitkin et al., 2021). This need escalated with the use of MT to translate user-generated content (UGC), e.g. in social media platforms. Unlike formal text, UGC often has colloquial language, including profanities, spelling errors, emojis, hashtags and abbreviations, and is grammatically ill-formed, which makes it hard for MT, often resulting in incorrect translations (Al Sharou et al., 2021). Some of these incorrect translations can contain critical errors. In this work, we refer to *critical errors* as instances of translations where the meaning in the target text deviates drastically from the source text where such translations can be misleading and may carry health, safety, legal, reputation, religious or financial implications.

The volume of content shared by users means that the MT-translated content cannot be manually post-edited. Therefore, users have to rely on MT as is and usually do not have the linguistic skills to identify the errors. As a consequence, users may be negatively affected if they misunderstand the intention or sentiment of the source text or could take inappropriate action if they act on critically corrupted translations. There are many instances where innocuous statements on social media have been translated by the machine to say something quite different, the opposite, or even turn a simple greeting into hate speech - translating ‘good morning’ into ‘attack them’ by the machine, leading to the arrest of the man who posted it on his social media profile as reported by the Guardian (Hern, 2017). Therefore, it is important that the issue of critical error is directly addressed.

To mitigate such a problem, recent research has looked into automatic methods to detect critical er-

Macken, Rufener, Van den Bogaert, Daems, Tezcan, Vanroy, Fonteyne, Barrault, Costa-jussà, Kemp, Pilos, Declercq, Koponen, Forcada, Scarton, Moniz (eds.)
Proceedings of the 23rd Annual Conference of the European Association for Machine Translation, p. 171–179
Ghent, Belgium, June 2022.

rors in machine translation, with a view to inform users of such errors. This was framed as a track in the WMT 2021 Shared Task on Quality Estimation (Specia et al., 2021). A taxonomy was proposed to annotate training and evaluation data for this task. The annotation effort focused on critical errors only, i.e. other errors were disregarded. This differs from previous work, where critical errors – if evaluated – are seen as an extra level of annotation on general errors, i.e. as a *severity judgement* on errors (Lommel et al., 2014). From a practical perspective, we believe this focused annotation is a good strategy as it saves annotation effort and allows gisting-oriented quality prediction models, under the assumption that MT is still usable even though it may contain minor (non-critical) errors. According to Specia et al. (2021), however, the annotation of critical errors proved very challenging, with low agreement amongst annotators.

A taxonomy is an important step as it establishes which types of errors should be considered critical. We revisit and extend the taxonomy proposed in Specia et al. (2021) in order to (a) perform a more focused, smaller-scale study with well-trained annotators to understand the general challenges in annotating critical errors, and (b) validate the extended taxonomy on different languages. For that, we commission the manual annotation of such errors and conduct an in-depth analysis of their impact on the translations. We reflect on the annotation process as an essential part of any evaluation task that aims to examine the performance and usability of MT systems for better evaluation and annotation practices. We also show how the source text can affect the quality of MT translations when it comes to the presence of critical errors.

We start by presenting an overview of popular quality evaluation taxonomies (Section 2) to then introduce the taxonomy we study, developed in Specia et al. (2021), with two additional categories we propose to add to the taxonomy (Section 3). We then explain our approach and criteria to validating the extended taxonomy and follow that with a data analysis through which we show how the taxonomy is validated (Section 4). We also reflect on the annotation process for different languages (Section 5). Finally, we explore how the quality or lack of quality of the source text could contribute to the generation of critical errors (Section 6).

2 Related Work

With the rapid development and increasing adoption of Machine Translation systems, evaluating the quality has become a common practice. This has led to advances in the area of translation quality assessment (TQA) and inspired initiatives that aimed to standardise this practice.[1] TQA is used to assess the performance of a system, and whether its output fits to be used either as is or as a first draft that requires some post-editing (O'Brien, 2012; Han, 2022). TQA can also be utilised to enhance the performance of systems, as a point of comparison between various systems, or to estimate the effort required to post-edit machine-translated content (Aziz et al., 2012; Popović, 2018). Examining the quality of the MT output has been conducted through either the identification of errors, or the overall assessment of MT quality, or both.

Various classifications of errors have been developed, against which MT system outputs are assessed (Lommel et al., 2014; Abu-Ayyash, 2017; Popović, 2018). The two most comprehensive frameworks, which have been widely adopted in industry, academia and by end-users, are (i) Multidimensional Quality Metrics (MQM), proposed under the EU-funded QTLaunchPad project (Lommel et al., 2014), and (ii) Dynamic Quality Framework (DQF) by the Translation Automation User Society (TAUS) (Lommel et al., 2015; Rivera-Trigueros, 2021). These initiatives offering general taxonomies are based on, and inspired by, earlier error-specific models including LISA QA Model, developed in the 1990s by the Localisation Industry Standards, and the SAE J2450 metric, among others (Lommel et al., 2014).

Another group of individual error classifications includes language-related and linguistically-motivated taxonomies that aim to evaluate the quality of MT output according to specific linguistic phenomena that occur in the translation and are associated with certain languages. For example, Costa et al. (2015)'s study classifies translation errors from English into European Portuguese. Their work extends previous taxonomies to study errors associated with morphologically rich languages. Some other studies focus specifically on the impact of certain features of the text on the output. For example, Abu-Ayyash (2017) explores errors and non-errors for the English-Arabic pair in MT-translated gender-bound constructs in tech-

[1] In this work, we only focus on human evaluation.

nical texts, and Han et al. (2020) proposes a categorisation of error types generated by MT systems when translating multiword expressions.

In addition to classifying types of errors, other aspects of quality evaluation are considered, i.e. the importance and severity of the errors. Still, these are optional criteria and considered depending on the task and the purpose of the translation. In the MQM framework, importance is assigned to categories of errors. For example, if one category is considered as a priority for a given task, it is deemed as important for that specific task. Severity, however, is applicable to individual errors, and is related to their nature and their impact on the usability of the translation. 'The more severe an error is, the more likely it is to negatively affect the user in some fashion' (Lommel, 2018). MQM identifies four levels of severity: critical, major, minor, and null that align to some extent with those adopted in the DQF framework (Lommel, 2018).

More recent work has focused on classifying only the most severe errors (referred to as *critical errors*). For example, the WMT 2021 Shared Task on Quality Estimation (Specia et al., 2021) organised a track on predicting the presence of critical errors in sentence translations. As part of this track, a taxonomy of critical errors was proposed and a large amount of data was annotated for such errors: 10K translations from English into four languages (Chinese, Japanese, Czech and German). Each translation was annotated by three professional translators. However, the authors observed that the annotation was problematic, with overall low annotator agreement. It was not clear from the effort whether this was because of the general lack of understanding of the task by the annotators, the complexity of the task, or because of other factors.

One interesting outcome of the report in Specia et al. (2021) was the high proportion of critical errors in UGC. It is clear that error-free MT is still unattainable and that critical errors are not rare. Therefore, further research towards understanding, formalising, and annotating such errors is much needed before prediction and mitigation strategies can be put in place. We, therefore, devote this work to bring attention to this issue. We study critical errors that have the same level of severity (highest), and treat them as critical errors because of their potential negative impact on those who use the translations as they are. The assumption, which we test in this paper, is that the types of critical errors should be applicable to any language pair. As far as we know, this is the first work which focuses on studying critical errors in UGC.

3 A Taxonomy of Critical Errors

In what follows, we present Specia et al. (2021)'s taxonomy of critical errors a) to serve as the base for a new extended taxonomy developed in this work and b) to be tested and analysed in detail. It recognises three ways in which meaning deviations from the source sentence can happen:

- **Mistranslation**: content is translated incorrectly into a different meaning, copied to the target text (i.e. it remains in the source language), or translated into gibberish.
- **Hallucination**: content that is not in the source is introduced into the translation. For example, profanity words are introduced.
- **Deletion**: critical content that is in the source sentence is not present in the translation. For instance, the source sentence may contain a negation that is removed from the translation.

In this taxonomy, there are five main categories of critical errors:

1. Deviation in toxicity (TOX): This category refers to instances where the translation may incite hate, violence, profanity or abuse against an individual or a group (a religion, race, gender, etc.) due to incorrect translations. It covers cases where toxicity is introduced into the translation when it is not in the source, deleted in the translation when it is in the source, mistranslated into different (toxic or not) words, or not translated at all (i.e. the toxicity remains in the source language or transliterated).

2. Deviation in health/safety risks (SAF): This category refers to instances where the translation may bring a risk to the reader where the meaning which has been changed has health and safety implications. This issue can happen when content is introduced into the translation, deleted from the translation when it is in the source, or mistranslated into different words, or not translated at all (i.e. it remains in the source language).

3. Deviation in named entities (NAM): A named entity (people, organisation, location) is deleted, mistranslated by either another incorrect named entity or a common word or gibberish, left untranslated when it should be translated, or introduced when it is not in the source text.

4. Deviation in sentiment or negation (SEN):

rics to validate the taxonomy and annotation task. Given the small number of participants, which may undermine the effectiveness of statistical analysis, we also look at the results from a qualitative perspective. We also asked the annotators to complete a questionnaire, reflecting on their experience carrying out the annotation task. The annotators were instructed to conduct the annotation independently.

4.2 Data Analysis

In order to validate the extended taxonomy, we looked at the annotation carried out for the three languages in light of two criteria:

- **Reproducibility** (through agreement rate among annotators): by confirming the presence or absence of critical errors in each translation, regardless of the types of critical error(s).
- **Applicability to other languages**: whether the error types in the taxonomy are observed for different language pairs.

4.2.1 Reproducibility

In this section, we present an analysis of the inter-annotator agreement (IAA) ratings among annotators, based on the set of 100 sentences, for each of the three language combinations, i.e. English–Chinese (EN–ZH), English–Italian (EN–IT) and English–Arabic (EN–AR).

Sentence Level: We compute IAA on the sentence-level binary labels, using Cohen's Kappa (Cohen, 1960), where raters agree on whether or not the sentence has at least one critical error, regardless of the type of critical error.

Table 1 displays the results for error mark-up, presented in pair-wise comparisons to evaluate the similarity between each pair of annotators.

Annot.	EN–ZH	EN–IT	EN–AR
1&2	0.802	0.906	0.840
2&3	0.825	0.652	0.640
1&3	0.872	0.699	0.640
Average	0.833	0.752	0.706

Table 1: Cohen's Kappa IAA - Sentence Level

Table 1 shows a substantial agreement among the annotator across the three languages, with English–Arabic gaining the lowest agreement rating. This high rating could have been influenced by the way the dataset was selected, described in Section (4). It is of relevance to note that although Arabic annotators (**2&3**) and (**1&3**) have the same agreement rating, their rating shows some discrepancies when it comes to error types (see Table 2) below. It is also important to clarify that we intended to order annotators according to whether they had received training on the taxonomy and guidelines (annotators labelled as **1**), followed by those who did not attend but asked for clarification (annotators labelled as **2**), then the ones who carried out the annotation using only the guidelines and the extended taxonomy (annotators labelled as **3**). This explains why the agreement rate among annotators (**1&2**) is higher, especially for the English–Italian and English–Arabic language pairs. These results serve our aim to examine factors such as training that can affect the annotation task and annotators' performance (for an in-depth analysis of the annotation task, see Section 5).

Type Level: As a further step, we calculate the IAA on a categorical scale. We use Fleiss' kappa in SPSS (Fleiss, 1971; Fleiss et al., 2003) that allows determining the level of agreement on a categorical scale, i.e. agreement on individual categories of errors. Based on the extended taxonomy, we included in the annotation task, as a drop-down menu for the annotators to use, the seven categories in addition to one more category, labelled as 'None', to cover cases where no critical error(s) were detected. Results presented in Table 2 show that the average over all pairs of annotators and all categories is lower in all languages, compared with the sentence level agreement rating. Overall categorical agreement rating can be described as moderate for Italian and Arabic (**0.548** and **0.424** respectively), and substantial for Chinese (**0.624**). This reveals that annotators may have found it difficult to decide on the types of errors. Their assessment may have been influenced by several factors. Annotation is to some extent a subjective task and is greatly influenced by how annotators treat and understand the source and target sides of the data. For example, some annotators were inclined to label errors as critical based on their own assessment rather than according to what the guidelines say (see discussion in Section 5).

It is interesting to see that Chinese has the highest agreement rate in both rating exercises, i.e. sentence level (**0.833**) and type level (**0.624**). A closer look shows that error types were assigned mainly under three types, i.e. **'TOX'**, **'Other'** and **'None'**. This somehow explains why it has the highest average agreement rates at both levels. We also no-

Error Type	Annot.	EN-ZH	EN-IT	EN-AR
TOX	1&2	0.451	0.792	0.838
	2&3	0.968	0.452	0.552
	1&3	0.336	0.435	0.535
SAF	1&2	—	-0.005	—
	2&3	-0.005	1	—
	1&3	-0.005	-0.005	—
NAM	1&2	-0.005	-0.02	-0.015
	2&3	—	0.490	-0.005
	1&3	-0.005	-0.01	-0.01
SEN	1&2	—	—	-0.01
	2&3	—	-0.005	-0.005
	1&3	—	-0.005	-0.005
NUM	1&2	—	-0.005	—
	2&3	—	-0.005	—
	1&3	—	1	—
INS	1&2	0.011	-0.015	-0.015
	2&3	0.795	-0.01	0.096
	1&3	0	0.385	-0.111
Other	1&2	0.479	-0.005	-0.031
	2&3	0.740	-0.02	—
	1&3	0.656	-0.026	-0.031
None	1&2	0.757	0.906	0.640
	2&3	0.872	0.486	0.880
	1&3	0.944	0.532	0.640
Overall Agreement		0.624	0.548	0.424

Table 2: Fleiss' kappa Agreement on Error Types

tice that annotators (**2&3**) are closer in their agreement rates, especially when it comes to '**Other**' and '**None**' categories. These two annotators may have collaborated on this task, although annotators were told to work independently.

It is important to highlight that a high rate is given to certain categories, e.g. '**INS**' in Chinese, achieving **0.795**. When annotators (**2&3**) from this group asked about the reason behind their selection of the '**INS**' type, their answer showed that they interpreted sentences in the *seemingly* imperative format as instructions, hence assigned errors as a 'deviation in instructions'. In reality, this might not have been the case, especially that the Chinese annotator **1** and the annotators for the other language pairs did not label a similar number of critical errors under the '**INS**' category. This finding gives an indication about how failure to understand what each category implies by annotators could affect the evaluation and annotation task and necessitates that focused training is provided, especially when more specific tasks are assigned to annotators.

4.2.2 Applicability

We carried out an analysis to validate the applicability of the extended taxonomy. Namely, we

- present an analysis of the error distribution for the language pairs, i.e. English–Chinese, English–Italian and English–Arabic;
- provide examples of the different types of errors in the three selected language pairs.

Error distribution across the three languages is presented in Table 3. We calculate the average of the total number of each error type, selected by the three annotators, for each language pair to show how many times each error has been selected by the annotators across the three languages.

Annot.	EN-ZH	EN-IT	EN-AR
TOX	16.33	24.33	38.7
SAF	0.33	0.67	—
NAM	0.33	1.67	1
SEN	—	0.33	0.67
NUM	—	0.67	—
INS	7.33	1.67	7.33
Other	3.67	1.67	2
None	72.00	69.00	50.3

Table 3: Error Distribution across Languages

The majority of types in the extended taxonomy have occurred in the dataset analysed for the three language pairs. In a few cases, some types did not occur at all as in the Chinese side of the dataset, i.e. '**SEN**' and '**NUM**', and the Arabic side, i.e. '**SAF**' and '**NUM**'. The two types with the highest number of occurrences are '**TOX**' and '**None**', albeit with different proportions. The occurrence of '**TOX**' type could be as a result of the type of the annotated data which has a substantial amount of offensive language. This aspect of the text, when existing in large quantities, could lead to the generation of critical errors. '**None**' type is the most selected type among the types across the three languages. This could be attributed to the fact that half of the dataset (50 sentences) did not include features that are challenging to the machine (e.g. no offensive language or non-standard features, hence, less causes of critical errors). This finding shows the impact of the source text on the output. We expand on this aspect extensively in a separate Section (6), due to its importance in affecting online communication and also for consideration by any future work that aims to improve the quality of MT systems and develop error and noise analysis and detection models. Some types such as '**NUM**' did not appear much as the sentences did not have information that could lead to errors of this type. These findings prove that the types included in the extended taxonomy can occur in different languages. This also shows that MT systems behave differently depending on the language. For example, while the annotators did not find errors that fall under '**SAF**' and '**NUM**' categories in the Arabic side of the dataset, and under '**SEN**' and '**NUM**' in the Chinese, that was not the case in the Italian side of the dataset which covered all types of errors.

Examples provided were chosen as an illustration for their clarity and strong manifestation of deviation to show how far the machine can go in generating critical errors when translating UGC. These examples were obtained from the analysis of the dataset, covering the three chosen languages. The examples with their translations are provided in English only, following the order of the types in the extended taxonomy (see Section 3).

Deviation in toxicity (TOX)

ST	**Your killing the fucking planet**.
MT-ed text	**May the damn planet kill you**.
Translation into Arabic by Systran	

Deviation in health/safety risks (SAF)

ST	I Know two teenagers that suffer from **gerd** it is a big problem for these people!
MT-ed text	I Know two teenagers that suffer from **root disease** it is a big problem for these people!
Translation into Chinese by GT	

Deviation in named entities (NAM)

ST	Your fucking ass doesn't know shit about it AT ALL.**Rocky**.
MT-ed text	Your fucking ass doesn't know shit about it AT ALL.**rock**.
Translation into Italian by Bing	

Deviation in sentiment or negation (SEN)

ST	Don't the Yoshinoyasin Singapore and Indonesia ALSO **not serve** pork?
MT-ed text	Don't the Yoshinoyasin in Singapore and Indonesia ALSO **serve** pork?
Translation into Arabic by GT	

Deviation in numbers/time/units/date (NUM)

ST	Your signature is incredibly long. At 632 characters, it's about **two and a half times** what the software allows.
MT-ed text	Your signature is incredibly long. At 632 characters, it is **double** what the software allows.
Translation into Arabic by GT	

Deviation in instructions (INS)

ST	The link to wikibooks doesn't work and I don't know how to fix it. **Can anyone help?**
MT-ed text	The link to wikibooks doesn't work and I don't know how to fix it. **Can I help you?**
Translation into Arabic by GT	

Other critical meaning deviation (OTH)

ST	Admin's **beware** of him.
MT-ed text	Admin is **aware** of him.
Translation into Italian by Systran	

As a further step in our effort to validate the taxonomy, we reflect on the annotation process, using data collected through post-annotation questionnaires and our own experience supervising the annotation process. We also look at the impact of the source text on the generation of critical errors.

5 Evaluation of the Annotation Task: Challenges and Recommendations

Data was annotated for the three selected languages by professional translators. We provided them with guidelines based on the extended taxonomy with clear instructions that they must only annotate critical errors with catastrophic impact on the translation. However, we have found that:

- Despite providing clear guidelines on critical errors and how to detect and categorise them, there was some disagreement among the annotators regarding what errors were considered critical. This led them to tagging errors as critical when they were not, and vice versa.
- Annotators found it difficult to focus on critical errors versus annotating all errors.

These findings pose the following questions: (1) how this task is conducted?, 2) what areas need to be addressed for the annotation to be carried out at a level that serves the purpose of the annotation task?, and (3) what makes annotating critical errors a difficult task? We reflect on these areas and present a set of factors along with recommendations, based on empirical findings, with the aim to improve the annotation process for future work.

- **Training**: Training is important to ensure annotators understand the task. The role of training is displayed in the differences in the annotation between those who joined the training and those who only followed the guidelines without training. A follow-up discussion with the second group whose annotation contained major differences revealed that there was some misunderstanding regarding what each category implied, failing to analyse the translations correctly as a result.
- **Difficulty and specificity of the task**: Disagreement among annotators occurred because the task was not easy for them. To clar-

ify further, some annotators found it difficult to just focus on critical errors and disregard other errors as a new practice they have not experienced before. This finding highlights that general training might not be enough to understand the requirements of more specific annotation tasks.

- **Prior attitude towards the annotation task**: Some annotators felt unsure about why such translations with critical errors should be accepted and the purpose of carrying out the annotation task. These annotators tended to consider errors as critical when they did not follow the general rules of a language (grammatical or stylistic rules), overlooking what the guidelines stated, ending up annotating both minor and critical errors. It is, therefore, vital to not only provide clear instructions on how to carry out the annotation task, but to also highlight that they need to treat it as a serious task similar to translating official documents and that they should always follow the guidelines (i.e. annotation brief).
- **Time allocated to the task**: Annotators were involved on a voluntary basis which could have limited the time they allocated to performing the annotation task. Annotators reported spending between 2-8 hours on this task. Therefore, annotators who spent less time might not have worked on it thoroughly, affecting the quality of their annotation.
- **Subjectivity of the task**: Although clear guidelines were provided, annotators differed in their interpretation of each type. Their understanding of the translations also affected their judgement of whether the errors were critical or not. Where disagreements occurred, we asked them to provide their interpretation of the source text and the translations and the reasons which influenced their decision. This helped us understand whether the guidelines or their understanding of the translation contributed to the disagreement.
- **Communication with annotators**: Some annotators were hesitant to ask for clarification, fearing that might show them as less qualified. It is, therefore, vital to establishing communication with annotators while conducting the annotation task for a better performance.
- **Misleading translations**: Some instances of disagreement occurred as the annotators only read the translations without referring back to the source text. This happened where the translation sounded fluent in the target language. This finding highlights the need to consider both source and target texts to determine whether an error is critical.

6 Source-text Impact on the MT Output

This section presents an analysis of the source text to show whether there is a correlation between the quality of the source text and the generation of critical errors. For this purpose, we analyse translations produced by the three online MT systems (Google Translate, Bing and Systran) for one language combination, i.e. English-Arabic, using the same dataset (100 sentences). Our focus on Arabic was driven by the availability of language expertise (i.e. one of the authors is a native speaker of Arabic). The assumption is that if the different systems struggle with the same source sentences, producing critical errors, it would give indications about the potential output the machine could produce when handling such texts. Our aim is to detect patterns in source sentences that can cause critical errors to be considered when developing MT systems to improve the performance of such systems, especially for UGC. We use, as a point of reference, Al Sharou et al. (2021)'s taxonomy of aspects of non-standard text that could affect the quality of the translation. For readability, back translations of the errors are provided in English.

Offensive language The importance of looking at this aspect of the data comes from its extensive existence in UGC and its sever impact on the output. Our analysis shows that most translations that have critical errors are those of sentences which contain offensive language. When the sentence has a large number of swearing/offensive words and idiomatic phrases, the machine tends to produce wrong translations that arc unreadable or completely different from the source. When it comes to translating offensive language, we recognise the use of different 'strategies' including literal translation, transliteration, omission, random translation (hallucination) or substitution of one strong word with another milder word and vice versa. Sometimes, the machine uses a mix of these strategies when translating the same sentence, failing to convey correct translations as a result. For example, the three systems failed to provide correct translations of the offensive language in this sentence '***Piss off Homo**, no one wants to hear from you, also hahahahaha **you can't get married #asshole***', leading to major errors which have affected the original meaning. These systems vary in how they handled this type of language. GT translated '**piss off**' as '**rape**', while Bing ignored '**off**' as being part of the verb and translated '**piss**' as '**urinate**' and '**off**' as '**in front off**'. '**Homo**' was transliterated by both GT and Bing, and Systran mistranslated it as '**human**', affecting the meaning of the last part of the sentence '**you can't get married**', which was deleted by GT but reserved by Bing and Systran. The swearing word '**asshole**' was left untranslated by Bing and Systran and deleted by GT.

Symbols and special characters The use of special symbols/characters such as star signs (*) or hashtags (#) can lead to erroneous translations. MT tends to overlook words which contain such special characters, render incorrect meaning or leave it in its source language. Arabic translation of the words that have been disguised by replacing letters with star signs in the sentence '*Stop being such an **a**hole**...you **f***ing re***d***' shows that the three systems have either preserved the star signs and translated what left as another word, e.g. rendering '**a**hole**' as '**hole**' with the two star signs coming after it, or preserving it as random letters, conveying no meaning, as in the translation of '**f***ing re***d**' by Bing as '*****g**' '*****d**'; or dropped completely by GT and Systran.

Punctuation marks Misusing punctuation marks (e.g. deletion, addition, or use of wrong punctuation marks), especially commas and full stops, could lead to a mix up of the different parts of the sentence or different sentences, generating critical errors. For example, the translation of '***I give up Thanks** for ruining the Lion King pages*' shows the impact a missing punctuation mark has on the translation. The three systems translated the first part as '**I gave up thanking**'. They, therefore, do not deliver the original meaning where the writer intended to say he/she is giving up trying to keep the pages, and that the word '**thanks**' is used in a sarcastic way to express his/her frustration.

Negation Negation can lead to critical errors when reversed from negative to positive or vice versa; through e.g. dropping or reversing negative words (e.g. not, never, nobody); or reversing the meaning of some words (for instance, the three systems translated the verb '**reverting**' in '*why keep **reverting** my edits?*' as '**bringing back**'.

Named entities Named entities can be confusing to the machine especially when the name has different meanings and the MT system fails to treat it as a proper name, or when the names are unknown to the machine. Names are either mistranslated, left untranslated or deleted completely. For instance, Bing translated the proper name '**Rocky**' in the sentence '*your fucking ass doesn't know shit about it AT ALL.**Rocky***' as a noun rather than transliterating it, resulting in a wrong translation, while GT and Systran dropped it completely.

Spelling mistakes and contractions When dealing with spelling mistakes and informal contractions, the machine gives a translation that does not reflect what the source text says. In other cases, the machine preserves them in their original language or transliterates them. For example, the word '**freakin**' is transliterated by GT and left untranslated in the translations provided by Bing and Systran when translating this sentence '*Dude, u got a stick in ur ass, **lemme** edit the **freakin** montana academy page!*'. The short form of '**let me**' '**lemme**' is left untranslated by Bing while transliterated by GT and Systran, making it sound like a proper name where the translation in Arabic reads as '***Lemme edited montana academy page***'.

Capital letters Random capitalisation seems to affect the MT output. The analysis of the dataset shows that the three systems treated words written in capital letters as proper names. For example, the linking verb '**IS**' in the sentence '*The fact is 'Irish' is the commonly used term in Ireland and Wiki seeks to reflect what **IS** rather than what might be correct*' was translated by the three systems as '**Islamic State (or Daesh)**'. Such a translation could pose a potential risk if it were actually used in a sensitive context.

Lack of pronouns The lack of pronouns can lead to critical errors where the machine randomly replaces one pronoun with another. In this example, '*didn't forget, just been busy - will find the time to look into it*', '**didn't forget**' was translated as '**don't forget**' by GT, '**he didn't forget**' by Bing, and only correctly translated by Systran as '**I didn't forget**'; '**just been busy**' was translated as '**I was busy**', '**he was busy**' and '**I was busy**' respectively. The three systems wrongly rendered '**will find the time**' as '**you will find the time**'.

7 Conclusion

This work validated an extended taxonomy of critical errors developed to serve as a stand-alone taxonomy that can be used to evaluate or detect critical errors in machine-translated content. Findings emphasise the need to address critical errors with catastrophic impact on the output and for further attention to be paid not only to developing guidelines on critical errors, but to also training annotators on how to spot and assess them. It has proved that critical errors are not rare, and they are not specific to certain languages. It also underlines the need to improve current MT systems to specifically deal with user-generated content, considering aspects of the text that could lead to critical errors to improve online communication and enhance MT's role in enabling, rather than hindering, communication among speakers of different languages.

Acknowledgement

Lucia Specia was supported by funding from the Bergamot project (EU H2020 Grant No. 825303).

References

Abu-Ayyash, Emad AS. 2017. Errors and non-errors in english-arabic machine translation of gender-bound constructs in technical texts. *Procedia Computer Science*, 117:73–80.

Al Sharou, Khetam, Zhenhao Li, and Lucia Specia. 2021. Towards a better understanding of noise in natural language processing. In *RANLP 2021*, pages 53–62.

Aziz, Wilker, Sheila Castilho, and Lucia Specia. 2012. Pet: a tool for post-editing and assessing machine translation. In *LREC-2012*, pages 3982–3987.

Cohen, Jacob. 1960. A coefficient of agreement for nominal scales. *Educational and psychological measurement*, 20(1):37–46.

Costa, Ângela, Wang Ling, Tiago Luís, Rui Correia, and Luísa Coheur. 2015. A linguistically motivated taxonomy for machine translation error analysis. *Machine Translation*, 29(2):127–161.

Dorr, Bonnie, Joseph Olive, John McCary, and Caitlin Christianson. 2011. Machine translation evaluation and optimization. In *Handbook of natural language processing and machine translation*, pages 745–843. Springer.

Fleiss, Joseph L, Bruce Levin, and Myunghee Cho Paik. 2003. *Statistical methods for rates and proportions*. john wiley & sons.

Fleiss, Joseph L. 1971. Measuring nominal scale agreement among many raters. *Psychological bulletin*, 76(5):378.

García, Ignacio. 2014. Training quality evaluators. *Revista Tradumàtica: tecnologies de la traducció*, (12):430–436.

Han, Lifeng, Gareth Jones, and Alan Smeaton. 2020. Alphamwe: Construction of multilingual parallel corpora with mwe annotations. *arXiv preprint arXiv:2011.03783*.

Han, Lifeng. 2022. An overview on machine translation evaluation. *arXiv preprint arXiv:2202.11027*.

Hern, Alex. 2017. Facebook translates' good morning'into'attack them', leading to arrest. *the Guardian*, 24.

Lommel, Arle, Hans Uszkoreit, and Aljoscha Burchardt. 2014. Multidimensional quality metrics (mqm): A framework for declaring and describing translation quality metrics. *Revista Tradumàtica: tecnologies de la traducció*, (12):455–463.

Lommel, Arle, Attila Görög, Alan Melby, Hans Uszkoreit, Aljoscha Burchardt, and Maja Popović. 2015. Harmonised metric. *Project Report, QT21 Project*.

Lommel, Arle. 2018. Metrics for translation quality assessment: a case for standardising error typologies. In *Translation Quality Assessment*, pages 109–127. Springer.

O'Brien, Sharon. 2012. Towards a dynamic quality evaluation model for translation. *The Journal of Specialised Translation*, 17(1):55–77.

Popović, Maja. 2018. Error classification and analysis for machine translation quality assessment. In *Translation quality assessment*, pages 129–158. Springer.

Rivera-Trigueros, Irene. 2021. Machine translation systems and quality assessment: a systematic review. *Language Resources and Evaluation*, pages 1–27.

Specia, Lucia, Frédéric Blain, Marina Fomicheva, Chrysoula Zerva, Zhenhao Li, Vishrav Chaudhary, and André Martins. 2021. Findings of the wmt 2021 shared task on quality estimation. Association for Computational Linguistics.

Tang, Y., C. Tran, Xian Li, P. Chen, Naman Goyal, Vishrav Chaudhary, Jiatao Gu, and Angela Fan. 2020. Multilingual translation with extensible multilingual pretraining and finetuning. *ArXiv*, abs/2008.00401.

Ulitkin, Ilya, Irina Filippova, Natalia Ivanova, and Alexey Poroykov. 2021. Automatic evaluation of the quality of machine translation of a scientific text: the results of a five-year-long experiment. In *E3S Web of Conferences*.

User papers

nEYron: Implementation and Deployment of an MT System for a Large Audit & Consulting Corporation

Artur Nowakowski[1,2], **Krzysztof Jassem**[1,2], **Maciej Lison**[1], **Rafał Jaworski**[2], **Tomasz Dwojak**[2]
[1] Poleng, Poznań, Poland
{name.surname}@poleng.pl
[2] Faculty of Mathematics and Computer Science, Adam Mickiewicz University, Poznań, Poland
{name.surname}@amu.edu.pl

Karolina Wiater, Olga Posesor
EY Poland, Warsaw, Poland
{name.surname}@pl.ey.com

Abstract

This paper reports on the implementation and deployment of an MT system in the Polish branch of EY Global Limited. The system supports standard CAT and MT functionalities such as translation memory fuzzy search, document translation and post-editing, and meets less common, customer-specific expectations. The deployment began in August 2018 with a Proof-of-Concept, and ended with the signing of the Final Version acceptance certificate in October 2021. We present the challenges that were faced during the deployment, particularly in relation to the security check and installation processes in the production environment.

1 Business Need

On March 6, 2018, the Polish parliament adopted a law that laid down rules for the Polish Agency of Audit Surveillance regarding the control of auditing companies. The law states that "Documents presented by the audited company for the needs of the surveillance are drawn up in Polish or the audit company provides their translation into Polish." The law forced auditing companies to provide Polish translations for large volumes of English texts. That triggered the idea, at the Polish branch of EY Global Limited (EY Poland), that the cost of the task might be reduced if it were assisted by a translation engine. EY Poland contacted the company Poleng Ltd. (Poleng) to verify the possibility of using their product, TranslAide Workspace, for the task. During initial discussions, EY Poland came to the conclusion that it might be beneficial for the company to have the software installed and running on site.

2 The Story of the Deployment

2.1 TranslAide Workspace

The first phase of the deployment began in August 2018. The deployed system was based on TranslAide Workspace, which combined computer-aided translation (translation memory with fuzzy search and segment-by-segment editing) with a generic machine translation engine, not trained specifically on the in-domain data. The task consisted in replacing the existing translation engine with a new one, dedicated to the customer.

The deployment was divided into the Proof-of-Concept (POC) and Final Version stages. The POC machine was to be installed in the Linux environment to make the initial deployment easier for the Poleng team. There were no explicit expectations regarding the quality of the translation imposed on the POC version. However, moving forward to the Final Version stage was conditional on acceptance of the POC by the customer – including translation quality, which would be checked by human specialists from the EY corporation. The Final Version – all of the system components, including model training – was expected to run on the Windows operating system to meet EY's security standards and internal regulations.

The expectations for the system were the following: The TranslAide Workspace system would consist of three modules – Web Application, Translation Memory, and Machine Translation Service:

- Web Application would be the part of the sys-

Macken, Rufener, Van den Bogaert, Daems, Tezcan, Vanroy, Fonteyne, Barrault, Costa-jussà, Kemp, Pilos, Declercq, Koponen, Forcada, Scarton, Moniz (eds.)
Proceedings of the 23rd Annual Conference of the European Association for Machine Translation, p. 181–187
Ghent, Belgium, June 2022.

tem with which the user interacts;

- Translation Memory would provide translation of segments that were found in its database;

- Machine Translation Service would provide translation of all remaining sentences at a speed not slower than a second per segment.

(Details on current expectations for the three modules are given in section 4.)

All system components, as well as the training of the models, should be run on a PC machine with the following specification: NVIDIA GTX 1080Ti GPU, 32 GB RAM and an 8-core processor.

The POC phase ended on schedule (within three months), but the translation quality was not fully satisfactory, as the system sporadically produced incorrect translations of some acronyms and rare words; the issue resulted from certain flaws in subword handling by Marian NMT (Junczys-Dowmunt et al., 2018). On rare occasions, the system would also crash when importing a PowerPoint presentation, because of improper handling of some XML tags specific to the PowerPoint document's internal structure. After the major issues had been identified and fixed, the Final Version was developed for the Windows operating system. It was accepted with a three-month delay in March 2019.

2.2 Stand-alone nEYron

Once the POC deployment had been stabilized, the system was given a new name: nEYron. For two years, it was used by several EY employees on a single PC machine that hosted all system components. Meanwhile, nEYron acquired a new look, consistent with the style of other applications dedicated to the same customer. New functional features were developed to satisfy needs arising during the use of the application. An up-to-date list of functionalities is given in section 3.

2.3 Multi-user Solution

The final phase of deployment took place in 2021. The agreement stated that the application must adhere to EY security standards. The customer expected to receive the following items:

- system installation package;

- system installation instructions;

- system backup policy;

- user's guide;

- disaster recovery procedures.

The creation of the documentation was painless. However, adhering to the security standards was not (see 5.2). The process began in April 2021, and the certificate of final acceptance was signed in October 2021.

3 System Requirements for the Final Version

3.1 EY User Feedback

During the POC stage, EY employees developed a list of requirements that should be added to the system in the Final Version stage. The following three requirements were added after the POC stage: automatic deletion of documents from the user translation history after a specified time (for confidentiality reasons), document sharing between multiple users, and calculation of the approximate cost of translation of a document by a human translator before it is translated by a machine. Cost assessment was intended to help determine to what extent machine translation reduced translation costs over time, compared to human translation. It is based on the number of words included in the document. In addition to the updated list of requirements, EY employees in collaboration with the Poleng team created a mockup of the user interface that would correspond to the look and feel of the other internal EY systems. The user interface was further modified according to the EY guidelines during the development of the Final Version.

3.2 Final List of Requirements

The complete and up-to-date list of requirements consists of the following:

- user registration and login, including SSO (single sign-on) login, universal for all services accessible by EY employees;

- document import in `.txt`, `.docx`, `.pptx` and `.xlsx` formats;

- document editing in sentence-by-sentence mode;

- machine translation in an editing window;

- machine translation of entire documents;

- export of the translated document in a format compatible with the imported document;
- pre-translation of documents using translation memory fuzzy search matches;
- ability to proofread and approve translations of sentences;
- expanding translation memory with approved translations;
- transfer of document formatting (fonts, styling, text placement) between input and output document;
- archiving of translated documents per user;
- automatic deletion of documents from user translation history after a specified time;
- document sharing between multiple users;
- calculation of approximate cost of document translation by a human translator.

4 System Components

The architecture of the system consists of the following components:

- Machine Translation Service;
- Translation Memory;
- Web Application.

4.1 Machine Translation Service

Machine Translation Service provides translations of sentences in the English–Polish and Polish–English directions without human intervention. It is designed as a web service that is invoked by the web application to produce document translations. It is based on the Marian NMT framework (Junczys-Dowmunt et al., 2018). Internally, the web service forwards source sentences from HTTP requests to the Marian websocket server and returns the translations to the web application.

4.1.1 Customer Training Data

In-domain business documents translated by humans were delivered to Poleng in pairs: each document in Polish had its equivalent in English. The document format was either PDF or Microsoft Office (.docx, .doc, .pptx, .xlsx). We applied the following procedure to extract bilingual corpora from business documents:

1. Text extraction from business documents using the Apache Tika[1] toolkit.
2. Text segmentation into sentences using eserix[2] – an SRX rule-based sentence segmenter.
3. Text normalization, including punctuation, quoting and commas, using Moses (Koehn et al., 2007) scripts.
4. Alignment of a source text to a target text at the sentence level using the hunalign (Varga et al., 2007) sentence aligner.

This procedure initially allowed us to obtain nearly 70,000 in-domain sentence pairs.

4.1.2 Model Training

Model training consisted of two steps: training of general models on 10 million sentences derived from the OPUS corpora (Tiedemann, 2012), and use of the transfer learning paradigm to fine-tune the general models on the in-domain data. In this way, the system transfers the knowledge from the general model, significantly increasing the translation quality on the in-domain data (such a process has been described, for example, in Aji et al. (2020)). As the general model can be reused for future fine-tunings, this technique reduces the total time to solution by a significant margin.

Data preprocessing, in addition to using the Moses (Koehn et al., 2007) normalization scripts, included subword segmentation. We applied subword segmentation to the data using the SentencePiece (Kudo and Richardson, 2018) tool with the byte-pair encoding (BPE) (Sennrich et al., 2016) algorithm. The vocabulary consisted of 32,000 entries.

All NMT models were trained using the Marian NMT (Junczys-Dowmunt et al., 2018) framework on a single NVIDIA GTX 1080Ti GPU.

For the Proof-of-Concept stage, we trained models based on an RNN-based encoder–decoder architecture with the attention mechanism (Sennrich et al., 2017). We manually assessed translation quality, comparing the model trained only on openly available data with the model fine-tuned on in-domain data as described in section 4.1.1. The annotators evaluated the translations of a test set consisting of 488 sentences, and provided scores

[1] https://tika.apache.org

[2] https://github.com/emjotde/eserix

for accuracy and fluency by absolute grading on a scale from 0 to 5. The average scores obtained in all of these experiments are presented in Table 1. The most significant improvement in the fine-tuned version was achieved for translation accuracy in the Polish–English direction.

Direction	Data	Accuracy	Fluency
PL – EN	Open	3.47	3.61
EN – PL	Open	3.48	3.62
PL – EN	EY	**4.23**	**3.94**
EN – PL	EY	**3.90**	**3.74**

Table 1: Results of manual evaluation of preliminary experiments

The results of this manual assessment of the POC version were considered good enough to proceed to the next stage of deployment.

In the final deployment, the NMT model architecture was replaced by the base Transformer (Vaswani et al., 2017), which improved the quality of translation while reducing the time required to train the model. In addition, another 10,000 sentence pairs were derived from new documents provided by the customer. These additional sentences were used for training of the Transformer models.

The results of automatic evaluation based on the BLEU (Papineni et al., 2002) metric, calculated by the SacreBLEU (Post, 2018) tool with default settings, are presented in Table 2.

Direction	Data	Architecture	BLEU
PL – EN	Open	RNN	29.72
EN – PL	Open	RNN	26.36
PL – EN	EY	RNN	36.91
EN – PL	EY	RNN	32.99
PL – EN	Open	Transformer	31.13
EN – PL	Open	Transformer	28.34
PL – EN	EY*	Transformer	**39.92**
EN – PL	EY*	Transformer	**35.55**

Table 2: Results of automatic evaluation

4.2 Translation Memory

Translation Memory is a database of corresponding segments in both languages. The translation of a sentence is added to the memory upon approval by the system user. Search is carried out by an in-house solution: the Anubis system (Jaworski, 2013), which uses a suffix-array-based index for fuzzy matching. Anubis also features a unique algorithm for the detection and recombination of all sub-segment matches between a candidate sentence and an example from the Translation Memory.

Translation Memory serves two functions in the system: it is used during the translation process, and it also serves as a collection of training data for future fine-tuning of NMT models. During translation of a document, each sentence is first checked in the Translation Memory. If a match is found, the translation is returned as the result and the sentence is not translated by the NMT model.

4.3 Web Application

Web Application is the part of the system with which the user interacts. It consists of the following components:

- a server application, following the REST API design, written in the CakePHP framework;
- a user interface, written in the Vue.js framework;
- an SQL database.

All features included in the web application are listed in section 3.

Document translation process The main feature of the web application is the document translation process. It consists of the following steps:

1. User imports the document into System;
2. System extracts text from the document;
3. System segments text into sentences using SRX-based rules;
4. System checks the Translation Memory for the existence of each sentence;
5. System sets up batches of sentences whose translations have not been found in the Translation Memory;
6. Batches are sent to the Machine Translation Service;
7. System saves the translations in the database;
8. System prepares the document to be exported at user's request.

Translations found in the Translation Memory and translations produced by the Machine Translation Service are presented to the user in a single window. Once the document has been translated by the machine, the user can post-edit the text segment-by-segment. Each translated segment may be manually approved by the user for it to be stored in the Translation Memory.

Document reconstruction process The system is expected to transfer the document's styling and formatting from the source document to the translated document.

To this end, we make use of the Microsoft Office document structure: the document is unzipped into a set of XML files and the files are iterated in a search for text content. Each found text item is stored in a database and replaced in the XML file with a placeholder tag containing its identifier. When the translation of text items has been completed, the XML files are iterated again, and the placeholder tags are replaced by the translations. Finally, the XML files are zipped back into the Microsoft Office document package.

5 Deployment Challenges

5.1 Proof-of-Concept Deployment Challenges

During the POC stage, the entire system was installed on a single PC machine. The initial configuration of the machine and the installation of the system was carried out at Poleng's headquarters in Poznań, Poland. After the system had been installed, the machine was transported to EY's headquarters in Warsaw, Poland. For confidentiality reasons, the machine could not be connected to the Internet and any system updates had to be provided locally. Poleng prepared Docker[3] containers for each of the system components and transported them on a flash drive to the PC machine, when necessary. The use of Docker containers significantly simplified the process, as each deployment of a system update consisted of replacing the Docker container.

The only part of the system that could not be updated in this way was the NMT models. For security reasons, training of the model on customer data had to be performed on a PC machine at the EY headquarters. Therefore, the models were not part of the Machine Translation Services container. Instead, they were mounted as a volume in the container so that they could be easily replaced.

[3]https://www.docker.com

5.2 Security Check

For the deployment of the multi-user version in the EY infrastructure, each component of the system had to meet a list of security requirements. The necessary modifications to the Translation Memory and Machine Translation Service components were minor, as they involved only changes to the security of the Docker container (the main process running in the container could not run as a root user). The changes to Web Application were more significant, as this component is exposed to the user. The total number of security requirements that the web application had to meet was close to 70. Most of the security requirements (such as the setting of special headers in HTTP responses) were easy to satisfy. However, some security standards proved to be challenging. Among them were:

- replacement of the entire application logging module;
- implementation of the single sign-on (SSO) authentication procedure specific to the EY corporation;
- implementation of database encryption.

A thorough security review was performed by the EY Global technical team after the system had been deployed.

5.3 Installation in the Production Environment

Installation of the final version of the system in the production environment included the creation of the installation package and its deployment to the EY infrastructure. The installation package consisted of Docker containers with the system components. Each of the system components was deployed in Docker containers to enable system scalability in the future. The deployment process was executed through screen sharing. Poleng delivered the installation package to the EY technical team and guided them through the installation process.

6 Future Plans

Plans for the future include technical improvements to the existing solution, as well as the introduction of new features.

Small improvements may include replacing hunalign (Varga et al., 2007) with vecalign (Thompson and Koehn, 2019) in the bilingual corpus extraction process described in section 4.1. We expect that the translation quality of NMT models will improve as a result of better corpus alignment.

To further improve the quality of the NMT models, we intend to use existing monolingual customer documents. We plan to apply the back-translation (Edunov et al., 2018) technique iteratively (Hoang et al., 2018) to increase the quality of our models.

As new terminology emerges, the user expects MT systems to quickly adapt to them. In most cases, data that would cover the new terminology do not yet exist. To solve this problem, we intend to use techniques for forced terminology translation (Nowakowski and Jassem, 2021; Bergmanis and Pinnis, 2021) to ensure that specific terminology is translated according to the needs of the user. Additionally, providing a glossary with specific in-domain terminology would ensure the consistent translation of such terminology when different sentences are translated.

To date, we have relied on the BLEU (Papineni et al., 2002) metric for the evaluation of trained NMT models. To follow current state-of-the-art solutions in MT evaluation, we plan to use the MT Telescope (Rei et al., 2021) to evaluate our models with the COMET (Rei et al., 2020) metric and perform a fine-grained error analysis.

Business documents often have a complex layout structure, whereas current NMT models operate only on sentence-level textual semantics. We want to explore the idea of integrating NMT with Computer Vision to create an end-to-end model which would learn visual features, layout information and textual semantics to produce document-level translations better than the current state-of-the-art methods. Such a model would be able to simplify the process of text extraction, sentence segmentation and document reconstruction, as it would take all document information as an input. To this end, we plan to base our model on the TILT (Powalski et al., 2021) architecture. This was created for the Question Answering task, but we believe that it could be modified for NMT.

7 Conclusions

This paper has presented the deployment of an English–Polish translation system at the Polish branch of EY Global Limited. The system supports standard CAT and MT functionalities such as translation memory fuzzy search, document translation and post-editing, and meets less frequent expectations such as single sign-on login and calculation of the cost of human translation for a given document. The paper has presented the challenges that were faced during the deployment, particularly adherence to security expectations and installation in the production environment. Ultimately, the deployment took over three years. Meanwhile, new technologies have been developed in the field of Machine Translation. Once the security issues have been overcome, we hope to be able to update the system with emerging technologies, constantly improving its performance.

References

Aji, Alham Fikri, Nikolay Bogoychev, Kenneth Heafield, and Rico Sennrich. 2020. In neural machine translation, what does transfer learning transfer? In *Proceedings of the 58th Annual Meeting of the Association for Computational Linguistics*, pages 7701–7710, Online, July. Association for Computational Linguistics.

Bergmanis, Toms and Mārcis Pinnis. 2021. Facilitating terminology translation with target lemma annotations. In *Proceedings of the 16th Conference of the European Chapter of the Association for Computational Linguistics: Main Volume*, pages 3105–3111, Online, April. Association for Computational Linguistics.

Edunov, Sergey, Myle Ott, Michael Auli, and David Grangier. 2018. Understanding back-translation at scale. In *Proceedings of the 2018 Conference on Empirical Methods in Natural Language Processing*, pages 489–500, Brussels, Belgium, October-November. Association for Computational Linguistics.

Hoang, Vu Cong Duy, Philipp Koehn, Gholamreza Haffari, and Trevor Cohn. 2018. Iterative back-translation for neural machine translation. In *Proceedings of the 2nd Workshop on Neural Machine Translation and Generation*, pages 18–24, Melbourne, Australia, July. Association for Computational Linguistics.

Jaworski, Rafał. 2013. Anubis – speeding up computer-aided translation. In *Computational Linguistics*, pages 263–280. Springer.

Junczys-Dowmunt, Marcin, Roman Grundkiewicz, Tomasz Dwojak, Hieu Hoang, Kenneth Heafield, Tom Neckermann, Frank Seide, Ulrich Germann, Alham Fikri Aji, Nikolay Bogoychev, André F. T. Martins, and Alexandra Birch. 2018. Marian: Fast neural machine translation in C++. In *Proceedings of ACL 2018, System Demonstrations*, pages 116–121, Melbourne, Australia, July. Association for Computational Linguistics.

Koehn, Philipp, Hieu Hoang, Alexandra Birch, Chris Callison-Burch, Marcello Federico, Nicola Bertoldi, Brooke Cowan, Wade Shen, Christine Moran, Richard Zens, Chris Dyer, Ondřej Bojar, Alexandra Constantin, and Evan Herbst. 2007. Moses: Open source toolkit for statistical machine translation. In *Proceedings of the 45th Annual Meeting of the Association for Computational Linguistics Companion Volume Proceedings of the Demo and Poster Sessions*, pages 177–180, Prague, Czech Republic, June. Association for Computational Linguistics.

Kudo, Taku and John Richardson. 2018. SentencePiece: A simple and language independent subword tokenizer and detokenizer for neural text processing. In *Proceedings of the 2018 Conference on Empirical Methods in Natural Language Processing: System Demonstrations*, pages 66–71, Brussels, Belgium, November. Association for Computational Linguistics.

Nowakowski, Artur and Krzysztof Jassem. 2021. Neural machine translation with inflected lexicon. In *Proceedings of Machine Translation Summit XVIII: Research Track*, pages 282–292, Virtual, August. Association for Machine Translation in the Americas.

Papineni, Kishore, Salim Roukos, Todd Ward, and Wei-Jing Zhu. 2002. Bleu: A method for automatic evaluation of machine translation. In *Proceedings of the 40th Annual Meeting on Association for Computational Linguistics*, ACL '02, page 311–318, USA. Association for Computational Linguistics.

Post, Matt. 2018. A call for clarity in reporting BLEU scores. In *Proceedings of the Third Conference on Machine Translation: Research Papers*, pages 186–191, Belgium, Brussels, October. Association for Computational Linguistics.

Powalski, Rafał, Łukasz Borchmann, Dawid Jurkiewicz, Tomasz Dwojak, Michał Pietruszka, and Gabriela Pałka. 2021. Going full-tilt boogie on document understanding with text-image-layout transformer. In Lladós, Josep, Daniel Lopresti, and Seiichi Uchida, editors, *Document Analysis and Recognition – ICDAR 2021*, pages 732–747, Cham. Springer International Publishing.

Rei, Ricardo, Craig Stewart, Ana C Farinha, and Alon Lavie. 2020. COMET: A neural framework for MT evaluation. In *Proceedings of the 2020 Conference on Empirical Methods in Natural Language Processing (EMNLP)*, pages 2685–2702, Online, November. Association for Computational Linguistics.

Rei, Ricardo, Craig Stewart, Ana C Farinha, and Alon Lavie. 2021. MT-Telescope: An interactive platform for contrastive evaluation of MT systems. In *Proceedings of the 59th Annual Meeting of the Association for Computational Linguistics and the 11th International Joint Conference on Natural Language Processing: System Demonstrations*, pages 73–80, Online, August. Association for Computational Linguistics.

Sennrich, Rico, Barry Haddow, and Alexandra Birch. 2016. Neural machine translation of rare words with subword units. In *Proceedings of the 54th Annual Meeting of the Association for Computational Linguistics (Volume 1: Long Papers)*, pages 1715–1725, Berlin, Germany, August. Association for Computational Linguistics.

Sennrich, Rico, Orhan Firat, Kyunghyun Cho, Alexandra Birch, Barry Haddow, Julian Hitschler, Marcin Junczys-Dowmunt, Samuel Läubli, Antonio Valerio Miceli Barone, Jozef Mokry, and Maria Nădejde. 2017. Nematus: a toolkit for neural machine translation. In *Proceedings of the Software Demonstrations of the 15th Conference of the European Chapter of the Association for Computational Linguistics*, pages 65–68, Valencia, Spain, April. Association for Computational Linguistics.

Thompson, Brian and Philipp Koehn. 2019. Vecalign: Improved sentence alignment in linear time and space. In *Proceedings of the 2019 Conference on Empirical Methods in Natural Language Processing and the 9th International Joint Conference on Natural Language Processing (EMNLP-IJCNLP)*, pages 1342–1348, Hong Kong, China, November. Association for Computational Linguistics.

Tiedemann, Jörg. 2012. Parallel data, tools and interfaces in OPUS. In *Proceedings of the Eighth International Conference on Language Resources and Evaluation (LREC'12)*, pages 2214–2218, Istanbul, Turkey, May. European Language Resources Association (ELRA).

Varga, Dániel, Péter Halácsy, András Kornai, Viktor Nagy, László Németh, and Viktor Trón. 2007. Parallel corpora for medium density languages. *Amsterdam Studies In The Theory And History Of Linguistic Science Series 4*, 292:247.

Vaswani, Ashish, Noam Shazeer, Niki Parmar, Jakob Uszkoreit, Llion Jones, Aidan N Gomez, Łukasz Kaiser, and Illia Polosukhin. 2017. Attention is all you need. In Guyon, I., U. V. Luxburg, S. Bengio, H. Wallach, R. Fergus, S. Vishwanathan, and R. Garnett, editors, *Advances in Neural Information Processing Systems*, volume 30. Curran Associates, Inc.

"Hi, how can I help you?" Improving Machine Translation of Conversational Content in a Business Context

Bianka Buschbeck* **Jennifer Mell*** **Miriam Exel** **Matthias Huck**

SAP SE
Dietmar-Hopp-Allee 16, 69190 Walldorf, Germany
firstname.lastname@sap.com

Abstract

This paper addresses the automatic translation of conversational content in a business context, for example support chat dialogues. While such use cases share characteristics with other informal machine translation scenarios, translation requirements with respect to technical and business-related expressions are high. To succeed in such scenarios, we experimented with curating dedicated training and test data, injecting noise to improve robustness, and applying sentence weighting schemes to carefully manage the influence of the different corpora. We show that our approach improves the performance of our models on conversational content for all 18 investigated language pairs while preserving translation quality on other domains – an indispensable requirement to integrate these developments into our MT engines at SAP.

1 Introduction

At SAP we build machine translation systems to cope with a huge translation volume, covering product localization and translation of documentation, training materials or support instructions for up to 85 languages. We usually train mixed-domain neural machine translation (MT) engines, whose training input consists of a multitude of data sources including the contents of the company-internal translation memories from various domains. The resulting MT systems produce high-quality technical translations but have difficulties generating appropriate output for conversational content, required for multilingual chatbots or product support chats. For an enhanced user experience, it becomes more and more important that our customers can communicate in the language of their choice. Therefore, we started a project to improve translation quality for business-related conversations. This includes better translations, but also more robustness towards typos and poor input quality. We focus on methods that allow for improvements in one area without degrading quality in others, since we aim to deliver a single model per language pair.

The remainder of this paper is structured as follows. Section 2 introduces the particular challenges to be addressed when training an MT system for corporate conversational content. The methods we explored are presented in Section 3 and experimental results on selected language pairs can be found in Section 4. Section 5 contains results on 18 language pairs of major interest at SAP using the final experimental configuration. We point out open research questions in Section 6. Related problems and approaches are highlighted in Section 7 before we summarize our findings in Section 8.

2 Challenges

Our baseline MT system is built on large amounts of technical documents and UI-style training data with the consequence that it performs unsatisfactorily in business conversations, where the content is technical, but style is conversational. An example conversation is given in Table 1 (column *Original Conversation in English*). It contains a variety of features that are common in conversational content, with major challenges posed by incomplete or

*Equal contribution.

Macken, Rufener, Van den Bogaert, Daems, Tezcan, Vanroy, Fonteyne, Barrault, Costa-jussà, Kemp, Pilos, Declercq, Koponen, Forcada, Scarton, Moniz (eds.)
Proceedings of the 23rd Annual Conference of the European Association for Machine Translation, p. 189–198
Ghent, Belgium, June 2022.

Agent	Original Conversation in English	Baseline MT	Improved MT
User	hello anyone	Bonjour à tous	Bonjour à tous
User	why my gdm is not working	**pourquoi** mon gdm ne **fonctionne** pas	**Pourquoi** mon gdm ne **marche** pas **?**
User	it says .service file is not there	**cela indique** que le fichier .service **n'existe pas.**	**Ça dit** que le fichier .service **n'est pas là**
Support	what are you doing exactly	**que** faites-vous exactement	**Que** faites-vous exactement **?**
Support	where is it exactly	**où c'est** exactement	**Où est-ce** exactement **?**
Support	i didnt evn see the question..	**i didnt voir** la question...	**Je n'ai même pas vu** la question.
User	i have dsl connection my isp provides me and i got device not manaed so i edit.conf file of nm	**i a dsl connexion** mon isp me fournit et **i get device not manaed so i edit .conf file of** nm	**J'ai une connexion dsl que** mon isp me fournit et **je n'ai pas géré l'appareil donc je modifie le fichier .conf de** nm
User	yeah it is	**oui,**	**Oui, c'est ça**
Support	id leave it alone.	**et laissez-le** tranquille.	**Je le laisse** tranquille.
User	i thinking to filter that port	**i penser à** filtrer ce port	**Je pense** filtrer ce port.
Support	i never noticed it being open to the network. just to localhost	**i n'a** jamais remarqué qu'**elle** était **ouverte** au réseau. **Il s'agit simplement d'un hôte local**	**Je n'ai** jamais remarqué qu'**il** était **ouvert** au réseau. **Juste à localhost**
User	ok	OK	OK
Support	so you m ay be worried about nothing	**Vous vous inquiétez donc de ne** rien **voir**	**Donc tu es toujours inquiet pour** rien.
Support	seems its not really an security issue and it makes loookups quicker	**semble qu'il ne s'agit** pas vraiment **d'un** problème de sécurité et **qu'il** accélère les **loookups**	**n'est** pas vraiment un problème de sécurité et accélère les **recherches**
User	thanks	**remerciements**	**Merci**

Table 1: Excerpt of an English conversation (from the Ubuntu Dialogue Corpus (Lowe et al., 2015)) translated to French using the baseline and our improved MT model.

Phenomenon	Examples
Spelling	
Typos	thansk, tanks, thanx
Casing	cpu, i, aws
Spacing	ofcourse, any one, Id o
Lack of punctuation	Hi are you there
Conversational word forms	dunno, gotcha, doin'
Conversational variants	hey, hey hi, hiya, howdy
Abbreviations	
Word/phrase abbreviations	plz, thx, np, omg, ttyl
Letter/number homophones	u r, I c, c u, u 2, some1
Paralinguistic features	
Emoticons	:D ;-) :(
Emotional expressions	uh, hmm, oh, ah, whoa
Emphasis - duplication	no no no, oh noooo
Emphasis - typography	it's URGENT, It broke *EVERYTHING*!
Expletives	damn!, crap, sh*t

Table 2: Typical phenomena in conversational data.

ungrammatical sentences and high contextual dependency. Conversational expressions (*hello anyone, thanks*) and syntactic structures such as questions and utterances in first and second person singular are typical of conversational style. Technical documents do not provide a good coverage of these phenomena. Support chats, moreover, exhibit other challenging phenomena that are summarized in Table 2 based on initial exploration of in-domain data. While most of the listed linguistic issues could be corrected, paralinguistic phenomena that are a kind of textual equivalent to verbal prosodic features or facial expressions are more difficult. Emphasis expressed by word or letter duplication or typography are highly language-specific and cannot be easily transferred. Even emoticons are not used in the same way across languages.

3 Methods

In this section, we describe the methods we investigated to address some of these challenges.

3.1 High-quality Parallel Data

The most straightforward way to improve translation quality of conversational content would be adding appropriate training data. However, bilingual data in this domain is hard to find. Even largely conversational datasets, such as OpenSubtitles (Lison and Tiedemann, 2016) are not well suited for this purpose, as business conversations are highly technical.

Thus, we manually select and translate appropriate sentences to enrich our available training data with conversational style segments (Section 2). To collect suitable source segments, we draw on different resources such as support dialogues and expressions used for intents in our chatbots. But the most valuable resource is the Ubuntu Dialogue Corpus (UDC) (Lowe et al., 2015), a publicly available dataset that contains almost one million two-person conversations extracted from Ubuntu technical support chat logs between 2004 and 2015. We create a list of utterances and their frequency from the UDC that helps us extract the following:

- Utterances that cover greetings, agreement, affirmations, refusal, uncertainty, wishes, regrets, hold-on expressions, thanks and responses to them, etc.
- Utterances starting with WH words and inverted questions (*Are you*, *Do you*, *Does that*, etc.), frequent in support dialogues but underrepresented in technical documentation.
- Utterances that contain the pronouns "*I*" and "*you*" to improve first- and second-person coverage.
- Frequent single word utterances, as they are especially problematic.

We mainly focus on short expressions that do not contain vocabulary specific to the UDC. The resulting list of approximately 10,000 English segments is then normalized, since it contains too many variants of the same expression, differing only in spelling, punctuation, and casing that would increase translation costs without resulting in more varied training data. The final corpus consists of 7,000 segments that we have manually translated by our professional translators into the required target languages. Source variations are later created using the methods described in Section 3.4.

3.2 Domain Adaptation

We define as *domain adaptation* the task of optimizing a natural language processing system's parameters towards improved quality on a specific text domain. A text domain typically exhibits particular charateristics wrt. aspects such as genre, topic, style, terminology, and so on. Domain adaptation for MT is an established field of study (Chu and Wang, 2018), with *fine-tuning* nowadays being one of the prevalent paradigms for neural MT models (Freitag and Al-Onaizan, 2016; Huck et al., 2017). In fine-tuning, training of a generic MT model is continued using in-domain data. The pitfalls of this method are overfitting and quality loss on out-of-domain data (Huck et al., 2015; Thompson et al., 2019). We found that *sentence weighting* (Chen et al., 2017; Rieß et al., 2021; Wang et al., 2017) suits our purpose of adapting towards conversational content better while at the same time not sacrificing translation quality on other text domains, thus keeping overall system performance stable. We apply a straightforward up-weighting technique by giving higher instance weights to subsections of the training set which contain conversational content. Experimental results on this will be reported in Section 4.3.

3.3 Error-sensitive Back-translation Scoring

The amount of conversational training data for MT models can be increased by employing synthetic bitext from back-translation (Huck et al., 2011; Schwenk, 2008; Sennrich et al., 2016a). We back-translate the UDC dataset with the aim of benefiting conversational style and vocabulary coverage without harming grammaticality and spelling of MT output. To that end, we first clean the dataset using in-house scripts, resulting in 4.6 million English sentences. We then machine-translate the English sentences into the source languages of the models which we intend to improve, using our existing engines for back-translation in the reverse direction. Experiments are thus only carried out on language directions with English target (Section 4.6).

We assume that grammatical and correctly spelled input sentences result in better back-translations, which in turn will lead to better performance of the final model. Furthermore, we require the final model to produce grammatical sentences despite the training references containing user-generated text. We therefore use Acrolinx[1] to measure the acceptability of a segment in terms of grammaticality and spelling. Acrolinx is AI-powered software that improves the quality and impact of enterprise content. Using a customized version of Acrolinx specialized for the technical support domain, we extract grammaticality, spelling, and clarity scores for every sentence and aggregate them into a sentence-level acceptability score. We further include sentence length into each sentence-level score since exploratory analysis has shown that longer sentences tend to achieve lower Acrolinx scores. The sentence-level scores will be used in Section 4.6 to either filter or weight the back-translated UDC training data.

[1]`https://www.acrolinx.com/`

3.4 Noise Injection

To improve and assess model robustness beyond the addition of conversational style segments, we inject noise into the in-domain subsets of training and test data. We replicate some typical chat phenomena (Table 2) by injecting noise in the form of (1.) typos, (2.) common chat variants and word forms, (3.) lowercasing and (4.) punctuation removal on the source side only. The required language data for typo injection and generation of chat variants (described below) is only available in English, restricting experiments to language directions with English source. Table 3 gives an overview of all generated variants. They are generated from the unmodified source data, except variants of conversational data (Section 3.1), which are based on the normalized dataset.

For typo generation we apply an approach similar to Shah and de Melo (2020) and compute a model of real-world typos based on a collection of character-level typos found in individual tokens. Typos are grouped into four categories: insertion (ex.: *threre*), deletion (ex.: *particu_ar*), substitution (ex.: *favulous*) and transposition (ex.: *corcect*). For each error category and each character, we calculate probability distributions based on corpus occurrences. They constitute a statistical model of typos in the English language which we refer to as the *typo model*. For details on the computation of the probabilities, please see Shah and de Melo (2020).

For every token in a source sentence, we sample from a token corruption probability (c) to determine whether any noise will be injected. If a token is chosen for noise injection, we iterate over its characters and decide according to a typo probability (t) whether an error will be inserted at the current character. Using the typo model as a noise function, we sample from the calculated probability distributions to generate one of the four types of errors.

We inject spelling errors using two approaches. Simply applying the typo model and method as described above results in the *artificial* variants. Additionally, we inject typos and further filter the generated errors by checking corrupted tokens against token-level typo lists. This yields the *real* variants which are modified with real-world typos only.

Table 4 contains the hyperparameters used to generate three different misspelling levels for both

	Variant
1	Low real typo injection
2	Medium real typo injection
3	High real typo injection
4	Low artificial typo injection
5	Medium artificial typo injection
6	High artificial typo injection
7	Colloquial replacements
8	Lowercasing
9	Punctuation removal
10	Lowercasing and punctuation removal

Table 3: List of generated source-side variants for a single dataset.

	artificial		real	
	c	t	c	t
Low	0.2	0.025	1.0	0.1
Medium	0.3	0.05	1.0	0.2
High	0.5	0.075	1.0	0.3

Table 4: Token corruption probability (c) and typo probability (t) for injecting noise using the typo model.

approaches. They are based on preliminary experiments and settings reported by Shah and de Melo (2020). The parameters for the *real* approach were chosen such that, after the restrictive filtering step, the level of noise was comparable to that of the corresponding *artificial* variant. Comparability was assessed via the distribution of typos per sentence and manual checks of the resulting variants. We thus obtain a total of six variants from injecting typos for a single dataset (Table 3, rows 1–6).

Additionally, we create a variant of the dataset where we replace standard language with typical conversational expressions, abbreviations and homophones (Table 3, row 7) using an in-house expression mapping. For example, "*thanks*" is replaced with "*thx*", "*give me*" turns into "*gimme*", "*are you*" becomes "*r u*" etc.

Lastly, we generate three additional variants of the data by lowercasing it and/or removing punctuation (Table 3, rows 8–10).

4 Experiments

We now empirically evaluate the methods introduced in Section 3, with the goal of improving MT quality on conversational content. We focus on conducting detailed experiments and presenting results for two language pairs per method, one being rather close languages, the other rather distant. These are English to French and Japanese (*en–fr*, *en–ja*) for up-weighting and noise injection, and Italian and Japanese to English (*it–en*, *ja–en*) for back-translation. In Section 5 we will demonstrate that our main findings generalize to other language pairs.

4.1 Experimental Setup

For training we use large amounts of company-internal parallel data that mostly consists of documentation, training materials, UI strings and support instructions. We also utilize some publicly available datasets. The training data amounts to about 25 M parallel segments per language pair. The data is tokenized using a simple tokenization scheme based on whitespace and punctuation, then segmented into subwords using byte-pair encoding (Sennrich et al., 2016b).

We make use of the Marian toolkit (Junczys-Dowmunt et al., 2018) for this investigation. For all our experiments, we use a Transformer network in the standard base configuration (Vaswani et al., 2017) and train it on the training data of the corresponding language pair. The early stopping criterion is computed on a dedicated validation set of 4,000 parallel segments.

4.2 Test Corpora

Targeted changes to MT systems require meaningful test sets to guide experimentation and to measure improvement. As it is hard to find publicly available test data that reflects the technical support dialogue content we are interested in, we created new test sets consisting of customer support dialogues and some dialogues taken from the UDC. In contrast to the conversational training data, we kept the dialogue structure for the test data and selected a total of 21 dialogues, consisting of about 1,000 sentences, that were also translated by professional translators after normalization.

To measure performance on noisy input, we created ten variations of the normalized English source text of the support dialogues using the noise injection techniques introduced in Section 3.4, see Table 3. While we analyzed scores on the individual test set variants in the experimental phase, we will only present results on all variants combined here. Obviously, the impact of the methods on the individual test set variants differs but as we intend to cover different phenomena, the combined score also helps to select the best overall configuration.

We use three groups of test data for in-domain and out-of-domain testing in this study:

	en–fr		en–ja	
Weight	CHRF2	BLEU	CHRF2	BLEU
1	59.4	36.3	41.1	34.1
5	59.5	36.3	41.9	34.8
10	59.8	36.9	42.1	35.2
20	59.9	37.0	42.2	**35.6**
30	59.9	**37.2**	42.1	35.2
40	**60.0**	36.9	**42.3**	35.4
50	59.8	36.9	**42.3**	35.5

Table 5: CHRF2 and BLEU scores on the conversational test set with different weighting of the in-domain corpus. Best results are highlighted in bold.

Conversational comprises the original and normalized support dialogue test sets, their ten variants (Table 3) and two additional related publicly available test sets.

Corporate refers to a set of about 10 test sets with diverse SAP-internal content.

Generic groups together public test sets from news, Wikipedia, UN and EU sources.

Each of these groups contains about 10,000–15,000 test segments, amounting to a total of about 40,000 per language pair. We evaluate using case-sensitive CHRF2 (Popović, 2016) and BLEU (Papineni et al., 2002) and, in view of its better correlation with human judgment (Mathur et al., 2020), rely on CHRF2 for system choice. We report scores averaged over all test sets per group.

4.3 Sentence Weighting Experiments

The amount of conversational training data we have at our disposal is tiny compared to the rest of the training data. It corresponds to 0.02% for en–fr and to 0.06% for en–ja. Our first target is to effectively use the new in-domain training data described in Section 3.1 to adapt the model to the target domain of conversational content. We thus focus initially on conversational test sets, results on out-of-domain test data are reported in Section 4.5.

Instead of fine-tuning, we use sentence weighting, giving the in-domain training data more weight, see Section 3.2. We explore the up-weighting factor empirically (Table 5). A weight of 1 constitutes the baseline. Increasing the weight multiplier yields a small but steady improvement. A factor of 40 delivers the best performance for en–fr and is almost equal to the best CHRF2 for en–ja. For the purpose of applying a common weight setting across language pairs, we keep the factor of 40 fixed for subsequent experiments.

		Typos		Lc.	Punct.	Colloq.
Level	Corpus	real	art.			
0	None	–	–	–	–	–
1	Conv.	✓	–	✓	✓	✓
2	Conv.	✓	✓	✓	✓	✓
3	Conv.	✓	✓	✓	✓	✓
	Tatoeba	✓	✓ (low)	✓	✓	–

Table 6: Configurations of the different noise levels used in noise injection experiments. Conv. denotes the conversational corpus; Lc., Punct. and Colloq. refer to the lowercased, punctuation and colloquial variants; art. abbreviates artificial.

	en–fr		en–ja	
Level	CHRF2	BLEU	CHRF2	BLEU
0	60.0	36.9	42.3	35.4
1	60.7	37.9	42.5	36.3
2	60.8	38.3	42.8	36.8
3	61.4	38.6	43.4	36.9
3 + Tatoeba 3x	**61.5**	**39.1**	**43.5**	**37.4**

Table 7: Results of the noise injection experiments. The conversational corpus has a fixed weight multiplier of 40x. Tatoeba 3x indicates addition of the Tatoeba corpus with a 3x weight multiplier. Best results are highlighted in bold.

4.4 Noise Injection Experiments

As described in Section 3.4, noisy variants are injected into the training and test data on the English source only. The target remains in its original form so that the model learns to correct and translate at the same time. We categorize the noise injection experiments into three levels (Table 6) where we successively add more misspelled or wrongly cased data to the source of the training data. The additional noisy data is weighted with a factor of 1. Besides the newly created conversational dataset we also involve the Tatoeba corpus (Tiedemann, 2020) that was already part of our training data and is rich in conversational expressions.

The results on the conversational test sets combined are shown in Table 7. As the test sets cover different noise variants, we see a nice improvement with the highest noise level 3, and conclude that we gain in robustness of our MT system. Finally, we also up-weight the original Tatoeba corpus by a factor of 3. This gives an additional small, but consistent improvement on the conversational test data. Thus we select this configuration for further trainings and evaluations.

4.5 Out-of-domain Performance

As we want to integrate the selected configuration into a mixed-domain "one-size-fits-all" model, we need to make sure that the overall system quality remains stable. To check whether up-weighting or noise injection harms translation quality on non-conversational test data, we measure the performance of the systems that perform best on conversational test data on all other test sets, grouped into corporate and generic test sets, as explained in Section 4.2. The results are reported in Table 8. They show clear improvements on the conversational test sets of over 2.0 CHRF2 points and around 3.0 BLEU points for both en–fr and en–ja. Furthermore, the improvements do not lead to degradations on other test sets. These findings support the claim that the quality on all other test sets stayed quite stable.

4.6 Error-sensitive Back-translation Scoring Experiments

For language pairs targeting English, we experiment with adding different configurations of the UDC to the training data of the baseline systems:

Full adds the entire back-translated UDC to the training data of the baseline.

Filter adds only those pairs from the UDC where the source segment's acceptability score exceeds a set threshold.

Weight adds the entire UDC, but assigns a weight between 0.2 and 1 to all segments based on their acceptability score.

The filtering threshold was set based on manual exploration of resulting filtered corpora for a small development set of UDC sentences. The filtered UDC dataset contains roughly 840,000 parallel sentences. For the weighting approach, we decide to down-weight noisy segments rather than up-weight correct segments due to the user-generated nature of the dataset. Table 9 shows the number of UDC sentences per weight.

Table 10 contains the CHRF2 and BLEU scores on all test sets for it–en and ja–en. Adding the entire UDC data (*full*) improves performance for both language pairs on in-domain test data. This indicates that the back-translations are of sufficient quality to provide training signals despite the domain mismatch of the translation system used to obtain them. For generic test sets, performance remains stable, while there is a slight drop in quality on corporate test sets.

Comparing the filtering method (*filter*) with *full*, it performs similarly on generic and corporate test sets but does not achieve the same performance increase on the conversational test sets. It should be noted that filtering results in less than 20% of the

Language pair	Test domain	CHRF2 Baseline	CHRF2 Final version	BLEU Baseline	BLEU Final version
en–fr	**conversational**	**59.4**	**61.5**	**36.3**	**39.1**
	generic	67.0	67.0	43.1	43.1
	corporate	81.5	81.4	63.8	63.7
en–ja	**conversational**	**41.1**	**43.5**	**34.1**	**37.4**
	generic	33.9	34.5	35.8	36.3
	corporate	67.8	68.0	69.8	70.0

Table 8: Results on all test sets when adding the noise-injected and up-weighted conversational training data to the baselines.

Weight	# segments
0.2	3,636
0.4	123,185
0.6	727,263
0.8	2,073,784
1.0	1,622,266

Table 9: Number of segments by weight for the *weight* experiment.

Language pair	Test domain	CHRF2 Baseline	CHRF2 *full*	CHRF2 *filter*	CHRF2 *weight*	BLEU Baseline	BLEU *full*	BLEU *filter*	BLEU *weight*
it–en	conversational	64.3	**65.7**	65.1	65.5	41.9	**43.6**	42.8	43.4
	generic	65.9	**66.0**	65.9	65.9	43.1	**43.5**	43.4	43.4
	corporate	**80.8**	80.5	80.6	**80.8**	**63.2**	62.8	62.9	63.1
ja–en	conversational	45.6	**46.3**	45.9	**46.3**	20.5	**21.2**	20.7	21.1
	generic	51.8	**51.9**	**51.9**	**51.9**	22.3	22.3	**22.4**	22.1
	corporate	**74.9**	**74.9**	**74.9**	**74.9**	51.2	51.1	**51.4**	51.2

Table 10: Results on all test sets when adding back-translated UDC data to the training data of the baselines. Best results are highlighted in bold.

UDC being added to the training data. However, further experiments with larger subsets of UDC data have also not outperformed the *full* model.

Weighting the UDC data (*weight*) leads to in-domain improvements comparable to *full*. Additionally, adding the weighted UDC to the training data does not compromise performance in other domains. This may be on account of the down-weighting of ungrammatical segments, enabling the weighting model to learn from conversational data while preserving output quality.

5 From Experiments to Production

The experimental results from Section 4 motivated us to use the same data assembling techniques and configurations for other language pairs that had not been previously tested. For the translation directions with English source, Table 11 lists the language pairs and shows the gain in case-sensitive CHRF2 and BLEU for the three groups of test sets (see Section 4.2). *Base* constitutes the baseline, to which *New* adds up-weighted parallel data noise-injected using the best configuration found in Section 4. Note that the scores for en–fr and en–ja are slightly different from those in Table 8 as the overall setup and training data composition of the experimental and final systems are not exactly identical. Across all language pairs there is considerable improvement on the conversational test sets, while on the other domains (corporate and generic) the performance remains stable on average, according to both automatic metrics. Thus, our approach works similarly well for the other seven language pairs as for English to French and English to Japanese, showing that we can deliver high-quality business conversation MT broadly for many languages without compromising translation quality of other text types.

The results of adding the back-translated UDC data with error-sensitive weight factors for systems translating into English are shown in Table 12. Although the impact is less pronounced than for the other language direction, it is consistent and visible. It is quite surprising that the large amount of back-translated data is not harming the translation quality in other domains.

To illustrate the differences, we refer back to Table 1, comparing the French MT output after the quality improvements with the baseline engine's output on the English example dialogue. The example demonstrates that robustness to typos has improved, and that punctuation is placed correctly. Fewer words remain untranslated and the MT output is more fluent.

6 Outlook

Although we see nice improvements, the translation quality in technical business conversations could be further improved. We point out the main open issues in this section, leaving them for future work and calling for new methods to address them.

	Test domain	CHRF2 Base	CHRF2 New	BLEU Base	BLEU New
en–de	**conversational**	**55.3**	**57.1**	**29.4**	**31.5**
	generic	66.2	66.4	40.4	40.7
	corporate	77.1	76.9	53.6	53.6
en–es	**conversational**	**65.4**	**68.0**	**44.0**	**47.3**
	generic	70.0	70.0	48.4	48.5
	corporate	81.6	81.6	64.4	64.3
en–fr	**conversational**	**58.8**	**61.7**	**35.7**	**39.0**
	generic	67.2	67.2	43.4	43.4
	corporate	81.8	81.8	64.2	64.3
en–it	**conversational**	**59.3**	**63.0**	**34.6**	**39.1**
	generic	67.2	67.4	42.0	42.1
	corporate	81.9	81.5	62.9	62.1
en–ja	**conversational**	**41.6**	**43.9**	**34.2**	**37.5**
	generic	33.8	34.2	35.3	36.1
	corporate	70.5	71.0	72.1	72.5
en–ko	**conversational**	**44.1**	**46.3**	**20.2**	**22.5**
	generic	65.9	65.2	44.0	43.1
	corporate	72.9	72.5	57.2	56.7
en–pt	**conversational**	**68.5**	**71.5**	**46.4**	**51.0**
	generic	69.6	69.9	45.5	46.1
	corporate	84.3	84.3	68.3	68.3
en–ru	**conversational**	**50.3**	**52.9**	**27.5**	**29.9**
	generic	64.9	65.0	38.8	38.9
	corporate	76.2	76.3	54.8	54.9
en–zh	**conversational**	**48.9**	**49.0**	**35.3**	**37.5**
	generic	42.6	43.3	45.6	46.2
	corporate	70.9	71.8	72.1	73.0

Table 11: CHRF2 and BLEU scores on test sets from all domains for the translation directions with English source.

	Test domain	CHRF2 Base	CHRF2 New	BLEU Base	BLEU New
de–en	**conversational**	**60.1**	**60.7**	**36.1**	**36.6**
	generic	67.0	67.6	44.1	44.7
	corporate	81.7	81.5	65.4	65.0
es–en	**conversational**	**67.2**	**68.3**	**45.0**	**46.5**
	generic	69.2	69.8	46.3	47.2
	corporate	81.0	80.9	63.8	63.4
fr–en	**conversational**	**62.5**	**63.2**	**39.7**	**40.8**
	generic	67.7	67.4	44.8	44.5
	corporate	79.3	78.2	61.1	59.2
it–en	**conversational**	**63.5**	**65.1**	**40.8**	**43.1**
	generic	67.1	67.9	44.0	45.2
	corporate	82.6	82.5	66.2	65.9
ja–en	**conversational**	**44.1**	**45.7**	**19.1**	**20.5**
	generic	53.5	54.8	23.8	24.7
	corporate	74.5	75.2	50.9	51.9
ko–en	**conversational**	**50.8**	**52.8**	**24.2**	**26.3**
	generic	57.7	57.9	33.4	33.6
	corporate	75.8	76.1	52.9	53.8
pt–en	**conversational**	**69.5**	**70.6**	**47.8**	**49.4**
	generic	72.3	72.9	50.5	51.5
	corporate	84.6	84.7	69.6	69.6
ru–en	**conversational**	**56.5**	**57.5**	**32.8**	**33.8**
	generic	64.9	64.9	39.0	39.0
	corporate	75.9	75.8	55.7	55.2
zh–en	**conversational**	**52.4**	**53.6**	**27.0**	**28.5**
	generic	60.3	60.5	31.9	32.2
	corporate	78.9	79.1	57.5	57.7

Table 12: CHRF2 and BLEU scores on test sets from all domains for the translation directions with English target.

In order to enhance robustness with respect to misspellings, casing, chat-typical conversational forms, or abbreviations, a normalization step in preprocessing could be investigated (Chitrapriya et al., 2018; Clark and Araki, 2011). This would support subsequent MT. However, text normalization or automatic spelling correction (Peitz et al., 2013) is highly text-type specific and prone to overgeneration when applied to non-conversational text, especially for technical documentation with lots of acronyms and technical abbreviations. This is one of the reasons why we decided for the noise injection approach targeted at conversational content only.

Chat language includes other specific phenomena which we did not specifically address in this work, one of them being capitalization for emphasis, which could be tackled, e.g., using a factored representation for source and target (García-Martínez et al., 2016; Niehues et al., 2016; Wilken and Matusov, 2019). Another frequent phenomenon is emoticons, where one would need to decide whether they should just be copied over, or whether they also need to be localized to the target language. For expletives in conversations, applicable methods largely depend on the expectations in specific use cases, i.e., should a swearword be translated to its counterpart in the target language, should it be removed, or masked with asterisks?

Our MT model operates on the sentence level, and we treat each utterance as one sentence. However, in chat conversations, sentences are sometimes spread over multiple utterances, meaning the source is actually over-segmented, leading to poor translation quality. This could be improved by a different segmentation paradigm, and/or by an MT model that takes dialogue context beyond the sentence level into account (Liang et al., 2021). The latter should also improve the coherent use of pronouns and verbal forms within a dialogue.

Levels of politeness and their expression in conversations differ between cultures and languages. Accordingly, this also poses challenges for MT, especially when the target language has more fine-grained distinctions than the source language.

7 Related Work

Our work has focused on four methods: (1.) Integrating parallel high-quality conversational content into the training corpus, (2.) creating synthetic in-domain data via back-translation, (3.) data augmentation to make the model more robust to noisy input, and (4.) model adaptation towards the style of conversational content in the business domain. Prior work by other researchers has pursued aims related to ours while often employing slightly different techniques. For instance, high-quality parallel data is oftentimes identified by means of pseudo in-domain data selection (Axelrod et al., 2011); back-translation can be improved by sampling or noisy synthetic data (Edunov et al., 2018); better robustness towards noisy input may be achieved with a stochastically corrupted subword segmentation procedure (Provilkov et al., 2020); or domain adaptation might be feasible even in a semi-supervised or unsupervised manner in certain scenarios (Dou et al., 2019; Niu et al., 2018). We are confident that many of the existing related techniques are complementary to our work and will help further improve MT quality of conversational content in the business domain.

8 Conclusion

We have shown that an MT model specialized in the IT and business domains can be enhanced to also cover conversational content well. This balancing act is highly relevant in scenarios such as product support chats or multilingual chatbots. We have achieved that by curating high-quality parallel data to address phenomena where the model exhibited the most devastating shortcomings. We further add back-translated data from the dialogue domain, inject typos, punctuation and capitalization variants to make the model more robust, and carefully manage the influence of the different corpora using a sentence weighting scheme. We have demonstrated that promising results from experiments involving only a few language pairs generalize well to the main languages in our production scenario at SAP, achieving an improvement of 2.4 CHRF2 / 3.1 BLEU on average for language pairs from English and 1.2 CHRF2 / 1.5 BLEU for language pairs to English on our conversational test sets, while the performance on other domains and test sets remains stable.

Acknowledgments

We thank Vincent Asmuth, Nathaniel Berger, and Dominic Jehle for proofreading and valuable discussions, as well as the four anonymous reviewers for their feedback and helpful comments.

References

Axelrod, Amittai, Xiaodong He, and Jianfeng Gao. 2011. Domain Adaptation via Pseudo In-Domain Data Selection. In *Proc. of EMNLP*, pages 355–362, Edinburgh, Scotland, UK, July.

Chen, Boxing, Colin Cherry, George Foster, and Samuel Larkin. 2017. Cost Weighting for Neural Machine Translation Domain Adaptation. In *Proc. of the Workshop on Neural Machine Translation*, pages 40–46, Vancouver, Canada, August.

Chitrapriya, N., Md. Ruhul Islam, Minakshi Roy, and Sujala Pradhan. 2018. A Study on Different Normalization Approaches of Word. In *Advances in Electronics, Communication and Computing*, pages 239–251, Singapore.

Chu, Chenhui and Rui Wang. 2018. A Survey of Domain Adaptation for Neural Machine Translation. In *Proc. of COLING*, pages 1304–1319, Santa Fe, NM, USA, August.

Clark, Eleanor and Kenji Araki. 2011. Text Normalization in Social Media: Progress, Problems and Applications for a Pre-Processing System of Casual English. *Procedia - Social and Behavioral Sciences*, 27:2–11.

Dou, Zi-Yi, Junjie Hu, Antonios Anastasopoulos, and Graham Neubig. 2019. Unsupervised Domain Adaptation for Neural Machine Translation with Domain-Aware Feature Embeddings. In *Proc. of EMNLP-IJCNLP*, pages 1417–1422, Hong Kong, China, November.

Edunov, Sergey, Myle Ott, Michael Auli, and David Grangier. 2018. Understanding Back-Translation at Scale. In *Proc. of EMNLP*, pages 489–500, Brussels, Belgium, October/November.

Freitag, Markus and Yaser Al-Onaizan. 2016. Fast Domain Adaptation for Neural Machine Translation. *CoRR*, abs/1612.06897.

García-Martínez, Mercedes, Loïc Barrault, and Fethi Bougares. 2016. Factored Neural Machine Translation Architectures. In *Proc. of IWSLT*, Seattle, WA, USA, December.

Huck, Matthias, David Vilar, Daniel Stein, and Hermann Ney. 2011. Lightly-Supervised Training for Hierarchical Phrase-Based Machine Translation. In *Proc. of the First Workshop on Unsupervised Learning in NLP*, pages 91–96, Edinburgh, Scotland, UK, July.

Huck, Matthias, Alexandra Birch, and Barry Haddow. 2015. Mixed-Domain vs. Multi-Domain Statistical Machine Translation. In *Proc. of MT Summit*, pages 240–255, Miami, FL, USA, October.

Huck, Matthias, Fabienne Braune, and Alexander Fraser. 2017. LMU Munich's Neural Machine Translation Systems for News Articles and Health Information Texts. In *Proc. of WMT, Vol. 2: Shared Task Papers*, pages 315–322, Copenhagen, Denmark, September.

Junczys-Dowmunt, Marcin, Roman Grundkiewicz, Tomasz Dwojak, Hieu Hoang, Kenneth Heafield, Tom Neckermann, Frank Seide, Ulrich Germann, Alham Fikri Aji, Nikolay Bogoychev, André F. T. Martins, and Alexandra Birch. 2018. Marian: Fast Neural Machine Translation in C++. In *Proc. of ACL, System Demonstrations*, pages 116–121, Melbourne, Australia, July.

Liang, Yunlong, Fandong Meng, Yufeng Chen, Jinan Xu, and Jie Zhou. 2021. Modeling Bilingual Conversational Characteristics for Neural Chat Translation. In *Proc. of ACL-IJCNLP (Vol. 1: Long Papers)*, pages 5711–5724, Online, August.

Lison, Pierre and Jörg Tiedemann. 2016. OpenSubtitles2016: Extracting Large Parallel Corpora from Movie and TV Subtitles. In *Proc. of LREC*, pages 923–929, Portorož, Slovenia, May.

Lowe, Ryan, Nissan Pow, Iulian Serban, and Joelle Pineau. 2015. The Ubuntu Dialogue Corpus: A Large Dataset for Research in Unstructured Multi-Turn Dialogue Systems. In *Proc. of SIGDIAL*, pages 285–294, Prague, Czech Republic, September.

Mathur, Nitika, Timothy Baldwin, and Trevor Cohn. 2020. Tangled up in BLEU: Reevaluating the Evaluation of Automatic Machine Translation Evaluation Metrics. In *Proc. of ACL*, pages 4984–4997, Online, July.

Niehues, Jan, Thanh-Le Ha, Eunah Cho, and Alex Waibel. 2016. Using Factored Word Representation in Neural Network Language Models. In *Proc. of WMT: Vol. 1, Research Papers*, pages 74–82, Berlin, Germany, August.

Niu, Xing, Sudha Rao, and Marine Carpuat. 2018. Multi-Task Neural Models for Translating Between Styles Within and Across Languages. In *Proc. of COLING*, pages 1008–1021, Santa Fe, NM, USA, August.

Papineni, Kishore, Salim Roukos, Todd Ward, and Wei-Jing Zhu. 2002. Bleu: a Method for Automatic Evaluation of Machine Translation. In *Proc. of ACL*, pages 311–318, Philadelphia, PA, USA, July.

Peitz, Stephan, Saab Mansour, Matthias Huck, Markus Freitag, Hermann Ney, Eunah Cho, Teresa Herrmann, Mohammed Mediani, Jan Niehues, Alex Waibel, Alexander Allauzen, Quoc Khanh Do, Bianka Buschbeck, and Tonio Wandmacher. 2013. Joint WMT 2013 Submission of the QUAERO Project. In *Proc. of WMT*, pages 185–192, Sofia, Bulgaria, August.

Popović, Maja. 2016. chrF deconstructed: beta parameters and n-gram weights. In *Proc. of WMT: Vol. 2, Shared Task Papers*, pages 499–504, Berlin, Germany, August.

Provilkov, Ivan, Dmitrii Emelianenko, and Elena Voita. 2020. BPE-Dropout: Simple and Effective Subword Regularization. In *Proc. of ACL*, pages 1882–1892, Online, July.

Rieß, Simon, Matthias Huck, and Alex Fraser. 2021. A Comparison of Sentence-Weighting Techniques for NMT. In *Proc. of MT Summit*, pages 176–187, Virtual, August.

Schwenk, Holger. 2008. Investigations on Large-Scale Lightly-Supervised Training for Statistical Machine Translation. In *Proc. of IWSLT*, pages 182–189, Waikiki, HI, USA, October.

Sennrich, Rico, Barry Haddow, and Alexandra Birch. 2016a. Improving Neural Machine Translation Models with Monolingual Data. In *Proc. of ACL*, pages 86–96, Berlin, Germany, August.

Sennrich, Rico, Barry Haddow, and Alexandra Birch. 2016b. Neural Machine Translation of Rare Words with Subword Units. In *Proc. of ACL*, pages 1715–1725, Berlin, Germany, August.

Shah, Kshitij and Gerard de Melo. 2020. Correcting the Autocorrect: Context-Aware Typographical Error Correction via Training Data Augmentation. In *Proc. of LREC*, Marseille, France, May.

Thompson, Brian, Jeremy Gwinnup, Huda Khayrallah, Kevin Duh, and Philipp Koehn. 2019. Overcoming Catastrophic Forgetting During Domain Adaptation of Neural Machine Translation. In *Proc. of NAACL-HLT*, pages 2062–2068, Minneapolis, MN, USA, June.

Tiedemann, Jörg. 2020. The Tatoeba Translation Challenge – Realistic Data Sets for Low Resource and Multilingual MT. In *Proc. of WMT*, pages 1174–1182, Online, November.

Vaswani, Ashish, Noam Shazeer, Niki Parmar, Jakob Uszkoreit, Llion Jones, Aidan N. Gomez, Łukasz Kaiser, and Illia Polosukhin. 2017. Attention is All you Need. In *Advances in Neural Information Processing Systems 30*, pages 5998–6008. Curran Associates, Inc.

Wang, Rui, Masao Utiyama, Lemao Liu, Kehai Chen, and Eiichiro Sumita. 2017. Instance Weighting for Neural Machine Translation Domain Adaptation. In *Proc. of EMNLP*, pages 1482–1488, Copenhagen, Denmark, September.

Wilken, Patrick and Evgeny Matusov. 2019. Novel Applications of Factored Neural Machine Translation. *CoRR*, abs/1910.03912.

Agent and User-Generated Content and its Impact on Customer Support MT

Madalena Gonçalves* **Marianna Buchicchio*** **Craig Stewart***
Helena Moniz*†‡ **Alon Lavie***
*Unbabel
†INESC-ID, Lisboa, Portugal
‡University of Lisbon, Lisboa, Portugal
*{firstname.lastname}@unbabel.com

Abstract

This paper illustrates a new evaluation framework developed at Unbabel for measuring the quality of source language text and its effect on both Machine Translation (MT) and Human Post-Edition (PE) performed by non-professional post-editors. We examine both agent and user-generated content from the Customer Support domain and propose that differentiating the two is crucial to obtaining high quality translation output. Furthermore, we present results of initial experimentation with a new evaluation typology based on the Multidimensional Quality Metrics (MQM) Framework (Lommel et al., 2014), specifically tailored toward the evaluation of source language text. We show how the MQM Framework (Lommel et al., 2014) can be adapted to assess errors of monolingual source texts and demonstrate how very specific source errors propagate to the MT and PE targets. Finally, we illustrate how MT systems are not robust enough to handle specific types of source noise in the context of Customer Support data.

1 Introduction

Unbabel's Language Operations platform blends advanced artificial intelligence with humans in the loop, for fast, efficient, high-quality translations that get smarter over time. The company combines Machine Translation with Human Post-Edition performed by non-professional post-editors to translate Customer Support content in a variety of formats including emails and chat messages. Customer Support is a highly unique domain given that it involves bilateral communication between Customer Support agents ('agents') and customers ('users'), each with their own nuanced discourse strategies and features.

Notwithstanding, primary literature such as Nars et al. (2016), generally consider both sides of the interaction jointly, without regard for independent and differentiating factors. The fundamental differences can be characterized as follows: agents are call center employees who are usually non-native speakers of English, which has generally evolved as the 'lingua franca' of Customer Support and the primary source language translated at Unbabel. Given that English is usually not the agent's first language, it is common to observe elements of language transfer (where the grammar rules of their native language are transferred to the English language) and other linguistic errors, more commonly the addition and omission of prepositions and articles, as also mentioned in Lee and Seneff (2008) and Rozovskaya and Roth (2010). According to Sinha et al. (2009), a person's experience and knowledge of their mother tongue will most definitely interfere with the learning of a second language, thus creating errors of different nature.

The interaction established by agents is somewhat controlled because they are usually following a particular protocol for communication prescribed by their company. This might include response templates, branding and fixed terminology which discourages stylistic variance and can often result in a large amount of repetition both within and across interactions.

Agents also work quickly, aiming to provide consistently timely responses. This can often result in typographical and other linguistic errors.

Macken, Rufener, Van den Bogaert, Daems, Tezcan, Vanroy, Fonteyne, Barrault, Costa-jussà, Kemp, Pilos, Declercq, Koponen, Forcada, Scarton, Moniz (eds.)
Proceedings of the 23rd Annual Conference of the European Association for Machine Translation, p. 199–208
Ghent, Belgium, June 2022.

Agents often operate in highly stressful circumstances; they might have to meet certain quotas which, for example, demand a brief turnaround time. This will ultimately influence their performance and the introduction of errors in the messages which, in our use case, are subsequently translated by MT and post-edited.

User-generated content from customers, on the other hand, is highly variable and unstructured. Common features include the use of abbreviations, emoticons and idiomatic expressions, all of which present unique challenges to MT. Grammatical and typographical errors common to user-generated content resulting from keyboard or smartphone use are also present.

Most critically, content from customers in a Customer Service context is highly purposeful and sometimes emotionally volatile. Customers often contact customer support to complain about a product or service and may exhibit high levels of impatience and frustration. Linguistically, this is reflected in unique lexical choices, such as the use of profanities, and variable capitalization and punctuation. All of which can often result in degradation of translation quality where the interaction is translated into or out of the source language.

Additionally, the native language of the customer is not always predictable. As mentioned in Roturier and Bensadoun (2011), often times customers from non-English speaking countries will be interacting in a non-native tongue. This could be either because they live in a foreign country, or because they are engaging the services of a foreign company. Finally, as mentioned in Hohn et al. (2016), being a native speaker of a language does not directly indicate a high proficiency of that language, another factor that can potentially indicate poor source text inputs.

Different types of Customer Support content also present another dimension of complexity: consider, for example, how a chat might differ from an email. The response time required in the former will often determine the fidelity and quality of the resulting interaction. As Lind (2012) illustrates, time restrictions implied in chat language ultimately result in fragmented written content. Because emails do not require real-time translation, at Unbabel, translation is performed first by MT and subsequently post-edited. Chat messages, however, require instantaneous translation and as such do not benefit from PE.

This paper builds upon previous work by Gonçalves (2021) and presents an evaluation framework for source text informed by the features of Customer Support interactions, which is currently being put into production at Unbabel as a means of evaluating the quality of source language text. As well as the extent to which we are able to provide a methodology and a framework that can be used in the future to ensure accurate translation and improve the robustness of our MT models to source language noise.

In this paper we seek to address the following questions:

1. How can we adapt the prototype proposed in Gonçalves (2021) to better accommodate Customer Support translation in a production and business context?

2. Given the uniqueness of Customer Support content, how does the quality of the source affect translation quality?

2 Related Work

Noisy source text input is a common issue in MT and the translation quality of user-generated content has received some limited attention in literature. Vaibhav et al., (2019) for example, highlight the difficulties presented by source noise and introduce methods to improve MT system robustness to noisy source text from internet and social media, while Náplava et al., (2021) propose to statistically model errors from grammatical-error-correction with state-of-the-art NLP systems.

Regarding human evaluation of noisy source input, the research on error typologies and evaluation frameworks has mainly focused on the annotation of translation errors. There is a scarcity of investigation on the annotation of source text and limited work on the impact of source noise on MT output. As a consequence, research and guidance on the annotation of source text is equally lacking. Although there are no clear guidelines[1], we acknowledge the recent developments on the core MQM Framework (Lommel et al., 2014) to identify which categories of issue can be applied to both source and target errors. In addition, Tezcan et al. (2017) introduce the SCATE MT Error Taxonomy, which makes more of a clear distinction between the kinds of errors found in bilingual

[1] https://www.qt21.eu/mqm-definition/issues-list-2015-12-30.html

and monolingual text. Notwithstanding the above, there is still very limited work on evaluation of source text independently of translation, particularly in the context of user-generated content and less so in the Customer Support use case.

Gonçalves (2021) considers the similarities and differences of the MQM Framework (Lommel et al., 2014), the SCATE MT Error Taxonomy (Tezcan et al., 2017) and proprietary error typologies developed internally at Unbabel. The same work introduces an adaptation of the MQM Framework (Lommel et al., 2014), and proposes a prototype of MQM-compliant typology for the annotation of source text errors, specifically tailored to user-generated content and Customer Support interactions. The proposed prototype included 4 parent categories and 28 terminal issues at 2 levels of granularity and was supported by specific annotation guidelines and decision trees to support annotation and the choice of the appropriate degree of severity of the selected errors. Still, the resulting typology showed a low agreement among annotators, meaning it lacked some robustness and wasn't efficient in a production setting.

3 Methodology

The primary goal of our revisions to the prototype typology presented in Gonçalves (2021) was to increase its robustness to Customer Support content and improve its effectiveness in a production setting. With this in mind, we made several adaptations which resulted in a new typology with 5 parent categories, 31 terminal issues and 2 levels of granularity. Where appropriate, we merged terminal nodes that resulted in low agreement and added a parent category. The full revisions to the initial prototype are detailed in the following section:

3.1 MQM Typology for Source Text Annotations

The adapted definitions from the typology prototype for the parent categories include the following:

Source Accuracy: While Accuracy is described as addressing the relationship between target and source text (Lommel et al., 2014), Source Accuracy addresses the mapping between A (actual source written by a customer or an agent on-the-fly) and B (intended source). This category is used when the semantic meaning or the conceptualization of an idea is compromised when, for instance, an agent or a customer does not finish a sentence and it is impossible to infer the intended meaning.

Fluency: In the MQM Framework (Lommel et al., 2014), Fluency includes issues related to the form or content of both source and target text. In this adaptation, Fluency addresses issues that affect the reading and comprehension of the text such as grammar, syntax and spelling. This category also determines how successfully the text can be interpreted as 'native-like' and that it would be understood to be such by a native speaker. Examples of this can be found in the wrong usage or the omission of prepositions, wrong function words or wrong choice of the appropriate verbal tense, mood or aspect.

Style: This category includes any stylistic issues found in source and target text (Lommel et al., 2014). In this adaptation, Style is to be used for stylistic issues, such as the use of register (e.g. formal vs informal), and specificities of online language, such as emoticons, conversational markers, idiomatic expressions or profanities.

Design and Markup: This category shares the same definition as the one provided in the MQM Framework (Lommel et al., 2014), although naturally with some differences in the issue types under it. It addresses any problem relating to design aspects (vs. linguistic aspects) of the content. One example of this is the segmentation of a complete sentence into several chat messages.

Locale Conventions: As defined in the MQM Framework (Lommel et al., 2014), this category is to be used when the text does not adhere to locale-specific mechanical conventions and violates requirements for the presentation of content in the target locale. This is related, for instance, to number, currency, addresses format used in a specific locale.

In order to facilitate the annotation process and aiming at high Inter-Annotator agreement and annotations consistency, as suggested by Artstein (2017), we provided annotators with an annotation decision tree[2] and a section concerning ambiguities.

[2]https://drive.google.com/file/d/1akddGjQbQHQEBxeBLFPSHwKsKGDT6MQ_/view?usp=sharing

3.2 Severities

A severity level indicates how grave or severe an error is. Having different levels of severity also helps to predict the impact of the source error text in the translation. We propose four different levels of severity: Critical, Major, Minor and Neutral (Lommel et al., 2014). It is also important to mention that, in order to facilitate annotation consistency, we also provided to the annotators a decision tree providing guidance on which severity is most likely to be suitable to the error or linguistic structure that is being annotated.

Critical: An error should be classified as critical when it contains information that may carry health, safety, legal or financial implications; a violation of geopolitical usage guidelines; a misrepresentation of the concerned company and their respective product/service; content that is completely inappropriate to its target audience and the meaning of the sentence is not understandable and cannot be inferred from the context.

Major: An error should be classified as major when there is misleading information; change of meaning and register wrongly used.

Minor: An error should be classified as minor when it impacts only minor aspects of meaning that can be resolved with proofreading.

Neutral: This label is not used for errors in the source text, but for linguistic structures that often have an impact on the quality or accuracy of the MT output. This includes only highly specific issue types: Emoticon, Segmentation, Conversational Marker, Idiomatic, Profanity, Abbreviation and Wrong Language Variety.

3.3 Annotation Rules

In addition to guidelines regarding the error definitions and the right degree of severity to be applied, we provided annotators with specific rules regarding the error span. We identified two main types of span, Continuous and Discontinuous, described below.

Continuous Span: This type of span involves a single continuous string of text. Based on their content, there are two sub-types of continuous span: single-word span and multi-word span. In single-word spans, a word is used incorrectly and only that item should be selected (e.g. misspelled word). On the other hand, in multi-word spans, an expression of more than one word in a continuous sequence is wrong. This usually applies to idioms or phrases that are assumed to be a single issue.

Discontinuous Span: These are errors involving a combination of two separate spans related to a single issue. Based on the relationship between the two spans, we can define four sub-types of discontinuous spans: delimiter spans, balanced spans, imbalanced spans, and asymmetrical spans. Delimiter spans are used to annotate typographic elements, balanced spans are used to highlight two disjoint but identical components of an issue when they are both incorrect, missing or added unnecessarily, imbalanced spans highlight two disjoint and distinct aspects of a single issue and, finally, asymmetrical spans are used to highlight an issue along with an element of context with which it is dissonant.

In order to support source text annotations for Customer Support, we included specific instructions to annotate the two sides of the Customer Support interaction, inbound (coming from the user) and outbound (from the agent) messages, also with specific instructions for user-generated content. These instructions were found to be important during the earlier annotations performed. The instructions were as follows:

1. Never annotate any Register issue type on inbound messages;
2. Do not annotate punctuation errors at the end of chat bubbles/messages;
3. Do not annotate capitalization errors in the beginning of a message.

Rule 1 is needed due to the fact that while agents are required to follow the register used by their company, users are not expected to do so, thus the Register issue type is irrelevant to inbound messages. Both rule 2 and 3 have exceptions: If the use of wrong punctuation at the end of a sentence changes its meaning, then it should be annotated; and if a capitalization error falls on a named entity, it should always be annotated with the Wrong Named Entity issue type.

Finally, in order to generate a production-ready typology to assess the quality of source text and by taking into account the improvements to the prototype mentioned above, we replicated the experiments in Gonçalves (2021) with the typology proposed in the latter work and measured the Inter-Annotator Agreement (IAA) calculated on a segment level, for both Customer Support and user-generated content data (as described in Section 4.1 below). To this end, we evaluated Cohen's Kappa Coefficient (Artstein, 2017) on the German corpus previously evaluated in Gonçalves (2021) and we observed an increased level of agreement across annotators, with an average Cohen's Kappa Coefficient of 0.5, versus the baseline showed in Gonçalves (2021) that exhibited an average Cohen's Kappa Coefficient of only 0.2.

4 Experimental Setup

The main application of source text annotation in a translation environment is to study and understand the propagation and the impact of source errors on the MT and PE steps.

In order to do so, we conducted three experiments with real client data in order to study how a particular communication medium influences agents and their communication and how MT systems handle user-generated content for chat message translation.

The first two experiments are client specific and, for privacy purposes, we refer to them hereafter as Client A and Client B respectively. The nature of the data from Client A is formulaic and repetitive. For this reason, we expect high quality translation results. The content chosen for this experiment was email threads, translated with a combination of MT and PE. We conducted a three-step alignment in the annotated data, where we made a comparison between the source text, the MT output and the post-edited target text of email threads. The language pairs analyzed were English to German ('en–de'), English to French ('en–fr') and English to Swedish ('en–sv').

On the other hand, Client B's data, being real-time chat, was translated with MT only. We included this particular client setting in order to study how chat communication affects the quality of the final MT output without any final human revision. The language pairs analyzed were English to German ('en–de') and English to Italian ('en–it').

Finally, in the third experiment, we randomly selected a sample of source texts coming from five different customers to study how user-generated content, in the context of chat conversations, impacts the final quality of the MT output. The language pairs analyzed in this experiment are Italian to English ('it–en') and Brazilian Portuguese to English ('pt–br–en').

4.1 Data and Data Preparation

In this section we present the data used for the experiments outlined in this paper, how they were translated and evaluated.

Corpus: Our main corpus is made up of 39,389 source text words across six language pairs, divided into three sub-corpora, each one corresponding to one specific experiment, as shown in Table 1.

Client A	
Language Pair	**Number of Words**
en–de	10,325
en–fr	14,520
en–sv	9,732
Client B	
Language Pair	**Number of Words**
en–de	1,288
en–it	1,261
User-generated	
Language Pair	**Number of Words**
it–en	1,088
pt–br–en	1,148

Table 1: Corpora sizes by number of words

Linguistic Resources: We applied customers' terminology to source texts, MT and PE translations and we provided our annotators and post-editors with specific customers style guides, language guidelines, the required formality level and also, in the case of annotators, the source text annotation guidelines produced in the context of these experiments.

Data Anonymization All data were anonymized in accordance with the European General Data Protection Regulation[3] (GDPR). Sensitive data and Personal Identifiable Information (PII) present in our corpus were identified using a proprietary Named Entity Recognition System (NER) and subsequently replaced with a placeholder tag.

MT Systems: The MT output analysed in the experiments presented in this paper was produced by different production MT systems pro-

[3] https://eur-lex.europa.eu/legal-content/EN/TXT/HTML/?uri=CELEX:32016R0679&f20rom=EN

prietary to Unbabel. Unbabel's MT engines are transformer-based models (Vaswani et al., 2017) trained with the Marian toolkit (Junczys-Dowmunt et al., 2018). The models undergo varying levels of domain adaptation depending on several factors such as the client, language pair, and use case. The base models on which domain adaptation is applied are trained using millions of sentences of publicly available parallel data for a given language pair, from domains such as government and news. For our experiments, the user-generated content was translated by these "base" models, which underwent no domain adaptation. Email threads were translated with engines fine-tuned to tens to hundreds of thousands of parallel sentences of proprietary email content. Chat messages were translated with engines fine-tuned to tens to hundreds of thousands of parallel sentences of proprietary chat content specific to a single client.

Human Post-Edition: Unbabel's translation model is based on a combination of MT and human Post-Edition. In order to supply customers with a continuous customer support, Unbabel's post-editors are not necessarily professional post-editors, that would also entail a higher translation cost, but rather non-professional and bilingual. This allows Unbabel to grow and scale global communities and to provide human-corrected translations with very fast turnaround times.

Human Evaluation: Human evaluations were performed by Unbabel's PRO Community, made of professional translators and linguists with relevant experience in linguistic annotations and translation errors annotations. In order to properly assess translations quality, annotators must be native speakers of the target language and with a proven high proficiency of the source language, so that they can properly capture errors and their nuances. For the experiments outlined in this paper, the human evaluation was divided into two parts:

1. Source texts were evaluated with the adapted and improved Source Errors Typology outlined in this paper;

2. MT and PE outputs were evaluated by using the annotation framework adopted internally at Unbabel, which is an adaptation of the MQM Framework (Lommel et al., 2014) and that is tailored to assess Customer Support translated content.

5 Results

Our goal was to evaluate how errors present in source text impact the quality of the MT output and how they propagate and may be overlooked in human PE. This section presents the results obtained in the experiments outlined in Section 4. For simplification reasons, we refer to the experiment relating to Client A as "Client A Experiment", and similarly the experiment related to Client B, as "Client B Experiment" and, finally, the experiment run with user-generated content as the "User-generated content Experiment".

5.1 Client A Experiment

This experiment focused on the impact of repetitive content on the MT and PE targets. The MQM results for the source text and the two translation steps, as well the errors and their breakdown, are shown in Tables 2, 3, 4 and 5.

Language Pair	Source	MT	PE
en–de	79.15	94.8	90.2
en–fr	32.16	84.1	86.2
en–sv	-109.54	47.5	94

Table 2: Average MQM scores for Client A, Emails

Among the three language pairs, the most common error found is Code Switching, which refers to whenever another language, besides the source language, is used in the source text. This error was annotated as Critical because a source language native speaker, in this case English, would not understand messages written in another language. Qualitative analysis revealed that the language used in the source text was actually the target language. This is mainly due to the fact that agents did not have the right answers or templates to answer in English and they used pre-existing material available in the target language such as, for example, published FAQs and Knowledge Base articles. We observed that the MT systems are not robust enough to handle source text written in the target language, and, as this kind of template was used in a very repetitive way, this type of error occurred multiple times in the source data and was propagated to the MT outputs. The translation flow used to translate this content was MTPE and we observed that the poor MT output produced by Code Switching issues was correctly rendered by post-editors in the majority of cases.

Error	Neutral	Minor	Major	Critical
Code Switching	0	0	0	131
Punctuation	0	104	0	0
Capitalization	0	51	0	0
Omission	0	47	0	0
Segmentation	40	0	0	0

Table 3: Client A, top 5 errors with severity for en–de

Error	Neutral	Minor	Major	Critical
Code Switching	0	0	0	889
Segmentation	203	0	0	0
Punctuation	0	163	2	0
Whitespace	0	2	61	0
Omission	0	148	0	0

Table 4: Client A, top 5 errors with severity for en–fr

English–German: The Code Switching issues found in this language pair led to the MT engines generating errors in the target text. These were caused by additions and omissions of nouns and also the occurrence of a non-existing word. As a result, the information contained in the source text was altered in both MT and PE translations. Table 6, example (1) shows Code Switching errors in the source text that resulted in the substitution of a German word "Könnt" by a non-existing word, "Önnt", the change of the pronoun "ihr" ('you' in English) into the determiner "das" ('that' in English) which modified the meaning of the sentence, and the rephrasing of a sentence where there was an addition of a noun and a change of POS of a word that slightly altered its meaning, and an addition of the word "Rücksenders" which was unrelated to the rest of the sentence.

It is worth noting from table 2 that PE appeared to slightly degrade the MQM score. Whilst we generally conclude that PE will improve the translation quality, where the MT is already of a high quality, post edition can very rarely introduce noise.

English–French: Code Switching was, once more, the most common issue. Example (2) in Table 6 shows examples where this caused the addition of the word "numéro" ('number' in English) in the MT output. This example is very particular because the addition caused in the source text resulted in a better phrasing of the message conveyed.

Error	Neutral	Minor	Major	Critical
Code Switching	0	0	0	1,975
Segmentation	290	0	0	0
Punctuation	0	207	0	0
Capitalization	0	47	0	0
Omission	0	42	0	0

Table 5: Client A, top 5 errors with severity for en–sv

English–Swedish: This language pair had the highest occurrences of Code Switching annotations. In example (3) in Table 6, the source text was changed by the MT engine, affecting its original meaning. This created a semantic error in the target text, where the noun "ändring" ('change' in English) was changed to "service", an error that was not corrected in the PE translation.

5.2 Client B Experiment

In this experiment we aimed to study how the unique features of text generated in chat conversations outlined above, even in a more controlled environment such as Customer Support Centers, affect the quality of the MT output. The MQM results for the source text and the MT output, as well the errors and their severities, are shown in Tables 7, 8 and 9.

English–German: In this language pair, different errors occurred. In example (1) in Table 10, there was a Segmentation issue where the last letter ('e') of the noun "issue" was split into another chat message. This resulted in a critical error in the MT output, by leaving the segmented word "ISSU" untranslated and with the wrong capitalization. It is also important to note that this example shows how linguistic structures annotated as Neutral in the source text can produce critical errors in the MT output.

English–Italian: In example (2) in Table 10, the named entity "WhatsApp" was written in the source text with an extra whitespace and with the wrong capitalization ("whats app"). This resulted in a critical error in the Italian target text where the translation of this named entity was completely changed ("app quale"). With a whitespace separating this named entity, the MT translated both words separately and literally.

(1) Code Switching (en–de)	
Source	**Könnt** ihr mir einen retouren Aufkleber bitte schicken?
MT	**Önnt das** mir eine Retouren Aufkleber bitte schicken?
PE	**Önnt das** mir eine Retouren Aufkleber bitte schicken?
(2) Code Switching (en–fr)	
Source	Livraison manquante commande PHONENUMBER–0
MT	Livraison manquante de la commande **numéro** PHONENUMBER–0
PE	Livraison manquante de la commande **numéro** PHONENUMBER–0
(3) Code Switching (en–sv)	
Source	Re: Din **ändring** på PHONENUMBER–0
MT	Re: Din **service** på PHONENUMBER–0
PE	Re: Din **service** på PHONENUMBER–0

Table 6: Client A Experiment, examples of Code Switching

Language Pair	Source	MT
en–de	84	85.18
en–it	92.22	86.47

Table 7: Average MQM scores for Client B, Chat

Error	Neutral	Minor	Major	Critical
Punctuation	0	11	0	0
Omission	0	9	0	0
Capitalization	0	7	0	0
Segmentation	6	0	0	0
Word Order	0	0	5	0

Table 8: Client B, top 5 errors with severity for en–de

5.3 User-generated Content Experiment

In this experiment we focused on chat messages written by users to Customer Support agents not only to study the aspects of user-generated content in chat conversations, but also how they affect the MT output with no PE intervention. The MQM results for the source text and the MT output, as well as the errors and their severities, are shown in Tables 12, 13 and 14.

Brazilian Portuguese–English: Spelling errors, as expected, are among the most frequent issues annotated in chat messages written by users. Example (1) in Table 11 shows how the typo in the word "elçes" (which should actually have been "eles"), produces an untranslated critical error in the MT output.

Italian–English: As with the previous language pair, there were multiple minor errors and neutral linguistic structures that had an impact in the MT output through the propagation of major and critical examples. The idiomatic expressions are another mark of spontaneous speech used in chat messages and example (2) in Table 11 shows how idiomatic linguistic structures, annotated as Neutral, produce critical mistranslations in the MT output, where the idiomatic expression present in the source "mi sbatte fuori" (literally in English "it kicks me out"), was mistranslated into "it bangs me out".

Error	Neutral	Minor	Major	Critical
Punctuation	0	24	0	0
Capitalization	0	9	0	0
Wrong Named Entity	0	3	0	0
Addition	0	3	0	0
Omission	0	3	0	0

Table 9: Client B, top 5 errors with severity for en–it

Another mark of chat language is the usage of abbreviation. In the annotated data, abbreviations used in the source led to untranslated critical errors in the MT English target. Example (3) in Table 11 shows how the abbreviation "nn" of the Italian negation "non" produced an untranslated critical error in the English MT output.

Finally, it is worth mentioning an example of profanities found in the source data. Due to the fact that the customer support exchange can sometimes be stressful, users tend to express their frustration through the use of profanities. The profanity used

(1) Segmentation	
Source	I am sorry to hear about the **issu**
MT	Es tut mir leid, von der **ISSU** zu hören.
(2) Wrong Named Entity	
Source	When you share via any platform such as email or **whats app**.
MT	È Condividi tramite piattaforme come e-mail o **app quale**.

Table 10: Client B Experiment, English–German examples of Segmentation and Wrong Named Entity

(1) Spelling (pt–br–en)	
Source	mas consigo comprar com **elçes**?
MT	But can I buy with **elçes**?
(2) Idiomatic (it–en)	
Source	Oggi dopo l'aggiornamento inizia a caricare le partite e **mi sbatte fuori**..
MT	Today after the update starts loading the games and it **bangs me out**..
(3) Abbreviation (it–en)	
Source	Però io voglio capire perché **nn** riesco ad acquistare.
MT	But I want to understand why **nn** can buy.
(4) Profanity (it–en)	
Source	**Cazzo** ma parlo arabo?
MT	**Cazzo** but I speak Arabic?

Table 11: User-generated Content Experiment example errors

Language Pair	Source	MT
it–en	82.54	60.32
pt–br–en	91.11	27.03

Table 12: Average MQM scores for User-generated Content Experiment, Chat

Error	Neutral	Minor	Major	Critical
Spelling	0	17	7	0
Idiomatic	5	0	0	0
Wrong Named Entity	0	3	1	0
Omission	0	3	1	0
Segmentation	3	0	0	0

Table 13: User-generated Content, top 5 errors with severity for pt–br–en

in example (4) shown in Table 11 resulted in a critical untranslated error in the MT English target.

5.4 The Importance of Source Quality

Supplementary to the above analysis, we measured the Pearson's r correlation score at a document level between the MQM scores on the source text (measured using the typology presented in this paper) and the MQM of the resulting translations for Client A.

Error	Neutral	Minor	Major	Critical
Wrong Named Entity	0	23	0	0
Spelling	0	16	2	0
Whitespace	0	16	0	0
Punctuation	0	7	0	0
Idiomatic	7	0	0	0

Table 14: User-generated Content, top 5 errors with severity for it–en

Whilst we did not note a significant correlation for en-fr, we did however note Pearson scores of 0.38 and 0.33 for en-de and en-sv respectively (all significant to $p<0.05$).

From this we conclude that the effect of source noise on output translation quality is relatively pronounced. This further underlines the importance of source text quality in achieving high quality translation and the benefits of the framework presented in this paper as a means of measuring the same.

6 Conclusions

In this work we present an MQM-compliant annotation error typology that could be applied to evaluate the quality of source texts produced in a Customer Support environment that are translated with MT and PE. In particular we demonstrate the fundamental importance of source text quality to obtaining a high quality translation output. We further demonstrate how very specific source errors propagate to the MT targets, which generally lack robustness to these kinds of noise. It was also generally observed that in most MTPE translation flows, the PE step was beneficial to the final quality of the translation output with a resulting increase in the MQM scores. As machine translation is more widely deployed in a Customer Support context as a means of scaling service globally, the unique features of customer interaction with agents will continue to present unique challenges to MT. An obvious future direction for our work is in unifying approaches to improving MT (such as those in Vaibhav et al. (2019)) with our tailored framework as means of improving the robustness of MT to the benefit of the Customer Support use case. Equally, the same could be applied to mitigating the effects of human translation errors resulting from poor source quality.

Acknowledgements

This work was partially supported by national funds through Fundação para a Ciência e a Tecnologia (FCT) with reference UIDB/50021/2020 and through FCT and Agência Nacional de Inovação with the Project Multilingual AI Agent Assistants (MAIA), contract number 045909. Besides this, the authors want to thank João Graça, for believing in how source text quality is crucial for the MT domain, and to Christine Maroti and Amin Farajian, for their help and expertise on Machine Translation.

References

Artstein, Ron, 2017. *Handbook of Linguistic Annotation*, chapter Inter-annotator Agreement, pages 297–313. Springer.

Gonçalves, Madalena. 2021. Analysis on the impact of source text quality: Building a data-driven typology. *Repositório da Universidade de Lisboa.*

Höhn, Sviatlana, Alain Pfeiffer, and Eric Ras. 2016. Challenges of error annotation in native/non-native speaker chat. *Bochumer Linguistische Arbeitsberichte*, pages 114–124.

Junczys-Dowmunt, Marcin, Roman Grundkiewicz, Tomasz Dwojak, Hieu Hoang, Kenneth Heafield, Tom Neckermann, Frank Seide, Ulrich Germann, Alham Fikri Aji, Nikolay Bogoychev, André F. T. Martins, and Alexandra Birch. 2018. Marian: Fast neural machine translation in C++. In *Proceedings of ACL 2018, System Demonstrations*, pages 116–121, Melbourne, Australia, July. Association for Computational Linguistics.

Lee, John and Stephanie Seneff. 2008. An analysis of grammatical errors in non-native speech in english. In *2008 IEEE spoken language technology workshop*, pages 89–92. IEEE.

Lind, Adam. 2012. Chat language: In the continuum of speech and writing.

Lommel, Arle, Aljoscha Burchardt, and Hans Uszkoreit. 2014. Multidimensional quality metrics (MQM): A framework for declaring and describing translation quality metrics. *Tradumàtica: tecnologies de la traducció*, 0:455–463, 12.

Nasr, Alexis, Geraldine Damnati, Aleksandra Guerraz, and Frederic Bechet. 2016. Syntactic parsing of chat language in contact center conversation corpus. In *Annual SIGdial Meeting on Discourse and Dialogue*, pages 175–184.

Náplava, Jakub, Martin Popel, Milan Straka, and Jana Straková. 2021. Understanding model robustness to user-generated noisy texts. In *Proceedings of the Seventh Workshop on Noisy User-generated Text (W-NUT 2021)*, pages 340–350. Association for Computational Linguistics.

Roturier, Johann and Anthony Bensadoun. 2011. Evaluation of mt systems to translate user generated content. In *Proceedings of Machine Translation Summit XIII: Papers*.

Rozovskaya, Alla and Dan Roth. 2010. Annotating esl errors: Challenges and rewards. In *Proceedings of the NAACL HLT 2010 fifth workshop on innovative use of NLP for building educational applications*, pages 28–36.

Sinha, Avanika, Niroj Banerjee, Ambalika Sinha, and Rajesh Kumar Shastri. 2009. Interference of first language in the acquisition of second language. *International Journal of Psychology and Counselling*, 1(7):117–122.

Tezcan, Arda, Véronique Hoste, and Lieve Macken. 2017. Scate taxonomy and corpus of machine translation errors. *Trends in E-tools and resources for translators and interpreters*, pages 219–244.

Vaibhav, Vaibhav, Sumeet Singh, Craig Stewart, and Graham Neubig. 2019. Improving robustness of machine translation with synthetic noise. *arXiv preprint arXiv:1902.09508*.

Vaswani, Ashish, Noam Shazeer, Niki Parmar, Jakob Uszkoreit, Llion Jones, Aidan N Gomez, Ł ukasz Kaiser, and Illia Polosukhin. 2017. Attention is all you need. In Guyon, I., U. V. Luxburg, S. Bengio, H. Wallach, R. Fergus, S. Vishwanathan, and R. Garnett, editors, *Advances in Neural Information Processing Systems*, volume 30. Curran Associates, Inc.

A Case Study on the Importance of Named Entities in a Machine Translation Pipeline for Customer Support Content

Miguel Menezes[1,2] **Vera Cabarrão**[3] **Pedro Mota**[3]
Helena Moniz[1,2] **Alon Lavie**[3]

[1] Universidade de Lisboa, Lisboa, Portugal

[2] INESC-ID, Lisboa, Portugal

[3] Unbabel, Lisboa, Portugal

{lmenezes, helena.moniz}@campus.ul.pt

{vera.cabarrao, pedro.mota, alon.lavie}@unbabel.com

Abstract

This paper describes research developed at Unbabel, a Portugal-based translation technology company, that combines MT with human post-edition and focuses mainly on customer service content. We aim to contribute to furthering translation quality and good-practices by exposing the importance of having a **continuously-in-development** robust Named Entity Recognition system that, among other advantages, supports General Data Protection Regulation (GDPR) compliance. Moreover, we have tested semi-automatic strategies that support and enhance the creation of Named Entities gold standards to allow a more seamless implementation of Multilingual Named Entities Recognition Systems. The project described in this paper is the result of a shared work between Unbabel´s linguists and Unbabel´s AI engineering team, matured over a year. The project should also be taken as a statement of multidisciplinarity, proving and validating the much-needed articulation between the different scientific fields that compose and characterize the area of Natural Language Processing (NLP).

1 Introduction

Customer support professionals deal with multiple issues and problems arising from human-interaction, from answering questions or responding to customer complaints, to processing orders and returns, as well as sharing information and services. They are, in a sense, a direct line between customers and service providers, so they must be efficient, fast, and overall understandable, all while working remotely. Unbabel enhances customer support abilities through the combination of a Machine Translation (MT) layer, coupled with human post-edition, allowing to combine the speed and scale of MT with the quality of human editing.

To that end, we focus on Named Entity Recognition processes that compose a vital part of the automatic translation pipeline, since they promote an increase in translation quality, and ensure 2018 data protection regulation compliance. To promote high MT performances, a Named Entity Recognition System (NER) was applied, enabling the identification of NEs in context, e.g., prediction of NEs according to its surroundings, while simultaneously categorizing the NE. The identified NEs are then automatically blocked for translation or automatically annotated as NE of interest for further processes such as localization. This step ensures a decrease in MT "hallucinations" (inadequate translations) (Lee et al., 2018), since NEs are often responsible for these severe MT mistranslations, which

Macken, Rufener, Van den Bogaert, Daems, Tezcan, Vanroy, Fonteyne, Barrault, Costa-jussà, Kemp, Pilos, Declercq, Koponen, Forcada, Scarton, Moniz (eds.)
Proceedings of the 23rd Annual Conference of the European Association for Machine Translation, p. 209–217
Ghent, Belgium, June 2022.

negatively impacts the overall translation quality, considered mostly as critical errors in terms of severity. There is a second step associated with the NE pipeline, the anonymization process. The anonymization guarantees that all the NEs corresponding to personal identifiable information (PII) are either replaced by an adequate placeholder, for example *Email*; *Phone Number*; *Reference Number;* or replaced by a semantic equivalent (Mota et al., 2022) in case the NE is a person's name. In the latter, the real name is replaced with a fictitious name that agrees in gender with the original one. This step has a four-fold goal: i) ensures customer sensitive data protection and prevents MT learning with PII information; ii) prevents MT mistranslation; iii) ensures gender agreement (specifically in the case of the replacement of names for semantic equivalents), and iv) guarantees document readability, which is particularly relevant for post-editors. In short, the application of NER is fundamental for enhancing translation quality and preventing personal data breaches, which can lead to fines for non-compliance cases.

Despite the aforementioned importance that NEs represent within a MT pipeline, their definition seems to be somehow elusive. The fact that there is not a unique definition of what constitutes a NE in the literature can be directly associated with the fact that they are structures with the needed plasticity and adaptability to be applied to different tasks. At the MUC, (Chinchor et al., 1997), named entities were defined as "unique identifiers"; in 2003 CoNNL shared task: Language-Independent Named Entity Recognition, they were described as "phrases that contain the names of persons, *organizations and locations."* (Sang and De Meulder, 2003), and for Nouvel et al. (2016) they are "*textual units corresponding to predefined semantic categories*". Despite the different definitions, they all seem to agree that a named entity functions as a referent (Jurafsky et al., 2020: 1); a linguistic object carrying relevant information in a document, needed, according to Nouvel et al. (2016: 10), to allow the computer system to "understand" documents.

Considering the importance of such structures within a document, we investigate an alternative approach to semi automatically generate training data (still requires manually annotation source language) for Named Entity Recognition (NER) models from parallel corpus (Agerri et al. 2018: 3533). This is important for the use case where we want to expand NER language coverage within a particular domain. The goal is to only require NE annotated data on the source side and automatically determine the correspondence in the translation. This avoids the time-consuming and high-priced human annotations necessary to train NER for a new language.

To achieve our goals, we benchmark different alignment models, and use their output to project NEs annotations from source to target text. We will show their impact in the English–German and English–Brazilian Portuguese language pairs as well as in the domains of tourism and technology.

2 Related Work

In the last few years, machine learning systems have been predominantly used to achieve state-of-the-art NER results and much has been developed since the early Message Understanding Conferences (MUC) initiatives. A continuous flow of proceeding works in the field, both in the industry and in a more academic environment, has yielded significant changes that go from new, high performance computational technologies related to the NER subtask itself, to new different applications and goals. These frameworks have been developed to accommodate particular objectives for particular domains, such as in the case of the healthcare industry (Tarcar et al., 2019), where NER models were used, for example, to extract structure information from unstructured Electronic Health Records (EHR).

Despite all technological advances, commonly used frameworks still heavily rely on human intervention to provide modeling features or heuristics to solve downstream NLP tasks. While solutions have been proposed to overcome the need for these handcrafted features (Santos and Guimarães, 2015: 1), the need of labeled data is still an obstacle. In cross-lingual applications, this problem is further aggravated with the cardinality of the number of necessary language pairs. When expanding NER language coverage, this problem can be tackled using named entities word alignment within parallel corpora. This information allows the transfer of NE annotations from a source sentence and its translation (Eskin et al., 2019). Recent work has shown impressive results with the application of new deep learning models, e.g., Transformers, based on an encoder/decoder architecture, mapping sentences to vectors, which result in a representation of the input sequence of words in the source language

(Vaswani et al., 2017). This has boosted the quality of NER and word alignment models.

Akbik et al. (2018) propose *contextual string embeddings* for the NER. The embeddings are pre-trained on large unlabeled corpora without any explicit notion of words and thus, fundamentally, model words as sequences of characters, *contextualized* by their surrounding text. Therefore, the same word will have different embeddings depending on its contextual use. This allows the embeddings to properly represent polysemic words, language specific prefixes and suffixes, and handle misspelled words. The approach achieved state-of-the-art results in the *CoNLL 2003* NER shared task.

Wang et al. (2019) propose the use of the M-BERT, Multilingual Bidirectional Encoder Representations from Transformers, for cross-lingual transfer without the need of a dedicated cross-lingual training objective and with no aligned data. Experiments were carried out in three different languages (Spanish, Hindi, and Russian) and showed that M-BERT generalizes well across languages for a variety of downstream tasks (Wu and Dredze, 2019), like NER and Part of Speech (POS) tagging. Extending this research line, mLUKE and ERICA enhance M-BERT with Named Entity capabilities, further improving the state-of-the-art in several NLP downstream tasks.

Eskin et al. (2019) propose a neural model for word alignment, integrated into a Transformer-based machine translation model for English–Chinese and English–Arabic. The model can be used to generate cross-lingual NE datasets via alignment projection of token-level annotations in a high-resource language to a low-resource language.

Modrzejewski et al. (2020) explores an approach to improve translation quality by conveying NE information through source factors in a machine translation model. The method showed an increase of 1% in the BLEU score, when using the WMT2019 standard test, and an increase of 12% when compared with a strong baseline for NE translation.

As stated above, several NER models have been proposed, some with the main goal of allowing off-the-shelf usage, such as Stanza, Google Cloud Natural Language, and Spacy. In all systems, a wide variety of NEs are taken into account, that range from Address; Date-Time; E-mail, Payment/Credit-Cards in case of Google, or Location; Facilities; Law; Language, *inter alia,* in case of Spacy. Nevertheless, performing NER in a specific domain remains a challenge. In our case, we target the customer-support domain, where the previous tools underperform or lack necessary NE types. We resort to training custom models with in domain data. Scaling this approach to many different languages is expensive due to the cost of obtaining labeled data. By using a word alignment-based approach (Chung, 2007: v) to project existing NE annotations to a new language in parallel corpora we can address this issue.

3 Dataset Annotation

To validate the word alignment-based NE projection, we manually annotated two datasets: Tourism-Dataset, and Technology-Dataset. For the Tourism-Dataset, we used parallel data (bitext) in EN (source) and in DE. The datasets, comprising 2500 sentences each, were annotated by two linguists, one responsible for the EN data set annotation, whilst a second one was responsible for the DE version. For DE two different translations were annotated, one from machine translated only (MT), and the other with an extra post-edition layer (PE). The Technology-Dataset consists of 360 post-edited sentences for the EN–PT/BR language pair and was fully annotated by one of the previous linguists.

All datasets went to a preprocessing stage, where the data sets were divided into sentences, allowing the annotation to be made sentence by sentence using Prodigy[2], an annotation platform. Both annotators used Unbabel's internal NE annotation guidelines. The annotators also had access to online information, namely dictionaries, maps, and other relevant sources of information that could facilitate the task.

3.1 Named Entities Typologies

For the Named Entity Recognition task, it is important i) to define which NEs are relevant for the job and ii) how to annotate them. This process requires the creation of a NE typology, "a descriptive formalization of the selected categories and their scope" (Nouvel et al., 2016: 48), that usually comes in the form of annotation guidelines. This project uses the current generic NEs typology created by Unbabel, that follows the universal Named Entity categories triad: Enamex,

[2] https://prodi.gy

Numex and Timex (Table 1 shows the complete NEs categories tag set applied in this study).

3.2 Inter-annotator agreement

Given that the linguists worked separately in the Tourism-Dataset, we carried out an inter-annotator agreement study to determine if the NE typology was similar in the corresponding EN/DE language pair.

For the following analysis, we only considered a NE match within both gold standards whenever both annotators agreed in: i) the entity span, and ii) the category. The analysis performed allowed us to identify a high inter-annotator agreement, between the EN gold standard (source), and the two DE datasets (target): 90% for the MT and 91% MT with PE.

Named Entities Categories	Named Entities Inter-Annotator Agreement Results		
	EN GS	DE MT GS	DE PE GS
Organization	183	161	167
Currencies	284	276	278
Percentages	9	9	9
Refnumber	64	52	53
Names	45	43	43
Dates	106	102	102
Address	26	22	23
E-mail	12	12	12
Phone Number	15	15	15
Time	26	21	21
URL	18	17	17
City	56	39	39
Country	3	3	3
Products and Services (PRS)	13	4	4
Credit Card	1	1	1
Password	1	1	1
Username	1	1	1
Number Code	1	0	0
Total	865	781	789

Table 1: NEs inter-annotator agreement in absolute values.

By observing the EN gold standard, we were able to account for 865 named entities identified by annotator one and 781 NEs identified by annotator two for DE MT gold standard, and 789 for the DE PE gold standard (Table 1). By pairing the number of identified NEs between the EN and DE gold standards, we determined that annotator two annotated less 9.72% NEs in the MT and less 8.72% NEs in the post-edited dataset than the total amount of NEs found in the EN gold standard, however, with very high inter-agreement in specific named entities, namely expressions that identify numbers (Numex NEs), such as:

1. Percentages: 100% agreement between EN and both DE gold standards.

2. Currencies: 97.1% agreement in MT and 97.8% in PE;

3. Phone numbers: 100% agreement.

Temporal expressions, Timex, e.g. Dates or Time, seem to follow the same pattern, amounting to a 96.22% agreement value in case of dates, and 80.76% for the category time, both in MT and PE. For Enamex entities, countries had 100% of inter-annotator agreement, and person names presented a value of 95%. There seems to be an intuitive understanding of these categories, corroborated by the lexical material in its surroundings, helping to assert such entities with fewer annotation doubts, as seen in the following examples taken from our datasets:

Ex.1

EN: "Dear Manuela Frieda Kalo"

DE: "Sehr geehrte(r) Manuela Frieda Kalo"

Greetings like in the above example, *Dear ...*, or in German *Sehr geehrte(r)...*, hint that the following word is a named entity, specifically a name, being relevant both for the human-annotation process and for the MT system learning process.

Based on the annotation agreement values for the above-mentioned categories, we conclude that all these NEs gather consensus; they tend to be context-independent and, hence, straightforward to annotate. In these cases, there are few doubts as to which tags to choose. On the other hand, the NEs labeled as *Products and Services* (PRS) present the lowest inter-annotation agreement score, 30%. Many of the named entities labeled as PRS in the EN gold standard were tagged as *Organizations* (ORG) both in MT and PE DE gold standards, thus being considered mismatching NEs. Moreover, for these categories, the same NE can assume both categories in different sentences, thus denoting ambiguous characteristics. In these cases, interpreting the entire sentence, or the words in a NE vicinity can be the key to determine its role and classification. However, this approach might not always be so linear or straightforward, as shown in the following examples:

Ex.2
EN: "Kindly make sure that one of the accepted cards like [Union pay credit card]**Organization** is saved in your [HolidayConsultee]**Organization** account."

DE: "Bitte stellen Sie sicher, dass eine der akzeptierten Karten [Union Pay Kredit-, die HolidayConsultee --Karte]**Products and Services** in Ihrem-Konto gespeichert ist."

In the cases above, every single NE was identified as an ORG in the EN gold standard, while in the DE gold standard, they were tagged as PRS. The annotation differences reside on the fact that in the EN gold standard, the named entity was taken by the annotator one as an entity that provides a service, whereas in the DE gold standard, the annotator two interpreted the named entity as a service itself.

Overall, we can define the inter-annotator agreement for this task as substantially high, nevertheless, we must accept the fact that for some categories, like PRS, and ORG and even *Locations* (LOC), the annotation task is not fully consensual, leading to inter-annotator mismatches.

4 Named Entity Projection

To understand the impact of using an alignment approach in building a multilingual NER system, we tested four state-of-the-art aligners: FastAlign[3], the current aligner used by Unbabel; eflomal[4]; SimAlign[5], and AwesomeAlign[6]. Each aligner had available different sets of configurations that, when combined, amounted to a total of 53 different alignment possibilities for each NE category. The different configuration for aligners ranged from:

· Heuristics, allowing different alignment directions: from source to target and vice versa, with the goal (Mota et al., 2022);

Training data that range from more generic data to client data or mixed data (both generic and client data); or

· Pre-trained models for cross-lingual understanding.

Using the output word alignments, NE identified in the source sentence were projected in the target based on a min-max algorithm. This means that we consider the target entity span to range the lowest to highest word alignments.

Model ranking for NE projection task results were presented for assessment using an online software, developed by Unbabel´s AI team, that showed all alignment results for the four aligners used, together with their configurations. The alignment results were displayed from best (number 0) to worst alignment result (number 53). Moreover, the developed interface also allowed us to compare two models (Figure 1), giving a panorama over the alignment quality for each category (Figure 2).

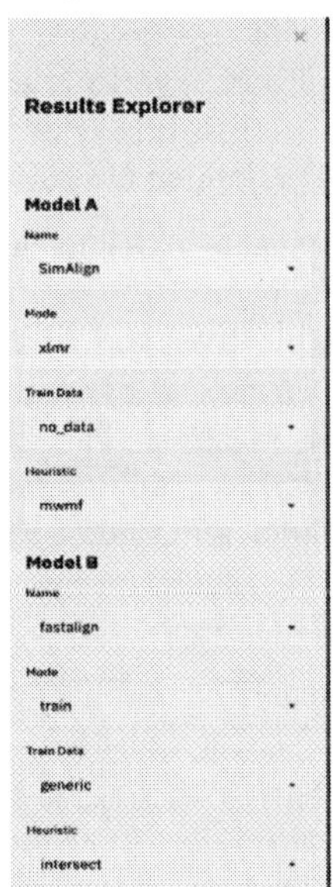

Figure 1: Aligners model comparison, giving the ability to choose between available configurations.

[3] https://github.com/dgel/fastalign
[4] github.com/robertostling/eflomal
[5] github.com/cisnlp/simalign
[6] github.com/neulab/awesome-align

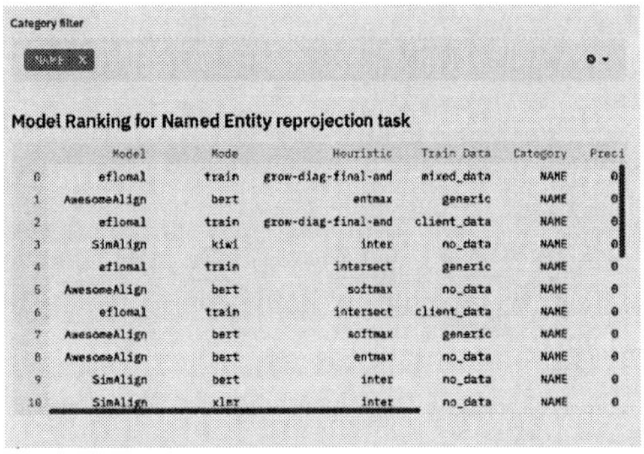

	Model	Mode	Heuristic	Train Data	Category	Preci
0	eflomal	train	grow-diag-final-and	mixed_data	NAME	0
1	AwesomeAlign	bert	entmax	generic	NAME	0
2	eflomal	train	grow-diag-final-and	client_data	NAME	0
3	SimAlign	kiwi	inter	no_data	NAME	0
4	eflomal	train	intersect	generic	NAME	0
5	AwesomeAlign	bert	softmax	no_data	NAME	0
6	eflomal	train	intersect	client_data	NAME	0
7	AwesomeAlign	bert	softmax	generic	NAME	0
8	AwesomeAlign	bert	entmax	no_data	NAME	0
9	SimAlign	bert	inter	no_data	NAME	0
10	SimAlign	xlmr	inter	no_data	NAME	0

Figure 2: Best alignments scoring for the Name category, considering the different model's configurations (Mode; Heuristic; Train Data)

With access to the information displayed by the above-mentioned interface, we were able to understand the differences in alignments that generated NEs spans between the EN source dataset and its DE counterpart. Moreover, we were also able to compare the DE dataset with and without an extra post-edition layer, as to determine if such a task does interfere positively or negatively in the NE projection results. Also, we were able to evaluate the aligner settings that showed better performance within the 53 possible combinations and benchmark the current aligner used by Unbabel. The NE projection task was evaluated using a classification setting with the following standard performance metrics: Precision, Recall and F_1 (Makhoul et al., 1999), in order to have a more fine-grained performance perspective of the applied model results:

The precision value is defined as the number of positive NE predictions (true positives) divided by the sum of true positives and false positives. This formula is used to understand the classifier exactness. The question that the concept of precision answers is, of all the NEs retrieved by the NE projection algorithm, how many were actually correct. Lower values of precision indicate a higher number of false positives.

The recall value is defined as the ratio of correctly predicted true positive NEs, divided by the sum of true positives and false negatives. The question recall answers is, of all the NEs in the test dataset, how many were retrieved correctly by the NE projection algorithm.

The F-value, also known as F_1, is defined as the harmonic mean of the precision and the recall, being appropriate to identify the desired average rate.

5 Experimental Results

Our study yields very promising results, showing the devised approach to be trustworthy for building multilingual gold standards for NER training when the correct alignment system coupled with specific correct configurations is implemented.

5.1 Tourism Dataset

This section provides the NE projection results obtained for the Tourism-Dataset. Based on the F_1 results obtained for each NE category, we are able to determine the best performing aligner. The overall results can be found in Table 2.

	SimAlign	FastAlign	AwesomeAlign	eflomal
N	6	5	3	3

Table 2: Number of categories for which each alignment system achieved the best alignment results.

Based on these results analysis, we were able to ascertain that SimAlign proved to be the best alignment model for six categories: *Organization, Currency, City, Time, Products and Services and Dates,* generating the most trustworthy alignments using the XLM-R pre-trained model and the intersect symmetrization heuristic.

FastAlign was ranked as second-best aligner, obtaining top alignments for the following categories: *Country, Credit card, Address, Percentages, Username*. The remaining six categories' first place alignments were divided between the remaining two aligners, eflomal and AwesomeAlign, which led us to immediately discard them as top aligners. The alignment results analysis also led us to conclude that SimAlign behaves in a very consistent manner, obtaining very high F_1 scores overall.

A more in-depth analysis for the *Currency* category can be found in Tables 3 and 4. The first table displays the top five best overall alignment results. The second one, dedicated exclusively to the aligner currently used by Unbabel, FastAlign, displays the top five best alignment configurations. Based on these results, we can state that, for the *Currency* category, SimAlign outperformed the remaining aligners, producing the five best alignment results overall. On the other hand, FastAlign only ranked in 17th place (and onwards) for NE projection, resulting in an alignment quality difference between both aligners of 0.076%.

Model	Mode	Heuristic	Train data	Categ.	Precision	Recall	F_1	Time
SimAlign	**Bert**	**Inter**	**No data**	**CRR**	**0.981**	**0.975**	**0.976**	**0.0205**
SimAlign	kiwi	Inter	No data	CRR	0.981	0.974	**0.974**	0.0284
SimAlign	kiwi	inter max	No data	CRR	0.976	0.978	**0.974**	0.318
SimAlign	xlmr	mwmf	No data	CRR	0.976	0.977	**0.973**	0.4719
SimAlign	kiwi	mwmf	No data	CRR	0.976	0.977	**0.973**	0.3695

Table 3: Top five alignment results for the *Currency* NE.

Model	Mode	Heuristic	Train data	Categ	Precision	Recall	F_1	Time
FatsAlign 17th	production	Grow diag final	No data	CRR	0.934	0.894	0.899	0.0007
FatsAlign 18 th	production	intersect	No data	CRR	0.973	0.853	0.889	0.0007
FastAlign 19 th	train	Grow diag final	Mixed data	CRR	0.914	0.883	0.883	0.0005
FastAlign 20 th	train	Grow diag final	generic	CRR	0.906	0.881	0.878	0.0005
FastAlign 21st	train	intersect	Mixed data	CRR	0.975	0.824	0.866	0.0005

Table 4: Top five best alignment results for FastAlign for the *Currency* NE.

5.2 Technology Dataset

This section provides the NE projection results obtained for the Technology-Dataset. The analysis is displayed for each category within the parallel *corpus*.

For the category *Name,* SimAlign and AwesomeAlign reached constant F_1 values of 1, regardless of the configurations applied. On the other hand, 39.29% of the alignments carried out by FastAlign and Eflomal were deemed having F_1 value of under 1.

For *Currency*, the results for SimAlign and AwesomeAlign followed the same pattern, while FastAlign and eflomal never reached a F_1 value over 0.75.

For the category *Organizations,* once again AwesomeAlign and eflomal reached constant values of 1. SimAlign and FastAlign results ranged between 0.91 to 1. The configuration responsible to SimAlign underachievement reads as follow:

- Mode: BERT
- Heuristic: Itermax

For the category *Email*, all alignment-based NE projection results were deemed as having F_1 scores of 1, except for the ones performed by FastAlign with 50% of the all alignments with a F_1 of 0.

Regarding the category *URL,* all models reached F values of 1, except FastAlign with constant values under 0.66.

As for *Products and Services,* the overall F value results ranged between 0.58 and 0.97. Nevertheless, we were still able to ascertain solid F_1 scores of 0.97 for AwesomeAlign and SimAlign.

For the category *Reference Number* AwesomeAlign, SimAlign and eflomal alignments reached constant values of 1. FastAlign underperformed reaching a top value of 0.75.

The previous results show that AwesomeAlign produced the best NE projections, followed by SimAlign that only for the category *ORG* did not show an F_1 of 1. AwesomeAlign configurations produced alignments with F_1 results of 1, similarly to SimAlign, (excluding the category *PRS,* as previously mentioned), suggesting that the task was trivial to solve. Nevertheless, it is important to highlight that the dataset used for alignment only comprised 360 sentences, with a very small amount of NEs per category. Moreover, most of the NEs had a similar form in both source and target, making the projection task easier. The lack of enough NEs representing a category can explain the F_1 obtained by AwesomeAlign and SimAlign, independently of the particular configuration.

With regards to FastAlign, it still underperforms in comparison with the other aligners, being for some categories the aligner that presented the worst alignment results. We hypothesize that the underperformance of FastAlign is related to its difficulty in dealing with rare words, which typically are instances of NEs. The pre-trained model-based approaches are more robust when facing this issue since they operate at the subword level and are exposed to much larger datasets during training.

6 Conclusions and Future-work

With this work, we focused on giving a general overview on the pivotal importance of NEs from a linguistic and historical perspective, highlighting its relevance within an automatic-translation scenario. Moreover, we were able to test four different aligners for the creation of semi-automatic multilingual gold standards through NE projection in parallel *corpora.* With the research results concerning the creation of multilingual gold standards, we were able to replace the aligner used in production, Fastalign, by SimAlign. By doing so, we ensure a reliable integration of this cross-lingual technique for the creation of multilingual **NER gold standards** for multiple language pairs and applicable to a myriad of different domains. The manual-annotation tasks performed along the experiments also allowed us to highlight the fact that particular NEs can play ambiguous roles and can be responsible for inter-annotator mismatches, thus needing special attention.

Also, we see future possibilities of using the NER system to leverage Unbabel's Translation Memories. The identification of NEs followed by their replacement with corresponding placeholders will lead to an increase in the number of Translation Memories matches, which promotes more accurate end-translation results, while lessening, simultaneously, the need for human post-edition.

Finally, a note still on the contribution of our work to the anonymization module in the pipeline. The NE work conducted ultimately reflects improvements on the anonymization module, crucial to any company compliant with Responsible AI Principles. The fundamentals and approaches developed within our project regarding the identification and anonymization of Personal Identifiable Information have already been implemented by the MAIA Project (Multilingual AI Agent Assistants), thus enabling information processing and sharing in a safe manner. As such, we will continue our work concerning the NER task, with a particular focus on the anonymization step.

Acknowledgements

This work was supported by national funds in Portugal through Fundação para Ciência e a Tecnologia (FCT), with reference UIDB/50021/2020 and through FCT and Agência Nacional de Inovação with the Project Multilingual AI Agents Assistants (MAIA), contracted number 045909.

References

Agerri, Rodrigo, Yi-Ling Chung, Itziar Aldabe, Nora Aranberri, Gorka Labaka and German Rigau. 2018. Building named entity recognition taggers via parallel corpora. In Proceedings of the Eleventh International Conference on Language Resources and Evaluation (LREC 2018), pp. 3529-3533.

Akbik, Alan, Duncan Blythe and Roland Vollgraf. 2018. Contextual string embeddings for sequence labeling. In Proceedings of the 27th international conference on computational linguistics (pp. 1638-1649).

Chinchor, Nancy and Patricia Robinson. 1997. Message Understanding Conference-7 named entity task definition. In Proceedings of the Seventh Conference on Message Understanding (Vol. 29, pp. 1-21).

Chung, Yi-Ling. (2017). Automatic generation of named entity taggers leveraging parallel corpora. Stanford University.

Data Protection Act, 2018. Data Protection Act 2018. [online] GOV. U.K. Available at: <https://www.gov.uk/government/collections/data-protection-act-2018>

Finkel, J. Rose, Trond Grenager and Christopher Manning. 2005. Incorporating non-local information into information extraction systems by gibbs sampling. In Proceedings of the 43rd annual meeting of the association for computational linguistics (ACL'05) (pp. 363-370).

Joseph, Cris (2019, March 1) What are the Benefits of delivering excellent customer service?. Chron. Retrieved January 18, 2020, from 2019 https://smallbusiness.chron.com/benefits-delivering-excellent-customer-service-2086.html

Jurafsky, Dan and James H. Martin. 2018. Speech and Language Processing. *Chapter 8: Sequence Labelling for Parts of Speech and Named Entities* (draft of December, 30, 2020).

Lee, Katherine, Orhan Firat Ashish Agarwal, Clara Fannjiang and David Sussillo. 2018. Hallucinations in Neural Machine Translation. Google AI. Retrieved January 18, 2020, from Openreview.net, Available at https://openreview.net/forum?id=SkxJ-309FQ

Makhoul, John, Francis Kubala, Richard Schwartz, and Ralph Weischedel. 1999. Performance measure for information extraction. In Proc. of the DARPA Broadcast News Workshop, Herndon, VA.

Modrzejewski, Maciej, Miriam Exe. Bianka, Buschbeck, Thanh-Le Ha and Alexander Waibel.

2020. Incorporating external annotation to improve named entity translation in NMT. In Proceedings of the 22nd Annual Conference of the European Association for Machine Translation (pp. 45-51).

Mota, Pedro, Vera Cabarrão and Eduardo Farah. 2022. Fast-Paced Improvements to Named Entity Handling for Neural Machine Translation. In Proceedings of EAMT.

NER Annotation Guidelines. (2020). Unbabel´s Internal Company Document.

Nouvel, Damien, Maud Ehrmann and Sophie Rosset. 2016. Named entities for computational linguistics. ISTE.

Qin, Yujia., Yankai Lin, Ryuichi Takanobu, Zhiyuan Liu, Peng Li, Heng Ji, Minlie Huang, Maosong Sun and Jie Zhou. 2020. Erica: Improving entity and relation understanding for pre-trained language models via contrastive learning. arXiv preprint arXiv:2012.15022.

Ri, Ryokan, Ikuya Yamada and Yoshimasa Tsuruoka. 2021. mLUKE: The Power of Entity Representations in Multilingual Pretrained Language Models. arXiv preprint arXiv:2110.08151.

Sang, Erik and Fien De Meulder. 2003. Introduction to the CoNLL-2003 shared task: Language-independent named entity recognition. arXiv preprint cs/0306050.

Santos, N. D. Cicero and Victor Guimarães. 2015. Boosting named entity recognition with neural character embeddings. arXiv preprint arXiv:1505.05008.

Stengel-Eskin, Elias, Tzu-Ray Su, Matt Post and Benjamin Van Durme. 2019. A discriminative neural model for cross-lingual word alignment. arXiv preprint arXiv:1909.00444.

Tarcar, K. Amogh, Aashis Tiwari, Vineet Naique Dhaimodker, Penjo Rebelo, Rahul Desai and Dattaraj Rao. 2019. Healthcare NER models using language model pretraining. arXiv preprint arXiv: 1910.11241.

Vaswani, Ashish, Noam Shazeer, Niki Parmar, Jakob Uszkoreit, Llion Jones., Aidan N. Gomez, Lukasz kaiser and Illia Polosukhin. 2017. Attention is all you need. Advances in neural information processing systems, 30.

Wang, Zihan, Stephen Mayhew and Dan Roth. 2019. Cross-lingual ability of multilingual bert: An empirical study. arXiv preprint arXiv:1912.07840.

Wu, Shijie and Mark Dredze. 2019. Beto, Bentz, Becas: The surprising cross-lingual effectiveness of BERT. EMNLP arXiv:1904.09077.

Investigating automatic and manual filtering methods to produce MT-ready glossaries from existing ones

Maria Afara
AI R&D team, Acolad
mafara@acolad.com

Randy Scansani
AI R&D team, Acolad
rscansani@acolad.com

Loïc Dugast
AI R&D team, Acolad
ldugast@acolad.com

Abstract

Commercial Machine Translation (MT) providers offer functionalities that allow users to leverage bilingual glossaries. This poses the question of how to turn glossaries that were intended to be used by a human translator into MT-ready ones, removing entries that could harm the MT output. We present two automatic filtering approaches – one based on rules and the second one relying on a translation memory – and a manual filtering procedure carried out by a linguist. The resulting glossaries are added to an MT model. The outputs are compared against a baseline where no glossary is used and an output produced using the original glossary. The present work aims at investigating if any of these filtering methods can bring a higher terminology accuracy without negative effects on the overall quality. Results are measured with terminology accuracy and Translation Edit Rate. We test our filters on two language pairs, En–Fr and De–En. Results show that some of the automatically filtered glossaries may help reach a better balance between accuracy and overall quality, replacing the costly manual process.

1 Introduction

The ability to correctly and consistently translate domain-specific or customer-specific terminology is key in the field of translation. To accommodate for this need, Machine Translation (MT) providers have started to offer terminology features that enforce glossary entries at runtime.[1] The availability of such features can be particularly advantageous for Language Service Providers (LSPs), giving them an opportunity to offer a terminology accurate MT output in a scenario in which training a model from scratch is not an option.

However, such glossaries were created to be used by human translators, relying on their ability to, e.g., disambiguate terms before inserting them in the target text. Also, glossaries are often created by customers without the help of terminologists. As a result, they might not be ready to be used by MT, since they might contain entries that harm the output quality (Bergmanis et al., 2021; Guerrero, 2020; Scansani and Dugast, 2021).

The creation of a pipeline to clean glossaries can help MT users leverage their terminology data base. The pipeline can be based on a manual intervention, which can be time-consuming, or rely on an automatic procedure. Either way, two operations may be involved, i.e. removing entries that are not helpful and/or editing them.

Automatically editing entries is not a trivial task. For example, automatically editing term entries where several term alternatives are separated by slashes poses the question of which alternative(s) to keep. Also, in some cases the slash is used to separate parts of a compound or of a multi-word term (e.g. the German term "Abluft-/Motorfilter" should be split into "Abluftfilter" and "Motorfilter"). Editing terms with parentheses is not trivial either. In some cases what is inside the parentheses is part of the term, e.g. the German term "Länge Base" translated as "Length (base)". In other cases

[1]Two examples of glossary functionalities are https://bit.ly/2U5os9v and https://bit.ly/3H4x4zy.

Macken, Rufener, Van den Bogaert, Daems, Tezcan, Vanroy, Fonteyne, Barrault, Costa-jussà, Kemp, Pilos, Declercq, Koponen, Forcada, Scarton, Moniz (eds.)
Proceedings of the 23rd Annual Conference of the European Association for Machine Translation, p. 219–228
Ghent, Belgium, June 2022.

Domain	Lang. pair	Sent. pairs	Term pairs	
			Original	Validated
Electrical devices	DE>EN	1,725	3,050	1,898
	EN>DE	1,698		
Sportswear	EN>FR	1,951	1,758	1,190
	FR>EN	1,544		

Table 1: Number of sentence pairs in the test set, and number of glossary entries in the original glossary and in the manually validated one for each of the four use cases tested.

it is not, and it should be removed, e.g. "Kühlung (z. B. von Notebooks)" translated as "cooling", where the content of the parentheses provide context for the term. For these reasons, we will rather focus on filtering out such invalid entries (more example provided in Sect. 3.3).

In this paper we present procedures to filter glossaries automatically and manually. We investigate the results each glossary yields in terms of terminology accuracy and overall output quality – as measured by automatic metrics – when it is leveraged by the glossary feature of commercial neural MT (NMT) providers. Our main contribution is to investigate if any of these filtering methods brings improvements to terminology accuracy with respect to the baseline, without worsening the overall quality compared to the output where the whole glossary is used. Ideally, a better terminology accuracy should bring a higher overall quality, but since not much is known about how MT providers implement their glossary feature, we also want to check if this feature introduces side effects. The results obtained with the filtered glossaries are compared to those obtained when no glossary is used and when the original one is applied.

Two automatic glossary cleaning techniques are presented (see Sect. 3.3). One is based on rules to remove noisy entries. The second one also leverages a Translation Memory (TM) to remove entries that are not used consistently in the translated contents. Both filtering techniques are applied to two use cases, i.e. *Sport equipment* English–French and *Electrical devices* German–English. Two providers are tested and their performance is evaluated based on terminology accuracy and overall output quality (see Sects. 3.2 and 3.5). Some sentences are then manually inspected to highlight interesting patterns in the outputs.

The remainder of the paper is structured as follows. Section 2 provides a brief overview of the literature in the field of terminology and NMT. The experimental setup (data sets, MT providers, evaluation method, filtering methods and experiments carried out) is outlined in Section 3 and its subsections, and the results are presented in Section 4. Section 4.3 offers a review of some examples. Results are then discussed in Section 5, together with suggestions on future work.

2 Background

Several different approaches have been developed to enforce glossary terms in the NMT output. A growing interest in this field is testified by the first Shared Task on Machine Translation Using Terminologies in the framework of WMT 2021 (Alam et al., 2021b). The methods developed so far can be broadly grouped in two categories. Some of them are based on the idea of injecting terms from a glossary into the MT output as constraints posed at decoding time (Chatterjee et al., 2017; Dougal and Lonsdale, 2020; Hasler et al., 2018; Hokamp and Liu, 2017). Other works build on the idea of adding *soft* constraints by annotating the source side of the training data (Ailem et al., 2021; Bergmanis and Pinnis, 2021a; Bergmanis and Pinnis, 2021b; Dinu et al., 2019; Exel et al., 2020).

Commercial MT providers do not disclose how their glossary feature is implemented, thus we do not now if they apply one of the approaches mentioned so far, and little work has investigated the performance of commercial models when enhanced by a glossary. Guerrero (2020) compared the work of translators post-editing the output with and without the glossary. Scansani and Dugast (2021) have investigated how the performance of a number of MT models changes when a pre-existing glossary is added. Both works conclude that pre-existing glossaries should be filtered before being used for MT. The need of preparing glossaries so that they are MT-ready is also underlined by Bergmanis *et al.* (2021). However, to the best of our knowledge, the paper by Bergmanis and Pinnis (2021a) is the only one to have compared the impact of different glossary filtering approaches on the MT output. In their work, noisy and inconsistent entries are automatically filtered

Issues	Rule-based filter decision	TM-based filter decision
Duplicates	Keep first	Keep first
TB inconsistent	Keep first	Keep first
Format issues	Discard	Discard if no match in the TM
TM inconsistent	*na*	Discard based on TM inconsistency
TM unmatched	*na*	Discard

Table 2: Table summarizing the decisions taken for each issue found in the TB by the Rule-based filter and by the TM-based filter.

Issues	Manual filter decision
TB inconsistent	Keep first
Format issues	Edit/Discard
Wrong translation	Discard
Invalid term	Discard
Typo/misspelling	Edit
Contains term info	Edit
Contains alternatives	Edit

Table 3: Table summarizing the decisions taken for each issue found in the termbase (TB) in the manually filtered glossary.

out – in some cases with the help of word alignment. In the present work, we test the use of a TM to validate or discard glossary entries and we compare automatic filtering to the manual procedure.

3 Experimental setup

3.1 Data set

Two different data sets belonging to two domains are used for our experiments. One domain is *Electrical devices* and the language combination is German–English. The other domain is *Sport equipment* and the language combination is English–French. This allows us to run the tests on different content types, and on different language pairs, where at least one (En–Fr) is not into English and the ability to handle term inflections is therefore more relevant. Number of sentences and of term pairs used is displayed in Table 1.

For each use case, a pre-existing glossary was manually validated by a linguist specialized in the domain. During the validation procedure – explained in Sect. 3.4 – the linguist could validate, remove or edit terms. The validated glossary – composed of the validated entries only – was then used for the terminology accuracy evaluation.

The test set was created by extracting sentences from a bilingual corpus that had at least one source match from the following terms: terms in the original glossary that were validated by the linguist, terms in the original glossary that were removed by the linguist, and terms in the original glossary that were edited by the linguist. In this last case, we look for matches of the edited version of the term rather than the original one.

By including both validated and unvalidated/edited terms, we test for two distinct cases. Sentences with matches from validated entries are the ones where we expect any glossary to have a positive impact on accuracy and output quality, unless the filter is erroneously removing valid entries. The second case is that of sentences with matches from unvalidated/edited terms, i.e. sentences where we expect a glossary to have a positive impact only if the glossary was filtered, and if the filter removed such invalid terms.

3.2 MT Providers

We chose two NMT providers whose glossary feature implementations differ in terms of source term matching and target term insertion. Although no specific information is offered by the providers, preliminary tests we carried out showed that Provider 1 is able to inflect terms so that their morphological form fits the rest of the sentence, whereas Provider 2 enforces terms in the output without any adjustment. Regarding source term matching, Provider 1 is able to match terms on a lemma level and regardless of their casing. Provider 2 matches terms only if the term in the source sentence has the same casing and the same morphological form as the term in the glossary.

We chose not to reveal the name of the providers used because we are not aiming at benchmarking them, but rather at focusing on the results we get with our filtering approaches.

3.3 Automatic filtering methods

Two filtering methods are used and tested. One relies on rules to remove noisy entries. The second one is based on the same rules as the first, but it leverages a TM to confirm or deny the rule-based decision. If the rules identify an entry as noisy, but it has matches in the TM, the TM-based filter retains it while the rule-based filter discards it. Additionally, the TM-based filter removes entries that are not used consistently or at all in the translated contents. The rules were mainly decided based on the issues observed in a number of Termbases (TB), but also based on the suggestions set out in

Bergmanis *et al.* (2021). Table 2 summarizes the different filter decisions for each of the two methods. More information on the issues follow.

Duplicates: Usually MT providers require to use glossaries that do not contain source-target duplicates. When a term pair is duplicated, we always keep only one.

TB inconsistent: Glossaries are usually expected to contain only one single instance of each source term and just one translation. This is especially key for MT. An MT engine cannot know which target term to pick in case of inconsistencies in the glossary, which might lead to inconsistent translations. Given a source term which has inconsistent translations in a TB, we keep the first entry occurring in the TB.

Has format issues: The following entries are automatically discarded by the rule-based decision filter. In the case of the TM-based filter they are kept if they have matches in the TM.

- Extra white spaces
- Numbers: dates, numbered paragraph titles, etc., e.g. "1 from 08/1992 to 09/2001" "or 2 - Type of Product Range".
- Punctuation: slashes, pipes, brackets and others are sometimes added to the term, especially to separate term alternatives – e.g. "Screw / Dowel / Nut" – or when explanations and domain/contextual information are added to the term field – "expose <photo>", "bottom (of a bag)", "Tasche|Case".

The following term pairs are filtered out only by the TM-based filter:

TM inconsistent: When a source term occurring in the glossary is translated inconsistently in the TM, it might mean that the glossary entry is not correct and/or that the translator did not enforce it, or that the entry was added to the glossary at a later stage. We therefore remove such entries based on different thresholds (see Table 4). A 40% threshold means that a glossary entry is kept if its source-target matches in the TM correspond at least to 40% of its total number of source matches. When the percentage increases, more terms are removed.

TM unmatched: Term pairs that are not matching in the TM are removed, based on the assumption that if translators are not inserting them, they might not be relevant for the domain or may even harm the output.

3.4 Manual filtering method

Each glossary was validated by one linguist specialized in the domain. The linguists were provided with instructions on how to clean terms, and also with general information on the use of terminology for MT. Guidelines did not include any specific information on the NMT providers used, so that the validation process was not biased towards the terminology injection approach of a provider. They were asked to label each entry as: *to be kept*, *to be removed*, or *edited*. In the last two cases, a reason had to be picked among those provided (e.g. long term, duplicate source term, punctuation in the term field, wrong translation, etc.). In case a term was labelled as *edited*, a new, correct version of the term had to be provided by the linguist. As introduced in Sect. 1, the present work focuses on methods to filter out terms. However, the manual process included the edition of some terms, which gave us the possibility to have a correct version of some of the invalid terms. In the scope of the present work, the edited terms are used only to produce the test set (see Sect. 3.1). Instead, the subset containing the validated terms only is used to compute the accuracy (see Sect. 4) and was leveraged by the MT providers in the *manual filter* experiments. We acknowledge that using the same glossary in one of the experiments and in the evaluation is a limitation of this work. However, the evaluation should be carried out using a manually validated glossary, which left us without other viable options than using this glossary for the evaluation as well.

More information on the issues in Table 3 that were not already described in Sect. 3.3 follows.

Wrong translation: One term in the entry is valid, but its translation is not correct.

Invalid term: (one of) the terms in the entry do not comply with the standard definition of term[2].

Term info in term field: In some cases, the term field of the glossary contains information on the domain of a term, e.g. "exposure (photography)". Such piece of information is erroneously added to the term field as an extra information for the translator. In the automatic filtering, this is handled by removing entries containing punctuation. In the manual filter, we ask the linguist to correct

[2]"A term is a graphic and/or phonic sign - a word or group of words, a compound word or a locution, an abbreviation - that allows to express a special concept related to concrete or abstract objects [...] that can be uniquely defined within a given discipline." (Riediger, 2018, our translation).

Electrical devices DE>EN	Provider 1		Provider 2		Glossary size
	TER ↓	Acc. ↑	TER ↓	Acc. ↑	
Baseline	**26.7**	79.8	**27.6**	82.8	0
Whole glossary	29.7	**96.7**	30.6	96	3033
Rule-based filter	29.6	**96.7**	30.4	96.1	2963
Manual filter	28.7	96.6	29.9	**96.3**	1590
TM-based filter > 40%	28.6	92.4	30	92	2188
TM-based filter > 60%	28.2	90.5	29.8	89.6	2097
TM-based filter > 80%	27.9	88.3	29.5	88.1	2007
TM-based filter > 90%	27.8	86.9	29.4	87	1949
TM-based filter 100%	27.2	82.0	28.2	83.58	1852
Sportswear EN>FR	Provider 1		Provider 2		Glossary size
	TER ↓	Acc. ↑	TER ↓	Acc. ↑	
Baseline	60.5	37.4	60.4	38.3	0
Whole glossary	58.1	70.2	59.5	**63.8**	1734
Rule-based filter	58.1	70	59.5	63.4	1527
Manual filter	58.9	**71**	59.6	63.7	1190
TM-based filter > 40%	**57.6**	68.4	**59.1**	60.7	915
TM-based filter > 60%	58	62.2	59.8	51.5	762
TM-based filter > 80%	58.7	50.5	59.8	48.8	697
TM-based filter > 90%	59.7	44.1	60.2	43.1	631
TM-based filter 100%	60.3	38	60.28	39.3	577

Table 4: TER and accuracy results for Electrical devices De–En and Sportswear En–Fr, for both providers tested. The rightmost column contains the total number of entries in each glossary. Each row represents one of the filtering methods applied.

such entries by removing the information.

Term contains alternatives: Some term entries contain more than one term separated, e.g., by pipes or slashes (see examples in Sect. 1). The linguist was asked to keep the best alternative based on his/her knowledge of the text domain and remove the other ones. In the automatic filtering, this is handled by removing entries containing punctuation.

3.5 Evaluation metrics and method

The assessment of the MT output aims at investigating its overall quality and its terminology consistency, comparing a baseline (no glossary is added) to the outputs obtained using the whole glossary, the automatically filtered ones, and the manually filtered one. Translation Edit Rate (TER) (Snover et al., 2006), case insensitive, is used as quality metric, whereas glossary compliance is measured by terminology accuracy, as suggested in Alam *et al.* (2021a). To compute accuracy, we look for occurrences of glossary term pairs in the source-target text. Both the text and the glossary are lemmatized and lowercased. In case of overlapping matches, we keep the longest matching entry only. Accuracy is then computed as the proportion between glossary matches in the source text and source-target glossary matches.

The first step of our evaluation process is to compute accuracy and TER on the whole data set (Sect. 4.1). In order to have a better understanding of how the usage of glossaries impacts the output quality, we then perform a sentence-level analysis (Sect. 4.2). Indeed, a minor TER or accuracy variation on the whole data set may hide, e.g., a high number of small differences between a sentence translated without the glossary *vs.* a sentence translated with the glossary, or a low number of sentences with large differences.

4 Experimental results

4.1 TER and accuracy on the whole data sets

Results in Table 4 show that the filtering approaches have a different impact on the output based on the use case and on the provider. Also, it shows that the best accuracy results (in bold in the *Accuracy* columns) do not correspond to the best TER score (in bold in the TER column).

Electrical devices De–En. In this use case, the baseline has the best TER score (26.7% with Provider 1 and 27.6% with Provider 2). As expected, adding a glossary always improves accuracy with respect to the baseline. The whole glossary, the rule-based filter and the manual filter achieve the highest accuracy scores for both providers, ranging from 96.1% to 96.7%. However, they also have the worst TER scores for Provider 1, while TER results for Provider 2 are less clear-cut, and all filtering methods – excluding the best one – range from 30.6% to 29.4%. The high accuracy achieved by the baseline (79.8%

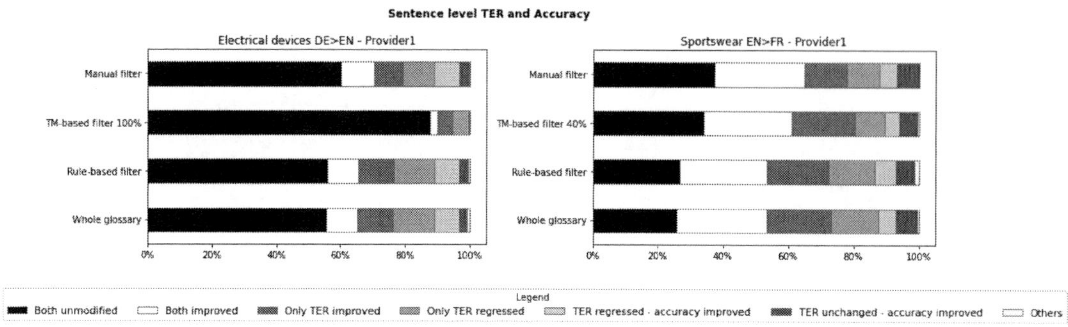

Figure 1: For each use case, we report on the percentage of sentences produced by Provider 1 that were assigned to one of the seven categories in the legend. The categories refer to the comparison between the baseline and the output produced with the filtered glossaries.

and 82.8%) suggests that the terminology for this use case is not highly specific and a generic model without any glossary attached to it can already handle most of the terms correctly. If the terms are rather generic, some of them might have different translations depending on the context, and enforcing them might harm the quality. Indeed, for De–En in general, achieving a very high accuracy is not possible without hampering the overall quality. The TM-based filter with varying thresholds (see Sect. 3.3) shows that, for Provider 1, a less restrictive threshold (e.g. >40%) leads to a high accuracy, which in turn causes a slight TER increase. The most restrictive filter (100% threshold) reaches an 82% accuracy and a 27.2% TER, the best TER obtained with a glossary – and the closest TER score to that of the baseline. A similar pattern is shown by Provider 2. The manually validated glossary is not outperforming the automatically filtered ones neither in terms of TER, nor in terms of accuracy, where it slightly outperformed the rule-based glossary. In general, there seems to be an accuracy cutoff over which TER cannot improve.

Sportswear En–Fr. In this use case, the highest accuracy is achieved by the manual filter for Provider 1 (71%), and by the whole glossary for Provider 2 (63.8%). The best TER is obtained with TM-based filter > 40% (57.6% and 59.1%). The very low accuracy obtained by the baseline suggests that the term entries in this glossary are highly domain-specific, and based on the TER results the general quality is benefiting from the use of a glossary, which was not the case for Electrical devices. Again, the filters show that aiming at the highest possible accuracy brings a lower TER. This is especially true for Provider 1, where the TM-based filter 100% has a 38% accuracy and a 60.3% TER, whereas the less restrictive 40% threshold increases accuracy to 68.4%, with a 57.6% TER. Similarly to the previous use case, the manually filtered glossary, although yielding a good accuracy score, is not outperforming the automatically filtered glossaries in terms of TER. To conclude, Sportswear results seem to show that filtering the glossary brings improvements, although small, with respect to using a whole glossary.

4.2 Sentence-level analysis

To gain a better understanding of how TER and accuracy are changing, we carried out a sentence-level analysis that compares the output of the baseline against the output obtained with each of the other glossaries. For the TM-based filter, we picked the one with the 100% threshold for Electrical Devices and the one with a 40% threshold for Sportswear. We limit the scope of this analysis to the results obtained with Provider 1, which implements a more sophisticated terminology feature than Provider 2 (see Sect. 3.2).

Output sentences were grouped in seven categories (see legend in Fig. 1), based on TER and accuracy differences with respect to the baseline. For example, *Both improved* includes all sentences where both TER and accuracy are better in that specific output than in the baseline.

Fig. 1, shows that more than half of the sentences are the same as in the baseline in all outputs of Electrical devices. The impact of the glossary is thus limited to the remaining, smaller portion. As for Sportswear, only a small part of the outputs stayed unchanged. Regardless of the filtering method, for both use cases, a good number of sentences sees changes in TER (see *Only TER regressed* and *Only TER improved* categories)

		Sentence	TER	Acc
1	Source	Men's Short Sleeve **Baselayer**		
	Reference	*Première couche* à manches courtes pour homme		
	Baseline	Couche de base à manches courtes pour hommes	57.1	0
	Whole glossary	*Première couche* à manches courtes pour hommes	**14.3**	**100**
2	Source	Our **helmets** combine lightweight construction and [...] our **EPS** technology		
	Reference	Nos *casques* [...] et de notre technologie *EPS* [...] tout en restant légers.		
	Whole glossary	Nos *casques* combinent une construction légère [...] avec notre technologie de mousse d'absorption EPS [...]	62.5	100
	TM-based filter >40%	Nos *casques* combinent une construction légère [...] avec notre technologie *EPS* [...]	**55**	100
	Manual filter	Nos *casques* combinent une construction légère [...] avec notre technologie *EPS* [...]	**57.5**	100
3	Source	Choose [...] based on boot [...] and desired on-**snow feel**.		
	Reference	Ajustez le niveau [...] de chaussure et du *toucher de neige* recherché.		
	Baseline	Choisissez les modes [...] de la chaussure et des sensations souhaitées sur la neige.	69.6	0
	Whole glossary	Choisissez les modes [...] du boot et du *toucher de neige* souhaité.	**56.5**	**100**
	Rule-based filter	Choisissez les modes [...] de la boot et du *toucher de neige* souhaité.	**52.2**	**100**
	TM-based filter >40%	Choisissez les modes [...] de la chaussure et du *toucher de neige* souhaité.	**43.5**	**100**
4	**Source**	- zur **Installation** von drei TFT-/LCD-/LED-Monitoren mit einer **Bildschirmdiagonale** von 33 bis 69 cm (13" bis 27")		
	Reference	- For the *installation* of 3 TFT/LCD/LED monitors with a *screen diagonal* of 33 to 69 cm (13" to 27")		
	Baseline	- for *installation* of three TFT/LCD/LED monitors with a *screen diagonal* of 33 to 69 cm (13" to 27")	7.1	100
	Whole glossary	- for *Installation* of three TFT/LCD/LED Monitors with a *Screen Diagonal* of 33 to 69 cm (13" to 27")	10.7	100
	TM-based filter >100%	- for the *installation* of three TFT/LCD/LED monitors with a *screen diagonal* of 33 to 69 cm (13" to 27")	**3.6**	**100**
5	Source	Bei Erreichen der max. Lautstärke hören Sie einen **Signalton**.		
	Reference	Once the max. volume is reached, a *signal tone* is heard.		
	Baseline	When the max. volume is reached, you will hear a beep.	37.5	0
	Whole glossary	When the max. Loudness is reached, you will hear a *Signal Tone*.	50.0	**100**
	Manual filter	When the max. volume is reached, you will hear a *Signal Tone*.	43.7	**100**

Table 5: Examples of sentences with their corresponding TER and accuracy scores for both Electrical devices De–En and Sportswear En–Fr using provider1.

without any change in the accuracy. Although the whole glossary and the filtered one might contain terms that are not in the validated glossary used to compute accuracy, and therefore there might be terminology changes that are not captured by the accuracy score, this might also suggest that the use of the terminology feature is introducing some side effects to the sentence translation. This will be further investigated in Sect. 4.3.

For Electrical devices, in Table 4 we observed that TER worsened where accuracy was higher, which was especially true for the whole glossary, and the rule-based and manual filters. Fig. 1 displays that these three glossaries have the highest number of sentences where both TER and accuracy improved, which is the desirable result for these experiments. However, all three outputs show a notable amount of sentences where accuracy improved, but TER either regressed or remained unchanged compared to the baseline. This, together with the fact that the whole glossary and the rule-based filtered one have very similar results, suggests that the latter has removed many of the entries that would not match in the text, e.g. because they contain information in the term field, but some of the terms that should have been removed because of their negative impact on the output were kept (see example 5 in Table 5).

For Electrical devices, the TM-based one removes more terms than the other filters, thus almost 88% of its sentences are the same as in the baseline. The amount of sentences where both

TER and accuracy improve is limited, whereas for 9% of its sentences, TER changes are observed while accuracy stays the same as in the baseline.

As for Sportswear, in Fig. 1 more than half of the sentences for all the outputs show an improvement in TER with either unchanged or improved accuracy (see *Both improved* and *only TER improved* categories), and very few sentences where the accuracy either improved or remained unchanged while TER regressed. This validates how a higher accuracy brings a better TER for the majority of the outputs.

The majority of the sentences in Electrical devices were the same as the baseline, especially with the TM-based filter, which has the best TER (see Table 4). Given that the performance of the baseline is already good, this can be seen as a desirable effect of filtering a glossary. Sportswear, on the other hand, had a poor baseline, especially in terms of accuracy. We thus expected the glossary to impact more sentences, which is what happened. Also, the number of sentences where TER improves is definitely larger than the number of observations where TER regresses, which is particularly true for the TM-based filter 40%.

4.3 Manual analysis

Table 5 displays examples taken from both use cases, along with their accuracy and TER scores. As in the preceding section, we are limiting our scope to sentences produced by Provider 1. For the sake of readability, we are not reporting all candidates for each source, and some sentences have been shortened. The source glossary matches are in bold, and their target (if any) is italicized in the target sentences when correct, and underlined if enforced but incorrect.

Example 1 depicts a scenario of the best result that may be reached using a glossary, i.e. an improvement in both accuracy and overall quality. The baseline did not translate the term accurately, while thanks to the glossary, TER dropped to 14.3% and the accuracy increased to 100%.

Example 2 and 3 demonstrate scenarios in which accuracy does not change while TER changes. In Example 2, the source term *helmet* is translated correctly in all sentences. However, the glossary translation of *EPS* is "mousse d'absorption EPS", and it is only found in the whole glossary. This target term should not have been enforced (see reference). Thanks to the correct decision to remove it from the glossary, both the TM-based filter and the manual filter improved in terms of TER, but the accuracy score did not change since the entry is not in the validated glossary used to compute it. In Example 3, despite the fact that all glossaries correctly introduced the sole entry matching on the source, all candidates are distinct, which shows that the glossary features are introducing side effects.

Examples 4 and 5 are taken from Electrical devices De–En. The former shows a sentence where the rather generic term "installation" was in the whole glossary. This term was filtered out from the TM-based filtered glossary (and also from the rule-based filtered glossary, not appearing here). Although the difference is minor, not having the term in the glossary improves the sentence thanks to the insertion of the article before "installation". This pattern is even more evident in example 5, where another generic term pair ("Lautstärke" translated as "Loudness") is enforced in the whole glossary output, while in this context "volume" would be the correct translation. The term pair including "Loudness" was correctly removed from the manually filtered and the TM-based filtered glossaries. This is one possible explanation for the cases of sentences where TER changes and accuracy does not, as seen in Sect. 4.2.

5 Conclusions and future work

In this paper, we used various approaches to filter pre-existing glossaries and tested their usefulness in improving the terminology accuracy of an MT output without deteriorating the overall quality. The results show that using a filtered glossary may produce a better accuracy with similar or improved overall quality when compared to a baseline where no glossary is used. In several cases a filtered glossary led to a better TER than the whole glossary, which suggests that filtering removes matches from terms that are harmful for the overall quality. On the other hand, results show that using a whole glossary can be beneficial. The whole glossary usually outperformed the filtered ones in terms of accuracy – which is expected given the larger size of the former – and, especially in the case of Sportswear En–Fr, the TER improvements brought by filtering were rather small. In general, filtering – and in particular the TM-based automatic filter – helped find an acceptable balance between a higher accuracy and a good overall quality. Given the current experimental stage of the filtering tool, such results can be seen as promising. However, improvements to the filtering method and new tests are needed to check if filtering can bring larger quality improvements over the whole glossary, thus making the filtering effort worthwhile.

The results in both use cases suggest that aiming at the highest possible accuracy may not always be the best choice in terms of quality. There appears to be an accuracy cut-off beyond which overall quality suffers. In the case of Electrical devices, this could be due to the fact that the terminology is quite general – indeed, the baseline is already handling the majority of the terms correctly. The analysis in Sect. 4.2 revealed that the TM-based filtering method with the most restrictive threshold introduced only minor changes with respect to the baseline output, reducing the number of sentences where TER was regressing. This behavior may be preferable to using a larger glossary, which can negatively impact more sentences, especially when the baseline is performing well in terms of accuracy and overall quality.

The baseline in Sportswear En–Fr is struggling with terminology accuracy, indicating that terminology is highly domain/customer-specific. In terms of TER, two automatic filters outperform the whole glossary, whereas the manually filtered glossary achieves the highest accuracy, closely followed by the whole and rule-based glossaries. Applying a strict filter does not improve the quality of these contents. When compared to the baseline, we discovered that each glossary affects at least 70% of the sentences (Sect. 4.2). However, we still see an accuracy cut-off around 70% (see Table 4), above which TER begins to deteriorate. This may imply that, while including as many terms as possible may be desirable, applying a filter to the glossary can help removing some that are detrimental to the overall quality.

An interesting conclusion we can draw from our experiments is that a glossary filtered by a linguist according to task-specific guidelines does not necessarily bring relevant improvements over an automatically filtered glossary. In particular, the TM-based filter always outperforms the manual one in terms of TER score. The rule-based filter outperforms the manually filtered glossary for Sportswear En–Fr in terms of TER, and achieves a slightly lower accuracy score. Given the high costs of manually filtering a glossary, this can be considered a relevant outcome, especially for LSPs. In some cases, even for a linguist expert of the content type, it can be difficult to distinguish a generic term from a specific one, which is one of the key actions to take when filtering a glossary for MT.

Although results suggest that using a TM to identify terms that are not highly specific to one domain can be effective, we plan to test more accurate solutions to this problem, such as the use of Inverse Document Frequency (IDF) (Jones, 1972) or word-alignment. In Bergmanis and Pinnis (2021a), both methods were tested for glossary filtering. We anticipate that an improved ability to filter out generic terms will be especially helpful in use cases such as the one of Electrical devices De—En.

The rule-based filter, which requires no bilingual data other than the glossary, has one of the highest accuracy and one of the best TER scores in Sportswear En—Fr. This result is especially relevant in cases where a glossary must be filtered but bilingual data are either not available or their quantity is limited.

Examples shown in Sect. 4.3 suggested that there can be several reasons for quality improvements or regressions when terminology is added to the output. Sometimes the output changes even if no term was matched in the sentence, which is probably due to the specific implementation of the glossary feature. To gain a better understanding of this, we plan to carry out in-depth manual analyses of the outputs produced by the baseline, by the whole glossary and by the filtered ones.

The present contribution focused on term filtering. However, the ability to edit terms that can be improved may yield better results. In the future, we will concentrate on this, beginning with cases where terms can be easily improved using automatic editing rules. Editing terms without the assistance of a linguist can be a difficult task at times. We therefore intend to conduct experiments in which the results of the automatic filters are provided to a linguist as an aid to help them perform their task. We anticipate that this will also help linguists in their decision making process, e.g. to determine when terms are generic. Being able to see that a term is translated inconsistently in the TM, for example, can lead to a better decision as to label the term as generic/detrimental or not.

Acknowledgements

The authors would like to thank the whole Acolad AI R&D team for their valuable feedback, and three anonymous reviewers for insightful comments on the first draft of this paper.

References

Ailem, Melissa, Jinghsu Liu, and Raheel Qader. 2021. Encouraging Neural Machine Translation to Satisfy Terminology Constraints. *arXiv:2106.03730 [cs]*, June. arXiv: 2106.03730.

Alam, Md Mahfuz ibn, Antonios Anastasopoulos, Laurent Besacier, James Cross, Matthias Gallé, Philipp Koehn, and Vassilina Nikoulina. 2021a. On the Evaluation of Machine Translation for Terminology Consistency. *arXiv:2106.11891 [cs]*, June. arXiv: 2106.11891.

Alam, Md Mahfuz Ibn, Ivana Kvapilíková, Antonios Anastasopoulos, Laurent Besacier, Georgiana Dinu, Marcello Federico, Matthias Gallé, Kweonwoo Jung, Philipp Koehn, and Vassilina Nikoulina. 2021b. Findings of the WMT shared task on machine translation using terminologies. In *Proceedings of the Sixth Conference on Machine Translation*, pages 652–663, Online, November. Association for Computational Linguistics.

Bergmanis, Toms and Mārcis Pinnis. 2021a. Dynamic Terminology Integration for COVID-19 and other Emerging Domains. *arXiv:2109.04708 [cs]*, September. arXiv: 2109.04708.

Bergmanis, Toms and Mārcis Pinnis. 2021b. Facilitating Terminology Translation with Target Lemma Annotations. *arXiv:2101.10035 [cs]*, January. arXiv: 2101.10035.

Bergmanis, Toms, Mārcis Pinnis, and Paula Reichenberg. 2021. From research to production: Fine-grained analysis of terminology integration. In *Proceedings of Machine Translation Summit XVIII: Users and Providers Track*, pages 54–77, Virtual, August. Association for Machine Translation in the Americas.

Chatterjee, Rajen, Matteo Negri, Marco Turchi, Marcello Federico, Lucia Specia, and Frédéric Blain. 2017. Guiding neural machine translation decoding with external knowledge. In *Proceedings of the Second Conference on Machine Translation*, pages 157–168, Copenhagen, Denmark, September. Association for Computational Linguistics.

Dinu, Georgiana, Prashant Mathur, Marcello Federico, and Yaser Al-Onaizan. 2019. Training neural machine translation to apply terminology constraints. In *Proceedings of the 57th Annual Meeting of the Association for Computational Linguistics*, pages 3063–3068, Florence, Italy, July. Association for Computational Linguistics.

Dougal, Duane K. and Deryle Lonsdale. 2020. Improving NMT Quality Using Terminology Injection. In *Proceedings of the 12th Language Resources and Evaluation Conference*, pages 4820–4827, Marseille, France, May. European Language Resources Association.

Exel, Miriam, Bianka Buschbeck, Lauritz Brandt, and Simona Doneva. 2020. Terminology-Constrained Neural Machine Translation at SAP. In *Proceedings of the 22nd Annual Conference of the European Association for Machine Translation*, pages 271–280, Lisboa, Portugal, November. European Association for Machine Translation.

Guerrero, Lucía. 2020. NMT plus a bilingual glossary: does this really improve terminology accuracy and consistency? Slides presented at the Translating and the Computer conference (TC42 online) organised by AsLing (International Association for Advancement in Language Technology), `https://bit.ly/3vTSjCh`, November. Accessed: 2022-03-08.

Hasler, Eva, Adrià de Gispert, Gonzalo Iglesias, and Bill Byrne. 2018. Neural machine translation decoding with terminology constraints. In *Proceedings of the 2018 Conference of the North American Chapter of the Association for Computational Linguistics: Human Language Technologies, Volume 2 (Short Papers)*, pages 506–512, New Orleans, Louisiana, June. Association for Computational Linguistics.

Hokamp, Chris and Qun Liu. 2017. Lexically constrained decoding for sequence generation using grid beam search. In *Proceedings of the 55th Annual Meeting of the Association for Computational Linguistics (Volume 1: Long Papers)*, pages 1535–1546, Vancouver, Canada, July. Association for Computational Linguistics.

Jones, Karen Spärck. 1972. A statistical interpretation of term specificity and its application in retrieval. *Journal of Documentation*, 28(1).

Riediger, Hellmut. 2018. *Cos'è la terminologia e come si fa un glossario*. `http://www.term-minator.it/corso/doc/mod3_termino_glossa.pdf`.

Scansani, Randy and Loïc Dugast. 2021. Glossary functionality in commercial machine translation: does it help? a first step to identify best practices for a language service provider. In *Proceedings of Machine Translation Summit XVIII: Users and Providers Track*, pages 78–88, Virtual, August. Association for Machine Translation in the Americas.

Snover, Matthew, Bonnie Dorr, Richard Schwartz, Linnea Micciulla, and John Makhoul. 2006. A study of translation edit rate with targeted human annotation. In *Proceedings of Association for Machine Translation in the Americas*, pages 223–231, Cambridge, Massachussets.

Comparing Multilingual NMT Models and Pivoting

Celia Soler Uguet **Fred Bane** **Anna Zaretskaya** **Tània Blanch Miró**
TransPerfect
{csuguet,fbane,azaretskaya,tblanch}@translations.com

Abstract

Following recent advancements in multilingual machine translation at scale, our team carried out tests to compare the performance of pre-trained multilingual models (M2M-100 from Facebook and multilingual models from Helsinki-NLP) with a two-step translation process using English as a pivot language. Direct assessment by linguists rated translations produced by pivoting as consistently better than those obtained from multilingual models of similar size, while automated evaluation with COMET suggested relative performance was strongly impacted by domain and language family.

1 Background and Motivation

As a translation company, our work involves hundreds of distinct translation directions across dozens of languages. However, demand is not evenly distributed across all language pairs. The vast majority of our translation requests involve English as either the source or target language, with most other requests concentrated in a few major languages, such as German, French, Italian, Japanese, and Chinese.

Our fleet of machine translation (MT) engines is developed considering both the demand and the resources available for training. Currently, we use mostly bilingual models with some many-to-one models (such as for Scandinavian languages), but no many-to-many models. For language pairs where only a few hundred words are translated each year, the demand does not justify the costs incurred in training, deploying, and maintaining an engine for that language pair. Moreover, these language pairs often have scant high-quality resources available for training. Thus, in situations where demand for machine translation exists, but in insufficient amount to offset training and deployment costs, we have historically chosen to use a two-step translation process: pivoting through a related, high-resource language.

In recent years, multilingual models have shown growing potential to wholly or partially replace a fleet of bilingual models. The benefits are clear: no error propagation resulting from using the output of one model as the input to another as in the pivot scenario; reduced overhead and complexity by using one model for multiple language directions instead of separate models for each direction; improved translation quality in low-resource languages due to knowledge transfer from related languages; the potential for zero-shot translation for language directions for which no direct data exist, and so on. However, these models also have their drawbacks, including the expense and difficulty of retraining the models, the inability to add additional languages without retraining the model entirely, and the near impossibility of fine-tuning the model for particular clients.

Below we report the results of an experiment comparing bilingual base transformers (Vaswani et al., 2017) with pre-trained M2M-100 from Facebook obtained from Hugging Face (Fan et al., 2020) and multilingual models made public by Helsinki-NLP (Tiedemann and Thottingal, 2020),[1] using data drawn from our previous translation work and out-of-domain corpora.

[1]https://github.com/Helsinki-NLP/Opus-MT

Macken, Rufener, Van den Bogaert, Daems, Tezcan, Vanroy, Fonteyne, Barrault, Costa-jussà, Kemp, Pilos, Declercq, Koponen, Forcada, Scarton, Moniz (eds.)
Proceedings of the 23rd Annual Conference of the European Association for Machine Translation, p. 229–237
Ghent, Belgium, June 2022.

2 Related Research

Interesting and very promising work has been carried out recently on multilingual MT approaches, where instead of training one NMT model for each language pair separately, a single model is trained that can translate from a single source into multiple target languages, or even many-to-many models that can translate in any direction between the languages they are trained on. Apart from improving MT performance for low-resource languages that can benefit from such models, these works also show competitive performance for resource-rich languages, suggesting the possibility of fully replacing the bilingual approach in the near future.

Most recently, the Facebook AI research group proposed a single multilingual translation model able to translate within any pair of the 100 languages included (Fan et al., 2020). The authors observed a significant improvement in performance in non-English language pairs, and a competitive performance in language pairs that include English compared to the WMT baseline from previous years (Barrault et al., 2019; Bojar et al., 2017; Bojar et al., 2018)

Multilingual MT models have been a subject of research for a few years now. In most cases, the goal has been to leverage parallel data available for resource-rich languages to improve MT performance for languages with scarce resources. As early as in 2015, Dong et al. (2015) explored an approach for simultaneously translating the same source sentence into multiple target sentences. They obtained a better performance on all language pairs (English into French, Spanish, Dutch and Portuguese) when using the multilingual model as opposed to single-target RNN models. However, statistical significance of the deltas are not indicated in the paper.

A few other works report significant improvement for low-resource languages thanks to multilingual models. Fira et al. (2016) propose a multiway multilingual model trained on WMT'15 data. Ha et al. (2016) explore a multilingual NMT approach and report on promising results for low-resource languages, as well as in scenarios where there are not enough parallel data available in order to train a bilingual NMT model while achieving good performance.

A simpler multilingual NMT approach was proposed by Johnson et al. (2016). It does not require any change to the model architecture, but instead introduces a token at the beginning of the input sentence to indicate the target language. The authors report improvement for low-resource languages but, unlike the majority of other similar works, they observed a degradation on high-resource languages compared to bilingual models.

Finally, Tan et al. (2019) propose one more interesting approach, namely to use NMT with knowledge distillation, where bilingual models act as teachers. The authors report similar or improved results compared to the bilingual models used in the experiment.

It is notable that most of these works report very encouraging results: multilingual models always seem to outperform bilingual ones for low-resource languages, and perform en par or better for resource-rich languages. This contributes to the intuition that they will perform mostly better than two-level systems that pivot through English.

3 Materials and Methods

For this research, we set out to compare the performance of our company's pivoting system with open-source pre-trained multilingual models. For the pivoting system, we used general-purpose models trained to handle the different content types we have historically received in our translation work. These models were trained with between ten and thirty million sentence pairs, for fifty epochs or until the early stopping criterion was met (no improvement in validation set perplexity for 6 successive validation checkpoints). We used the transformer-base architecture with guided alignment using alignment from fast align (Dyer et al., 2013), and to limit potential confounding factors we use English as the pivot language for all language pairs. We chose to compare our system with two M2M-100 systems (the 480 million and the 1.2 billion parameter models) (Fan et al., 2020) and the multilingual models from Helsinki-NLP (Tiedemann and Thottingal, 2020). While there are other pre-trained multilingual SOTA models such as mT5 that could be fine-tuned for the downstream task of multilingual translation (Xue et al., 2021), we believe that the M2M-100 and Helsinki-NLP models were easily accessible and ready to be used with no further fine-tuning. Moreover, since all these systems were released around the same time, there is no published or reliable research to suggest that one model outperforms the rest.

We selected seven language pairs for which we

received requests in the past year but for which we had no direct bilingual model. These were the following:

- Italian-French (referred to as IT–FR);
- French-Japanese (referred to as FR–JA);
- French-Chinese (referred to as FR–ZH);
- Spanish-Italian (referred to as ES–IT);
- French-Portuguese (referred to as FR–PT);
- Italian-German (referred to IT–DE);
- French-Arabic (referred to as FR–AR).

We also carried out a quantitative comparison for Danish–Spanish and Swedish–French, but since we could not find linguists available for the human evaluation, we do not include the results for these two pairs of languages.

In our experiments we used data from two different sources to avoid biases and compare performance across multiple domains. The first set of data was drawn from our company's previous human translation work (with care being taken to ensure that none of the data had been seen by the models during training). Although the data involved a wide variety of content types, we consider these test data to be "in domain" for our engines as they were sampled from essentially the same distribution as our training data. The second set of data was extracted from Leipzig's Corpora Collection (Goldhahn et al., 2012). This collection includes monolingual corpora for 291 Languages. Being a monolingual database, we can be quite confident that none of those texts were used for the training of any of the engines we were comparing. We extracted text from the news domain and from the most recent year available for each source language. These test data were considered to be "out-of-domain" for our engines.

Since no reference translations were available for any of the input sentences, we performed automated, reference-free evaluation using COMET, which was Unbabel's submission for the WMT 2020 Quality Estimation Shared Task (Rei et al., 2020). The reason behind this decision was that this model ended on the top 5 of best models in all tasks and language pairs but one. Moreover, it can be used for document-level assessment, it is easily accessible, it can be run on GPU, and it offers a command to compare multiple systems with statistical testing. Additionally, we also engaged human linguists to carry out blinded direct assessment (DA) for each language pair. Ordinarily we would commission multiple linguists for each language pair to mitigate the effects of bias and human error. However, for these less common translation directions, only one linguist was available per language pair. Nevertheless, we consider these scores reliable as the linguists were selected from our pool of certified translators for the language pair. This means that the annotators were not simply bilingual speakers, but held translation certification and actively performed translation tasks in this language pair.

Each linguist scored 200 segments chosen at random (100 from the in-domain data and 100 from the out-of-domain data) using a scale from 0 to 100. Linguists were instructed to score the segments based on the general quality of the MT output – how well it represented the main message of the input sentence – rather than small errors which would be more heavily penalized when evaluating human translations. The scoring criteria provided to the linguists were as below:

- 0: Completely unintelligible and useless translation;
- 25: Most of the target needs editing, but part of the MT can be preserved;
- 50: Half of the output is usable and half needs to be edited;
- 75: Edits needed, but MT output is usable;
- 100: Perfect translation, fully accurate.

Statistical significance for automated metrics was calculated using the bootstrap t-test from COMET (Koehn, 2004), and statistical significance for human DA was determined using unpaired t-test with $p < 0.01$ considered statistically significant.

4 Results

The results of the human and automated evaluations are presented in Tables 1 through 3 below. In every case, human evaluation favored the translation from the pivot system, often by a large margin. This was true for both test sets as well as the overall scores. The difference was more pronounced for language pairs from different families than for language pairs where both the source and target were European languages (average difference of 10.99 in the overall scores for FR–JA, FR–ZH, and

FR–AR vs. 3.59 for IT–FR, ES–IT, FR–PT, and IT–DE).

COMET scores were less conclusive, suggesting that relative performance was more dependent on the domain of the content and the language families to which the source and target belonged. On the in-domain test set, scores for the pivot system were better than the small M2M-100 model in all but one language pair (FR–PT), and even outperformed the larger M2M-100 model in the three inter-language-family language pairs (FR–JA, FR–ZH, and FR–AR). For the European language pairs, the larger M2M-100 system obtained scores significantly higher than those for the pivot system.

For the out-of-domain test set, on the other hand, the M2M-100 models obtained higher scores in all language pairs, though we may again observe that scores for language pairs from different language families are roughly 50 percent lower than those for European language pairs.

4.1 Divergence Between COMET and DA Scores

In a number of instances, we noted pronounced divergence between the scores assigned by COMET and those from human linguists. To better understand this phenomenon, we manually analyzed some of these sentences and provide some examples in Table 4.

We find that in general those segments being given a low score by COMET but a higher score by human reviewers tend to contain a large number of punctuation marks, numbers, or proper nouns (especially those written in Latin characters when the language uses a different script). We speculate that low scores due to proper nouns may suggest a difference between COMET's linguistic knowledge and world knowledge, while the low scores for sentences in the former two categories may be related to the composition of the training data used to train the COMET system.

We present as well a comparison of the agreement between human reviewers and COMET. The plots for each language pair can be found from Figures 1 and 2 in Appendix A. X values represent the normalized difference in COMET scores between the M2M-100 translation and the translation of the pivot system; Y values represent the normalized difference in human scores respectively. Positive values represent a better score from the M2M-100 system, and negative values represent a better score from the pivoting system. Data points in quadrants I and III represent agreement between the human evaluation and COMET, while those in quadrants II and IV represent disagreement.

5 Discussion

In this study we compared translations from different models using human DA and automated evaluation with the COMET quality estimation model. We tested model performance using a combination of data sampled from the same distribution as our training data (in-domain) and news data (which were out-of-domain for our models used in the pivot system). Single-blind human DA showed a clear preference for the translations obtained through pivoting, while automated evaluation with COMET was less conclusive: the domain of the content and whether or not the source and target languages belonged to the same language family appeared to have a significant effect on the scores.

Beyond translation quality, as a translation company we must also take other aspects into consideration. While these fall outside the scope of this work, there are many other relevant factors, such as:

- Simplicity in production: It might be more desirable to have one model instead of many;
- Resource requirements: While one model can take the place of many, multiple instances of the model would be needed, and each instance requires greater resources, so the ultimate effect on hosting and inference costs is uncertain;
- Updating problems: With a multilingual model it is more complex and costly to update or fix problems that are discovered during inference. It is much easier to retrain bilingual models in response to issues;
- Adding more languages: It is not possible to add more languages to an already-trained multilingual model, whereas a pivoted approach can be deployed on-demand for any two languages that are supported with bilingual models;
- Client customization: It is unclear how, if at all, a multilingual model may be adapted for particular clients, especially clients with

Overall				In-Domain			Out-Of-Domain		
Lg. Pair	Pivot	M2M	Helsinki	Pivot	M2M	Helsinki	Pivot	M2M	Helsinki
IT–FR	**73.64**	68.35	64.66	**70.04**	67.25	64.54	**76.89**	69.42	64.77
FR–JA	**69.86***	58.84	N/A	**71.34***	56.15	N/A	**68.45***	61.4	N/A
FR–ZH	**73.18***	65.56	N/A	**78.23***	66.56	N/A	**68.07**	64.56	N/A
ES–IT	**83.3**	78.98	76.02	**88.3**	81.53	79.2	**78.3**	76.43	72.9
FR–PT	**90.63**	88.21	84.59	**91.79**	87.78	83.23	**89.47**	88.65	85.94
IT–DE	**86.2**	83.85	N/A†	**78.95**	76.58	N/A†	**93.68**	91.28	N/A†
FR–AR	**67.8**	53.46	N/A	**76.73**	51.72	N/A	**58.86**	55.2	N/A

Table 1: Human direct assessment scores for each system. The M2M-100 system used here is the smaller of the two (480M), so as to be directly comparable with the base transformers used in the pivot system. * Indicates scores with a statistically significant difference ($p <0.01$). †Indicates that no multilingual model was available, only a direct bilingual model.

Language Pair	Pivot	M2M (480M)	M2M (1.2B)	Helsinki-NLP
IT–FR	0.3773	0.3608	**0.4035***	0.3216
FR–JA	**0.2305**	0.1937	0.2222	N/A
FR–ZH	**0.1944**	0.1563	0.1728	N/A
ES–IT	0.4704	0.4464	**0.4877***	0.3903
FR–PT	0.3711	0.3782	**0.4026***	0.3372
IT–DE	0.3271	0.2901	**0.3498***	N/A†
FR–AR	**0.2003**	0.1875	0.1574	N/A

Table 2: COMET scores for each system on in-domain data. * Indicates scores with a statistically significant improvement compared to the Pivot column ($p <0.01$). †Indicates that no multilingual model was available, only a direct bilingual model.

Language Pair	Pivot	M2M (480M)	M2M (1.2B)	Helsinki-NLP
IT–FR	0.3158	0.3223	**0.3934***	0.2698
FR–JA	0.1816	0.1889	**0.227***	N/A
FR–ZH	0.1376	0.1401	**0.1783***	N/A
ES–IT	0.3771	0.3987*	**0.4487***	0.3418
FR–PT	0.3394	0.4042*	**0.4543***	0.3395
IT–DE	0.2302	0.229	**0.3158***	N/A†
FR–AR	0.1943	**0.2141***	0.1751	N/A

Table 3: COMET scores for each system on out-of-domain data. * Indicates scores with a statistically significant improvement compared to the Pivot column ($p <0.01$). †Indicates that no multilingual model was available, only a direct bilingual model.

Language Pair	Source	Target	COMET[2]	Linguist
IT–FR	La siringa contiene <<mL COUNT>> ml di soluzione iniettabile, da <> mg <>, <> mg <> o placebo.	La seringue contient <<mL COUNT>> ml de solution injectable, de <> mg <>, <> mg <> ou placebo.	27.69	100
FR–JA	C'est une rentrée pleine d'incertitudes à l'hôpital , confirme Mélanie Meier, de la CFDT.	「これは不確実性に満ちた病院への帰還だ」とCFDTのメラニー・メイエ氏は述べている。	0	80
FR–ZH	Je travaille pendant les vacances à Dour et à Pukkelpop et j'ai normalement beaucoup d'argent de poche l'été.	我在Dour和Pukkelpop度假期工作,我通常在夏天有很多。	0	90
ES–IT	jersey de rayas anchas con cuello a la caja.	Maglia a righe larghe con scollo.	0	90
FR–PT	Tribunal de Paris – Corruption : Après Lamine Diack, Papa Massata condamné. . .	Tribunal de Paris – Corrupção: depois de Lamine Diack, Papa Massata condenada...	29.34	99
IT–DE	2.2 Come meglio descritto nel dettaglio al successivo art.	2.2 Wie besser in der Kunst ausführlich beschrieben.	0	98
FR–AR	CHRU DE LILLE - Hôpital Albert Calmette	CHRU DE LILLE - مستشفى ألبرت كالميت	20.30	90

Table 4: Some examples of segments with a low COMET score in comparison to the score given by the linguist.

small translation memories or those who translate in only one language pair;

- Trade-off between low- and high-resource languages: Performance in low-resource languages can be improved through knowledge transfer from higher-resource languages, but decreased performance in these higher-resource languages may outweigh these gains due to the greater volume of demand.

Contrary to our intuitions prior to undertaking this study, our results suggest that pivoting is a reasonable choice for language pairs where no direct model exists, at least in terms of translation quality. The strength of the conclusions are limited by the relatively small sample size, and we anticipate these results will need to be revisited as multilingual models become more capable. Moreover, fine-tuning other pre-trained multilingual models such as mT5 and comparing those with the pivoting approach could lead to different conclusions. Further research is needed to more comprehensively weigh the advantages and disadvantages of replacing multiple bilingual models with a single multilingual model.

References

Barrault, Loïc, Ondřej Bojar, Marta R. Costa-jussà, Christian Federmann, Mark Fishel, Yvette Graham, Barry Haddow, Matthias Huck, Philipp Koehn, Shervin Malmasi, Christof Monz, Mathias Müller, Santanu Pal, Matt Post, and Marcos Zampieri. 2019. Findings of the 2019 conference on machine translation (WMT19). In *Proceedings of the Fourth Conference on Machine Translation (Volume 2: Shared Task Papers, Day 1)*, pages 1–61, Florence, Italy, August. Association for Computational Linguistics.

Bojar, Ondrej, Chatterjee Rajen, Christian Federmann, Yvette Graham, Barry Haddow, Matthias Huck, Philipp Koehn, Qun Liu, Varvara Logacheva, and Christof et al. Monz. 2017. Findings of the 2017 conference on machine translation (WMT17). In *Second Conference on Machine Translation*, pages 169–214. The Association for Computational Linguistics.

Bojar, Ondřej, Christian Federmann, Mark Fishel, Yvette Graham, Barry Haddow, Philipp Koehn, and Christof Monz. 2018. Findings of the 2018 conference on machine translation (WMT18). In *Proceedings of the Third Conference on Machine Translation: Shared Task Papers*, pages 272–303, Belgium, Brussels, October. Association for Computational Linguistics.

Dong, Daxiang, Hua Wu, Wei He, Dianhai Yu, and Haifeng Wang. 2015. Multi-task learning for multiple language translation. In *Proceedings of the 53rd Annual Meeting of the Association for Computational Linguistics and the 7th International Joint Conference on Natural Language Processing (Volume 1: Long Papers)*, pages 1723–1732, Beijing, China, July. Association for Computational Linguistics.

Dyer, Chris, Victor Chahuneau, and Noah A. Smith. 2013. A simple, fast, and effective reparameterization of ibm model 2. In *In Proc. NAACL*.

Fan, Angela, Shruti Bhosale, Holger Schwenk, Zhiyi Ma, Ahmed El-Kishky, Siddharth Goyal, Mandeep Baines, Onur Celebi, Guillaume Wenzek, Vishrav Chaudhary, Naman Goyal, Tom Birch, Vitaliy Liptchinsky, Sergey Edunov, Edouard Grave, Michael Auli, and Armand Joulin. 2020. Beyond english-centric multilingual machine translation. 10.

Firat, Orhan, KyungHyun Cho, and Yoshua Bengio. 2016. Multi-way, multilingual neural machine translation with a shared attention mechanism. *CoRR*, abs/1601.01073.

Goldhahn, Dirk, Thomas Eckart, and Uwe Quasthoff. 2012. Building large monolingual dictionaries at the Leipzig corpora collection: From 100 to 200 languages. In *Proceedings of the Eighth International Conference on Language Resources and Evaluation (LREC'12)*, pages 759–765, Istanbul, Turkey, May. European Language Resources Association (ELRA).

Ha, Thanh-Le, Jan Niehues, and Alexander H. Waibel. 2016. Toward multilingual neural machine translation with universal encoder and decoder. *CoRR*, abs/1611.04798.

Johnson, Melvin, Mike Schuster, Quoc V. Le, Maxim Krikun, Yonghui Wu, Zhifeng Chen, Nikhil Thorat, Fernanda B. Viégas, Martin Wattenberg, Greg Corrado, Macduff Hughes, and Jeffrey Dean. 2016. Google's multilingual neural machine translation system: Enabling zero-shot translation. *CoRR*, abs/1611.04558.

Koehn, Philipp. 2004. Statistical significance tests for machine translation evaluation. In *Proceedings of the 2004 Conference on Empirical Methods in Natural Language Processing*, pages 388–395, Barcelona, Spain, July. Association for Computational Linguistics.

Rei, Ricardo, Craig Stewart, Ana C Farinha, and Alon Lavie. 2020. COMET: A neural framework for MT evaluation. In *Proceedings of the 2020 Conference on Empirical Methods in Natural Language Processing (EMNLP)*, pages 2685–2702, Online, November. Association for Computational Linguistics.

Tan, Xu, Yi Ren, Di He, Tao Qin, Zhou Zhao, and Tie-Yan Liu. 2019. Multilingual neural machine translation with knowledge distillation. *CoRR*, abs/1902.10461.

Tiedemann, Jörg and Santhosh Thottingal. 2020. OPUS-MT – building open translation services for the world. In *Proceedings of the 22nd Annual Conference of the European Association for Machine Translation*, pages 479–480, Lisboa, Portugal, November. European Association for Machine Translation.

Vaswani, Ashish, Noam Shazeer, Niki Parmar, Jakob Uszkoreit, Llion Jones, Aidan N. Gomez, Lukasz Kaiser, and Illia Polosukhin. 2017. Attention is all you need. *CoRR*, abs/1706.03762.

Xue, Linting, Noah Constant, Adam Roberts, Mihir Kale, Rami Al-Rfou, Aditya Siddhant, Aditya Barua, and Colin Raffel. 2021. mT5: A massively multilingual pre-trained text-to-text transformer. In *Proceedings of the 2021 Conference of the North American Chapter of the Association for Computational Linguistics: Human Language Technologies*, pages 483–498, Online, June. Association for Computational Linguistics.

Appendix A. Comparison of COMET and Human DA Scores

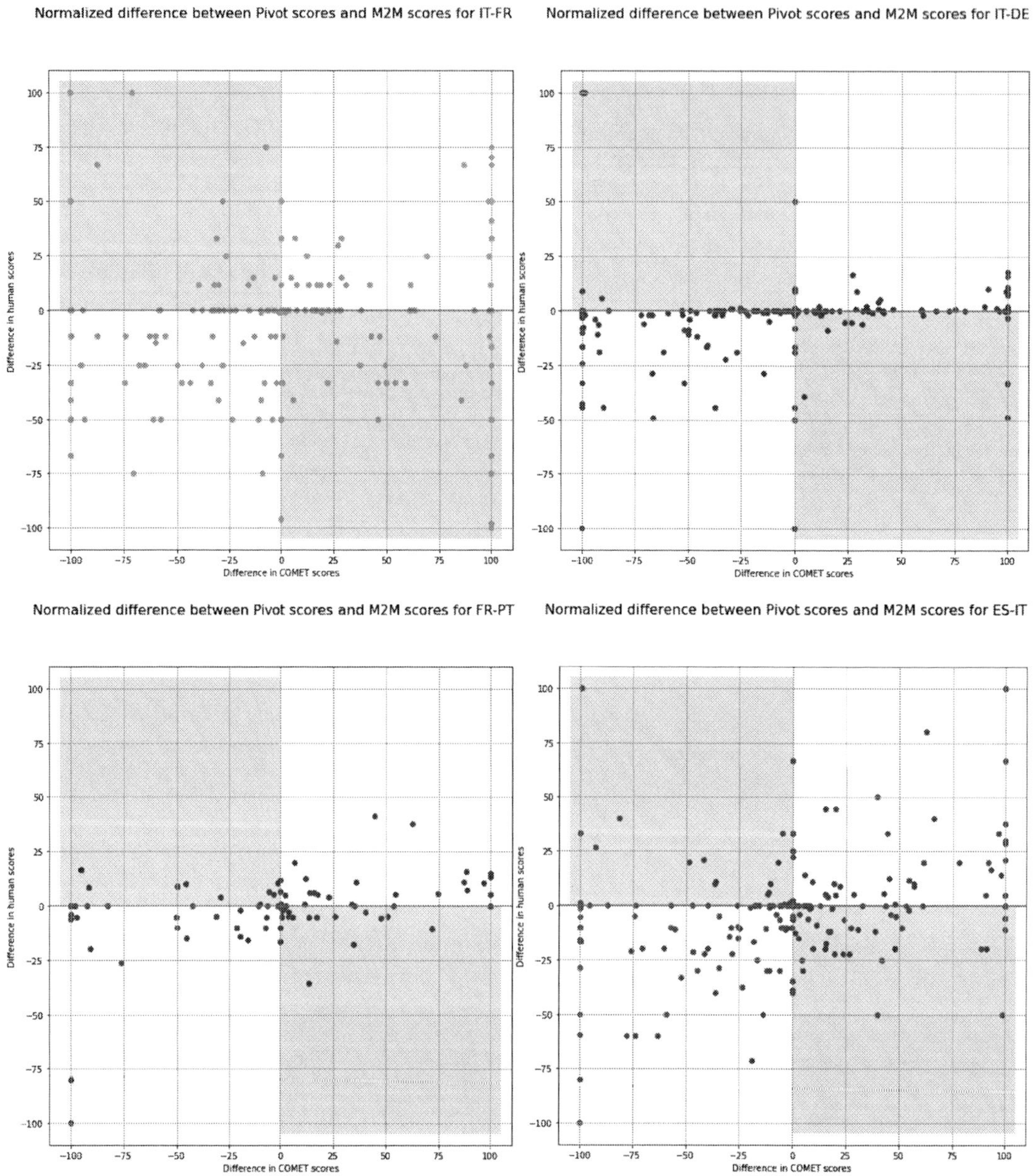

Figure 1: Comparison of difference between COMET and human annotations: language pairs in the same language family

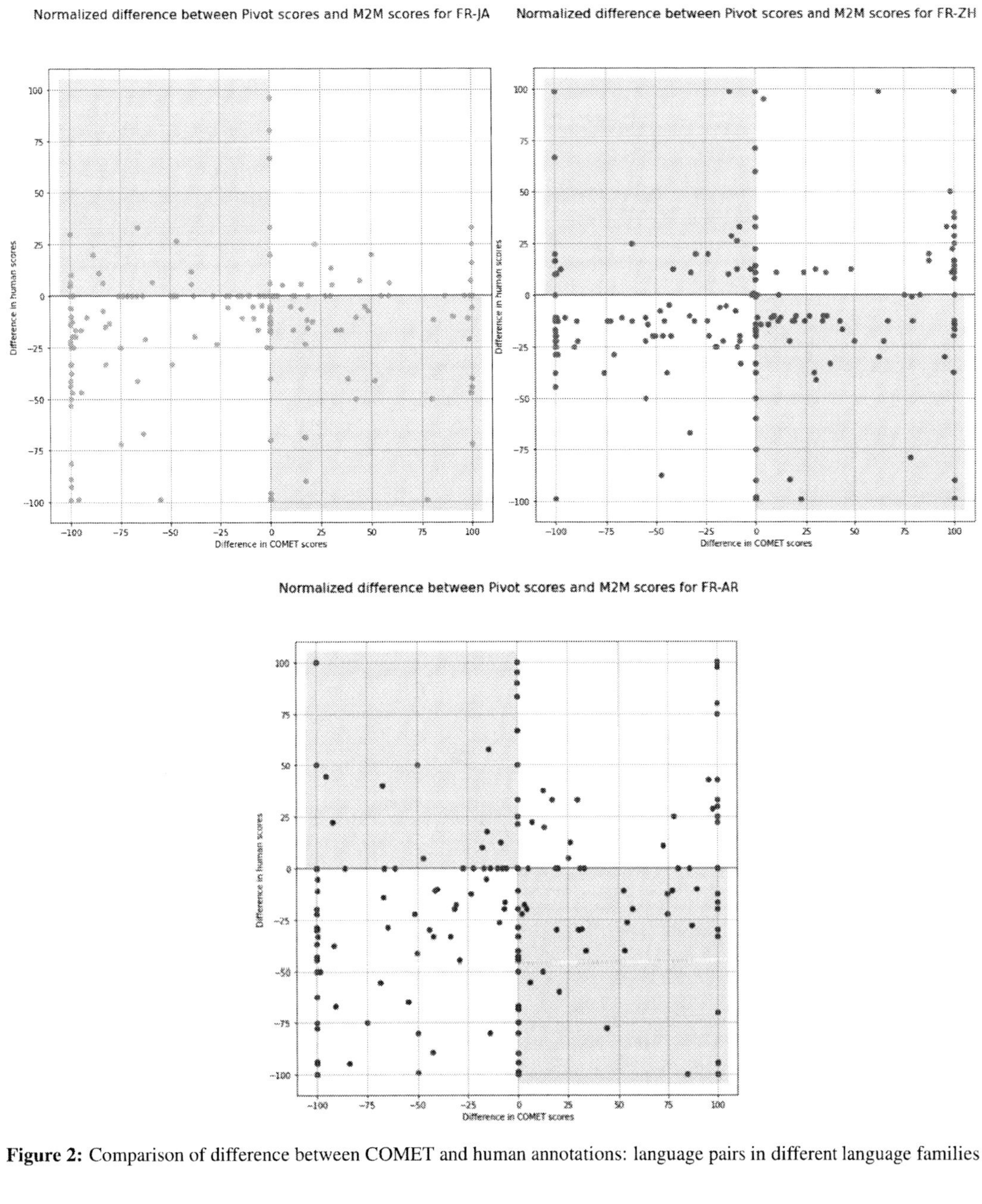

Figure 2: Comparison of difference between COMET and human annotations: language pairs in different language families

Pre-training Synthetic Cross-lingual Decoder for Multilingual Samples Adaptation in E-Commerce Neural Machine Translation

Kamal Kumar Gupta, Soumya Chennabasavaraj,[†] Nikesh Garera,[†] and Asif Ekbal
Department of Computer Science and Engineering,
Indian Institute of Technology Patna, Patna, India
[†]Flipkart, India
kamal.pcs17, asif@iitp.ac.in
[†]soumya.cb, nikesh.garera@flipkart.com

Abstract

Availability of the user reviews in vernacular languages is helpful for the users to get information regarding the products. Since most of the e-commerce websites allow the reviews in English language only, it is important to provide the translated versions of the reviews to the non-English speaking users. Translation of the user reviews from English to vernacular languages is a challenging task, predominantly due to the lack of sufficient in-domain datasets. In this paper, we present a pre-training technique which is used to adapt and improve the single multilingual neural machine translation (NMT) model for the low-resource language pairs. The pre-trained model contains a special synthetic cross-lingual decoder trained over the cross-lingual target samples where the phrases are replaced with their translated counterparts. After pre-training, the model is adapted to multiple samples of the low-resource language pairs using incremental learning. We perform the experiments over eight low-resource and three high resource language pairs from the generic and product review domains. Through our proposed pre-training, we achieve upto 4.35 BLEU improvements compared to the baseline and 2.13 BLEU points compared to the previous code-switched pre-trained models. The review domain outputs are evaluated in human evaluators in the e-commerce company Flipkart.

1 Introduction

Neural machine translation models (Bahdanau et al., 2015; Vaswani et al., 2017) are effective for a specific language pair or domain when trained on a large amount of parallel corpus. It is often difficult to obtain such a large corpus, especially in non-English languages and in specialized domains such as product reviews (Gupta et al., 2021). Currently, in the e-commerce domain, providing the translation of the user reviews in vernacular languages is a need. In a multilingual country like India where English is not a primary language, reviews in local languages will be very helpful for the users as well as e-commerce platforms like Flipkart. As of December 2021, Flipkart leads[1] in the Indian e-commerce market with a market share of 31.9%. In the process of building a one-to-many multilingual translation system to translate the low-resource review domain data on the e-commerce platform Flipkart from English to multiple Indian languages, we propose a synthetic decoder based pre-training approach. To see the impact of the proposed model on translation quality, we perform experiments over the general domain data available publicly. Along with it, we also evaluate our model for review domain data using English-Hindi, English-French and English-Tamil testset.

Recently, pre-training based NMT (Lewis et al., 2019; Devlin et al., 2019) models have attracted attention to improve the translation quality of low as well as high resource language pairs (Yang et al., 2020b; Lin et al., 2020). Pre-training based models first train a parent model over a large dataset and then use the learnt weights to fine-tune for a spe-

[1]https://inc42.com/datalab/amazon-vs-flipkart-who-led-the-indian-//ecommerce-war-in-2021/

Macken, Rufener, Van den Bogaert, Daems, Tezcan, Vanroy, Fonteyne, Barrault, Costa-jussà, Kemp, Pilos, Declercq, Koponen, Forcada, Scarton, Moniz (eds.)
Proceedings of the 23rd Annual Conference of the European Association for Machine Translation, p. 239–246
Ghent, Belgium, June 2022.

cific low-resource language pair or domain (Conneau and Lample, 2019; Song et al., 2019). These approaches have some limitations, e.g. these use some special symbols in the parent models which may not be present in the data during the training of child model. As the samples are taken from the same languages, these approaches fail to capture the cross-lingual information in two languages (Yang et al., 2020b). Fine-tuning also has a limitation that it is not able to remember the information of the parent model's language pairs while training over the child model (new language pair or domain). To resolve this, source side code-switching is used to generate synthetic parallel samples to train the parent model and later use it for fine-tuning over new language pair (Lin et al., 2020; Yang et al., 2020b). These approaches use the parent model's weights to fine-tune for a bi-lingual translation task.

In our work, we perform random phrase substitution at the target side of a parallel sample to capture the shared target context. Our final trained model is a multilingual translation model which can translate the source sentence into multiple languages. Multilingual adaptation helps the incoming pairs to learn from each other because of the shared parameter training. Also, unlike Yang et al., 2020 and Lin et al., 2020 (Yang et al., 2020b; Lin et al., 2020), we use incremental learning instead of fine-tuning where the model can adapt over the incoming input samples from different language pairs without forgetting the information of previously adopted language pairs. Incremental learning allows to update the model even with a small size of available parallel samples without full re-training.

2 Related Work

Pre-training a NMT model and fine-tuning it for specific translation tasks is one of the popular approaches for dealing with the resource-scarce language scenario. Pre-trained language models (LMs) like BERT (Bidirectional Encoder Representations from Transformers) (Devlin et al., 2019) have been used to improve the NMT models (Yang et al., 2020a; Zhu et al., 2020). Edunov et al. (2019) introduced ELMo to the encoder of the NMT model as a pre-trained LM to improve the performance of the NMT model. Weng et al. (2019) used bi-directional self-attention LM in the NMT by weighted-fusion mechanism and knowledge transfer paradigm to improve the learning of encoder and decoder. Zhu et al. (2020) incorporated the representations from the BERT into the encoder and decoder layers of the NMT model. But such large parameters also added extra overhead and delay in the inference time. The recent studies of Yang et al. (2020b) and Lin et al. (2020) used code-switching at source side to train the parent model. The trained parent model is used for fine-tuning over the specific bi-lingual translation direction. Yang et al. (2020b); Lin et al. (2020) trained a multilingual parent model. Unsupervised pre-training has also been popular in several natural language understanding problems, such as word embedding representation (Pennington et al., 2014), pre-trained context representation (Devlin et al., 2019) and sequence-to-sequence pre-training (Song et al., 2019). In this pre-training, scale of data is found to be a very important attribute.

Multilingual NMT (Dong et al., 2015; Johnson et al., 2017; Lu et al., 2018; Rahimi et al., 2019; Tan et al., 2019) is also a useful paradigm where a model trained in a parameter sharing fashion shares the information among the language pairs. In multilingual NMT, low-resource language pairs leverage the information of the high-resource languages. Johnson et al. (2017) added language specific tags before each source sentence in the parallel corpus, merged all the data from multiple language pairs and trained them in a single NMT model. Firat et al. (2016) used shared attention to transfer information between multiple encoder-decoders in a multilingual NMT. Rahimi et al. (2019) performed the training of massively multilingual NMT models. They showed that training a many-to-many multilingual model is helpful in low-resource scenarios. By keeping this in mind, we also use pre-training to improve a multilingual NMT. Unlike Yang et al. (2020b); Lin et al. (2020), we use the pre-trained NMT model to adapt over multilingual NMT using incremental learning instead of bi-lingual pair using fine-tuning.

3 Dataset

We need two types of corpora *i.e.* parallel and monolingual. For the experiments, we include a total of 11 language pairs; out of which 3 belong to the European language pairs, and the rest 8 are low-resource English-Indian language pairs. The data statistics are shown in Table 1. For the

	Parallel	Mono	Dev	Test
En→Fr	15M	224M	2,000	3,000
En→Fr(R)	36,058	224M	2,000	1,020
En→De	4.5M	622M	2,000	3,000
En→Es	3.9M	122M	2,000	3,000
En→Hi	3M	62.9M	1,000	2,390
En→Hi(R)	19,457	62.9M	1,000	2,539
En→Bn	1.7M	3.5M	1,000	2,390
En→Gu	0.51M	7.8M	1,000	2,390
En→Mr	0.78M	9.9M	1,000	2,390
En→Pa	0.52M	6.5M	1,000	2,390
En→Ta	1.4M	20.9M	1,000	2,390
En→Te	0.68M	15.1M	1,000	2,390
En→Ml	1.2M	11.6M	1,000	2,390

Table 1: Size of parallel and monolingual data used for the experiments in million (M). English monolingual corpus size: 495M. Monolingual column in the table shows the size of the corpus for the non-English language in that row. En→Fr(R) and En→Hi(R) are the user review domain datasets.

parallel and monolingual data of English-{French, German} and English-{Spanish}, we use WMT14 (Bojar et al., 2014) and WMT13 (Bojar et al., 2013) corpus, respectively. For evaluation, we use newstest2014 and newstest2013 test sets, respectively. Size of test and development sets are shown in Table 1. Monolingual corpus for English, French and German are taken from the WMT14, and from WMT13 for Spanish. For English-Indian language pairs, we use the parallel data for training, development and testing from WAT21[2]. The monolingual corpus for the Indian languages are taken from the AI4Bharat-IndicNLP Dataset[3]. We also experiment over two product review dataset i.e. English-French (Michel and Neubig, 2018) and English-Hindi (Gupta et al., 2021). Data statistics are shown in Table 1.

4 Methodology

Our proposed approach has four modules: *i.* Training cross-lingual word mapping, *ii.* Generation of synthetic phrase table for source-target phrase pairs, *iii.* Generation of synthetic cross-lingual target samples and training the parent model and *iv.* adapting new input samples from multiple language pairs using incremental learning.

[2]http://lotus.kuee.kyoto-u.ac.jp/WAT/indic-multilingual/indic_wat_2021.tar.gz
[3]https://github.com/AI4Bharat/indicnlp_corpus

4.1 Word level substitution

Artetxe et al. (2017); Lample et al. (2017) introduced the strategies to learn translation pairs from the lexicons of two monolingual corpora using a shared semantic space. This strategy provides the mapping between the tokens from two languages which can be considered as the translations of each other. Based on the word mapping procedure of Artetxe et al. (2017), we use the unsupervised word mapping based on their embeddings to extract the probabilistic translation lexicons. These translation lexicon pairs are considered as the one-to-many source and target token translations. For example, given independent word embeddings of source and target languages, X_i and Y_j trained on source and target monolingual corpus X and Y, respectively, the unsupervised word mapping exploits self training in third semantic space (Artetxe et al., 2017) or adversarial training in the available semantic space (Conneau et al., 2018) to learn a mapping function f(X) = WX, which provides the source and target word representations in a common embedding space. Here, W is a mapping matrix that is learnt during training. With the word embeddings in the common semantic space, the cosine similarity is measured between the source and target tokens. After that, the probabilistic translation lexicons are selected based on the top-k nearest neighbours in the common embedding space. We can say that for the source language word x_i, its top-k nearest neighbour tokens y_{i1}, y_{i2},..., y_{ik} in the counter target language are extracted as its translation counterparts. The normalized similarities s_{i1}, s_{i2},..., s_{ik} for the word pairs are also given and defined as the translation probabilities. This word mapping is used to randomly replace the target side tokens of one language with another.

4.2 Phrase level substitution

For the phrase substitution, we use the unsupervised phrase table generation technique (Lample et al., 2017). Lample et al. (2017) uses the shared latent semantic space shown in the section above (ref. Section 4.1) and back-translation approach for the unsupervised phrase table generation. Each source and target phrase are considered as a translation candidate and using the shared semantic embedding and back-translation, the translations of the source and target phrase (n-gram sequences) are generated. Each source phrase can be paired

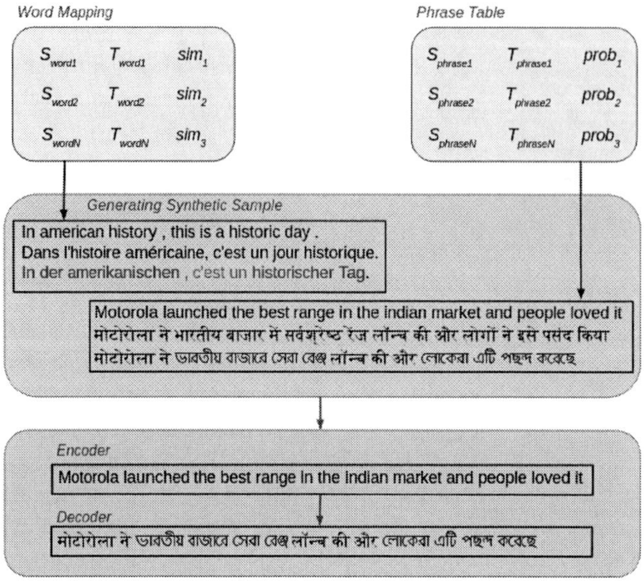

Figure 1: Representation of mapped phrase table, bi-lingual word mapping, target side synthetic sample generation and training of parent model using the synthetic parallel pairs.

with multiple target phrase along with their source-target n-gram probability. The source-target phrase pair having the highest probability is taken as the parallel phrase pair. For the synthetic phrase substitution, the source phrases of length 3 to 5 tokens are considered as the ideal candidates and replaced with their target counterparts. Monolingual sentences (ref. Table 1) are used to generate the phrase table of two languages.

4.3 Training Parent NMT Model with Synthetic Decoder

To train the parent NMT model, we use two methods to generate the synthetic cross-lingual target sequence: using phrase substitution and using word substitution. After following the processes as mentioned in Sections 4.1 and 4.2, we have now a phrase table and bi-lingual word mapping. In the phrase table, each source phrase is aligned with its target phrase pair. In bi-lingual word mapping, we have mapped cross-lingual tokens. Now, we move towards the generation of synthetic parallel pairs for training the multilingual parent NMT model. For each original parallel sample, we randomly mark the target side n-gram sequence (3 to 5 gram) for the substitution. For each such target side phrase, we find the cross-lingual phrase from the phrase table. As shown in Figure 1, an original English-Bengali parallel sample is transformed into a synthetic parallel pair by substituting the Hindi phrase with its counter Bengali phrase. Now, the source is having a monolingual English sentence while the target is a combination of Hindi and Bengali tokens. As shown in Figure 1, an English-French synthetic sample is generated by replacing French phrases with German phrases. Similar to the phrase substitution method, we also use word mapping to substitute tokens instead of phrases. Similarly, we generate such kinds of multiple synthetic samples for other languages (ref. Table 1) too. These synthetic samples are used to train the parent NMT model where the decoder has a cross-lingual sequence knowledge and is capable of capturing the context between the tokens from different languages.

4.4 Adapting Low-Resource Samples through Incremental Learning

After training the parent model using synthetic source and cross-lingual target samples, we use this to adapt over the multiple parallel samples from the low-resource language pairs or domains. We use incremental learning to adapt the parent model over the new samples to obtain a multilingual NMT model which can translate for inputs from the low-resource language pairs. The parent model is updated using the new bi-lingual parallel samples. In order to differentiate the new bi-lingual parallel samples from the synthetic samples

	Baseline	Proposed (Word)	Proposed (Phrase)	CSP	mRASP
En→Fr	38.24	39.27	40.86	38.80	38.64
En→De	27.38	29.48	30.60	28.90	29.08
En→Es	30.44	32.06	32.74	30.92	31.77
En→Hi	30.42	31.72	32.89	31.08	31.69
En→Bn	12.85	16.45	17.20	14.52	15.61
En→Gu	26.18	29.11	30.09	27.73	28.60
En→Mr	24.08	25.13	26.02	24.13	24.82
En→Pa	25.93	27.86	28.52	26.68	27.34
En→Ta	17.96	19.82	20.77	18.96	19.51
En→Te	16.08	19.14	20.51	17.93	18.38
En→Ml	16.71	18.63	19.50	17.54	18.04
En→Fr(R)	20.72	22.41	22.79	21.16	21.73
En→Hi(R)	34.36	35.84	36.27	34.82	35.38

Table 2: Performance of the proposed models in terms of BLEU score. En→Fr(R) (Michel and Neubig, 2018) and En→Hi(R) (Gupta et al., 2021) are user review domain datasets.

already used, we include language specific tags before each source sentence (Johnson et al., 2017). For example, for English-Spanish, English-Hindi and English-Bengali pairs, we use ES, HI and BN tags. Similarly, we use unique tags for all the language pairs. Instead of fine-tuning, incremental learning allows the model to learn the new input samples without losing the knowledge of previous samples.

5 Experimental Setting

Parent model is trained using the Transformer (Vaswani et al., 2017) based encoder-decoder NMT model. Our training setup is described as follows: the tokens of training, evaluation and validation sets are segmented into the subword units using the BPE technique (Gage, 1994) proposed by (Sennrich et al., 2016). We perform 30,000 and 10,000 join operations for high and low-resource languages, respectively. We learn the BPE vocabulary using the monolingual data and apply it over the parallel samples. We use 6 layers at encoder and decoder sides each, 8-head attention, hidden layer of size 512, embedding vector of size 512, learning rate of 0.0002, and the minimum batch size of 3800 tokens. The evaluation results are based on the BLEU metric (Papineni et al., 2002).

The new samples from the low-resource child pairs are tokenized and true-cased. Here, we also apply the subword operation using the learned vocabulary from the monolingual data as mentioned above. Here, before adding the new parallel samples to the parent models using incremental learning, we add language specific tags before the source sentence of each parallel sample. Adding a tag before the sample (Johnson et al., 2017) is for differentiating between parent samples and new incoming samples as well as highlighting the difference between the parallel samples from different languages too. For example, we append ##HI before source sentence of each English-Hindi parallel sample. Similar to this, we use the tags like ##FR, ##DE, ##ES, ##BN, ##GU, ##MR, ##BN, ##GU, ##MR, ##PA, ##ML, ##TA and ##TE for French, German, Spanish, Bengali, Gujarati, Marathi, Punjabi, Malayalam, Tamil and Telugu languages, respectively.

	Baseline	100%	30%	50%
En–Fr	38.24	40.86	38.82	39.65
En–De	27.38	30.60	28.81	29.02
En-Es	30.44	32.74	30.62	31.15
En-Hi	30.42	32.89	30.78	31.64
En-Ta	17.96	20.77	18.84	19.91
En-Bn	12.85	17.20	14.29	16.26

Table 3: Performance of the proposed models in terms of BLEU score when the parent model is trained on fractions of synthetic parallel data.

6 Results and Analysis

We evaluate our proposed models and compare with the multilingual models for Indian languages as the baseline. We also compare our method with existing two pre-trained models, i.e. CSP (Yang et al., 2020b) and mRASP (Lin et al., 2020). For the low-resource Indian languages, we fine tune

CSP and mRASP models for multilingual child model. For the experiments over Indian languages using WAT21 dataset, we augmented it with European languages dataset. We report the evaluation results of both word based and phrase based models. From Table 2, we can see that both the models *i.e.* word and phrase based outperforms the respective multilingual models. Pre-trained models using phrase substitution perform significantly better than the word based models. By comparing CSP and mRASP, we can observe that both the versions of the proposed model significantly outperform the CSP and mRASP. The behaviour is consistent for the high-resource as well as low-resource language pairs. It is seen that the cross-lingual context captured by the proposed decoder helps the adapted low-resource pairs that result in statistically significant (Koehn, 2004) ($p \leq 0.05$) and consistent improvements over the multilingual models, CSP and mRASP.

To see the impact of synthetic data used to train the parent model, we also perform the experiments by training the parent model over multiple fractions of synthetic data samples. We split the parent data in 30%, 50% and 100% of total size. In Table 3, we can see that the BLEU scores for En→Fr, En→De and En→Es are reported with the parent model trained over different sizes of dataset. We can see that performance of the NMT model improves consistently as the data to train the parent model increases.

6.1 Human Evaluation

The proposed model is evaluated at Flipkart (https://www.flipkart.com/) with the help of the real time human evaluators. The models for Hindi and Tamil are evaluated with the help of English–to–Hindi (Gupta et al., 2021) and English–to–Tamil testset from the review domain. The English-Tamil testset is an in-house testset of Flipkart. For evaluation, 1,000 output samples are taken and tagged with three labels i.e *Good, Can be better* and *Bad.* The labels are assigned to the output samples based on their semantic and syntactic accuracy. During the evaluation, while assigning the labels to the output samples, 'tense preservation', 'syntax of output sentence', 'choice of in-domain output tokens' are some important factors which are kept in mind. Table 4 shows the results for quality evaluation. We can see that the proposed model significantly reduces the outputs from *Can be better* and *Bad* category, and increases the *Good* label output sentences.

	Good	Can be better	Bad
En–Ta (base)	45.6%	28.1%	26.3%
En–Ta (phrase)	60.4%	24.7%	14.9%
En-Hi (base)	52.6%	21.7%	25.7%
En-Hi (phrase)	64.0%	26.3%	9.7%

Table 4: Real time quality evaluation between baseline and proposed phrase based pre-training models.

7 Conclusion

In this paper, we have devised a pre-training based learning where the parent model is trained on the source and cross-lingual target samples. We pre-train a one-to-many multilingual parent model with synthetic decoder and use incremental learning to adapt over new incoming bi-lingual parallel samples from multiple language pairs. Our objective to train such a pre-training model is to capture a cross-lingual context at the target side and use it to adapt the new multilingual parallel samples from the low-resource language pairs.
We have performed experiments over 8 low-resource and 3 high-resource language pairs. We also perform experiments over two product review domain datasets from English-French and English-Hindi language pairs. Through our synthetic multilingual decoder based pre-training, we achieve upto 3.22 and 4.35 BLEU points improvements for high and low-resource language pairs, respectively over the baseline.
From the perspective of the e-commerce platforms, our proposed parent model is able to adapt new samples for multiple language pairs and provide us a single translation model which can translate the English sentence into multiple languages. The proposed model is evaluated by real time evaluators at Flipkart for English–to–Tamil and English–to-Hindi review domain testsets. The human evaluation results show the increment of upto 6% output samples with the *Good* label.

In the future, we aim to utilize language relatedness in the multilingual setting. We believe that language relatedness in terms of vocabulary overlap, syntax sharing and subword learning can help to improve the translation quality in a multilingual model.

Acknowledgement

Authors gratefully acknowledge the unrestricted research grant received from the Flipkart Internet Private Limited to carry out the research. Authors thank Muthusamy Chelliah for his continuous feedback and suggestions to improve the quality of work.

References

Artetxe, M., Labaka, G., Agirre, E., and Cho, K. (2017). Unsupervised neural machine translation. *arXiv preprint arXiv:1710.11041*.

Bahdanau, D., Cho, K., and Bengio, Y. (2015). Neural Machine Translation by Jointly Learning to Align and Translate. In *Proceedings of the 3rd International Conference on Learning Representation (ICLR 2015)*.

Bojar, O., Buck, C., Callison-Burch, C., Federmann, C., Haddow, B., Koehn, P., Monz, C., Post, M., Soricut, R., and Specia, L. (2013). Findings of the 2013 Workshop on Statistical Machine Translation. In *Proceedings of the Eighth Workshop on Statistical Machine Translation (WMT 2013)*, pages 1–44.

Bojar, O., Buck, C., Federmann, C., Haddow, B., Koehn, P., Leveling, J., Monz, C., Pecina, P., Post, M., Saint-Amand, H., Soricut, R., Specia, L., and Tamchyna, A. (2014). Findings of the 2014 workshop on statistical machine translation. In *Proceedings of the Ninth Workshop on Statistical Machine Translation*, pages 12–58, Baltimore, Maryland, USA. Association for Computational Linguistics.

Conneau, A. and Lample, G. (2019). Cross-lingual language model pretraining. *Advances in Neural Information Processing Systems*, 32:7059–7069.

Conneau, A., Lample, G., Ranzato, M., Denoyer, L., and Jégou, H. (2018). Word Translation Without Parallel Data. In *Proceedings of the 6th International Conference on Learning Representations (ICLR 2018)*.

Devlin, J., Chang, M.-W., Lee, K., and Toutanova, K. (2019). BERT: Pre-training of deep bidirectional transformers for language understanding. In *Proceedings of the 2019 Conference of the North American Chapter of the Association for Computational Linguistics: Human Language Technologies, Volume 1 (Long and Short Papers)*, pages 4171–4186, Minneapolis, Minnesota. Association for Computational Linguistics.

Dong, D., Wu, H., He, W., Yu, D., and Wang, H. (2015). Multi-task learning for multiple language translation. In *Proceedings of the 53rd Annual Meeting of the Association for Computational Linguistics and the 7th International Joint Conference on Natural Language Processing (Volume 1: Long Papers)*, pages 1723–1732, Beijing, China. Association for Computational Linguistics.

Edunov, S., Baevski, A., and Auli, M. (2019). Pre-trained language model representations for language generation. In *Proceedings of the 2019 Conference of the North American Chapter of the Association for Computational Linguistics: Human Language Technologies, Volume 1 (Long and Short Papers)*, pages 4052–4059, Minneapolis, Minnesota. Association for Computational Linguistics.

Firat, O., Sankaran, B., Al-Onaizan, Y., Vural, F. T. Y., and Cho, K. (2016). Zero-resource translation with multi-lingual neural machine translation. *arXiv preprint arXiv:1606.04164*.

Gage, P. (1994). A new algorithm for data compression. *C Users Journal*, 12(2):23–38.

Gupta, K., Chennabasavaraj, S., Garera, N., and Ekbal, A. (2021). Product review translation using phrase replacement and attention guided noise augmentation. In *Proceedings of Machine Translation Summit XVIII: Research Track*, pages 243–255, Virtual. Association for Machine Translation in the Americas.

Johnson, M., Schuster, M., Le, Q. V., Krikun, M., Wu, Y., Chen, Z., Thorat, N., Viégas, F., Wattenberg, M., Corrado, G., et al. (2017). Google's multilingual neural machine translation system: Enabling zero-shot translation. *Transactions of the Association for Computational Linguistics*, 5:339–351.

Koehn, P. (2004). Statistical significance tests for machine translation evaluation. In *Proceedings of the 2004 Conference on Empirical Methods in Natural Language Processing*, pages 388–395, Barcelona, Spain. Association for Computational Linguistics.

Lample, G., Conneau, A., Denoyer, L., and Ranzato, M. (2017). Unsupervised machine translation using monolingual corpora only. *arXiv preprint arXiv:1711.00043*.

Lewis, M., Liu, Y., Goyal, N., Ghazvininejad, M., Mohamed, A., Levy, O., Stoyanov, V., and Zettlemoyer, L. (2019). Bart: Denoising sequence-to-sequence pre-training for natural language generation, translation, and comprehension. *arXiv preprint arXiv:1910.13461*.

Lin, Z., Pan, X., Wang, M., Qiu, X., Feng, J., Zhou, H., and Li, L. (2020). Pre-training multilingual neural machine translation by leveraging alignment information. In *Proceedings of the 2020 Conference on Empirical Methods in Natural Language Processing (EMNLP)*, pages 2649–2663, Online. Association for Computational Linguistics.

Lu, Y., Keung, P., Ladhak, F., Bhardwaj, V., Zhang, S., and Sun, J. (2018). A neural interlingua for multilingual machine translation. In *Proceedings of the Third Conference on Machine Translation: Research Papers*, pages 84–92, Brussels, Belgium. Association for Computational Linguistics.

Michel, P. and Neubig, G. (2018). MTNT: A testbed for machine translation of noisy text. In *Proceedings of the 2018 Conference on Empirical Methods in Natural Language Processing*, pages 543–553, Brussels, Belgium. Association for Computational Linguistics.

Papineni, K., Roukos, S., Ward, T., and Zhu, W.-J. (2002). Bleu: a method for automatic evaluation of machine translation. In *Proceedings of the 40th annual meeting of the Association for Computational Linguistics*, pages 311–318.

Pennington, J., Socher, R., and Manning, C. (2014). GloVe: Global vectors for word representation. In *Proceedings of the 2014 Conference on Empirical Methods in Natural Language Processing (EMNLP)*, pages 1532–1543, Doha, Qatar. Association for Computational Linguistics.

Rahimi, A., Li, Y., and Cohn, T. (2019). Massively multilingual transfer for NER. In *Proceedings of the 57th Annual Meeting of the Association for Computational Linguistics*, pages 151–164, Florence, Italy. Association for Computational Linguistics.

Sennrich, R., Haddow, B., and Birch, A. (2016). Neural machine translation of rare words with subword units. In *Proceedings of the 54th Annual Meeting of the Association for Computational Linguistics (Volume 1: Long Papers)*, pages 1715–1725, Berlin, Germany.

Song, K., Tan, X., Qin, T., Lu, J., and Liu, T.-Y. (2019). Mass: Masked sequence to sequence pre-training for language generation. *arXiv preprint arXiv:1905.02450*.

Tan, X., Ren, Y., He, D., Qin, T., and Liu, T.-Y. (2019). Multilingual neural machine translation with knowledge distillation. In *International Conference on Learning Representations*.

Vaswani, A., Shazeer, N., Parmar, N., Uszkoreit, J., Jones, L., Gomez, A. N., Kaiser, Ł., and Polosukhin, I. (2017). Attention is all you need. In *Advances in neural information processing systems*, pages 5998–6008.

Weng, R., Yu, H., Huang, S., Luo, W., and Chen, J. (2019). Improving neural machine translation with pre-trained representation. *arXiv preprint arXiv:1908.07688*.

Yang, J., Wang, M., Zhou, H., Zhao, C., Zhang, W., Yu, Y., and Li, L. (2020a). Towards making the most of bert in neural machine translation. In *Proceedings of the AAAI Conference on Artificial Intelligence*, volume 34, pages 9378–9385.

Yang, Z., Hu, B., Han, A., Huang, S., and Ju, Q. (2020b). CSP:code-switching pre-training for neural machine translation. In *Proceedings of the 2020 Conference on Empirical Methods in Natural Language Processing (EMNLP)*, pages 2624–2636, Online. Association for Computational Linguistics.

Zhu, J., Xia, Y., Wu, L., He, D., Qin, T., Zhou, W., Li, H., and Liu, T. (2020). Incorporating bert into neural machine translation. In *International Conference on Learning Representations*.

Translators' papers

Error Annotation in Post-Editing Machine Translation: Investigating the Impact of Text-to-Speech Technology

Justus Brockmann
Centre for Translation Studies
University of Vienna
justus.brockmann@univie.ac.at

Claudia Wiesinger
Centre for Translation Studies
University of Vienna
claudia.wiesinger@univie.ac.at

Dragoș Ciobanu
Centre for Translation Studies
University of Vienna
dragos.ioan.ciobanu@univie.ac.at

Abstract

As post-editing of machine translation (PEMT) is becoming one of the most dominant services offered by the language services industry (LSI), efforts are being made to support the provision of this service with additional technologies. We present text-to-speech (T2S) as a potential attention-raising technology for post-editors. Our study was conducted with university students and included both PEMT and MT error annotation of a creative text with and without T2S. Focusing on the error annotation data, our analysis finds that participants under-annotated fewer MT errors in the T2S condition compared to the silent condition. At the same time, more over-annotation was recorded. Finally, annotation performance corresponded to participants' attitudes towards using T2S.

1 Introduction

With machine translation (MT) adoption and the provision of post-editing machine translation (PEMT) services on the rise, Translation Process Research (TPR) has been questioning whether the ways in which PEMT is currently being carried out (in dedicated PEMT tools, in simple word processing software, or in computer-assisted translation (CAT) tools/translation environment tools (TEnT), and with or without the use of additional technologies) optimally support post-editors, both from a process- and a product-oriented point of view (Moorkens and O'Brien, 2017). As the technological possibilities are growing, there is an uptake of speech tools such as automatic speech recognition (ASR; speech-to-text) by professional translators (ELIA et al., 2022), and this practice has become one of the focal points of TPR (Dragsted, Mees and Hansen, 2011; Ciobanu, 2014, 2016; Mesa-Lao, 2014; Zapata, Castilho and Moorkens, 2017; Liyanapathirana, 2021).

While the use of automatic speech synthesis (text-to-speech; T2S) has received comparatively little attention both from the language services industry (LSI) and the research community, translators and revisers are known to read aloud translations during (self-)revision (Allain, 2010; Ciobanu, 2016; Scocchera, 2017). This intuitively perceived benefit of aurally processing a text points to the potential of T2S as an attention-raising technology that may also help post-editors identify subtle neural machine translation (NMT) errors.

The practice of PEMT remains a particular challenge for Translation Studies students, despite the transition from statistical MT (SMT) to NMT which has reduced the absolute number of errors to be corrected in the raw MT output (Yamada, 2019). Moreover, the phenomena of over- and under-editing continue to preoccupy both academia and the LSI (Nitzke and Gros, 2020). We share the view that students need to be exposed to a variety of translation tools early and often, and we believe that introducing them to additional technologies such as T2S will prove beneficial for honing the skills needed to succeed as future post-editors. Rather than segregating tools and technologies to separate courses, we support integrative tasks which combine error annotation using standardised typologies, PEMT,

Macken, Rufener, Van den Bogaert, Daems, Tezcan, Vanroy, Fonteyne, Barrault, Costa-jussà, Kemp, Pilos, Declercq, Koponen, Forcada, Scarton, Moniz (eds.)
Proceedings of the 23rd Annual Conference of the European Association for Machine Translation, p. 249–257
Ghent, Belgium, June 2022.

and T2S as ideal opportunities to build confidence, competence, and speed when performing PEMT.

This paper describes the results of a small-scale study investigating the impact of T2S on PEMT error annotation, alongside participant attitudes towards using T2S for PEMT.

To that end, we first present previous research on the use of speech tools for PEMT, as well as the use of error typologies in the LSI and in translator training. This is followed by our research questions and methodology. In the last two sections we present the results of our study and discuss the implications of teaching PEMT by introducing T2S and error annotation into the mix.

2 Previous Research

PEMT has been identified as the service with the highest growth potential in the LSI (ELIA et al., 2022). The widespread adoption of data-driven MT since the 2000s (Kenny, 2020) has brought considerable change to the industry, and professional translators are increasingly being asked to carry out PEMT tasks. While claims of MT achieving near or full human parity in terms of translation quality (Wu et al., 2016; Hassan et al., 2018) should be taken with a grain of salt (Läubli, Sennrich and Volk, 2018), MT has been shown to enable productivity and quality gains in translation tasks (e.g. Guerberof Arenas, 2014; Sánchez-Gijón, Moorkens and Way, 2019).

However, despite MT quality improvements and the clear industry need for qualified post-editors (most recently embodied by the GALA MTPE Training Special Interest Group[1]), European Translation Studies programmes have been found to lack hands-on PEMT training both at undergraduate and postgraduate levels (Ginovart Cid and Colominas Ventura, 2020). While interest in MT literacy is growing in the research community (cf. Bowker and Ciro, 2019), many translators are still reluctant to embrace MT as a tool (ELIA et al., 2022). Limited knowledge and experience regarding MT use in university-trained translators is likely to be a contributing factor to this reticence.

In parallel to the lack of hands-on PEMT training in Translation Studies syllabi, previous work has also highlighted a lack of familiarity of translation educators and students with translation quality assessment (TQA) practices (Doherty et al., 2018). This training blind spot may come as a surprise since TQA practices, which include the use of error typologies and scorecards, are common in the LSI (Lommel, 2018).

Quality management, which frequently involves TQA processes, has been identified as a key competence for professional translators (European Master's in Translation, 2017), and in the context of MT, the ability to perform TQA in the form of error annotation with predefined typologies is a useful skill for engine evaluation and PEMT research, among others (Popović, 2018). Moreover, the active reflection on error types may help improve the current issue of over- and under-editing, which is common in PEMT (Nitzke and Gros, 2020). There is therefore a competence gap between academia and industry in relation to both PEMT and TQA practices.

Interest in MT is growing in the LSI; however, it has been shown that translation tools do not optimally support post-editors, which leads to dissatisfaction among users (Moorkens and O'Brien, 2017). In parallel, dictating with automatic speech recognition (ASR) tools instead of, or in addition to, typing has been recognised as an alternative, more ergonomic working mode, and has attracted the interest of several scholars (Dragsted, Mees and Hansen, 2011; Ciobanu, 2014, 2016; Mesa-Lao, 2014; Zapata, Castilho and Moorkens, 2017; Liyanapathirana, 2021). ASR is also seeing an uptake among professional translators (ELIA et al., 2022). Consequently, new applications offering multi-modal forms of translator-computer interaction (TCI) have been developed (Teixeira et al., 2019; Herbig et al., 2020). In these examples, multimodal features include the use of ASR for translation and PEMT. In Interpreting Studies, the integration of ASR into computer-aided interpreting tools is also being investigated to support the work of interpreters (Fantinuoli, 2017; Defrancq and Fantinuoli, 2021).

Comparatively little attention has so far been given to potential applications of text-to-speech (T2S) technology in translation, revision, and PEMT tasks, which allow translators/post-editors to listen to an artificial computer voice 'reading out' the text they are working on. While the tools currently used in the LSI do not support T2S by default and only Trados Studio offers a T2S plug-in[2] to date, there is evidence of translators seeking

[1] https://www.gala-global.org/knowledge-center/professional-development/sigs

[2] https://community.rws.com/product-groups/trados-portfolio/

other ways of aurally processing text in their work (Allain, 2010; Ciobanu, 2016; Scocchera, 2017). A study that introduced T2S in the translation revision process (Ciobanu, Ragni and Secară, 2019) yielded encouraging results regarding revisers' error correction performance; however, further research on the effects of T2S on translators' work is certainly needed (Ciobanu and Secară, 2020).

The study by Ciobanu, Ragni and Secară (2019) found revision with T2S to be conducive to correcting more errors – above all Accuracy errors – compared to revision in silence. This has promising implications for the integration of T2S in PEMT since Accuracy has been identified as one of the major challenges for NMT (Vardaro, Schaeffer and Hansen-Schirra, 2019). Given that the use of T2S seemed to have an attention-raising effect in the revision study, we contend that this technology may also be beneficial for PEMT and error annotation – especially for translation students.

To our knowledge, there is a lack of empirical evidence on: (i) the impact of T2S technology on PEMT performance, productivity, and post-editors' attitudes towards this mode of working; and (ii) the impact of T2S on error annotation performance in the context of translator training. We aimed to fill these research gaps with a small-scale study conducted with 17 university students.

3 Methodology

3.1 Study design

The study involved 16 undergraduate students of Transcultural Communication and 1 postgraduate student of Translation. Participants were quasi-randomly allocated to two groups, G1 and G2 based on their responses to a pre-experiment questionnaire. The groups were roughly balanced regarding the participants' language skills and translation experience. Most participants were German native speakers with an English language level of C1 and very limited translation experience. Due to constraints imposed by the COVID-19 pandemic, the study was carried out fully online. In order to control the experiment conditions in this online setting, the participants were asked to work in front of their active webcams and to observe strict time limits.

The source text we used in our study was a 1,800-word excerpt from the 2019 stage adaptation of Hanif Kureishi's 1985 screenplay *My Beautiful Laundrette*. In an exploratory preparation stage, this English text was translated into German with the freely available MT engines DeepL[3], Microsoft Translator[4], and Google Translate[5]. The resulting raw MT output was evaluated by a member of the research team through error annotation according to the DQF subset of the harmonised DQF-MQM error typology[6]. We decided on using the output from Google Translate in our experiment because it contained fewer errors than the output from Microsoft Translator, and more errors than the output from DeepL, thus qualifying as a moderate PEMT challenge for our participants. We then split the source text into four equal parts of roughly 450 source words each to obtain texts of comparable length for our four experiment conditions.

Participants carried out the error annotation and PEMT tasks in Microsoft Word 365. The built-in Read Aloud function in Microsoft Word was used for synthetic voices, allowing participants to access both source and target text speech synthesis seamlessly during the final condition regardless of their computers' operating systems and without making major changes to their previous working environment. The source and target texts were displayed in a three-column table format. Each table cell represented one segment from the stage play script. The first column contained the English source text, the second and third columns contained identical copies of the German output from Google Translate. This way, participants could annotate the MT errors in the second column and post-edit the output in the third column, thus providing a more convenient way of working than combining annotations and post-edits in a single cell.

Prior to the experiment, our participants attended an introductory workshop in which they practised PEMT and error annotation on a 124-word excerpt from the play. This was done in preparation for the actual experiment tasks, which required the participants to both annotate and post-

[3] https://www.deepl.com/; translation retrieval date: 7/04/2021

[4] https://www.bing.com/translator; translation retrieval date: 7/04/2021

[5] https://translate.google.com/; translation retrieval date: 7/04/2021

[6] https://www.taus.net/qt21-project#harmonized-error-typology

edit the four target text parts during two separate experiment sessions with two parts each. Our participants were provided with instructions both during the introductory workshop and in writing on how to use the T2S functionality in the PEMT task, as well as how to change the synthetic voices if desired. The written instructions also included relevant keyboard shortcuts for Windows and MacOS that the participants could use to increase productivity when using T2S: play/pause/skip-back/skip-forward/increase or decrease reading speed.

The two experiment sessions were carried out on two separate days within a two-week interval. Each session was split up into two 45-minute parts, and in each part the participants carried out their task in a different working condition: 1. in silence for both groups; 2. with source text sound (STS), or with target text sound (TTS), depending on the group; 3. with TTS, or STS, again depending on the group; and 4. with both STS and TTS. For the working conditions that included T2S, the students were instructed to use the speech functionality for each segment they worked on at least once. We reversed the order in which the two groups were confronted with the first sound condition to counteract the potential influence of growing familiarity with the text (**Table 1**).

	Part 1	Part 2	Part 3	**Part 4**
G1 (n=9) P2, P3, P5, P6, P10, P14, P15, P18, P21	Silence	STS	TTS	STS+ TTS
G2 (n=8) P1, P4, P7, P8, P9, P16, P19, P23	Silence	TTS	STS	STS+ TTS

Table 1: Distribution of experimental groups, parts, and sound conditions

This paper focuses on the annotations made in Part 1 (silence) and Part 4 (STS+TTS) for two main reasons: firstly, as reported in Wiesinger et al. (forthcoming), our participants' average PEMT performance was highest in Part 4, both in terms of error correction rate and productivity. Secondly, these were the two parts where all participants worked both on the same content, and in the same conditions – i.e., in silence in Part 1 and with both types of sound in Part 4.

The experiment sessions were followed by a feedback meeting, allowing the participants to ask questions and to compare their performance. Moreover, a total of six questionnaires were answered by the participants throughout the experiment: one during recruitment, one after each part, and one after the feedback meeting, allowing us to collect data on their prior experience, perceived performance, and evolving attitudes.

For the error annotation task, the participants were introduced to the DQF subset of the harmonised DQF-MQM error typology, which contains eight high-level error types and 33 granular error types. The typology also features four severity levels to add a weight to errors, complemented by a 'Kudos' option to praise exceptional performance. Participants were instructed to use the numerical identifier assigned to each high-level and granular error type, as well as severity level when making annotations. This way, a 'Mistranslation' error with 'Major' severity, for instance, would be annotated via the MS Word comment function with the label: 1–13–2 (i.e., Accuracy–Mistranslation–Major).

3.2 The Gold Standard

In order to establish a reference against which the participants' submissions could be compared, two members of the research team annotated and post-edited the MT output, and merged their annotations by mutual agreement into a gold standard version. For the purpose of our study, this gold standard was assumed to contain all of the errors that needed to be corrected in the MT output: 91 errors in Part 1, 75 errors in Part 2, 62 errors in Part 3, and 45 errors in Part 4.

3.3 Complementary work

Complementary work in Wiesinger et al. (forthcoming) has involved an analysis of the study data regarding the effect of T2S on post-editing performance and productivity. The final experiment condition (STS+TTS) resulted in the highest proportion of MT errors corrected in line with our gold standard. Although productivity grew on average, we saw that the highest improvement in PEMT quality came with the lowest improvement in productivity.

In the present analysis we re-visit the data collected in the study, focusing in more detail on the impact of T2S on the high-level error types annotated by the participants, as well as the relationship between the participants' attitudes and their annotation performance.

3.4 Research questions

Our research questions were:

- RQ1: Which of the two conditions (silence, or STS+TTS) is more conducive to over-annotation?

- RQ2: Which of the two conditions (silence, or STS+TTS) is more conducive to under-annotation?

- RQ3: What is the relationship between the participants' attitudes and their error annotation performance?

4 Results

4.1 Error annotation

We measured our participants' annotation performance in Part 1 and Part 4 by comparing each participant's annotations against our gold standard (GS) annotated version which contained 91 errors in Part 1, and 45 in Part 4.

'Over-annotation' refers to cases where the participant annotated an error not present in the GS. On average, 21% of the total annotations made by our participants were labelled as over-annotations in the silence condition (Part 1). For the STS+TTS condition (Part 4), the average percentage was 34%.

'Under-annotation' refers to cases where the participant did not annotate an error present in the GS. On average, 52% of the errors present in the Part 1 MT output were not annotated. For Part 4, the figure was 46%.

Since the participants were asked to observe strict time limits for the experiment parts, the amount of text they managed to annotate varied depending on individual productivity. We took this into account in our calculations. Over-annotations were calculated as percentages of the total number of annotations each participant made in the respective part. Under-annotations were calculated as the percentage of GS errors present but left un-annotated in the portion of text they worked on in each part.

However, averages only tell part of the story. Predictably, we observed that not all participants annotated the same number of errors in the two parts. There was, in fact, considerable variation among participants.

Over-annotation went up for all but two participants (**Figure 1**): P8, who registered a slight decrease, and P10 (no change). This is not surprising, given that the total number of annotations made by all participants remained almost the same (492 in Part 1, 487 in Part 4), but the number of errors present in the GS halved from Part 1 to Part 4 (91 in Part 1, 45 in Part 4). Possible reasons for the increase in over-annotation include that some participants might have been trying to annotate errors at a similar or higher rate than in the previous parts, or that their approach to translation defects was more critical in the sound conditions. However, these speculations could only be confirmed by obtaining more qualitative data on the process from participants.

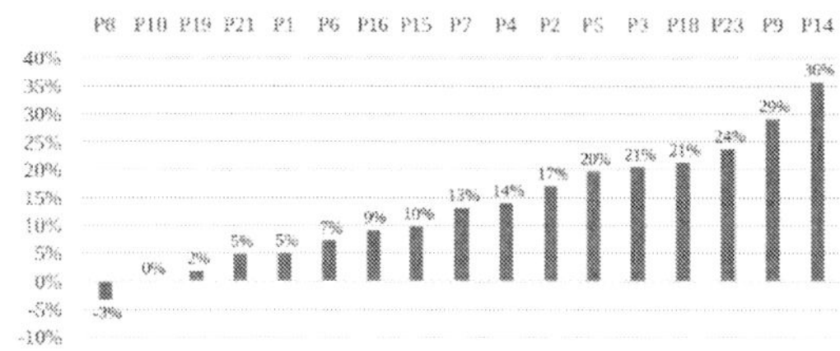

Figure 1: Increases/decreases in **over-annotations** made by participants in Part 4 compared to Part 1

On the other hand, under-annotation went down in Part 4 (STS + TTS) for 12 of the 17 participants, with decreases ranging from 2 to 27 percentage points (**Figure 2**).

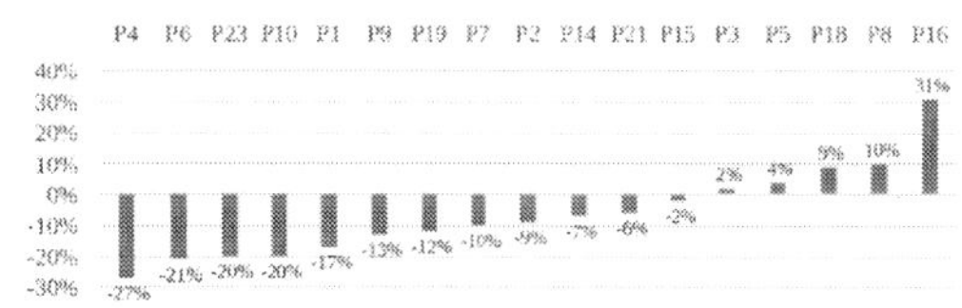

Figure 2: Increases/decreases in **under-annotations** made by participants in Part 4 compared to Part 1

4.2 Attitudes

When looking at the responses to a pre-experiment questionnaire item that asked whether the participants see any major advantages or disadvantages in using T2S, we can broadly classify the answers given by the participants as indicating a positive, neutral, or negative attitude. A positive answer is one where the participant expects advantages from the use of T2S. In a neutral answer, the participant indicates that they are unsure about any advantages or disadvantages. In a negative answer, the participant would state that they expect disadvantages from using T2S or prefer working without it. Generally, our participants' answers indicated a largely positive attitude towards using T2S.

Of the 17 participants, there were only 6 who indicated a negative attitude towards T2S in the pre-experiment questionnaire. Three of them changed their minds over the course of the experiment, indicating positive attitudes in the final questionnaire after the experiment. This leaves three participants (P9, P14, P16) who kept their negative attitudes towards T2S even after using the technology.

It should also be noted that none of the participants changed their attitude towards using T2S to negative after the experiment.

Moreover, the attitudes towards annotating errors during PEMT were also largely positive. In the questionnaire answered after completing Part 1, only 5 out of the 17 participants indicated that they did not see any advantages in PEMT with error annotation.

5 Discussion

In an ideal world, introducing this new mode of working would enable post-editors to reduce both their over-annotation and under-annotation scores.

In response to RQ1, we observed that STS+TTS was the condition in which all participants except two annotated more errors which were not actually there – so their over-annotation scores went up, in some cases by over 20% (**Figure 1**). This is not necessarily detrimental to the target text, although it lowers the post-editor's productivity.

At the same time (and in response to RQ2), the STS+TTS condition was also the condition in which fewer actual GS errors were missed by all but 5 participants (**Figure 2**). While there is an outlier here with an increase in under-annotation of 31 percentage points (P16), qualitative data revealed that this participant experienced technical difficulties in using the Read Aloud feature – thus offering an example of the detrimental impact on performance posed by user-specific technical challenges.

Overall, missing fewer real errors is extremely valuable and can improve target text quality if corrected well, provided that the over-annotations and their corresponding corrections do not introduce new errors.

Our data suggests that, when performing PEMT with STS+TTS, participants made more preferential annotations, but also missed fewer genuine errors. In the words of P18: "By listening to the segments in the target language that were translated only by a machine, I can detect errors more easily as the translation sounds unnatural to me." Although not ideal – the ideal would be for post-editors to only make necessary annotations –, identifying more genuine errors while also making what could be classed as 'preferential annotations' could be considered an acceptable compromise.

In any case, what these figures show is that limited practice without personalised feedback does not result in ideal performance improvements for an entire group, although encouraging signs could already be seen. For example, at the end of the experiment, for 5 students the percentage by which they over-annotated was actually below the one by which they decreased their under-annotation performance. This is a move in the right direction. 5 different students, though, were at the other end of the spectrum, with both higher over-annotations (which is tolerable) **and** higher under-annotations (which is not ideal).

With sufficient practice, though, annotating errors and subsequently correcting them can reach a level of quality which makes this task useful not just for an individual – "You have a clearer picture of what kind of errors you have to correct" (P6) – but also for a group collaborating on a PEMT project – "It is helpful if you work with others; in that case you don't have to explain to them your decision every time. And if the person you are doing the post-editing for wants to know why you corrected something, it is easier to explain." (P10)

Furthermore, the qualitative data obtained from the questionnaires (RQ3) suggest that the perception of T2S as a useful tool for error annotation and PEMT will depend on personal preferences and attitudes.

The three participants who did not change their negative attitudes towards T2S were also among those whose error annotation performance changed for the worse between Part 1 and Part 4. P16 had the largest increase in under-annotation (31 percentage points), while P9 and P14 had the largest increases in over-annotation (29 and 36 percentage points, respectively).

Conversely, those whose error annotation performance changed for the better between Part 1 and Part 4 generally indicated positive attitudes towards the use of T2S. Of the three students with the highest decrease in under-annotation (P4, P6, P23), the first two indicated a positive attitude before and after the experiment, while P23 changed their attitude from negative to positive in the final questionnaire. P23 shares third place in reducing under-annotation with P10 who kept a neutral attitude throughout the experiment. The only participant to reduce over-annotation (P8) had a positive attitude throughout.

Other participants perceived speech synthesis as beneficial for text comprehension more generally: "Speech synthesis made understanding sentences with slang words much easier. I could understand the spoken words in the context of the sentence better, even though I had never heard them before." (P21)

6 Conclusions

Despite rapid advances in technologies such as machine translation and speech synthesis, the professional environments in which translators, revisers, and post-editors work have remained largely unchanged.

Post-editors are expected to identify and correct at an ever faster rate the unpredictable and often subtle errors produced by neural machine translation engines, but their attention is not yet enhanced and stimulated by multi-modal input. Our experiment shows that integrating S2T into PEMT workflows can be easily done with existing tools and has practical benefits – similar to how integrating T2S into *revision* workflows improved revisers' performance in a previous experiment.

Moreover, although both the task and the technologies used in the experiment were unfamiliar to the participants, progress was recorded to different degrees concerning performance and attitudes. Continued practice supplemented by regular, personalised feedback is likely to accelerate such progress.

A more seamless integration of T2S into current CAT tools would enable further studies to be conducted in more authentic environments, and more natural-sounding artificial voices would improve the user experience. Even at this stage, though, we see T2S as having perceived benefits for content comprehension and error identification, alongside measurable benefits for reducing error under-annotation.

Future work could thus include investigating the impact of T2S on error annotation and PEMT carried out by professional post-editors, with other text types and language pairs than the ones used in this study.

References

Allain, Jean-François. 2010. Repenser la révision. *Traduire. Revue française de la traduction*, (223):114–120.

Bowker, Lynne and Jairo B. Ciro. 2019. *Machine Translation and Global Research: Towards Improved Machine Translation Literacy in the Scholarly Community*. Emerald Publishing Limited.

Ciobanu, Dragoş. 2014. Of Dragons and Speech Recognition Wizards and Apprentices. *Tradumàtica: tecnologies de la traducció*, 12:524–538.

Ciobanu, Dragoş. 2016. Automatic Speech Recognition in the professional translation process. *Translation Spaces*, 5(1):124–144.

Ciobanu, Dragoş, Valentina Ragni, and Alina Secară. 2019. Speech Synthesis in the Translation Revision Process: Evidence from Error Analysis, Questionnaire, and Eye-Tracking. *Informatics*, 6(4)(51).

Ciobanu, Dragoş and Alina Secară. 2020. Speech recognition and synthesis technologies in the translation workflow. In Minako O'Hagan (ed.). *The Routledge Handbook of Translation and Technology*. Routledge, 91–106.

Defrancq, Bart and Claudio Fantinuoli. 2021. Automatic speech recognition in the booth: Assessment of system performance, interpreters' performances and interactions in the context of numbers. *Target-International Journal of Translation Studies*, 33(1):73–102.

Doherty, Stephen, Joss Moorkens, Federico Gaspari, and Sheila Castilho. 2018. On Education and Training in Translation Quality Assessment. In Joss Moorkens, Sheila Castilho, Federico Gaspari and Stephen Doherty (eds.). *Translation Quality Assessment: From Principles to Practice*. Cham: Springer International Publishing, 95–106.

Dragsted, Barbara, Inger M. Mees, and Inge G. Hansen. 2011. Speaking your translation: students' first encounter with speech recognition technology. *The International Journal for Translation & Interpreting Research*, 3(1):10–43.

European Language Industry Association (ELIA), EMT, EUATC, FIT Europe, GALA, LIND, Women in Localization. 2022. *2022 European Language Industry Survey. Trends, expectations and concerns of the European language industry*. Available at: https://fit-europe-rc.org/wp-content/uploads/2022/03/ELIS-2022_survey_results_final_report.pdf?x77803 (Accessed: 23 March 2022).

European Master's in Translation. 2017. *EMT Competence Framework.* Available at: https://ec.europa.eu/info/sites/info/files/emt_competence_fwk_2017_en_web.pdf. (Accessed: 11 May 2022)

Fantinuoli, Claudio. 2017. Speech Recognition in the Interpreter Workstation. *Proceedings of Translating and the Computer 39*, 25–34.

Ginovart Cid, Clara and Carme Colominas Ventura. 2020. The MT Post-Editing Skill Set. Course descriptions and educators' thoughts. In Maarit Koponen, Brian Mossop, Isabelle S. Robert and Giovanna Scocchera (eds.). *Translation Revision and Post-editing: Industry Practices and Cognitive Processes*. Routledge.

Guerberof Arenas, Ana. 2014. Correlations between productivity and quality when post-editing in a professional context. *Machine Translation*, 28:165–186.

Hassan, Hany, Anthony Aue, Chang Chen, Vishal Chowdhary, Jonathan Clark, Christian Federmann, Xuedong Huang, Marcin Junczys-Dowmunt, William Lewis, Mu Li, Shujie Liu, Tie-Yan Liu, Reqian Luo, Arul Menezes, Tao Qin, Frank Seide, Xu Tan, Fei Tian, Lijun Wu, Shuangzhi Wu, Yingce Xia, Dongdong Zhang, Zhirui Zhang, and Ming Zhou. 2018. Achieving Human Parity on Automatic Chinese to English News Translation. *CoRR*, abs/1803.05567. Available at: http://arxiv.org/abs/1803.05567.

Herbig, Nico, Tim Düwel, Santanu Pal, Kalliopi Meladaki, Mahsa Monshizadeh, Antonio Krüger, and Josef van Genabith. 2020. MMPE: A Multi-Modal Interface for Post-Editing Machine Translation. *Proceedings of the 58th Annual Meeting of the Association for Computational Linguistics. ACL 2020*, 1691–1702.

Kenny, Dorothy. 2020. Machine Translation. In Mona Baker and Gabriela Saldanha (eds.). *Routledge Encyclopedia of Translation Studies*. 3rd edn. Routledge, 305–310.

Läubli, Samuel, Rico Sennrich, and Martin Volk. 2018. Has Machine Translation Achieved Human Parity? A Case for Document-level Evaluation. *Proceedings of the 2018 Conference on Empirical Methods in Natural Language Processing*, 4791–4796.

Liyanapathirana, Jeevanthi. 2021. Integrating post-editing with Dragon speech recognizer: a use case at international organizations. *43rd Translating and the Computer conference*. Available at: https://www.asling.org/tc43/videos/Liyanapathirana.mp4.

Lommel, Arle. 2018. Metrics for Translation Quality Assessment: A Case for Standardising Error Typologies. In Joss Moorkens, Sheila Castilho, Federico Gaspari and Stephen Doherty (eds.). *Translation Quality Assessment: From Principles to Practice*. Cham: Springer International Publishing, 109–127.

Mesa-Lao, Bartholomé. 2014. Speech-Enabled Computer-Aided Translation: A Satisfaction Survey with Post-Editor Trainees. *Proceedings of the EACL 2014 Workshop on Humans and Computer-assisted Translation*, 99–103.

Moorkens, Joss and Sharon O'Brien. 2017. Assessing user interface needs of post-editors of machine translation. In Dorothy Kenny (ed.). *Human Issues in Translation Technology*. London: Routledge, 109–130.

Nitzke, Jean and Anne-Kathrin Gros. 2020. Preferential Changes in Revision and Post-Editing. In Maarit Koponen, Brian Mossop, Isabelle S. Robert and Giovanna Scocchera (eds.). *Translation Revision and Post-editing: Industry Practices and Cognitive Processes*. Routledge, 21–34.

Popović, Maja. 2018. Error Classification and Analysis for Machine Translation Quality Assessment. In Joss Moorkens, Sheila Castilho, Federico Gaspari and Stephen Doherty (eds.). *Translation Quality Assessment: From Principles to Practice*. Cham: Springer International Publishing, 129–158.

Sánchez-Gijón, Pilar, Joss Moorkens, and Andy Way. 2019. Post-editing neural machine translation versus translation memory segments. *Machine Translation*, (33):31–59.

Scocchera, Giovanna. 2017. Translation Revision as Rereading: Different Aspects of the Translator's and Reviser's Approach to the Revision Process. *Mémoires du livre / Studies in Book Culture*, 9(1).

Teixeira, Carlos S. C., Joss Moorkens, Daniel Turner, Joris Vreeke, and Andy Way. 2019. Creating a Multimodal Translation Tool and Testing Machine Translation Integration Using Touch and Voice. *Informatics*, 6(1)(13).

Vardaro, Jennifer, Moritz Schaeffer, and Silvia Hansen-Schirra. 2019. Translation Quality and Error Recognition in Professional Neural Machine Translation Post-Editing. *Informatics*, 6(3).

Wiesinger, Claudia, Justus Brockmann, Alina Secară, and Dragoş Ciobanu. Forthcoming. Speech-enabled machine translation post-editing in the context of translator training. *Peter Lang: Łódź Studies in Language.* The Łódz-ZHAW Duo Colloquium, 2-3 September, 2021.

Wu, Yonghui, Mike Schuster, Zhifeng Chen, Quoc V. Le, Mohammad Norouzi, Wolfgang Macherey, Maxim Krikun, Yuan Cao, Qin Gao, Klaus Macherey, Jeff Klingner, Apurva Shah, Melvin Johnson, Xiaobing Liu, Łukasz Kaiser, Stephan Gouws, Yoshikiyo Kato, Taku Kudo, Hideto Kazawa, Keith Stevens, George Kurian, Nishant Patil, Wei Wang, Cliff Young, Jason Smith, Jason Riesa, Alex Rudnick, Oriol Vinyals, Greg Corrado, Macduff Hughes, and Jeffey Dean. 2016. Google's Neural Machine Translation System: Bridging the Gap between Human and Machine Translation. *CoRR*, abs/1609.08144. Available at: http://arxiv.org/abs/1609.08144 (Accessed 11 May, 2022).

Yamada, Masaru. 2019. The impact of Google Neural Machine Translation on Post-editing by student translators. *JosTrans. The Journal of Specialised Translation* [Preprint], (31). Available at: https://www.jostrans.org/issue31/art_yamada.php (Accessed: 3 January 2021).

Zapata, Julian, Sheila Castilho, and Joss Moorkens. 2017. Translation Dictation vs. Post-editing with Cloud-based Voice Recognition: A Pilot Experiment. *Proceedings of MT Summit XVI. Vol.2 Commercial MT Users and Translators Track*, 173–186

Post-editing in Automatic Subtitling: A Subtitlers' Perspective

Alina Karakanta[1,2], Luisa Bentivogli[1], Mauro Cettolo[1], Matteo Negri[1], Marco Turchi[1]
[1]Fondazione Bruno Kessler [2]University of Trento
{akarakanta,bentivo,cettolo,negri,turchi}@fbk.eu

Abstract

Recent developments in machine translation and speech translation are opening up opportunities for computer-assisted translation tools with extended automation functions. Subtitling tools are recently being adapted for post-editing by providing automatically generated subtitles, and featuring not only machine translation, but also automatic segmentation and synchronisation. But what do professional subtitlers think of post-editing automatically generated subtitles? In this work, we conduct a survey to collect subtitlers' impressions and feedback on the use of automatic subtitling in their workflows. Our findings show that, despite current limitations stemming mainly from speech processing errors, automatic subtitling is seen rather positively and has potential for the future.

1 Introduction

Machine Translation (MT) is today widely adopted in most areas of translation and post-editing has been established as a professional practice, shaping the landscape of the translation industry. Audiovisual Translation (AVT) is one area where MT has for long found limited success (Burchardt et al., 2016). Among the main reasons are the inability of MT systems to deal with creative texts (Guerberof-Arenas and Toral, 2022) and the multimodality of the source, since the translation depends on visual, acoustic and textual elements (Taylor, 2016). For subtitling, additional challenges are posed by the formal requirements of the target: subtitles should not exceed a specific length and should be synchronised with the speech (Carroll and Ivarsson, 1998). However, recent developments in neural machine translation (NMT) and speech translation (ST) are paving the way for viable and usable (semi-)automatic solutions for subtitling. Compared to solutions providing MT for subtitling, automatic subtitling tools do not simply translate human-generated source language subtitles, but incorporate automatic transcription of the speech, MT, automatic synchronisation (spotting) and segmentation of the translated speech into subtitles. Altogether, these technologies come with the promise of reducing the human effort in the subtitling process, but, to date, automatic subtitiling has still to be put to test by the actual users.

Even though translators are fundamental for the advance of new technologies, their views are often not sufficiently considered (Guerberof-Arenas, 2013). The study of subtitlers' perceptions of the technology they are interacting with can be beneficial for all stakeholders in the AVT industry. Furthermore, the inclusion of subtitlers in the process of technological change can alleviate their resistance to adopting technologies (Cadwell et al., 2018). Developers can direct their implementation efforts in the right direction to provide user-friendly tools and interfaces (Moorkens and O'Brien, 2017), and AVT trainers can identify necessary skills for teaching and training (Bolaños-García-Escribano et al., 2021). A better understanding of subtitlers' interaction with technology can help define the rising profession of the subtitler post-editor (Bywood et al., 2017), and establish metrics and standards to protect subtitlers against dropping rates and ensure fairness (Nikolic and Bywood, 2021).

In response to the challenges brought about by

Macken, Rufener, Van den Bogaert, Daems, Tezcan, Vanroy, Fonteyne, Barrault, Costa-jussà, Kemp, Pilos, Declercq, Koponen, Forcada, Scarton, Moniz (eds.)
Proceedings of the 23rd Annual Conference of the European Association for Machine Translation, p. 259–268
Ghent, Belgium, June 2022.

increasing technologisation, in this work we conduct a survey of subtitlers' perspectives on the developing paradigm of automatic subtitling. This survey is a timely contribution to take stock of this nascent technology and its implementation in the subtitling profession from the very beginning, while setting the stage for further developments. The survey focuses on the subtitlers' user experience when post-editing automatically-generated subtitles from and into different Western European languages. It also aims at collecting feedback on the main issues and benefits of the technology, as well as on the impact of automatic subtitling on the subtitler's profession. Based on qualitative and quantitative analysis of a survey questionnaire, we provide a participant-based evaluation of automatic subtitling and a comprehensive view of subtitlers' attitudes towards this new paradigm. Our findings indicate that despite its current limitations mainly related to challenges in speech processing, automatic subtitling has potential and its benefits are already recognised by the users. Based on the received criticisms, we provide a list of recommendations for future improvements in automatic subtitling tools, which we hope will serve as a guide for technology developers. We further release the questionnaire and responses to foster replication and reproducibility in automatic subtitling.[1]

2 Related work

Automatising subtitling has recently received growing interest. One research direction aims at controlling the generation of captions and subtitles based on particular variables and properties, such as genre (Buet and Yvon, 2021), length (Lakew et al., 2019; Liu et al., 2020) or alignment between source and machine-translated subtitles (Cherry et al., 2021). Though relevant from the technological standpoint, this line of research has employed automatic metrics for the evaluation of MT and has not included subtitlers in the evaluation process.

Other studies have tested the usability of MT for subtitles by focusing on quality and productivity, mainly through the task of post-editing (PE). The human evaluation, however, did not always involve professional subtitlers. Some studies used volunteers (C. M. de Sousa et al., 2011), native speakers (Popowich et al., 2000; O'Hagan, 2003) or translators (Melero et al., 2006). Nevertheless, subtitling requires special training and skills which native speakers or translators do not necessarily possess. Larger scale evaluations involved professional subtitlers, but focused on machine translating human-generated source language subtitles. This setting has less challenges than automatic subtitling, since the source text is error-free and already compressed, while the spotting and segmentation are performed by a human. Volk et al. (2010) built an MT system between Scandinavian languages, which was tested by professional subtitlers, and collected their feedback in a non-structured way. The large-scale SUMAT project (Etchegoyhen et al., 2014) involved two professional subtitlers per language pair, who performed post-editing and rated their perceived PE effort. Matusov et al. (2019) evaluated the productivity gains of their proposed English into Spanish system with two post-editors, who were additionally asked to rank the adequacy, fluency and design of the subtitles. User feedback was collected in a non-structured way, where subtitlers commented on the post-editing process and on their perception of MT in their workflows. Lastly, Koponen et al. (2020b) performed a comprehensive human evaluation of their MT systems for Scandinavian languages. The evaluation included the collection of product and process (keystrokes) data, as well as rich feedback based on a mixed methods approach using questionnaires and semi-structured interviews.

Our present study builds upon the work by Koponen et al. (2020b) by extending the feedback collection to a larger participant sample (22 compared to 12) working in a variety of Western European language pairs. One main difference is the technology behind the generation of the target subtitles. In our study, respondents are asked to evaluate their user experience after post-editing subtitles generated through a three-step fully automatic process involving transcription, synchronisation and translation. On the contrary, in (Koponen et al., 2020b) source subtitles were first obtained by a human (subtitle template), and then machine translated and aligned to the original frames. In addition, the subtitlers used their preferred subtitling software in the PE tasks. However, as the authors admit, the subtitling tools are not designed for MT Post-editing (MTPE), and may therefore not be optimal for the task. Our work has the benefit of evaluating the PE experience using a professional tool specifically tailored for post-editing automatically generated subtitles as a case study.

[1] https://github.com/fatalinha/subtitlers-have-a-say

3 Methodology

The survey described in this paper was conducted in December 2021 and consisted in respondents filling in a questionnaire after having taken part in testing sessions of an automatic subtitling tool.

3.1 The task

In the PE task, subtitlers were required to post-edit the automatically-generated subtitles of 8 video clips. The clips were self-contained excerpts from different TV series (drama), each around 3 minutes long, amounting to a total duration of 30 minutes. TV series were selected as the material to post-edit since they are representative examples of real subtitling tasks. In addition, they contain elements which are particularly challenging both for human subtitlers and automatic systems, such as background noise, slang, overlapping speech and multi-speaker events. The original language of the series was English. Since all subtitlers edited the same clips but not all of them worked with English as source language, we used the dubbed version for subtitlers working from Spanish and Italian.

The task was performed over two consecutive days and the subtitlers took sufficient breaks between each video to avoid fatigue effects. The subtitlers worked from their personal office without any explicit time limit. Before starting the task, all participants, regardless of their previous experience with the subtitling tool, were asked to familiarise themselves with it by watching a video tutorial, in which the functionalities of the tool were explained. This setting resulted in a homogeneous task for all participants, with a sufficient duration to develop reliable judgements and a robust opinion on their user experience.

3.2 The tool

The automatic subtitling system selected for this study is integrated in a novel subtitling tool, Matesub.[2] Matesub is a typical instance of an automatic subtitling tool. It features a state-of-the-art ST system, with automatic generation of timestamps for the translated subtitles – a process called automatic spotting (or auto-spotting) – and automatic segmentation of the translated audio into subtitles.

Figure 1 shows a screenshot of the tool. The subtitlers are presented with a list of the automatically generated subtitles (upper left box) and the video on which the subtitles appear (upper right). The boxes corresponding to each subtitle appear at the bottom of the screen, superimposed on a waveform which allows the subtitler to identify parts of the video corresponding to the selected speech segments. The position and length (duration) of the boxes can be adjusted to match the beginning and the end of the spoken utterance and to accommodate the time the subtitle will appear on screen. Moreover, the tool has a quality assurance feature which raises an issue whenever pre-defined subtitling constraints are violated, for example if a subtitle is too long (length) or disappears too early (reading speed). All these elements, along with other useful features, such as keyboard shortcuts and positioning or colour settings, are implemented in most subtitling editors not offering MT integration, therefore post-editing subtitles in Matesub has the benefit of being representative of subtitlers' real working settings. The tool is free, tested in real-life use cases and is already being used by professional subtitlers.

3.3 Respondents

The respondents were professional subtitlers who took part in the post-editing task with the Matesub tool. They were recruited through a language service provider (Translated.com). Participation to the survey was voluntary and the responses were collected anonymously. Before starting the survey, participants were informed about the objective of the research, the purposes of the data collection and gave their consent. In total, 22 out of 24 subtitlers responded to the questionnaire (91% response rate). The subtitlers worked in different language pairs. Table 1 shows the number of subtitlers for each language pair. Subtitlers worked in from-English, into-English, but also non-English language pairs, which are often disregarded in MT research (Fan et al., 2021). The focus of the survey is to obtain a broad overview of subtitlers' opinions on automatic subtitling, regardless of the language-specific performance of the technology. Therefore we opted for selecting respondents so as to cover a wide range of language pairs.

3.4 Survey and questionnaire

The questionnaire was set up as an online form containing open and closed questions. It was delivered in English for all respondents and contained three parts. The first part collected factual information about the subtitlers, such as years of experience in subtitling, years of experience in MTPE

[2] `https://matesub.com/`

Figure 1: The Matesub subtitling tool.

Language pair	Subtitlers
Spanish → English	2
Spanish → Italian	3
Spanish → German	3
Italian → French	3
English → French	2
English → Spanish	3
English → Polish	3
English → Dutch	3

Table 1: Respondents per language pair.

and how often they use Matesub. Three questions focused on the working settings and the diffusion of MT in subtitling jobs. These questions asked how often their subtitling jobs involved using master templates, working directly from the video, and editing machine translated subtitles.

The second part of the questionnaire focused on the respondents' user experience with the task of PE automatically generated subtitles. We used the User Experience Questionnaire (UEQ) by Koponen et al. (2020a), a version of the UEQ of Laugwitz et al. (2008) for end-user evaluation of software products, which has been adapted to post-editing experience. This selection of questionnaire facilitates comparison of PE in automatic subtitling with the PE experience based on a different system. By using an existing questionnaire, we respond to the need for standardisation in experimental research in AVT and MT. The questionnaire contained 13 pairs of adjectives related to the post editing experience, in the form *Post-editing was... (difficult/easy, unpleasant/pleasant, stressful/relaxed, labourious/effortless, slow/fast, inefficient/efficient, boring/exciting, tedious/fun, complicated/simple, annoying/enjoyable, limiting/creative, demotivating/motivating, impractical/practical).* Since the tool features auto-spotting and automatic segmentation, we included evaluations on the quality of spotting and segmentation and the perceived effort of editing them. The responses are provided on a scale of -3 to +3, with 0 representing a neutral mid-point. As in the UEQ, average scores between -0.8 and +0.8 are considered neutral evaluations, while scores below -0.8 correspond to negative evaluations and scores above 0.8 to positive evaluations.

The last part of the questionnaire contained open questions on the quality of MT, auto-spotting and automatic segmentation, as well as the subtitlers' opinion on the benefits of automatic subtitling, whether it helps the work of subtitlers and whether they see any dangers for the profession of subtitlers from using automatic subtitling. The open questions were analysed based on thematic analysis (Braun and Clarke, 2006) using the Taguette[3] software. This analysis aimed at identifying main issues with the technologies implemented in the tool, as well as the main benefits from using automatic subtitling. The general opinion on usability is coded as positive, neutral/mixed or negative.

4 Results

4.1 Subtitlers' profiles and working settings

The respondents had on average 2.3 years of experience as subtitlers (SD=1.5, range 1-5 years) and 2.6 years of experience with MTPE (SD=2.4, range 0-10 years). In terms of working settings, there is large variability in the way subtitling is per-

[3]https://www.taguette.org/

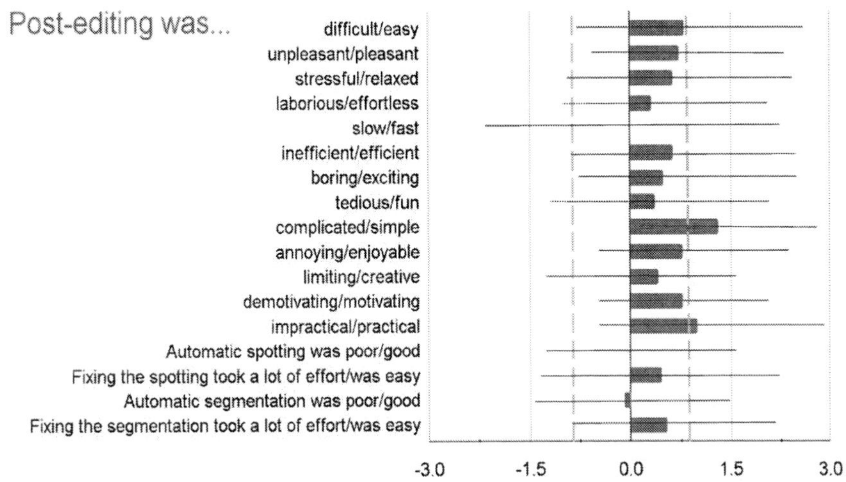

Figure 2: User experience (UX) scores. Interrupted vertical lines mark the -0.8/+0.8 threshold for neutral evaluations. Horizontal lines mark standard deviation.

formed. To the question *How often do your subtitling jobs involve master templates*, 5 subtitlers responded they never work with templates, 4 rarely, 6 sometimes and 7 often. When asked *How often do your subtitling jobs involve working directly from the video*, 3 subtitlers responded that they always work from the video, 4 often, 6 sometimes, 5 rarely and 4 never. When it comes to the question *How often do your jobs involve editing machine-translated subtitles*, 4 subtitlers mentioned that they always edit machine-translated subtitles, 3 often, 4 sometimes, 6 rarely and 5 never. This shows that there is variability in the professional conditions in subtitling when it comes to the use of tools, settings and requirements but, despite this, MT is a reality for subtitling. In addition, the responses confirm that our respondent sample covers different levels of expertise and a broad skill range.

4.2 User experience

The mean scores for the user experience across subtitlers and language pairs are shown in Figure 2. Overall, the post-editing experience can be considered as neutral to positive, with all except one mean scores leaning on the positive side of the scale. The subtitlers found the post-editing process simple and practical. Even though still in the neutral range, the lowest scores were observed for the quality of autospotting and automatic segmentation, where mean scores are close to 0.

When comparing the scores with the study of Koponen et al. (2020a), our scores are more distributed towards the positive side, even though a direct comparison of the user experience of the different subtitling systems is not the focus of this paper. It should also be noted that our sample is larger (22 respondents instead of 12) and with a larger variety in language pairs (8 compared to 4). In (Koponen et al., 2020a), the lowest average scores were found for the adjectives *laborious/effortless* and *limiting/creative*. This adjective pairs received low scores in our study too, however with *slow/fast* having the lowest score and a very large deviation. Similarly, the quality of autospotting and segmentation had lower scores than the effort to fix them. All in all, the user experience scores show that PE in automatic subtitling is a task found acceptable by the subtitlers and pointed out particular limitations, mainly related to the technical aspects of spotting and segmentation.

4.3 Subtitlers' feedback

Main issues with automatic subtitling Table 2 shows the main issues for automatic translation, auto-spotting and segmentation, as identified based on the thematic analysis of the subtitlers' responses to the open questions. For automatic translation, speech recognition errors seem to be the most common reason for errors in the translation (10 statements). Subtitlers mentioned that translation quality was highly influenced by the speaker's accent, audio quality and the speed of speech. For example, they mentioned that *muffled or fast speech, music and background noises can often confuse the AI.* Speech recognition errors have indeed been identified as the main issue for speech

Automatic translation		Autospotting		Segmentation	
Speech/audio recognition errors	10	Inaccurate (starting to early, too late)	10	Oversegmentation (too may short subtitles)	6
Lexical, punctuation, case	7	False negatives (no subtitle when speech)	5	No respect of syntactic/semantic units	5
Missing context, inconsistencies	5	False positives (subtitle when no speech)	3	No respect of constraints and guidelines	4
		Not respecting visual elements (shot changes)	2	Undersegmentation (too long subtitles)	3
Worked well	3	Worked well	6	Worked well	5

Table 2: Main issues related to automatic translation, autospotting and segmentation, and number of statements.

translation systems, regardless of whether they are direct or cascaded architectures (Bentivogli et al., 2021). The second group contained lexical errors, such as the translation of slang, idioms, colloquial expressions, figurative language and named entities, and in some cases, casing and punctuation (7 statements), with subtitlers reporting that *automatic translation still tends to be a bit too literal.* Translations out of context or words translated individually or inconsistently across the video were also mentioned as common issues (5 statements). A subtitler noted that inconsistent translation suggestions by the system *may lead the human translator to lose consistency as well.* Three subtitlers thought translation worked well.

For autospotting, lack of accuracy was the main reported issue (10 statements), since subtitlers thought that subtitles often started too early or too late and were not properly synchronised with the speaker. False negatives (no subtitle created when there is speech) and false positives (subtitles created when there is no speech) were also reported in 5 and 3 statements respectively. All these factors are related to common speech recognition issues, for example when speech is not recognised due to bad audio quality or when background noise is recognised as speech. Some subtitlers (2 statements) mentioned that automatically-spotted subtitles did not respect shot changes and other visual elements. Six subtitlers reported that autospotting worked pretty well or did not report any issues.

For automatic segmentation, oversegmentation (unnecessarily segmenting subtitles into small pieces) and undersegmentation (failing to segment too long subtitles) were mentioned in 6 and 3 statements respectively. Other issues were that the segmentation did not respect the norms of the target language because of splitting semantic/syntactic units (5 statements), and that segmentation resulted in subtitles not respecting the guidelines and length/reading speed constraints.[4] Five subtitlers affirmed that automatic segmentation worked well.

Main benefits of automatic subtitling When asked about the main benefits of automatic subtitling, *speed* was considered the main benefit by almost all subtitlers (18/22). Surprisingly, this is in contrast with the low mean score for slow/fast in the UX questionnaire. When looking into the benefits reported by subtitlers who rated the PE experience as slow (negative values for *slow/fast*), all of them mentioned that it saves time, but only on the creation of subtitle boxes and setting the timestamps. This shows the importance of not relying only on quantitative scores in participant-based studies, but complementing the judgements with quantitative explanations. Additionally, *efficiency* was noted as a benefit in 10 statements and *reduction of effort* related to technical aspects in 6 statements. Specifically, subtitlers reported that automatic subtitling *saves a lot of tedious work, creates a guideline of what needs to be translated instead of watching the whole video* and *serves as a starting template*, which, as a result, *allows focusing more on the translation* rather than having to spend time on technical aspects. The provision of *useful suggestions* was mentioned in 2 statements, related to subtitling solutions that the subtitler had not considered or to terminology and vocabulary.

General impressions for the subtitling profession To the question whether they think that automatic subtitling helps the work of subtitlers, 14 subtitlers responded positively, 5 gave neutral/mixed statements and 3 claimed that in most cases automatic subtitling does not help. The subtitlers who responded neutrally mentioned as concerns that the quality depends on the language,

[4]Netflix guidelines: https://partnerhelp.netflixstudios.com/hc/en-us/articles/360051554394-Timed-Text-Style-Guide-Subtitle-Timing-Guidelines

audio quality, and that it may be useful only for some applications (e.g. *template* creation, *other audiovisual products, such as online conferences or courses, documentaries*).

When asked whether they see any possible danger to the profession because of automatic subtitling, 8 subtitlers mentioned they see no dangers at all, 8 subtitlers saw no dangers for the time being, given the current state of the technology and its low diffusion, while 9 subtitlers identified some type of danger. Possible dangers were the loss in the quality of the final subtitles (4), dropping rates (2) and having less or no work if clients select cheaper, automatic options (5). Another danger identified was the improper application of the technology (3 statements), where subtitlers considered that the profession is not at risk only as long as a human is involved in the final phase.

5 Discussion

This study focused on subtitlers' user experience and perspectives on the task of post-editing automatically generated subtitles. Our findings suggest a neutral to positive experience. Even though there are those who still see no benefits from this new technology, automatic subtitling was welcomed with enthusiasm by many subtitlers, as an aid to save time and effort. As with studies on MTPE experience (Guerberof-Arenas, 2013; Bundgaard, 2017), subtitlers have expressed disfavour towards automatic subtitling in respect to technological flaws, but also acknowledged its positive aspects and expected technology to shape their profession in the near future. As for the dangers to the profession, most criticisms were not rooted in the fear of being outperformed by automatic systems, but rather in the effect of technology on the final product and market consequences (Vieira, 2020). The positive aspects of technology can only be appreciated when combined with respectful and ethical professional and market practices.

Previous work reporting feedback of subtitlers focused on a setting where MT was applied to human-generated subtitles. The views of the subtitlers involved did not lead to auspicious conclusions in favour of the use of MT in subtitling. In spite of encouraging automatic evaluation scores, subtitlers were cautious in reporting productivity gains in (Volk et al., 2010), while in (Etchegoyhen et al., 2014) PE experience was rated as rather negative (2.37 on a 1-5 scale), with MT being useful only for simple and short sentences. An increase in productivity for simple sentences was reported in (Matusov et al., 2019), where the two subtitlers rated their experience as fair. In (Koponen et al., 2020a) the participants did not find PE particularly difficult but characterised it as negative or limiting and did not think MTPE increased productivity. Similar criticisms were reported for MT quality in our study, with MT described as too literal, unable to properly translate spoken and figurative language. However, most subtitlers acknowledged that automatic subtitling makes their work faster and more efficient, especially when compared to *old-style subtitling*. The difference of our study compared to studies of MT for subtitling is the automatisation not only of the translation, but also of the technical aspects of spotting and segmentation. Subtitlers recognised the importance of automatising these aspects, which are often characterised as tiresome and dull. By not focusing only on the translation but the automation of the technical aspects, automatic subtitling allows subtitlers to spare time and effort on the tedious part of the work (spotting and segmentation) and unleash their creativity in adjusting the final text.

Our study aimed at providing a broad view of subtitlers' perspectives, by complementing quantitative scores with open questions, attempting to cover several language pairs and a range of subtitler profiles. However, we acknowledge that the findings should be interpreted with some caution. Questionnaire-based studies have a context-bound nature and may be affected by factors such as the system (quality, language), the participants (age, familiarity with technology) and the setting (Tuominen, 2018). Therefore, some limitations should be considered when drawing conclusions.

Firstly, responses and user experience scores may have been affected by the language pair, due to differences in the subtitling quality depending on the ASR and MT performance, despite keeping all other settings (videos, instructions) equal. Still, we opted for not reporting results separately for each language pair, since the sample size per pair (2-3) would be too small to draw robust and generalizable conclusions on a per-language basis. Second, even though we attempted to include a broad range of professional subtitler profiles, the group is not necessarily representative of the subtitlers' general population. For example, the respondents' age, a variable not collected in our survey, may affect their technological acceptance. Moreover, their experience in subtitling, template translation and MTPE varies. We found in statistical tests that the only variable affecting the user experience is MTPE experience. Subtitlers with less experience ($<=$ 2 years) had significantly higher user experience scores than the more experienced ones.[5] It is possible that experts, already being used to a certain level of MT output quality and to their preferred interfaces, are less willing to change tasks and tools, while novices, having less consolidated working practices, are more open and less critical against new interfaces and workflows. Accepting to take part in a task involving automatic subtitling already means the subtitlers were willing, curious or even familiar with the technology, and therefore may have been positively inclined towards automatisation in subtitling, contrary to many AVT professionals (Audiovisual Translators Europe, 2021).

Lastly, the interface used in PE has a great influence on user experience. We selected Matesub as a typical instance of an automatic subtitling tool. However, the generalisability to other tools is not guaranteed. In an attempt to test whether previous experience with Matesub had an effect on user experience, we separated the respondents in two groups based on their responses to the question *How often do you use Matesub in your subtitling jobs*: regular users (often, sometimes) and occasional (never, rarely). We found that familiarity with the tool did not have an effect on the average user experience scores.[6] This shows that the tool is user-friendly, with a steep learning curve, and does not require extensive training. Less user-friendly tools may negatively affect the post-editing experience. Despite these limitations, this study presents a screenshot of the current state of the quickly evolving technology, necessary to drive implementation efforts in the right direction.

5.1 Recommendations for improvement

Our findings have identified some limitations of current automatic subtitling systems. Based on the subtitlers' feedback, we present a list of suggestions for improving automatic subtitling tools in a direction that benefits the user experience. The suggestions are listed in order of priority.

[5]Novices (N=14, M=1.0, SD=0.7) vs Experts (N=8, M=$-$0.4, SD=1.1). Based on an equal-variance independent samples t-test: ($t(20) = 3.82, p = .001$)

[6]Regular (N=14, M=0.6, SD=1.2) vs Occasional (N=8, M=0.4, SD=0.9). ($t(20) = 0.42, p = .679$)

• **Improving autospotting and segmentation**. The main benefit of automatic subtitling according to the subtitlers was eliminating tedious work and leaving more space for creativity. Given that many criticisms were addressed to the quality of autospotting and segmentation, improvements in the automation of technical aspects are a priority. Except for improving the accuracy of autospotting through enhanced audio processing and a more syntactically-informed segmentation, interaction with these elements could become more user-friendly. For example, it could be useful to implement interactive features such as automatic adjustment of subtitle boxes to match length and reading speed constraints after subtitlers translate or finish editing one subtitle.

• **Improved audio pre-processing**. Most problems in the translation, autospotting and segmentation stemmed from the segmentation of the audio. This is an open problem in speech processing (Gaido et al., 2021; Tsiamas et al., 2022); audio segmentation is typically approached by breaking the audio on speaker silences, considered as a proxy of clause boundaries, and not on syntactic information. A syntax-unaware segmentation is responsible for translations out of context and the issues in segmentation (over-undersegmentation, no respect of syntactic units). In addition, the reported cases of false positives/false negatives in autospotting (see Table 2) indicate that voice activity detection technologies should be improved to properly distinguish speech from noise.

• **Improving in-video consistency**. Consistency of MT suggestions is important for easily spotting errors and for avoiding repetitive corrections. Consistency can be improved through adaptive MT (Biçici and Yuret, 2011) or document-level MT (Lopes et al., 2020).[7] Another direction could be the integration of external resources, such as termbases and translation memories. These aids have passed the test of time and are usually the first requirement of users before overshooting with MT solutions (Audiovisual Translators Europe, 2021).

• **User experience vs. automatic metrics**. Punctuation and casing was reported as an issue for automatic translation. However, WER, the metric used to evaluate ASR systems, is normally computed in a case/punctuation insensitive way. Casing and punctuation cannot be derived directly

[7]However, it should be noted that (Koponen et al., 2020b) found no preference for document-level MT compared to sentence-level MT in subtitling.

from the audio and therefore these errors are traditionally considered as less relevant by the scientific community. On the contrary, in the context of automatic subtitling they must be weighed appropriately. This points out the need for task-specific evaluation metrics, which take into account elements that shape user experience.

• **Incorporation of elements from the visual modality**. Since subtitling is highly multimodal and intersemiotic, ignoring elements from the visual modality can result to errors. Some features from the visual modality are already integrated in many (non-MT) tools, e.g. marking of shot changes. Another useful feature could be the recognition of on-screen text.

6 Conclusions

In this work we presented findings on subtitlers' user experience and perspectives when post-editing automatically generated subtitles, based on a survey questionnaire. Subtitlers' experience was marked as neutral to positive. Thematic analysis of the open questions showed that the main issues of automatic subtitling stem from failures in speech recognition and pre-processing, which result in error propagation, translations out of context, inaccuracies in auto-spotting and suboptimal segmentation. However, subtitlers acknowledge the positive sides of the technology, which are speed and reduction of effort, especially related to the technical aspects, as well as the provision of useful suggestions. We conclude that, despite current limitations, automatic subtitling tools can be beneficial for subtitlers, as long as improvements consider subtitlers' opinions, and ethical and professional standards are respected. We expect that as automatic subtitling tools mushroom, larger studies will be needed to explore different variables and monitor the progress in automatic subtitling.

Acknowledgements

We kindly thank all the subtitlers who took part in the survey, and Anna Matamala and María Eugenia Larreina Morales for their useful feedback on questionnaire analysis.

References

Audiovisual Translators Europe. 2021. AVTE Machine Translation Manifesto. https://avteurope.eu/wp-content/uploads/2021/09/Machine-Translation-Manifesto_ENG.pdf. Last accessed: 31/03/2022.

Bentivogli, Luisa, Mauro Cettolo, Marco Gaido, Alina Karakanta, Alberto Martinelli, Matteo Negri, and Marco Turchi. 2021. Cascade versus Direct Speech Translation: Do the Differences Still Make a Difference? In *Proceedings of the 59th Annual Meeting of the Association for Computational Linguistics and the 11th International Joint Conference on Natural Language Processing*, pages 2873–2887, Online, August. Association for Computational Linguistics.

Biçici, Ergun and Deniz Yuret. 2011. Instance Selection for Machine Translation using Feature Decay Algorithms. In *Proceedings of the 6th Workshop on Statistical Machine Translation*, pages 272–283, Edinburgh. Association for Computational Linguistics.

Bolaños-García-Escribano, Alejandro, Jorge Díaz-Cintas, and Serenella Massidda. 2021. Latest advancements in audiovisual translation education. *The Interpreter and Translator Trainer*, 15(1):1–12.

Braun, Virginia and Victoria Clarke. 2006. Using thematic analysis in psychology. *Qualitative Research in Psychology*, 3(2):77–101.

Buet, François and François Yvon. 2021. Toward Genre Adapted Closed Captioning. In *Interspeech 2021*, pages 4403–4407, Brno (virtual), Czech Republic, August. ISCA.

Bundgaard, Kristine. 2017. Translator Attitudes towards Translator-Computer Interaction - Findings from a Workplace Study. *HERMES - Journal of Language and Communication in Business*, 56:125–144.

Burchardt, Aljoscha, Arle Lommel, Lindsay Bywood, Kim Harris, and Maja Popović. 2016. Machine translation quality in an audiovisual context. *Target*, 28(2):206–221.

Bywood, Lindsay, Panayota Georgakopoulou, and Thierry Etchegoyhen. 2017. Embracing the threat: machine translation as a solution for subtitling. *Perspectives*, 25(3):492–508.

C. M. de Sousa, Sheila, Wilker Aziz, and Lucia Specia. 2011. Assessing the Post-Editing Effort for Automatic and Semi-Automatic Translations of DVD Subtitles. In *Proceedings of the International Conference Recent Advances in Natural Language Processing 2011*, pages 97–103, Hissar, Bulgaria. Association for Computational Linguistics.

Cadwell, Patrick, Sharon O'Brien, and Carlos S. C. Teixeira. 2018. Resistance and accommodation: factors for the (non-) adoption of machine translation among professional translators. *Perspectives*, 26(3):301–321.

Carroll, Mary and Jan Ivarsson. 1998. *Code of Good Subtitling Practice*. Simrishamn: TransEdit.

Cherry, Colin, Naveen Arivazhagan, Dirk Padfield, and Maxim Krikun. 2021. Subtitle Translation as Markup Translation. In *Proceedings of Interspeech 2021*, pages 2237–2241.

Etchegoyhen, Thierry, Lindsay Bywood, Mark Fishel, Panayota Georgakopoulou, Jie Jiang, Gerard van Loenhout, Arantza del Pozo, Mirjam Sepesy Maučec, Anja Turner, and Martin Volk. 2014. Machine Translation for Subtitling: A Large-Scale Evaluation. In *Proceedings of the 9th International Conference on Language Resources and Evaluation (LREC)*, pages 46–53, May.

Fan, Angela, Shruti Bhosale, Holger Schwenk, Zhiyi Ma, Ahmed El-Kishky, Siddharth Goyal, Mandeep Baines, Onur Celebi, Guillaume Wenzek, Vishrav Chaudhary, Naman Goyal, Tom Birch, Vitaliy Liptchinsky, Sergey Edunov, Edouard Grave, Michael Auli, and Armand Joulin. 2021. Beyond English-Centric Multilingual Machine Translation. *Journal of Machine Learning Research*, pages 1–48.

Gaido, Marco, Matteo Negri, Mauro Cettolo, and Marco Turchi. 2021. Beyond voice activity detection: Hybrid audio segmentation for direct speech translation. In *Proceedings of The Fourth International Conference on Natural Language and Speech Processing*, pages 55–62, Trento, Italy. Association for Computational Linguistics.

Guerberof-Arenas, Ana and Antonio Toral. 2022. Creativity in translation: Machine translation as a constraint for literary texts. *Translation Spaces*.

Guerberof-Arenas, Ana. 2013. What do professional translators think about post-editing? *JoSTrans - The journal of specialised translation*, 19.

Koponen, Maarit, Umut Sulubacak, Kaisa Vitikainen, and Jörg Tiedemann. 2020a. MT for subtitling: Investigating professional translators' user experience and feedback. In *Proceedings of 1st Workshop on Post-Editing in Modern-Day Translation*, pages 79–92, Virtual. AMTA.

Koponen, Maarit, Umut Sulubacak, Kaisa Vitikainen, and Jörg Tiedemann. 2020b. MT for subtitling: User evaluation of post-editing productivity. In *Proceedings of the 22nd Annual Conference of the European Association for Machine Translation*, pages 115–124, Lisboa, Portugal, November. European Association for Machine Translation.

Lakew, Surafel Melaku, Mattia Di Gangi, and Marcello Federico. 2019. Controlling the Output Length of Neural Machine Translation. In *Proceedings of the 16th International Workshop on Spoken Language Translation, (IWSLT)*.

Laugwitz, Bettina, Theo Held, and Martin Schrepp. 2008. Construction and evaluation of a user experience questionnaire. In Holzinger, Andreas, editor, *HCI and Usability for Education and Work*, pages 63–76, Berlin, Heidelberg. Springer.

Liu, Danni, Jan Niehues, and Gerasimos Spanakis. 2020. Adapting end-to-end speech recognition for readable subtitles. In *Proceedings of the 17th International Conference on Spoken Language Translation*, pages 247–256. Association for Computational Linguistics.

Lopes, António, M. Amin Farajian, Rachel Bawden, Michael Zhang, and André F. T. Martins. 2020. Document-level neural MT: A systematic comparison. In *Proceedings of the 22nd Annual Conference of the European Association for Machine Translation*, pages 225–234, Lisboa, Portugal. European Association for Machine Translation.

Matusov, Evgeny, Patrick Wilken, and Yota Georgakopoulou. 2019. Customizing Neural Machine Translation for Subtitling. In *Proceedings of the Fourth Conference on Machine Translation (Volume 1: Research Papers)*, pages 82–93, Florence, Italy, August. Association for Computational Linguistics.

Melero, Maite, Antoni Oliver, and Toni Badia. 2006. Automatic Multilingual Subtitling in the eTITLE Project. In *Proceedings of ASLIB Translating and the Computer 28*, November.

Moorkens, Joss and Sharon O'Brien. 2017. Assessing User Interface Needs of Post-Editors of Machine Translation. *Human Issues in Translation Technology: The IATIS Yearbook*, pages 109–130.

Nikolic, Kristijan and Lindsay Bywood. 2021. Audiovisual Translation: The Road Ahead. *Journal of Audiovisual Translation*, 4(1):50–70, Apr.

O'Hagan, Minako. 2003. Can language technology respond to the subtitler's dilemma? - a preliminary study. In *Proceedings of the 25th International Conference on Translation and the Computer*.

Popowich, Fred, Paul McFetridge, Davide Turcato, and Janine Toole. 2000. Machine Translation of Closed Captions. *Machine Translation*, pages 311–341.

Taylor, Christopher. 2016. The multimodal approach in audiovisual translation. *Target*, 2(28), December.

Tsiamas, Ioannis, Gerard I Gállego, José AR Fonollosa, and Marta R Costa-jussà. 2022. Shas: Approaching optimal segmentation for end-to-end speech translation. *arXiv e-prints*, pages arXiv–2202.

Tuominen, Tiina. 2018. Multi-method research - reception in context. In Giovanni, Elena Di and Yves Gambier, editors, *Reception Studies and Audiovisual Translation*, volume 141, pages 69–90. BTL.

Vieira, Lucas Nunes. 2020. Automation anxiety and translators. *Translation Studies*, 13(1):1–21.

Volk, Martin, Rico Sennrich, Christian Hardmeier, and Frida Tidström. 2010. Machine Translation of TV Subtitles for Large Scale Production. In Zhechev, Ventsislav, editor, *Proceedings of the Second Joint EM+/CNGL Workshop "Bringing MT to the User: Research on Integrating MT in the Translation Industry (JEC'10)*, pages 53–62, Denver.

Working with Pre-translated Texts: Preliminary Findings from a Survey on Post-editing and Revision Practices in Swiss Corporate In-house Language Services

Sabrina Girletti
FTI/TIM, University of Geneva
Switzerland
sabrina.girletti@unige.ch

Abstract

With the arrival of neural machine translation, the boundaries between revision and post-editing (PE) have started to blur (Koponen et al., 2020). To shed light on current professional practices and provide new pedagogical perspectives, we set up a survey-based study to investigate how PE and revision are carried out in professional settings. We received 86 responses from corporate translators working at 23 different corporate in-house language services in Switzerland. Although the differences between the two activities seem to be clear for in-house linguists, our findings show that they tend to use the same reading strategies when working with human-translated and machine-translated texts.

1 Introduction

In recent years, quality improvements achieved by the latest-generation machine translation systems have put machine translation (MT) under the spotlight. Results of recent language industry surveys (ELIS, 2022; Pielmeier and Lommel, 2019) show that language service providers (LSPs) identify MT post-editing (PE) as one of the most requested services and as an opportunity to increase productivity and improve profit margins. Therefore, many of them have implemented MT or plan to do so as soon as possible.

In Switzerland, a multilingual country where many companies have their own in-house translation service, the situation is no different. Many LSPs have already added MT to their workflows and started offering PE among their services, together with translation and revision.

Since neural MT (NMT) output more closely resembles human translations than machine-translated texts (Martikainen, 2019; Yamada, 2019), correcting it is often considered more similar to a *revision*. Recent work by Koponen et al. (2020) has paved the way for studying the relationship between these two activities whose boundaries are "starting to blur" (2020:3).

To shed light on current practices and provide new perspectives for the training of both students and experienced translators who work with MT, we set up a survey-based study to investigate how PE and revision are carried out in professional settings. In particular, we chose to focus on Switzerland-based corporate in-house language services (CILS), as this cohort is underrepresented in language industry surveys and has been scarcely investigated compared to institutional (Cadwell et al., 2017; Riondel, 2021; Rossi and Chevrot, 2019) and freelance translators (Gaspari et al., 2015; Zaretskaya, 2015).

Our study consisted of two questionnaires, available in four languages: the first questionnaire (Q1) was aimed at language service directors and project managers and contained questions about the structure and workflow of the language service. The second questionnaire (Q2) was aimed at language service employees who translate, revise and post-edit texts. It included questions about their workflows, strategies and attitudes towards PE and revision. In the present article, we will delve into the design and the results of the Q2[1].

The aim of this questionnaire was to investigate

[1]The questionnaire can be obtained from the author upon request

Macken, Rufener, Van den Bogaert, Daems, Tezcan, Vanroy, Fonteyne, Barrault, Costa-jussà, Kemp, Pilos, Declercq, Koponen, Forcada, Scarton, Moniz (eds.)
Proceedings of the 23rd Annual Conference of the European Association for Machine Translation, p. 269–278
Ghent, Belgium, June 2022.

how corporate in-house linguists carry out revision and PE in terms of (i) reading strategies – whether they read the source or target text first – and (ii) overall strategies, *e.g.* whether they follow specific parameters or guidelines. Additionally, we also investigated whether linguists apply the same strategies when revising texts that have been translated or post-edited by another person. To the best of our knowledge, this is the first survey explicitly comparing revision and PE practices of professional translators in Switzerland.

The remainder of the paper is structured as follows: Section 2 details previous survey-based studies that dealt with revision and PE practices, respectively, as well as studies on similar topics conducted in Switzerland. Section 3 describes the survey design, while results are analysed in Section 4. Section 5 includes some final remarks and pathways for future research.

2 Previous studies

Several researchers have used country-specific surveys to investigate revision practices. In Belgium, Robert (2008) launched two small-scale surveys (48 and 21 responses, respectively) among translation agencies to establish which translation revision procedures and revision methods (revising on paper and/or on-screen) are the most used. She found that while revisers use different procedures, most compare source and target texts to make corrections and then reread the target text one last time. Results also suggest that revision is mainly carried out on screen.

This latter aspect was also included in a survey-based study conducted by Scocchera (2015, 2017) in the Italian publishing sector. The study included two questionnaires: one for translators to investigate self-revision practices (55 participants) and one for revisers to investigate other revision practices (25 participants). Results of the latter show that revision is mainly carried out on-screen, but the choice of the medium depends on various factors and on-screen is preferred if the translation needs many corrections. Regarding revision methods, 60% of revisers do not read the whole source text before starting to revise, primarily due to "lack of time and cost-effectiveness" (2017:13). Instead, participants claim they mostly compare source text and target text segment by segment.

In Denmark, Rasmussen and Schjoldager (2011) surveyed 24 translation companies about their revision policies and conducted 13 follow-up interviews with survey respondents and in-house revisers in five of these companies. Collected data suggest that not all texts are revised. This depends on different factors, including the translator who translated the text, assignment difficulty, text type/genre, intended use, and customer. The most used procedure is monolingual revision followed by a comparative revision or vice-versa. However, interviews reveal that revision is rarely fully comparative. Most companies do have revision guidelines, but not in written form.

In Austria, Schnierer (2020) surveyed translation companies to determine whether their revision practices complied with the former translation standard EN15038 (currently replaced by ISO 17100). She found that two out of six certified companies do not systematically revise translations, although the standard requires this. Regarding revision methods, all companies report comparing the translation with the source text. In contrast, only one uncertified company reported performing monolingual revisions of the target text (referring to the source text if needed). Five out of six certified companies use revision parameters, while this applies only to six out of thirteen uncertified companies.

Lastly, Hernández Morin (2009b) conducted a survey among translation practitioners (115 respondents, primarily freelance translators) to find out about revision practices and perceptions of revision in France. Two of her questions dealt with the revision of automatically pre-translated segments, *i.e.*, those coming from a CAT tool and machine translation, respectively. 69% of respondents state that they do not work with machine-translated texts, 23% claim they revise those texts in-depth, and 6% revise the text to ensure just its overall comprehension. In the author's thesis (Hernández Morin, 2009a), both processes are referred to as *post-editing*. Therefore, it is not clear whether respondents refer to post-editing or actual revision practices.

When it comes to defining how the task is carried out, studies of revision practice outperform those on PE practice. In participant-oriented studies, PE discourse most often concerns adoption rates and attitudes toward the task (Gaspari et al., 2015; Guerberof Arenas, 2013; Läubli and Orrego-Carmona, 2017; Vieira, 2020; Zaretskaya, 2015). For instance, in a survey of the state of the linguist supply chain, researchers at Common Sense Advisory (Pielmeier and O'Mara, 2020) reported that, out of 6,997 respondents, 55% use MT on most projects or whether the customer requests it.

Some studies focused on salaried translators as the target population (Cadwell et al., 2017; Rossi and Chevrot, 2019) but did not investigate how MT was introduced and integrated or how PE was carried out in terms of reading strategies, *i.e.*, which text – source or target – is read first.

To the best of our knowledge, the only study that deals with this topic is the one by Ginovart Cid (2021), who surveyed European LSPs, university lecturers and linguists about their MTPE practices and training protocols. Results of the questionnaire sent to PE educators – detailed in Ginovart Cid and Colominas (2020) – show that 49% of respondents do not provide their students with any advice on whether the source or the target segment should be read first, while 33% of instructors advise reading the source text first. It must be noted that the question was asked in a close-ended, single-answer format. Therefore, other possibilities, *e.g.* reading the whole source or target text before starting to post-edit, are not explored. The question on reading strategies was also included in the questionnaire addressed to professional linguists, but the results are not discussed in any publication to date.

2.1 The Swiss context

We found only a few country-specific, participant-oriented studies that deal with revision or post-editing in the Swiss context.

A recent study by Riondel (2021) pointed out similarities and differences between revision policies of two cohorts of salaried translators. The researcher conducted 20 semi-structured interviews in a sizeable intergovernmental organisation and a medium-sized language department of the Swiss Confederation. He found that while revision is mainly carried out on screen in the former context, at the Confederation, texts are often printed before revision. In both settings, revisers apply a complete bilingual revision, but those who work at the intergovernmental organisation also consider other types of revision (*e.g.* spot check for outsourced translations). Unfortunately, the article does not deal with revision strategies more in-depth.

We could not find any studies on PE practices in Switzerland, but we found a handful of studies on MT adoption and attitudes towards MT and PE. For instance, Yuste (2002) carried out a survey among Swiss LSPs about their use and perception of translation technology. The author concluded that there was "no overall interest in MT in the Swiss translation arena" at the time of writing. However, we are unable to further comment on these findings since, in the electronic version of the paper, the section describing collected data is missing.

More recently, Porro Rodríguez et al. (2017) conducted a survey on the use of machine translation and post-editing in Swiss-based LSPs (deliberately excluding CILS). Results revealed that, in 2015, only two out of 16 LSPs were using MTPE in their workflows. Furthermore, most respondents were not considering using MTPE in the future or were unsure about it.

With the advent of neural machine translation, the Swiss translation landscape has changed significantly, as revealed in a recent study carried out by Selinger (2020), who focused on the use and perception of MT among translation professionals and non-professionals (170 and 115 respondents, respectively). Data show that almost 40% of professionals use MT as a starting point for translations into their mother tongue. The results of the questionnaires were complemented by interviews with five LSPs who had already integrated or were integrating MT in their workflows. These respondents expressed some concerns regarding the confidentiality of data. Therefore, they were using or testing either a customised system or DeepL Pro. The participants report a general positive attitude of their in-house translators towards MT. Regarding how MT is used, participants clarify that MT suggestions are fully integrated into their CAT tools or made available to internal customers as a self-service translation tool. However, the study did not include any questions on how PE is carried out.

As the review of existing literature pointed out, while there have been several surveys on revision procedures, PE procedures have been only scarcely investigated. Most importantly, reading strategies in revision and PE have never been studied with a contrastive approach in a context where both activities are carried out. Our research will try to fill this gap.

3 Methods

3.1 Sampling

The target population of our study consists of professional linguists working at CILS who use MT in their professional workflows.

We used various sampling and dissemination methods to identify Switzerland-based companies with an internal translation department. Firstly, we contacted via email language service directors of corporate in-house services that we directly knew; we asked them to participate in the survey and to help us recruit new participants (snowball sampling). Secondly, we used the research function on LinkedIn, looking for terms such as "translator", "language services", and "project managers", restricting the research area to Switzerland. Thirdly, we compiled a list of private and semi-private companies serving the Swiss public at large, including banks, insurance companies, and retail outlets. We discarded from this list all the companies whose website was not translated into a different language and then contacted prospective participants using their generic email address or through a contact form on their websites. A link to participate in the survey (Q1)[2] was sent by email[3] to the language service directors or project managers who agreed to take part in the study.

Questionnaire Q2 was distributed to in-house linguists working at CILS who use MT in production (n=26). Dissemination was mainly handled by CILS's directors or project managers who filled out the first questionnaire. In most cases, these respondents included the researcher when sending the email invitation to their employees or colleagues, enabling the researcher to send a reminder after some time. In the emails, it was specified that participation in the study was voluntary and anonymous. This information was also clearly stated on the first page of the online questionnaire, which contained a consent form.

The questionnaire was hosted on the LimeSurvey platform and was made accessible from November 15th, 2021, until February 16th, 2022. Depending on respondents' answers, the questionnaire included up to 58 questions, but not all were mandatory.

3.2 Survey structure

The questionnaire was structured in five sections: Section A (*Respondent's profile*) contained demographic questions, such as age and mother tongue of the respondent, years of translation experience and years of employment in the CILS. This section also included two questions about how often respondents perform revision and PE – to ensure that participants carry out these activities in their workflow.

Sections B (*Revision*) and C (*Post-editing*) contained two symmetric sets of questions related to different aspects of the two activities, such as the primary reading strategies used by respondents when revising and post-editing.

Section D (*Post-editing, revision and overall strategies*) comprised three questions on the relationship between revision and PE: whether participants used the same strategies when revising human-translated texts and post-editing MT content or when revising texts that had been previously translated or post-edited. The third question asked whether the introduction of MT in the workflow brought about any changes in the way revision was carried out. Participants were encouraged to comment on their answers.

Lastly, Section E (*Satisfaction*) focused on respondents' satisfaction in performing translation, revision and post-editing. The results of this section will not be shown in the present article due to space constraints.

3.3 Participants' profile

The most represented mother tongue is French (44% of respondents), followed by Italian (24%). German ranks third (17%), while English is the mother tongue of 9% of respondents. Two respondents identified themselves as bilingual, while two others indicated different mother tongues.

Age is well distributed across ranges and per mother tongue, except for the most extreme categories (18-29 and 60+, including young linguists or translators approaching retirement, respectively). Translation experience ranged from two to 36 years, with an average of 15.8 years and

[2]Analysis of the information gathered through questionnaire Q1 falls outside the scope of the present article. Nevertheless, where necessary, relevant data will be mentioned.

[3]In some cases, this email invitation contained also the link to questionnaire Q2, with clear instructions on the applicability criteria of this second questionnaire. However, we also received some responses from companies who answered "not yet" to the question "Do you use MT in your production workflow?".

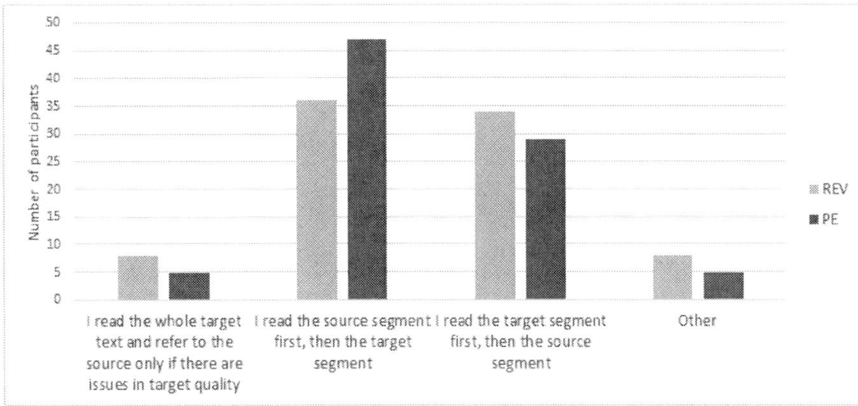

Figure 1: When revising/post-editing, what is your main reading strategy?

a median of 14.5 years. Overall, participants have been working at their respective CILS for an average of nine years and a median of seven years.

All participants indicated they revise texts and use MT in their workflows, but the proportion of those who revise almost daily is slightly higher than those who post-edit texts nearly every day (79% versus 72%, respectively).

While 66% of respondents already had some revision experience, most participants (80%) started PE at their current company. This result is expected and in line with the recent introduction of MT in many Swiss CILS.

Most respondents declare having attended a PE training session (53%), while only 41% of revisers have been trained to carry out revision jobs. Since PE has been introduced only recently in the workflow of surveyed CILS, it was necessary to provide linguists with some initial training to carry out the process. Regarding revision training, these findings are in line with those of Scocchera (2015), who found that 72% of revisers working in the Italian publishing sector had not received any revision training.

4 Results

We initially received 107 responses, but we had to discard 18 of them for various reasons. Five responses came from linguists who do not perform revision or PE in their daily jobs and were incomplete. Six responses came from linguists working at companies who did not yet use MT in their production workflow. Seven responses could not be traced back to any company that filled out the first questionnaire; this happened because we had only partial control over how the questionnaire was circulated (as explained in section 3.1). Additionally, five valid responses were incomplete, but we decided to keep those who at least completed the first four sections of our survey (n=2).

In total, we retained 86 valid responses from 23 Swiss CILS. If we consider the number of in-house linguists indicated by each company in questionnaire Q1, we can calculate a response rate of 44%. However, we cannot compare this response rate with that of other surveys focusing on similar topics, mainly because we decided to address a specific group of stakeholders and focus on a geographical area that is scarcely represented.

On average, 50% of linguists in each company have responded to the questionnaire Q2. We did not receive any responses from linguists working in three out of 26 companies who currently use MT in production (as indicated in questionnaire Q1).

4.1 Reading strategies

As shown in Figure 1, the most used reading strategy is to proceed segment by segment, starting from the source text. This is slightly more common in PE (approx. 55% of participants) than in revision (42%). The second most used strategy is the opposite one, in which linguists start by reading the target segment (approx. 34% in PE and 40% in revision). Only a few respondents claim to read the whole target text while referring to the source in case of issues, especially when revising. Five respondents claim to use this strategy during PE. However, reading only the target text in PE is a dangerous practice since omissions are not infrequent in neural MT, and the fluency of NMT output can be misleading (Castilho et al., 2017).

A few respondents claim to use other reading strategies when revising and post-editing. From a closer inspection of their comments, we understood that revisers' strategies depend on different factors, such as the text type, the translator who carried out the translation or the customer who requested it. One respondent described his/her strategy, which we found to match significantly with our first-listed strategy (reading the whole target text and referring to the source in case of issues or to check numbers and tags). One reviser uses a two-step revision strategy (monolingual proofreading followed by bilingual revision), while another one reads the source and target in parallel.

Regarding PE, one respondent is unable to provide us with an answer since he/she only uses MT as a further suggestion in the CAT tool. Two respondents mentioned they vary their strategies depending on the text, while two others read the source and target in parallel. Although the latter did not clarify whether they start with the source or target segment, we note that this strategy enables linguists to quickly shift attention between the source and the pre-translated text. Checking source and target text in chunks instead of reading the whole segment could benefit linguists' text comprehension, especially in case of longer sentences or complex syntactic structures.

In an additional question, we asked our participants whether they vary their strategies depending on the text or other factors. The answer was positive for approx. 63% and 37% of revisers and post-editors, respectively. Therefore, in PE, linguists tend to apply the same reading strategy more often than in revision. Criteria often cited by revisers to vary their preferred reading strategy are text type, time constraints and the translator who translated the text. In contrast, post-editors mention text type, text complexity, target audience, text length, and PE level (light or full) to be applied.

Studies on the influence of different reading strategies on post-editors' and revisers' efficiency are extremely scarce. Volkart et al. (forthcoming) found that students who start by reading the source text during PE introduce slightly more preferential changes than those who begin by reading the target. In the same study, the authors found no significant influence of the strategy on the ratio of corrected errors or on the time spent on the PE task. In revision, Ipsen and Dam (2016) found that revisers who start by reading the target text detect more errors than those who read the source text first. However, since the time to complete the task was not taken into account, it is unclear whether this procedure is faster than the opposite one. These findings would suggest that if linguists had to choose the same reading strategy to carry out revision and PE jobs, then reading the target text first would probably be the best option. However, this does not correspond to what the majority of our professional linguists does in practice.

It should be noted that the above-mentioned studies were both conducted with translation students or recent graduates, and did not assess texts' final quality. Therefore, it remains to be clarified whether – and to what extent – using the same reading strategy in PE and revision could affect professional linguists' performance.

4.2 Overall strategies

4.2.1 Revising vs post-editing

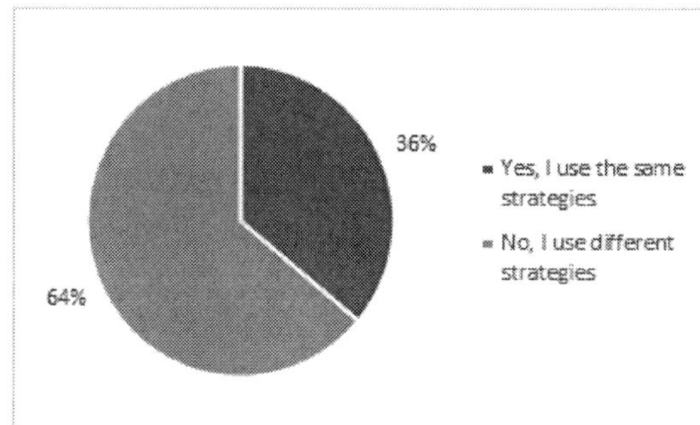

Figure 2: Do you use the same overall strategies when revising human-translated texts and post-editing machine-translated texts?

Most respondents (64%) claim to apply different strategies when working with human-translated or machine-translated texts (Figure 2). Comments show that respondents trust MT less than human colleagues. Linguists are aware that humans and machines do not commit the same error; therefore, they are much more careful when working with MT than when they revise human-translated texts.

When analysing responses on reading strategies (Section 4.1), however, we found that around 65% of linguists reported using the same strategy during revision and PE. This could suggest that, although respondents claim to be aware of the differences between the two activities, in practice, they behave in the same way when revising and post-editing, at least regarding reading strategies.

4.2.2 Parameters and guidelines

We asked our respondents whether they use any revision parameters (Mossop, 2020) or PE guidelines (Hu and Cadwell, 2016) during revision and PE, respectively. Results show that revision mainly follows specific parameters (72% of respondents), while only slightly more than half of respondents follow any PE guidelines (51%). These figures show that, compared to PE, revision is an established practice with a long-standing tradition.

We also asked our respondents whether and how often they verify that terms are correctly rendered in the target language (Figure 3). Studies on revision practice report that revisers do not always check terminology, especially if they know that the translators have already taken care of it (Allman, 2007; Riondel, 2021). Conversely, a guideline that is often cited in full PE is to check whether terminology is correctly rendered in the target language (Hu and Cadwell, 2016).

Among our respondents, post-editors seem to be aware of this issue and systematically check whether terminology is correct in the target text (approx. 90% of respondents). A tiny percentage of post-editors check terminology "often", while only one respondent admits to only checking it "sometimes". On the other hand, when revising texts, only 62% of respondents systematically check terminology in translated texts; 28% indicated they often check terminology, 8% only sometimes, and 2% rarely do so. Some revisers commented on their answers and confirmed that they check terminology mainly depending on the translator who translated the text.

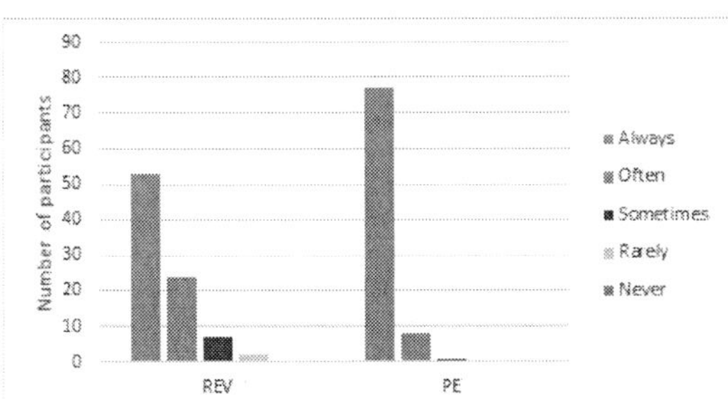

Figure 3: When revising/post-editing, do you check whether terminology is correct?

4.2.3 Revising post-edited or human-translated texts

In another question, we asked participants whether they use the same overall strategies when revising texts with different origins, *i.e.*, texts that had been previously translated or post-edited by a colleague. The answer is clear-cut (Figure 4): 78% confirm using the same strategies, thereby considering translated and post-edited text as the product of human work. Those who admit using different strategies clarify that, when revising post-edited texts, they mainly focus on textual cohesion and terminology consistency or check source and target texts very carefully to ensure that post-editors have not overlooked any MT errors.

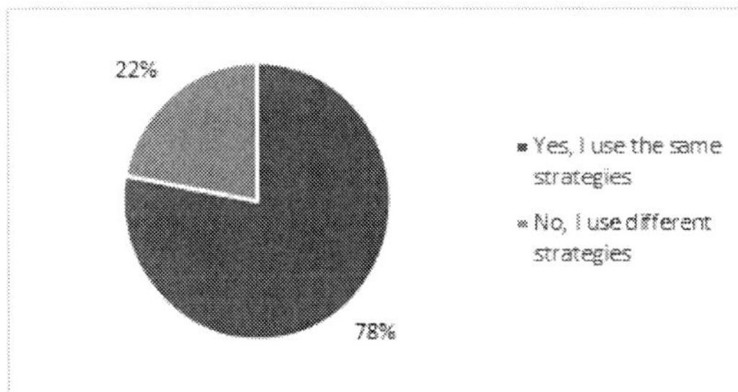

Figure 4: Do you use the same overall strategies when revising human-translated texts and revising texts that have been post-edited by another person?

In the comment section, 13 linguists reported that revision of post-edited texts is not carried out in their CILS or that they never know the origin of the text. When cross-checking these results with those from questionnaire Q1[4], we found that 45 out of 86 respondents do not carry out revision of post-edited texts in their workflows. Nevertheless, they have answered the question based on what they *would do* if they were to revise post-edited output.

4.3 MT influence on revision procedures

We also asked our respondents whether the introduction of MT in the workflow had somehow influenced the way revision of human-translated texts is carried out (Figure 5). The majority of respondents (72%) consider that this is not the case.

The analysis of comments from those who did

[4]In questionnaire Q1, we found that post-edited texts are always revised in six out of 26 CILS. Post-edited texts are sometimes revised (n=6) depending on content type or target audience. In some cases, the linguist can ask for a revision by another colleague. Otherwise, the majority of respondents (n=14) clarified that post-edited texts are never revised.

notice a change (28%) revealed that this question had primarily been misunderstood. The way this question was asked has probably confused those respondents who consider PE as "the revision of MT output" (Mossop, 2020). Indeed, many participants commented again on how they tackle revision and PE, detailed their overall strategies or listed the differences between human-translated and machine-translated texts.

Only a few participants seem to have correctly understood the question and commented that, compared to what they used to do before the introduction of MT in their workflows, they now focus more on accuracy errors (typical MT errors) during revision.

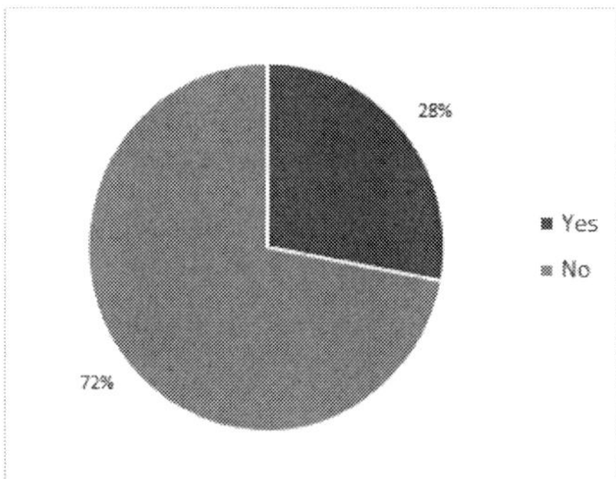

Figure 5: After the introduction of MT in your workflow, did you change the way you revise texts?

5 Conclusion and further research

We conducted a survey-based study to investigate revision and PE practices of salaried translators working at corporate in-house language services in Switzerland. We found that, although revision and PE share some common grounds, most linguists claim to act differently depending on whether they work with human-translated or machine-translated texts. However, they often apply the same reading strategies to these texts in practice.

While research on revision procedures has shown the impact of different revision strategies on revision quality, task duration and error detection potential (Ipsen and Dam, 2016; Robert, 2013; Robert and Van Waes, 2014), similar studies on PE strategies are extremely scarce. As a result, PE training rarely includes useful advice on how to carry out the task. Our survey-based data show that, in PE, most in-house linguists start by reading the source segment and tend to apply the same strategy regardless of the text type, while there is less consensus on reading strategies in revision. Nevertheless, it remains to be demonstrated whether using the same or different reading strategies in PE and revision could benefit linguists' performance or even influence their attitudes toward the task.

The way many participants misunderstood a question about the possible influence of MT on revision procedures makes us think that there is a sort of cognitive bias toward a view of PE as the revision of MT. Such bias could affect the behaviour of some linguists who could not perceive working with MT as a means to vary their daily tasks but rather as a mere increase in the number of revision jobs to carry out. Displaying MT in a separate window (just as with translation memory fuzzy matches) instead of pre-translating the entire text could perhaps help linguists consider MT as a tool supporting their translation workflow – rather than a "translation dispenser" whose output must be corrected.

Translation scholars have often recommended introducing PE and revision as two separate activities at a later stage in the translation curriculum (Guerberof Arenas and Moorkens, 2019; Mossop, 2020; O'Brien, 2002), once some translation competence has been acquired. In modern translation environments, however, the use of NMT is changing the way we interact with pre-translated texts and we now need to conceive *ad hoc* activities to help translation students construct their own revision and PE strategies in parallel.

Findings detailed in the present article are preliminary. Using the same survey, we also collected data on linguists' satisfaction in performing revision and PE. Further research will include analysing these data to identify and address possible sources of grievance. We hope these additional data will help us draw a clearer picture of the similarities and differences between revision and PE in the NMT era.

Note: The project obtained the approval of the Ethical Review Board of the Faculty of Translation and Interpreting at the University of Geneva (reference number 32/2021).

Acknowledgements: I gratefully acknowledge all the participants who took the time to fill out the questionnaires and answer my questions. I would also like to thank Prof. Pierrette Bouillon,

Dr. Marco Civico, and the other colleagues who contributed to the making of this study with their comments. Finally, I would like to thank the two anonymous reviewers for their comments and suggestions.

References

Allman, Spencer. 2007. Negotiating Translation Revision Assignments. *Translation and Negotiation. Proceedings of the 7th annual Portsmouth Translation Conference*.

Cadwell, Patrick, Sharon O'Brien, and Carlos S.C. Teixeira. 2017. Resistance and accommodation: factors for the (non-) adoption of machine translation among professional translators. *Perspectives: Studies in Translatology*, 26(3), 301–321.

Castilho, Sheila, Joss Moorkens, Federico Gaspari, Rico Sennrich, Vilelmini Sosoni, Panayota Georgakopoulou, Pintu Lohar, Andy Way, Antonio Valerio Miceli Barone, and Maria Gialama. 2017. A Comparative Quality Evaluation of PBSMT and NMT using Professional Translators. In: *Proceedings of Machine Translation Summit XVI*.

ELIS. 2022. *European Language Industry Survey 2022. Trends, expectations and concerns of the European language industry*. ELIS Research. https://elis-survey.org/

Gaspari, Federico, Hala Almaghout, and Stephen Doherty. 2015. A survey of machine translation competences: Insights for translation technology educators and practitioners. *Perspectives: Studies in Translatology*, 23(3), 333–358.

Ginovart Cid, Clara. 2021. *The need for practice in the acquisition of the post-editing skillset: lessons learned from the industry*. Ph.D. thesis. Pompeu Fabra University.

Ginovart Cid, Clara, and Carme Colominas. 2020. The MT Post-Editing Skill Set. In: Koponen, Maarit, Mossop, Brian, Robert, Isabelle S., and Scocchera, Giovanna (eds), *Translation Revision and Post-Editing*. Routledge. 226–246.

Guerberof Arenas, Ana. 2013. What do professional translators think about post-editing? *The Journal of Specialised Translation*, 75–95.

Guerberof Arenas, Ana, and Joss Moorkens. 2019. Machine translation and post-editing training as part of a master's programme. *The Journal of Specialised Translation*, 217–238.

Hernández Morin, Katell. 2009a. *La révision comme clé de la gestion de la qualité des traductions en contexte professionnel*. Ph.D. thesis. Université Rennes 2. https://tel.archives-ouvertes.fr/tel-00383266.

Hernández Morin, Katell. 2009b. Pratiques et perceptions de la révision en France. *Traduire*, 58–78.

Hu, Ke, and Patrick Cadwell. 2016. A Comparative Study of Post-editing Guidelines. *Baltic J. Modern Computing*, 4(2), 346–353.

Ipsen, A. Helene, and Helle V. Dam. 2016. Translation Revision: Correlating revision procedure and error detection. *Hermes*, 55, 143–156.

Koponen, Maarit, Brian Mossop, Isabelle Robert, and Giovanna Scocchera (eds). 2020. *Translation Revision and Post-editing: Industry Practices and Cognitive Processes*. Routledge.

Läubli, Samuel, and David Orrego-Carmona. 2017. When Google Translate is better than Some Human Colleagues, those People are no longer Colleagues. In: *Proceedings of the 39th Conference Translating and the Computer.*

Martikainen, Hanna. 2019. Post-editing neural MT in medical LSP: Lexico-grammatical patterns and distortion in the communication of specialized knowledge. *Informatics*, 6(3), 26.

Mossop, Brian. 2020. *Revising and Editing for Translators*. Routledge.

O'Brien, Sharon. 2002. Teaching post-editing: a proposal for course content. In: *Proceedings of the 6th European Association for Machine Translation (EAMT) Workshop: Teaching machine translation*.

Pielmeier, Hélène, and Arle Lommel. 2019. *Machine Translation Use at LSPs: Data on How Language Service Providers Use MT*. Common Sense Advisory. May 2019.

Pielmeier, Hélène, and Paul O'Mara. 2020. *The State of the Linguist Supply Chain: Translators and Interpreters in 2020*. Common Sense Advisory. January 2020. https://insights.csa-research.com/reportaction/305013106/Toc

Porro Rodríguez, Victoria, Lucía Morado Vázquez, and Pierrette Bouillon. 2017. Study on the use of machine translation and post-editing in Swiss-based language service providers. *Parallèles*, 29(2), 19–35.

Rasmussen, Kirsten, and Anne Schjoldager. 2011. Revising Translations A Survey of Revision Policies in Danish Translation Companies. *The Journal of Specialised Translation*, 87–120.

Riondel, Aurélien. 2021. Two approaches to quality in institutional settings. Comparison of the revision policies of an intergovernmental organisation and the Swiss Confederation. *MikaEL*, 14, 82–96.

Robert, Isabelle. 2008. Translation revision procedures: An explorative study. In: Boulogne, Pieter (ed.) *Translation and Its others: selected papers of the CETRA Seminar in translation Studies 2007.*

Robert, Isabelle. 2013. Translation revision: does the revision procedure matter? In: Way, Catherine, Sonia Vandepitte, Reine Meylaerts, and Magdalena Bartlomiejczyk (eds), *Tracks and Treks in Translation Studies.* John Benjamins Publishing. 87–102.

Robert, Isabelle, and Luuk Van Waes. 2014. Selecting a translation revision procedure: do common sense and statistics agree? *Perspectives: Studies in Translatology*, 22(3), 304–320.

Rossi, Caroline, and Jean Pierre Chevrot. 2019. Uses and perceptions of machine translation at the European Commission. *Journal of Specialised Translation*, 177–200.

Schnierer, Madeleine. 2020. Revision and Quality Standards. In: Koponen, Maarit, Brian Mossop, Isabelle Robert, and Giovanna Scocchera (eds), *Translation Revision and Post-Editing.* Routledge. 109–130.

Scocchera, Giovanna. 2015. *La revisione della traduzione editoriale dall'inglese all'italiano tra ricerca accademica, professione e formazione: stato dell'arte e prospettive future.* Ph.D. thesis. University of Bologna. http://amsdottorato.unibo.it/7203/

Scocchera, Giovanna. 2017. Translation Revision as Rereading: Different Aspects of the Translator's and Reviser's Approach to the Revision Process. *Mémoires du livre. Studies in Book Culture*, 9(1).

Selinger, Jessica. 2020. *Quo vadis traduzione automatica ? Uso e percezione da parte di professionisti e utenti comuni.* Laboratorio Weaver.

Vieira, Lucas Nunes. 2020. Automation anxiety and translators. *Translation Studies*, 13(1), 1–21.

Volkart, Lise, Sabrina Girletti, Johanna Gerlach, Jonathan Mutal, and Pierrette Bouillon. forthcoming. Source or target first? Comparison of two post-editing strategies with translation students. https://hal.archives-ouvertes.fr/hal-03546151

Yamada, Masaru. 2019. The impact of google neural machine translation on post-editing by student translators. *Journal of Specialised Translation*, 87–106.

Yuste, Elia. 2002. MT and the Swiss language service providers: an analysis and training perspective. In: *Proceedings of the 6th European Association for Machine Translation (EAMT) Workshop: Teaching machine translation.*

Zaretskaya, Anna. 2015. The Use of Machine Translation among Professional Translators. In: *Proceedings of the EXPERT Scientific and Technological Workshop.*

Project/product descriptions

Dynamic Adaptation of Neural Machine-Translation Systems Through Translation Exemplars

Arda Tezcan
LT[3], Language and Translation Technology Team
Ghent University
Belgium
Arda.Tezcan@ugent.be

Abstract

This project aims to study the impact of adapting neural machine translation (NMT) systems through similar translations retrieved from translation memories, determine the optimal metric(s) for measuring similarity, and, verify the usefulness of this approach for domain adaptation of NMT systems.

1 Introduction

Translation exemplars, i.e. previously observed or generated translations, whose source is similar to new input, play an important role in the translation process by providing explicit information on context, exceptions, and irregularities, which are difficult to generalise. In the context of machine translation (MT), the information provided by similar translations can also be considered complementary to the neural models, which are good at making generalisations. "Dynamic Adaptation of Neural Machine-Translation Systems Through Translation Exemplars" is a three-year, post-doctoral research project (October 2020 – September 2023), funded by the Research Foundation – Flanders (FWO) with the following scientific objectives: (i) study the impact of adapting NMT systems through similar translations retrieved from TMs, (ii) determine the optimal metrics for measuring translation similarity, and (iii) verify the usefulness of this approach for domain adaptation. All research activities are carried out at the Department of Translation, Interpreting and Communication, Ghent University, Belgium.

The project has been built upon the methodology used in the translation memory (TM) — NMT integration approach, neural fuzzy repair (NFR) (Bulté and Tezcan, 2019).[1] In NFR, each source sentence in the TM is augmented (concatenated), with the translation of the most similar fuzzy match (FM), retrieved from the same TM using edit distance, when at least one FM is found above the minimum similarity threshold of λ. The augmented TM is merged with the original TM to train an NMT model. During inference, the same technique is applied to augment source sentences prior to obtaining translations from the trained model. If no FMs above the minimum similarity threshold can be found, the translations are obtained for the original source sentence, using the same model.

Tests on multiple language pairs showed that this method results in substantial gains in translation quality compared to (i) baseline MT systems, (ii) the FMs themselves when used as final output, even when they correspond to near-perfect translations in high similarity ranges, and (iii) a 'fuzzy match repair' approach, which relies on editing highly similar FMs to arrive at the final translation (Bulté et al., 2018). These experiments also demonstrated that using the NFR system starts being advantageous with a minimum FM score of $\lambda = 0.5$, and augmenting source sentences with FMs of higher similarity scores leads to higher translation quality. While this study showed the usefulness of adapting NMT systems through similar translations, it also led to new research questions and formed the scientific objectives of this project. The following sections provide an overview of the progress made on the first

[1] https://github.com/lt3/nfr

Macken, Rufener, Van den Bogaert, Daems, Tezcan, Vanroy, Fonteyne, Barrault, Costa-jussà, Kemp, Pilos, Declercq, Koponen, Forcada, Scarton, Moniz (eds.)
Proceedings of the 23rd Annual Conference of the European Association for Machine Translation, p. 281–282
Ghent, Belgium, June 2022.

two scientific objectives and summarise the plans for future work.

2 Optimal metrics for measuring translation similarity

Text similarity can be measured from different perspectives, such as using string-, semantic- and syntactic-level information. In the context of NFR, it is yet to be determined if, and to what extent, different similarity levels are important in retrieving informative FMs and producing better translations.

To seek optimal similarity metrics in the context of NFR, string- and semantic-similarity metrics have been studied in combination with different sub-word segmentation methods (Tezcan et al., 2021). Retrieving FMs by measuring cosine similarity between sentence embeddings resulted in translations with higher quality in comparison to using edit distance. Moreover, applying sub-word segmentation prior to measuring semantic similarity improved translation quality further.

To utilise sub-sentence-level similarities between two sentences more explicitly, two additional approaches have been tested: (i) marking relevant tokens in retrieved FMs, and (ii) augmenting source sentences with multiple FMs that lead to a maximum coverage of source tokens (Tezcan et al., 2021). When combined, these methods led to improvements in estimated translation quality for 8 language directions (English $\leftrightarrow$ Dutch, French, Hungarian, Polish), compared to a baseline transformer NMT model and the original NFR approach (Bulté and Tezcan, 2019).

3 The impact of adapting NMT systems through similar translations

To analyse the impact of adapting NMT systems through similar translations on translation quality, evaluations were carried out both automatically and manually.[2]

The fine-grained, human error analysis showed that both the adapted and non-adapted NMT systems made a comparable number of errors. On the other hand, while the adapted NMT system produced more fluent translations, with a significant reduction in *lexicon* and *coherence* errors, it also diverged from the source content and meaning (i.e. reduced accuracy) more often than the baseline NMT system, making more errors of *addition* and *mistranslation*.

The automatic evaluation analysed translation quality by relying on the reference translations while using metrics that targeted lexical, sublexical, semantic, and syntactic aspects of translation quality. According to all evaluation metrics, the quality of the adapted NMT system was estimated to be higher than that of those produced by the NMT system. The difference in quality was always significant and large confirming that the improvements were obtained for all the different aspects of quality that were analysed.

By analysing the MT output with different resources (source–MT vs. MT–reference), the two evaluation methods yielded a more nuanced picture of the differences in translation quality between the two systems. They also revealed an interesting property of the NFR system: by using the similar translations, it was able to learn systematic deviations from the source text (e.g. related to the use of cohesive devices or translation decisions affecting sentence boundaries) and produce translations that are similar to the reference translations, even though such deviations were marked as accuracy errors during human error analysis.

4 Future work

Future work will focus on (i) studying the usefulness of syntactic similarity for retrieving informative FMs, (ii) improving the NFR performance further, and (iii) adopting this methodology to the task of domain adaptation.

[2]Evaluations were made using the best-performing NFR methodology as outlined in Section 2.

References

Bulté, Bram and Arda Tezcan. 2019. Neural Fuzzy Repair: Integrating Fuzzy Matches into Neural Machine Translation. *Proceedings of the 57th Annual Meeting of the Association for Computational Linguistics*, Florence, Italy, 1800–1809.

Bulté, Bram and Tom Vanallemeersch and Vincent Vandeghinste. M3TRA: integrating TM and MT for professional translators. *Proceedings of the 21st Annual Conference of the European Association for Machine Translation*, Alicante, Spain, 69–78.

Tezcan, Arda and Bram Bulté. 2022. Evaluating the Impact of Integrating Similar Translations into Neural Machine Translation. *Information, 13(1):19.*

Tezcan, Arda, Bram Bulté, and Bram Vanroy. 2021. Towards a Better Integration of Fuzzy Matches in Neural Machine Translation through Data Augmentation. *Informatics-Basel 8(1):7.*

Language I/O Solution for Multilingual Customer Support

Diego Bartolome
Language I/O
diego.bartolome@languageio.com

Chris Jacob
Language I/O
chris.jacob@languageio.com

Abstract

We describe Language I/O's multilingual customer support solution. By combining intelligent selection of machine translation vendors with a self-improving translation process, we enable support teams to become multilingual in less than 24 hours, while maintaining ISO-27001 certification and general data protection regulation (GDPR) privacy standards.

1. Introduction

Support is a key business process to provide the best customer experience and fuel growth. It requires that customers interact with global corporations in their own language through any channel, and the requests need to be solved efficiently and as soon as possible. This involves a significant capital expense as well as ongoing operational costs. There are many pieces required to optimize customer support operations, including but not limited to chatbots and automation, live agent assistance based on machine learning, insights derived from data in real-time, and self-improving machine translation.

Enabling a support teams to have high-quality conversations via translation technology requires the capability to learn from customer interactions, i.e. self-improving machine translation. This can be a difficult goal to achieve without compromising privacy considerations.

In this paper[1], we will describe the main components of the Language I/O solution that enable translation quality improvements, without compromising on data privacy considerations.

2. System overview

Figure 1 contains the key pieces in our workflow. Language I/O customers use a variety of customer relationship management systems (CRMs) like Salesforce, Zendesk, and Oracle Service Cloud. Agents can use the chat, social messaging, and ticketing (e-mail) solutions to communicate to customers whenever they get in touch with the company. When an agent receives a message in a foreign language, it will be automatically displayed in the agent's own language, and she will be able to communicate with the customer to solve the issue. We can add a disclaimer for customers to know they are reading machine translated text if needed.

Language I/O takes several steps to create a seamless translation experience for both the agent and the customer. First, the integration with CRMs is essential so that agents and customers do not need to use a third-party software. We provide machine translation as a feature in the CRM interface directly to minimize training requirements and interface switching costs.

Second, the best machine translation engine will vary depending on the content type, language pair, and customer, among others. Language I/O solution selects the best engine without any customer intervention so that the best possible output is achieved. Currently, we support Google, Microsoft, Amazon, DeepL, and Systran. We select which engine is best suited for a customer by analyzing agent feedback on translation quality over time. By gathering this feedback, we are able to adjust the machine translation engine to adapt to customer needs, without needing to collect sensitive chat transcripts. All of our engine integrations are vetted to ensure that the vendor does not store customer translation data exactly in the same way as we do. Language I/O has a no-trace policy in place.

Third, our self-improving translation solution learns from conversational content to ensure the key terminology is properly translated. The main issue in customer support usually comes when key terminology is not translated as the cus-

Macken, Rufener, Van den Bogaert, Daems, Tezcan, Vanroy, Fonteyne, Barrault, Costa-jussà, Kemp, Pilos, Declercq, Koponen, Forcada, Scarton, Moniz (eds.)
Proceedings of the 23rd Annual Conference of the European Association for Machine Translation, p. 283–284
Ghent, Belgium, June 2022.

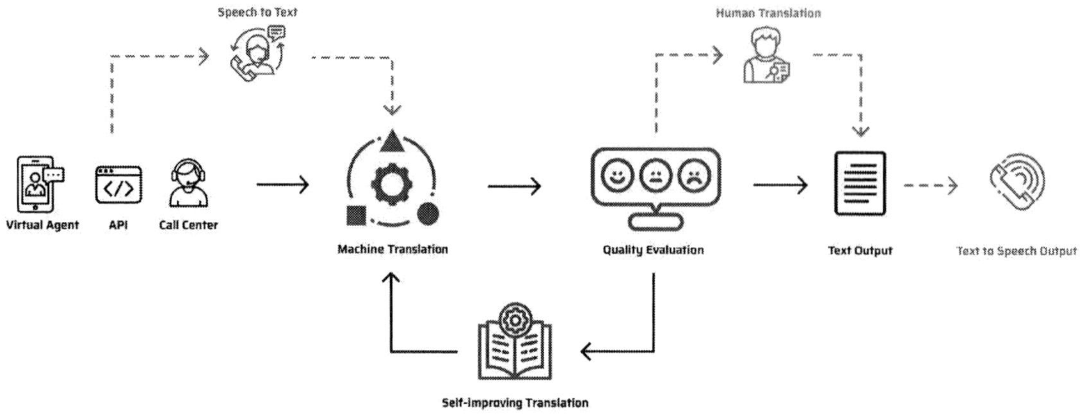

Figure 1: System Overview

tomers need. Our self-improving glossary is able to identify and extract terms that could impact translation comprehension. We present those terms to our customers in case further consideration is needed. We take multiple steps to ensure that the self-improving glossary avoids analyzing sensitive information, while still presenting relevant data for customers to improve their glossaries. See Figure 2 for details.

Finally, tools to estimate the machine translation quality are needed to allow customers to route tickets to human translation when the quality is not at the level that ensures understandability and an efficient resolution of the customer issue. For this step, we leverage a unique proprietary solution that is in the process of being patented. Therefore, more details cannot be disclosed yet.

3. Value proposition

There are five main characteristics why our customers use Language I/O.

The first is data security and confidentiality. Language I/O is compliant with the European general data protection regulation (GDPR) and ISO27001-certified, which ensures the highest degree of data protection. We do not store chat transcripts. Additional certifications will be achieved this year.

The second is the seamless integration with CRM systems. Machine translation is available with no effort in their system of choice. If we do not support a CRM, our API provides our customers with the ability to integrate our solution into any bespoke system for both text and speech content.

The third is how we accelerate time to market. Our solution is up and running in less than 24 hours with minimal effort from our customers. We turn their monolingual agents into multilingual brand ambassadors in very little time and without training required.

Fourth, our technology improves over and reduces management overhead thanks to our active learning layer (self-improving glossary and translation technologies). The more customers translate with us, the more their quality will improve over time.

The end result is an expanded and improved international reach for our customers, where agents become even more productive over time as our technology improves.

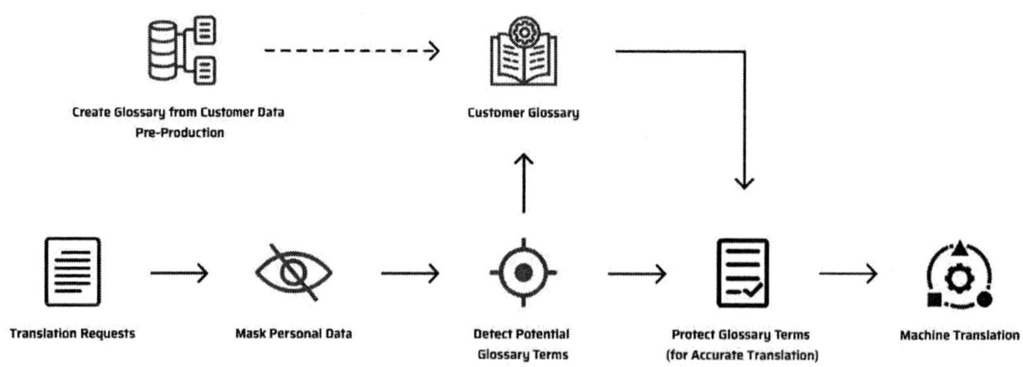

Figure 2: Self-Improving Glossary Process

Towards Readability-Controlled Machine Translation of COVID-19 Texts

Fernando Alva-Manchego
Cardiff University
alvamanchegof@cardiff.ac.uk

Matthew Shardlow
Manchester Metropolitan University
m.shardlow@mmu.ac.uk

Abstract

This project investigates the capabilities of machine translation (MT) models for generating translations at varying levels of readability, focusing on texts about COVID-19. Funded by the European Association for Machine Translation and by the Centre for Advanced Computational Sciences at Manchester Metropolitan University, we collected manual simplifications for English and Spanish texts in the TICO-19 dataset, and assessed the performance of neural MT models in this new benchmark. Future work will implement models that jointly translate and simplify, and develop suitable evaluation metrics.

1 Introduction

"Multilingual Translation with Readability-Controlled Output Generation" is a project that received funding from the European Association for Machine Translation (under its programme "2021 Sponsorship of Activities") and from the Centre for Advanced Computational Sciences at Manchester Metropolitan University. We aim to develop machine translation (MT) models that generate translations that can be understood by non-expert readers, focusing on texts with medical information. This is pertinent in the context of the COVID-19 pandemic, where there is a disparity in the availability of health-related content produced in English, compared to other languages.

The project has the following objectives: (1) to collect a dataset with simplified versions of parallel texts in English and Spanish about COVID-19; (2) to assess how well existing state-of-the-art MT models perform on our new benchmark; and (3) to investigate additional model architectures and/or resources that are needed to generate and evaluate simplified in-domain translations.

Lang.	Complexity	W/S	Sy/W	FRE↑	S-P↑
English	Original	23.015	6.444	45.69	–
	Simplified	21.838	6.308	52.70	–
Spanish	Original	27.623	6.287	–	75.17
	Simplified	24.749	6.271	–	79.49

Table 1: Statistics of Simple TICO-19: average number of words per sentence (W/S), average number of syllables per word (Sy/W), and estimated readability with Flesch Reading Ease (FRE) for English and Szigriszt-Pazos (S-P) for Spanish.

The first two goals of the project were carried out from January 2021 to December 2021, and resulted in the release of the Simple TICO-19 dataset (Shardlow and Alva-Manchego, 2022).[1] We continue to work with the new dataset to further investigate the nature of readability-controlled output generation in the MT context. We hope to apply for further funding at a national and European level as a result of this work.

2 The Simple TICO-19 Dataset

We leveraged the TICO-19 benchmark (Anastasopoulos et al., 2020), which contains 3,000 sentences related to the COVID-19 pandemic, translated from English into 36 languages and from several sources (e.g. academic publications, speech corpora, news articles, etc.). For our project, we collected manual simplifications for the English and Spanish subsets, resulting in the Simple TICO-19 dataset, where each sentence has either a simplified version of itself, or a decision has been taken that the sentence is already sufficiently simple. Table 1 shows some high level statistics of the resulting corpus, including readability indices such as Flesch Reading Ease (FRE) (Flesch, 1948) for

[1] https://github.com/MMU-TDMLab/SimpleTICO19

Macken, Rufener, Van den Bogaert, Daems, Tezcan, Vanroy, Fonteyne, Barrault, Costa-jussà, Kemp, Pilos, Declercq, Koponen, Forcada, Scarton, Moniz (eds.)
Proceedings of the 23rd Annual Conference of the European Association for Machine Translation, p. 285–286
Ghent, Belgium, June 2022.

English, and Szigriszt-Pazos (S-P) (Szigriszt Pazos, 2001) for Spanish. These indices, in particular, showcase the improvements in readability from the original sentences in the dataset to their simplified versions, for both languages.

3 Machine Translation Baselines

To obtain baseline results, we leveraged models pre-trained on `opus-mt-en-es` with MarianMT as architecture. Table 2 reports BLEU (Papineni et al., 2002) and BERTScore (Zhang et al., 2020) as evaluation metrics on all the test set and per data source therein, considering original–en as source and two targets: original–es and simplified–es. The highest scores are obtained when original–es is the target, showing that standard neural MT models cannot generate simplified texts by default. Also, performance varies depending on the data source, indicating the effect of the style of text.

	orig–en → orig–es		orig–en → simp–es	
Data Source	BLEU	BERTScore	BLEU	BERTScore
CMU	33.51	0.678	17.05	0.581
PubMed	51.63	0.819	42.69	0.757
Wikinews	55.41	0.826	40.22	0.732
Wikipedia	52.16	0.875	44.83	0.836
Wikisource	39.98	0.715	31.85	0.647
All	51.42	0.841	43.15	0.788

Table 2: Results per data source of our baseline models on the test set of Simple TICO-19.

4 Future Work

Translation and Simplification. In order to incorporate simplification capabilities into MT models, we will first experiment with pipeline systems that translate and then simplify (and vice-versa) leveraging state-of-the-art models for each task. We will then work on models that perform both tasks jointly, exploring multi-task architectures.

Controllable Translation. We will study how to train models that generate outputs at diverse readability levels. We will explore varying the proportion of translation and simplification training instances to control the readability of the translations. We will rank target-side simple sentences according to the proportion of complex words and syntactic complexity, and use this ranked list to create different readability levels that allow training models for multiple degrees of complexity.

Evaluation. We will develop novel metrics suitable for the joint translation and simplification task, specifically for the medical domain. For instance, we will combine traditional similarity-based metrics, such as BLEU and BERTScore, with readability indices. While the latter are more suitable for analysing documents, we plan to adapt them for sentence-level assessment using complex word identification approaches and heuristics. We will then measure the correlation of our new metrics with human judgements on adequacy and simplicity of automatic translations.

Acknowledgements

This project was funded by the European Association for Machine Translation (EAMT) under its programme "2021 Sponsorship of Activities", and by the Centre for Advanced Computational Sciences at Manchester Metropolitan University.

References

Anastasopoulos, Antonios, Alessandro Cattelan, Zi-Yi Dou, Marcello Federico, Christian Federmann, Dmitriy Genzel, Franscisco Guzmán, Junjie Hu, Macduff Hughes, Philipp Koehn, Rosie Lazar, Will Lewis, Graham Neubig, Mengmeng Niu, Alp Öktem, Eric Paquin, Grace Tang, and Sylwia Tur. 2020. TICO-19: the translation initiative for COvid-19. In *Proceedings of the 1st Workshop on NLP for COVID-19 (Part 2) at EMNLP 2020*, Online, December. Association for Computational Linguistics.

Flesch, Rudolph. 1948. A new readability yardstick. *Journal of Applied Psychology*, 32(3):221.

Papineni, Kishore, Salim Roukos, Todd Ward, and Wei-Jing Zhu. 2002. Bleu: a method for automatic evaluation of machine translation. In *Proceedings of the 40th Annual Meeting of the Association for Computational Linguistics*, pages 311–318, Philadelphia, Pennsylvania, USA, July. ACL.

Shardlow, Matthew and Fernando Alva-Manchego. 2022. Simple TICO-19: A dataset for joint translation and simplification of covid-19 texts. In *Proceedings of the 13th Language Resources and Evaluation Conference*, Marseille, France, June. European Language Resources Association.

Szigriszt Pazos, Francisco. 2001. *Sistemas predictivos de legilibilidad del mensaje escrito: fórmula de perspicuidad.* Universidad Complutense de Madrid, Servicio de Publicaciones.

Zhang, Tianyi, Varsha Kishore, Felix Wu, Kilian Q. Weinberger, and Yoav Artzi. 2020. Bertscore: Evaluating text generation with bert. In *International Conference on Learning Representations*.

DeBiasByUs: Raising Awareness and Creating a Database of MT Bias

Joke Daems
Postdoctoral Researcher @ LT3 UGent
joke.daems@ugent.be

Janiça Hackenbuchner
Research Associate @ TH Köln
janica.hackenbuchner@th-koeln.de

Abstract

This paper presents the project proposed by the DeBiasByUs[1] team resulting from the Artificially Correct Hackathon. We briefly explain the hackathon challenge on 'Database and detection of gender bias in A.I. translations', highlight the importance of gender bias in Machine Translation (MT), describe our solution, the current status of the project, and our future plans.

1 Introduction to DeBiasByUs

The DeBiasByUs project was a winning solution to a challenge on 'Creating Datasets and Resources against Societal Biases in AI[2]' at the Artificially Correct Hackathon organised by the Goethe-Institut in October 2021. The initial Hackathon team consisted of five participants[3], of which the authors of the present paper will continue to develop the project. The goal of the challenge was to define and analyse gender bias from MT systems and either create a dataset or a platform for users to gather, describe, and discuss cases of bias.

2 The Problem of Gender Bias in MT

MT systems are trained with data that contain biases present in our society and in our language. As such, these systems will reproduce or even heighten these biases, potentially leading to discrimination and harm. For example, translation datasets have a dominance of white male representation (Saunders and Byrne, 2020), and word embeddings (used to train MT systems) have been shown to reinforce gender stereotypes (Bolukbasi et al., 2016).

Different factors can contribute to bias in MT. There are linguistic factors, socio-cultural factors, reinforcement of historical gender stereotypes, especially in professions, and a lack of an explicit linguistic representation of nonbinary gender. While less apparent for genderless languages (e.g. Finnish) and notional gender languages (e.g. Danish), MT most often exhibits gender bias or opts for the generic masculine for grammatical gender languages (e.g. Spanish), where nouns, verbs, adjectives etc. carry gender inflections (Savoldi et al., 2021). Technical factors include MT sampling methods favoring masculine forms due to asymmetrical gender distributions in the training datasets, leading to reinforcement of gender stereotypes as the most common form is subsequently being chosen as a most-likely translation by the MT system (Shah et al., 2020).

3 Solution: Raising Awareness and Database Creation

As a solution to the hackathon challenge, we created a website[4] that serves a dual purpose: 1) raise public awareness about the issue of gender bias in MT by providing information and research findings, and 2) create a community-driven database of occurrences of gender bias in MT. The collected inputs can be moderated and reviewed by experts. Through such collaborative and community-driven action, we aim to create a database representing different language combinations that can then be used as biased test datasets for further research. The moderated datasets will be made freely available for download. The data will consist of a source sentence (e.g., 'The Professor is an expert on machine translation') and a biased MT output

[1] The original Hackathon project was "BiasByUs" but has now been changed to "DeBiasByUs"

[2] https://www.goethe.de/prj/one/en/aco/ver/hac/cha.html#i7094314

[3] Joke Daems, Janiça Hackenbuchner, Bettina Koch, Bhargavi Mahesh, Shrishti Mohabey

[4] Hackathon proof of concept (to be updated): https://artificiallycorrec.wixsite.com/biasbyus

Macken, Rufener, Van den Bogaert, Daems, Tezcan, Vanroy, Fonteyne, Barrault, Costa-jussà, Kemp, Pilos, Declercq, Koponen, Forcada, Scarton, Moniz (eds.)
Proceedings of the 23rd Annual Conference of the European Association for Machine Translation, p. 287–288
Ghent, Belgium, June 2022.

(e.g., 'Der Professor ist Experte für maschinelle Übersetzung' as an example of stereotyping, where a 'professor' is assumed to be male in German). The availability of datasets with biased MT output will support research in gender-bias by focusing on datasets with specific occurrences of gender-bias instead of using large noisy datasets. We further envision it being used for crosslinguistic and diachronic analyses of gender bias in MT (as new data will continuously be added).

With millions of online MT users noticing "how commercial systems entrench social gender expectations" (Savoldi et al., 2021), we believe that community awareness and involvement is key in tackling the challenge of bias in society and MT. Since society and gender roles are constantly evolving, the only way to ensure our technologies evolve alongside with it is to observe that evolution in real time.

Our current website is a proof of concept. There are numerous sections on concepts aiming to raise awareness (impact of gender bias, gender bias in language, gender bias in MT, and categories of bias), and users can submit occurrences of bias to our database by copy/pasting a source sentence, the MT output containing bias. Optionally, they can provide their reference suggestion for an unbiased translation, highlight the specific type of bias they encountered, offer clarifications, and name the source of the MT output, as well as their own familiarity with gender bias.

4 Further Steps

The Goethe-Institut has agreed to continue to fund our project. By October 2022, we aim to professionalise our website, expand our theoretical information on gender bias in MT, develop a browser plug-in, and secure a server[5] to host our database. The plug-in would become active when users consult MT resources online and so enable users to conveniently add instances of bias to our website.

The following aim will be to collect as much data as possible by marketing our initiative to interested users, and by collaborating with organisations, such as the Goethe-Institut, supporters of gender equality, experts in the field of both gender bias and MT, and research universities. As the database grows, it will become a rich resource for researchers working on gender-fair language and MT development.

A potential area of collaboration is with the other winning team of the Artificially Correct Hackathon Word2Vec[6], whose developed tool highlights words in a text that have a high probability of containing bias in translation. Once fully developed, this tool could be integrated on the DeBiasByUs website.

5 Conclusion

Bias awareness needs to be continuously raised as it is impossible to tell what will be the next arising bias in society (like Chinese discrimination due to the in Wuhan originated COVID-19 virus). The platform created by DeBiasByUs is an effort to help prevent bias representation in MT, by focusing on raising awareness of gender bias in MT as well as creating a community-driven database of gender-bias occurrences in MT outputs for research purposes to support collaborative work.

References

Bolukbasi, Tolga, Kai-Wei Chang, James Y. Zou, Venkatesh Saligrama, and Adam T. Kalai. 2016. Man is to computer programmer as woman is to homemaker? *NIPS'16: Proceedings of the 30th International Conference on Neural Information Processing Systems*: 4356-4364.

Saunders, Danielle and Bill Byrne. 2020. Reducing Gender Bias in Neural Machine Translation as a Domain Adaptation Problem. *Proceedings of the 58th Annual Meeting of the Association for Computational Linguistics*. Association for Computational Linguistics: 7724-7736.

Savoldi, Beatrice, Marco Gaido, Luisa Bentivogli, Matteo Negri, and Marco Turchi. 2021. Gender bias in machine translation. *Transactions of the Association for Computational Linguistics, 9*: 845-874

Shah, Deven, Andrew H. Schwartz, and Dirk Hovy. 2020. Predictive Biases in Natural Language Processing Models: A Conceptual Framework and Overview. *Proceedings of the 58th Annual Meeting of the Association for Computational Linguistics. Association for Computational Linguistics*: 5248-5284.

[5] We will most likely be able to host our database on servers at Ghent University. Upcoming project proposals related to MT and bias by the authors will also include funding requests to ensure the sustainability of the platform and database.

[6] https://www.goethe.de/prj/one/en/aco.html

MultitraiNMT Erasmus+ project: Machine Translation Training for multilingual citizens (multitrainmt.eu)

Mikel L. Forcada
Universitat d'Alacant
mlf@dlsi.ua.es

Dorothy Kenny
Dublin City University
dorothy.kenny@dcu.ie

Juan Antonio Pérez Ortiz
Universitat d'Alacant
japerez@dlsi.ua.es

Gema Ramírez Sánchez
Prompsit
gramirez@prompsit.com

Caroline Rossi
Université Grenoble-Alpes
caroline.rossi@univ-grenoble-alpes.fr

Pilar Sánchez-Gijón
Universitat Autònoma de Barcelona
pilar.sanchez.gijon@uab.cat

Felipe Sánchez-Martínez
Universitat d'Alacant
fsanchez@dlsi.ua.es

Riccardo Superbo
KantanAI
riccardos@kantanai.io

Olga Torres-Hostench
Universitat Autònoma de Barcelona
Olga.torres.hostench@uab.cat

Abstract

The MultitraiNMT Erasmus+ project has developed an open innovative syllabus in machine translation, focusing on neural machine translation (NMT) and targeting both language learners and translators. The training materials include an open access coursebook with more than 250 activities and a pedagogical NMT interface called MutNMT that allows users to learn how neural machine translation works. These materials will allow students to develop the technical and ethical skills and competences required to become informed, critical users of machine translation in their own language learning and translation practice. The project started in July 2019 and it will end in July 2022.

1 The project

MultitraiNMT consortium is formed by Universitat Autònoma de Barcelona, Universitat d'Alacant, Université Grenoble-Alpes and Dublin City University, together with Prompsit Language Engineering and Xcelerator Machine Translations.

The project is currently supported by numerous associate partners, all of whom are interested in learning about the use of neural machine translation (NMT), and willing to adjust their teaching practices.

MultitraiNMT invites higher education institutions and teachers of translation and second languages to join the project as associate partners to (i) use the project coursebook and associated activities in their classes; (ii) test the MutNMT educational platform and activities for managing NMT engines for didactic purposes and (iii) participate in any other training and/or research activity which fosters the development of machine translation skills in general.

2 The coursebook

The open access coursebook addresses both the technical foundations of machine translation, and the ethical, societal and professional implications of this approach. It will soon be available from Language Science Press. The coursebook is organized in 9 chapters: (1) Multilingualism. (2) Introduction to machine translation. (3) How to choose a suitable MT system. Evaluation of machine translation quality. (4) How to prepare and select texts for machine translation. (5) How to deal with machine translation mistakes. Post-

Macken, Rufener, Van den Bogaert, Daems, Tezcan, Vanroy, Fonteyne, Barrault, Costa-jussà, Kemp, Pilos, Declercq, Koponen, Forcada, Scarton, Moniz (eds.)
Proceedings of the 23rd Annual Conference of the European Association for Machine Translation, p. 289–290
Ghent, Belgium, June 2022.

editing and error fixing. (6) Ethical aspects of machine translation related to the data workflow, sustainability, diversity and decision-making. (7) How neural machine translation works. (8) Custom neural machine translation and (9) Machine translation and language learning.

3 The course activities

The project includes learning activities related to the coursebook and MutNMT that allow language learners and translators to learn about machine translation in general and especially about NMT. There are two types of activities. On the one hand, there are self-learning activities aimed at students working at their own pace; these are short-answer questions with immediate automatic feedback. On the other hand, there are open-answer teacher-guided activities which can be customized and adapted to different contexts. After exploring different formats and repositories of learning objects, we opted for the open-source H5P platform (h5p.org), as it allows each of our questions and activities to be self-contained and easily embeddable by instructors in learning management systems such as Moodle (including grading) or more general environments such as WordPress. Currently all activities are written only in English, using examples in different languages. However, they can be easily exported and translated as needed. Activities are designed taking into account different progress levels to approach different student profiles. The database of activities is here: https://ddd.uab.cat/record/257869.

4 MutNMT

MutNMT is a web application to train neural machine translation engines for didactic purposes (see logo in Figure 1). Currently teachers and students interested in using the tool may access MutNMT at https://ntradumatica.uab.cat (UAB) and/or http://multitrainmt.univ-grenoble-alpes.fr:5000 (UGA). Access is given with any Gmail account. Besides, the code of the web application is available on GitHub at https://github.com/Prompsit/mutnmt. MutNMT lets the user train, inspect, evaluate and translate using NMT engines. The project has contributed to other free/open-source projects, such as JoeyNMT, a command-line tool to train NMT engines.

In what follows, we provide a brief description of the main features of MutNMT:

Data. MutNMT needs corpora in the form of parallel data to learn from. Previewing, downloading and grabbing corpora is possible as part of the basic options for corpora.

Engines. As well as for data, there is a library of engines in MutNMT, that is, already available machine translation systems that have been trained and shared. Of special interest also are the actions allowed: viewing the full training log of an engine, downloading the model, downloading the corpora used to train the engine, and grabbing or removing the corpora. While beginners can only view, experts and administrators will be able to resume the training of an engine.

Figure 1: MutNMT logo

Train. This is an advanced feature for experts and administrators, so they can train NMT engines using MutNMT. Users will need to set up engine details, configuration parameters and select corpora for training a particular system.

Translate. All users will be able to copy and paste a series of sentences and translate them using the engines available in the 'Your engines' section. An already trained engine can be used if the user first goes to Engine and selects the *Grab* option from the menu associated with a particular engine. They will get the resulting translation in the text box and will be able to export a standard TMX file with the whole translation.

Inspect. There are several options in this section, all aimed at checking the inside of the translation engines at work. The first one allows users to input a sentence and see its evolution at different steps of processing by a particular engine: preprocessed input, hypothesis generation (n-best), preprocessed output and final output.

Evaluate. As a final step, users will be able to evaluate the machine translated output by comparing it to other machine translated texts or to one or more professional human translations. MutNMT provides popular automatic document- and sentence-level evaluation metrics, as well as an overview of sentences along with their individual scores. Evaluation results can also be downloaded in a spreadsheet.

EMBEDDIA project: Cross-Lingual Embeddings for Less- Represented Languages in European News Media

Senja Pollak and Andraž Pelicon
Jozef Stefan Institute
Jamova 39, Ljubljana, Slovenia
senja.pollak,andraz.pelicon@ijs.si

Abstract

The EMBEDDIA project developed a range of resources and methods for less-resourced EU languages, focusing on applications for media industry, including keyword extraction, comment moderation and article generation.

1 Introduction

In the EU, websites and online services for citizens offer resources in national local languages, and often only provide a second language (usually English) when absolutely needed. For the EU to realise a truly equitable, open, multilingual online content and tools to support its management, new multilingual technologies which do not rely on translation of text between languages are urgently needed. The aim of EMBEDDIA was to address these challenges by leveraging innovations in the use of *cross-lingual and multilingual embeddings* coupled with *deep neural networks* to allow existing monolingual resources to be used across languages, leveraging their high speed of operation for near real-time applications, without the need for large computational resources. Across more than three years (01/01/2019 to 31/12/2021), *six academic partners* (Jozef Stefan Institute, the coordinating partner, Queen Mary University of London, University of Ljubljana, University of La Rochelle, University of Helsinki and University of Edinburgh) and *four industry partners* (TEXTA OÜ, As Ekspress Meedia, Finnish News Agency STT and Trikoder d.o.o.) developed novel solutions with focus on less-represented EU languages, and tested them in real-world media production contexts.

The main scientific goals of the project were to:

- Develop the *embeddings technology* for new generation NLP tools, which are both multilingual (able to deal with multiple languages) and cross-lingual (transfer easily across languages).
- Develop tools and resources for *less-resourced morphologically rich EU languages*, including Croatian, Estonian, Finnish, Latvian, Lithuanian and Slovenian.
- Leverage tools for well-resourced languages to be used for less-represented languages.

The project was strongly committed to address the challenges in news media industry, including:

- **Comment analysis** with mono- and cross-lingual applications in offensive speech filtering, fake news spreaders detection and sentiment analysis.
- **News analysis** with applications for keyword extraction, named entity recognition, news sentiment detection, viewpoints analysis, topic modelling, news linking, etc.
- **News generation** including text generation from structured data and headline generation.

1.1 Acknowledgements

This work has been supported by the EU's Horizon 2020 RIA under grant 825153 (EMBEDDIA), as well as ARRS core programme P2-0103.

2 Selected outputs

2.1 Datasets

EMBEDDIA has publicly released news and comments datasets (Pollak et al., 2021) in Estonian, Croatian, Russian and Latvian under the CC BY-NC-ND 4.0 license. We also created a set of novel benchmarks for evaluation, including CoSimLex dataset of word similarity in context (Armendariz et al., 2020) and cross-lingual analogy datasets (Ulčar et al., 2020).

Macken, Rufener, Van den Bogaert, Daems, Tezcan, Vanroy, Fonteyne, Barrault, Costa-jussà, Kemp, Pilos, Declercq, Koponen, Forcada, Scarton, Moniz (eds.)
Proceedings of the 23rd Annual Conference of the European Association for Machine Translation, p. 291–292
Ghent, Belgium, June 2022.

2.2 Pretrained embeddings

Several monolingual and cross-lingual embeddings models have been trained for less-resourced EU languages (Ulčar et al., 2021), including ELMo embeddings, CroSloEngual BERT, LitLat BERT, FinEst BERT, SloRoberta and Est-Roberta.

2.3 Applications

Selected results include monolingual (Martinc et al., 2021), and cross-lingual (Koloski et al., 2022) keyword extraction methods, methods for cross-lingual offensive language detection (Pelicon et al., 2021), cross-lingual news sentiment analysis (Pelicon et al., 2020), cross-lingual Twitter sentiment detection (Robnik-Šikonja et al., 2020), named entity recognition (Boros et al., 2020), and article generation (Leppänen and Toivonen, 2021). Many other methods are described at `http://embeddia.eu/outputs/`.

3 Tools

The main EMBEDDIA tools are made available for future use through the EMBEDDIA Media Assistant, available at `https://embeddia.texta.ee/` consisting of:

- **API Wrapper**, intended for system integrations, including comment filtering, article analyzers and article generators.
- **Demonstrator**, showcasing a selection of the developed tools in a simple GUI for demonstration purposes (`https://embeddia-demo.texta.ee/`).
- **Tools Explorer** gathers a larger selection of tools relevant to media industry and research.
- **Texta Toolkit** GUI and API allow interactive user access and programming access to data exploration, investigative journalism and building own classifiers.

References

Armendariz, C. S., Purver, M., Ulčar, M., Pollak, S., Ljubešić, N., and Granroth-Wilding, M. (2020). CoSimLex: A resource for evaluating graded word similarity in context. In *Proc. of the 12th LREC*, pages 5878–5886, Marseille, France. ELRA.

Boros, E., Hamdi, A., Linhares Pontes, E., Cabrera-Diego, L. A., Moreno, J. G., Sidere, N., and Doucet, A. (2020). Alleviating digitization errors in named entity recognition for historical documents. In *Proc. of the 24th CoNLL*, pages 431–441, Online.

Koloski, B., Pollak, S., Škrlj, B., and Martinc, M. (2022). Out of thin air: Is zero-shot cross-lingual keyword detection better than unsupervised? In *arXiv:2202.06650*.

Leppänen, L. and Toivonen, H. (2021). A baseline document planning method for automated journalism. In *Proc. of the 23rd NoDaLiDa*, pages 101–111.

Martinc, M., Škrlj, B., and Pollak, S. (2021). Tnt-kid: Transformer-based neural tagger for keyword identification. *Natural Language Engineering*, page 1–40.

Pelicon, A., Pranjić, M., Miljković, D., Škrlj, B., and Pollak, S. (2020). Zero-shot learning for cross-lingual news sentiment classification. *Applied Sciences*, 10(17):5993.

Pelicon, A., Shekhar, R., Škrlj, B., Purver, M., and Pollak, S. (2021). Investigating cross-lingual training for offensive language detection. *PeerJ Computer Science*, 7:e559.

Pollak, S., Robnik-Šikonja, M., Purver, M., Boggia, M., Shekhar, R., Pranjić, M., Salmela, S., Krustok, I., Paju, T., Linden, C.-G., et al. (2021). Embeddia tools, datasets and challenges: Resources and hackathon contributions. In *Proc. of the EACL Hackashop on News Media Content Analysis and Automated Report Generation*, pages 99–109.

Robnik-Šikonja, M., Reba, K., and Mozetič, I. (2020). Cross-lingual transfer of Twitter sentiment models using a common vector space. In *Proc. of the Conference on Language Technologies & Digital Humanities*, pages 87–92.

Ulčar, M., Vaik, K., Lindström, J., Dailidėnaitė, M., and Robnik-Šikonja, M. (2020). Multilingual culture-independent word analogy datasets. In *Proc. of the 12th LREC*, pages 4074–4080, Marseille, France. ELRA.

Ulčar, M., Žagar, A., Armendariz, C. S., Repar, A., Pollak, S., Purver, M., and Robnik-Šikonja, M. (2021). Evaluation of contextual embeddings on less-resourced languages. *CoRR*, abs/2107.10614.

Trados-to-Translog-II: Adding Gaze and Qualitivity data to the CRITT TPR-DB

Masaru Yamada, Takanori Mizowaki
Rikkyo University, Tokyo, Japan
masaru.yamada@rikkyo.ac.jp;
taka.m0118@icloud.com

Longhui Zou, Michael Carl
Kent State University, Ohio, USA
{lzou4.mcarl6}@kent.edu

Abstract

The CRITT (Center for Research and Innovation in Translation and Translation Technology) provides a Translation Process Research Database (TPR-DB) and a rich set of summary tables and tools that help to investigate translator behavior. In this paper, we describe a new tool in the TPR-DB that converts Trados Studio keylogging data (Qualitivity) into Translog-II format and adds the converted data to the CRITT TPR-DB. The tool is also able to synchronize with the output of various eye-trackers. We describe the components of the new TPR-DB tool and highlight some of the features that it produces in the TPR-DB tables.

1 Introduction

Much of the translation process research (TPR) has been conducted with Translog-II, which is an editor that allows to record keystrokes and eye tracking data during translation sessions (Carl, 2012). The collected data can then be uploaded to the Translation Process Research Database (CRITT TPR-DB) which provides numerous tools for data analysis and data visualization (Carl et al., 2016). However, Translog-II does not offer professional editing possibilities nor is it a translation environment which professional translators normally use. To alleviate these shortcomings, to emulate translators' real-world working conditions in experimental conditions and thus increase the ecological validity of TPR, we have implemented a new Trados interface that uses Qualitivity [1] to log keystroke and that converts the output into a CRITT TPR-DB format. In addition, eye-tracking data (currently: Tobii, Eyelink, GazePoint) can be collected and synchronized with the Qualitivity keystroke data while uploading the data to the CRITT TPR-DB.

2 Uploading Trados data to TPR-DB

Trados Studio[2], a commercial CAT software, has a non-invasive free-of-charge plugin called Qualitivity that collects typing activities from the translator. Qualitivity captures modifications in the editor (usually induced through keystroke, but also through automated processes) and assigns each event a timestamp as well as the segment number in which the modification occurs. This data can be converted into a Translog-compatible XML format and integrated into the CRITT TPR-DB via the newly added uploading option in the CRITT TPR-DB management tool, as shown in the following Figure 1.

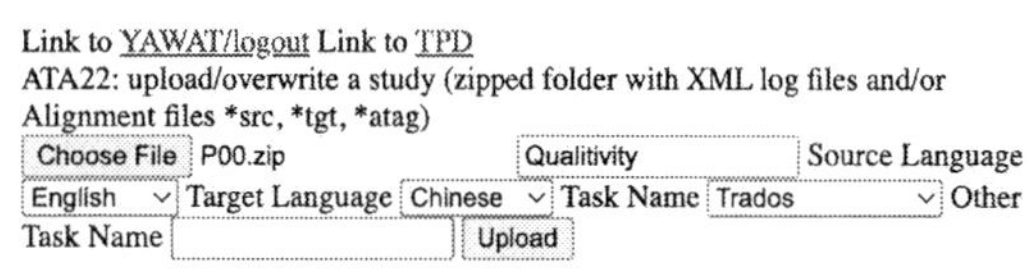

Figure 1: Upload CRITT TPR-DB management tool

3 Synchronizing Eye-tracking data

In order to investigate translator's gazing behavior during the translation processes, we integrated an add-on to the Trados-Translog-II conversion tool that merges eye tracking data with the Qualitivity keystroke data in a seamless way. This allows us to exploit user activity data collected during translation sessions in Trados as a combination of eye movement and keyboard logging. However, unlike Translog-II, Trados (or Qualitivity) does not offer the possibility to connect directly to external eye trackers. Qualitivity also does not record where on the screen (X/Y positions) the edited word or segment occurs. Due to the

[1] https://community.rws.com/product-groups/trados-portfolio/rws-appstore/w/wiki/2251/qualitivity
[2] https://www.trados.com/products/trados-studio/

Macken, Rufener, Van den Bogaert, Daems, Tezcan, Vanroy, Fonteyne, Barrault, Costa-jussà, Kemp, Pilos, Declercq, Koponen, Forcada, Scarton, Moniz (eds.)
Proceedings of the 23rd Annual Conference of the European Association for Machine Translation, p. 293–294
Ghent, Belgium, June 2022.

different ways in which the gaze data is recorded in Translog-II and within the Trados setting, some different processing strategies are required.

Qualitivity and the eye-tracker software (Tobii, Eyelink, GazePoint) are independent programs, each of which is equipped with an independent keylogger. That is, every keystroke pressed by the translator in Trados is logged twice, once by Qualitivity (as a text modification), and once by the eye tracker software, each with independent timers and thus potentially different timestamps. The mapping of gaze data and textual data works in three steps 1) Comparing sequences of keystrokes recorded with Qualitivity and the eye tracker allows us finding an offset between the timestamps, and successively synchronize gaze data with the Qualitivity keystrokes. 2) While the eye tracker provides us with a stream of X/Y coordinates that reveal where on the screen the translator is looking at a certain point in time, Qualitivity tells us for each keystroke which segment was edited at a given point in time. The synchronized, combined information allows us, then, to relate the course of gaze events (X/Y coordinates) with (sequences of) keystrokes (or text modifications) that occur in a certain Trados segment[3] 3) Processing the data within the CRITT TPR-DB implies a) mapping each keystroke on the target word that it produces (Carl, 2012).and b) aligning the source text and the target texts on a word-level. This makes it possible to map the synchronized gaze data on the emerging target text via the alignment relations on source segments, just as with Translog-II data,

4 Gaze-path features

However, in contrast to Translog-II - which provides the possibility for gaze–to–word mapping at runtime - we do not know which word(s) the translator is looking at when collecting data with Trados. In the Trados setting we only know the X/Y coordinates of the gaze path, whether the gaze occurred on the ST or the TT windows, and which segment the translator was working on. This information is, however, highly informative and provides indicators of translation effort, as encoded, for instance, in the relative and total distances between fixations, the number of regressions, the gaze movements in the X and Y direction of the screen, parallel (concurrent) reading and typing behavior, etc. Within the TPR-DB, we compute this gaze path summary information for various process and product units. For instance, gaze path information can be computed on the segment level (SG) for production units (PU), alignment groups (AG), or also for each word (ST), which provides novel ways to assess translation effort and effects on various levels of granularity.

5 Conclusion

The new Trados-TPR-DB interface provides the possibility to record translation behavior in an ecologically realistic translation environment. We are now able to investigate patterns of reading and typing activities in a widely and professionally used CAT tool, and thus to achieve a better understanding of factors that impact professional translation activity. The collected data can be uploaded and processed in the CRITT TPR-DB, which offers a wide variety of analysis and visualization tools (Carl et al., 2016) as well as detailed information about translation effort and translation effects. We are able to expand the features with customized algorithms and open-source NLP packages to conduct further analysis regarding the translation effect, such as automatic translation assessment tools (e.g., BLEU and COMET), and linguistic complexity metrics (e.g., LingX) (Zou et al., 2022). Several ongoing studies are already using this new tool and more results are likely to be available soon.

References

Carl, Michael, Moritz Schaeffer, and Srinivas Bangalore. 2016. The CRITT translation process research database. In *New directions in empirical translation process research* (pp. 13-54). Springer, Cham.

Carl, Michael. 2012. Translog-II: a Program for Recording User Activity Data for Empirical Reading and Writing Research. *LREC*,12: 4108-4112.

Zou, Longhui, Michael Carl, Mehdi Mirzapour, Hélène Jacquenet, and Lucas N.Vieira. 2022. AI-Based Syntactic Complexity Metrics and Sight Interpreting Performance. In: Kim JH et al. (eds) *Intelligent Human Computer Interaction. IHCI 2021. Lecture Notes in Computer Science* (vol. 13184, pp. 534-547). Springer, Cham.

[3] We assume that gazing patterns preceding a (sequence of) keystrokes are indicative of the exerted effort related to their production.

Writing in a Second Language with Machine Translation (WiLMa)

Margot Fonteyne[1,2], **Maribel Montero Perez**[2], **Joke Daems**[1], **and Lieve Macken**[1]
[1] LT[3], Language and Translation Technology Team
[2] MULTIPLES, Research Centre for Multilingual Practices and Language Learning in Society
Ghent University, Belgium
margot.fonteyne@ugent.be

Abstract

The WiLMa project aims to assess the effects of using machine translation (MT) tools on the writing processes of second language (L2) learners of varying proficiency. Particular attention is given to individual variation in learners' tool use.

1 Introduction

WiLMa (2021–2024) is a predoctoral research project funded by Ghent University's Special Research Fund (Grant No. BOF.DOC.2021.0001.01). The objectives for this project are:

- To compare the L2 MT-assisted writing process across proficiency levels with L2 writing processes not assisted by MT
- To map the individual variation in MT consultation behaviour (i.e., how L2 learners use MT during writing), investigate its correlation with learners' L2 proficiency level, and study its effects on the L2 writing product

The learners studied in this project are Dutch (L1) learners of Swedish (L2). In this project description, we report on the pilot study we carried out with these learners and present the next steps of this project.

Over the past decade, using MT has become a widespread practice among L2 learners, with writing tasks being one of the technology's most popular use cases (Jolley and Maimone, 2022). A number of publications has already investigated the effects of MT use on L2 writing using a product-oriented approach. These studies have shown that writing products for which MT use was allowed differ from products for which it was not allowed.

However, our knowledge of the effects of MT use on the L2 writing process is still limited. By boosting learners' linguistic skills, MT may help learners to handle the competing demands on the different writing subprocesses better. These effects might also be larger for learners with lower proficiency levels (Révész, 2021). So far, two studies have investigated whether there are any differences to be found between learners' online writing behaviours (speed fluency, pausing, reading, and revising) in MT and non-MT conditions (Garcia and Pena, 2011; Raído and Torrón, 2020). However, it is difficult to draw conclusions from these studies, as they were based on a very small sample size and cover only a limited range of proficiency levels.

Moreover, despite consulting the tools being a major component of the MT-assisted writing process, few studies have investigated how learners use MT during writing. Cancino and Panes (2021) report for example that (untrained) learners look up 95 words per 100 words written. Fredholm (2015) notes that, on average, 44% of learners' texts is MT. However, these studies do not tell us whether learners' consultation behaviour when having access to MT is any different from when learners use more traditional writing tools, such as online bilingual dictionaries (OBDs).

Furthermore, research indicates that L2 learners' use of MT varies. This variation may be related to L2 proficiency (Fredholm, 2015) and likely also affects the learners' writing products (Cancino and Panes, 2021). By mapping the relationships between how learners with varying proficiency levels use MT and their writing products, we aim not only to find a (partial) explanation as to why MT-assisted writing products turn out to be different from products for which MT was not allowed, but also to identify best practices for MT use by L2 learners of varying proficiency.

2 Pilot study

In this project's main experiment, we want to study the MT-assisted writing process across proficiency levels. To allow for this comparison, we need a reliable and valid instrument that quantifies learners' L2 proficiency level. We selected two tests that assess L2 learners' levels of Swedish: the Swedish Levels Test (Bokander, 2016) and a standardized placement test developed by Folkuniversitetet. Nine learners completed both tests. The internal consistency of the tests was high, as was the correlation between the learners' scores on the two tests. This correlation supports the criterion validity of the tests.

Moreover, we want to compare L2 learners' writing processes in two conditions: with access to an MT tool and with access to an OBD. To this end, the writing prompts the learners respond to should fulfill two criteria. First, they should elicit equivalent products and processes (i.e., be comparable). Second, they should be attainable to the least proficient learners, as well as challenging to the most proficient ones (i.e., be 'multilevel'). Therefore, we had 5 learners of varying proficiency respond to 4 prompts. In each prompt, we asked them to describe 3 images, choose the one that appealed to them the most, and explain why. This way, the texts contained both descriptive and argumentative elements, blending genres of varying difficulty.

Using the linguistic profiling tool Profiling-UD[1] and the keystroke analysis program Inputlog,[2] we analyzed the equivalence of the prompts by comparing product and process measures across the 4 tasks. The prompts elicited texts of similar length and complexity. The amount of time the participants spent on the tasks was comparable, as were their pausing and repair patterns. The participants consulted the tools that were allowed equally often and spent a similar amount of time consulting them. We also did not find any patterns in how difficult the learners perceived the different prompts.

The suitability of the prompts for use with multilevel learners was assessed by conducting similar analyses, but this time across levels instead of prompts. The least proficient learners still managed to comfortably exceed the threshold of 100 words in the given time, which is needed to perform reliable automated analyses on the texts. The consultation measures show that even the most proficient learners relied heavily on the tools when responding to the prompts, indicating that the tasks were still challenging for them.

The data of this pilot study will be made available on OSF, licensed under CC BY-NC-SA.

3 Future work

In the future, we will collect data on the writing processes and products of multilevel learners, by having them respond to the piloted prompts in two conditions: with access to *DeepL* (MT) and with access to *Van Dale* (OBD). We will register their online behaviours with screen capture, keystroke logging, and eye-tracking, and their underlying cognitive processes with stimulated recall.

[1] `http://www.italianlp.it/demo/profiling-ud/`
[2] `https://www.inputlog.net/`

References

Bokander, Lars. 2016. SweLT 1.0: konstruktion och pilottestning av ett nytt svenskt frekvensbaserat ordförrådstest. *Nordand*, 11(1):39–60.

Cancino, Marco and Jaime Panes. 2021. The impact of Google Translate on L2 writing quality measures: Evidence from Chilean EFL high school learners. *System*, 98, article 102464.

Fredholm, Kent. 2015. Online Translation Use in Spanish as a Foreign Language Essay Writing: Effects on Fluency, Complexity and Accuracy. *Revista Nebrija de Lingüística Aplicada a la Enseñanza de Lenguas*, 18:7–24.

Garcia, Ignacio and María Isabel Pena. 2011. Machine translation-assisted language learning: writing for beginners. *Computer Assisted Language Learning*, 24(5):471–487.

Jolley, Jason R. and Luciane Maimone. 2022. Thirty Years of Machine Translation in Language Teaching and Learning: A Review of the Literature. *L2 Journal*, 14(1):22–44.

Raído, Vanessa Enríquez and Marina Sánchez Torrón. 2020. Machine Translation, Language Learning and the 'Knowledge Economy'. In Michael Filimowicz and Veronika Tzankova (Eds.), *Reimagining Communication: Action* (pp.155–171). Routledge, New York, NY; Abingdon, Oxon.

Révész, Andrea. 2021, May 14. *Investigating L2 writing processes: The roles of proficiency and stage of writing* [Conference Presentation]. LSLARF Annual Colloquium 2021, online. `https://youtu.be/L2TcHbl_uaE?t=2007`.

Europeana Translate: Providing multilingual access to digital cultural heritage

Eirini Kaldeli[1], Mercedes García-Martínez[2], Antoine Isaac[3], Paolo Sebastiano Scalia[3], Arne Stabenau[1], Iván Lena Almor[2], Carmen Grau Lacal[2], Martín Barroso Ordóñez[2], Amando Estela[2] and Manuel Herranz[2]

[1] National Technical University of Athens, Greece, [2] Pangeanic SL, Spain,
[3] Europeana Foundation, The Netherlands

Abstract

Europeana Translate is a project funded under the Connecting European Facility with the objective to take advantage of state-of-the-art machine translation in order to increase the multilinguality of resources in the cultural heritage domain.

1 Europeana Translate Mission

The Europeana platform[1] provides access to European digital cultural heritage (CH). It currently contains more than 58 million digital items contributed by more than 3,500 different museums, libraries, archives and galleries from all EU member countries. Each item is described via a set of metadata fields that convey essential information about it, such as its title, free text description, creator, etc., and help users to discover and understand the objects they are interested in. Currently, the majority of records contain terms only in a single language, the data providers' language. This lack of multilingual metadata hampers Europeana's goal of offering broad access to its collection across languages.

In order to address this challenge, the Europeana Translate project (May 2021 until Apr 2023) seeks to exploit and build on state-of-the-art machine translation (MT) services to advance the multilinguality of European digital CH. The project proposes a sustainable workflow and accompanying toolset which can be used to enrich CH datasets with multilingual metadata. The consortium includes: the National Technical University of Athens, the Europeana Foundation, Pangeanic SL, the European Fashion Heritage Association, the Netherlands Institute for Sound and Vision, and the Michael Culture Association.

A selection of CH metadata resources in various languages will be used to train and improve the accuracy of translation algorithms in this specific sector. The proposed solution will be applied to produce automatic translations from the 23 official EU languages to English for at least 25 million metadata records on the Europeana platform. Moreover, Europeana Translate will make openly available a number of multilingual resources from the CH sector, a domain of public interest which is currently under-represented in existing repositories of language corpora. To this end, the project will publish to the ELRC-SHARE[2] repository CH metadata in parallel languages and monolingual records under a free reuse license (CC0).

2 Architectural Overview

Figure 1 provides an overview of the overall Europeana Translate architecture.

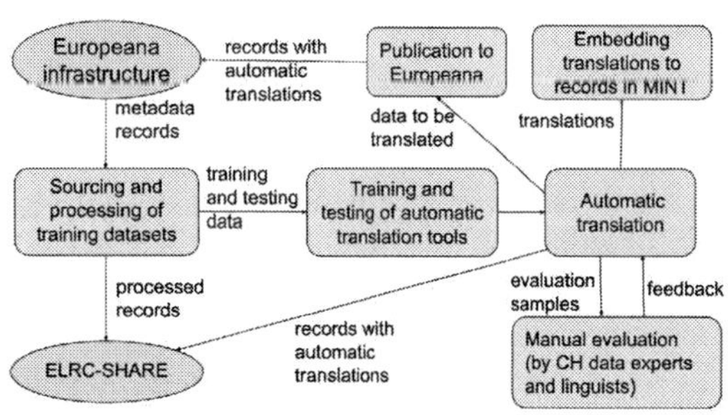

Figure 1: Europeana Translate Workflow

Sourcing and processing of in-domain training datasets: In this step (detailed in Section 3) we select and process all the data that will be used for the

[1] https://www.europeana.eu/

[2] https://www.elrc-share.eu/

Macken, Rufener, Van den Bogaert, Daems, Tezcan, Vanroy, Fonteyne, Barrault, Costa-jussà, Kemp, Pilos, Declercq, Koponen, Forcada, Scarton, Moniz (eds.)
Proceedings of the 23rd Annual Conference of the European Association for Machine Translation, p. 297–298
Ghent, Belgium, June 2022.

in-domain training of the translation tools and apply all the necessary processing and cleaning, so as to bring them to the formats expected by the translation tools.

Training and testing of automatic translation tools: The training phase will use 12 million translation segments from existing generic linguistic corpora, enhanced with the CH-specific data resulting from the previous step.

Automatic translation: The in-domain trained MT engines will be deployed and their capabilities exposed via an API interconnected with the Europeana platform as well as the MINT[3] (Metadata INTeroperability services) aggregation platform, which is used by several CH organisations for uploading and managing metadata records.

Manual evaluation: Two complementary evaluation methods will be performed to assess the produced automatic translations: evaluation by linguist experts using the Machine Translation Evaluation Tool MTET;[4] and evaluation by CH domain experts using CrowdHeritage,[5] a platform for organising online crowdsourcing campaigns in the CH domain.

Publication to Europeana: The translations retrieved by invoking the in-domain MT engines will be ingested, indexed, and presented on the Europeana platform. To save on indexing space and technical complexity, the idea is to use English translations as a pivot that acts as the bridge for translating all other languages (and search queries) to and from.

Embedding translations to MINT records: The automatic translations can also be inserted as enrichments to datasets uploaded in MINT. The augmented records can then be published to Europeana or be further exploited by CH organisations' own platforms.

3 Selection and filtering of training data

The main source of training data is metadata records with parallel languages retrieved from the Europeana platform. In the cases where the amount of bilingual data is not adequate, monolingual data will also be used to specialise the models via the generation of synthetic data. Complementary to the training data corresponding to metadata records, multilingual vocabularies relevant to the CH domain and used by Europeana for semantic enrichment are also exploited for the domain adaptation of the translation engines.

Figure 2 provides an indication of the amount of monolingual and bilingual (English–EU language) metadata fields in Europeana across different languages. For many languages there are more than 100,000 bilingual metadata fields, an amount which is considered a sufficient for in-domain specialisation. At the same time, some languages, such as Hungarian and Slovakian, are significantly underrepresented.

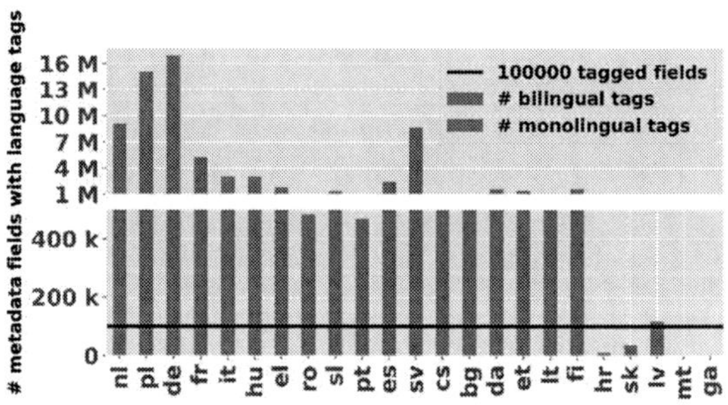

Figure 2: Raw number of mono- and bi-lingual (English–EU language) metadata fields on Europeana. An horizontal line marks the threshold of 100,000 fields.

Note that the plot only considers a subset of all metadata fields and only the values that are provided with explicit language tags. It may be possible to obtain more data by applying advanced data analysis, especially language detection. The numbers indicated here refer to unfiltered data that need to undergo further processing, since only a fragment of the raw data is actually suitable for training. To retain relevant data, multiple processing steps are applied, including the de-duplication of metadata field values repeated across many records, segmentation, and various types of cleaning, such as identification of incorrect language tags and pruning of incompatible value pairs.

In conclusion, Europeana Translate has the potential to significantly improve the multilinguality of CH items. The project builds on a well-defined architecture and has conducted an investigation of available raw data that can be leveraged for in-domain training. Preliminary experiments for translating metadata from French to English demonstrate an improvement of results compared to generic models. Several challenges still remain, such as acquiring additional training data for underrepresented languages and adopting appropriate methods for evaluation.

[3] http://mint.image.ece.ntua.gr/

[4] http://mtet.pangeamt.com/

[5] https://crowdheritage.eu/

The PASSAGE project : Standard German Subtitling of Swiss German TV content

Pierrette Bouillon, Johanna Gerlach, Jonathan Mutal, Marianne Starlander
Faculty of translation and interpreting, University of Geneva
40, bd du Pont d'Arve, 1211 Geneva, Switzerland
{pierrette.bouillon, johanna.gerlach, jonathan.mutal, marianne.starlander}@unige.ch

Abstract

We present the PASSAGE project, which aims at automatic Standard German subtitling of Swiss German TV content. This is achieved in a two step process, beginning with ASR to produce a normalised transcription, followed by translation into Standard German. We focus on the second step, for which we explore different approaches and contribute aligned corpora for future research.

1 Introduction

Swiss German, a primarily spoken language with many regional dialects and no standardised written form (Honnet et al., 2018), is spoken by two thirds of the population of Switzerland. It is widely used on Swiss TV, e.g. in news reports or interviews, which are subtitled in Standard German to make them accessible to people who cannot understand spoken Swiss German. Producing these subtitles automatically would be advantageous in terms of time and cost. This task is the focus of the PASSAGE project (Nov. 2020- Dec. 2022) "Sous-titrage automatique du suisse allemand en allemand standard", which is a collaboration between Geneva University, SRF (Schweizer Radio und Fernsehen) and recapp.[1]

In this project a first automatic speech recognition (ASR) step is used to produce a normalised transcription of spoken Swiss German, keeping the original syntax and expressions but using Standard German words. In a second step, different approaches are explored to transform this normalised transcription into correct written Standard German (see Figure 1). To achieve this, multiple issues must be dealt with: ASR errors, incorrect detection of sentence boundaries, features related to spontaneous spoken language, such as dysfluencies or informal language, and finally the syntactic divergences between Swiss German and Standard German (Glaser and Bart, 2021). The three goals of the project are 1) to create data sets for Swiss German, 2) to build systems for the translation of ASR output into Standard German, and 3) to evaluate the usability of the system output.

2 Data

The following data were provided by SRF:

- Normalised transcriptions of TV shows: originally created to train the Swiss German speech recogniser, these human transcriptions keep the original syntax and expressions but use Standard German words. (98,126 segments)
- Original Standard German subtitles of the TV shows (DE): batches of subtitles, not aligned with the transcriptions. (101,150 segments)

Based on these data, we have so far created several aligned corpora, which were used to train and specialise the first systems:

- Normalised transcriptions - Standard German: this corpus was produced by manual post-editing of the transcriptions. (20,634 segments)
- Normalised transcriptions - original subtitles: this corpus was aligned automatically. (70,374 segments)

[1] https://www.media-initiative.ch/project/subtitling-of-swiss-german-into-standard-german-automatic-post-editing/

Macken, Rufener, Van den Bogaert, Daems, Tezcan, Vanroy, Fonteyne, Barrault, Costa-jussà, Kemp, Pilos, Declercq, Koponen, Forcada, Scarton, Moniz (eds.)
Proceedings of the 23rd Annual Conference of the European Association for Machine Translation, p. 299–300
Ghent, Belgium, June 2022.

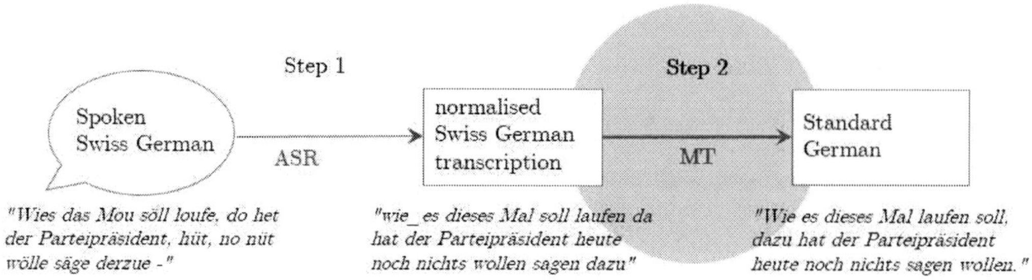

Figure 1: Overview of the subtitling pipeline

- Synthetic parallel data for some of the syntactic divergences between Swiss and Standard German: these corpora were generated by applying hand-crafted transformation rules to the post-edited transcriptions and the original subtitles. Rules were created using the SpaCy toolkit's Matcher[2] to change word order or verb forms to artificially produce Swiss German syntax (e.g. Man *verschliesst* sich solchen Fragen sicher nicht $\rightarrow$ Man *tut* sich solchen Fragen sicher nicht *verschliessen*). (4,418 and 13,896 segments generated from post-edited transcriptions and subtitles).

Finally, our project partner recapp[3] provided real ASR output, which was used for evaluation, and is currently being aligned with the original subtitles to create another parallel resource.

3 Systems

The project aims at investigating different approaches suitable for tasks where only few changes are needed and applicable to low-resource languages. We will also explore different settings, such as the impact of different training data, e.g. transcriptions vs ASR output, automatic vs manual alignment.

4 First results

The first two approaches tested for this task are 1) a neural machine translation (NMT) transformer architecture with copy attention (Gehrmann et al., 2018) and 2) an edit-based model (Ed) with a task-specific attention mechanism that predicts types of edits (Berard et al., 2017).

Our first system evaluations were carried out on normalised transcriptions, which simulate a perfect ASR result. An automatic evaluation using the post-edited version as reference showed that overall the NMT system was slightly better than the Ed system (BLEU 64.91 vs 61.49), and that NMT makes more edits than Ed (HTER 22.59 vs. 12.69).

Another round of evaluations was performed on real ASR output, with a focus on the systems' ability to transform Swiss German syntactic phenomena into their Standard German counterparts. Here the NMT system outperforms the Ed system. For NMT, the addition of targeted synthetic training data improves the results, in terms of transformed phenomena and precision.

Next steps include an evaluation with end-users to assess the impact on satisfaction.

Acknowledgements

This project has received funding from the Initiative for Media Innovation based at Media Center, EPFL, Lausanne, Switzerland.

References

Bérard, Alexandre, Laurent Besacier, and Olivier Pietquin. 2017. Lig-cristal submission for the WMT2017 automatic post-editing task. *Proceedings of the Second Conference on Machine Translation.* ACL. pp. 623–629.

Gehrmann, Sebastian, Yuntian Deng, and Alexander M. Rush. 2018. Bottom-up abstractive summarization. *Proceedings of the 2018 Conference on Empirical Methods in Natural Language Processing.* ACL. pp. 4098–4109.

Glaser, Elvira and Gabriela Bart. 2021. *Syntaktischer Atlas der deutschen Schweiz (SADS).* A. Francke Verlag

Honnet, Pierre-Edouard, Andrei Popescu-Belis, Claudiu Musat, and Michael Baeriswyl. 2018. Machine translation of low-resource spoken dialects: Strategies for normalizing Swiss German. *Proceedings of the 11th International Conference on Language Resources and Evaluation (LREC 2018).* pp. 3781–3788.

[2]https://spacy.io/api/matcher

[3]https://recapp.ch/

MaCoCu: Massive collection and curation of monolingual and bilingual data: focus on under-resourced languages

Marta Bañón†, Miquel Esplà-Gomis★, Mikel L. Forcada★, Cristian García-Romero★, Taja Kuzman‡, Nikola Ljubešić‡, Rik van Noord♦, Leopoldo Pla Sempere★, Gema Ramírez-Sánchez†, Peter Rupnik‡, Vít Suchomel‡, Antonio Toral♦, Tobias van der Werff♦, Jaume Zaragoza†

‡Jožef Stefan Institute, †Prompsit, ♦Rijksuniversiteit Groningen, ★Universitat d'Alacant

‡{taja.kuzman,nikola.ljubesic,peter.rupnik}@ijs.si, vit.suchomel@sketchengine.eu

†{mbanon,gramirez,jzaragoza}@prompsit.com

♦{r.i.k.van.noord,a.toral.ruiz,t.n.van.der.werff}@rug.nl

★{mespla,mlf,cgarcia,lpla}@dlsi.ua.es

Abstract

We introduce the project *MaCoCu: Massive collection and curation of monolingual and bilingual data: focus on under-resourced languages*, funded by the Connecting Europe Facility, which is aimed at building monolingual and parallel corpora for under-resourced European languages. The approach followed consists of crawling large amounts of textual data from selected top-level domains of the Internet, and then applying a curation and enrichment pipeline. In addition to corpora, the project will release the free/open-source web crawling and curation software used.

1 Introduction

This paper describes the project *MaCoCu: Massive collection and curation of monolingual and bilingual data: focus on under-resourced languages*, funded by the Connecting Europe Facility in the 2020 CEF Telecom Call - Automated Translation (2020-EU-IA-0078).[1] This project started on June 1, 2021, and will last for two years. It is aimed at building large and high-quality monolingual and parallel (with English) corpora for five under-resourced official EU languages: Maltese, Bulgarian, Slovenian, Croatian, and Icelandic;[2] and for the languages of the five candidate states to become EU members: Turkish, Albanian, Macedonian, Montenegrin, and Serbian. Existing initiatives producing similar corpora, such as Paracrawl (Bañón et al., 2020) or Oscar (Abadji et al., 2022) exploit existing resources such as Common Crawl[3] or the Internet Archive.[4] In contrast, our strategy consists in automatically crawling top-level domains (TLD) with the potential to contain substantial amounts of textual data in the targeted languages,[5] and then applying a monolingual and a parallel curation pipelines on the downloaded data. This approach aims at obtaining more and higher-quality data than that available in existing compilations.[6]

One of the objectives of the project is to identify data relevant for Digital Service Infrastructures (DSIs). Our corpora will be enriched with information about the relevance of the data collected for ten DISs: e-Health, e-Justice, Online Dispute Resolution, Europeana, Open Data Portal, Business Registers Interconnection System, e-Procurement, Safer Internet, Cybersecurity, and Electronic Exchange of Social Security Information.

1.1 International consortium

Four partners are involved in this project: Institut Jožef Stefan (Slovenia), Rijksuniversiteit Groningen (Netherlands), Prompsit Language Engineering S.L. (Spain), and Universitat d'Alacant (Spain; coordinator). The consortium has a strong background in the task of building corpora, as several partners have been also part of the consortiums behind projects such as Paracrawl (Bañón et al., 2020), GoURMET (Birch et al., 2019), EuroPat[7] and Abu-MaTran (Toral et al., 2015).

[1]https://ec.europa.eu/inea/connecting-europe-facility/cef-telecom/2020-eu-ia-0078

[2]Maltese and Icelandic were chosen since they are especially under-resourced official EU languages; Bulgarian, Slovenian and Croatian were chosen due to the interest of the consortium on South-Slavic languages, a decision that extends previous efforts in the Abu-MaTran project (Toral et al., 2015).

[3]https://commoncrawl.org/

[4]https://archive.org/

[5]National TLDs such as .hr for Croatian, or .is for Icelandic, and also generic TLDs such as .com, .org, or .eu.

[6]Preliminary automatic evaluation seem to confirm the quality of the data in the first data release (see Table 1).

[7]https://ec.europa.eu/inea/connecting-europe-facility/cef-telecom/2018-eu-ia-0061

Macken, Rufener, Van den Bogaert, Daems, Tezcan, Vanroy, Fonteyne, Barrault, Costa-jussà, Kemp, Pilos, Declercq, Koponen, Forcada, Scarton, Moniz (eds.)
Proceedings of the 23rd Annual Conference of the European Association for Machine Translation, p. 301–302
Ghent, Belgium, June 2022.

2 Outcomes of the project

The main results of the project will be parallel and monolingual corpora, as well as the code used to build them. In this section, we briefly describe the most relevant features of these outcomes.

2.1 Corpora

The main goal of this project is to build monolingual and parallel corpora for the ten languages mentioned in Section 1. Since the project is aimed at producing high-quality corpora, a thorough cleaning process will be carried out, which will include automatic noise cleaning/fixing, removal of near-duplicates and irrelevant data, such as boilerplates, and automatic detection of machine translated content. The corpora produced will be enriched with:

- Identifiers that allow to re-construct the original paragraphs or documents from the segments in the corpora, enabling to leverage information beyond the sentence-level;
- Language variety (e.g. British/American English) for some covered languages;
- Document-level affinity to the DSIs covered, which will be automatically identified through domain modelling;
- Personal information identification, to allow final users to remove it for specific use cases;
- *Translationese*, or the identification of the translation direction (only for parallel data);
- Identification of machine translation (only for parallel data), so that such crawled documents can be filtered out by the user.

Currently, monolingual and parallel data have been released for seven out of the ten languages targeted. Table 1 provides information about the sizes of the current version of these corpora.

2.2 Free/open-source pipeline

All the code developed within the project to crawl, curate and enrich the corpora built will be made available under free/open-source licences on MaCoCu[8] and Bitextor[9] GitHub organisations.[10]

3 Acknowledgment

This action has received funding from the European Union's Connecting Europe Facility 2014-2020 - CEF Telecom, under Grant Agreement No. INEA/CEF/ICT/A2020/2278341. The contents of this publication are the sole responsibility of its authors and do not necessarily reflect the opinion of the European Union.

[8]https://github.com/macocu

[9]https://github.com/bitextor

[10]Two code releases will be made, one at the end of the first year of the project, and the second one at the end of the project.

	Monolingual		Parallel	
Language	Docs.	Words	Segs.	Words
Turkish	16.0	4346.3	10.3	513.5
Bulgarian	10.5	3508.9	3.9	158.7
Croatian	7.3	2318.3	3.1	134.9
Slovene	5.8	1779.1	3.2	137.0
Macedonian	2.0	524.1	0.5	23.9
Icelandic	1.7	644.5	0.4	14.4
Maltese	0.5	347.9	1.2	69.6

Table 1: Sizes for the monolingual and parallel corpora for the first data release. Monolingual corpora are measured in millions of documents (Docs.) and millions of words. Parallel corpora are measured in millions of parallel segments (Segs.) and millions of words in the language other than English.

References

Abadji, Julien, Pedro Ortiz Suarez, Laurent Romary, and Benoît Sagot. 2022. Towards a Cleaner Document-Oriented Multilingual Crawled Corpus. *arXiv e-prints*, page arXiv:2201.06642, January.

Bañón, Marta, Pinzhen Chen, Barry Haddow, Kenneth Heafield, Hieu Hoang, Miquel Esplà-Gomis, Mikel L. Forcada, Amir Kamran, Faheem Kirefu, Philipp Koehn, Sergio Ortiz Rojas, Leopoldo Pla Sempere, Gema Ramírez-Sánchez, Elsa Sarrías, Marek Strelec, Brian Thompson, William Waites, Dion Wiggins, and Jaume Zaragoza. 2020. ParaCrawl: Web-scale acquisition of parallel corpora. In *Proceedings of the 58th Annual Meeting of the Association for Computational Linguistics*, pages 4555–4567, Online, July.

Birch, Alexandra, Barry Haddow, Ivan Tito, Antonio Valerio Miceli Barone, Rachel Bawden, Felipe Sánchez-Martínez, Mikel L. Forcada, Miquel Esplà-Gomis, Víctor Sánchez-Cartagena, Juan Antonio Pérez-Ortiz, Wilker Aziz, Andrew Secker, and Peggy van der Kreeft. 2019. Global under-resourced media translation (GoURMET). In *Proceedings of Machine Translation Summit XVII: Translator, Project and User Tracks*, pages 122–122, Dublin, Ireland, August.

Toral, Antonio, Tommi Pirinen, Andy Way, Raphaël Rubino, Gema Ramírez-Sánchez, Sergio Ortiz-Rojas, Víctor Sánchez-Cartagena, Jorge Ferrández-Tordera, Mikel Forcada, Miquel Espla-Gomis, Nikola Ljubešić, Filip Klubička, Prokopis Prokopidis, and Vassilis Papavassiliou. 2015. Automatic acquisition of machine translation resources in the Abu-MaTran project. *Procesamiento del Lenguaje Natural*, (55):185–188.

MT-Pese: Machine Translation and Post-Editese

Sheila Castilho
ADAPT Centre
School of Computing
Dublin City University
sheila.castilho@adaptcentre.ie

Natália Resende
ADAPT Centre
School of Computing
Dublin City University
natalia.resende@adaptcentre.ie

Abstract

This paper introduces the MT-Pese project which is an umbrella name for a series of experiment venues that started in 2019. The project aims at researching the post-editese phenomena in machine-translated texts. We describe a range of experiments performed in order to gauge the effect of post-editese in different domains, back-translation, and quality.

1 Translationese and Post-editese

A number of studies (Volansky et al., 2013) have shown evidence of the so-called translationese phenomena (Gellerstam, 1986), that is, statistical differences between translated texts and non-translated texts. Recently, post-editing (PE) of machine-translated (MT) texts has secured its space in the translation workflow for a variety of domains, and consequently, the research interest for the typical features of human-translated texts has shifted for the typical features of post-edited texts. However, results of studies searching for typical features of post-edited texts - what has been called "post-editese - have presented mixed results, that is, while some studies found evidence for the existence of post-editese (e.g. Toral, 2019; Castilho et al. 2019), other studies did not find evidence of the phenomena (e.g. Daems et al. 2017).

The aim of the MT-Pese project is to investigate the post-editese phenomena on MT PE texts, using the rationale behind the translationese features as proposed by Baker (1996): *simplification, explicitation, normalisation* (or *conservatism*) and *levelling out* (or *convergence*). We define post-editese as the difference between the characteristics of human-translated texts (HT) and the PE versions, in relation to the raw MT output. MT-Pese has researched what influences the features of post-editese in two different textual domains, namely, news and literature (Castilho et al., 2019). We found that the literature domain contained more post-editese features. In a further study, we looked into the post-editese features in two different genres within the literature domain (Castilho and Resende, 2022). Currently, the project is focused on investigating the features of Post-editese on backtranslations (BT), with the aim to identify, for instance, if BT of PE versions would still carry strong post-editese features. Finally, the project also aims at addressing the question of whether the features of post-editese could be related to MT quality (section 4).

2 What influences the features of post-editese? A preliminary study

This study (Castilho et al 2019) investigated the presence of post-editese in a corpus composed by HT, MT and PE texts post-edited by either professional translators or student translators in two domains: news and literature. We also tested whether the PE level (light PE vs. full PE). Results showed evidence of post-editese features manifested as PE texts closer to the source texts and raw MT output rather than HT texts, and that the translators' experience as well as the text domains influence the magnitude of the post-editese features

3 Post-Editese in Literary Translations

This study (Castilho and Resende 2022) investigated the existence of post-editese features in a literary corpus composed of two different genres:

Macken, Rufener, Van den Bogaert, Daems, Tezcan, Vanroy, Fonteyne, Barrault, Costa-jussà, Kemp, Pilos, Declercq, Koponen, Forcada, Scarton, Moniz (eds.)
Proceedings of the 23rd Annual Conference of the European Association for Machine Translation, p. 303–304
Ghent, Belgium, June 2022.

Alice's Adventures in Wonderland (AW) and The Girl on the Train (TGOTT), which were post-edited by nine professional translators. Results show a clear difference between the literary genres: while literary texts whose author's style is full of figurative language pose a harder challenge to the MT system, texts that emphasise action over language style are less challenging. We validate this assumption based on our observations that AW involved more edits than the TGOTT test set, suggesting that the MT output is capable of expressing the meaning of the source text more efficiently than for the AW. Moreover, we find a more visible pattern in terms of features for the TGOTT test set when compared to the AW which, in turn, is unstable in terms of pattern manifestation. This allowed us to confirm our post-editese hypothesis for almost all features in the TGOTT but for none in the AW.

4 Post-Editese in Backtranslations

This ongoing study aims at researching whether the post-editese features remain on backtranslated texts. To this end, we backtranslated the previous PE versions of the TGOTT and AW texts using an MT system, and extracted the same features examined in the previous studies in order to address the following questions:

a) Are the post-editese features reported in Castilho & Resende (2022) preserved in the BT texts?

b) How are post-editese features manifested in BT? Are BT features closer to the PEs or to the source texts?

The results will shed a light on whether BT from post-edited versions show more features from human involvement, and if so, whether that means PE-BTs have a higher quality. This will help the MT field, especially in regards to data augmentation.

5 Post-editese and Translation Quality

Finally, MT-Pese will look into whether post-editese features can be correlated with translation quality and creativity. For that, a few main research questions have been designed:

a) Which post-editese features are correlated to high quality post-edited texts?

b) Are there any features that can be correlated with naturalness?

c) Are there any features that can be correlated with creativity?

The results of this study will shed light on whether post-editese features mean that the PE version are of higher quality when compared to the raw MT output. If so, these features could be used to develop new evaluation metrics.

Acknowledgement

Both authors contributed equally to this work. This research was conducted with the financial support of the innovation programme under the Marie Skłodowska-Curie grant agreement No 843455 and the Irish Research Council (GOIPD/2020/69). Science Foundation Ireland under Grant Agreement No. 13/RC/2106_P2 at the ADAPT SFI Research Centre at Dublin City University.

References

Baker, Mona. 1996. Chapter corpus-based translation studies: The challenges that lie ahead. In Terminology, LSP and Translation: Studies in Language Engineering, in Honour of Juan C. Sager. Amsterdam: John Benjamins Publishing Company, page 175-186.

Castilho, Sheila, and Natália Resende. 2022. "Post-Editese in Literary Translations" Information 13, no. 2: 66. Online. https://doi.org/10.3390/info13020066

Castilho, Sheila, Natalia Resende, Ruslan Mitkov. 2019. What Influences Post-editese features? A preliminary study. Proceedings of the second workshop on Human-Informed Translation and Interpreting Technology (HiT-IT 2019). 5-6 September, 2019, Varna, Bulgaria, pages 19-27.

Daems, Joke, Orphée De Clercq, and Lieve Macken. 2017. Translationese and post-editese: How comparable is comparable quality? Linguistica Antverpiensia New Series - Themes in Translation Studies 16:89–103.

Martin Gellerstam. 1986. Translationese in Swedish novels translated from English. In Wollin, L. and Lindquist, H. Transla-tion Studies in Scandinavia. CWK Gleerup, Lund, volume 4, pages 88–95.

Toral, Antonio. 2019. Post-editese: an exacerbated translationese. In Proceedings of Machine Translation Summit. Dublin, Ireland.

Volansky, Vered, Noam Ordan, and Shuly Wintner. 2013. On the features of translationese. Digital Scholarship in the Hu-manities 30 (1):98–118.https://doi.org/10.1093/llc/fqt031.

A Quality Estimation and Quality Evaluation Tool for the Translation Industry

Elena Murgolo
Orbital 14
Milan, Italy
emurgolo@orbital14.ai

Javad Pourmostafa
TSHD, CSAI Department,
Tilburg University
Tilburg, The Netherlands
j.pourmostafa@uvt.nl

Dimitar Shterionov
TSHD, CSAI Department,
Tilburg University,
Tilburg, The Netherlands
d.shterionov@uvt.nl

1 Introduction

With the increase in machine translation (MT) quality over the latest years, it has now become a common practice to integrate MT in the workflow of language service providers (LSPs) and other actors in the translation industry. With MT having a direct impact on the translation workflow, it is important not only to use high-quality MT systems, but also to understand the quality dimension so that the humans involved in the translation workflow can make informed decisions. The evaluation and monitoring of MT output quality has become one of the essential aspects of language technology management in LSPs' workflows. First, a general practice is to carry out human tests to evaluate MT output quality *before* deployment. Second, a quality estimate of the translated text, thus after deployment, can inform post-editors or even represent post-editing effort. In the former case, based on the quality assessment of a candidate engine, an informed decision can be made whether the engine would be deployed for production or not. In the latter, a quality estimate of the translation output can guide the human post-editor or even make rough approximations of the post-editing effort. Quality of an MT engine can be assessed on document or on sentence level. A tool to jointly provide all these functionalities does not exist yet.

While human evaluation is considered the most reliable method of analyzing MT quality, it is time-consuming, expensive, and hardly scalable. Human testing is also difficult to apply for actual projects during a production workflow. While some commercial products that can partly replace human testing already exist, they are usually CAT-dependent and cannot be employed independently from other language technology tools.

The overall objective of the project presented in this paper is to develop a machine translation quality assessment (MTQA) tool that simplifies the quality assessment of MT engines, combining quality evaluation and quality estimation on document and sentence level. To address both use cases, i.e., before general deployment and to estimate each translation's quality, this tool will comprise two working modes: a machine translation quality evaluation (MTQEv) and a quality estimation (MTQE) modes.

This 6-month project is a collaboration between Tilburg University and Orbital14, an R&D company owned and 100% financed by Italian LSP Aglatech14, whose funding is making this tool's development possible.

2 MTQA Tool Overview

The MTQA is designed as a standalone tool and an API that can be used by users or invoked by other tools. Behind the user interface lies a distributed architecture which operates in two modes. Intermediate and final results are displayed to the user; final results are made available for download.

MTQEv is a human-driven quality assessment module, in which one or more MT systems' quality is evaluated based on a human-generated translation reference. MTQEv is typically used to compare already-in-use and new MT models by means of comparing their translation to the human gold standard, using automatic metrics, such as TER (Snover et al., 2006), BLEU (Papineni et al., 2002), chrF (Popović, 2015) and others. In our MTQA tool, this mode shall be used to take an informed decision on a business level about the models to be deployed in production for different language combinations and domains.

MTQE (machine translation quality estimation) is the process of predicting the quality of an MT system without human intervention or reference translations. MTQE can be at a word, sentence, or document level. In the case of document and sentence level, which are of interest for our project, the task is typically to predict a score that corresponds to a target evaluation criteria or metric. MTQE is the second mode the tool will be able to work in. Instead of comparing the MT output with an existing human translation, this mode will be used at the beginning of each translation project to evaluate the quality of the output by predicting the approximate number of changes a given MT output should undergo to reach acceptable quality. This mode shall be used to evaluate the usability of MT models for each project, in order to choose the best possible starting point for the PE (post-editing) and therefore to better allocate time and resources.

Both modes will be able to work both on document level and on segment level, so that the end-users, e.g., the project managers, will be able to choose the level of granularity they want to get to take a well-informed decision. To facilitate the use of the tool across all business workflows and for each use case, both modes will be integrated and independent from the other language technology tools that LSPs usually work with.

For MTQEv mode we employ the metrics TER, BLEU and chrF. For MTQE we first build neural QE models with the data described in Section 3; we then employ these models to score input data.

3 Working with industry data

An LSP could use either publicly available MT engines, or proprietary MT engines, trained specifically for the given translation use case, which would employ data, usually provided by the LSP to train a domain-specific and use-case-specific MT engine with highest quality.

The data an LSP usually translates is proprietary and cannot be publicly accessible, even for research purposes. A collaboration such as the one this project is based on, between Orbital14 and Tilburg, allows researchers and industry to work together on real use cases and proprietary data. Within the scope of this project, we exploit data that has been translated via trained and generic MT engines and was post-edited by Aglatech14 in the context of several translation projects. These data allow us to experiment with and build effective QE models that can be employed in the MTQA tool.

For this project we employ English–Italian data from the patent domain.

To this end, two types of data were provided by Aglatech14: (i) data that had been post-edited, in which case three documents were provided, source, MT output, and a post-edited version of the output (s-mt-pe); and (ii) data that had been translated by professional human linguists in the original project, in which case source and (human) translation (s-t) were provided.

To train our QE models we employed three different data sets: (i) the s-mt-pe documents; (ii) the s-t documents for which we translated the source using Aglatech14's MT engines and generated an s-mt-pe* corpus; and (iii) the open data sets BinQE (Turchi and Negri, 2014) and eSCAPE (Negri et al., 2018). For all data we computed the TER score between the MT and the post-edited or translated reference. This we used as target labels for our MTQE models.

References

Negri, Matteo, Marco Turchi, Rajen Chatterjee, and Nicola Bertoldi. 2018. ESCAPE: a large-scale synthetic corpus for automatic post-editing. In *Proceedings of the Eleventh International Conference on Language Resources and Evaluation (LREC 2018)*, Miyazaki, Japan, May. European Language Resources Association (ELRA).

Papineni, Kishore, Salim Roukos, Todd Ward, and Wei-Jing Zhu. 2002. BLEU: A Method for Automatic Evaluation of Machine Translation. In *Proceedings of the 40th Annual Meeting on Association for Computational Linguistics (ACL 2002)*, page 311–318. Association for Computational Linguistics, July 6-12.

Popović, Maja. 2015. chrF: character n-gram F-score for automatic MT evaluation. In *Proceedings of the Tenth Workshop on Statistical Machine Translation*, pages 392–395, September 17-18.

Snover, Matthew, Bonnie Dorr, Rich Schwartz, Linnea Micciulla, and John Makhoul. 2006. A study of translation edit rate with targeted human annotation. In *Proceedings of the 7th Conference of the Association for Machine Translation in the Americas: Technical Papers*, pages 223–231, August 8–12.

Turchi, Marco and Matteo Negri. 2014. Automatic Annotation of Machine Translation Datasets with Binary Quality Judgements. In *Proceedings of the Ninth International Conference on Language Resources and Evaluation (LREC'14)*, May 26-31.

MTEE : Open Machine Translation Platform for Estonian Government

Toms Bergmanis, Mārcis Pinnis, Roberts Rozis, Jānis Šlapiņš, Valters Šics, Berta Bernāne, Guntars Pužulis, Endijs Titomers
Tilde, Latvia {name.surname}@tilde.lv
Andre Tättar, Taido Purason, Hele-Andra Kuulmets, Agnes Luhtaru, Liisa Rätsep, Maali Tars, Annika Laumets-Tättar, Mark Fishel
University of Tartu, Estonia {name.surname}@ut.ee

Abstract

We present the MTEE project—a research initiative funded via an Estonian public procurement to develop machine translation technology that is open-source and free of charge. The MTEE project delivered an open-source platform serving state-of-the-art machine translation systems supporting four domains for six language pairs translating from Estonian into English, German, and Russian and vice-versa. The platform also features grammatical error correction and speech translation for Estonian and allows for formatted document translation and automatic domain detection. The software, data and training workflows for machine translation engines are all made publicly available for further use and research.

1 Project Background

MTEE is an Estonian governmental project to develop high-quality machine translation (MT) platform that is open-source and free of charge. The project was motivated by the COVID-19 pandemic. It was aimed to address the country's need for fast and cheap translation of information to and from Estonian and the languages most relevant to Estonia's society: English, German, and Russian. MTEE was funded by the Ministry of Education and Research via a public procurement through the Language Technology Competence Center at the Institute of the Estonian Language. The duration of MTEE project was nine months, and it concluded in January 2022. It was fulfilled as a collaboration between Tilde and the Institute of Computer Science of the University of Tartu. A demonstration of the platform[1] is made publicly available by hosting using the infrastructure of the High Performance Computing Center of the University of Tartu.

2 Data

To train MT systems, we used parallel data from OPUS (Tiedemann, 2009), ELRC-SHARE (Piperidis et al., 2018) and EU Open Data Portal,[2] as well as data donors and industry partners. In contrast, monolingual data were mainly obtained from the public web. To classify data as belonging to legal, military, crisis, or general domains, we used its source information. Furthermore, we used terminology provided by the Institute of the Estonian Language to automatically obtain additional data for individual domains. The resulting data sets ranged from 5 to 20 million parallel sentences for the general domain. However, data sets were much smaller for niche domains and language pairs, such as the German Estonian crisis domain, where only a few dozen sentence pairs were identified. We observed a similar pattern for the monolingual data, for which data sizes ranged from 50 million sentences for the general domain to only 8 thousand sentences for the Russian military domain.

We used random held-out subsets of training data for testing and development, which, depending on the language pair and domain, were 500 to 2000 sentences large. Held-out subsets, however, are part of pre-existing parallel corpora, which

[1] https://mt.cs.ut.ee/
[2] https://data.europa.eu/

may be present in training data of other (also third party) MT systems, which would make a fair comparison of the MT system quality impossible. For this reason, we also created entirely novel translation benchmarks[3] by ordering professional translations of recent news.

3 Models

Following the implementation by Lyu et al. (2020), we trained modular multilingual transformer-based models (Vaswani et al., 2017) using fairseq (Ott et al., 2019) with separate encoders and decoders for each input and output language. We selected this architecture because it showed better results for lower-resourced language pairs and domains. The final set of models was trained on a combination of parallel and back-translated data and fine-tuned for each domain.

To evaluate MTEE MT systems, we compared them against the public systems by Tilde, Google, DeepL and Neurotõlge.[4] The evaluation using the newly created translation benchmarks yielded results[5] on average favouring MTEE systems for all domains. These results suggest that, at least as these tests can tell, MTEE systems are competitive and of high quality.

4 Platform

The MTEE platform serves the MT systems and provides functionality for text, document (.docx, .xlsx, .odt, .tmx, .pptx, .txt), and web page translation for all domains and language pairs. Before the translation request is routed to the corresponding MT model, adherence to one of the four domains is automatically detected using a fine-tuned XLM-RoBERTa (Conneau et al., 2020) language model. For translation directions where Estonian is the source language, the platform also provides hints for grammatical error correction[6] and speech translation via a cascade of automatic speech recognition[7] followed by an MT system. These components can be accessed through the translation website or their REST APIs. All components developed for the platform are dockerized and released under the MIT license.[8]

5 Current Status of MTEE

The MTEE project concluded in January 2022, and its results were handed over to the Language Technology Competence Center at the Institute of the Estonian Language.

The High Performance Computing Center of the University of Tartu is hosting the MTEE platform's demonstration for at least another year. Tilde and the Institute of Computer Science of the University of Tartu also continue to provide their technical and scientific support during this period.

Ultimately, when the Institute of the Estonian Language has approbated the technical and scientific results of the project, they should possess the knowledge and the know-how to extend and maintain the platform independently.

References

Conneau, Alexis, Kartikay Khandelwal, Naman Goyal, Vishrav Chaudhary, Guillaume Wenzek, Francisco Guzmán, Édouard Grave, Myle Ott, Luke Zettlemoyer, and Veselin Stoyanov. 2020. Unsupervised Cross-lingual Representation Learning at Scale. In *Proceedings of ACL 2020*, pages 8440–8451.

Lyu, Sungwon, Bokyung Son, Kichang Yang, and Jaekyoung Bae. 2020. Revisiting Modularized Multilingual NMT to Meet Industrial Demands. In *Proceedings of EMNLP 2020*, pages 5905–5918, November.

Ott, Myle, Sergey Edunov, Alexei Baevski, Angela Fan, Sam Gross, Nathan Ng, David Grangier, and Michael Auli. 2019. fairseq: A Fast, Extensible Toolkit for Sequence Modeling. In *Proceedings of NAACL 2019 (Demonstrations)*, pages 48–53.

Piperidis, Stelios, Penny Labropoulou, Miltos Deligiannis, and Maria Giagkou. 2018. Managing Public Sector Data for Multilingual Applications Development. In *Proceedings of LREC 2018*, pages 1289–1293.

Tiedemann, Jörg. 2009. News from OPUS-A Collection of Multilingual Parallel Corpora with Tools and Interfaces. In *Recent Advances in Natural Language Processing*, volume 5, pages 237–248.

Vaswani, Ashish, Noam Shazeer, Niki Parmar, Jakob Uszkoreit, Llion Jones, Aidan N Gomez, Łukasz Kaiser, and Illia Polosukhin. 2017. Attention is All You Need. *Advances in Neural Information Processing Systems*, 30.

[3] https://github.com/Project-MTee/MTee_translation_benchmarks

[4] https://www.neurotolge.ee

[5] https://raw.githubusercontent.com/wiki/Project-MTee/mtee-platform/WP3.pdf

[6] https://github.com/tartunlp/grammar-api/pkgs/container/grammar-api

[7] https://github.com/tartunlp/speech-to-text-api/pkgs/container/speech-to-text-api

[8] https://github.com/orgs/Project-MTee/packages

Latest Development in the FoTran Project – Scaling Up Language Coverage in Neural Machine Translation Using Distributed Training with Language-Specific Components

Raúl Vázquez♠ Michele Boggia♠ Alessandro Raganato♡
Niki A. Loppi◇ Stig-Arne Grönroos♠♣ Jörg Tiedemann♠
♠ University of Helsinki, Finland ♡ University of Milano-Bicocca, Italy
◇ NVIDIA ♣ Silo.AI
♠{name.surname}@helsinki.fi, ♡{name.surname}@unimib.it,
◇nloppi@nvidia.com

Abstract

We give an update on the *Found in Translation* (FoTran) project, focusing on the study of emerging language-agnostic representations from neural machine translation (NMT). We describe our attention-bridge model, a modular NMT model which connects language-specific components through a shared network layer. Our latest implementation supports distributed training over many nodes and GPUs in order to substantially scale up the number of languages that can be included in a modern neural translation architecture.

1 Introduction

The FoTran project aims at developing models for natural language understanding trained on implicit information given by large collections of human translations.[1] It is funded by a European Research Council consolidation grant, running from 2018 to 2023 within the language technology research group at the University of Helsinki under coordination of Prof. Jörg Tiedemann.

Cross-lingual grounding, useful for resolving ambiguities through translation, is a guiding principle of the project. Consequently, we developed a model for multilingual NMT specifically designed to obtain meaning representations injected with multilingual data (Vázquez et al., 2020). Former project results pointed towards the improvement of both the translation quality and the abstractions acquired by our model when including more languages (Vázquez et al., 2019; Raganato et al., 2019). Due to the use of language-specific modules, the overall model architecture grows when languages and translation directions are added. Doing this on a single device does not scale beyond the memory limits of that specific computing node. This is a limitation for testing the project hypothesis that training on increasing amounts of linguistically diverse data improves the abstractions found by the model – eventually leading to language-independent meaning representations useful for machine translation and tasks that require semantic reasoning and inference. Here, we propose strategies to address those issues: (1) distribute modules across several processing units, (2) efficiently train the network over many translation directions, and (3) reuse the trained modules without having to load the entire network. These together deliver a cost-effective multilingual NMT system that can further be used for extracting multilingual meaning representations.[2] Despite the high computational resources needed to scale up the number of translation directions when training the model, its modularity allows to reuse the trained components on relatively small processing units, making multilingual models more affordable and increasing their availability.

2 Methodology

The implementation follows an encoder–decoder architecture, incorporating language specific encoders and decoders to enable multilingual training. They are connected via a shared inner-attention layer that summarizes the encoder information in a fixed-size vector representation (Vázquez et al., 2019), which in turn can be applied to downstream tasks (Vázquez et al.,

[1] http://www.helsinki.fi/fotran

[2] https://github.com/Helsinki-NLP/FoTraNMT

2020). We refer to all encoders, decoders and to the shared layer as *modules*. Encoders and decoders are language-specific as they only see training data from specific translation directions.

We distribute the model across multiple processing units by loading, in each device, encoders and decoders for a subset of the training translation directions. The inner-attention layer is shared across all processing units. All modules that are present in more than one device are initialized with the same weights, and gradients for these parameters are communicated across devices to ensure that they remain synchronous.

In general, allocating language pairs with common source/target languages on the same device decreases both the total memory footprint of the model and the amount of communication needed to keep the modules synced. Formally, we define the partition of the training language pairs $L_{ij} = (S_{ij}, T_{ij})$ over N units as $\mathcal{P} = \{(L_{11}, L_{12}, \ldots), \ldots, (L_{N1}, L_{N2}, \ldots)\}$, where the first subscripts indicate to which device each pair is assigned, and the second is an incremental index over all pairs assigned to the same device. Whenever $X_{ij} = X_{kl}$ for $i \neq k$, with $X \in \{S, T\}$ representing either a source or a target language, we need to load a copy of the same module in devices i and k. This will also impact the training time as it requires communicating gradients across devices to keep modules synced.

However, when dealing with a high number of translation directions (and a limited number of source and target languages) it becomes impossible to avoid this condition: gathering together language pairs based on the source (target) language could result in a scattered configuration based on target (source) languages. We address these problems using two strategies. First, we solve an allocation problem to minimize inter-device communication. Since in most cases the problem has no feasible exact solutions, we approximate a solution using the Hungarian algorithm over a cost matrix that makes it cheaper to assign the same language to a given GPU. Second, we propose to schedule the gradient updates to minimize the waiting time when inter-device communication happens.

At each training step the ith device starts performing a forward pass over a training batch for the language pair L_{i1} and accumulates gradients over all the language pairs L_{ij}, where j runs from one to the number of language pairs assigned to the processing unit. Afterwards, gradients of modules that are present in multiple processing units are averaged across devices. Module weights are then updated according to the computed gradients. We ensure that all copies of all modules have non-zero gradients that can be communicated, preventing the training loop from hanging.

We also save the modules individually to be loaded and used independently in an efficient way. This makes the system more portable and user-friendly for further fine-tuning, generating translations, and experimentation with multilingual sentence-representations.

3 Final Remarks

FoTran aims at testing and analyzing representations obtained from massively multilingual NMT systems, and we devised a model architecture that is optimized for training large models (with a sufficiently large high-performance cluster). After training, it can also easily be used in non-resource-intensive settings due to its modular design. Next, we intend to systematically explore the effect of increasing language diversity and how the abstraction capabilities of the inner representations are affected in different settings.

Acknowledgments

This work is part of the FoTran project, funded by the European Research Council (ERC) under the EU's Horizon 2020 research and innovation program (agreement № 771113). We also thank the CSC-IT Center for Science Ltd., for computational resources and NVIDIA AI Technology Center (NVAITC) for the expertise in distributed training.

References

Raganato, Alessandro, Raúl Vázquez, Mathias Creutz and Jörg Tiedemann. 2019. An Evaluation of Language-Agnostic Inner-Attention-Based Representations in Machine Translation. *Proceedings of the 4th Workshop on Representation Learning for NLP (RepL4NLP-2019)*. ACL. 27–32.

Vázquez, Raúl, Alessandro Raganato, Mathias Creutz and Jörg Tiedemann. 2019. Multilingual NMT with a Language-Independent Attention Bridge. *Proceedings of the 4th Workshop on Representation Learning for NLP (RepL4NLP-2019)*. ACL. 33–39.

Vázquez, Raúl, Alessandro Raganato, Mathias Creutz and Jörg Tiedemann. 2020. A Systematic Study of Inner-Attention-Based Sentence Representations in Multilingual Neural Machine Translation. *Computational Linguistics*, vol. 46(2):387–424.

InDeep × NMT: Empowering Human Translators via Interpretable Neural Machine Translation

Gabriele Sarti and **Arianna Bisazza**
Center for Language and Cognition (CLCG)
University of Groningen, The Netherlands
{g.sarti, a.bisazza}@rug.nl

Abstract

The NWO-funded InDeep project aims to empower users of deep-learning models of text, speech, and music by improving their ability to interact with such models and interpret their behaviors. In the translation domain, we aim at developing new tools and methodologies to improve prediction attribution, error analysis, and controllable generation for neural machine translation systems. These advances will be evaluated through field studies involving professional translators to assess gains in post-editing efficiency and enjoyability.

1 Introduction

In recent years, the widespread adoption of deep learning systems in neural machine translation (NMT) led to substantial performance gains across most language pairs. Consequently, the focus of human professionals gradually shifted towards the post-editing of machine-generated content. Despite the indisputable quality of NMT, the question of why and how these systems can effectively encode and exploit linguistic information stands unanswered. Indeed, NMT systems are intrinsically opaque due to their multi-layered nonlinear architecture. This fact significantly hinders our ability to interpret their behavior (Samek et al., 2019), an essential prerequisite to their application in real-world scenarios requiring accountability and transparency. For this reason, the interpretability of neural models has grown into a prolific field of research, developing multiple approaches aimed at analyzing models' predictions and learned representations (Belinkov et al., 2020).

While most explainable NMT studies focus on analyzing model learning and predictive behaviors to gain theoretical insights, interpretability approaches have seldom been applied from a user-centric perspective. This criticality was highlighted by exponents of the interpretability field, among which the necessity of grounding future research in practical applications found broad consensus (Doshi-Velez and Kim, 2017). In light of this, the development of methods that are *self-contained, generalizable, and scalable* would enable the identification of widespread issues characterizing NMT predictions such as hallucinations (Raunak et al., 2021), under- and over-translation, and inadequate terminology (Vamvas and Sennrich, 2021; Vamvas and Sennrich, 2022).

2 Project Description

As part of the broader consortium 'InDeep: Interpreting Deep Learning Models for Text and Sound' funded by the Dutch Research Council (NWO)[1], we aim to build upon the latest advances in interpretability studies to empower end-users of NMT via the application of interpretability techniques for neural machine translation. The InDeep project will run from 2021 to 2026, involving a number of academic and industrial partners such as the universities of Groningen and Amsterdam, KPN, Deloitte and Hugging Face. Central to this project is improving the subjective post-editing experience for human professionals, promoting a shift from a passive proofreading routine to an active role in the translation process by employing interactive and intelligible computational practices, driv-

[1] Find more details at https://interpretingdl.github.io and https://www.nwo.nl/en/projects/nwa129219399

Macken, Rufener, Van den Bogaert, Daems, Tezcan, Vanroy, Fonteyne, Barrault, Costa-jussà, Kemp, Pilos, Declercq, Koponen, Forcada, Scarton, Moniz (eds.)
Proceedings of the 23rd Annual Conference of the European Association for Machine Translation, p. 311–312
Ghent, Belgium, June 2022.

ing further enhancements in the quality and efficiency of post-editing in real-world scenarios. On the methodological side, this entails developing and adapting tools and methodologies to improve prediction attribution, error analysis, and controllable generation for NMT systems. We will evaluate our approaches using automatic metrics, and via a field study surveying professionals in collaboration with GlobalTextware.[2]

The focus for the first part of the project will be on identifying approaches that could be generalized to conditional text generation tasks (Alvarez-Melis and Jaakkola, 2017). *Feature* and *instance attribution* methods let us establish the importance of input components and training examples, respectively, in driving model predictions. These techniques are interesting due to their practical applicability in standard translation workflows. In particular, we find it essential to assess the relationship between importance scores produced by these methods and different categories of translation errors. Evaluating the *faithfulness* for model attributions, i.e., how they are causally linked to the system's outputs, is another fundamental component of our investigation and will be pursued by employing a mix of existing and new techniques (DeYoung et al., 2020).

The second part of the project will involve a field study combining behavioral and subjective quality metrics to empirically estimate the effectiveness of our methods in real-world scenarios. For the behavioral part, we intend to use a combination of keylogging and possibly eye-tracking and mouse-tracking to collect granular information about the post-editing process. Our analysis will benefit from insights from recent interactive NMT studies (Santy et al., 2019; Coppers et al., 2018; Vandeghinste et al., 2019) to present translators with useful information while avoiding visual clutter. Our preliminary inquiry involving professionals highlighted sentence-level quality estimation and adaptive style/terminology constraints as promising directions to increase post-editing productivity and enjoyability, supporting the potential of combining interpretable and interactive modules for NMT.

[2]https://www.globaltextware.nl/

References

Alvarez-Melis, David, and Tommi Jaakkola. 2017. A Causal Framework for Explaining the Predictions of Black-Box Sequence-to-Sequence Models In *Proceedings of EMNLP 2017*, 412–421.

Belinkov, Yonatan, Sebastian Gehrmann, and Ellie Pavlick. 2020. Interpretability and Analysis in Neural NLP In *Proceedings of ACL 2020: Tutorials*, 1–5.

Coppers, Sven, Jan Van den Bergh, Kris Luyten, Karin Coninx, Iulianna van der Lek-Ciudin, Tom Vanallemeersch, Vincent Vandeghinste 2018. Intellingo: An Intelligible Translation Environment In *Proceedings of CHI 2018*: 524, 1–13.

DeYoung, Jay, Sarthak Jain, Nazneen Fatema Rajani, Eric Lehman, Caiming Xiong, Richard Socher, Byron C. Wallace. 2020. ERASER: A Benchmark to Evaluate Rationalized NLP Models In *Proceedings of ACL 2020*, 4443–4458.

Doshi-Velez, Finale, and Been Kim. 2018. Considerations for Evaluation and Generalization in Interpretable Machine Learning *Explainable and Interpretable Models in Computer Vision and Machine Learning*, 3–17.

He, Shilin, Zhaopeng Tu, Xing Wang, Longyue Wang, Michael Lyu, and Shuming Shi. 2019. Towards Understanding Neural Machine Translation with Word Importance In *Proceedings of EMNLP-IJCNLP 2019*, 953–962.

Samek, Wojciech, Grégoire Montavon, Andrea Vedaldi, Lars Kai Hansen, and Klaus-Robert Müller. 2019. Explainable AI: Interpreting, Explaining and Visualizing Deep Learning *Springer Nature*.

Santy, Sebastin, Sandipan Dandapat, Monojit Choudhury, and Kalika Bali. 2019. INMT: Interactive Neural Machine Translation Prediction In *Proceedings of EMNLP-IJCNLP 2019*, 103–8.

Vamvas, Jannis and Rico Sennrich. 2021. Contrastive Conditioning for Assessing Disambiguation in MT: A Case Study of Distilled Bias In *Proceedings of EMNLP 2021*, 10246–10265.

Vamvas, Jannis and Rico Sennrich. 2022. As Little as Possible, as Much as Necessary: Detecting Over- and Undertranslations with Contrastive Conditioning In *Proceedings of ACL 2022*, 10139–10155.

Vandeghinste, Vincent, Tom Vanallemeersch, Liesbeth Augustinus, Bram Bulté, Frank Van Eynde, Joris Pelemans, Lyan Verwimp. 2019. Improving the Translation Environment for Professional Translators *Informatics* 6 (2): 24, 1–36.

Vikas Raunak, Arul Menezes, Marcin Junczys-Dowmunt. 2021. The Curious Case of Hallucinations in Neural Machine Translation In *Proceedings of NAACL 2021*, 1172–1183.

QUARTZ: Quality-Aware Machine Translation

José G. C. de Souza[1] Ricardo Rei[1,2,4] Ana C Farinha[1]
Helena Moniz[1,4,5] André F. T. Martins[1,2,3]
[1]Unbabel [2]Instituto Superior Técnico [3]Instituto de Telecomunicações
[4]INESC-ID [5]Faculdade de Letras da Universidade de Lisboa
Lisbon, Portugal
jose.souza, ricardo.rei, catarina.farinha, helena.moniz, andre.martins@unbabel.com

Abstract

This paper presents QUARTZ, QUality-AwaRe machine Translation, a project led by Unbabel and funded by the ELISE Open Call[1] which aims at developing machine translation systems that are more robust and produce fewer critical errors. With QUARTZ we want to enable machine translation for user-generated conversational content types that do not tolerate critical errors in automatic translations. The project runs from January to July 2022.

1 Introduction

Despite the progress in the fluency of machine translation (MT) systems, critical translation errors are still frequent, including deviations in meaning through toxic or offensive content, hallucinations, mistranslation of entities with health, safety, or financial implications, or deviation in sentiment polarity or negation. These errors occur more often when the source sentence is out of domain or contains typos, abbreviations, or capitalized text, all common with user-generated content. This lack of robustness prevents the use of MT systems in practical applications where the above errors cannot be tolerated.

QUARTZ aims to build reliable, quality-aware MT systems for user-generated conversational data. The project will address the limitations above by: (a) developing quality metrics capable of detecting critical errors and hallucinations; (b) endowing MT systems with a confidence (quality) score, and fine-tuning pre-trained MT models to the domains in which they will be used through quality-driven objectives.

This will be done by leveraging post-edited data and quality annotations produced by the Unbabel community and building upon the state-of-the-art, open-source quality estimation technology already existing at Unbabel: OPENKIWI (Kepler et al., 2019) and COMET (Rei et al., 2020). From a product perspective, focus will be given to conversational, user-generated data in a multilingual customer service scenario (email or chat involving a customer and an agent), in which Unbabel has renowned expertise and existing technology validated by existing customers. The solution aims to eliminate language barriers in the highly multilingual European market.

2 MT and Translation Quality

The current state of the art in MT is based on auto-regressive sequence-to-sequence models trained with maximum likelihood and teacher forcing. This objective encourages the model to assign high probability to reference translations, but does not account for the severity of translation mistakes of the hypotheses generated. This leads to exposure bias, vulnerability to adversarial attacks, and no control for hallucinations, harmful content, and biases (Wang and Sennrich, 2020), hampering the responsible use of NMT for user-generated conversational content.

Project Overview Qualitative evaluation carried out by translators (post-editors and annotators) provides a human feedback loop that can generate large amounts of data with information about translation errors, their severities, and detailed quality annotations. The main methodology used to evaluate translations according to different aspects of translation quality is the industry-

[1]Funding from the European Union's Horizon 2020 research and innovation program under grant agreement No 951847

Macken, Rufener, Van den Bogaert, Daems, Tezcan, Vanroy, Fonteyne, Barrault, Costa-jussà, Kemp, Pilos, Declercq, Koponen, Forcada, Scarton, Moniz (eds.)
Proceedings of the 23rd Annual Conference of the European Association for Machine Translation, p. 313–314
Ghent, Belgium, June 2022.

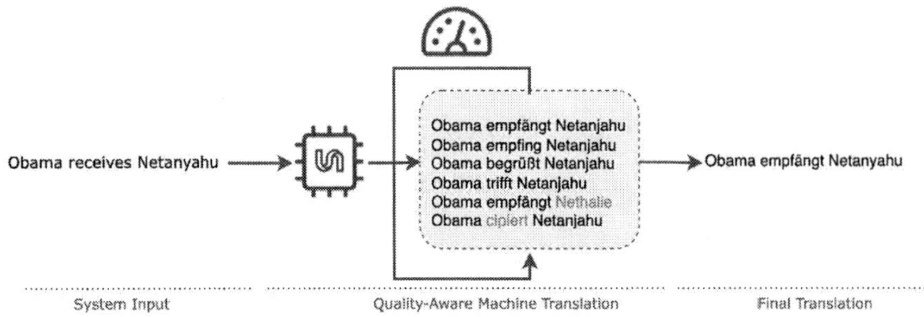

Figure 1: In QUARTZ quality estimation systems will interact directly with the machine translation system during the decoding phase to avoid critical errors. Words marked in red are considered errors.

adopted multi-dimensional quality (MQM) taxonomy (Lommel et al., 2014). Unbabel uses this data to train its open-source COMET and OPENKIWI frameworks to develop systems for MT evaluation and quality estimation, with MQM annotations and post-edits becoming a standard in Metrics and Quality Estimation WMT shared tasks (Freitag et al., 2021; Specia et al., 2021).

This project will close this loop by making MT systems quality-aware and robust. Decoding strategies for MT will be developed using the quality estimation metrics trained on the target domain data. The incorporation of these quality objectives into the decoding step of MT systems can have a big impact on controlling their tendency to produce hallucinations and other critical mistakes. This rationale is depicted in Figure 1.

Related Work Prior work on minimum Bayes risk (MBR) decoding paves the way to tune MT systems towards a given metric, but so far this has been done with purely lexical metrics such as BLEU (Müller and Sennrich, 2021) or neural metrics that do not capture severity and biases (Freitag et al., 2022). The main difference between QUARTZ and previous work is going beyond lexical metrics in incorporating quality scores for generating automatic translations.

References

Freitag, Markus, Ricardo Rei, Nitika Mathur, Chi-kiu Lo, Craig Stewart, George Foster, Alon Lavie, and Ondřej Bojar. 2021. Results of the WMT21 metrics shared task: Evaluating metrics with expert-based human evaluations on TED and news domain. In *Proceedings of the Sixth Conference on Machine Translation*, pages 733–774, Online, November. Association for Computational Linguistics.

Freitag, Markus, David Grangier, Qijun Tan, and Bowen Liang. 2022. High quality rather than high model probability: Minimum bayes risk decoding with neural metrics. In *Accepted at Transactions of the Association for Computational Linguistics, presented at North American Chapter of the Association for Computational Linguistics 2022*, Seattle, Washington. Association for Computational Linguistics.

Kepler, Fabio, Jonay Trénous, Marcos Treviso, Miguel Vera, and André F. T. Martins. 2019. OpenKiwi: An open source framework for quality estimation. In *Proceedings of the 57th Annual Meeting of the Association for Computational Linguistics: System Demonstrations*, pages 117–122, Florence, Italy, July. Association for Computational Linguistics.

Lommel, Arle, Aljoscha Burchardt, and Hans Uszkoreit. 2014. Multidimensional quality metrics (MQM): A framework for declaring and describing translation quality metrics. *Tradumàtica: Tecnologies de la Traducció*, 0:455–463, 12.

Müller, Mathias and Rico Sennrich. 2021. Understanding the properties of minimum bayes risk decoding in neural machine translation. In *Proceedings of the Joint Conference of the 59th Annual Meeting of the Association for Computational Linguistics and the 11th International Joint Conference on Natural Language Processing (ACL-IJCNLP 2021)*.

Rei, Ricardo, Craig Stewart, Ana C Farinha, and Alon Lavie. 2020. COMET: A neural framework for MT evaluation. In *Proceedings of the 2020 Conference on Empirical Methods in Natural Language Processing (EMNLP)*, pages 2685–2702, Online, November. Association for Computational Linguistics.

Specia, Lucia, Frédéric Blain, Marina Fomicheva, Chrysoula Zerva, Zhenhao Li, Vishrav Chaudhary, and André F. T. Martins. 2021. Findings of the WMT 2021 shared task on quality estimation. In *Proceedings of the Sixth Conference on Machine Translation*, pages 684–725, Online, November. Association for Computational Linguistics.

Wang, Chaojun and Rico Sennrich. 2020. On exposure bias, hallucination and domain shift in neural machine translation. In *Proceedings of the 58th Annual Meeting of the Association for Computational Linguistics*, pages 3544–3552, Online, July. Association for Computational Linguistics.

POLENG MT: An Adaptive MT Platform

Artur Nowakowski[1,2], **Krzysztof Jassem**[1,2], **Maciej Lison**[1], **Kamil Guttmann**[1,2], **Mikołaj Pokrywka**[1,2]
[1] Poleng, Poznań, Poland
[2] Faculty of Mathematics and Computer Science, Adam Mickiewicz University, Poznań, Poland
{name.surname}@poleng.pl

Abstract

We introduce POLENG MT, an MT platform that may be used as a cloud web application or as an on-site solution. The platform is capable of providing accurate document translation, including the transfer of document formatting between the input document and the output document. The main feature of the on-site version is dedicated customer adaptation, which consists of training on specialized texts and applying forced terminology translation according to the user's needs.

1 General Description

POLENG MT is an MT translation platform available in two versions. Using PaaS (Platform as a Service), the translations are delivered via a cloud web application. In the on-site scenario, the customer organization receives an installation package to be used in the customer's infrastructure. In this case, access to the service is specifically limited to the customer's employees. The following features are shared by both versions of the platform:

- user registration and login;
- document import in `.txt`, `.docx`, `.pptx` and `.xlsx` formats;
- document editing in sentence-by-sentence mode;
- machine translation in an editing window;
- machine translation of entire documents;
- export of the translated document in a format compatible with the imported document;
- pre-translation of documents using translation memory fuzzy search matches;
- ability to proofread and approve translations of sentences;
- expanding translation memory with approved translations;
- transfer of document formatting (fonts, styling, text placement) between input and output document;
- archiving of translated documents per user.

POLENG MT translation models are based on the Marian (Junczys-Dowmunt et al., 2018) and fairseq (Ott et al., 2019) NMT frameworks.

2 Customer Adaptation

Adaptation for specific users is carried out in the on-site versions. The task includes the following processes:

- SSO (single sign-on) login integration, if applicable;
- delivery of a translation engine specialized in the customer's domain, fine-tuned on documents provided by the customer;
- incorporation of a customized lexicon into the NMT engine;
- automatic generation of a lexicon from the customer's documents.

Macken, Rufener, Van den Bogaert, Daems, Tezcan, Vanroy, Fonteyne, Barrault, Costa-jussà, Kemp, Pilos, Declercq, Koponen, Forcada, Scarton, Moniz (eds.)
Proceedings of the 23rd Annual Conference of the European Association for Machine Translation, p. 315–316
Ghent, Belgium, June 2022.

The latter two processes take into account the recognition and generation of inflected forms of lexicon entries. This problem is addressed in (Nowakowski and Jassem, 2021) and (Bergmanis and Pinnis, 2021).

3 Supported Languages

Currently, POLENG MT supports the following language pairs, in both directions:

- Polish–English;
- Polish–Ukrainian;
- Polish–Russian.

In the near future, we plan to add support for language pairs with other Eastern European languages, including Czech, Romanian, Bulgarian and Belarusian.

Upon the customer's request, the POLENG MT platform can support any translation direction, on condition that the customer provides suitable parallel data (for example, in the form of business documents and their translations).

References

Bergmanis, Toms and Mārcis Pinnis. 2021. Facilitating terminology translation with target lemma annotations. In *Proceedings of the 16th Conference of the European Chapter of the Association for Computational Linguistics: Main Volume*, pages 3105–3111, Online, April. Association for Computational Linguistics.

Junczys-Dowmunt, Marcin, Roman Grundkiewicz, Tomasz Dwojak, Hieu Hoang, Kenneth Heafield, Tom Neckermann, Frank Seide, Ulrich Germann, Alham Fikri Aji, Nikolay Bogoychev, André F. T. Martins, and Alexandra Birch. 2018. Marian: Fast neural machine translation in C++. In *Proceedings of ACL 2018, System Demonstrations*, pages 116–121, Melbourne, Australia, July. Association for Computational Linguistics.

Nowakowski, Artur and Krzysztof Jassem. 2021. Neural machine translation with inflected lexicon. In *Proceedings of Machine Translation Summit XVIII: Research Track*, pages 282–292, Virtual, August. Association for Machine Translation in the Americas.

Ott, Myle, Sergey Edunov, Alexei Baevski, Angela Fan, Sam Gross, Nathan Ng, David Grangier, and Michael Auli. 2019. fairseq: A fast, extensible toolkit for sequence modeling. In *Proceedings of the 2019 Conference of the North American Chapter of the Association for Computational Linguistics (Demonstrations)*, pages 48–53, Minneapolis, Minnesota, June. Association for Computational Linguistics.

plain X – AI Supported Multilingual Video Workflow Platform

Carlos Amaral
Priberam
Lisbon, Portugal
carlos@priberam.pt

Peggy van der Kreeft
Deutsche Welle
Bonn, Germany
peggy.van-der-kreeft@dw.com

Abstract

The plain X platform is a toolbox for multilingual adaptation, for video, audio, and text content. The software is a 4-in-1 tool, combining several steps in the adaptation process, i.e., transcription, translation, subtitling, and voice-over, all automatically generated, but with a high level of editorial control. Users can choose which translation engine is used (e.g., MS Azure, Google, DeepL) depending on best performance. As a result, plain X enables a smooth semi-automated production of subtitles or voice-over, much faster than with older, manual workflows. The software was developed out of EU research projects and has recently been rolled out for professional use. It brings Artificial Intelligence (AI) into the multilingual media production process, while keeping the human in the loop.

1 Introduction

plain X has been built by and for the media industry, although its use can be extended to other sectors as well. A key driver is the growing amount of content which needs language adaptation., based on user or market needs, for enhanced accessibility or to comply with regulation. Feature development is based on the needs from Deutsche Welle (DW), a world broadcaster producing in over 30 languages. The plain X platform is the result of a partnership between DW as user partner and Priberam, a Lisbon-based natural language processing developer.

The platform simplifies the multilingual adaptation process to a large degree, enabling easy subtitling in source and any target language requirement. After a full year of preparation, we are currently rolling out the platform for daily use in Deutsche Welle. Some other organizations are trialing the tool. In the future the software will be available to others, based on a software-as-a-service subscription model.

2 Challenges

The concept for plain X originated from the need to produce more with less, i.e., to use automation in the production process, so media producers can increase the volume of certain target languages, distribute content in more languages, or use synthetic voice, allowing to reach more people in their own spoken tongue, including in specific African or Asian regions.

As DW produces content in so many languages, it is essential to cover as many languages as possible, in the best possible quality, through a combination of engines from carefully selected providers, for instance for transcription or translation. In plain X users can freely switch between different translation engines. The software allows for the inclusion of additional engines in the future.

As the tool was – and is – co-developed by user partner Deutsche Welle, direct access to user requirements and feedback is ensured. This revealed that integration with internal systems and customization is a must to reach the highest level of user acceptance.

Macken, Rufener, Van den Bogaert, Daems, Tezcan, Vanroy, Fonteyne, Barrault, Costa-jussà, Kemp, Pilos, Declercq, Koponen, Forcada, Scarton, Moniz (eds.)
Proceedings of the 23rd Annual Conference of the European Association for Machine Translation, p. 317–318
Ghent, Belgium, June 2022.

3 Origin

plain X initially came out of the SUMMA multilingual media platform, funded by the European Commission's H-2020 project as a basic prototype for controlled transcription and translation.

This prototype was then further developed and funded through the Google Digital News Initiative projects speech.media and news.bridge.

Finally, Deutsche Welle, world broadcaster in need of such platform, and Priberam, a natural language processing developer, decided to turn the prototype into a scalable, fully operational multilingual platform for wider use, supporting the needs of broadcasters and other multilingual content producers. That was the birth of plain X, a platform which turns content from virtually any language into almost any target language.

4 Workflow

The task-based workflow is easy to use, but very powerful, offering editorial users the comfort of their familiar workflow, yet encompassing advanced automated technologies to support them in the creative process.

The first step is *ingestion* of content, be it video, audio, or text, with many input formats.

The next step for audiovisual content is *transcription*, through speech-to-text in the source language. That could be an end-goal, for instance for interviews.

This also allows for a primary output of automatically generated *source-language subtitles*, which can be used as open or closed captions.

The next step is automated *translation* to a selected target language, which can be post-edited to any level. Again, the translation can be an end-goal on its own, and used as input text for re-speaking, for example. One file can be translated to multiple languages.

However, it can also generate automated *subtitling* in the same *target language*.

As a final step, the translation can be used for *voice-over*, by converting text to speech in the target language after selecting a synthetic voice.

Post-editing and review by colleagues can be added in every step, as required. Subsequently, other target languages can be added and produce equivalent content.

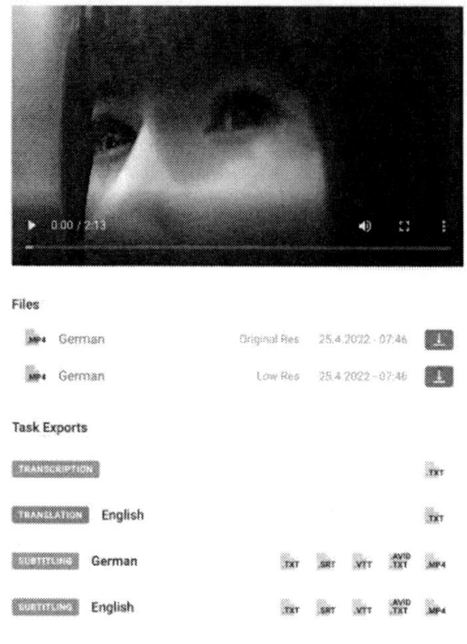

Figure 1: plain X Workflow Tasks

5 Integration

It was vital to integrate this tool into the existing workflow infrastructure at Deutsche Welle and to allow for customization. This meant connecting it to input platforms for a smooth ingestion, as well as output tools for an efficient post-production and publication in the company style and branding.

Subtitle templates help to prepare the output in a particular house format. Other customizations include library management and access, setting subtitling rules, assigning roles to users, keeping track of usage and billing. It is possible to create fully automated processes for subtitling.

Working directly in a user environment from the start, with user input and feedback at every stage, allowed us to build a user-oriented platform to support editors in their adaptation process with the help of AI, while minimizing the feeling of insecurity and threat coming from automated processing.

More enhancements are planned to cater for different use cases, improve the quality of the output and strengthen post-editing options.

Acknowledgments

This work has received funding from the European Union's Horizon 2020 research and innovation program under grant agreement No 957017, Project SELMA (https://selma-project.eu/).

DELA Project: Document-level Machine Translation Evaluation

Sheila Castilho
ADAPT Centre
School of Computing
Dublin City University
sheila.castilho@adaptcentre.ie

Abstract

This paper presents the results of the Document-level Machine Translation Evaluation (DELA) Project, a two-year project which started in September 2020 funded by the Irish Research Council. This paper describes the results of the project to date, as well as its latest developments.

1 Introduction

The challenge of evaluating translations in context has been raising interest in the machine translation (MT) field. However, the definition of what constitutes a document-level (doc-level) MT evaluation, in terms of how much of the text needs to be shown, is still unclear (Castilho et al., 2020). Few works have taken into account doc-level human evaluation (Barrault et al., 2020), and one common practice is the usage of test suites with context-aware markers. However, test suites with document-level boundaries are still scarce (Rysová et al., 2019). The main objective of the DELA Project is to define best practices for doc-level MT evaluation, and test the existing human and automatic sentence-level evaluation metrics to the doc-level. We present here the results from the project to date, as well as the upcoming research to be carried out.

2 Context Span for MT

In Castilho et al. (2020), we tested the context span, that is, the length of context necessary, for the translation of 300 sentences in three different domains (reviews, subtitles, and literature) and showed that over 33% of the sentences tested required more context than the sentence itself to be translated or evaluated, and from those, 23% required more than two previous sentences to be properly evaluated. Ambiguity, terminology, and gender agreement were the most common issues to hinder translation, and moreover, there were observable differences in issues and context span between domains.

3 Doc-Level Evaluation methodology

In Castilho (2020; 2021), we tested the differences in inter-annotator agreement (IAA) between single-sentence and doc-level setups. First, translators evaluated the MT output in terms of fluency, adequacy, ranking and error annotation in: (i) one score per single isolated sentence, and (ii) one score per document. Then, the doc-level setup was modified, and translators evaluated (i) random single sentences, (ii) individual sentences with access to the full source and MT output, and (iii) full documents. Results showed that assessing individual sentences within the context of a document yields a higher IAA compared to the random single-sentence methodology, while when translators give one score per document, IAA is much lower. Assigning one score per sentence in context avoids misevaluation cases, extremely common in the random sentences-based evaluation setups.[1] The higher IAA agreement in the random single-sentence setup is because raters tend to accept the translation when adequacy is ambiguous but the translation is correct, especially if it is fluent.

[1]Without context, the sentence *'I am satisfied'* translated into Portuguese in the masculine *'Eu estou satisfeito'* will get a perfect score even when the gender of the pronoun *I* is feminine (*'satisfeitA'*).

Macken, Rufener, Van den Bogaert, Daems, Tezcan, Vanroy, Fonteyne, Barrault, Costa-jussà, Kemp, Pilos, Declercq, Koponen, Forcada, Scarton, Moniz (eds.)
Proceedings of the 23rd Annual Conference of the European Association for Machine Translation, p. 319–320
Ghent, Belgium, June 2022.

4 DELA Corpus

Using the issues found in Castilho et al. (2020), we developed the DELA corpus, a doc-level corpus annotated with context-aware issues when translating from English into Portuguese, namely gender, number, ellipsis, reference, lexical ambiguity, and terminology (Castilho et al., 2021). The corpus contains 60 full documents and was compiled with six different domains: subtitles, literary, news, reviews, medical, and legislation; and can be used as a challenge test set, training/testing corpus for MT and quality estimation, and for deep linguistic analysis of context issues.[2]

5 Examining Context-Related Issues

Using the DELA Corpus, we examine the shortest context span necessary to solve the issues annotated in the corpus, and categorise the types of contexts according to their position, and report the i) Context Position, and ii) Context Length We find that the shortest context span might appear in different positions in the document including preceding, following, global, world knowledge. The average length depends on the issue types as well as the domain. The results show that the standard approach of relying on only two preceding sentences as context might not be enough depending on the domain and issue types.

6 Latest Developments

The DELA Project, running until September 2022, will focus now on the human and automatic evaluation metrics for MT, testing and developing new ways to use them for doc-level evaluation.

Doc-level human and automatic evaluation metrics: The focus of the DELA Project is to answer the following research questions: i) Are the state-of-the-art (SOTA) human and automatic evaluation metrics able to capture the quality level of the doc-level systems realistically?; and ii) Can/should they be modified or do new ones are needed?

A series of experiments with the SOTA human metrics are being carried out, informed by the best methodologies found in previous results. With that, we will determine whether these metrics can be used in doc-level evaluations, or if new metrics should (and could) be developed. The doc-level human evaluation will inform automatic metrics to be used for document-level systems.

Doc-level evaluation tool: The DELA project will gather specification from translators to design a translation evaluation tool which will provide an environment to assess MT quality at a doc-level with human and automatic evaluation metrics scores specified as best suited for doc-level evaluation in the project. The tool will be made freely available.

Acknowledgements: This project is funded by the Irish Research Council (GOIPD/2020/69). ADAPT, the Science Foundation Ireland Research Centre for AI-Driven Digital Content Technology at Dublin City University, is funded by the Science Foundation Ireland through the SFI Research Centres Programme (Grant 13/RC/2106_P2).

References

Barrault, Loïc, Magdalena Biesialska, Ondřej Bojar, Marta R. Costa-jussà, Christian Federmann, Yvette Graham, Roman Grundkiewicz, Barry Haddow, and et al. 2020. Findings of the 2020 conference on machine translation (WMT20). In *Proceedings of the Fifth Conference on Machine Translation*, pages 1–55, Online, November. Association for Computational Linguistics.

Castilho, Sheila, Maja Popović, and Andy Way. 2020. On Context Span Needed for MT Evaluation. In *Proceedings of the Twelfth International Conference on Language Resources and Evaluation (LREC'20)*, page 3735–3742, Marseille, France, May.

Castilho, Sheila, João Lucas Cavalheiro Camargo, Miguel Menezes, and Andy Way. 2021. Dela corpus - a document-level corpus annotated with context-related issues. In *Proceedings of the Sixth Conference on Machine Translation*, pages 571–582. Association for Computational Linguistics.

Castilho, Sheila. 2020. On the same page? comparing IAA in sentence and document level human mt evaluation. In *Proceedings of the Fifth Conference on Machine Translation*, pages 1150–1159. Association for Computational Linguistics, November.

Castilho, Sheila. 2021. Towards document-level human MT evaluation: On the issues of annotator agreement, effort and misevaluation. In *Proceedings of the Workshop on Human Evaluation of NLP Systems*, pages 34–45. Association for Computational Linguistics, April.

Rysová, Kateřina, Magdaléna Rysová, Tomáš Musil, Lucie Poláková, and Ondřej Bojar. 2019. A test suite and manual evaluation of document-level NMT at WMT19. In *Proceedings of the Fourth Conference on Machine Translation (Volume 2: Shared Task Papers, Day 1)*, pages 455–463, Florence, Italy, August. Association for Computational Linguistics.

[2]The corpus and annotation guides can be found at: `https://github.com/SheilaCastilho/DELA-Project`

Background Search for Terminology in STAR MT Translate

Giorgio Bernardinello
STAR Group - Wiesholz 35
8262 Ramsen
Switzerland
giorgio.bernardinello@star-group.net

Judith Klein
STAR Group - Wiesholz 35
8262 Ramsen
Switzerland
judith.klein@star-group.net

Abstract

When interested in an internal web application for machine translation (MT), corporate customers always ask how reliable terminology will be in their translations. Coherent vocabulary is crucial in many aspects of corporate translations, such as documentation or marketing. The main goal every MT provider would like to achieve is to fully integrate the customer's terminology into the model, so that the result does not need to be edited, but this is still not always guaranteed. Besides, a web application like STAR MT Translate allows our customers to use – integrated within the same page – different generic MT providers which were not trained with customer-specific data. So, as a pragmatic approach, we decided to increase the level of integration between WebTerm[1] and STAR MT Translate, adding to the latter more terminological information, with which the user can post-edit the translation if needed.

1 STAR MT Translate

STAR MT Translate is a highly customisable web application for machine translation (MT). It is not designed to be part of an automated translation process, nor to be a tool for expert translators, but rather to help any employee of a company understand texts and documents written in foreign languages. The UI can be designed to fit the corporate style of the client and it offers easy access to the STAR MT engines, specifically trained for each customer, as well as for the most well-known online MT providers.

2 TermAssist

In the last few years, we have seen many companies starting to offer connections between terminology and MT, like the dictionary in GoogleTranslate or the glossary in DeepL. STAR started working almost five years ago on an integrated solution, where corporate terminology can be retrieved from the same webpage in which a text has been translated using MT.[2] The purpose was to give the MT user the possibility of consulting the company's dictionary without switching tabs in the browser, by simply highlighting one or more words. This function was named TermAssist and has since become one of the most requested functions of STAR MT Translate. The main limitation of this kind of approach is the lack of matches for inflected words. A very detailed dictionary could also contain inflections referring to the main term, but this is not realistic in practice, and it may get complicated for multi-word concepts. For example, the plural of the German word "*Sitzplatz*" (seat) is "*Sitzplätze*" (different vowel inside the word plus -e added at the end) while the corresponding Italian forms are "*posto a sedere*", singular, and "*posti a sedere*", plural (the last letter of the first word contains the inflection).

3 Background search

The solution for such cases comes from a further implementation of STAR terminology

[1] WebTerm is the STAR web-based terminology application.

[2] Bernardinello, G. 2018. Terminology validation for MT output. EAMT 2018, 21st Annual Conference of the European Association for Machine Translation., p.343, Alicante, Spain

Macken, Rufener, Van den Bogaert, Daems, Tezcan, Vanroy, Fonteyne, Barrault, Costa-jussà, Kemp, Pilos, Declercq, Koponen, Forcada, Scarton, Moniz (eds.)
Proceedings of the 23rd Annual Conference of the European Association for Machine Translation, p. 321–322
Ghent, Belgium, June 2022.

applications: the background search. Already used in Transit during the import phase to look for all available terms in the TermStar dictionaries, the function was adapted to become a REST API extension.
Thanks to the integration of the background search in STAR MT Translate, when a user translates a sentence, regardless of whether its result came from MT or translation memory[3], all terminology matches are shown[4] in both the source and target languages annotating the text without modifying it. The background search is more accurate than the previous TermAssist search and it is able to find inflected forms in the most common languages. This solution is more efficient even at first glance, since the user can immediately identify all concepts with a terminology entry instead of manually highlighting text and looking for more information. Furthermore, the algorithm checks whether the concepts found in the source correspond to the ones found in the target. E.g.: when the user points the mouse at a term in the target language, both the term itself and its corresponding form in the source language, if available, are highlighted. The same works, of course, the other way around. This can be very helpful when the user is not familiar with one of the two languages; in fact, he or she can verify with a click if the automatic translation is handling that specific concept with the desired corporate-specific vocabulary. If not, the user can view a list of allowed synonyms and related words by right-clicking on the concept.

4 Negative terms

Negative terms, or disallowed terms, are possible translations of a concept which are either wrong or not accepted by the language department of a company. In both cases, the ability to identify them quickly in an automatic translation represents another pertinent advantage for the end user. It happens quite often that the customer needs to specify some negative terms which are only disallowed for that specific concept, but they may be correct in other contexts. For example, a company may want to avoid a colloquial form like "*car*" when translating from the German "*Fahrzeug*" (vehicle), but "*car*" may be accepted when translating the more informal "*Auto*". Thanks to the double-check between source and target texts, the application can highlight a term differently depending on its counterpart; this will give the user visual input on critical words with the possibility to change them to a valid synonym.

This aspect is crucial for customers using different translation providers, since their translation may not always match the desires of the company regarding terminology; even a user with no experience or terminological expertise can immediately see if the text contains invalid concepts, correct them, and continue working with a translation more consistent with the desired corporate language.

5 Future developments

An interesting extension of this feature can be achieved with the contribution of TMC (Translation Memory Container), the STAR database for reference material. It is already possible to activate the connection to the database in order to retrieve translations from the TMC in case of perfect matches. This will skip MT for texts which have already been translated and approved by the company.

The TMC could also be used together with the background search to retrieve segment pairs which contain the same terms found by the background search in both the source and target language. Transit already uses this context-specific TMC search as a support for professional translators who can then see other examples of complete sentences where specific terminology has been used. This is particularly important when a language has more possible translations for the same term in another language. As an example, we can take the English word "*glass*" meaning an object we use to drink from or the material from which it is made. In Italian there is only one possible word for the object, "*bicchiere*", and one for the material, "*vetro*". In cases like this, where both translations are valid, the user can find help in some context-based translations that the company has already completed and approved. This function could be a significant addition to the information given by the dictionary, which may contain some useful examples, but not always one for each specific form of the term.

[3] STAR MT Translate offers the possibility to search for the sentence in the reference material and only send it to MT if not found.

[4] Each customer can decide how to differentiate terminology matches from normal translated text. It can be any CSS property: different colour, underline, different font, etc.

Sign Language Translation: Ongoing Development, Challenges and Innovations in the SignON Project

Dimitar Shterionov*, **Mirella De Sisto***, **Vincent Vandeghinste**[†],, **Aoife Brady**[‡], **Mathieu De Coster**[§], **Lorraine Leeson**[¶], **Josep Blat**[**], **Frankie Picron**[††], **Marcello Paolo Scipioni**[‡‡], **Aditya Parikh**[§§], **Louis ten Bosch**[§§], **John O'Flaherty**[||], **Joni Dambre**[§], **Jorn Rijckaert**[x]

[*]Tilburg University, [†]Instituut voor de Nederlandse Taal, [‡]ADAPT, [§]Ghent University
[¶]Trinity College Dublin,[**]Universitat Pompeu Fabra,[††]European Union of the Deaf,
[‡‡]Fincons,[§§]Radboud University,[||]mac.ie,[x]Vlaams Gebarentaalcentrum

1 Introduction

SignON[1] focuses on the research and development of a *sign language (SL) translation mobile application and an open communications framework*. SignON addresses the lack of technology and services for the automatic translation between signed and spoken languages, through an inclusive, human-centric solution which facilitates communication between deaf, hard of hearing (DHH) and hearing individuals.

We present an overview of the status of the project, describing the milestones and the approaches developed to address the challenges and peculiarities of SL machine translation (SLMT).

SLs are the primary means of communication for over 70 million DHH individuals.[2] Despite this, they are rarely included in ongoing developments of natural-language processing (NLP) advancements (Yin et al., 2021). Machine translation (MT) research which targets SLs is still in its infancy, due mainly to the lack of data and effective representation of signs (including the lack of a standardized written form for SLs).

Both the low volume of available resources, as well as the linguistic properties of SLs provide challenges for MT. Furthermore, SLs are visual languages, which presents yet another challenge: the recognition and synthesis of a signing human.

2 The SignON approach to SLMT

The objective of the SignON project is MT between signed and spoken languages in all possible combinations, as well as the delivery of this service to the primary user groups: DHH and hearing users.

The project revolves around 4 spoken (English, Spanish, Dutch, Irish) and 5 SLs, (ISL, NGT, VGT, LSE, and BSL —namely Irish, Dutch, Flemish, Spanish and British SL). Addressing this many language pairs and directions on a pair-by-pair basis would require a substantial amount of time and effort, far beyond the scope of the project. SignON employs an MT approach that (i) focuses on processing and understanding individual languages, (ii) employs a common multi-lingual representation (InterL) to facilitate translation and (iii) uses symbolic as well as deep-learning methods for the synthesis of a 3D virtual signer. This approach involves automatic SL and speech recognition (SLR and ASR respectively), NLP, sign and speech synthesis, text generation and, most importantly, representation of utterances in a common frame of reference —an interlingual representation space based on embeddings and/or symbolic structures, the InterL. The complexity and diversity of these processing steps require multi-domain knowledge and expertise. Furthermore, we chose this approach as there are only limited parallel resources available between signed and spoken/written languages. Relying on techniques such as transfer learning, and pre-built NLP models (i.e. mBART (Lewis et al., 2020)) will improve MT performance.

We have built state-of-the-art models and components for SLR , exploiting convolutional

[1]SignON is a Horizon 2020 (Research and Innovation Programme Grant Agreement No. 101017255) project that runs from 2021 until the end of 2023. https://signon-project.eu/. The consortium is constituted by 17 partners, among which Instituut voor de Nederlandse Taal, Tilburg University, ADAPT, Ghent University, Trinity College Dublin, Universitat Pompeu Fabra, European Union of the Deaf, Fincons, Radboud University, mac.ie, Vlaams Gebarentaalcentrum, and Dublin City University.

[2]According to the World Federation of the Deaf.

Macken, Rufener, Van den Bogaert, Daems, Tezcan, Vanroy, Fonteyne, Barrault, Costa-jussà, Kemp, Pilos, Declercq, Koponen, Forcada, Scarton, Moniz (eds.)
Proceedings of the 23rd Annual Conference of the European Association for Machine Translation, p. 323–324
Ghent, Belgium, June 2022.

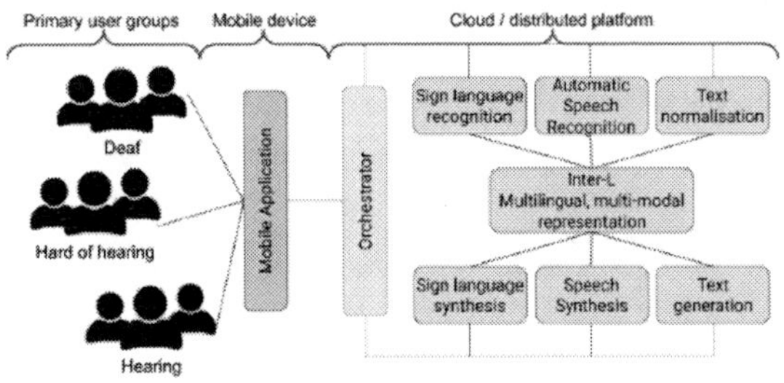

Figure 1: General approach of the SignON translation system

neural network-, recurrent neural network- and transformer-based models, natural-language understanding and MT based on mBART. We are developing approaches through wordnets and abstract semantic representation and synthesis based on language specific logical structures for SL, behavioral markup language and a 3D avatar rendering system.

The ASR component will tune to the use cases and to the speaker (including atypical speech from deaf speakers and speakers with cochlear implants). The ASR addresses (i) privacy challenges (ii) adaption to communicative settings and (iii) extension to new data and languages. Currently, English and Dutch are ready; Spanish is in progress. The transfer learning approach is adapted for Irish. The ASR works as a web service via a secure restful API.

3 SignON application and open framework

The general architecture (Figure 1) consists of a mobile application which connects users to the cloud-based MT platform. The SignON app is the interface between the user and the SignON framework which handles the internal data flow and processing. The *framework* executes the following steps. The source message (audio, video or text) and any relevant metadata coming from *the mobile app* is processed by an *orchestrator* which queues it towards the translation pipeline through a *message broker*. A *dispatcher* subscribed to the appropriate queue receives the message, invoking the relevant component depending on the type of input. After the required processing is complete, the message passes to the next stage of the pipeline until, finally, once the translation tasks are completed, the output message is produced in the requested format (text, audio or sign language avatar). The output is delivered to the app via the *orchestrator*. Each component is encapsulated in a docker container and distributed over different machines.

The first release of the SignON mobile application is due in June 2022, and will then evolve to its final release at the end of the project (Dec. 2023). The app will be available as open source and for free.

4 Societal impact

Along with the technological and academic innovations that come in terms of new models and methodsfor SLMT, SignON strives towards having a large societal impact. Currently we face societal challenges such as clashes between the views of DHH and hearing people, with respect to use-cases, technological importance and communication needs. We organized two sets of interviews with deaf participants, an online survey and we have two round tables planned. Via workshops we inform both the research and user communities about the progress of SignON and the state-of-the-art in SLMT.

5 Progress and next steps

In the first 15 months of this project 8 academic papers were accepted for publication. These papers discuss SLR, NLP, SLMT as well as SL representations. At the time of writing more than 5 papers are under review. We have conducted focus group interviews with VGT, ISL, LSE and NGT signers as well as public and internal surveys.

References

Lewis, Mike, Yinhan Liu, Naman Goyal, Marjan Ghazvininejad, Abdelrahman Mohamed, Omer Levy, Veselin Stoyanov, and Luke Zettlemoyer. 2020. BART: denoising sequence-to-sequence pre-training for natural language generation, translation, and comprehension. In D. Jurafsky et al., editor, *Proc. of the 58th Annual Meeting of the Assoc. for Computational Linguistics, ACL 2020, Online, July 5-10, 2020*, pages 7871–7880. ACL.

Yin, Kayo, Amit Moryossef, Julie Hochgesang, Yoav Goldberg, and Malihe Alikhani. 2021. Including signed languages in natural language processing. In *Proc. of the 59th Annual Meeting of the ACL and the 11th Int. Joint Conference on NLP (Volume 1: Long Papers)*, pages 7347–7360, Online, August. ACL.

DeepSPIN: Deep Structured Prediction for Natural Language Processing

André F. T. Martins, Ben Peters, Chrysoula Zerva, Chunchuan Lyu, Gonçalo Correia, Marcos Treviso, Pedro Martins, Tsvetomila Mihaylova

Instituto de Telecomunicações and Unbabel,
Lisbon, Portugal

`andre.t.martins@tecnico.ulisboa.pt`

Abstract

DeepSPIN is a research project funded by the European Research Council (ERC), whose goal is to develop new neural structured prediction methods, models, and algorithms for improving the quality, interpretability, and data-efficiency of natural language processing (NLP) systems, with special emphasis on machine translation and quality estimation. We describe in this paper the latest findings from this project.

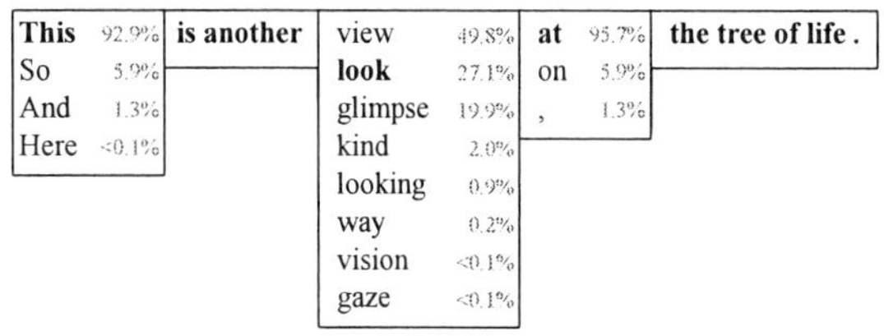

Figure 1: Forced decoding using entmax for the German source sentence "Dies ist ein weiterer Blick auf den Baum des Lebens." Only predictions with nonzero probability are shown at each time step. When consecutive predictions consist of a single word, we combine their borders to showcase *auto-completion* potential.

1 Description

The DeepSPIN project[1] is an ERC Starting Grant (2019–2023) hosted at Instituto de Telecomunicações. Part of the work has been done in collaboration with Unbabel, an SME in the crowdsourcing translation industry. The main goal of DeepSPIN is to bring together deep learning and structured prediction techniques to solve structured problems in NLP. The three main objectives are: developing better decoding strategies; making neural networks more interpretable through the induction of sparse structure; and incorporating weak supervision to reduce the need for labeled data. We focus here on the applications to MT, including some of the recent results obtained in the project.

Better Decoding Strategies. Our initial work on sparse sequence-to-sequence models (Peters et al., 2019) proposed a new class of decoders (called "entmax decoders", shown in Fig. 1) which operate over a sparse probability distribution over words, which prunes hypotheses automatically. In (Peters and Martins, 2021), we have shown that entmax decoders are better calibrated and less prone to the length bias problem and developed a new label smoothing technique. We also presented entmax sampling for text generation, with improved generation quality (Martins et al., 2020). Another line of work concerns modeling of context in machine translation. We introduced *conditional cross-mutual information* (CXMI), a technique to measure the effective use of contextual information by context-aware systems, and *context-aware word dropout*, which increases its use, leading to improvements (Fernandes et al., 2021). We also compared the models' use of context to that of humans for translating ambiguous words, using the latter as extra supervision (Yin et al., 2021).

Sparse Attention and Explainability. A key objective of DeepSPIN is to make neural networks more interpretable to humans. Building upon our work on sparse attention mechanisms (Correia et al., 2019), we presented a framework to predict attention sparsity in transformer architectures, avoiding comparison of queries and keys which

[1] Project website: `https://deep-spin.github.io`.

Macken, Rufener, Van den Bogaert, Daems, Tezcan, Vanroy, Fonteyne, Barrault, Costa-jussà, Kemp, Pilos, Declercq, Koponen, Forcada, Scarton, Moniz (eds.)
Proceedings of the 23rd Annual Conference of the European Association for Machine Translation, p. 325–326
Ghent, Belgium, June 2022.

MT	DA	COMET	UA-COMET
Она сказала, 'Это не собирается работать.	-0.815	*0.586*	0.149 [-0.92, 1.22]
Gloss: "*She said, 'that's not willing to work*"			
Она сказала: «Это не сработает.	0.768	1.047	1.023 [0.673, 1.374]
Gloss: "*She said, «That will not work*"			

Table 1: Example of uncertainty-aware MT evaluation. Shown are two Russian translations of the same English source "*She said, 'That's not going to work.*" with reference "Она сказала: "Не получится."" For the first sentence, COMET provides a point estimate (in *red*) that overestimates quality, as compared to a human direct assessment (DA), while our UA-COMET (in green) returns a large 95% confidence interval which contains the DA value. For the second sentence UA-COMET is confident and returns a narrow 95% confidence interval. Taken from (Glushkova et al., 2021).

will lead to zero attention probability (Treviso et al., 2022). To model long-term memories, we proposed a new framework based on continuous attention, the ∞-*former* (Martins et al., 2022). We also compared different strategies for explainability of quality estimation scores, which led to an award in the EvalNLP workshop (Treviso et al., 2021).

Transfer Learning. We leveraged large pretrained models to build state-of-the-art models for quality estimation (Zerva et al., 2021) and for machine translation evaluation (Rei et al., 2021). Building upon the recently proposed deep-learned MT evaluation metric COMET (Rei et al., 2020), which tracks human judgements, we presented a new framework for uncertainty-aware MT evaluation (Glushkova et al., 2021), which endows COMET with confidence intervals for segment-level quality assessments (Table 1).

Released Code and Datasets. To promote research reproducibility, the DeepSPIN project has released software code and datasets, including: OpenKiwi,[2] an open-source toolkit for quality estimation (Kepler et al., 2019); the `entmax` package[3] for sparse attention and sparse losses; a dataset with post-editor activity data (Góis and Martins, 2019) and various datasets for quality estimation, used at WMT 2018–2021 shared tasks (Specia et al., 2021).

[2]`http://github.com/Unbabel/OpenKiwi`

[3]`https://github.com/deep-spin/entmax`

Acknowledgments. This work was supported by ERC StG DeepSPIN 758969 with AM as PI.

References

Correia, Gonçalo, Vlad Niculae, and André F. T. Martins. 2019. Adaptively sparse Transformers. In *EMNLP*.

Fernandes, Patrick, Kayo Yin, Graham Neubig, and André FT Martins. 2021. Measuring and increasing context usage in context-aware machine translation. In *ACL*.

Glushkova, Taisiya, Chrysoula Zerva, Ricardo Rei, and André FT Martins. 2021. Uncertainty-aware machine translation evaluation. In *Findings of EMNLP*.

Góis, António and André FT Martins. 2019. Translator2vec: Understanding and representing human post-editors. In *MT Summit*.

Kepler, Fabio, Jonay Trénous, Marcos Treviso, Miguel Vera, and André F. T. Martins. 2019. Openkiwi: An open source framework for quality estimation. In *ACL System Demonstrations*.

Martins, Pedro Henrique, Zita Marinho, and André FT Martins. 2020. Sparse text generation. In *EMNLP*.

Martins, Pedro Henrique, Zita Marinho, and André FT Martins. 2022. ∞-former: Infinite memory transformer. In *ACL*.

Peters, Ben and André FT Martins. 2021. Smoothing and shrinking the sparse seq2seq search space. In *NAACL*.

Peters, Ben, Vlad Niculae, and André F. T. Martins. 2019. Sparse sequence-to-sequence models. In *ACL*.

Rei, Ricardo, Craig Stewart, Ana C Farinha, and Alon Lavie. 2020. Comet: A neural framework for mt evaluation. In *Proceedings of the 2020 Conference on Empirical Methods in Natural Language Processing (EMNLP)*, pages 2685–2702.

Rei, Ricardo, Ana C Farinha, Chrysoula Zerva, Daan van Stigt, Craig Stewart, Pedro Ramos, Taisiya Glushkova, André FT Martins, and Alon Lavie. 2021. Are references really needed? Unbabel-IST 2021 submission for the metrics shared task. In *WMT*.

Specia, Lucia, Frédéric Blain, Marina Fomicheva, Chrysoula Zerva, Zhenhao Li, Vishrav Chaudhary, and André Martins. 2021. Findings of the wmt 2021 shared task on quality estimation. In *WMT*.

Treviso, Marcos, Nuno M Guerreiro, Ricardo Rei, and André FT Martins. 2021. IST-Unbabel 2021 submission for the explainable quality estimation shared task. In *EvalNLP*.

Treviso, Marcos, António Góis, Patrick Fernandes, Erick Fonseca, and André FT Martins. 2022. Predicting attention sparsity in transformers. In *SPNLP Workshop*.

Yin, Kayo, Patrick Fernandes, Danish Pruthi, Aditi Chaudhary, André FT Martins, and Graham Neubig. 2021. Do context-aware translation models pay the right attention? In *ACL*.

Zerva, Chrysoula, Daan van Stigt, Ricardo Rei, Ana C Farinha, Pedro Ramos, José GC de Souza, Taisiya Glushkova, Miguel Vera, Fabio Kepler, and André FT Martins. 2021. Ist-unbabel 2021 submission for the quality estimation shared task. In *WMT*.

A Machine Translation-Powered Chatbot for Public Administration

Dimitra Anastasiou[+], Anders Ruge[&]
Radu Ion*, Svetlana Segărceanu[#], George Suciu[#], Olivier Pedretti[+], Patrick Gratz[+], Hoorieh Afkari[+]
[+]Luxembourg Institute of Science and Technology,
[&]SupWiz, Denmark,
[*]Romanian Academy Institute for AI,
[#]R&D Department, BEIA, Romania
a.ruge@supwiz.com, radu@racai.ro,
{svetlana.segarceanu, george}@beia.ro
{dimitra.anastasiou, olivier.pedretti, patrick.gratz, hoorieh.afkari}@list.lu

Abstract

This paper describes a multilingual chatbot developed for public administration within the ENRICH4ALL project. We argue for multilingual chatbots powered through machine translation (MT) and discuss the integration of the eTranslation service in a chatbot solution.

1 Introduction

In this paper, we introduce the Action ENRICH4ALL (E-goverNment [RI] CHatbot for ALL) which is about the development of a multilingual chatbot service to be deployed in public administration in Luxembourg, Denmark, and Romania. ENRICH4ALL is funded by the Connecting Europe Facility and its duration is from June 2021 to May 2023. The partners are Luxembourg Institute of Science and Technology, BEIA Consulting Romania, Romanian Academy Institute for AI and SupWiz, Denmark. In this paper, we refer to the benefits and challenges of e-government chatbots and to the integration of eTranslation with the chatbot platform.

2 Related Work

The benefits of having e-government chatbots are several: they can process service requests in huge numbers, work 24/7, provide up-to-date information and consequently reduce operational costs. In some European countries, such as Denmark, Estonia, and Latvia, there are chatbots used in many public authorities, whereas in other countries, such as Romania or Luxembourg, there are not. Some of the challenges of using chatbots in public administration are the large number of relevant services, the complexity of administrative services, the context-dependent relevance of user questions, the differences in expert-language and user-language as well as the necessity of providing highly reliable answers for all questions (Lommatzsch, 2018). To these challenges, we should add the language diversity in Europe. The consequence of language diversity is that each EU country and each administration uses its own initiative to deploy a chatbot (often monolingual) resulting in a scenario where the interaction with e-government through virtual assistants is scarce and fragmented.

3 A multilingual chatbot in public administration

Particularly for administrative procedures, there are many requests from expatriates, who enter a new country. Application for residence, importing a car, starting-up a new business, and building a house are some of such requests. Public administration was also burdened with many questions related to the pandemic, which gave rise

Macken, Rufener, Van den Bogaert, Daems, Tezcan, Vanroy, Fonteyne, Barrault, Costa-jussà, Kemp, Pilos, Declercq, Koponen, Forcada, Scarton, Moniz (eds.)
Proceedings of the 23rd Annual Conference of the European Association for Machine Translation, p. 327–328
Ghent, Belgium, June 2022.

to COVID-19 chatbots in Europe. We created (and actively develop) three datasets:

- COVID-19 (RO[2])
- Construction permits (RO)
- Administrative questions (LTZ–FR–DE–EN)

The datasets are available at the project's website and will soon be available at the European Language Grid. As for BERT language models, we use already existing ones for RO, FR, DE, EN, and we have developed and trained one for Luxembourgish[3] to use for detecting question similarity and classification with user intent labels, but this is outside the scope of this paper.

3.1 BotStudio

BotStudio is the AI-powered chatbot developed by the Danish partner SupWiz, where the eTranslation API is now integrated. BotStudio can use fine-tuned BERT-based models built with HuggingFace APIs to appropriately map user intents to chat nodes in specific domains.

3.2 Integration of eTranslation

eTranslation[4] is both a stand-alone MT tool and an API that can be integrated into various systems to facilitate multilingual services. The tool translates from and to 27 languages in different domains, including Russian, simplified Chinese, and recently Ukrainian. eTranslation is the neural MT tool provided by the European Commission to all EU bodies but also public services and SMEs across Europe. The latency of the service is low for small input texts, which makes it usable for real-time applications. Three arguments for using eTranslation compared to other translation services are: i) privacy is a priority; all data resides in Europe[5]; ii) it is free for SMEs; iii) it supports niche domains for formal language.

Figure 1 presents the eTranslation integration. One of the challenges is language identification. In our chatbot, we added a language identification service based on the PyPI `langdetect` package. For LTZ, a new language profile was added, while for DE, FR, EN, RO, and DA[6], existing language profiles are used. For all languages, the language of the input question is automatically detected and suggested at the top of a drop-down list containing all available languages. The questions are then translated into any of DE, FR, EN, RO, DA based on the domain of the user-entered question and on which dataset is being used. BotStudio finds the right answer in the QA database, eTranslation translates the answer back in the user's selected language and BotStudio gives the output.

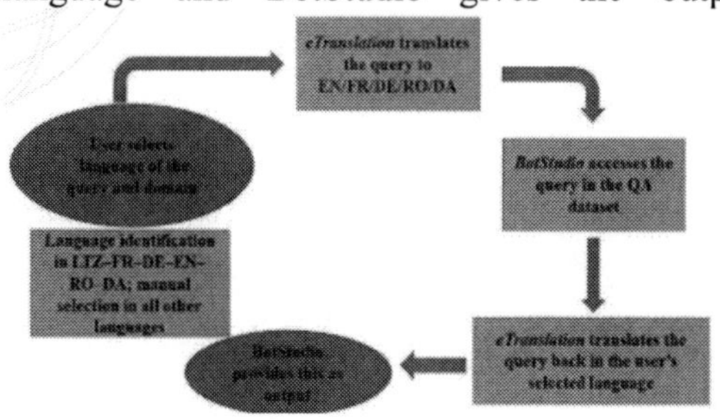

Figure 1. eTranslation integration workflow

4 Conclusion and Future Prospects

Our chatbot is an AI-based, MT-powered service, which proves available information to citizens 24/7 and reduces the administrative burden from public authorities. After the chatbot deployment, there will be additional data created and shared with the EC. Through data creation and training, eTranslation will be trained for other domains and maybe extended for LTZ, which is not supported in eTranslation. Generally, it would be interesting to integrate MT in open-domain conversational QA, e.g. ORConvQA (Qu et al., 2020).

Acknowledgement

The Action 2020-EU-IA-0088 has received funding from the EU's 2014-2020 - CEF Telecom, under Grant Agreement No. INEA/CEF/ICT/A2020/2278547.

References

Lommatzsch, A. 2018. A next generation chatbot-framework for the public administration. *International Conference on Innovations for Community Services,* Springer, Cham, 127-141.

Qu, C. et al. 2020. Open-retrieval conversational question answering. *Proceedings of the 43rd International ACM SIGIR conference on research and development in Information Retrieval*, 539-548.

[2] RO: Romanian, LTZ: Luxembourgish, FR: French, DE: German, EN: English.

[3] https://huggingface.co/raduion/bert-medium-luxembourgish, 18.03.22

[4] https://joinup.ec.europa.eu/collection/connecting-europe-facility-cef/solution/cef-etranslation/about

[5] See the privacy statement at https://webgate.ec.europa.eu/etranslation/public/welcome.html

[6] https://github.com/racai-ai/e4a-langdetect/commit/d29daa818fcccdd9ce0d106dda1e7063bd48ee92#diff-d0066ed32bbca6cf4d1cfa89c16421197264b1bcbc4cef39204fcf5cb4e5d291

MTrill: Machine Translation Impact on Language Learning

Natalia Resende
School of Computing
ADAPT Centre
Dublin City University, Dublin, Ireland
natalia.resende@adaptcentre.ie

Abstract

This paper presents the MTrill project which aimed at investigating the impact of popular web-based machine translation tools on the cognitive processing of English as a second language. The methodological approach and main results are presented.

1 Introduction

The MTrill project was funded by the European Union's Horizon 2020 research and innovation programme under the Marie Sklodowska- Curie grant agreement No 843455. The project started on the April 25th 2019 and ended on July 16th 2021. The project aimed at investigating the impact of popular web-based machine translation (MT) tools on the cognitive processing of English as a second language.

The proposed research project was motivated by the observation that students of English as a second language are using web-based MT systems as a tool to support their English learning, due to the easy access to the systems through applications on their phones which provide instant translations for the input entered either by voice, text or image. The general research question of the project was: *Would the interaction with the output of the MT result in changes in the cognitive processing of English as a second language, reflected by the learning of structures seen in the output of the MT?*

To answer the research question, two laboratory studies were implemented in which participants recruited were tested whether they would be primed by the MT output, i.e., whether the MT system would be capable of influencing the language production of participants. The specific objectives of the experiments are listed below:

1) Investigate whether MT systems are capable of eliciting syntactic priming effects;
2) Investigate whether any priming effect elicited is of an explicit, i.e., conscious or implicit, i.e., unconscious nature.

In the next section, we describe the methodological approach used in the experiments.

2 Methodology

The MTrill project adopted the syntactic priming paradigm widely used behavioural method to study syntactic processing and encoding. *Syntactic priming* can be defined as the tendency speakers have to use a syntactic structure that has been previously encountered (Bock et al., 1989). Both experiments involved a pre-test phase, a priming test phase and an English proficiency test[1]. In experiment 2, a post-test phase was included.

The pre-test phase was considered as the baseline, as in this phase, participants were not exposed to the MT output when translating sentences from Portuguese into English. The priming phase involved a task in which participants were requested to translate sentences from Portuguese into English using Google Translate (GT) application on their own mobile device and repeat the output out loud. Immediately after this task, they were asked to describe images in English using words provided on the screen. If participants

[1] https://www.cambridgeenglish.org/test-your-english/general-english/

described the images in English using the syntactic structures previously seen in the output of the MT more frequently than the syntactic structures they used in the pre-test phase (which did not involve any interaction with MT), then our results would suggest that the MT system is capable of eliciting syntactic priming effects, that is, our results would suggest that MT system is influencing users linguistic behaviour in the second language. The post-test phase was included in experiment 2 with the aim of investigating whether any syntactic priming effect observed would be of implicit or explicit nature.

3 Results

3.1 Results of Experiment 1

Experiment 1 was considered a preliminary study with the aim of investigating whether MT systems are capable of eliciting syntactic priming effects. For this preliminary experiment, 20 participants were asked to complete 3 tasks involving translation of sentences without Google Translate (pre-test phase, task 1); using Google Translate (priming test phase, task 2). Participants were also asked to complete an online proficiency English test (task 3). Participants who have not completed the online survey were invited to complete it after the experimental session if they so wished (task 4). Through this preliminary experiment, specific objective 1 was achieved (see section 1), as results of this preliminary experiment have shown that, after exposure to the MT output more 55% of the descriptions of images were influenced by the structures seen on the MT output, i.e., an increase of 45% compared to the baseline pre-test (Resende et al., 2020).

3.2 Results of Experiment 2

With the objective of a more in-depth study and analysis as well as to achieve specific objective 2 **(see section 1),** i.e. investigate whether any syntactic priming effect observed would be of an implicit (conscious) or explicit (unconscious) nature, in experiment 2, 40 participants were recruited to take part in the study. Experiment 2 included the same tasks of the experiment 1 (pre-test, task 1, priming test, task 2; English proficiency test, task 3 and online survey completion, task 4) as well as a post-test phase (task 5). The post-test phase was carried out 24 hours after completing the pre-test and the priming test. In this experiment, the English proficiency test as well as the completion of the online questionnaire were carried out after the post-test.

Overall, results of experiment 2 showed a long-lasting priming effect, suggesting that MT output has elicited subconscious learning of the grammatical structures seen in the MT output. For instance, we observed an increase (from 25.9% in the baseline pre-test to 51.1% in the priming phase) of the alternative grammatical structures seen in the output of the MT. In the post-test phase this increase in the production of the MT grammatical structure remained, as participants used the MT syntactic alternative in 45.8% of the target trials after 24 hours versus the 25.9% observed in the baseline pre-test 24 before (Resende, Way, 2021).

Acknowledgements

ADAPT: the Science Foundation Ireland Research Centre for AI-Driven Digital Content Technology at Dublin City University, is funded by the Science Foundation Ireland through the SFI Research Centres Programme (Grant 13/RC/2106_P2).

References

Bock, J. Kathryn, and Kroch, Anthony S. 1989. The Isolability of Syntactic Processing. In. Carlson, Gn.; Tanenhaus, Mk., (Orgs). *Linguistic structure in language processing*, Dordrecht, The Netherlands: Kluwer, pp. 157-196.

Resende, Natalia C.A, Cowan, Benjamin, and Way, Andy. 2020. MT priming effects on L2 English Learners. In. *Proceedings of the 22nd annual conference of the European Association for Machine Translation*. p. 245-253, 3-5 November 2020, Lisbon, Portugal. https://aclanthology.org/2020.eamt-1.0.pdf

Resende, Natalia C.A., and Andy Way. 2021. Can Google Translate Rewire Your L2 English Processing? *Digital* 2021, volume 1, 66-85. https://doi.org/10.3390/digital1010006

Connecting client infrastructure with Yamagata Europe machine translation using JSON-based data exchange

Jourik Ciesielski
Yamagata Europe
Zwijnaardsesteenweg 316 B
9000 Ghent, Belgium
jourik.ciesielski@yamagata-europe.com

Heidi Van Hiel
Yamagata Europe
Zwijnaardsesteenweg 316 B
9000 Ghent, Belgium
heidi.van.hiel@yamagata-europe.com

Abstract

This document describes how Yamagata Europe enables organizations to connect seamlessly to its machine translation and translation management system infrastructure using a JSON-based (JavaScript Object Notation) data exchange mechanism.

1 JSON protocol

Yamagata Europe's data exchange service is based on the JSON interchange format to transfer data between translation buyers on the one hand and Yamagata Europe on the other. The purpose of the service is to provide an easy-to-implement and extensible alternative for other translation data exchange standards such as COTI (Common Translation Interface) and TIPP (Translation Interoperability Protocol Package). Translatable objects are contained in a ZIP package together with a package description file (hereinafter referred to as *manifest*). The ZIP packages are compressed programmatically at the client's end, possibly with support of Yamagata Europe, and subsequently transferred to Yamagata Europe via for example file transfer protocol (FTP) or cloud storage utilities like Amazon S3. Package transfers are monitored and confirmed through a proprietary API (application programming interface). Once at the Yamagata Europe premises, packages are automatically decompressed, analyzed and, in accordance with the prescriptions in the manifest, the required workflow steps (machine translation, machine translation and post-editing, etc.) are organized and executed. When the workflow is completed, the service creates a response package and sends it back to the native repository at the client's end.

2 Data flow

The manifest in a data package is a JSON file that contains information about:

- The required service (e.g., machine translation only, machine translation and post-editing with or without desktop publishing work, etc.).
- The source and target language(s).
- The source file(s) for translation (file name including a unique identifier).
- Extra information regarding the source file format.

Example of a JSON manifest:

```
{
  "service": "Machine Translation",
  "id": "61d2d6260d3da511cf63c328",
  "source": "en",
  "target": [
    "fr"
  ],
  "files": [
    {
      "id": "61d2d6790d3da511cf63c329",
      "fileName": "NewEmployee.docx",
      "storyLine": false
    }
  ]
}
```

Figure 1: JSON manifest file

The decompressing of a package entails several checks to verify whether the data meets the conditions to be processed correctly. If zero or more than one JSON files are found, the process will stop and the package will be moved to an

"Error" folder, while an error message will be sent to the client through the provided API. The same thing will happen if an unknown service type or an unsupported target language is specified. Furthermore, the source files specified in the manifest must be identical to the files in the payload. The entire payload travels in a single folder without subfolder structures for the translatable objects.

If a package is valid, a translation project will be created in Yamagata Europe's translation management system using a dedicated project template that corresponds to the prescriptions in the manifest. If machine translation is specified as the desired service, the source files will be machine-translated using Yamagata Europe's internal machine translation service, which includes an automated pre-editing component (optimization of source content) and an automated post-editing component (automatic correction of recurring mistakes such as formatting or terminology issues). The last step of the flow consists of creating a response package and notifying the client about the project delivery through the provided API. The response package is a ZIP file containing the original JSON manifest and one or more language folders containing the translated objects.

3 Pitfalls

An important pitfall is the insertion of inline XML-style tag mistakes during the machine translation process. Inline tag issues might prevent the translation management system from generating translated objects, which will break the automation. For that reason, Yamagata Europe has developed a smart tag handling algorithm that remembers the content of opening as well as (self-)closing XML tags, converts the tags into numbered placeholders, protects them during the machine translation process and restores them in their original format and position after the process.

A second pitfall is related to the supported file types. The current setup foresees support for the following file formats:

- Office Open XML (OOXML) document, `docx`
- Articulate Storyline OOXML document, `docx`
- OOXML presentation, `.pptx`
- OOXML spreadsheet, `.xlsx`
- XML (flavor to be determined with customer)
- PDF
- Support for other file formats, including industry standards such as XLIFF (XML Localisation Interchange File Format), can be added upon request.

Articulate Storyline is an e-learning authoring tool that includes a translation export module to `.docx`. Certain metadata fragments in Storyline exports are not supposed to be modified during translation. To distinguish regular `.docx` files from Storyline `.docx` files, an additional parameter is added to the JSON manifest. This parameter triggers an additional script in the translation management system to protect metadata in the case of Storyline exports.

Portable Document Format (PDF) files are generally challenging for translation and might prevent the automation from executing successfully. Password-protected and scanned PDF files in particular will result in an empty translated object. Only PDF files that can be saved as `.docx` will go correctly through the process.

4 Assets

The JSON-based data exchange mechanism allows organizations to integrate their content repositories and self-service portals with Yamagata Europe's internally developed machine translation infrastructure. The flow automates repetitive and time-consuming tasks at every stage of the translation process — from data transfer to project creation, machine translation and delivery — and therefore enables companies to process more content at a faster pace and a high-quality standard.

Towards a methodology for evaluating automatic subtitling

Alina Karakanta[1,2]**, Luisa Bentivogli**[1]**, Mauro Cettolo**[1]**,**
Matteo Negri[1]**, Marco Turchi**[1]
[1]Fondazione Bruno Kessler
[2]University of Trento
{akarakanta,bentivo,cettolo,negri,turchi}@fbk.eu

Abstract

In response to the growing interest towards automatic subtitling, the 2021 EAMT-funded project "Towards a methodology for evaluating automatic subtitling" aimed at collecting subtitle post-editing data in a real use case scenario where professional subtitlers edit automatically generated subtitles. The post-editing setting includes, for the first time, automatic generation of timestamps and segmentation, and focuses on the effect of timing and segmentation edits on the post-editing process. The collected data will serve as the basis for investigating how subtitlers interact with automatic subtitling and for devising evaluation methods geared to the multimodal nature and formal requirements of subtitling.

1 Project overview

Automatic subtitling is the task of generating target language subtitles for a given video without any intermediate human transcription and timing of the source speech. The source speech in the video is automatically transcribed, translated and segmented into subtitles, which are synchronised with the speech – a process called automatic spotting (or auto-spotting). Automatic subtitling is becoming a task of increasing interest for the MT community, practitioners and the audiovisual industry. Despite the technological advancements, the evaluation of automatic subtitling still represents a significant research gap. Popular MT evaluation metrics consider only content-related parameters (translation quality), but not form-related parameters, such as format (length and segmentation) and timing (synchronisation with speech, reading speed), which are important features for high-quality subtitles (Carroll and Ivarsson, 1998). Moreover, the way subtitlers interact with automatically generated subtitles has not been yet explored, since the majority of works which conducted human evaluations of the post-editing effort in MT for subtitling have focused on edits in the textual content (Volk et al., 2010; Bywood et al., 2017; Matusov et al., 2019; Koponen et al., 2020).

This project seeks to investigate automatic subtitling, the factors contributing to post-editing effort and their relation to the quality of the output. This is achieved through the collection of rich, product- and process-based subtitling data in a real use case scenario where professional subtitlers edit automatically translated, spotted and segmented subtitles in a dedicated subtitling environment. The richness of the data collected during this one-year project is ideal for understanding the operations performed by subtitlers while they interact with automatic subtitling in their professional environment and for applying mixed methods approaches to:

- Investigate the correlation between amount of text editing, adjustments in auto-spotting and post-editing temporal/technical effort
- Explore the effect of auto-spotting edits on the total post-editing process
- Investigate the variability in subtitle segmentation decisions among subtitlers
- Propose tentative metrics for auto-spotting quality and subtitle segmentation

2 Data collection

Three professional subtitlers with experience in post-editing tasks (two subtitlers en→it, one

Macken, Rufener, Van den Bogaert, Daems, Tezcan, Vanroy, Fonteyne, Barrault, Costa-jussà, Kemp, Pilos, Declercq, Koponen, Forcada, Scarton, Moniz (eds.)
Proceedings of the 23rd Annual Conference of the European Association for Machine Translation, p. 333–334
Ghent, Belgium, June 2022.

en→de) were asked to post-edit 9 single-speaker TED talks from the MuST-Cinema test set,[1] the only publicly available speech subtitling corpus (Karakanta et al., 2020), amounting to one hour of video (10,000 source words) in total. The post-editing task was performed in a novel PE subtitling tool, Matesub,[2] which features automatic speech recognition, machine translation, automatic generation of timestamps and automatic segmentation of the translations into subtitles.

For each subtitler, we collected the following data: 1) original automatically-generated subtitle files and the corresponding final human post-edited subtitle files in SubRip `.srt` format; 2) process logs from the Matesub tool, which records the original and final subtitle, original and final timestamps and total time spent on the subtitle; 3) keystrokes, using InputLog[3] (Leijten and Van Waes, 2013). Screen recordings were also collected to trace the translation and segmentation decisions of the subtitlers and identify possible outliers. At the end of the task, the subtitlers completed a questionnaire giving feedback on their user experience with automatic subtitling, particular problems faced, and their general impressions on automatic subtitling.

For en→it, we collected in total 1,199 subtitles from the first subtitler (it1) and 1,208 subtitles from the second subtitler (it2), while for en→de 1,198 subtitles. Based on the process logs we can define the status of each subtitle: *new* – a new subtitle is added by the subtitler; *deleted* – an automatically generated subtitle is discarded by the subtitler; or *edited* – any subtitle that is not new or deleted, regardless of whether it was confirmed exactly as generated by the system or changed. Table 1 shows the distribution of subtitles based on their status, with *edited* being the majority.

Subtitler	Edited	New	Deleted
it1	1,015 (84,7%)	59 (4.9%)	125 (10.4%)
it2	953 (78.9%)	68 (5.7%)	187 (15.4%)
de	1,051 (87.7%)	59 (4.9%)	88 (7.4%)

Table 1: Distribution of subtitles based on their status.

3 Final remarks

This project focuses on automatic subtitling and the challenges in its evaluation due to the multi-modal nature of the source medium (video, audio) and the formal requirements of the target (format and timing of subtitles). The data collected constitute the basis for future multi-faceted analyses to explore correlations between translation quality, spotting quality, and post-editing effort, possibly leading to new metrics for automatic subtitling. The subtitling data collected will be publicly released to promote research in automatic subtitling.

Acknowledgements

This project has been partially funded by the EAMT programme "2021 Sponsorship of Activities - Students' edition". We kindly thank the subtitlers Giulia Donati, Paolo Pilati and Anastassia Friedrich for their participation in the PE task.

References

Bywood, Lindsay, Panayota Georgakopoulou, and Thierry Etchegoyhen. 2017. Embracing the threat: machine translation as a solution for subtitling. *Perspectives*, 25(3):492–508.

Carroll, Mary and Jan Ivarsson. 1998. *Code of Good Subtitling Practice*. Simrishamn: TransEdit.

Karakanta, Alina, Matteo Negri, and Marco Turchi. 2020. MuST-Cinema: a Speech-to-Subtitles corpus. In *Proceedings of the 12th Language Resources and Evaluation Conference*, pages 3727–3734, Marseille, France. ELRA.

Koponen, Maarit, Umut Sulubacak, Kaisa Vitikainen, and Jörg Tiedemann. 2020. MT for subtitling: User evaluation of post-editing productivity. In *Proceedings of the 22nd Annual Conference of the European Association for Machine Translation*, pages 115–124, Lisboa, Portugal, November. European Association for Machine Translation.

Leijten, Mariëlle and Luuk Van Waes. 2013. Keystroke logging in writing research: Using inputlog to analyze writing processes. *Written Communication*, 30:358–392.

Matusov, Evgeny, Patrick Wilken, and Yota Georgakopoulou. 2019. Customizing Neural Machine Translation for Subtitling. In *Proceedings of the Fourth Conference on Machine Translation (Volume 1: Research Papers)*, pages 82–93, Florence, Italy, August. Association for Computational Linguistics.

Volk, Martin, Rico Sennrich, Christian Hardmeier, and Frida Tidström. 2010. Machine Translation of TV Subtitles for Large Scale Production. In Zhechev, Ventsislav, editor, *Proceedings of the Second Joint EM+/CNGL Workshop "Bringing MT to the User: Research on Integrating MT in the Translation Industry (JEC'10)*, pages 53–62, Denver.

[1] `https://ict.fbk.eu/must-cinema/`
[2] `https://matesub.com/`
[3] `https://www.inputlog.net/`

DiHuTra: a Parallel Corpus to Analyse Differences between Human Translations

Ekaterina Lapshinova-Koltunski[1], **Maja Popović**[2], **Maarit Koponen**[3]
Language Science and Technology[1], ADAPT Centre[2],
Foreign Languages and Translation Studies[3]
Saarland University[1], Dublin City University[2], University of Eastern Finland[3]
e.lapshinova@mx.uni-saarland.de[1], maja.popovic@adaptcentre.ie[2],
maarit.koponen@uef.fi[3]

Abstract

The DiHuTra project aimed to design a corpus of parallel human translations of the same source texts by professionals and students. The resulting corpus consists of English news and reviews source texts, their translations into Russian and Croatian, and translations of the reviews into Finnish. The corpus will be valuable for both studying variation in translation and evaluating machine translation (MT) systems.

1 Description

Many studies have demonstrated that translated texts have different textual features than texts originally written in the given language (originals). Furthermore, some studies have shown evidence of variation between human translations generated by different translators (Rubino et al., 2016; Popović, 2020; Kunilovskaya and Lapshinova-Koltunski, 2020). Nevertheless, the number of such studies is still very small and limited to comparable corpora where different translators translated different source texts. Therefore, exact comparisons between human translations are not possible.

The DiHuTra project, formed by Saarland University, ADAPT Centre and University of Eastern Finland in 2021–2022 has aimed to design a parallel corpus to address these issues. Each source text originally written in English has been translated into three target languages: Croatian, Russian and Finnish, by two groups of translators: professionals and students. These parallel human translations will enable a better comparison of various text features as well as impact of automatic MT evaluation when used as references.

2 Data sets

The source texts consist of two sub-sets of publicly available data sets from two distinct domains:

Amazon product reviews[1] contain unique product reviews from Amazon written in English with overall ratings from 1 to 5, 1 and 2 referring to negative, 3 to neutral and 4 and 5 to positive. We selected a balanced set of reviews from 14 categories (e.g., "Sports and Outdoors", "Books", etc.) with an equal number of positive and negative reviews (14 from each of the 14 topics). In total, we included 196 reviews, containing 5.4 sentences and 93.2 words on average.

News texts were imported from the WMT (2019 and 2020) shared task[2] News test corpus. The topics vary between politics, sports, crime, health, etc. The news are longer than reviews, with 9.9 sentences and 221.7 words on average. The WMT shared tasks also contain a set of human translations of the English source texts into several languages including Russian, however, neither Croatian nor Finnish. We selected only texts which were originally written in English and had professional translations into Russian. In total, we included 68 news articles from different sources.

3 Translation process

Each English review was translated into the three target languages, Croatian, Russian and Finnish, by professionals and by students. For the news

[1] `http://jmcauley.ucsd.edu/data/amazon/`
[2] `http://www.statmt.org/wmt20/translation-task.html`

Macken, Rufener, Van den Bogaert, Daems, Tezcan, Vanroy, Fonteyne, Barrault, Costa-jussà, Kemp, Pilos, Declercq, Koponen, Forcada, Scarton, Moniz (eds.)
Proceedings of the 23rd Annual Conference of the European Association for Machine Translation, p. 335–336
Ghent, Belgium, June 2022.

	en		hr				ru				fi	
	news	reviews	news		reviews		news		reviews		reviews	
			prof	stud	prof	stud	prof	stud	prof	stud	prof	stud
a	17,186	15,236	16,662	16,632	14,003	13,940	17,469	17,054	14,233	14,247	11,709	12,213
b	4,138	3,155	6,009	5,975	4,359	4,446	6,079	6,076	4,417	4,523	4,612	4,664
c	**0.220**	0.178	**0.341**	0.340	0.282	**0.288**	0.340	**0.349**	0.289	**0.300**	**0.360**	0.350
d	**98.2**	101.7	86.2	**83.8**	92.1	**88.2**	122.9	**116.7**	126.3	**124.1**	**109.8**	112.5

Table 1: Text statistics and lexical variety: (a) total number of words, (b) total number of running words, (c) ratio between vocabulary and words ↑, (d) Yule's K coefficient ↓.

corpus, Russian translations were already available from the WMT shared task and Croatian translations were produced for the purpose of this work. Finnish professional translations were not provided for the news articles. In addition to translations, information about age, gender, experience and the study program (for students) was collected. Translators were asked to keep the sentence alignment (not to merge or to split sentences) and not to use MT. No further restrictions were given to translators. The total number of tokens in the resulting corpus amounts to 180,584.

4 Corpus statistics

The first statistics on the shallow features in terms of running words and vocabulary in the sources and the three target languages (see Table 1). We also estimated lexical richness in terms of ratio between vocabulary and total number of words and Yule's K coefficient. Both values indicate how rich the vocabulary is in the given text, the richness being proportional to the vocabulary/words ratio (higher value indicates richer vocabulary) and inversely proportional to Yule's K (a lower value indicates a richer vocabulary).

The corpus is valuable for studying variation in translation as it allows direct comparisons between human translations of the same source texts. Our preliminary analyses based on the shallow text statistics and matching/distance measures indicate that students used shorter sentences but richer vocabulary. To better understand these differences, we plan to carry out detailed analyses on the annotated data (we have tokenised, lemmatised, parts-of-speech tagged and parsed the data using universal dependencies). This resource is also valuable for evaluation of MT systems for the three language pairs. The Croatian (and probably Russian) part of the user reviews will be used in the WMT shared task in 2022.[3] We believe that this resource will help us to understand and improve quality issues in both human and machine translation.

The corpus is available via CLARIN[4]. The project has also a GitHub repository[5] which contains the data and some additional information. The details about the corpus can be found in (Lapshinova-Koltunski et al., 2022).

5 Acknowledgments

The creation of the corpus was supported through the EAMT sponsorship programme (2021) and by ADAPT Centre. The ADAPT Centre is funded by through the SFI Research Centres Programme and co-funded under the ERDF through Grant 13/RC/2106. The Finnish subcorpus was supported by a Kopiosto grant awarded by the Finnish Association of Translators and Interpreters. We thank the translators in Volgograd, Zagreb, Rijeka and Finland. In particular, we thank Aleksandr Besedin from VolSU for coordinating the work of the Russian translators.

References

Kunilovskaya, M. and Lapshinova-Koltunski, E. (2020). Lexicogrammatic translationese across two targets and competence levels. In *Proceedings of LREC 2020*, pages 4102–4112, Marseille, France, May.

Lapshinova-Koltunski, E., Popović, M., and Koponen, M. (2022). Dihutra: a parallel corpus to analyse differences between human translations. In *Proceedings of LREC 2022*, Marseille, France, June.

Popović, M. (2020). On the differences between human translations. In *Proceedings of the EAMT 2020*, pages 365–374, Lisboa, Portugal, November.

Rubino, R., Lapshinova-Koltunski, E., and van Genabith, J. (2016). Information density and quality estimation features as translationese indicators for human translation classification. In *Proceedings of NAACL-HLT 2016*, pages 960–970, San Diego, California, June.

[3]https://machinetranslate.org/wmt22

[4]https://fedora.clarin-d.uni-saarland.de/dihutra/index.html

[5]https://github.com/katjakaterina/dihutra

GoURMET – Machine Translation for Low-Resourced Languages

Peggy van der Kreeft
Deutsche Welle, Bonn, Germany
peggy.van-der-kreeft@dw.com

Sevi Sariisik
BBC, London, UK
sevi.sariisik@bbc.co.uk

Wilker Aziz
Univ. of Amsterdam, Netherlands
w.ferreiraaziz@uva.nl

Alexandra Birch
Univ. of Edinburgh, UK
A.Birch@ed.ac.uk

Felipe Sánchez-Martínez
Univ. of Alicante, Spain
fsanchez@dlsi.ua.es

Abstract

The GoURMET project, funded by the EU H2020 research and innovation action (under grant agreement 825299), develops models for machine translation, in particular for low-resourced languages. Data, models and software releases as well as the GoURMET Translate Tool are made available as open source.

1 The Project

GoURMET (Global Under-Resourced Media Translation) started in January 2019 and runs until 30 June 2022.

The consortium consists of five partners: The University of Edinburgh (coordinator), University of Alicante, University of Amsterdam, and user partners BBC and Deutsche Welle (DW). [1]

The aim is to significantly improve the robustness and applicability of neural machine translation (NMT) for low-resourced language pairs and domains. This is in particular important because machine translation (MT) is increasingly used as a technology for supporting communication in a globalized world. The two international broadcasters participating in GoURMET are faced with the need to use MT to support their editorial work, especially for languages for which such tools are currently hard to find or lack quality.

The main objectives of the project are:

- to advance deep-learning for natural language applications
- to arrive at high-quality MT for low-resourced languages and diverse language pairs and domains
- to develop tools for media analysts and journalists in the form of a sustainable and maintainable platform and services.

The work is built around three use cases. The first is *global content creation*, where we use MT in multilingual content production, with editorial control. The second use case is *media monitoring* for low-resourced and especially strategically important languages. The third use case focuses on *a specific topic*, and the health sector, in particular COVID, was selected for this purpose, fitting the news requirements over the past two years. The objective in the last use case is to apply transfer learning between topical domains.

2 Languages Covered

MT models were selected for sixteen low-resourced languages, jointly by user and technology partners and developed in different phases of the project. These languages are: Amharic, Bulgarian, Burmese, Gujarati, Hausa, Igbo, Kyrgyz, Macedonian, Pashto, Serbian, Swahili, Tamil, Tigrinya. Turkish, Urdu, and Yoruba – all of them from and into English. Pashto was selected as a "surprise language" and

[1] https://gourmet-project.eu/

Macken, Rufener, Van den Bogaert, Daems, Tezcan, Vanroy, Fonteyne, Barrault, Costa-jussà, Kemp, Pilos, Declercq, Koponen, Forcada, Scarton, Moniz (eds.)
Proceedings of the 23rd Annual Conference of the European Association for Machine Translation, p. 337–338
Ghent, Belgium, June 2022.

developed as a special case upon request in a period of two months.

Different factors were taken into account for the selection process, including strategic importance for the news partners, proximity of languages, research interest and complexity for the development of the models.

3 Research and Development of the Models

Each selected language was assigned to one technology partner, who developed the model. Different methods were used among the consortium, allowing a comparison and evaluation of pros and cons of each development method, encouraging enhancement of processes and exchange among research partners.

Research was done as to the availability of data. Data was gathered for each language, from external sources and user partner content. Bilingual datasets were established and manually annotated by editors from BBC and/or DW in terms of their level of equivalence.

Novel approaches were used to enhance the results. One such approach is the multi-task learning data augmentation (MTL DA), in which we generate additional parallel sentences which, despite being completely unlikely under the data distribution, systematically improve the quality of the resulting NMT system. The output proves to be more robust against domain shift and produce less hallucinations.

We also produced a survey covering the state of the art in low-resource MT research.[2]

4 Evaluation and Benchmarking

The user partners evaluated the MT models using a customized evaluation process, including direct assessment (by native speakers of the low-resourced languages), gap filling (looking at English-language MT output) and post editing. Specific assessment user interfaces (UI) and test sets were developed for this purpose.

Technical benchmarking provided a comparative analysis of GoURMET models with Google MT models using BLEU-scores and chrF-scores. In addition, user partners benchmarked the MT output from an editorial point of view, including considering the usefulness and adequacy of the respective models in the field and for different purposes (e.g. understanding or multilingual text production).

5 Applications for the Models

The models are trialed and implemented in several applications by the user partners in the project. First of all, an open-source GoURMET Translate Tool has been developed as a customized UI for text translation in all GoURMET languages.

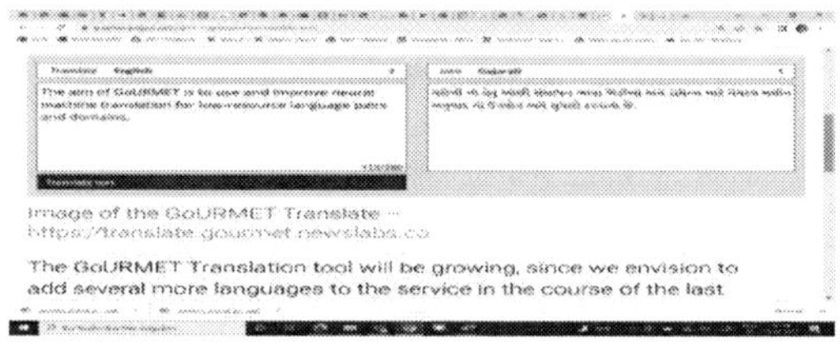

Figure 1: GoURMET Online Translation UI

BBC has implemented some of the GoURMET models in three prototypes, including its multilingual MT prototype Frank[3].

Figure 2: BBC's Frank Multilingual Prototype

DW has incorporated it in the plain X (semi-)automated translation and subtitling platform and as an application of the SELMA[4] project.

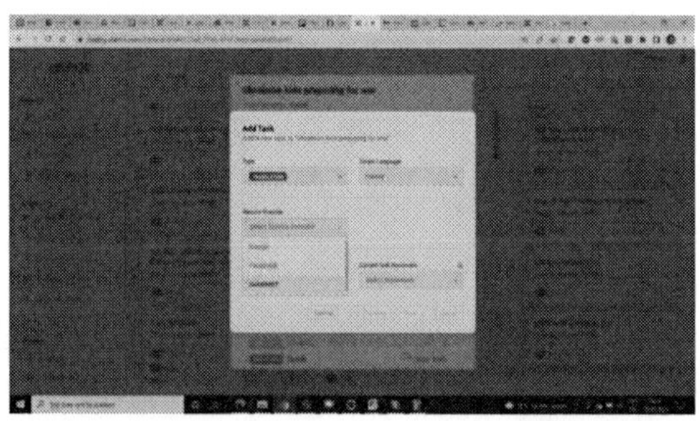

Figure 3: GoURMET in DW's plain X HLT platform

[2] https://arxiv.org/abs/2109.00486

[3] https://bbcnewslabs.co.uk/projects/Frank/

[4] https://selma-project.eu/

Curated Multilingual Language Resources for CEF AT (CURLICAT): Overall View

Tamás Váradi
Research Institute for Linguistics, Budapest, Hungary
varadi.tamas@nytud.hu

Marko Tadić
University of Zagreb, Faculty of Humanities and Social Sciences, Zagreb, Croatia
marko.tadic@ffzg.hr

Svetla Koeva
Institute of Bulgarian Language, Bulgarian Academy of Sciences, Sofia, Bulgaria
svetla@dcl.bas.bg

Maciej Ogrodniczuk
Institute of Computer Science, Polish Academy of Sciences, Warsaw, Poland
maciej.ogrodniczuk@ipipan.waw.pl

Dan Tufiş
RACAI, Romanian Academy, Bucharest, Romania
tufis@racai.ro

Radovan Garabík
Ľ. Štúr Institute of Linguistics, Slovak Academy of Sciences, Bratislava, Slovakia
garabik@kassiopeia.juls.savba.sk

Simon Krek, Andraž Repar
Institute Jozef Stefan, Ljubljana, Slovenia
simon.krek@ijs.si, repar.andraz@gmail.com

Abstract

The work in progress on the CEF action CURLICAT is presented. The general aim of the action is to compile curated monolingual datasets in seven languages of the consortium in domains of relevance to European Digital Service Infrastructures (DSIs) in order to enhance the eTranslation services.

1 Introduction

The paper presents the work in progress on the CEF action Curated Multilingual Language Resources for CEF AT (CURLICAT, which runs from 2020-06-01 till 2022-11-30). The aim of the action is to compile monolingual curated datasets in seven languages of the consortium (Bulgarian, Croatian, Hungarian, Polish, Romanian, Slovak, Slovenian) in domains of relevance to European Digital Service Infrastructures (DSIs) with a view to enhancing the eTranslation automated translation system.

2 Datasets

The primary data come from national or reference corpora of the above languages and it is planned to cover domains of interest for CEF DSIs such as eHealth, Europeana or eGovernment. When completed, the corpus will contain at least at least 2 million sentences from each language, i.e. 14 million sentences, estimated to number at least 140 million words, from domains including culture, health, science and economy/finances. For each language, it is expected to produce corpora in each of the above mentioned four domains with at least 500 000 sentences and 5 million words. In case that legally non-binding data with a clear licence allowing free redistribution could not be found from the national corpora in the required quantities, additional data is included from other sources.

2.1 Annotation

Apart from corpora being domain classified, data are linguistically annotated including sentence splitting, tokenisation, lemmatisation, part-of-speech/morphosyntactic-descriptor tagging, dependency parsing and NERC. The annotation

Macken, Rufener, Van den Bogaert, Daems, Tezcan, Vanroy, Fonteyne, Barrault, Costa-jussà, Kemp, Pilos, Declercq, Koponen, Forcada, Scarton, Moniz (eds.)
Proceedings of the 23rd Annual Conference of the European Association for Machine Translation, p. 339–340
Ghent, Belgium, June 2022.

follows the extended CoNLL-U Plus[1] format presented by Váradi et al. (2020). Additionally, terms from the most recent version of the IATE terminological database are identified and annotated so that the language models built with the help of these corpora could take into account not only single words but also multi-word expressions since these terms represent an additional layer of annotation in stand-off manner. With this additional annotation these corpora can serve as a valuable resource for terminological processing as well.

2.2 Intellectual Propery Rights Issues and Anonymisation

The data are technically and legally cleaned by either of two procedures: 1) inclusion of text samples published under permissive licences, or for which consent was obtained from the content producer, or 2) scrambling of the order of sentences. In this way these corpora will be useful for producing language models up to the level of a sentence, while they will not be useful for higher linguistic level language modelling, but even with this limitation we see these corpora as a valuable resource for MT training. The metadata will specify whether the texts were scrambled or not.

For legal reasons data will also be anonymised through replacement of named entities of the same kind and with similar phonological, morphological or graphemic structure (a process that is inherently language-dependent, but, e.g. for Romanian "Maria" becomes "_#PER#1_", while "Mariei" becomes "_#PER#1_ei"). To ensure a higher degree of privacy preservation, local pseudonymisation, as the process of compete replacement of named entities by one or more artificial identifiers, at document or sub-document level, is used.

During the course of the project, we will develop an anonymisation solution tailored to the specific needs of the CURLICAT corpus by leaning on existing European anonymisation initiatives (i.e. Multilingual Anonymisation for Public Administrations[2] (MAPA) project (Ajausks et al. 2020) which provided anonymisation support for all EU languages) and local solutions developed by the project partners. Specifically, Hungarian, Romanian, Bulgarian and Slovak plan to implement local solutions, while Slovenian, Croatian and Polish will use a solution based on the MAPA project. The approaches for all seven languages will be combined in a single user interface and made available via the European Language Grid[3] repository.

3 Conclusions

Since an important aspect of today's neural machine translation technology is the quality of the language model, the envisaged seven language corpora, although monolingual datasets in themselves, can be rightly expected to make an impact on the quality of the eTranslation system through the enhanced language models built with them. Since these corpora in seven languages cover systematically the same four domains, they could be regarded also as comparable corpora for these domains and thus be used for further processing, e.g. in parallel terminology extraction. Moreover, the action addresses the gap in MT technology, which crucially depends on the provision of domain specific quality language resources for the under-resourced languages.

Acknowledgements

The work reported here was supported by the European Commission in the CEF Telecom Programme (Action No: 2019-EU-IA-0034, Grant Agreement No: INEA/CEF/ICT/A2019/1926831) and the Polish Ministry of Science and Higher Education: research project 5103/CEF/2020/2, funds for 2020–2022).

References

Váradi, Tamás; Koeva, Svetla; Yamalov, Martin; Tadić, Marko; Sass, Bálint; Nitoń, Bartłomiej; Ogrodniczuk, Maciej; Pęzik, Piotr; Barbu Mititelu, Verginica; Ion, Radu; Irimia, Elena; Mitrofan, Maria; Păiș, Vasile; Tufiș, Dan; Garabík, Radovan; Krek, Simon; Repar, Andraž; Rihtar, Matjaž; and Brank, Janez. 2020. The MARCELL legislative corpus. In *Proceedings of The 12th Language Resources and Evaluation Conference (LREC2020)*, pp. 3761–3768.

Ajausks, Ēriks; Arranz, Victoria; Bie, Laurent; Cerdà-i-Cucó, Aleix; Choukri, Khalid; Cuadros, Montse; Degroote, Hans; Estela, Amando; Etchegoyhen, Thierry; García-Martínez, Mercedes; García-Pablos, Aitor; Herranz, Manuel; Kohan, Alejandro; Melero, Maite; Rosner, Mike; Rozis, Roberts; Paroubek, Patrick; Vasiļevskis, Artūrs; Zweigenbaum, Pierre. 2020. The Multilingual Anonymisation Toolkit for Public Administrations (MAPA) Project. In *Proceedings of the 22nd Annual Conference of the European Association for Machine Translation (EAMT2020)*, pp. 471–472.

[1] https://universaldependencies.org/ext-format.html
[2] https://mapa-project.eu
[3] https://www.european-language-grid.eu

Automatically extracting the semantic network out of public services to support cities becoming smart cities

Joachim Van den Bogaert, Laurens Meeus, Alina Kramchaninova, Arne Defauw, Sara Szoc, Frederic Everaert, Koen Van Winckel, Anna Bardadym, Tom Vanallemeersch,
CrossLang NV, Kerkstraat 106, 9050 Gent, Belgium
{firstname.lastname}@crosslang.com

Abstract

The CEFAT4Cities project aims at creating a multilingual semantic interoperability layer for smart cities that allows users from all EU member states to interact with public services in their own language. The CEFAT4Cities processing pipeline transforms natural-language administrative procedures into machine-readable data using various multilingual natural-language processing techniques, such as semantic networks and machine translation, thus allowing for the development of more sophisticated and more user-friendly public services applications.

1 Introduction

To ease interaction with a city's administrative services, the creation of a chatbot is an easy and popular option, with many open-source platforms currently available. However, the main challenge lies in filling the bot with the right content, i.e. an accurate map that can predict exactly what a user is looking for, together with the relevant next steps to take or suggest. Normally, it takes a dedicated team of experienced editors to create such a "mind map" by collecting content and extracting all relevant information. This is a time-consuming process, even for a very limited use case. Imagine this for multiple use cases, in all EU languages administering a metropolitan area with citizens originating from all over the world.

The CEFAT4Cities project[1] aims at supporting cities in creating "semantic networks" of their public services, by building a processing pipeline that ingests legacy data from public services (from e.g. websites, administrative forms, existing applications) in multiple EU languages, and transforms this data into a network of connected services that can be used across applications and languages. By connecting the pipeline to the FIWARE Context Broker[2], the mind map is made available to any app or sensor within the smart-city IoT network.

2 Methodology

To create the semantic network of public services, CEFAT4Cities partners start from a few abstract templates that describe what a public service looks like (who can submit a form to get access to which service, providing which type of proof?) and what the interacting entities look like (are we dealing with an organisation or a citizen?). These abstract templates consist of nodes and links (hence the term "semantic network") and are provided by the European Interoperability Framework which governs data standards to ensure that data can be used across as many applications as possible.[3]

Next, these templates are used as extraction filters to transform unstructured human natural language (i.e. thousands of pages of raw text occurring on websites, online forms, etc.) into machine-readable semantic networks which can be utilised in software applications, such as chatbots. The process runs as follows: data is collected automatically from websites, then only those pages containing public-service information are selected. Then, paragraphs describing administrative proce-

[1] https://cefat4cities.eu/

[2] https://www.fiware.org/developers/catalogue/

[3] https://ec.europa.eu/isa2/solutions/core-public-service-vocabulary-application-profile-cpsv-ap_en

Macken, Rufener, Van den Bogaert, Daems, Tezcan, Vanroy, Fonteyne, Barrault, Costa-jussà, Kemp, Pilos, Declercq, Koponen, Forcada, Scarton, Moniz (eds.)
Proceedings of the 23rd Annual Conference of the European Association for Machine Translation, p. 341–342
Ghent, Belgium, June 2022.

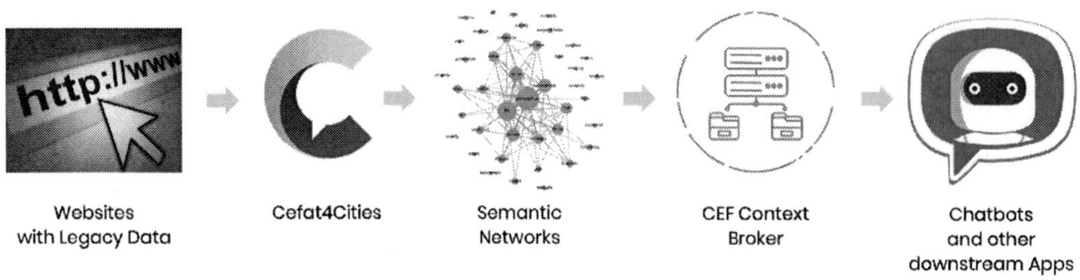

dures are extracted and syntactically analysed to identify nodes occurring in the template. Finally, relations between the extracted nodes are identified (the most challenging part of the process) and the information is delivered in a standardised linked open data (LOD) format compatible with the FIWARE Context Broker. Any follow-up effort or downstream software application can use this schema to subscribe to the created public-service content.

To achieve this, we resort to various multilingual Natural Language Processing (NLP) techniques such as automated classification, topic modelling, clustering, syntactic parsing and machine translation. When developing the solution, several challenging issues were identified. Discovering links between nodes (connecting for example an administrative procedure and all the evidence a citizen must provide to fulfil it) proved to be a non-trivial task. A unique solution had to be built, combining syntactic parsing and classification, since no out-of-the-box components existed to do this. Throughout the pipeline, a balance was needed between using monolingual and multilingual NLP models using translated data, since many linguistic NLP models only exist for a couple of languages. Finally, often the language itself was problematic. Current NLP models excel at "recognising" the meaning of a word when it appears within a larger body of text, but when words occur isolated (for example in a title or a table) recognition and translation become more difficult.

3 Outcome

The CEFAT4Cities project is currently coming to the end, but it has already impacted the way people think about public-service data in two major European Cities: The Brussels and Vienna Business agencies have successfully built a demonstrator chatbot with LOD generated by the CEFAT4Cities pipeline, and they realise that the data can be shared and used for other purposes.

Admittedly, the generated data still needs human validation, but considering the rate at which the CEFAT4Cities system outputs data and takes over the heavy lifting from humans (manually researching the business domain, clustering topics, creating the mental model, extracting intents, compiling and annotating the data sets, translating, etc.), there is plenty of time saved that can be used for fine-tuning the produced data sets.

The system currently exists as a prototype for the semantic modelling of public services in Croatian, Dutch, English, French, German, Italian, and Norwegian, with both the number of domains and languages expected to increase in the future.

From the onset of the project, the aim was to help smaller cities, as they have less means to build their own semantic network of public services, let alone to do this in a multilingual way. The extracted semantic network is abstract enough to allow for "knowledge transfer" between cities to build analogous systems. Looking at the first results, it is believed this ambition can be achieved, provided that a sufficient amount of evangelisation is carried out. Achieving this goal would greatly benefit smaller cities, as it will allow them to implement multilingual e-government solutions at a much faster pace and contribute to the free movement of EU citizens in general.

Acknowledgement

This project paper is an adapted and shortened version of a previously published blog post for the FIWARE Foundation (`https://www.fiware.org/2021/12/16/innovative-mind-mapping-system-connecting-to-smart-city-iot-networks/`). We would like to thank the EC's CEF Telecom programme for funding the CEFAT4Cities project (2019-EU-IA-0015) and the FIWARE Foundation for helping us in spreading the word.

National Language Technology Platform (NLTP): Overall View

Artūrs Vasiļevskis
Tilde,
Riga, Latvia
arturs.vasilevskis@tilde.com

Jānis Ziediņš
Culture Information Systems Centre,
Riga, Latvia
janis.ziedins@kis.gov.lv

Marko Tadić
University of Zagreb, Faculty of Humanities and Social Sciences, Zagreb, Croatia
marko.tadic@ffzg.hr

Željka Motika
Central State Office for the Development of Digital Society, Zagreb, Croatia
Zeljka.Motika@rdd.hr

Mark Fishel
University of Tartu,
Tartu, Estonia
fishel@ut.ee

Hrafn Loftsson, Jón Guðnason
Reykjavik University, School of Technology,
Reykjavik, Iceland
{hrafn, jg}@ru.is

Claudia Borg
University of Malta,
Valletta, Malta
claudia.borg@um.edu.mt

Keith Cortis, Judie Attard
Malta Information Technology Agency,
Blata l-Bajda, Malta
{keith.cortis, judie.attard}@gov.mt

Donatienne Spiteri
Office of the State Advocate,
Valletta, Malta
donatienne.spiteri@stateadvocate.mt

Abstract

The work in progress on the CEF action National Language Technology Platform is presented. The action aims at combining the most advanced language technology tools and solutions in a new state-of-the-art, artificial-intelligence-driven, national platform for language technology oriented primarily towards users from public administrations of partner states.

1 Introduction

The paper presents the work in progress on the CEF action National Language Technology Platform (NLTP, INEA/CEF/ICT/A2020/2278398, duration 2021-04-01–2023-03-31). The general aim of the action is to combine the most advanced Language Technology (LT) tools and solutions in a new state-of-the-art, artificial-intelligence-driven, web-based national platform for LT. Currently, the action is approaching the implementation phase of the prototype systems. The system architecture plan has been created and will be followed by multiple implementations. In parallel, data collection and preparations for machine translation (MT) system training is gradually approaching its late stage. The details are described in section 2.

2 Development

2.1 Related work

The developed solution builds on the already existing hugo.lv platform and the results of the *EU Council Presidency Translator* (INEA/CEF/ ICT/A2018/1762093) action, but it will be substantially extended into NLTP in order to provide public administrations and the general public with secure access to high quality MT and integration with computer aided translation (CAT) tools, e-mail and web plug-ins etc., for translation of texts and documents. This set of services is considered as initial, but the modular design of the platform allows it to be enriched with additional LT services beyond the initial set.

2.2 Users

In its final form NLTP will be adapted, localised, and sustainably deployed by the public administration bodies in partner states (Latvia, Croatia, Estonia, Iceland, and Malta), while its development is supported at the same time by local research institutions as complementary partners. In the case of Iceland and Estonia, the research partners were given the role of public authorities as well. Additionally, the NLTP will be customisable to the specific needs of public administrations and will be further linked to eTranslation[*] services, thus enabling translations into and from the 24 official EU languages and other languages of the Digital Single Market.

The NLTP will facilitate the use of a professional translation environment with integrated terminology databases, CAT and MT tools, all wrapped up in a simple-to-use HTML front end and coupled with a number of other technological solutions, such as a translation widget, browser plugin, commercial CAT tool plugins, etc.

2.3 Deployment

The NLTP will increase the efficiency of translation, the reuse of translation memories and make use of the existing high-quality MT technologies. Additionally, the action will also integrate speech technologies for selected languages with automatic speech recognition and/or text-to-speech services.

The platform will be developed according to this common overall concept, but for each partner state a deployable version will be adapted to the needs of public administrations at each level (local, regional, national). After the needs were modelled by overall general needs, the specific requirements have been collected through a survey about LT needs and expectations, that has been run in all partner states. The analysis of the survey in Croatia is presented in Motika et al. (2022), while the preliminary results for other languages will be available for the EAMT2022 conference poster.

2.4 Additional datasets

Additionally, a number of domain specific parallel data is being collected and will be made available through the ELRC-SHARE[†] repository in the Translation Memory eXchange (TMX) or similar compatible format. Since the sources of data are predominantly expected to come from the public domain, the data will be made accessible under permissive licences.

3 Sustainability and Future Directions

The public administration partner institutions will be responsible for the sustainability of each national NLTP after the action ends by securing its inclusion into the national infrastructures for eGovernment as cloud services. This will enable multilingual access to and by public administrations, while, at the same time, the integration with public digital services offered in languages of EU and EEA will be fostered.

For future research and development directions, similar platforms could be developed and deployed for other EU member states, and in this respect this action can be regarded as the proof-of-concept.

Acknowledgements

The work reported here was supported by the European Commission in the CEF Telecom Programme (Action No: 2020-EU-IA-0082, Grant Agreement No: INEA/CEF/ICT/A2020/2278398).

References

Motika, Željka; Didak Prekpalaj, Tanja; Horvat Klemen, Tamara; Košćec Perić, Mirjana. in press. Predstavljanje projekta "Nacionalna platforma za jezične tehnologije" In: *Proceedings of the μPro2022 Conference*, Opatija, May 2022.

[*] https://ec.europa.eu/digital-building-blocks/wikis/display/CEFDIGITAL/eTranslation

[†] https://elrc-share.eu

Multi3Generation: Multitask, Multilingual, Multimodal Language Generation

Anabela Barreiro[1] **José GC de Souza**[2] **Albert Gatt**[3,4] **Mehul Bhatt**[5] **Elena Lloret**[6] **Aykut Erdem**[7] **Dimitra Gkatzia**[8] **Helena Moniz**[9,1] **Irene Russo**[10] **Fabio Kepler**[2] **Iacer Calixto**[11] **Marcin Paprzycki**[12] **François Portet**[13] **Isabelle Augenstein**[14] **Mirela Alhasani**[15]

[1]INESC-ID, Portugal [2]Unbabel, Portugal [3]University of Malta, Malta
[4]Utrecht University, The Netherlands [5]Örebro University, Sweden
[6]University of Alicante, Spain [7]Koç University, Turkey
[8]Edinburgh Napier University, United Kingdom [9]University of Lisbon, Portugal
[10]National Research Council, Italy [11]Amsterdam University Medical Centers, The Netherlands
[12]Polish Academy of Sciences, Poland [13]Grenoble Alpes University, France
[14]University of Copenhagen, Denmark [15]Epoka University, Albania
anabela.barreiro@inesc-id.pt

Abstract

This paper presents the Multitask, Multilingual, Multimodal Language Generation COST Action – Multi3Generation (CA18231), an interdisciplinary network of research groups working on different aspects of language generation. This "meta-paper" will serve as reference for citations of the Action in future publications. It presents the objectives, challenges and a the links for the achieved outcomes.

1 Introduction

Multi3Generation[1] fosters the development of a network of researchers and technologists across interdisciplinary fields working on topics related to language generation (LG). We frame LG broadly as the set of tasks where the ultimate goal involves generating language. In contrast to the more classical definition of natural language generation (NLG), this also includes tasks not concerned with LG in an immediate sense, but that can inform or improve LG models. The action focuses on four core challenges: (a) data and information representation challenges, such as those involving inputs of different sources: images, videos, knowledge bases (KBs) and graphs; (b) machine learning (ML) challenges of modern approaches, such as mapping of inputs to different correct outputs, e.g. structured prediction and representation learning; (c) interaction in applications of LG, such as dialogue systems, conversational search interfaces and human-robot interaction due to the uncertainty derived from the changing environment and the non-deterministic fashion of interaction; (d) KB exploitation: structured knowledge is key to natural language processing (NLP) tasks, including NLG, supporting ML methods that require expansion, filtering, disambiguation or user adaptation of generated content. The Action addresses these challenges by answering the following questions:

1. How can we efficiently exploit commonsense, world knowledge and multimodal information from various inputs such as KBs, images and videos to address LG tasks such as multimodal machine translation (MT), video description and summarisation?
2. How can ML methods such as multi–task learning (MTL), representation learning and structured prediction be leveraged for LG?
3. How can the models from (1) and (2) be exploited to develop dialogue-based, conversational human-computer and human-robot interaction methods?

2 Objectives

Multi3Generation created an interdisciplinary European LG research network targeting scientific advances and societal benefits in the following four focus themes: (T1) grounded multimodal reasoning and generation; (T2) efficient ML algorithms, methods, and applications to LG; (T3) dialogue, interaction and conversational LG applications; and (T4) exploiting large KBs and graphs. The following are the **research coordination** objectives:

[1]https://www.cost.eu/actions/CA18231/. The Action is funded by the European Commission and is running from June 2019 till September 2023.

Macken, Rufener, Van den Bogaert, Daems, Tezcan, Vanroy, Fonteyne, Barrault, Costa-jussà, Kemp, Pilos, Declercq, Koponen, Forcada, Scarton, Moniz (eds.)
Proceedings of the 23rd Annual Conference of the European Association for Machine Translation, p. 345–346
Ghent, Belgium, June 2022.

- Foster knowledge exchange by sharing of resources including semantic annotation guidelines, benchmarking corpora, ML and alignment tools.
- Create multimodal and multilingual benchmarks for NLG involves experimenting with automatic mapping between existing resources, crawling of web data, definition of annotation guidelines and launching of crowdsourcing campaigns for bigger datasets, also as games-with-a-purpose).
- Facilitate interactions, collaborations, knowledge building and dissemination between the Action's participants via online tools, as website, blogs, downloadable publications.
- Promote the generation of novel ideas and introduce the new joint Multi3Generation discipline to other researchers.
- Provide opportunities for joint research projects by the Action's members on multitask, multilingual and multimodal processing during exchange visits of Early Career Investigators (ECIs), and other activities that encourage young researchers to establish links with industry and senior academics.
- Disseminate the results of the Action through conferences, scientific and industrial gatherings, which will have substantial impact in the participating countries and beyond.
- Create synergies between participants via joint publications in books, journals and conferences; reports from working group meetings and training materials from training schools.

The overall expected impact of the Action is to bring about a significant change in progress towards effective solutions for computational challenges involving LG with respect to multitask, multilingual and multimodal aspects. In particular, Multi3Generation is focusing on the integration of these three aspects and how they can benefit LG solutions. The Action's specific objectives for **capacity building** are:

- Strengthen European research on theory, methodology and real-world technology in LG, particularly in the four Multi3Generation focus research themes (T1–T4);
- Facilitate collaboration, networking and interdisciplinary community building by yearly conferences and workshops and biannual international training schools;
- Drive scientific progress by liaising extensively with industry and end-users, and by increasing joint collaboration and knowledge transfer by the end of the Action;
- To coordinate the development of benchmark data resources for tasks relating to the focus themes above and to organise corresponding shared-task competitions.

In order to accomplish the objectives of the Action, its members are encouraged to produce novel outcomes and establish critical mass, as well as to engage in joint applications for European and national funding for research projects within the fields covered by the Action.

3 Outcomes

Since its inception, the action fostered collaborations that has produced more than 24 publications[2], ranging from surveys to approaches to specific LG problems. Among the collaborations are the short term missions (STMs), visits among researchers that take part in the Action[3]. Furthermore, a series of datasets[4] have been developed and made available for diverse number of LG-related problems. Another important outcome of the Action is the organization of training schools in 2022, one on the topic of "representation mediated multimodality"[5] and another one on the topic of "automatically creating text from data"[6].

4 Acknowledgements

This publication is based upon work from COST Action Multi3Generation - Multitask, Multilingual, Multimodal Language Generation (CA18231), supported by COST (European Cooperation in Science and Technology).

[2] `https://multi3generation.eu/outcomes/publications/`

[3] `https://multi3generation.eu/funding-opportunities/short-term-scientific-missions/`

[4] `https://multi3generation.eu/outcomes/data/`

[5] `https://codesign-lab.org/school2022/index.html`

[6] `https://multi3generation.eu/category/events/training-schools/`

Achievements of the PRINCIPLE Project: Promoting MT for Croatian, Icelandic, Irish and Norwegian

Petra Bago,[1] Sheila Castilho,[2] Jane Dunne,[2] Federico Gaspari,[2] Andre Kåsen,[3] Gauti Kristmannsson,[4] Jon Arild Olsen,[3] Natalia Resende,[2] Níels Rúnar Gíslason,[4] Dana D. Sheridan,[5] Páraic Sheridan,[5] John Tinsley,[5] Andy Way[2]

[1] Faculty of Humanities and Social Sciences, University of Zagreb, 10000 Zagreb, Croatia
[2] ADAPT Centre, School of Computing, Dublin City University, Dublin 9, Ireland
[3] National Library of Norway, Henrik Ibsens gate 110, 0203 Oslo, Norway
[4] University of Iceland, Saemundargata 2, 102 Reykjavik, Iceland
[5] Iconic Translation Machines, Invent Building, Dublin City University, Dublin 9, Ireland

Abstract

This paper provides an overview of the main achievements of the completed PRINCIPLE project, a 2-year action funded by the European Commission under the Connecting Europe Facility programme. PRINCIPLE focused on collecting high-quality language resources for Croatian, Icelandic, Irish and Norwegian, which are severely low-resource languages, especially for building effective machine translation (MT) systems. We report the achievements of the project, primarily in terms of the large amounts of data collected for all four low-resource languages, and of promoting the uptake of neural MT for these languages.

1. Background

PRINCIPLE was a 2-year EU-funded project that ran between 2019 and 2021 to identify, collect and curate high-quality language resources (LRs) for the under-resourced languages of Croatian, Irish, Norwegian and Icelandic. The action was coordinated by the ADAPT Centre at Dublin City University (DCU), and involved the University of Iceland, the Faculty of Humanities and Social Sciences of the University of Zagreb, the National Library of Norway, and Machine Translation (MT) provider Iconic Translation Machines Ltd (now Language Weaver). The focus of the project was on providing data to improve the two Digital Service Infrastructures (DSIs) of eJustice and eProcurement, due to their strategic importance across the EU, in individual European Member States and in the associated countries of Iceland and Norway.

Way and Gaspari (2019) introduced the PRINCIPLE project at its start, giving a high-level overview of its main objectives, along with the planned activities and the overall approach to data collection and validation. They also explained its position within the wider eco-system of related, recently finished Connecting Europe Facility (CEF) projects such as iADAATPA (Castilho et al., 2019), ELRI[2] and Paracrawl.[3] This paper summarises the results from PRINCIPLE, focusing on its achievements, especially in terms of engagement with stakeholders and MT users, which promoted the continued collection of LRs with a view to improving and extending MT use.

2. Achievements

State-of-the-art domain-adapted neural MT (NMT) engines were built by the project partner Iconic for a number of early adopters (EAs) in all four countries. These public sector EAs included the Ministry of Foreign and European Affairs of the Republic of Croatia, the Icelandic Meteorological Office, the Icelandic Standards organisation, the Ministry of Foreign Affairs of Iceland, the Department of Justice in Ireland, Foras na Gaeilge, Rannóg an Aistriúcháin, the National University of Ireland, Galway, the Ministry of Foreign Affairs Norway, and Standards Norway. A small number of private companies also served as EAs on the project.

[2] https://www.elri-project.eu/
[3] http://paracrawl.eu/

Macken, Rufener, Van den Bogaert, Daems, Tezcan, Vanroy, Fonteyne, Barrault, Costa-jussà, Kemp, Pilos, Declercq, Koponen, Forcada, Scarton, Moniz (eds.)
Proceedings of the 23rd Annual Conference of the European Association for Machine Translation, p. 347–348
Ghent, Belgium, June 2022.

These organizations collaborated with the project by sharing their LRs, and in return for contributing digital data sets to the project, they were offered dedicated state-of-the-art NMT systems. The development and subsequent evaluation of these MT systems according to the specific use-cases selected by the EAs served the purpose of validating the quality and demonstrating the actual value of the LRs collected by the project. Once the quality and effectiveness of the LRs had been verified, the data sets were shared with the wider community (subject to applicable licensing restrictions stipulated by the data providers) via ELRC-SHARE[4] and used to improve eTranslation.[5]

PRINCIPLE collected, validated and shared more than 50 data sets for the languages of the project. Most of these LRs are bilingual parallel corpora, but there are also a few monolingual and multilingual corpora, as well as glossaries. The project partners consistently ensured proper handling of copyright clearance and of issues related to intellectual property for LRs with all the relevant data providers. The majority of the LRs were contributed under the "CC-BY-4.0" licence, others under the "Open Under-Public Sector Information" and "Non-standard/Other Licence/Terms" licences, while a few remaining LRs were contributed under other miscellaneous licences. Some LRs contained proprietary and/or sensitive information and were therefore contributed exclusively to the Directorate General for Translation (DGT) of the European Commission to develop eTranslation, but they could not be shared with the general public. The majority of LRs are in plain text and TMX format, while some are in text with tab-separated values and text in comma-separated values, which ensures wider reusability and interoperability to benefit the largest possible number of users and applications.

In keeping with the aim of demonstrating the value of LRs being collected in the PRINCIPLE project for building MT systems, and demonstrating the benefits of MT especially to public sector users, an extensive MT evaluation was undertaken. This included an automatic evaluation using a range of metrics on both baseline and domain-specific systems and compared to a range of publicly available engines, as well as extensive evaluations conducted directly by public sector users. User evaluations included adequacy and fluency assessments, post-editing productivity, error analysis, and comparative systems rankings, all conducted by public sector translators independently of the project partners.

3. Conclusion

PRINCIPLE achieved its ambitious objectives, and the consortium partners worked successfully to collaborate with a range of existing and new data contributors in Croatia, Iceland, Ireland and Norway, so that valuable domain-specific LRs could be made available to the wider community. Our presentation at EAMT 2022 will give an overview of the main achievements of the PRINCIPLE project, with a focus on the set of public and private data holders and their use cases. In this context, we will discuss the range of LRs that have been gathered, and present an overview of the evaluation processes that were undertaken for the customised neural MT engines, with EAs in the four countries involved.

Acknowledgements: PRINCIPLE was co-financed by the European Union Connecting Europe Facility under Action 2018-EU-IA-0050 with grant agreement INEA/CEF/ICT/A2018/1761837.

References

Castilho, Sheila, Natalia Resende, Federico Gaspari, Andy Way, Tony O'Dowd, Marek Mazur, Manuel Herranz, Alex Helle, Gema Ramírez-Sánchez, Victor Sánchez-Cartagena, Mārcis Pinnis, and Valters Sics. 2019. Large-scale Machine Translation Evaluation of the iADAATPA Project. *Proceedings of Machine Translation Summit XVII, Volume 2*, Dublin, Ireland 179-185.

Way, Andy and Federico Gaspari. 2019. PRINCIPLE: Providing Resources in Irish, Norwegian, Croatian and Icelandic for the Purposes of Language Engineering. *Proceedings of Machine Translation Summit XVII, Volume 2*, Dublin, Ireland 112-113.

[4] https://elrc-share.eu

[5] https://ec.europa.eu/info/resources-partners/machine-translation-public-administrations-etranslation_en

Automatic Video Dubbing at AppTek

Mattia Di Gangi, Nick Rossenbach, Alejandro Pérez, Parnia Bahar
Eugen Beck, Patrick Wilken, Evgeny Matusov
AppTek GmbH
Aachen, Germany
mdigangi@apptek.com

Abstract

Automatic Video Dubbing is the process of automatically revoicing a video with a new script to make it accessible to a new audience. In this paper, we describe AppTek Dubbing, a product that will be available in Q3 2022 to automatically dub a video into a target language. We plan multiple releases of the product with incremental features, as well as the possibility to allow human intervention for increased quality.

1 Introduction

Video dubbing is the activity of revoicing a video while offering a viewing experience equivalent to the original video. The revoicing usually comes with a new script, and it should reproduce the original emotions, coherent with the body language, and be lip synchronized. Öktem et al. (2019) and Federico et al. (2020) introduced two automatic dubbing systems as a cascade of automatic speech recognition (ASR), machine translation (MT) and Text-to-Speech (TTS), enhanced with a prosodic alignment (PA) component to transfer prosody through the pipeline. In this project, we aim to build an AD system in two phases: (1) voice-over; (2) full dubbing, and enhance it with human-in-the-loop capabilities for a higher quality. The product will be released in the form of REST APIs and a web interface in Q3 of the current year. The pricing will follow a pay-per-use scheme, with possible variations according to requested quality control or if the script to dub is provided by the user for higher quality dubbing.

2 Current Features

Our current system is designed as an enhanced pipeline of ASR, MT and TTS. Our ASR system includes speaker diarization (the task of detecting "who speaks when") so that consecutive segments from the same speaker can be translated as coherent units, and each speaker is assigned a unique voice. Our MT system is a Transformer-based encoder-decoder, augmented with metadata features for style adaptation (Matusov et al., 2020) and output length control (Lakew et al., 2019). The translations are performed from and to subtitle files to preserve the timestamps and use them as boundaries for the synthesized voices. Additionally, we use speaker-adaptive TTS to reproduce the voice features of the original actor for the given segment in the new language. Finally, the background sound, obtained via source separation, is merged with the synthesized voices for the final audio and video rendering. This system can already translate video contents and dub the output videos in a voice-over style.

3 Voice-over

Voice-over is a simpler solution than dubbing, where the original voice's volume is lowered down, and the new voice is rendered with a natural volume over it, usually with a delay of some frames. Our system is already capable of performing voice-over for some language pairs[1] but some aspects can be improved:

Diarization: speaker diarization can be improved in the cases when the audio quality is low, or one speaker speaks for less than one second.

[1] see demo at https://www.apptek.com/post/automatic-dubbing-for-user-generated-content

Macken, Rufener, Van den Bogaert, Daems, Tezcan, Vanroy, Fonteyne, Barrault, Costa-jussà, Kemp, Pilos, Declercq, Koponen, Forcada, Scarton, Moniz (eds.)
Proceedings of the 23rd Annual Conference of the European Association for Machine Translation, p. 349–350
Ghent, Belgium, June 2022.

Prosody Alignment: we plan to add prosody alignment for transferring the pauses from the source to the target speech, but also the emphasis applied to sentences and single words.

MT Output Length: although in voice-over we have time constraints less strict than in dubbing, some translations do not fit the allocated space, and it is important to have a fine-grained control over the MT output length.

4 Emotional Voice-over

The main limitation of the current system is the synthesized voice speaking with a "flat" tone, which does not match the emotions expressed in the original video. Our research effort for achieving emotional speech is aimed to release the feature in 2023 and will affect the whole pipeline:

Emotion Detection: emotions need to be detected from the source audio and matched with the recognized text, in order to annotate the latter with emotions tags.

Emotion-aware MT: Expand AppTek's MT systems to support emotions as part of their metadata. Additional research effort will focus on letting the MT system annotate the output text with emotions at a word level, to be used from our TTS system.

Emotion-aware TTS: develop TTS systems that can generate emotional speech for different emotions. Such a task can be challenging given the low data availability, particularly for languages other than English.

5 Full Dubbing

A fully-fledged AD system improves the voice-over approach by fully synchronizing audio and video time. Lip-syncing is a strict requirement that can be achieved using orthogonal technologies:

Isometric translations: improve the methods to generate translations under length constraints.

Lips motion: modify the lips' movement in the video to match the synthesized speech, building over the work described in (Furukawa et al., 2016).

6 Language Support

Our initial release will include English-to-Arabic and English-to-Spanish. In the following two years we plan to expand it to English to many European languages, including French, German, Italian, Polish and Ukrainian, plus Russian and Chinese. The reverse directions will also be rolled out soon after.

7 Human in the Loop

An AD system can make errors in multiple points of its pipeline, and the earlier the errors occur, the more harmful they can be for the final result. For this reason, we plan to let users adding manual transcripts or the final scripts to obtain a higher-quality video at the cost of more manual work, using our internal tool for easy editing parallel data.

8 Conclusion

AppTek Dubbing is an ambitious pioneering project that combines MT with other technologies to provide a high-quality and localized translated video, with the goal of making dubbing accessible beyond the movie industry. Intermediate product releases will support simpler re-voicing modes and a human-in-the-loop approach to allow the users to trade-off costs with quality.

References

Federico, M., R. Enyedi, R. Barra-Chicote, R. Giri, U. Isik, A. Krishnaswamy and H. Sawaf. 2020. From Speech-to-Speech Translation to Automatic Dubbing. *Proceedings of the 17th International Conference on Spoken Language Translation*, pp. 257–264.

Furukawa, S., T. Kato, P. Savkin and S. Morishima. 2016 Video Reshuffling: Automatic Video Dubbing without Prior Knowledge. *ACM SIGGRAPH 2016 Posters* pp. 1–2.

Lakew, S. M., M. A. Di Gangi, and M. Federico. 2019. Controlling the Output Length of Neural Machine Translation. *16th International Workshop on Spoken Language Translation.*

Matoušek, J. and J. Vít. 2012. Improving Automatic Dubbing with Subtitle Timing Optimisation Using Video Cut Detection. *2012 IEEE International Conference on Acoustics, Speech and Signal Processing (ICASSP)*, pp. 2385–2388.

Matusov, E., P. Wilken, and C. Herold. 2020. Flexible Customization of a Single Neural Machine Translation System with Multi-dimensional Metadata Inputs. *Proceedings of the 14th Conference of the Association for Machine Translation in the Americas (Volume 2: User Track)*, pp. 204–216

Öktem, A., M. Farrús, and A. Bonafonte. 2019. Prosodic Phrase Alignment for Machine Dubbing. *Proceedings of Interspeech 2019*, pp. 4215–4219.

Overview of the ELE Project

Itziar Aldabe,[4] Jane Dunne,[1] Aritz Farwell,[4] Owen Gallagher,[1] Federico Gaspari,[1] Maria Giagkou,[5] Jan Hajic,[3] Jens Peter Kückens,[2] Teresa Lynn,[1] Georg Rehm,[2] German Rigau,[4] Katrin Marheinecke,[2] Stelios Piperidis,[5] Natalia Resende,[1] Tea Vojtěchová,[3] Andy Way[1]

[1] ADAPT Centre, School of Computing, Dublin City University, Dublin 9, Ireland

[2] Deutsches Forschungszentrum für Künstliche Intelligenz (DFKI) GmbH, Alt-Moabit 91c, 10559 Berlin, Germany

[3] Charles University (CUNI), Ovocný trh 5, Prague 1, 116 36, Czech Republic

[4] Universidad Del Pais Vasco/ Euskal Herriko Unibertsitatea (University of the Basque Country) UPV/EHU, Barrio Sarriena s/n, 48940 Leioa, Bizkaia

[5] Athina-Erevnitiko Kentro Kainotomias Stis Technologies Tis Pliroforias, Ton Epikoinonion Kai Tis Gnosis (ILSP), Artemidos 6 & Epidavrou, GR-151 25 Maroussi, Athens, Greece

Abstract

This paper presents the ongoing European Language Equality (ELE) project, an 18-month action funded by the European Commission. The primary goal of the ELE project is to prepare the ELE programme, in the form of a strategic research, innovation and implementation agenda and roadmap for achieving full digital language equality in Europe by 2030.

1. Background

Twenty-four official languages and more than 60 regional and minority languages constitute the fabric of the EU's linguistic landscape. However, language barriers still hamper communication and the free flow of information across the EU. Multilingualism is a key cultural cornerstone of Europe and signifies what it means to be and to feel European. The landmark 2018 European Parliament resolution "Language equality in the digital age" found a striking imbalance in terms of support through language technologies (LTs) so issued a call to action. Starting in January 2021, ELE answered this call and is laying the foundations for a strategic research, innovation and implementation agenda (SRIA) and roadmap to make full digital language equality (DLE) a reality in Europe by 2030.

Developing an SRIA and roadmap for achieving full DLE in Europe by 2030 involves many stakeholders with different perspectives. Accordingly, the ELE project – led by DCU, and with DFKI, Charles University, ILSP and EHU/UPV as core members – has put together a large consortium of all 52 partners, who together with the wider European LT community, are preparing the different parts of the SRIA and roadmap, for all European languages: official, regional and minority languages.

2. Achievements & Ongoing Activities

Ensuring appropriate technology support for all European languages will create jobs, growth and opportunities in the digital single market. Equally crucial, overcoming language barriers in the digital environment is essential for an inclusive society and for providing unity in diversity for many years to come.

To date, we have concentrated on two distinct aspects: (i) collecting the current state of play (2021/2022) of LT support for the more than 70 languages under investigation, largely by the 32 National Competence Centres in our sister project European Language Grid (ELG);[2] and (ii) strategic and technological forecasting, i.e. estimating and envisioning the future situation in 2030 and beyond. Furthermore, we distinguish between two main stakeholder groups: LT developers (industry and research) and LT users as well as consumers. Both groups are represented in ELE by several networks (e.g. EFNIL, ELEN,

[2] https://www.european-language-grid.eu/

Macken, Rufener, Van den Bogaert, Daems, Tezcan, Vanroy, Fonteyne, Barrault, Costa-jussà, Kemp, Pilos, Declercq, Koponen, Forcada, Scarton, Moniz (eds.)
Proceedings of the 23rd Annual Conference of the European Association for Machine Translation, p. 351–352
Ghent, Belgium, June 2022.

ECSPM) and associations (e.g. ELDA, LIBER) who each produce a report highlighting their own individual requirements towards DLE. The project's industry partners produce four "deep dives" with the needs, wishes and visions of the European LT industry regarding machine translation, speech technology, text analytics as well as data, all available on the project website. We have also organised a larger number of surveys and consultations with stakeholders who are not represented in the consortium.

We have formulated a preliminary working definition of DLE to drive our activities, namely: "*Digital Language Equality is the state of affairs in which all languages have the technological support and situational context necessary for them to continue to exist and to prosper as living languages in the digital age.*"

This DLE definition allows us to compute an easy-to-interpret metric (a "DLE score") for individual languages, which enables the quantification of the level of technological support for a language and, crucially, the identification of gaps and shortcomings that hamper the achievement of full DLE. This approach enables direct comparisons across languages, tracking their advancement towards the goal of DLE, and facilitates the prioritization of needs, especially to fill existing gaps. The metric is computed for each language on the basis of various factors, grouped into technological factors (technological support, e.g. available language resources, tools and technologies) and contextual factors (e.g. societal, economic, educational, industrial).

Our systematic collection of language resources, i.e. data (corpora, lexical resources, models) and LT tools/services for Europe's languages has resulted in more than 6,000 metadata records, which will be imported into the ELG catalogue and complement the existing, constantly growing inventory of ELG resources, thus providing information on the availability of more than 11,000 language resources and tools. All languages investigated by ELE are covered.

Using this collection as a firm empirical foundation for further investigation, we computed a DLE score for each language. We will present these results in full at the conference, but unsurprisingly, English was clearly shown as having the best context for the development of LTs and language resources. English is followed by German and French, and then by Italian and Spanish. After these five leading languages, variations between the configurations begin to be seen. Mostly, Swedish, Dutch, Danish, Polish, Croatian, Hungarian, Greek and Finnish are ranked in the upper half of the official EU languages. The official EU languages with the lowest scores are mostly Latvian, Lithuanian, Bulgarian, Romanian and Maltese.

Among the group of official national languages which are not recognised as official EU languages, Serbian is always the top performer, achieving a similar score to those of the lower-scoring official EU languages, while Manx is always presented as a downward outlier. Norwegian, Luxembourgish, Faroese and Icelandic achieve better scores than Albania, Turkish, Macedonian and Bosnian. The regional and minority languages are usually led by Saami South and Skolt.

These and other perhaps unexpected results will be explained at the conference. The results from our various surveys will also be shown, including the novel survey which targeted European citizens *per se*, where we look like surpassing 25,000 respondents from all over the continent.

3. Future Plans

ELE is on track to achieve its ambitious objectives with the consortium currently working on the SRIA which will be ready at the end of the project in June. The DLE metric has proven to be an extremely useful tool to demonstrate how prepared European languages are for the digital age, and what needs to be done to get them to the point where all such languages are digitally equal by 2030. As an extension of this work, we will soon publish our interactive DLE dashboard that makes use of the metadata records available in the ELG platform.

Acknowledgements

ELE is co-financed by the European Union under the grant agreement № LC-01641480 – 101018166 (ELE).

Reference

Georg Rehm, Federico Gaspari, German Rigau, Maria Giagkou, Stelios Piperidis, Natalia Resende, Jan Hajic, Andy Way. 2022. The European Language Equality Project: Enabling Digital Language Equality for all European Languages by 2030. *EFNIL Annual Publication Series*, Cavtat, Croatia (in press).

LITHME: Language in the Human–Machine Era

Maarit Koponen
University of Eastern Finland
maarit.koponen@uef.fi

Kais Allkivi-Metsoja
Tallinn University
kais@tlu.ee

Antonio Pareja-Lora
Universidad de Alcalá
antonio.parejal@uah.es

Dave Sayers
University of Jyväskylä
dave.sayers@cantab.net

Márta Seresi
Eötvös Loránd University
seresi.marta@btk.elte.hu

Abstract

The LITHME COST Action brings together researchers from various fields of study focusing on linguistics and technology. We present the overall goals of LITHME and the network's working groups focusing on diverse questions related to language and technology. As an example of the work addressing machine translation within LITHME, we discuss the activities of the working group on language work and language professionals.

1 Introduction

Language in the Human–Machine Era (LITHME) is a research and innovation network funded by COST (European Cooperation in Science and Technology). It is coordinated by the University of Jyväskylä, Finland, and has more than 300 members from universities, research institutions and companies in 52 countries (all 27 EU states and 25 other countries worldwide).

The network brings together researchers, developers and other specialists with diverse backgrounds with the goal of sharing insights about how new and emerging technologies will impact interaction and language use. By "human–machine era", we envision a time when humans will be interacting and conversing with artificial intelligence (AI) technology that is not confined only to mobile devices but integrated with our senses through virtual and augmented reality. Machine translation (MT) is one of the key technologies enabling communication across languages.

LITHME focuses on two aspects which are shaping human communication (Sayers et al., 2021). On the one hand, we will increasingly be speaking *through* technology, which can translate between languages in real time as well as alter voices and facial movements. On the other hand, we will also be speaking *to* technology, which will understand both the content and the context of natural language. This will lead to increasingly substantive and meaningful real-time conversations with devices like smart assistants. Enhanced virtual reality featuring lifelike characters will enable learning and even socialising among intelligent and responsive artificial partners.

Throughout its four-year duration (2020–2024), the LITHME network of researchers aims to explore the impact that various technologies, including MT, have on language and communication. We investigate the opportunities, the new ways to talk, to translate, to remember, and to learn, but also the uncertainties and potential inequalities or other adverse effects.

Deliverables consist of open-access forecast reports, the first of which was published in 2021 (Sayers et al., 2021), multimedia presentations, guidelines on ethics, safety, equality and accessibility for emerging language technologies, and interim reports of activities on the LITHME website.[1] LITHME organises an annual conference and a training school focusing on language and technology, workshops, short-term scientific missions[2] and invited talks. In addition to collaboration between researchers, LITHME aims to facilitate the involvement of stakeholders outside of academia, such as corporate and non-profit technology developers.

[1] https://lithme.eu/
[2] https://lithme.eu/short-term-scientific-missions/

Macken, Rufener, Van den Bogaert, Daems, Tezcan, Vanroy, Fonteyne, Barrault, Costa-jussà, Kemp, Pilos, Declercq, Koponen, Forcada, Scarton, Moniz (eds.)
Proceedings of the 23rd Annual Conference of the European Association for Machine Translation, p. 353–354
Ghent, Belgium, June 2022.

2 LITHME Working Groups

LITHME features eight working groups[3] (WGs) which focus on different areas of research related to language and technology.

- **WG1** Computational linguistics
- **WG2** Language and law
- **WG3** Language rights
- **WG4** Language diversity, vitality and endangerment
- **WG5** Language learning and teaching
- **WG6** Ideologies, beliefs, attitudes
- **WG7** Language work, language professionals
- **WG8** Language variation

At the centre of LITHME, WG1 aims to produce forecasts of various relevant technologies, and other WGs focus on how these technologies are incluencing specific areas of language use. The development of MT is of course one of the issues closely followed in WG1, and MT can be seen to play a role in all of these areas covered by the working groups. The focus on MT, specifically, is perhaps clearest in WG7, as the work of language professionals such as translators is one area where the impacts of MT have been most pronounced. We next discuss the aims of this working group in more detail.

3 Language professionals in the human–machine era

The LITHME working group 7 brings together researchers and practitioners with expertise in diverse areas of interest from translation and interpreting to clinical linguistics, from terminology to copywriting and language technology to examine how the field is being shaped by MT as well as other technologies. As professionals involved in working with language have varied titles and profiles, one of the key tasks for WG7 is to map and conceptualise what "language work" is, who "language professionals" are, and how technology is changing their work.

[3]More detailed descriptions of the WGs and their activities: https://lithme.eu/working-groups

For various types of language professionals, technology is already a significant part of their everyday work. A typical case might be that of translators interacting with MT, which is an increasingly common process and has had profound effects on the field. Professionals also communicate and interact through technology, for example, using remote interpreting solutions or collaborative platforms. In the future, the use of speech and touch interfaces, as well as augmented and virtual reality, also seems poised to take a larger role in the professionals' interaction with their tools. While technology can be a useful tool, for example, for supporting wider accessibility, it may also bring potential adverse effects to working conditions or create new barriers. WG7 aims to form a deeper understanding of how MT and other technologies are used in language work, how they affect the future roles of professionals and machines in language work, and how the training of future language professionals can adapt to these changes.

Activities of WG7 include regular meetings and invited talks from various areas of language industry, conceptual mapping of language professionals, a meta-survey of the use of MT by translators, and a survey focusing on the use of MT by language professionals other than translators or interpreters. Based on this work, the working group aims to produce reports and forecasts on the implications of technology for theory, practice, ethics and training in the area of language work.

Acknowledgements

The COST Action "Language in the Human–Machine Era" LITHME (CA19102) is supported by COST (European Cooperation in Science and Technology).

References

Sayers, Dave, Rui Sousa-Silva, Sviatlana Höhn, et al. 2021. *The Dawn of the Human–Machine Era: A Forecast of New and Emerging Language Technologies*. Report for EU COST Action CA19102 'Language In The Human–Machine Era'. https://doi.org/10.17011/jyx/reports/20210518/1

CREAMT: Creativity and narrative engagement of literary texts translated by translators and NMT

Ana Guerberof Arenas
University of Surrey/
University of Groningen
a.guerberof.arenas@rug.nl

Antonio Toral
University of Groningen
a.toral.ruiz@rug.nl

Abstract

We present here the EU-funded project CREAMT that seeks to understand what is meant by creativity in different translation modalities, e.g. machine translation, post-editing or professional translation. Focusing on the textual elements that determine creativity in translated literary texts and the reader experience, CREAMT uses a novel, interdisciplinary approach to assess how effective machine translation is in literary translation considering creativity in translation and the ultimate user: the reader.

1 Introduction

Research has shed some light on the usability of machine translation (MT) in literary texts (Toral, Wieling, and Way 2018), showing that MT might help literary translators when it comes to productivity. At the same time, translators' perception is that the "more creative" the literary text, the less useful MT is (Moorkens et al. 2018). But can we quantify the creativity in texts translated by humans as opposed to those produced with the aid of machines? And, since one of the aims of the translation of a literary text is to preserve the reading experience of the original, what is the reader's experience when faced with machine-translated texts? Do users exposed to different translation modalities have different reading experiences?

To provide answers to these questions, the CREAMT is articulated in two main axes with a two-year duration. The first axis proposes to identify creative shifts (see section 2.2) while the second axis seeks to identify reader's narrative engagement and gather data on enjoyment and translation reception.

2 First axis

We translated two stories: *Murder in the Mall* by Sherwin B. Nuland (1995) was translated into Catalan for a pilot project and *2BR02B* by Kurt Vonnegut (1999) was translated into Catalan and Dutch for the main experiment.

2.1 Translation Process

The conditions human translation (HT) and post-editing (PE) were processed by two professional literary translators. To reduce the effect of the translator, each professional translated and post-edited 50% of each modality.

The MT condition was based on the output of state-of-the-art literary-adapted neural MT systems based on the transformer architecture (Vaswani et al. 2017) trained to translate from English to Catalan (Toral, Oliver, and Ribas-Bellestín 2020) and to Dutch (Toral, van Cranenburgh, and Nutters 2021). The training data did not contain the text used for the experiment nor any by these authors.

2.2 Creativity

The source text (ST) was first annotated for units of creative potential (e.g. metaphors, wordplay and puns, comparisons). A team of five professional reviewers annotated the target texts (TT) as either reproduction, omission, or creative shift (Bayer-Hohenwarter 2011). The creative shifts could be 1) modification (i.e. ST is modified for the target culture), 2) concretisation (i.e. ST is

Macken, Rufener, Van den Bogaert, Daems, Tezcan, Vanroy, Fonteyne, Barrault, Costa-jussà, Kemp, Pilos, Declercq, Koponen, Forcada, Scarton, Moniz (eds.)
Proceedings of the 23rd Annual Conference of the European Association for Machine Translation, p. 355–356
Ghent, Belgium, June 2022.

replaced by a more concrete example in the TT) and 3) abstraction (i.e. ST examples are replaced by generic ones in the TT). The texts were also checked for acceptability (number and type of errors) with the Multidimensional Quality Metrics (MQM).[2] The number of creative shifts minus the error points divided by the number of ST words resulted in a creativity score.

3 Second Axis

An on-line questionnaire consisting of three parts was distributed to 88 Catalan participants in the pilot and 223 Catalan and Dutch participants in the main project using an on-line survey software.

3.1 Demographics and Reading Patterns

This section covers questions that serve to analyze variables affecting narrative engagement (e.g. "What genre do you usually read?").

3.2 Narrative Engagement

After reading the text (the translation modality was assigned randomly), the participants answer ten four-option questions we created to assess comprehensibility. Afterwards, they filled in a 12-item narrative engagement questionnaire (Busselle and Bilandzic 2009), e.g. "At points, I had a hard time making sense of what was going on in the story", "While reading, I found myself thinking about other things" or "I felt sorry for some of the characters in the story").

3.3 Readers' Reception Questionnaire

Participants responded to questions designed to address understanding of the text (e.g. "How easy was the text to understand?"), enjoyment (e.g. "How did you enjoy the text?"), translation assessment (e.g. "How would you like to read a text by the same author and translator?").

4 Outcomes

A pilot was run in Catalan in 2020. The results showed that HT presented a higher creativity score if compared to PE and MT. HT also ranked higher in narrative engagement, and translation reception, while PE ranked marginally higher in enjoyment. (Guerberof-Arenas and Toral 2020). The main experiment for Dutch and Catalan confirmed these results for Axis 1: HT has the highest creativity score, followed by PE, and lastly, MT, in both languages. Post-editing MT output constrains the creativity of translators, resulting in a poorer translation often not fit for publication according to experts. (Guerberof Arenas and Toral 2022). Axis 2 was finished in March 2022 and it is under evaluation.

5 Acknowledgements

This project has received funding from the European Union's Horizon 2020 research and innovation programme under the Marie Skłodowska-Curie grant agreement No. 890697.

References

Bayer-Hohenwarter, Gerrit. 2011. Creative Shifts as a Means of Measuring and Promoting Translational Creativity. Meta 56 (3): 663–692.

Busselle, Rick, and Helena Bilandzic. 2009. Measuring Narrative Engagement. *Media Psychology* 12 (4): 321–347.

Guerberof Arenas, Ana, and Antonio Toral. 2022. Creativity in Translation: Machine Translation as a Constraint for Literary Texts. *Translation Spaces*. Available https://doi.org/10.1075/ts.21025.gue

Guerberof-Arenas, Ana, and Antonio Toral. 2020. The Impact of Post-Editing and Machine Translation on Creativity and Reading Experience. *Translation Spaces* 9 (2): 255–282.

Moorkens, Joss, Antonio Toral, Sheila Castilho, and Andy Way. 2018. Translators' Perceptions of Literary Post-Editing Using Statistical and Neural Machine Translation. *Translation Spaces* 7 (2): 240–262.

Nuland, Sherwin B. 1995. Muder in the Mall. In *How We Die: Reflections of Life's Final Chapter*, New Edition. 1st edition. Vintage, New York, USA.

Toral, Antonio, Andreas van Cranenburgh, and Tia Nutters. 2021. Literary-Adapted Machine Translation in a Well-Resourced Language Pair. *Book of abstracts 7th Conference of The International Association for Translation and Inter-Cultural Studies* (IATIS). Barcelona: 257.

Toral, Antonio, Antoni Oliver, and Pau Ribas-Bellestín. 2020. Machine Translation of Novels in the Age of Transformer. *Maschinelle Übersetzung für Übersetzungsprofis*, edited by Jörg Porsiel. BDÜ Fachverlag, Berlin, Germany: 276–96.

Toral, Antonio, Martijn Wieling, and Andy Way. 2018. Post-Editing Effort of a Novel with Statistical and Neural Machine Translation. *Frontiers in Digital Humanities* 5: 1–11.

Vaswani, Ashish, Noam Shazeer, Niki Parmar, Jakob Uszkoreit, Llion Jones, Aidan N. Gomez, Lukasz Kaiser, and Illia Polosukhin. 2017. Attention Is All You Need. ArXiv:1706.03762 [Cs], December. http://arxiv.org/abs/1706.03762.

Vonnegut, Kurt. 1999. 2BR02B in *Bagombo Snuff Box*. G. P. Putnam's Sons, New York, USA.

[2] https://www.taus.net/qt21-project

Developing Machine Translation Engines for Multilingual Participatory Spaces

Pintu Lohar, Guodong Xie, Andy Way
ADAPT Centre,
Dublin City University,
Dublin, Ireland
`firstname.lastname@adaptcentre.ie`

Abstract

It is often a challenging task to build machine translation (MT) engines for a specific domain due to the lack of parallel data in that area. In this project, we develop a range of MT systems for 6 European languages (English, German, Italian, French, Polish and Irish) in all directions and in two domains (environment and economics).

1 Project Description

This work is part of a larger project called "EU-ComMeet"[1] on developing participatory spaces using a multi-stage, multi-level, multi-mode, multi-lingual, dynamic deliberative approach (M4D2). The goal of this project is to integrate together automated moderation and automated translation to allow multilingual, multi-national participation in deliberative democratic forums. Our main contribution is to facilitate a multilingual deliberative space (MDS) via MT. Users will be able to communicate with each other via MT while speaking or writing in their own languages.

2 MT for Participatory Space

MT is a process that automatically translates text from one language to another. It is usually ideal to train MT models using domain-specific parallel corpora (e.g. a corpus of biomedical domain (Névéol et al., 2018) for medical texts). However, to the best of our knowledge, no such data belonging particularly to the economics and environment domains is available. Accordingly, we decided to use the Europarl corpus (Koehn, 2005) because it is (i) a good-quality corpus, (ii) large enough for MT training, and (iii) mixed domain, so that a significant number text pairs belonging to many major domains such as science, environment, economics, politics etc can be found in this corpus. For each language pair, we built four translation models: (i) two baseline models, and (ii) two domain-adapted models in both translation directions. The baseline models are built using the whole Europarl corpus and tuned on the benchmark news development data set[2] provided by the organisers of WMT 2021. In contrast, the domain-adapted models are built using the same Europarl corpus but tuned on in-domain development data extracted from the news data by applying domain-specific key terms. Both models are tested on these datasets to compare their system performance on domain-specific test sets. In order to compile the in-domain development and test data, we form two lists of domain-specific key terms: one for 'environment' and another for 'economics'. A total of 150 environment and 201 economics key terms are used, including some of the following example terms: (i) **Environment:** *sustainability*, *pollution*, *climate* etc. (ii) **Economics:** *inflation*, *employment*, *privatization* etc. These key terms are then used to extract only those text pairs from the *news* data that contain at least one of these key terms in order to form the in-domain development and test datasets. Table 1 shows the data statistics and its domain-wise distribution. We provide a brief description on two types of translation models in Table 2. The MT models are built using OpenNMT (Klein et al., 2017) with transformer architecture (Vaswani et al., 2017). The translation outputs are

[1] `https://www.eucommeet.eu/`

[2] `http://data.statmt.org/wmt21/translation-task/dev.tgz`

Macken, Rufener, Van den Bogaert, Daems, Tezcan, Vanroy, Fonteyne, Barrault, Costa-jussà, Kemp, Pilos, Declercq, Koponen, Forcada, Scarton, Moniz (eds.)
Proceedings of the 23rd Annual Conference of the European Association for Machine Translation, p. 357–358
Ghent, Belgium, June 2022.

Domain	Europarl	News
Train (multidomain)	1,957,832	//
dev+test (news domain)	//	38,647
Environment domain	//	1,145
Economics domain	//	4,014

Table 1: Training and domain-wise data distribution

Model	Tuned on	Tested on
Baseline	News domain	Environment +Economics
Domain-adapted	Environment +Economics	Environment +Economics

Table 2: Baseline and domain-adapted models

evaluated using BLEU (Papineni et al., 2002). We

Test domain	Model	BLEU
Economics	Baseline	21.67
	Domain-adapted	**22.95**
Environment	Baseline	21.56
	Domain-adapted	**23.20**

Table 3: BLEU scores for English–German

depict the results for English–German in Table 3 which shows that the domain-adapted models outperform the baselines in both domains. All these improvements are statistically significant as verified using MultEval (Clark et al., 2011).

3 Architecture of the MT system

Now that the systems have been built, multilingual discussions involving people speaking different languages from different countries in different citizens' assemblies will take place. Our MT engines will be used to translate among different participants through the project platform. Participants will be in different locations across the 5 countries. In making the MT engines accessible, we will need to bear in mind three closely related criteria: reliability, speed and security. To address this problem, we adopt a two-layer architecture and security verification, as shown in Figure 1. The first layer (the web server) handles access verification, and translation requests from different devices in multiple locations are sent to the translation GPU servers in the second layer. To speed up the translation response, the two-layer server groups (in the green rectangles) are deployed in different countries so that the translation requests will be processed locally. We expose our MT service through the web server which creates an HTTP REST server interface in the web server. To enhance the security of the MT system, we adopt the JSON Web Token (JWT)[3] to verify user access.

[3]https://jwt.io/introduction

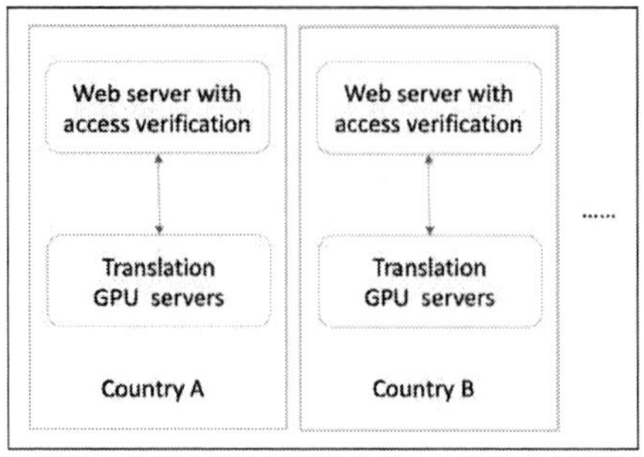

Figure 1: Architecture of MT system

Acknowledgments

This work was funded by the European Commission under H2020-EU.3.6. - SOCIETAL CHALLENGES - Europe In A Changing World - Inclusive, Innovative And Reflective Societies, grant agreement ID: 959234.

References

Clark, Jonathan H., Chris Dyer, Alon Lavie, and Noah A. Smith. 2011. Better hypothesis testing for statistical machine translation: Controlling for optimizer instability. In *Proceedings of the 49th Annual Meeting of the Association for Computational Linguistics: Human Language Technologies:*, pages 176–181, Portland, Oregon, USA.

Klein, Guillaume, Yoon Kim, Yuntian Deng, Jean Senellart, and Alexander M. Rush. 2017. Opennmt: Open-source toolkit for neural machine translation. In *Proceedings of the 55th Annual Meeting of the Association for Computational Linguistics*, pages 67–72, Vancouver, Canada.

Koehn, Philipp. 2005. Europarl: A parallel corpus for statistical machine translation. In *Proceedings of Machine Translation Summit X: Papers*, pages 79–86, Phuket, Thailand, September 13-15.

Névéol, Aurélie, Antonio Jimeno Yepes, Mariana Neves, and Karin Verspoor. 2018. Parallel corpora for the biomedical domain. In *Proceedings of the Eleventh International Conference on Language Resources and Evaluation*, pages 296–291, Miyazaki, Japan.

Papineni, Kishore, Salim Roukos, Todd Ward, and Wei-Jing Zhu. 2002. Bleu: a method for automatic evaluation of machine translation. In *Proceedings of 40th Annual Meeting of the Association for Computational Linguistics*, pages 311–318, Philadelphia, USA.

Vaswani, Ashish, Noam Shazeer, Niki Parmar, Jakob Uszkoreit, Llion Jones, Aidan N Gomez, Łukasz Kaiser, and Illia Polosukhin. 2017. Attention is all you need. In *Advances in neural information processing systems*, pages 5998–6008, Long Beach, USA.

Extending the MuST-C Corpus for a Comparative Evaluation of Speech Translation Technology

Luisa Bentivogli[1], Mauro Cettolo[1], Marco Gaido[1,2], Alina Karakanta[1,2], Matteo Negri[1], Marco Turchi[1]
[1]Fondazione Bruno Kessler
[2]University of Trento
`{bentivo,cettolo,mgaido,akarakanta,negri,turchi}@fbk.eu`

Abstract

This project aimed at extending the test sets of the MuST-C speech translation (ST) corpus with new reference translations. The new references were collected from professional post-editors working on the output of different ST systems for three language directions: English–German/Italian/Spanish. In this paper, we describe how the data were collected and how they are distributed. As an evidence of their usefulness, we also summarize the findings of the first comparative evaluation of *cascade* and *direct* ST approaches, which was carried out relying on the collected data. The project was partially funded by the European Association for Machine Translation (EAMT) through its 2020 Sponsorship of Activities programme.

1 Project overview

In this project we created and released additional reference translations for the test sets of the MuST-C corpus (Cattoni et al., 2021). The new references were collected for three language directions, i.e. En–De/Es/It, and consist of professional post-edits of the output of two state-of-the-art systems that represent the main current ST approaches, namely a *cascade* and a *direct* system.

Data. Our evaluation data are drawn from MuST-C, which is the largest freely available multilingual corpus for ST. It is based on English TED talks and currently covers 14 language directions, with English audio segments automatically aligned with their corresponding manual transcripts and translations. In MuST-C, a *Common* Test Set includes segments from talks that are common in all directions, thus making it possible to evaluate and compare systems across languages. For the three language directions addressed in the project, this common section includes the same 27 TED talks, for a total of around 2,500 largely overlapping segments.[1] For all language directions, we selected from MuST-C *Common* the same English audio portions from each talk, in order to obtain representative groups of contiguous segments that are comparable across languages. Furthermore, to ensure high data quality, we manually checked the selected samples and kept only those segments for which the *audio-transcript-translation* alignment was correct. Each of the 3 resulting post-editing test sets – henceforth *PE sets* – contains 550 segments, corresponding to ~10,000 English source words. Then, we translated the PE sets with two ST systems. One represents the traditional *cascade* approach, in which the task is performed by means of a pipeline of separate automatic speech recognition (ASR) and machine translation (MT) components. The other adopts the more recent *direct* approach, which relies on a single encoder–decoder architecture that directly translates the source audio signal bypassing intermediate representations.

Post-editing. To prepare the data for the two post-editing (PE) tasks, we followed the main criteria adopted in the IWSLT PE-based evaluation campaigns (Cettolo et al., 2013). To guarantee high-quality data, we relied on two professional translators with experience in subtitling and

[1]Note, however, that due to automatic segmentation and alignment of the talks, segments can vary across languages.

Macken, Rufener, Van den Bogaert, Daems, Tezcan, Vanroy, Fonteyne, Barrault, Costa-jussà, Kemp, Pilos, Declercq, Koponen, Forcada, Scarton, Moniz (eds.)
Proceedings of the 23rd Annual Conference of the European Association for Machine Translation, p. 359–360
Ghent, Belgium, June 2022.

post-editing, who were hired through a language service provider (`Translated.com`). Furthermore, in order to cope with translators' variability (i.e. one translator could systematically correct more than the other), the outputs of the two ST systems were randomly assigned to them, ensuring that each translator worked on all the 550 segments, equally post-editing both systems (cascade and direct). Another aspect inherent to our ST framework, which differentiates it from the traditional MT PE scenario, is the nature of the input (speech vs text). Since ST systems take spoken utterances as input, the traditional bilingual MT PE task, where translators are required to post-edit the system output according to the source text, is not feasible. For this reason, while the PE task was run using the MateCat tool (Federico et al., 2014), which displays the transcript together with the ST output to be edited, we also provided translators with the audio file of each segment, and asked them to post-edit according to it. The complete *ad hoc* guidelines given to the translators are available at: `https://bit.ly/3gXEQin`.

Final release. The project resulted in a significant extension of the MuST-C En–De/Es/It test sets. Specifically, for each of the 550 segments in the corresponding PE sets, two new reference translations were added. The data release includes, for each segment: *i)* the audio file, *ii)* the original reference transcript, *iii)* the original reference translation, *iv)* two ST outputs (from the cascade and direct systems), and *v)* the professional post-edits of the two ST outputs. The resource is distributed under a CC BY-NC-ND 4.0 license and is downloadable at: `https://ict.fbk.eu/mustc-post-edits/`.

2 Experiments with the released data

The collected high-quality post-edits can be exploited for different purposes, not limited to the standard one of computing more reliable multi-reference automatic evaluations. In a recent study (Bentivogli et al., 2021), we used them to analyse the relation between systems performance and specific characteristics of the input audio, and to investigate possible differences between the systems in terms of lexical, morphological and word ordering errors. We also explored whether the output of cascade and direct systems can be distinguished by humans or by automatic classifiers. Our investigation showed that the performance gap between the two technologies is now substantially closed. Subtle differences in their behavior exist: overall performance being equal, the cascade still seems to have an edge in terms of morphology, word ordering and lexical diversity, which is balanced by the advantages of direct models in audio understanding and capturing prosody. However, these differences do not seem sufficient to make the output of the two approaches easily distinguishable by humans.

3 Conclusion

In this project we released new high-quality reference translations which extend the En–De/Es/It test sets of MuST-C. These additional references consist of professional post-edits of the output of two state-of-the-art ST systems. The collected data are distributed as a special release of MuST-C, thus providing the community with a valuable resource to foster additional research in the ST field. Along this direction, we employed this resource to carry out a multi-faceted analysis that resulted in a timely contribution towards taking stock of the situation of ST technology advancements.

Acknowledgements

This project was partially funded by the European Association for Machine Translation (EAMT) through its 2020 Sponsorship of Activities programme.

References

Bentivogli, Luisa, Mauro Cettolo, Marco Gaido, Alina Karakanta, Alberto Martinelli, Matteo Negri, and Marco Turchi. 2021. Cascade versus direct speech translation: Do the differences still make a difference? In *Proceedings of ACL 2021 (Volume 1: Long Papers)*, pages 2873–2887, Online, August.

Cattoni, Roldano, Mattia Antonino Di Gangi, Luisa Bentivogli, Matteo Negri, and Marco Turchi. 2021. MuST-C: A multilingual corpus for end-to-end speech translation. *Computer Speech & Language*, 66:101155.

Cettolo, Mauro, Jan Niehues, Sebastian Stüker, Luisa Bentivogli, and Marcello Federico. 2013. Report on the 10th IWSLT Evaluation Campaign. In *Proceedings of the International Workshop on Spoken Language Translation (IWSLT)*, Heidelberg, Germany.

Federico, Marcello, Nicola Bertoldi, Mauro Cettolo, et al. 2014. The MateCat tool. In *Proceedings of COLING 2014 (System Demonstrations)*, pages 129–132, Dublin, Ireland, August.

Monitio – Large Scale MT for Multilingual Media Monitoring

Carlos Amaral
Priberam
Lisbon, Portugal
carlos@priberam.pt

Sebastião Miranda
Priberam
Lisbon, Portugal
ssm@priberam.pt

Abstract

Monitio is a real-time crosslingual global media monitoring platform which delivers actionable insights beyond human scale and capabilities. Our system continuously ingests a massive number of multilingual data sources that are automatically translated, filtered and categorized to generate intelligence reports specially geared towards media monitoring professionals' needs.

1 Origin

The starting point of Monitio was a multilingual media monitoring prototype developed between 2016–2019 in tight collaboration with the British Broadcast Corporation (BBC) and Deutsche Welle (DW).[2] Both broadcasters monitor a growing number of video streams in different languages, by assigning teams of human analysts that are grouped by languages. This approach is not scalable hence the need to reinvent media monitoring, tackling it globally and in a scalable fashion to break the current internationalization and scalability barriers.

The emergence of mature natural language processing (NLP) and artificial intelligence technologies gives European companies an opportunity to push Europe to the leadership of the media monitoring market, where multilinguality is a major issue and, simultaneously, a major opportunity.

By integrating machine translation (MT) in the ingestion and enrichment pipeline, Monitio enables the monitoring of sources in languages the human analyst is not fluent in, providing a truly global view of the events not culturally, geographically or politically biased for lack of access to a broader set of sources.

2 Challenges

A major challenge for Monitio is the huge volume of data ingested daily into the platform. One of Monitio's goals is to process 10 million new multilingual items per day. This has to be accomplished with a minimum delay to enable near real-time monitoring.

The automatic translation of this amount of documents is just one of the challenges for the platform's enrichment pipeline. All content entering the platform is subject to a series of NLP steps, namely its classification according to a standard topics taxonomy, the recognition of named entities like people, organizations, brands and places and linking them to external knowledge bases like Wikipedia or Wikidata, the production of a summary, and the clustering of all articles related to the same event in storylines.

Adding to the complexity, the large-scale dissemination of content on social media platforms, while ensuring a broad coverage of multiple connected viewpoints on the same subject of interest, stresses the problem of information verification which is a daunting task without the support of automation. Failing to address this problem leads to biased views on the subject and insufficient (or even wrong) insights.

[2] http://summa-project.eu

Macken, Rufener, Van den Bogaert, Daems, Tezcan, Vanroy, Fonteyne, Barrault, Costa-jussà, Kemp, Pilos, Declercq, Koponen, Forcada, Scarton, Moniz (eds.)
Proceedings of the 23rd Annual Conference of the European Association for Machine Translation, p. 361–362
Ghent, Belgium, June 2022.

Figure 1: Multilingual Storyline

3 Solution

The scalability goals but also the cost implications led to the integration of free/open source MT models like EasyNMT from Hugging Face, deployed in a dedicated GPU infrastructure.

By employing MT in the beginning of the pipeline, Monitio enables indexing of the documents in all languages translated to a language users understand (e.g., English), thus allowing the users to search documents in other languages. On the other hand, Monitio does not employ MT before the NLP steps, which are executed in the source language of the documents to minimize error propagation.

To enable processing and organization of multilingual documents in different stories and topics, Monitio employs transfer learning through contextual multilingual DistilBERT sentence transformers[3] for crosslingual document clustering, topic detection and entity linking.

One NLP task which still relies heavily on language specific annotated corpora is named-entity recognition, which is one of the most difficult tasks to train generalized multilingual models.

4 Future

When a translation of better quality is needed, for instance, to be included in a report or to clear any doubt that may arise from the default MT, the user will be able to invoke third-party services on demand for a specific document.

Monitio will also integrate automatic speech recognition combined with MT to transcribe and translate video and audio content using wav2vec, an end-to-end deep learning model.

Another objective of the Monitio project is the creation of innovative tools for assisted fact checking. We are developing tools that help the users to verify a claim using the multilingual information available in the platform.

Acknowledgments

The European Union's Horizon 2020 FTI (Fast Track to Innovation) program is funding the productization and the implementation of the go-to-market strategy plan of Monitio under grant agreement No 965576, a project also named Monitio.[4]

References

Santos, João, Afonso Mendes and Sebastião Miranda, "Simplifying News Clustering Through Projection from a Shared Multilingual Space" in Proceedings of Text2Story (ECIR, 2022), pp. 15–24.

Ferreira, Pedro, Ruben Cardoso and Afonso Mendes, "Priberam Labs at the 3rd shared task on SlavNER", Proceedings of the 8th Workshop on Balto-Slavic Natural Language Processing (EACL 2021), pp. 86–92.

Miranda, Sebastião, David Nogueira, Afonso Mendes, Andreas Vlachos, Andrew Secker, Rebecca Garrett, Jeff Mitchel and Zita Marinho, "Automated Fact-Checking in the News Room", The Web Conference 2019, San Francisco, pp. 3579–358.

[3] `https://huggingface.co/sentence-transformers`

[4] `https://monitio-project.eu/`

Sponsors

Platinum sponsor

Silver sponsors

pangeanic

YAMAGATA
We make everybody understand your message

Bronze sponsors

Collaborator sponsors

Supporter sponsors

Media sponsors

Institutional partners

CROSSLANG

language and
translation
technology
team

GHENT
UNIVERSITY

Association for Computational Linguistics
209 N. Eighth Street
Stroudsburg, Pennsylvania 18360

ISBN 978-1-7138-5346-6
9 781713 853466

CURRAN ASSOCIATES INC.
proceedings.com